THE HISTORICAL ATLAS OF

AMERICAN CRIME

THE HISTORICAL ATLAS OF
AMERICAN CRIME

Fred Rosen

Checkmark Books®
An imprint of Facts On File, Inc.

The Historical Atlas of American Crime

Checkmark Books
An imprint of Facts On File, Inc.
132 West 31st Street
New York NY 10001

Library of Congress Cataloging-in-Publication Data

Rosen, Fred.
The historical atlas of American crime / Fred Rosen.
p. cm.
Includes bibliographical references and index.
ISBN 0-8160-4841-X (hc : alk. paper) — ISBN 0-8160-4842-8 (pb : alk. paper)
1. Crime—United States—History. 2. Crime—United States—History—Maps. I. Title.
HV6779.R67 2004
364.973—dc22   2004011346

Checkmark Books are available at special discounts when purchased in bulk quantities for businesses, associations, institutions or sales promotions. Please call our Special Sales Department in New York at (212) 967-8800 or (800) 322-8755.

You can find Facts On File on the World Wide Web at http://www.factsonfile.com

Text design by James Scotto-Lavino
Cover design by Cathy Rincon
Maps by Sholto Ainslie

Printed in the United States of America

VB FOF 10 9 8 7 6 5 4 3 2 1

This book is printed on acid-free paper.

To Sara, who inspires me

Say, what was your name in the States?
Was it Johnson or Thompson or Bates?
Did you murder your wife and flee for your life?
Say, what was your name in the States?
Did you have to change your name?
Was it Miller or Benton or James?
Did you spend time in jail or ride on a rail?
Say, what was your name in the States?

—A song of the Gold Rush, by "Anonymous"

Contents

Preface

The summer of 1992 was a hot one in Brooklyn. The temperature frequently went into the 90s, hot enough, as the locals like to say, to fry an egg on the sidewalk.

In Brooklyn Heights, a once-sedate neighborhood of turn-of-the-century brownstones now yuppie chic, David Bosse was sweating. Bosse was the map curator at the William L. Clements Library at the University of Michigan in Ann Arbor. He was trudging up and down the steps to the third floor of a brownstone, carrying heavy boxes that contained the largest and most historically accurate assemblage of American crime literature: the Medler Collection.

James Vincent Medler was a retired printer and lithographer who had long been fascinated by what is termed today *true crime*—that is, actual accounts of crimes. Over 30-plus years, Medler amassed what is described in *Quarto,* the journal of the Clements Library, as "a magnificent collection of American crime literature dating from the mid-eighteenth century up to the early 1900's." When it came on the market, Clements director John Dann immediately recognized the breadth and quality of materials and went for them on the spot.

Dann acquired the collection and sent Bosse to Brooklyn to collate it. Bosse did his job, and soon the Medler Collection took up its permanent home in Michigan. At the Clements Library, curators assessed the 900 or so items, repairing where necessary—some of the material was more than three centuries old—cataloging, and shelving.

With the job done, the collection was opened to the public in 1994. For the first time, much of its assets have been put into their proper context as the absolutely vital cog in American crime literature. Much literature exists on late 19th-century and 20th-century crime, but little is available to the

researcher on crime in the Americas during the 17th, 18th, and 19th centuries. It is that gap that the Medler Collection fills.

Not always does the writer of crime literature have the actual, and thoughtful, words of the "bad guys" to guide him. And yet, those words do exist in the James E. Medler Crime Collection. Much of it consists of first-person accounts that the criminals delivered to ministers, reporters, and others that were duly recorded and published in pamphlets that swept through the colonies and, later, the states. Often, the stories were embellished by the writers to provide some sort of moral. That is interesting now as a window into our ancestors' notions of what life should really be like.

At the heart of this collection is the absolute historical accuracy of what took place—the crimes, the criminals, and the aftermath. In the process, as we trace crime branching out west from the original 13 colonies along the highways and byways of an emerging nation, a picture is painted of the dark side of a culture that was raw to begin with. Murderers, thieves, rogues, and highwaymen are all here. These are the men and women who formed the most powerful subculture in every generation since before colonial times. As far back as the first white settlers stepping ashore, these criminals had enough strength to strangle a grown man, yet a touch sensitive enough to pick a pocket.

As in any good story, there should be a "through line." The through line is the westward development of roads, riverways, and the railroad.

Before the first decade of the 19th century, white settlers—and crime—lived only east of the Mississippi River. After Lewis and Clark blazed their path westward, criminals were among the first white settlers to pour into the new land. This, in turn, formed an exigency to set up a national force to police the new territories. Thus the U.S. Marshals Service was born in the late 1700s.

Similarly, the development of the Ohio River as a major north/south route led to the rise of a different type of crime. Cave-in-Rock, a limestone opening in a bluff above the Ohio River at its junction with the Saline River, was a well-known natural landmark throughout the 18th century, a rest stop for river travelers migrating west. Beginning in the 1790s and until the 1830s, it was home base to an entire corporation of river pirates.

Post–Civil War, the coming of the railroads to the West led to train robbery, a crime first performed by the James/Younger Gang. By 1900 every conceivable kind of crime had occurred as far west as California. With no place to go except a new territory, crime moved north and so did the criminal.

Soapy Smith, the prototype of the modern gangster, controlled Denver's rackets until reformers kicked him out. Seeking new fortune, he followed the Gold Rush and established his own criminal fiefdom in Alaska.

The 20th century saw crime imploding. Having gone beyond U.S. geological borders, crime came back for round two, this time with modern firepower and modern methods. Criminals employed machine guns and other automatic weapons, hand grenades, and every other conceivable type of weapon in the 20th century.

And then there was the old standby, the rope. Whether it was Ralph Lane in the 16th century killing an Indian chief or Sheriff Shipp in the 20th allowing a black man to be lynched, white supremacy was at the heart of many crimes.

The Thompson submachine gun became the weapon of choice for depression-era gangsters like the vicious Baby Face Nelson, the much maligned Pretty Boy Floyd, the cowardly Machine Gun Kelly, and of course that blazing star of the gangster era, John Dillinger. These men and their gangs began to realize that robbing banks was not the only way to make money, and so they adopted a new method: kidnapping. The government responded by making kidnapping a federal crime punishable by the death penalty.

Were it not for the rapidly expanding road system, these gangs would not have been able to traverse the countryside. Likewise, New York's Murder, Inc., of the 1930s could not have hired out their executioners to crime families nationwide were it not for the rail system, the fastest and most efficient method of transportation then in existence.

As the 20th century drew to a close, the terrorism practiced by the Ku Klux Klan since the century's beginning became an art form. Whether it was Arab terrorists trying to blow up the World Trade Center in 1993, in which my college professor John DiGiovanni lost his life, or Osama bin Laden's successful attack on the World Trade Center on September 11, 2001, terrorists became the criminals to fear. How ironic that the greatest criminal act in U.S. history could not have been done were it not for the terrorists' brilliant criminal use of the airplane, one of the greatest inventions of the millennium.

A true account of a crime should also include the real, fascinating personalities of the people involved. So in *The Historical Atlas of American Crime,* the reader will meet such vivid characters as Micajah (Big) Harp, Wiley (Little) Harp, Julian Carlton, and Chester Gillette.

America's first known serial killers, Big Harp and Little Harp, terrorized what are now North Carolina, Ohio, Tennessee, and Kentucky from 1775 to 1798. Their combined kill total has been conservatively estimated at 50.

Chester Gillette and Grace Brown worked together in 1905 at a skirt factory in Cortland, New York that was owned by Gillette's uncle. In spring 1906 Grace found herself pregnant with Gillette's child. He promised to marry her. On the morning of July 11, 1906, they took a rowboat out onto Moosehead Lake in the Adirondack Mountains. Grace never came back, and Gillette claimed she committed suicide because of her condition.

The Brown murder case became the basis for the first U.S. novel based on a true crime, Theodore Dreiser's *An American Tragedy,* which in turn became the basis for the 1952 Montgomery Clift/Elizabeth Taylor film *A Place in the Sun.* But what has been all but lost to history is that in the rush to execute Gillette, one journalist stood up for him. He was William Barclay "Bat" Masterson, the famous western marshal turned journalist for the *New York Morning Telegraph.*

Julian Carlton was Frank Lloyd Wright's butler at Taliesin, Wright's magnificent home in the Wisconsin countryside. On August 14, 1914, Carlton, in a seeming fit of rage, burned the place down and chopped the survivors to death with an ax. On that day, Wright lost his one true love, his common-law wife Mamah Borthwick, her two children, and several of his draftsmen.

Wright and Borthwick had become what today would be called "media stars." Because of the development of wireless telegraphy and the wire services, their romance received coast-to-coast newspaper coverage, making them the first modern media celebrities. The murders received even more ink.

By the time readers finish *The Historical Atlas of American Crime,* they will not only understand how a monster like Carlton could commit his crimes, but how the contemporary social and economic circumstances create crime and criminals.

Any good story begins at the beginning, and the story of crime in America starts when the English first attempted to colonize the Americas.

Acknowledgments

My editor, James Chambers, conceived the idea for this book. I am profoundly grateful for the opportunity he gave me to realize his vision. During the actual writing of the book, he provided unqualified support and then brilliant editing. Every writer should be as lucky as to one time in their lives work for an editor like Jim.

Thanks, too, to associate editor Sarah Fogarty, Dale Williams and Sholto Ainslie (black-and-white maps), art director Cathy Rincon, production director Rachel Berlin, James Scotto-Lavino and Elizabeth Margiotta (design and production), Michael Laraque and Laura Magzis (copyediting), and editorial assistant Vanessa Nittoli.

It is my agent Lori Perkins, herself an accomplished writer, who put Jim and me together. She made it possible. I am profoundly grateful to her as well.

My friend Jim DeFelice took the time to discuss many of the entries in this book and lend his considerable expertise. Jim, who had previously written about Lincoln, helped me hone in on crime during the Civil War years and how the war and the social conditions of the time affected crime. I thank him for that and the wonderful cigars we smoked along the way.

My wife Leah lent personal support in taking on a lot of the personal responsibilities normally left to me. She suffered through many a dinner table conversation where I waxed ad infinitum about the minutiae of criminal history. I thank her for her love and patience.

Greg Rose helped out by tuning me into the Pacific Northwest. Janet and Rob Garratt lent encouragement and provided many a wonderful meal.

Most of all, I feel a profound debt of gratitude to those chroniclers of American history who have come before me. I am acutely conscious that I am building on what they have already done.

In particular, I want to mention Robert Coates, whose book *The Outlaw Years: The History of the Land Pirates of the Natchez Trace,* and Frank Leslie, whose *Frank Leslie's Illustrated Newspaper* provided many of the sketches of 19th-century crime well before photography became popular. They have been an inspiration.

How to Use This Book

The Historical Atlas of American Crime presents a new way of looking at the evolution of crime in America.

From 1592 to 2003, crime and criminals adapted to geography, population shifts, and new methods of communication, transportation, and weapons technology. The entries presented here detail this progression in a way crime has rarely been considered. They are topical, geographical, and biographical, depending upon which element is most important to that piece of the story.

Certain cases are labeled "firsts," with a caveat. These are the earliest cases for which the author's research revealed documentation. Any of these crimes may well have been committed in the New World and gone unrecorded prior to the date of the accounts presented here.

Some little-known cases, such as that of the Confederate spy Martha "Matt" Sanders, have been chosen to illustrate the connections between American history and American crime. Complex, dichotomous figures, both hero and villain, provide many of the insights into the period in which they lived. Jean Lafitte, John Brown, Jesse James, and John Dillinger fit into this category.

Some locations appear repeatedly in connection with criminal cases, such as the Natchez Trace, Cave-in-Rock, and Harper's Ferry. Particular emphasis has been placed on the period prior to, during, and after the Civil War, which the author sees as a pivotal event in the evolution of crime in America.

It became clear during the writing that including modern organized crime as an "American first" was historically inaccurate. In the early part of the 19th century in the United States, John A. Murrel established himself as the American "Napoleon of crime." For most of his career, Murrel was unknown to law enforcement authorities. He organized his criminal network throughout the West without a line in newspapers, magazines, or pamphlets. He used the Natchez Trace in particular and the subsidiary transportation systems of plantation railroads, newly developed state roads, and, of course, the river to spread his vast criminal empire. It is a testament to his criminal brilliance that few in his own time knew who he was.

In the annals of crime, Murrel remains the single most brilliant architect of a criminal conspiracy bigger than anything even the modern Mafia could imagine. Murrel was as ruthless as Capone, as deadly as Siegel, and as smart as Lansky.

Murrel was the original.

As for serial killers, none in modern times—not Ted Bundy, not John Wayne Gacy, not Richard Speck—could match the ferocity and "kill total" of Big Harp and Little Harp of the late 18th and early 19th centuries.

A few crimes of note are not included because they do not illustrate a greater trend in American society or are not the first of their kind, though they may be the best known.

The St. Valentine's Day massacre, for example, has no historical significance beyond the fact that two rival Prohibition gangs had a falling out. As for Sacco and Vanzetti, they may have been discriminated against because of their ethnicity and personal beliefs, but they weren't the first, even the second. They would have to stand in a line that begins with William Ledra, who was hanged in the Massachusetts Bay Colony in 1660 because he dared to be a Quaker in a colony run by Puritans. In subsequent centuries he was followed by thousands of African Americans lynched because of their skin color and at least one Jewish American, Leo Frank, who was lynched in 1916 because of his religion.

Finally, this book can be read in two ways, either skipping around from entry to entry and century to century, or as a whole from start to finish. Either way, the reader will see the commonality that binds the criminal side of American culture through centuries of American history.

PART ONE

THE COLONIES

ONE
1587-1650

Introduction

The Americas were "discovered" in 1492 by Christopher Columbus, but for 80 years, no country had done anything to exploit the northern part of the continent. The English decided to do something about it.

The roots of crime in America really begin in 1578 in England. That year, England's Queen Elizabeth granted Sir Gilbert Humphrey the right to search out and find undiscovered lands "not inhabited by civilized Christian people." With the Virgin Queen's imprimatur in hand, Sir Humphrey mounted an expedition to the New World. It soon failed. Some of his ships abandoned the mission due to harsh conditions, while others turned back, allegedly for "repairs." In 1583 the dogged Sir Humphrey tried and failed again, only this time, he died near the coast of New England. Considering the difficulties he had encountered, it would take no less than a visionary to continue. It so happened that such a man, Walter Raleigh, had sailed with Sir Humphrey during his first voyage.

Raleigh envisioned a country emerging from the wilderness. Raleigh the explorer could make that happen, and Raleigh the dashing suitor of Queen Elizabeth I could get permission to do it.

After Sir Humphrey died, Raleigh petitioned Queen Elizabeth to allow him to mount a new exploratory expedition to the New World. Raleigh charmed Elizabeth into granting his request, and in 1584 his ships departed for the New World. One of the commanders of the voyage was a man named Arthur Barlowe.

After three months of sailing across the stormy Atlantic, Barlowe saw land through his spyglass. He proceeded to describe the area, which would later be identified as Roanoke Island off the present state of North Carolina: ". . . so full of grapes, as the very beating, and the surge of the sea overflowed them, of which we founde such plentie . . . that I thinke in all the world the like aboundance is not to be founde." Barlowe and his explorers formed such good relations with the Indians that Raleigh, now Sir Raleigh, once again petitioned the queen.

3

This time Raleigh was not interested in a voyage of exploration; he wanted to make money. He planned to colonize the New World and establish a permanent settlement in the name of the queen. Once again Elizabeth granted her favorite his request.

In 1585 seven vessels under Raleigh's patent made ready to sail to the New World. Under the command of Sir Richard Grenville, the party included approximately 600 men with full provisions. They set sail for the Americas that spring. A transatlantic voyage in leaky wooden ships was a dangerous proposition. Grenville's fleet ran into a bad storm off the African coast that grounded some ships while the rest were forced to sail to the Spanish territory of Puerto Rico. There, Grenville settled in to await the rest of the fleet. Within two weeks, all but one of the seven ships had reunited with Grenville, and they continued on their voyage.

Reaching the shores of Wococon Inlet in what is now North Carolina, the lead ship grounded and most of the cargo was destroyed. But the rest made it, and by fall 1585, a fort had been built. Sir Grenville, meanwhile, was due back to England to report on the colony's progress to Raleigh. The man he left in charge was about to assume a dubious place in American history.

Roanoke Colony (1587) first documented murder in the English New World

Captain Ralph Lane was left to command the 107 men in the Roanoke colony. He was a military man who knew nothing of human relations and in fact considered the Indians, who had been friendly and helpful to the colonists, as less than human. The Indians, meanwhile, had readily shared their stores of food and the colonists assumed they would continue to do just that.

Unfortunately, the Roanoke colony had the misfortune to attempt colonizing the New World during the worst drought in 800 years. It was so bad that the Indians began to go hungry, and it became a battle just to stay alive.

On one flank were the settlers, determined to stay despite the long odds of their survival. On the other was the drought. How could the Indians feed the colonists when their own children were going hungry? The answer, of course, was they could not. Friction between settlers and natives worsened during the winter of 1585–86, when the colonists spread diseases to the Indians, who had no immunity to European sicknesses. Many died. During spring 1586, relations between the English and the Indians continued to further deteriorate. All the Indians knew was that the Europeans wanted their food stores; all the Europeans knew was that the Indians refused to share. As far as Ralph Lane was concerned, that was cause enough to act.

Lane led an attack on the Indians, and the colonists killed not only the Indian chief and his warriors, but women and children as well. Lane and his men had become the New World's first documented murderers, a capital offense even in the 16th century, but Lane had picked his victims well: Europeans considered Indians inferior. As far as Lane was concerned, his men had killed in self-defense—the Indians would not help them, so they were killed for their provisions.

Lane's victory should have been short-lived in the face of retaliation by the Indians, but before they had a chance to respond, Sir Francis Drake came to the rescue. Drake, the era's most famous swashbuckling sea captain, was returning from the West Indies, his ships heavily laden with booty. He offered to transport the starving colonists back to England. Rather than wait for Grenville, who was already late with reinforcements and supplies, Lane and the colonists all left with Drake. "Two ships passing in the night," Drake and Grenville literally passed each other in the North Atlantic fog.

Barely a month after Lane and his men had left, Grenville arrived back in the Americas with fresh supplies. After learning of the departure of his colonists, he left only 15 men to stay on Roanoke Island and stake Elizabeth's claim, then returned to England, with most of his men and supplies still on board.

Upon his arrival in England, Lane was hailed a hero for his treatment of the Indians. No one thought his actions were unjust, because he was dealing with people they considered to be savages. It was an argument that murderers would subsequently use over and over again to explain their crimes in the New World. Only the definition of a savage would change from era to era. (Americans in the 19th century looked at the Irish as savages; the Ku Klux Klan in the 19th, 20th, and 21st century labeled blacks, Jews, and Catholics as savages.) The murders Ralph Lane and his men committed had set the precedent for many more to come.

As for the second Roanoke colony, it disappeared. When Grenville came back to reprovision it, it was gone. There were no signs of a struggle, no signs of survivors. The second Roanoke colony had been wiped off the map of memory.

Crime in America had begun in the grand, age-old style of murder.

See also MONTANA (1876).

Jamestown, Virginia (1607) the colonies' first kidnapping

Twenty-one years after he first sent his expedition to the New World, Sir Walter Raleigh found himself a prisoner in the Tower of London. It must have hurt Raleigh to learn that while he languished helplessly in jail, the even more dashing Captain John Smith had accomplished what he could not and established a beachhead in an area that today is called Jamestown, Virginia. It was here that a bright 12-year-old Indian girl named Pocahontas befriended Smith, commander of the settlement.

Pocahontas was an Indian princess, born in 1595. Her father was Powhatan, the powerful chief of the Algonquin tribe in Virginia's Tidewater region. Years after their first meeting, Smith described her as "a child of tenne yeares old, which not only for feature, countenance, and proportion much exceedeth any of the rest of his (Powhatan's) people, but for wit and spirit (is) the only non-pareil of his countrie."

Though lively commercial relations were established, the Virginia settlers with their superior ways, alienated their hosts. As political relations worsened, the two sides continued to engage in the mutually beneficial trading of goods. But by 1609, when John Smith was injured in a gunpowder explosion and had to return to England for proper treatment, relations between the Indians and Europeans were openly hostile.

Pocahontas found herself at wit's end. She had come to love visiting Smith at the settlement but now that pleasure was denied her. The colonists told her Smith had been killed, and so their relationship ended.

In 1610 Pocahontas married an Indian named Kocoum and went with him to live in the Potomac country, where she could lead an anonymous existence among her people. She never suspected that she was about to become America's first kidnapping victim. An enterprising member of the beleaguered

Artist's rendering of Sir Walter Raleigh, the man responsible for the white settlement of America (Library of Congress)

Jamestown settlement, Captain Samuel Argall, discovered where she was and devised a plan to kidnap and hold her for ransom. Using another Indian tribe as a go-between, Argall tricked Pocahontas into boarding his ship, where he told her she had been kidnapped and would not be allowed to leave.

Word was quickly passed to Chief Powhatan that the settlers were holding his daughter as their captive and demanding as ransom Powhatan's English prisoners, the guns the Indians had stolen from the settlers, and some corn. Powhatan sent part of the ransom immediately and asked that his daughter be treated well. But he never delivered the rest of it, so Pocahontas stayed a prisoner.

While held in Jamestown, she met and fell in love with a planter named John Rolfe. They planned to marry but were separated when Pocahontas was moved to the settlement of Enrico, which was under the leadership of Sir Thomas Dale.

Dale grew tired of Powhatan's procrastination. Accompanied by the hostage Pocahontas and 150 armed men, he marched into Powhatan's camp, confronted the chief, and he demanded the balance of the ransom. The chief replied by ordering his men to open fire with the weapons they had stolen from the settlers.

With their superior firepower, the Englishmen fought back with ferocity and quickly gained the upper hand. They burned Indian villages and killed Indian braves, but ultimately Pocahontas was set free in order to bring about peace. Returning to her village, she told her father that the English had kept her well—so well, in fact, that she had fallen in love with one of them and wanted to marry him. An astute politician, Powhatan realized that such a marriage would bring peace to the region and readily granted his daughter permission. Ironically, America's first kidnapping victim married the man who later would help make slavery the vital economic heart of the South. In 1612 John Rolfe came up with the idea that saved struggling Jamestown and ultimately led to the successful settlement of Virginia: Use slave labor to farm a crop of tobacco on plantations.

Tobacco had become a popular luxury among Europeans, but tobacco plants require a special kind of climate to grow, one nonexistent in Europe. However, tobacco thrived in the mild Virginia climate, and John Rolfe's plantations succeeded in saving the Virginia colony and laying the foundation for what became the southern United States. Ironically, in the late 20th century, some cigarette manufacturers, the virtual descendants of those first tobacco growers,

An early rendering of the myth that Pocahontas saved John Smith's life (Library of Congress)

would eventually admit to participating in a criminal conspiracy to make tobacco products addictive.

Virginia (1622) the colonies' first death sentence

The first execution in the American colonies took place in the colony of Virginia in 1622. Daniel Frank was found guilty of burglary and sentenced to death. The Virginian colonists executed him by hanging Frank "by the neck until he was dead." In those days, a death sentence meant swift execution. There was no delay after sentencing with lengthy appeals.

That burglary, considered a minor felony today, was then punishable by death only serves to show how isolated the colonists were. Though there were "gaols," there were no such things as prisons for long-term incarceration, and the idea that a criminal could be reformed was centuries away. The colonists could simply not tolerate any deviance within their society. Living in the wilderness of America was a matter of sheer survival. The only way in was by ship. The only way out was by ship. There were only rough-hewn roads north and south. If someone disobeyed the colonial laws, who knew if they might not do it again, only next time worse? Daniel Frank had to die to maintain order. Arguments about the death penalty would have to wait for another century.

TWO
1650-1700

Introduction

It was an uncertain time for the future republic. Europeans established a beachhead on the eastern coast of North America and were gazing upon the virgin wilderness. Along with their natural fondness for all things new, the intrepid settlers brought with them morals and a justice system often barbaric by modern standards.

Many criminal offenses were resolved by a quick trial, if the defendant got one at all, and often followed by a quick death. Burglary, highway robbery, rape, and murder were all capital offenses punishable by hanging. Lesser crimes merited the pillory, branding, and tar-and-feathering. Distinctions between sanity and insanity did not exist, and mitigating factors such as mental retardation or youth were given no consideration. The harsh code of justice stretched to the stifling of dissent. Religious or political, those who went against the majority were often beaten down and sometimes paid the ultimate price for their personal beliefs.

Massachusetts (1660) religious repression

The mere fact Massachusetts was a bay colony meant that it was a trading ground for ideas delivered through merchants and travelers coming and going from the colonies. Whether they traveled the waves from Europe or traversed a series of rough roads cut by muscle and steel through the virginal mountains and forests of the colonies, travelers converged on Boston to make money. Banking, shipping, provisioning, all the comforts of commerce were in the city that would help to define the soul of a nation.

The colony was run by a theocracy that brooked no questioning of its divinely inspired mission to spread the word of God. Its leaders were the Puritans who had landed at Plymouth Rock in 1607 and whose faith remained the colony's controlling religion into the middle of the century.

The Puritans saw themselves as guardians of a strictly defined religious doctrine that expressed the true spirit of Christianity. Two members of the Society of Friends (also called Quakers), Ann Hutchinson and Roger Williams, publicly questioned them, and the Puritans responded by banishing them from the colony and into the wilderness. This was no small matter.

The only city south of Boston was New York, 250 miles away. Everything in between was wilderness, most of it controlled by Indian tribes. The colonies of Connecticut and Rhode Island had not yet been founded. Williams settled in a place that would eventually become the Rhode Island colony. Hutchinson would drifted farther south and found the colony of Connecticut. Both colonies, of course, would become founding members of the Republic. How ironic, then that they should have been born from religious intolerance.

Williams and Hutchinson were the lucky ones. Some of their Quaker brothers and sisters met grimmer fates. One such man was William Ledra, the last person executed in America by the government purely for his religious beliefs.

The Puritans had executed several members of the Society of Friends who refused to leave the colony or conform to established Congregational practice. But records of the Court of Assistants from this period disappeared in the 18th century, leaving only documentation of Ledra's trial and sentence. The document of Ledra's death sentence, dated March 5, 1660, contains a transcription of the verbal exchange between the prisoner and his prosecutors. It showed Ledra to be a persuasive champion of freedom of conscience in a world that did not yet respect that idea.

The document, a copy, was apparently made in 1716 and is entirely in the hand of Elisha Cook (1678–1737), an important leader in the movement to increase popular control over the institutions of colonial government. This is the only documentation that still exists of Ledra's trial and sentence.

[Ledra] sayd I know your Ministers are deluders & yourselves Murderers as you are, let all this Company say I have turned from God which is Salvation of his People & this I will seal with my blood.

It was told him he might save his life & be at libertie if he would. He Answered I am willing to dy for it, saying he spake the truth.

It was sayd do you believe the Scriptures to be Gods Word. How dare you then Revile Magistrates and Ministers. He sayd it is not Reviling to Speak the truth. You are Such as I affirm you to be. Was it not the Spirit of Christ beated in Stephen when he told the People they were Murtherers? He was bid prove himself to be such as an one as Stephen. He sayd We must go where the Lord draws us.

Shortly after this exchange, Ledra was led to the gallows. In the full view of those in Massachusetts Bay Colony who chose to attend, the hangman sprung the trap and Ledra's feet dangled out into space and eternity. The execution fueled tension mounting within the colony.

It was only a matter of time before frontiersmen would be setting off south for New York on a regular basis. Their travels into the wilderness allowed the country to grow and ideas to spread. Religious tyranny would eventually be defeated. But until it was, there were those criminals who would take advantage of the social situation.

New Jersey (1691) murder

William Bradford was a printer who set up shop in Salem, New Jersey. He began a pamphlet that chronicled a major murder case in the colony of "West Jarsey" in this way: "Blood will out, or An example of justice in the trial, condemnation, confession and execution of Thomas Lutherland, who barbarously murthered the body of John Clark of Philadelphia and was executed at Salem in West Jarsey the 23d of February 1691/2."

The story of the Clark murder case is as much a story of the settling of the colony of New Jersey as a tale of violence, and it begins in the early part of the 17th century.

Interior waterways allowed colonists to settle in what would become the powerful northeastern cities. No river in the East helped out more in this capacity than the Delaware. Running from Hancock in northern Pennsylvania, it skirts the New York State southern border until, at Port Jervis, New York, it cuts south through the heart of New Jersey, defining its border with Pennsylvania on the western bank. Sailing down the Delaware's waters in flatboats, the colonists came, some religious refugees from New England, some businessmen from New York seeking further wealth, some just farmers looking for fertile land.

The history of New Jersey goes back to Dutch claims to the Hudson and Delaware Valleys based on the voyages of Henry Hudson, who sailed into Newark Bay in 1609, as well as the subsequent explorations of the lower Delaware by Cornelis Jacobsen in May 1614. The Dutch West India Company then offered patroonships for settlement. Subsequently, small colonies were established in Hoboken, Jersey City, and Gloucester City.

By 1664 the New Yorkers across the bay in the Dutch land grant of New Netherland found themselves under new "sponsorship" when Richard Nicholls, acting for James, Duke of Berkeley—later James II—seized New Netherland. Suddenly, the colonists had new masters. Moving swiftly to annex the rest of the Dutch claim to the New World, James granted proprietorship of the land west of the Hudson, what today is New Jersey, to Lord John Berkeley and Sir George Carteret.

Carteret and Berkeley encouraged settlement. They gave out free land grants and provided the framework for an appointed council and an elected assembly. Unfortunately, the original grants to Carteret and Berkeley that had divided the future state between the two men was not properly defined, which led to confused land titles, crooked business transactions, and changes in authority. The Wintipartite Deed of 1676 clarified the split. Under the deed, the province was defined into East and West Jersey, or "Jarsay" as it was spelled at that time.

In West Jersey the Berkeley interest was sold in 1674 to John Fenwick, who was serving as agent for Edward Byllynge. The following year, Fenwick and other Quakers founded a settlement at Salem. Like its more famous New England cousin, Salem is a town on the water, the Delaware River south of Philadelphia. Across the banks of the river lay the colony of Delaware.

Not three years went by before Fenwick found himself in financial difficulties. He had overextended himself. In 1677 William Penn of Pennsylvania and Quakers under his aegis purchased Fenwick's rights in West Jersey, with the exception of Salem, which remained under Fenwick's economic control. The colonists at Salem followed the laws of England, which promised a trial by jury to anyone accused of a crime—which all leads back to Thomas Lutherland and John Clark.

On February 16 and 17, 1691, John Worlidge presided over a three-judge panel and a jury of Lutherland's peers. Worlidge read the indictment. Taking it all down was reporter William Bradford, who would later publish a pamphlet, distributed throughout the colony, chronicling the proceedings.

The indictment alleged that on November 12, 1690, Lutherland, formerly of Pennsylvania, "wickedly, maliciously, feloniously entered the boat of John Clark, then residing near Salem Landing. He broke open and took away the goods of said John Clark to the full value of 15 pounds, 8 shillings and 11 pence." Then he murdered Clark.

The prisoner Lutherland was standing at the bar when Justice Worlidge asked him for his plea. He replied that he was guilty of the robbery but innocent of the murder. The trial then commenced with an account of the crime: "In the beginning of November last, John Clark, late of the city of Philadelphia, was trading at Salem with several forts of goods. Upon the 12th day of the said month, his boat was found on shore at Sandy Point near the mouth of Salem Creek."

The ship was secured and the justices and sheriff began to investigate what had happened. At the scene where the boat was found, "were several persons that were with John Clark the day before in his boat."

The supposition was that Clark was murdered for his goods. Based on Lutherland's reputation, "he was a person conversant in English, at sea and at Philadelphia, and being of evil name and fame in Salem." The court issued a search warrant. The constable went to Thomas Lutherland's house and, in executing the warrant, "found the late John Clark's goods." Lutherland, who was not home at the time, was captured a short time later.

When the constable asked him how he got the goods, he replied, "I bought the goods of John Clark the same night he went away from Salem Land and they cost me 1 pound, 55. I paid him all but 35 shillings that I owe him full and he gave me credit for so much in his book."

Despite Lutherland's insistence, no credit could be found for him in any of six books recovered from

Clark's possession. Still Lutherland went on to testify that "in the morning before the day I was at Salem's Landing to buy some tape when I came there to John Clark's boat, he was gone."

So concerned was Lutherland in giving Clark the 35 shillings he owed him that, "[t]hinking to overtake the boat, I did see it at Sandy point. Then I took a canoe from Widhma Land and went to the boat where I found nobody. Then I went into the boat, took the goods and brought them on shore and came to my own house. By that time, the sun was half an hour high in the morning."

The court then called his wife, Mary Lutherland, to the stand. The right of a spouse to refuse to testify against a spouse would become law in all 50 states many years hence, but in 1691, if Mary Lutherland did not testify, she herself would have been subject to criminal charges and penalties. She had no choice.

"My husband went from home in the evening and came not until almost morning then he came to bed and lay until the usual time that he used to go to work," Mary Lutherland testified.

William Bradford wrote that Lutherland could not account for his time, "whereupon he was committed to prison from hence he made his escape but the Sheriff soon recaptured him." Bradford then recounts the crime and its investigation. His account reads like the tough prose of a modern police beat reporter, except it was written 350 years ago:

On January 11, 1691, at 2 in the afternoon, the body of John Clark was found near Windham Landing. The Coroner impaneled an inquest who upon viewing the Corpse and diligently searching the same, they found his neck was very limber and much shriveled upon the skin and seemed more blew than other parts of his body.

After Lutherland was taken into custody, "they sent for the prisoner. When he was brought, he was bid to touch the corpse, which he did do, and wished most execrable wishes that God would send some sudden judgment upon him if ever he murdered John Clark, saying if he had murdered him, he would bleed fresh."

Again, Lutherland was asked how he came by the aforementioned goods. He told a story about his wife wanting some bitters, a medicinal substance at the time. Yet he could produce no corroboration from witnesses that he had actually taken a canoe out to the boat where Clark was. The case then went to trial, and the prosecutor reviewed the facts as established by the crown: "I am fully satisfied the prisoner

deserves to die. And it is a special rule of justice to condemn one that is accustomed to wickedness."

Presaging future "three strikes" laws that would put repeat offenders in jail for life if they were convicted of three felonies, the prosecutor was saying that the prisoner's past should be held against him at sentencing.

"If this wickedness should escape with impunity, it will be hazardous for a single person to travel the land or by water, especially in the night," claimed the prosecution.

Lutherland was then asked to formally plead. He responded, "I am guilty of the felony but not of the murder."

The jury then went out to consider its verdict. The court adjourned until 8 A.M., February 17, 1671. When it reconvened, they jury delivered the verdict:

"Guilty." And so the jury said all, one by one distinctly. A case of this nature never happening in this part of the country before, the court was very cautious in passing sentence of death. Whereupon the Grand Inquest, the Jury of Life and Death and the Coroner's Inquest and the most part of the country present a petition to 'pass sentence of death' on the said Lutherland according to law and government order for the execution thereof.

On the fifth day of the week after his condemnation, the prisoner sent for the High Sheriff, confessed to him that he had murdered John Clark, and said he would make an open confession at the place of execution. The next morning, February 23, the prisoner sent for the clerk to take his confession in writing.

In it, Lutherland said: "I have been a great sinner and have continued in my sins until the 40th year of my age. I was convicted of felony in England for which I was transported into Pennsylvania."

Lutherland's "punishment," becoming a settler in the colony of Pennsylvania, could have been viewed as luck because the colony that William Penn had established was a place where religious freedom was guaranteed to everyone, slavery was discouraged, and even a humane penal code was established. Instead, Lutherland used his transportation to America as a license to steal.

Once in Pennsylvania, he wrote, "I consented to the stealing of several parcels of foods in shipboard which is the same as doing the fact. In Pennsylvania, I was convicted of several thefts but could take no warning by all this."

He then went on to talk of the murder of John Clark: "When I touched the murdered corps of John

Clark, I was afraid the blood would have flown in my face. Pray take heed young and old, this hard heart of mine is the greatest enemy I have."

He decided to rob Clark knowing that he "could not take away the goods without killing the man."

On the pretense that he had some goods to sell, he arrived at Clark's boat and Clark congenially invited him into his cabin to warm up. What Lutherland was actually doing was casing the place, planning his robbery and murder.

Later that same evening, he went back to the boat, his collar turned up and his hat pulled low on his forehead so he would not be recognized so easily. Lutherland duped Clark into believing he was a traveler seeking passage to New Castle. Clark offered to take him for a fee, but Lutherland leapt onto the boat and overpowered Clark. He wound a rope around Clark's neck and proceeded to choke him.

Lutherland's account of the killing is bloodless and unemotional. When a person is strangled, the victim does not die instantly. Most likely, Clark was conscious for at least a minute and a half, knowing he was being strangled. When he finally sagged, due to his brain being deprived of oxygen, he would still not have been dead. Had Lutherland stopped strangling him, he would have eventually revived. Instead, Lutherland kept pulling the rope until he heard the hyoid, or throat bone, crack. At that point, Clark would have been dead.

Lutherland took the keys "out of Clark's pocket, unlocked his goods and put them into a sack" that he had brought. Just then, some of Clark's friends, including a man named William Benton, arrived at the dock outside.

They called for Clark, so Lutherland lay down in the waste of the boat and covered himself with some sacks. When the men left, he removed the goods into George Hazelwood's sloop and rowed Clark's boat down to Wyndham. He hauled Clark's body overboard but could not make him sink, so he jumped on shore, left the boat, returned to the sloop, removed the goods, and hid them in a haystack. Two to three days later, he removed them into his open haycart and afterward, brought them into his home, where they were found by the authorities.

Lutherland also confessed to bigamy. He had a wife and child in England and yet he had married his current wife in Pennsylvania.

Not long after the clerk had taken his confession, he was carried in a cart to his place of execution.

Guarding him were the sheriff and his deputies. As he was carried, he made a repetition of his confession and warned those present to keep the Sabbath and be dutiful to their parents and thus avoid his fate.

When he reached the scaffold, he was given time to pray.

"I desire all there present to join with me in prayer," he announced.

And so the condemned man prayed with the people who had condemned him. Fifteen minutes later, the cart was positioned under a tree from which the hangman's noose had already been suspended. The executioner put the rope around his neck.

"I forgive you," he said to the black-masked executioner.

The cart moved away and Lutherland's neck snapped.

Salem, Massachusetts (1692) the Salem witch hunt murders

Since its founding 85 years before, Massachusetts had shown itself to be resistant to new religious ideas. Imagine then, what would happen if these same insular people encountered what they believed was the supernatural.

Much has been written about the Salem witch trials, most of it unreliable. Apologists have presented all kinds of sociological and psychological reasons to explain the actions that led to the Salem Witch Trials, but it is more useful to go back to the facts and see the witch trials for what they were.

Samuel Parris was the pastor of Salem Village. During the cold winter of 1691–92, strange things began happening in Parris's home.

Parris had a West Indian slave named Tituba. Tituba performed magic tricks for Parris's daughter, niece, and "an ever widening circle of curious friends," but Tituba's magic had "a curious effect" on some of the young girls: They began to act irrationally. A local physician was called for assistance, and he diagnosed the girls as bewitched. That made it a matter for the church.

The girls were intensely questioned by the town's clerics. When asked who had bewitched them, they accused Tituba "and two derelict women in the community." The three were arrested on February 29, 1692, and examined the next day. Tituba informed on the other two.

Historian Charles Upham described the three judges at this examination as "the two leading

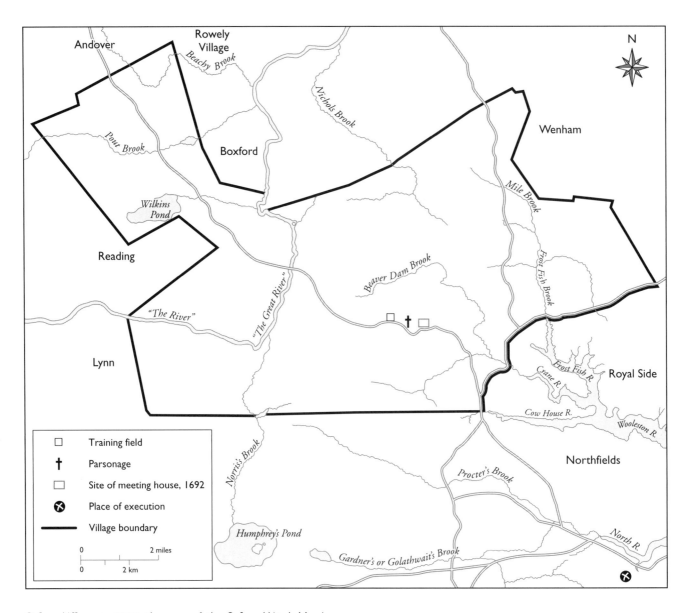

Salem Village in 1692, the year of the Salem Witch Murders

magistrates of the neighborhood, men of great note and influence, whose fathers had been among the chief founders of the settlement, and who were Assistants, that is, members of the highest legislative and judicial body in the colony, John Hathorne and Jonathan Corwin."

Three months went by, during which many women and a few men were accused of witchcraft. Thus was convened "A Special Court of Oyer and Terminer" in May, appointed by the governor of the colony to try the defendants.

The first of what would come to be known as the Salem Witch Trials took place June 2, 1692. The defendant, Bridget Bishop, was found guilty of witchcraft and hanged on June 10 at Gallows Hill. Three mass executions followed on July 19, August 19, and September 22; a total of 18 people were hanged under the charge of performing witchcraft. One defendant, Giles Cory, who refused to speak at all during his trial, was pressed to death under the weight of the heavy rocks used to extract his confession. Two others died "due to unfavorable prison conditions."

A total of 20 people lost their lives as a result of the state-sponsored Salem witch trials. In the following years, those responsible for the prosecutions began to reconsider their actions. One apologized, saying: "We walked in clouds and could not see our way."

The law of attainder in the colony at the time declared a condemned person already legally dead and therefore not worthy of any civil rights. The "witches" and their heirs tried, therefore, to destroy all written proof of the whole affair, but at least one document remained. That document, in the Medler Collection, is a warrant for the arrest of two of those accused of witchcraft. Specifically addressed to the sheriff of Essex County, July 28, 1692, it calls for the arrest of Mary Green and Hanah Bromage (Brumidge) both of Haverhill, for witchcraft, and is countersigned by Constable William Sterling.

The transcription is as follows:

[To the] Sherriff of Essex or his dep't. or [Con]stable in Haverhill

You are theire Majes's names herreby Required to apprehend and forthwith or as soon as may be bring before us Mary Green ye wife of Peter Green of Haverhill weaver and Hanah Bromage the wife of Edward Bromage of Haverhill husbandman who both stand charged on behalfe of theire Majes's with heaving committed sundry acts of Witchcraft on the Bodys of Timothy Swan of Mary Walcott Ann Putnam &c whereby great hurt hath been donne them, In order to theire, examination Relateing to the above s'd premise fale not. Date Salem the 28th 1692

Barth'o Gedney
John Hathorne
Jonathan Corwin
John Higginson

By virtue of this warrant I have seased Hanah Brumidge and Mary Green the persons mentioned by me.
William Sterling, Constable.

Green and Bromage were among the 18 executed for witchcraft. No one in the colonies, or the United States, would ever again be legally murdered by the state for their religious beliefs, but the Salem witch trials, alongside the hanging of William Ledra and the other Quakers, remain an indelible black mark on the burgeoning society.

THREE
1700-1750

Introduction

West of the colonies that hugged the eastern coast of the New World, present-day Tennessee and Kentucky represented an unexplored frontier for white settlers in the early 18th century. How far the continent stretched west or what was out there, no frontiersman knew. It was within this New World that criminals found a place to flourish.

Some of the earliest writing about crime in pre-colonial America details the development of the criminal personality in almost direct correlation to the expansion of the country. Looked at from the perspective of more than three centuries of criminal history, it is clear that the farther the nation expanded, the more crime seized hold of society.

By the end of the 17th century, piracy was easily the most profitable crime in the New World. Pirates in command of ships that rivaled those of any navy plundered ships throughout the Caribbean. North Carolina, because of its shallow inlets and sounds, became a haven for many of these pirates. According to the Museum of North Carolina, "Restrictive laws passed by the British Parliament had made smuggling acceptable and even desirable in North Carolina and other American colonies. Preying upon lightly armed merchant ships, the pirates seized their contents and sometimes killed those who resisted."

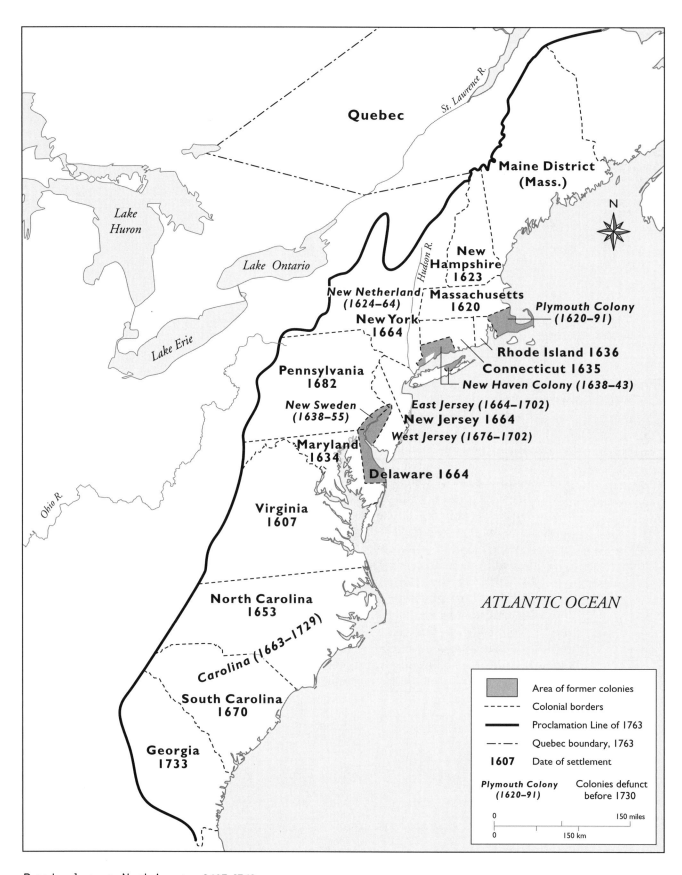

Quebec

St. Lawrence R.

Lake Huron

Lake Ontario

Lake Erie

Maine District (Mass.)

N

New Hampshire 1623

New Netherland (1624–64)

New York 1664

Hudson R.

Massachusetts 1620

Plymouth Colony (1620–91)

Rhode Island 1636
Connecticut 1635

New Haven Colony (1638–43)

Pennsylvania 1682

New Sweden (1638–55)

East Jersey (1664–1702)
New Jersey 1664
West Jersey (1676–1702)

Maryland 1634

Delaware 1664

Ohio R.

Virginia 1607

North Carolina 1653

Carolina (1663–1729)

South Carolina 1670

Georgia 1733

ATLANTIC OCEAN

▨	Area of former colonies
- - -	Colonial borders
▬▬	Proclamation Line of 1763
—·—·—	Quebec boundary, 1763
1607	Date of settlement
Plymouth Colony (1620–91)	Colonies defunct before 1730

0   150 miles
0   150 km

British colonies in North America, 1607–1763

Natchez Trace, Mississippi Territory (1701) early merchant trail

The Natchez Trace began as a series of Indian trails through the present states of Kentucky, Tennessee, and Mississippi. In the early 18th century, they began to be used extensively by the French, English, and Spanish, all of whom had designs on colonizing the continent. Frontiersmen could float their goods down the Ohio and Mississippi Rivers, sell them in New Orleans, then trek home north on the trace from Natchez to Nashville.

Of course, travelers with heavy purses were an ideal target for highwaymen, a few of whom began to haunt the trace in search of ill-gotten gain. But it would not be until the later part of the century that the era of the highwayman, celebrated in song and story, would come into full bloom.

See also JOSEPH HARE; SAMUEL "BLOODY SAM" MASON; THE WESTERN FRONTIER.

Edward Teach, a.k.a. Edward Thatch (d. 1718) Blackbeard the Pirate

Blackbeard the Pirate was the first quintessentially American criminal to command the fear of the American public. His origins are murky. Historians are not certain if he was born in England, Jamaica, Philadelphia, or elsewhere. What is known for certain is that he emerged as a pirate around 1713, under the name Edward Teach or Edward Thatch. Serving as a crewman under the command of Benjamin Hornigold, by 1716 he so distinguished himself in battle that his captain gave him command of a captured ship. By June 1717 Teach and Hornigold sailing together inspired fear throughout the Caribbean.

In November 1717 the two pirates captured a French 26-gun ship loaded with riches from the Caribbean. In response, the British offered Hornigold amnesty to stop his criminal activities. He accepted, but Teach rejected the offer. Instead, he took the French ship, fitted it with 14 more guns for a total of 40 and renamed it *Queen Anne's Revenge*.

Throughout winter 1717–18, Teach sailed the seas. His cutlass and pistols and, most of all, his big guns brought him four more vessels and untold riches until, in spring 1718, he made his fatal error of sailing up the American coastline.

By that time, Teach's fame as Blackbeard the Pirate had preceded him. His criminal alias came from the black beard that covered his face, which he cleverly braided with gunpowder-laced wicks that he

would light in battle. The flashing light from his beard, his crimson coat, cutlasses in each hand, bandoliers stuffed with pistols, and knives across his chest all added to his general appearance as a man as wicked as they come.

Much like successful gunfighters who would come on the scene in the 19th century, Teach relied on his reputation and appearance to avoid taking life. If his victims surrendered, he would often let them escape with their lives. Resistance meant battle. Survival meant being marooned on some Caribbean atoll, the worst thing for a sailor.

Blackbeard's career was sailing to its end when, along with four ships and 300 pirates, he blockaded the port of Charlotte, North Carolina, in May 1718. Just one week later, he lost the *Queen Anne's Revenge* when it ran aground in Beaufort Inlet, then called Topsail Inlet. Another of Blackbeard's ships, the 10-gun sloop *Adventure*, was lost in trying to come to the *Queen Anne's* assistance.

Before sailing away on one of his last remaining ships, Blackbeard marooned 25 pirate acolytes who were dissatisfied with his rule. Whether Blackbeard and any of his other pirate associates actually buried treasure during these activities on American soil is questionable, since none has ever been found.

Later in 1718 Blackbeard showed up in Bath, which was then the colony's capital, where the pirate was granted a pardon by Governor Charles Eden. Like most pirates, though, Blackbeard got greedy. He knew that he was pardoned for old sins, not new ones, yet he continued his privateering ways into Virginia's waters. Virginia's governor Alexander Spottswood sent the Royal Navy after him.

During the battle at Ocracoke Inlet on November 22, 1718, Blackbeard was killed, but it took the British a lot of effort to accomplish it. Reportedly, he was shot five times and run through with a sword 20 times before he went down. Blackbeard had captured more than 40 ships during his piratical career, and his death represented the end of an era in the history of piracy in the New World.

Cave-in-Rock, Illinois (1729) sinister landmark

Located in southern Illinois near the border with Kentucky, it is a natural limestone formation that centuries of erosion have made into a 55-foot-wide, deep, dark cave that overlooks the Ohio River.

In 1729 French explorer M. De Lery encountered the formation and called it *caverne dans le roc*. For some, it became a natural wonder to visit while passing through the country. But others had darker purposes in mind for its beauty. More than one passing brigand noted how secure the place seemed, sitting atop its high bluffs overlooking the river where it turned south. The question was, how could it be exploited for criminal potential?

That question remained unresolved for the better part of the 18th century. In fact, it would take another 68 years before a veteran of the Revolutionary War, Samuel Mason, would name the place in the English language and subsequently use it to further his nefarious criminal enterprises.

See also BIG HARP; LITTLE HARP; SAMUEL "BLOODY SAM" MASON.

Daniel Boone (1734–1820) pioneer and frontiersman

With a road being cut out of the wilderness allowing highwaymen to ply their trade and a wonderful hideout provided by the uncharted land, the only thing left was for the thieves and murderers to make their way into the new country. The story of how crime spread beyond the original 13 colonies really begins with Daniel Boone.

Boone was born near Reading, Pennsylvania, in 1734 to a family of English Quakers. They left the colony in 1750, when Daniel was 16 years old, and settled in the Yadkin Valley of North Carolina. Boone became a frontiersman, serving with various military expeditions to Fort Duquesne in Pittsburgh. He thought about moving to Florida, but his wife, Rebecca Bryan, whom he married in 1755, refused to go there. Instead, the peripatetic Boone decided to push out west and south.

It was Boone who found the path, known to every schoolchild as the Cumberland Gap, through the mountains of Tennessee and into Kentucky. Boone blazed his trail on the boulders and trees he passed, putting his sign on them for those who would come after. The country he found is described in Robert Coates's book *The Outlaw Years* as follows:

He found it netted with buffalo paths, hunting trails— the Tennessee Path, the Bison Street, the Warrior's Path—which the roaming [Indians] from time immemorial, had been weaving through the forest. Boone went zigzagging through the maze. He blazed fording-places at the rivers, felled trees to make "raccoon bridges," across the creeks: thousands of other men, abandoning the comfortable prosperous East, came groping westward after him.

By 1771 Boone had explored the Kentucky region entirely. It was time to colonize. Like Ralph Lane before him, he considered the Indians to be savages not worthy of survival. Boone battled them in 1773 to establish his colony but was repulsed. Undaunted, Boone came back for more. This time, he won.

With a band of 30 armed men, acting as advance agent for Richard Henderson and the Transylvania Company, Boone fought the Indians back and blazed Boone's Trace through Kentucky, the path followed by most of the brave settlers who came after him. It led upward through Virginia's Great Smoky Mountains, down along the Wautaga River, then across to its juncture with the Clinch River. Here, the path forked.

One branch went south to Knoxville and then westward through Tennessee. The second fork went sharply northward, climbing through the Cumberland Gap, descending into Kentucky and curving west and south again. It was this trail that became known as the Wilderness Road.

The two forks met at Nashville, which by the late 17th century had already become what Coates describes as "the metropolis of the middle valley, with a population of about 1,000 inhabitants, all commodiously housed in cabins 'built of cedar logs with stone or mud chimneys.' With a post-office and a general store run by Larder Clark, Esq., Merchant and Ordinary Keeper."

The metropolis of Nashville had what one contemporary account said were "more wheeled vehicles than any other frontier town." The town's founder, Timote DeMonbreun, an old French Canadian trader, could be seen in the public square wearing keen breeches with silver belt buckles and "even to the end he favored the old time clothes."

Life on the frontier was dangerous. Between hostile Indians and the wilderness, many, many people died violent deaths. Life expectancy was very limited. And yet, showing the rootlessness that would characterize the American consciousness for centuries, the settlers continued to come in. As they did, the danger from the Indians diminished. By sheer force of numbers, they would eventually be defeated and forced to give up their land.

That very large tide of immigration also brought crime to the wilderness. The Ohio River cut through the forests that the settlers felled and flowed south, emptying into the Mississippi, which flowed further south to Natchez, Mississippi and finally the crowded port of New Orleans. The river was used to transfer goods from farms to settlements where they were sold if they reached the settlements. For with the immigrations came not just law abiding folk but criminals who would prey upon them. Farmers and merchants who survived the river pirates would sell their goods in New Orleans. Then, taking their money, they would ride home on horseback on the Natchez Trace.

With the increasing settlement in Ohio, Kentucky, Tennessee, and Mississippi, the time was now ripe for the highwaymen to reap the greatest gains in their brief history. But even as their primacy among the criminal underworld came into full bloom, murder was on the minds of the colonists back east.

PART TWO

THE REVOLUTIONARY PERIOD

FOUR
1750–1800

Introduction

The latter half of the 18th century was a crucial period in the development of crime. For the first time, reports appeared of children murdering children, executions of children for crimes, and infanticide. The first known case of serial murder inspired fear across the American frontier, and in the everyday criminal world, the daring highwayman held sway. The Revolutionary War provided the early training for one of the century's most notorious highwaymen, Samuel Mason. As the century drew to a close, criminals became proficient with all manner of modern firearms, including flintlocks and pistols.

Patterns that would later be repeated began to form, of criminals preceding emigration and then preying upon unsuspecting pilgrims. These are the stories of the criminals themselves who, upon the day of their impending execution, told their life stories to the clergymen and others who had come to offer them succor before their sentence was carried out.

Connecticut (1780) the confession of Barnett Davenport

A brief narrative of the life and confession of Barnett Davenport: under sentence of death for a series of the most horrid murders ever perpetrated in this country, or perhaps any other, on the evening following the 3d of February 1780: is to be executed at Litchfield [Connecticut]. On the 8th of May.

Barnett Davenport's story is one of the more interesting in the annals of American criminal justice because it provides a window into life in colonial Connecticut, where Davenport became the state's most infamous murderer. Here, then, is his dying confession.

As they tell me, I was born at New Milford [Connecticut] the 25th of October, 1760 and lived with my parents until I was about nine years of age. By this time, I was becoming quite an expert on using language. How early was the infernal dialect become habitual?

The next winter, my father bound me to Mr. John Stilwell, to live with him til I was of age. While I lived there, I once laid a plan to murder Mr. Stilwell. But my heart then failed me not being yet hardened to my horrid plan to perpetuate the shocking crime. It is a maxim as old as ancient Rome, that no man becomes a devil in a minute.

Davenport then stole Stilwell's horse. The following winter he enlisted for three years in Colonel Brewer's Massachusetts regiment.

I went to Ticonderoga and in March 1777, tarried there till the fort was evacuated. I retreated with our forces [from the British] and was at the Battle of Hobart when we retreated to Stilwater. Here, I one day became enraged at a soldier in my passion. I threw a club at him which missing him wounded an officer and I was punished.

When our Army after General Burgoyne's surrender came down to Albany, I was there visited with sore sickness, went home on a 12 day furlough and relapsed with a fever.

Davenport appears to have exited the army for good. The next spring, he showed up in Danbury, Connecticut, "where I stole hens, geese, and wine. From there, I went to Valley Forge and joined the Army but on the road, stole some sugar. I was at the Battle of Monmouth and remained with the Army until General Patterson's brigade came to

Woodbury the following October. Then I got a pass for one day to go see my brother and was then to rejoin the Army. But I never rejoined that Brigade again."

Instead, Davenport went to his brother and "on the road stole a pair of stockings. I lived in Cornwall and Canaan for the next four months. I was then hired by a man in Marbletown to go into the service for nine months [a common practice at the time] and went to Albany and joined Captain Bovit's company."

After nine months, the man who had hired him as a substitute to war refused to pay.

I tried to desert and get back to father. I was caught and brought back.

During the next year, I stole small items for fellow soldiers: shirts, cloth, and a frock coat. I finally was released and returned to Connecticut where I went to live at Caleb Mallory's. Just at the close of the month of January, 1780, about 5 or 6 days before my perpetuating the blackest crimes that evil mortals committed, I determined upon the murder of Mr. Mallory and his family at the first opportunity; and this merely for the sake of plundering his houses with the least provocation or prejudice against any of them.

The crime he was planning had eerie similarities to one that would be committed in 1959 by Perry Smith and Dick Hickok: the murder of the Clutter family in Kansas that became the basis for Truman Capote's classic *In Cold Blood*.

The family in which I now lived consisted of Mr. Mallory, Mrs. Mallory, a daughter-in-law, a daughter and 3 grandchildren. I was haunted and possessed with the thoughts of murder from the time of my first entertaining them both day and nite. Nor could I get rid of them even when I attempted to do it.

On the third of February, it was a nite big with uncommon horror. Mr. Mallory and his wife with one of the children went to bed in the same room, he lying on one bed and the other two on the other. Upon this, I took a piece of cloth and made me a knapsack and then went to plundering the daughter-in-law's room, searching for some hard money which I understood she had but could not find. After putting some things in my knapsack, I went into the room where Mr. Mallory, his wife and one grandchild lay asleep.

First, I smote him with my might once or twice on the head; upon this, Mrs. Mallory awakened and attempted to rile up; I turned and struck her 1 or 2

blows. Mr. Mallory then sprung up. I struck immediately at him but he partly warded off the blow with his arms and then struck the candle out of my hand. I then pushed him back and down upon the bed belabored him with the club.

He asked me, "Who are you? What did I mean? Why was I doing it for?" Then he called to his wife repeatedly to come and help him. Mrs. Mallory made no answer, only shrieks and cries and doleful lamentations.

Davenport was not finished. He hit Mallory so hard that the club split in half. Then he got a gun from behind the door and hit him with that. He turned and did the same to Mrs. Mallory.

She cried out bitterly. She called out for me by name. But I continued paying on, feeling no remorse at killing my aged patrons and benefactors. Finally, she lay still as well. The children, who were 7 years and 8 months old, woke at the screams and commotion. For the children, I seemed to feel some small relentings without remitting in the least my execrable exertions.

Davenport looked for the key to a chest that he thought contained money; he couldn't find it. Then Mrs. Mallory "gave a few terrible shrieks and then lay still fighting and groaning in the most affecting manner."

With remarkable strength, Mr. and Mrs. Mallory had not yet died. They were mortally wounded, so Davenport went to finish the job. He beat Mr. Mallory's head "to pieces. I smote her also and she tumbled behind the bed. Before this, I saw her face swollen to twice its common size, disfigured with wounds and covered with gore and streaming blood."

Searching the home further, Davenport found some paper currency and coin.

Then I put on some of the dying man's clothes and went into the room where the two grandchildren lay. They had woken up by the preceding blows or cries and asked for their clothes to get up. I told them to lay down and go to sleep for it was not morning. They cried and asked what was the matter with their grandmother? Then they lay down sobbing.

Davenport plundered the rest of the house and set the place on fire. He left for Blue Swamp, about eight miles away, and stayed from Friday morning to Wednesday afternoon. Before he left, he set his hideout on fire, hoping people would think he had died in the second fire. He recalled, "On Wednesday afternoon, I set off and went to Cornwall where I put up for the nite."

That very night, he was captured in his bed at the inn. He confessed, claiming he had an accomplice, then recanted his statement entirely. It was too late. After being jailed, he was arraigned on April 25 before the Superior Court of the State of Connecticut. He pleaded guilty to the indictment of murder. Two days later, on April 27, sentence of death was publicly pronounced. He wrote:

Upon the 8th of May next, I am to be executed. O that others may take warning by my dreadful example and fearful end! And avoid those sins which I have committed and which by a series of wickedness have led me to the most awful crimes that were ever perpetrated in this land and for which I must suffer a violent death and I greatly fear, everlasting burning horror and despair.

Barnett Davenport, Litchfield Gaol, this 29th day of April, Anno Domini, 1780

On May 8, 1780, Barnett Davenport was hanged by the neck until he was dead.

Connecticut (1786) youngest child ever executed

The story of Hannah Occulish presages by more than 200 years the modern day story of a British au pair charged with murdering an infant in her care in Massachusetts in 1996.

In 1786 Hannah Occulish, "a Mulatto girl aged 12 years and 9 months, was convicted of the murder of a child in her care, Eunice Bolles, 6 years and 6 months." Before Hannah was taken to the gallows, she was forced to sit through a sermon preached at New London, Connecticut, on December 20, 1786, by the Reverend Henry Channing.

"The beginning of an amiable disposition should be cultivated," the reverend admonished his parish. "Everything that favours of impropriety or a contempt of God and his service should not been so much as named among children."

Then he pointed to Hannah.

There behold, my young brethren, the fate of one who with a mind not below the common level, has been left untrained to the guidance of guilty passions and a corrupt heart.

Hannah, the time for you to die is come. Yes, poor girl, in about two hours, your eyes will be shut by death and you will not see the light of this sun again forever.

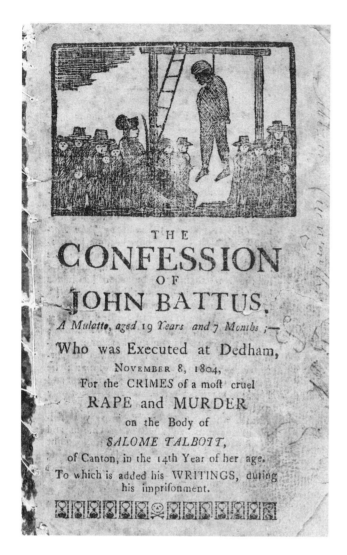

This woodcut illustrates the typical punishment for murder, which even young Hannah Occulish received. (Clements Library, University of Michigan)

This is the last time you will hear my voice from this place.

You are now going to be hanged until you are dead. O, Hannah! Repent of your wickedness. Be ashamed before God. Remember if he has mercy upon you, it will be from his own goodness, not from any good that he sees in you.

Poor girl! I must say no more. Farewell. God in his abundant goodness gives you repentance until life and have mercy on your soul. Amen and amen.

And with that, Hannah was taken to the gallows and hanged, proving that while Anne Hutchinson had founded a colony more moderate than Massachusetts

in its religious beliefs, in criminal matters it made no difference who committed murder. Adult and child alike would be put to death.

Pennsylvania (1786) infanticide

A faithful narrative of Elizabeth Wilson who was executed at Chester, January 3d, 1786; charged with the murder of her twin infants containing some account of her dying sayings with some serious reflections drawn up at the request of a friend unconnected with the deceased.

"Was found by a person crossing the fields in a piece of woods a little distance from the road leading from Brandywin to Turk's Head, two dead infants." So begins the sad story of Elizabeth Wilson, the first fully recorded narrative in Pennsylvania colony of a woman charged with murdering her own children. The account continues:

Upon inquiry and from concurring circumstances, there was reason to deduce they were Elizabeth Wilson's who some time before was delivered of two children not far from the place where they were found and who about 8 weeks before had left the house with the children having a design as she said of going to Philadelphia.

Wilson was arrested and, after a brief arraignment, sent to jail pending trial, which occurred on October 17, 1785. With Judge Atlee presiding before a jury, "Wilson denied her guilt and acted innocent," according to the unknown writer of the narrative. "She did not appear to be the kind of insensible hardened creature and did not expect to die for this crime."

Wilson did seem to have knowledge of what the court established was two counts of infanticide. Even after the jury convicted her on two counts of murder and sentenced her to death, she said nothing more about the crime other than that she knew nothing until she sent a note pleading with her brother to come and see her.

The brother arrived only to be thrown into his sister's web; Wilson tried to implicate him. The brother denied complicity and since there was no evidence to show he was involved, he was allowed to leave. The next day, before she was to be executed, two Baptist ministers visited her and she made the following confession. It oozes with religious piety typical of the time, but offers real details on the plight of an unmarried woman with children, forced into a criminal conspiracy.

From sixteen to 21 years of age, I had a rel. concern but thro' the subtly of Satan and the corruption of nature was led away to the foul sin of fornication wich I believe to be my predictable evil.

I had three children in an unlawful way before I fell into the wretched company of Joseph Deshong. At the time I fell in company with him, I lived in Philadelphia at the Sign of the Crossways, in Chestnut Street at the Corner of 3rd Street. He [Deshong] said he was single and he'd marry me.

That was good enough for Wilson, although she would soon learn the truth.

"In a short time after I proved with child, the two dear innocents for which I must shortly suffer an ignominious death," she remembered. Upon hearing of her pregnancy, Deshong disappeared. It was easy enough to just ride out of the city and into the countryside. Anyone who kept to the back roads would never be seen again.

After the twins were born, Wilson decided to find their father. Deshong had made the mistake of coming back to Philadelphia, figuring that Wilson would have grown tired of looking for him. But Wilson did find him at an inn and told him "of my deplorable situation." She threatened to go to the law if he did not help her financially, and he agreed.

Wilson asked Deshong for money for only one child, "one of the dear children I nursed," and he gave her some, then told her to meet him later, at a prearranged place in a secluded area, where he would give her more. Deshong met her instead "within two miles of the aforesaid Wilkinson's house where she was staying."

They went into the woods. Wilson remembered sitting on a rotten log "with both my children in my arms. He asked me if I would let him look at one of the children in order to see if it looked like him. He held it in his arms, asked me what I thought I would do with them?"

Wilson said it was his place "to accord and promise to do for them."

After a little pause, he placed "the dear infant on the ground and taking the other one out of arms, led it beside its dear little fellow sufferer."

"I have no money for you nor your bastards," he said.

He then requested me to take their dear lives which I would by no means consent to, but required him to let me have them and I would beg for them. He then arose up, put a pistol to my breast, forbid me to make any

noise, then he wickedly stamped on their dear little breasts upon which the dear infants gave a faint scream and expired.

He still kept the pistol at my breast forcing me to most solemnly vow that I would never disclose the dreadful act to which I through fear consented. He then required me to strip my dear, dead infants naked. I know I deserve not only death but hell.

Elizabeth's Wilson's confession fails to explain many things. It seems that Wilson sacrificed her children's lives out of fear for her own. For this reason the court, faced with no evidence to prove remorse, sentenced her to death.

Wilson's brother, holding no grudge that his sister had tried to implicate him, rode to Philadelphia. Using her confession, he hoped to get the appeals court to grant a stay or reprieve of sentence.

Back at Chester, she was led to the gallows, where she recited her confession. But "the execution was prolonged to give time for her brother's returned from Philadelphia." The executioner waited and, when the brother failed to arrive, he was given the go-ahead by the sheriff to proceed.

The moment before the execution, the sheriff asked her if she sealed her confession with her dying breath.

"I do, for it is the truth," Wilson replied.

"And in a moment, she was turned off and quickly left the world, we hope, for a better one. But here, we must drop a tear!" the unknown narrator of her story writes. "What heart so hard as not to melt at human woe!"

"Her brother came in all haste from Philadelphia with a respite or letter from the Honorary President and the Council to delay the execution, but through unexplained and unavoidable hindrances on the road, did not arrive until 23 minutes after the solemn scene was closed."

Once again, the frontier had encroached on events. Had the road been clear, Wilson's brother would have arrived in time and changed her fate.

"When he came with the respite in hand and saw his sister irretrievably gone, he held her motionless and sunken in death. He took her body home and some efforts were made to restore her to life in vain."

Elizabeth Wilson was buried and "a large number of respectable people attended her funeral. Thus ended the life of Elizabeth Wilson in the 27th year of her age, innocent we believe, of the crime for which she suffered, but guilty in attempt to conceal a crime of a horrid nature which she was privy to.

May others reflect that a few years past, she was esteemed and had a virtuous character."

Joseph Deshong would later be tried, convicted, and hanged for the murders of the infants. In contrast, 21st-century case law shows that the penalties imposed for infanticide are rarely, if ever, the same as for killing an adult.

Washington, D.C. (1789) U.S. Marshals office created

With the approval of the U.S. Constitution in 1788 by all 13 of the original colonies, a nation was finally created out of the wilderness that Sir Walter Raleigh's colonists had tried and failed to conquer 200 years before.

In 1789 George Washington took office as the first U.S. president. A wily man—Washington's surprise attack on the Hessian garrison in Trenton in 1776 is legendary—he knew that if the government were to succeed, it would have to fill a major gap in the Constitution: the framers did not make any provision for a regional administrative structure stretching throughout the country. Both the Congress and the executive branch were housed at the national capital. No agency was established or designated to represent the federal government's interests at the local level. The need for a regional organization quickly became apparent. Congress and the president solved part of the problem by creating specialized agencies, such as customs and revenue collectors, to levy tariffs and taxes. Yet, there were numerous other jobs that needed to be done.

Washington then championed the Judiciary Act of 1789. Not only did the act establish a federal judicial system, it also created the offices of U.S. Marshal and Deputy Marshals. Under this legislation, the marshals were given extensive authority to support the federal courts within their judicial districts and to carry out all lawful orders issued by judges, Congress, or the president.

The marshals also provided local representation for the federal government within their districts. They took the national census every 10 years through 1870. They distributed presidential proclamations, collected a variety of statistical information on commerce and manufacturing, supplied the names of government employees for the national register, and performed other routine tasks needed for the central government to function effectively. But what distinguished the Marshals Service was the legal authority to back up the government with force when necessary.

The marshals and their deputies served subpoenas, summonses, writs, warrants, and other documents issued by the federal courts, made arrests, and handled prisoners. Forevermore, whenever criminals committed crimes within federal jurisdiction, the marshals would be dispatched to track them down and bring them to justice.

By the next century, the U.S. Marshals would become the scourge of criminals on the western frontier.

Connecticut (1789) execution of highwayman Joseph Mountain

It was common practice in the late 18th and early 19th centuries for a man or woman condemned to death for "unspeakable" crimes to confess to a clergyman or reporter prior to going to the gallows. It was seen as a way of expiating their sins and sending them into the next realm with a clean conscience.

These accounts provide a window into not only the criminals and the crimes themselves but also into the social, racial, and economic mores of the times. While the accounts were embellished to provide a moral, they nevertheless stand as compelling documents that provide a historical record of the early days of the United States seen through the eyes of the country's greatest criminals at the time.

One such criminal who confessed before he met his maker was Joseph Mountain. Mountain was one of the premier highwaymen in the late 18th century who preyed on the unsuspecting and operated on no less than three continents. Born as an indentured servant, Mountain recounted his origins:

I, Joseph Mountain, was born on the 7th Day of July, A.A. 1758, in the house of Samuel Mifflin, Esq. Of Philadelphia, father of the present Governor of Pennsylvania.

My mother is a Negro and was a slave till she was twenty-one years of age. She now resides at Reading, in Pennsylvania. The first seventeen years of my life were spent in Mr. Mifflin's family. As a servant in the house, I acquired the reputation of unusual sprightliness and activity. My master was industrious to instruct me in the Presbyterian religion which he professed, teach me to read and write, and improves my mind with sentiments of virtue.

With his master's consent, at the age of 17, Mountain took a ship to Downs, England, in March 1775. From there he quickly made his way to London, where before long he succumbed to the temptations of the big city.

One day, at an ale house in London, I accidentally became acquainted with one Francis Hyde, originally from Middlesex, and one Thomas Wilfon, of Staffordshire in England. They were travelling the country with a hand organ and various other musical instruments, pretending to great art in numerous performances and really possessing surprising knowledge in every specis of juggling. This was their employment in the day time, for the purpose of executing more effectually, the principle business of their lives, viz highway robbery.

Highway robbery was rampant on English roads at the time. The two men readily recruited Mountain, and the trio set out from London that evening each armed with a hanger (sword) and a brace of pistols. Dressed suitably for their criminal endeavor and equipped with a "dark lanthorn," they planned to attack the mail coach, which would start at 12 midnight from the ship tavern, between Woolwich and Gravesend, about nine miles form London.

We were on the spot at the hour agred [sic] upon, and disguised ourselves for the adventure. Hyde and Wilson were dressed in white frocks and boots with their faces painted yellow to resemble Mulattos.

Mountain was dressed in the same manner, with the addition of a large tail wig, white gloves, and a black mask over his face.

When the stage arrived, I started and caught the leading horses by their bridles, while Hyde and Wilson each presented a brace of pistols in at the coach window, and demanded of the passengers their money. There were four gentlemen and one lady in the coach. They denied having any money.
Wilson said, "Deliver or death."

The passengers handed over their money.

We then retired to an unfrequented place, shifted out dresses and prepared to prosecute our journey to Chatham in the county of Kent. In the day time, Hyde and Wilson commonly played upon their instruments and performed various feats of sleight of hand, as tho' that was their sole occupation.

Hyde and Wilson would thus become history's only known juggling highwaymen: "In October 1786, we committed a burglary upon the house of General Arnold, who then resided in London."

Mountain and his associates, having no political leanings, had robbed the house of the most famous traitor of the American Revolution, Benedict Arnold. Arnold had escaped to England after he betrayed America.

We entered his house about 2 o'clock at night, with a dark lanthern and from a bureau in the room where the General and lady were asleep, we stole about 150£ sterling in cash and a pair of stone show buckles.

Three years later Mountain came back to America to try his luck in his home country. He arrived in Boston on May 2, 1789, and 12 days later headed for New York on foot. Along the way he stopped in Hartford, Connecticut, to steal five dollars from the cabin of a sloop on the Connecticut River, but he was immediately apprehended. Taken before George Pitkin, Esquire, he was sentenced to be whipped five times.

Mountain was absolutely humiliated that "a highwayman of the first eminence, who had robbed most of the capital cities of Europe, who had attacked gentlemen of the first distinction with success; who had escaped King's bench prison and Old Bailey, that he should be punished for such a petty offence in such an obscure part of the country."

A week later, being the 26th of May, about 3 o'clock in the afternoon, I set out for New York. At the distance of one mile, I met the unhappy girl whom I have so wantonly injured. She was in company with an elder sister and going into New Haven. I began a conversation with them and attempted by persuasion, to effect my purpose [robbery].
They were terrified at my conduct and endeavored to avoid me. Upon this I seized the eldest girl; she however, struggled with me. I then caught the younger and threw her on the ground. I have uniformly thought that the witnesses were mistaken in swearing to the commission of Rape; That I abused her in most brutal and savage manner—that her tender years and pitiable shrieks were unavailing—and that no exertion was wanting to ruin her, I frankly confess.

Mountain disclaimed responsibility to defiling a virgin, a most heinous crime punishable by death in Massachusetts. In saying, "No exertion was wanting to ruin her," Mountain was, in effect, saying that she had already had sex. Mountain was trying to do what so many defense lawyers have ever since: put the victim of a sexual offense on trial.

Mountain claimed that the only excuse he had for the rape was "intoxication."

Today, if Mountain used the same defense and could prove he was drunk at the time of the rape, many a Massachusetts jury would have no choice but to either convict on a lesser charge or acquit because the alcohol caused him not to be responsible for his actions. But to Massachusetts in 1789, there was no excuse. Yet, Mountain's defense of drunkenness would seem to be borne out by his irrational behavior. Nothing in his professed confession exhibits such depravity. If anything, he is a pragmatic, meticulous man who made sure to attack with neatness and efficiency. Such a professional criminal, then or now, is unlikely to let his sexual urges get the better of him, unless they are released some way, such as through substance abuse.

Knowing death was upon him, Mountain got reflective. He was "surprized that I did not attempt my escape. Yet by some unaccountable fatality, I loitered unconcerned [after the assault] as tho' my conduct would bear the strictest scrutiny." The highwayman took note how. "At four o'clock, I was brought before Mr. Justice Daggett for examination. The testimony was so pointed, that I was ordered into immediate confinement, to await the approaching session of the Superior Court."

Mountain was arraigned before a magistrate on the rape charge and held without bail pending trial.

On the 5th of August last, I was arraigned before the Bar of the Superior Court. My trial was far more favoureable than I expected. There was every indulgence granted me which I could have wished; and the court, jurors and spectators appeared very differently from those I had seen at the Old Bailey [London's famous criminal court].

The jury, though, had little hesitation. "They pronounced me guilty." Mountain pleaded for his life, and told the court "No man's life can be unjustly taken from him." His pleas fell on deaf ears.

"On the Tuesday following, the Chief Justice pronounced Sentence of Death against me." The custom of the time was that the condemned prisoner would have access to a cleric not just to mitigate his sins, but to see those sins paraded throughout the entire community in a sermon by an area minister.

The sermon preached at Mountain would later be published in a pamphlet widely circulated through the state. It is perhaps the first recorded indictment against the death penalty in one of the original 13 states. It reads:

Dr. Dana's Sermon at the Execution of Joseph Mountain On the Conviction of Rape. October 20, 1790.

Shall crimes so different in their nature as murder and a trifling theft be subjected to the same penalty? Policy, justice, and humanity alike remonstrate against it.

There is a distinct difference between the forfeiture of liberty and the forfeiture of life. But the criminal whose atrocious conduct hath merited imprisonment for life doth not differ materially in his moral character from one whom all will allow to have merited death. I have never considered that I preached to moral men but was never called to preach to one doomed to death by public justice and but a few hours before his launch into eternity.

Once more I am called to address you, Joseph Mountain. No more will you hear the counsel of God from any of his ministers. The judge, your eternal judge, now stands before the door. This day, in about three hours, you must die, must be hanged as a spectacle to the world as a warning to the vicious.

[Y]ou have been almost in all evil for 15 years past. That is even since you were 17 years old and left your master's family. You have personally and in cooperation with others, been guilty of highway robbery in about 20 instances; of burglary at least once; of theft repeat; and for rape you are now to be executed.

How many have you seduced? How many have you ruined in their character and estate?

But Dana believed he did not deserve death.

Yet the execution of a member of society can be justified only for crimes of magnitude. It is putting a period, a reproachful and excruciating period to the probation of a fellow creature. A just and human government will resort to it only in cases where the sovereign life has declared his will or the public safety clearly requires it.

Dr. James Dana, DD, of First Church in New Haven.

Mountain himself wrote of his reaction less than an hour before he died: "The address of the Rev. Dr. Dana was calculated to awaken every feeling of my heart. Much gratitude is due from me to this gentlemen who has exhibited such a tender concern for my immortal interest."

An hour later, Joseph Mountain was led from the jail into the prison courtyard, where a gallows had been set up. Quietly, he mounted the steps. At the top, the masked executioner gently thrust his head into the noose and tightened it. A few moments later, the executioner pulled a lever, the trap door opened, and Joseph Mountain, as the state had promised, fell into eternity.

See also CHARLES ARTHUR FLOYD; JOSEPH HARE.

Western Frontier (1790–1800) Big Harp and Little Harp: America's first serial killers

Modern-day Ohio, Kentucky, Tennessee, and Mississippi were once a savage environment yet to be tamed. Justice was meted out swiftly and mercilessly by the appropriate legal system or by vigilantes. The problem was that some of America belonged to the French, some to the Spanish, and some to the United States. Who had jurisdiction? All a criminal had to do was commit a crime in one jurisdiction and flee into another to avoid capture. The United States would have a similar problem in the 20th century with the dawn of autos, which allowed criminals to move easily between jurisdictions. Between criminals, Indians, wild animals, and bad weather, death was an ever-present threat on the frontier.

Enter the Harps. It is hard to imagine murdering machines as efficient and cold-blooded as Big Harp and Little Harp. Their actions practically define the conscienceless serial killer. They were the first in American history.

Their real names were Micajah and Wiley Harp. They passed for brothers but were cousins, the sons of brothers John and William Harpe, Scottish immigrants to Orange County, North Carolina. (Micajah and Wiley spelled their surname without the "e.") Young men with a hankering to see the world and make their mark, they left home in 1775 with the goal of becoming overseers of slaves in Virginia. In the South, that was a respectable occupation, but the Harps had a dark side to their personality. They had not wanted to be slave overseers simply because they liked the money. What they enjoyed even more was the excitement of inflicting pain.

But, as with many young men with a plan for their lives throughout history, war intervened. During the Revolutionary War, the cousins Harp, who like many Americans at the time had no loyalty to the American cause, sided with the Tories. The Harps did not become soldiers in the king's cause, or Tory sympathizers, for that matter. Instead, they became outlaws and joined a Tory gang that plundered the North Carolina countryside. They pillaged livestock and crops, burned farmhouses, and raped farmers' daughters. Attempting to kidnap and rape a young girl as he had so many times, Little Harp was shot and wounded by a local patriot, Captain James Wood. The Harps escaped but swore revenge.

By 1780 the British were so desperate for help that they took the Tory outlaws into their ranks. For the next few months, Big Harp and Little Harp fought under General Tarleton's command at King's Mountain near the Carolinas' border in October, in the battle of Blackstocks in November, and in January 1781 in the battle of Cowpens.

Shortly after the battle of Cowpens the Harps grew weary of having to fight in a civilized manner. They deserted and joined up with a renegade group of Cherokees, taking part in an Indian raid on Nashville, Tennessee. But they longed for home, female companionship and, most of all, revenge against one man.

Returning to North Carolina, they kidnapped Captain Wood's daughter, Susan, and another local girl, Maria Davidson. Along with Sally Rice, a third woman they snatched, these victims became the Harps' "wives." They were never formally married.

The Harps and their women fled civilization across the Appalachians, making their way into central Tennessee. Along the way, a member of their gang, Moses Doss, objected to their brutal treatment of the women. The Harps killed him, then took refuge in the outlaw Cherokee-Chickamauga town of Nickjack, near present-day Chattanooga, Tennessee.

For the next 10 years, Nickjack was their home base. During that decade, two of the Harp wives gave birth twice. But the Harps did not want babies around, so they murdered the infants. Soon after, the Harps once again threw in their lot with their erstwhile British allies, participating in British-backed Indian raids on Kentucky settlers west of the mountains.

In 1794 American settlers finally grew sick and tired of the outlaw sanctuary and razed Nickjack to the ground. The Harps, though, had quite a good intelligence network; they received warning of the raid and escaped with their women before the Americans came. By 1797 Big Harp and Little Harp and their wives had settled in a cabin on Beaver's Creek, near the frontier capitol of Knoxville, Tennessee.

The Harps' criminal reputation had grown throughout the frontier. They were credited with five known killings, but they had greater aspirations. Two more random killings of farmers who made the mistake of crossing the Harps' path finally drove Tennesseans to come after them.

In December 1798 the Harps hightailed it to Kentucky, where they killed two traveling men from Maryland. The Harps' modus operandi was to gut their victims, fill the stomach cavities with rocks to weigh them down, and then throw them in a river, where evidence of the crime would disappear with the bodies below the waters.

On December 12, 1798, they stopped to breakfast at John Farris's Wayside House near the Big Rock Castle River. Hungry and broke, dirty and bedraggled, the Harps and their wives appeared destitute. John Langford, a generous Virginian traveling to visit a friend in Kentucky, invited them to be his guests at his table. Like many wilderness travelers, Langford preferred facing the dangers of the road with company, but he had no idea who the Harps were.

Two days after the party departed the inn, cattle drovers discovered Langford's mutilated corpse on the trail. The Harps were captured soon after but managed to make their escape, leaving their wives to face what little law the wilderness offered.

Eventually, the Harp wives were freed, but not before they birthed three babies in prison. Traveling by canoe, the wives went west toward the Ohio River and a reunion with their husbands at Cave-in-Rock on the Illinois side of the river. The Harps had decided to make the limestone cave their headquarters, from which they would launch their criminal forays into Kentucky.

The Harps murders had not gone unnoticed by the Kentucky authorities. Kentucky governor James Garrard ordered out a posse after them, and the lawmen came close to getting them in a cane field in central Kentucky. The posse came upon the Harps in an open clearing. Seeing immediately that their pursuers had no stomach for violence, the harps shamed them by riding boldly through their ranks without a word being said. The posse skulked back to civilization, but one man, Henry Scaggs, had had enough. Scaggs turned for help to a Revolutionary War veteran and wilderness pioneer, Colonel Daniel Trabue.

Trabue and Scaggs were in the middle of a discussion about the Harps at Trabue's home in Adair County, Kentucky, when Trabue's young son's dog came limping into the yard alone, covered in blood. The dog had left the house earlier with 13-year-old John Trabue, who had been sent on an errand. Two weeks later, the boy's decomposed, dismembered body was found dumped in a sinkhole, where the Harps had left him. Horrified at young Trabue's awful death, the governor issued a $300 reward on each of the Harp heads, but the Harps continued moving, one step ahead of the law.

Headed north, the cousins left two more dead men in their wake. Reaching a plantation near the mouth of the Saline River, they discovered three men sitting around a campfire. By that time, the posse that was after them stopped just short of Cave-in-Rock on the Illinois side of the Ohio River, or they might have had the Harps that day.

Through the years, Cave-in-Rock had become a rest stop for river travelers migrating west and, not coincidentally, home to an entire corporation of river pirates. These pirates, the most famous among them being a Revolutionary War veteran named Samuel Mason, would lure unwary victims to the cave where they would be beaten and robbed. With the arrival of the Harps and their wives, their crimes would escalate to murder.

The Harps took their victims to the top of the bluff, stripped them naked, and threw them in the river. The river pirates did not want the Harps' murdering ways to bring them any more attention from the authorities, so they kicked them out. The Harps were on the move again.

In July 1798 in eastern Tennessee, the Harps continued the slaughter. They killed a farmer named Bradbury, a man named Hardin, and a boy named Coffey. Another man, William Ballard, was gutted and his innards filled with stones and dumped in the Holston River. James Brassel was found with his throat ripped apart on Brassel's Knob. John Tully, a father of eight in south central Kentucky, was also killed by the peripatetic Harps. Then there were John Graves and his teenaged son, out planting crops, when the Harps came upon them and cut off their heads with axes. Moving toward Logan County, the Harps encountered a little girl. They killed her and a young slave on his way to the mill. Near the Whippoorwill River, they butchered an entire migrating family asleep in their camp, but for one son who survived.

Stopping to rest in a clearing near the Mud River in Russellville, wife Sally's four-month-old daughter kept crying and refused to be consoled. Big Harp took the baby from her mother's arms, swung her by her ankles, and hit her head against the trunk of a tree, killing her instantly.

Moving on, they killed a man named Trowbridge who had gone for salt at Robertson's Lick. Then they invaded the Stegall home in Webster County. They killed Major William Love, an overnight guest; the Stegalls' baby, who made the mistake of crying; and Mrs. Stegall, who screamed when she saw her infant's throat being slit.

Later, pretending to be the posse after the Harps, the Harps caught two men who they accused of being them, "arrested," and executed them. Just as they were about to kill a third man, the posse finally sighted them far down a valley on the Natchez Trace.

The two Harps had stopped a stranger on the road. They were chatting, moving closer to him, getting ready to kill him and steal his money. But the Harps heard the posse approaching and leapt on their horses to escape, splitting up as they went. Little Harp rode into the forest and vanished. Big Harp kept going on the trace and the posse decided it was easier to follow him.

Riding over one hill after another, the posse got within rifle range. A man named Samuel Leiper, one of the county's best marksmen, had taken the point. He reined his horse in, pulled his flintlock rifle from his scabbard, took careful aim, and fired. The musket ball shot out of the barrel, but Leiper missed. Big Harp kept going.

Trying to reload, the weapon jammed. James Tompkins, a second member of the posse, threw him his rifle and Leiper fired again. This bullet struck Big Harp in the middle of his spine. He dropped the reins and his arms jerked spasmodically upward. Now free, his horse decided to turn toward the thicket of branches that grew on both sides of the trail.

When the posse finally caught up with him, Big Harp's horse was cantering slowly through the woods. The serial killer lolled in the saddle, semiconscious. Leiper and Tompkins rolled up alongside and yanked him from his mount. Then Big Harp's luck changed from bad to worse.

The previous day, he and his brother had killed the wife and baby of Moses Stegall. Stegall had subsequently joined the posse when he found out what had happened. Now, Stegall came riding up, vowing revenge. Dismounting, Stegall kicked Big Harp in the face. He took out his hunting knife and waved it furiously announcing to one and all, "I'm going to cut your head off with that!" The other members of the posse pulled him back.

They were content to wait and see if Big Harp died from his wounds. If not, they'd bring him in for trial.

Big Harp knew he was done for. His legs had been paralyzed by the gunshot. He began muttering about his murders, confessing to many of them, without regret. His homicidal nature had evidently taken a religious bent because he purportedly said, "I have seen a vision and the All Wise has forged me as a scourge to humanity."

As he died, Big Harp said that the one murder he did regret was the Stegall baby. He admitted that in a fit of pique, he had "slung it by the heels against a large tree by the path-side . . . thrown it from me . . . into the woods" and then slashed its throat.

Stegall waited with the rest for Harp to give out. Angry at the delay, he turned his gun barrel on Big Harp, but when Big Harp saw that, he just laughed. Stegall then resorted to his knife and pulled Big Harp's head up as he slowly pulled the knife across the back of Harp's neck, cutting it to the bone.

"You are a God damned rough butcher. But cut on and be damned!" Big Harp was heard to whisper.

Stegall worked until he had severed Big Harp's neck, and then tossed his head in a bag he had brought for the occasion.

Revenge was a much-prized commodity on the frontier. While trial by jury existed and was a constitutional right, revenge existed too—only revenge required others to look the other way, just as the posse did that night.

They left Harp's body on what forevermore would be called Harp's Hill and took his head to the crossroads, where they hung it from an oak tree. Subsequently, the three Harp wives were freed.

Sally Rice returned to her family in Knoxville, remarried and migrated west with her new husband and her father. Maria Davidson, a.k.a. Betsey Roberts, remarried too, moved to Illinois, and had a large family. Susan Wood became a weaver and raised her surviving daughter in Tennessee, where she later died.

That left Little Harp to be accounted for. Smarter than his big cousin, he had retreated to Cave-in-Rock and the company of "Bloody Sam" Mason.

See also CAVE-IN-ROCK, ILLINOIS (1729); H. H. HOLMES; SAMUEL "BLOODY SAM" MASON.

Samuel "Bloody Sam" Mason (1750–1804)
highwayman and murderer

"Bloody Sam" Mason was the first of the great criminal masterminds of the frontier, Mason organized a gang that terrorized the Ohio River and Natchez Trace country. But for a criminal, he had a strange background. Mason was a Revolutionary War hero who had so distinguished himself as an officer in battle against the British that the Kentucky legislature later rewarded him for his service by appointing him justice of the peace.

Born in Virginia in 1750 he joined the rebels in 1775. Burly and strong, he became a member of explorer/soldier George Rogers Clark's "Long Knives." It was Clark and his men who floated down the Ohio, went through swamps, and pushed into the wilderness to Illinois where they captured the British general Hamilton at Vincennes. Clark's nephew William Clark would, in just a few years, be the coleader of the great expedition to the West.

After the war Mason settled in Kentucky where the legislature set him up in his political sinecure. His fighting legend continued to grow. Along with a group of 28 men, Mason withstood an Indian onslaught for a day and a night, holding off 300 attackers. When the smoke cleared, Mason and another man were the only survivors.

By 1790 he was middle-aged and married with four children. A contemporary account describes Mason this way: "He weighed about two hundred pounds and was a fine-looking man." His face, however, was odd. He had a "a tooth which projected forwards and could only be covered with his lip by effort." Mason was affluent and respected. In a Greek tragedy, he would be ripe for a fall. For a change, life imitated art.

One of Mason's daughters took up with a scoundrel named Kuykendall. After having sex in Mason's house, the couple flaunted their freedom and ran off together, prompting Mason to threaten the man's life. But he soon came to his senses and got word to the worried couple that he no longer bore them ill will. They returned to a joyous wedding celebration. But that night, after the guests had dispersed, Kuykendall was killed and his body tossed in the underbrush. Who did it is unknown, though it was widely suspected that Mason's two sons had done the deed on orders from their father.

The next day, Mason and his sons fled westward with a companion, Henry Havard. Captain John Hall, "the only recognized officer of the law in all this territory" rode out to bring them back. He was shot and his body left for the buzzards in a cornfield. Mason was accused of this second murder, but there appeared to be reasonable doubt that he had done it. Instead, blame fell on young Havard, the man who had accompanied the Masons into the wilderness.

A few months later, Havard showed up at his father's Tennessee farm with a friend, Samuel Mays. News of his arrival had preceded him and an armed posse was waiting for him. The "regulators" stormed the farmhouse and shot Havard as he lay in bed. They let Mays go. As for Mason, he was long gone and taking refuge at Cave-in-Rock.

By then, in 1799, the place had become infamous. For years pirates had waylaid boats on the river and then escaped with impunity into the cave. No longer. Around the time of Mason's arrival, a fleet of flatboats, loaded stern to keel with armed volunteers, prepared to attack.

Mason and the other bandits heard of the invasion plan and quickly fled. Mason went south on the river to Wolf Island, on the Mississippi a few miles below the mouth of the Ohio. By chance, John Audubon, the naturalist, happened to be on the river at the same time and took special note of Mason and his gang of cutthroats. Audubon wrote, "He formed a line of worthless associates from the eastern part of Virginia to New Orleans."

In 1800 Mason showed up in New Madrid, a town in the Spanish Territory near the Tennessee state line. Using a Spanish passport, he could easily escape from one pursuing agency by slipping into another. And as Mason moved through the country, his notoriety as a highwayman grew.

The following year, Colonel Joshua Baker, a merchant and planter in Hardin County, Kentucky, left for New Orleans. He formed a packet of several flatboats laden with crops to be sold for gold in the Spanish city. By midsummer, they reached New Orleans, sold the crops, and proceeded back up the Natchez Trace. The party consisted of Baker and two other men. On August 14, 1801, they were 90 miles up the trace at Twelve-Mile Creek. A local paper, the *Kentucky Gazette*, describes what happened next. It is the first newspaper coverage of Mason's thievery on the Natchez Trace:

We are informed that on the fourteenth of August, about sixty miles on this side of the Big Biopiere River, Colonel Joshua Baker, a Mr. William Baker and a Mr. Rogers of Natchez were robbed of their horses, traveling utensils and about $2,300 cash.

In 1801, that was a huge amount of money.

It seems that the company had halted in the morning at a small clear stream of water in order to wash. As soon as they had dismounted and gone to the water, four men appeared, blacked, between them and their horses and demanded surrender of their money and property which they were obliged to comply with.

Mr. W. Baker was more fortunate than his companions. A packhorse, on which was a considerable sum of money, being frightened at the appearance of the robbers, ran away, and they being in haste to escape did not pursue. Mr. W. Baker recovered his horse and money. He, however, lost his riding-horse, etc.

Colonel Baker and Mr. Rogers came to the first settlement, where they procured assistance and immediately went in pursuit of the villains. It is to be hoped they will be apprehended.

One of them [Mason] was described by Colonel Baker, formerly resided at Red Bank. A brother of Colonel Baker, our informant, contained this information from Mr. W. Baker, who lodged at his house in Lexington on Thursday night last.

Mason's reputation as a highwayman was growing. Men moved warily through the wilderness, in fear they would encounter him on the trace or some other trail. Things were so bad that many a traveler would wait at the trace's beginning outside Natchez and not proceed up the trace unless in the company of fellow travelers.

Mason himself would often stop the mail carrier, John Swaney, whose route took him north on the trace. "He was always anxious to know what was said of him by the public," Swaney would later recall. Mason wanted to know what was happening in the towns on the frontier.

The highwayman and the mailman chatted amicably on many an occasion. Mason seemed like a respectable businessman, concerned that his reputation was being tarnished. Many murders and robberies were attributed to his efforts, and yet no law enforcement body came after him, not just because the evidence of his complicity was circumstantial but because Mason was just too difficult to track in the wilderness.

By 1801 Mason had been a highwayman on the Natchez Trace for more than a year. It is possible he was still not committed to the wrong side of the law. Perhaps he still thought he could find a way back to respectability. In those days, with communication poor, it was possible for a man to be a villain in one settlement but a hero in the next. Clearly, from his conversations with Swaney, Mason still hungered for respectability and put up an excellent facade constantly protesting how he was being labeled a bad man when all he craved was justice.

In fall 1801 Mason and one of his sons rode down to Natchez to try and clear his name. Natchez, at the beginning of the 19th century, was second only to New Orleans in beauty. It was a handsome city of commerce and romance, of big and little men, rich and poor. It was a city cut out of the virgin wilderness that surrounded it in a ring of dogwood, locust, black oak, which flowered in spring. Where the trace, the Spanish Road and a few roads from the plantations came together, that was Natchez.

Anthony Glass lived in the city. His reputation as an honest merchant hid his real occupation as Mason's "fence" for his stolen goods. He would send word to Mason on the trace when a richly laden caravan was coming up from Natchez and the highwayman would then be ready to strike.

It was Glass who got Mason and his son who accompanied him, their rooms at a local inn, Glass who took Mason around Natchez and introduced him to the town elders as a planter from upstate. Mason enjoyed his renewed respectability. He was in a local tavern, sipping some beer, when a stranger pointed at him. "That's the man! The man that robbed Baker!"

Mason and his son were immediately thrown in jail, an old one from the days when the Spanish controlled the town. A few days later, he came to trial. His attorney did his best for his clients but in the end, Mason and his son were found guilty of robbery by the presiding magistrates. The sentence was 39 lashes each, to be administered in the Town Square, followed by another 12 hours in the town pillory.

For Mason, it was the end of any hopes he had had for regaining his respectability. Still, the punishment was mild compared to what he could have gotten. At that time, there were at least 11 crimes punishable by death, including murder, arson, rape, forgery, manslaughter, slave stealing, and horse stealing (second offense). Mason was getting off easy with his life. The whole town turned out to watch. The whip caught Mason square in the back, over and over. According to a contemporary account of someone who witnessed the flogging. "I shall never forget the cries of 'Innocent!' at every blow of the cowhide. Until the last lash was given, they shrieked with the same despairing cry of 'Innocent! Innocent!'"

After the whipping, Mason and his son were locked neck and wrist in the pillory. Author Robert Coates believes "this was the bitterest punishment of all. No one can tell what savage thoughts he had, clamped in the uncouth device while the townsmen gawked, but by his future actions, they must have been savage indeed."

After 12 hours of this indignity, he and his son were released. Their debt to frontier society had been paid. To celebrate, "The elder Mason and his son shaved their heads and stripped themselves naked, mounted their horses and yelling like Indians, rode through and out of the town," out onto the trace where they seemingly vanished.

A few days later, one of the jurors who had found them guilty rode out onto the trace, alone. Mason, who was standing there, armed to the teeth, stopped him just beyond the town limits. The juror pleaded for his life, telling Mason he had a wife and children, who would starve if he died.

Mason raised his gun as if to fire and reportedly said, "Did I ever do you any harm? Did you ever hear of me murdering anybody?"

The man said no twice and Mason replied, "You ain't worth killing," then proceeded to kick him around. When he was satisfied that the man's ribs were sufficiently broken, he turned and spurred his horse away at a gallop.

If Mason had been an effective highwayman before his public punishment, he was even more so after. He began to rob and kill with wild abandon. Anyone who came by his path was a victim, and his path was the trace, so he had many victims. He took to hanging placards on their necks with his name scrawled in their own blood upon it.

Few saw him now, for he realized that he would be shot on sight if they did. Mason took the time to build up his criminal gang, which allowed him to commit simultaneous robberies on the river and the trace. On February 10, 1802, the new governor of the Mississippi Territory, William C. C. Claiborne, wrote to the Spanish governor general of the province of Louisiana, asking for assistance in policing the frontier and ridding it of the bandits.

On February 28 Manuel de Salcedo, the Spanish governor general, wrote back that he had given his officers "the most positive orders to take the most efficacious means of discovering and apprehending the criminals that can be adopted, and I assure your Excellency that if the criminals are taken, they will be punished in such manner as to serve as an example to others."

In other words, every country for itself. There would be no international cooperation in capturing Mason.

About a month and a half later, Colonel Baker, who had already been a victim of Mason once, again faced the big man, this time on the river. As Baker was flatboating his produce to market in New Orleans, his boat was boarded by Mason and his pirates. A battle ensued; Mason escaped unharmed.

In response, the governor sent letters to all commanders of military outposts along the river and the

Cave-in-Rock on the Ohio River, the criminal sanctuary of "Bloody" Sam Mason and Wiley Harp. Engraving from Barber and Howe's 1861 book *Our Whole Country: Or the Past and Present of the United States, Historical and Descriptive.* (Author's Collection)

trace, informing them that Baker and many others had been attacked "near the mouth of the Yazou River." He urged the military men to capture the robbers. The letters contained one detail that spread further terror into the countryside.

An informant had claimed that among Mason's gang was "a certain Wiley Harp." If the informant was to be believed, Little Harp was not only alive but still at his criminal mischief. The news spread like a dark pall over the frontier.

Big Harp was dead but his brother was worse. It was like a supernatural terror gripped the people. The reality was that a serial killer was still out there in the trace's canebrake, ready to kill again without the slightest provocation.

A few months later, a stranger married the sister of a Tennessee farmer named Bass. After the wedding, the newly married couple set out for North Carolina. A few days later, the groom returned to the settlement from which he had just come, claiming that his young wife's horse had bolted. The girl was thrown from the saddle but her foot stuck in the stirrup and she was dragged to her death.

It would be months before Bass suspected that the man who had married his sister was Wiley Harp. When he finally did, he traveled out on the trace and opened his sister's grave. He found that she had been beaten to death and horribly mutilated.

So now, Mason had teamed up with Harp to make as deadly a pair of killers as any in the history of American crime. The robberies and murders continued. The *Frankfort* (Kentucky) *Palladium* quoted from "A letter dated Natchez, June 11 [1802], containing the following intelligence: 'We were attacked by robbers near the mouth of the White River. They hailed us from the shore, telling us they wished to purchase rifles, and on our refusing to land, they commenced the pursuit, in pirogues [small boats], having in each six men well armed. They were commanded by a person named Mason, who scours the road through the wilderness.'"

This kind of con, posing as a trader to lure his prey into a trap, was a standard strategy of Mason's that worked time and again. Two nations and countless police forces now hunted Mason, and his name was infamous throughout the wilderness. Such audacity as he displayed can never be tolerated by a civilized government. Not only is it a danger to the populace, it is bad for business.

On January 11, 1803, a man named Pierre Dapron appeared before the Spanish magistrate in the town of New Madrid. He claimed that he had just come from the settlement of Little Prairie, 20 miles downstream, where a friend had told him of four men loitering near the town's outskirts. The friend believed these men to be members of the Mason Gang. The magistrates asked around and found one Georges Ruddell, who claimed to have seen the newcomers.

According to Ruddell, eight men and one woman comprised the party. Well armed and mounted, they had arrived the week before and rented 10 acres and a house from a farmer named Lesieur. Strangely, they always had one heavily armed man posted as guard at the cabin door.

The magistrates wisely turned the investigation over to Don Robert McCoy, captain of the militia. McCoy and a dozen regulars rode down to Little Prairie. They had no sooner dismounted in the village square than they ran right into Mason.

The Revolutionary War hero did not deny his identity, and in fact flaunted it. He said he had heard that people were talking about him in New Madrid, saying bad things about him. He claimed to be a decent, honorable man, saying "I'm going up there myself and set matters square. I want to live in peace."

McCoy did what any good law enforcement officer would do—he decided to play it coy. He asked Mason if he had his Spanish passport and Mason replied in the affirmative.

"Well," McCoy continued, "I'm just down here on an inspection tour and it's no affair of mine, but I did hear that there was a complaint about you. Now, I've got some business to attend to about town first, but if you want to, after that, you can get your people together and I'll come over to your cabin and check your papers. Then I can report back to the Commandant tonight and if everything's all right, you won't have to go to town at all."

Mason thought it a good idea. A few hours later, McCoy rode up alone to the cabin, where Mason and his sons and the rest of his party gathered to have their passports checked in the kitchen. McCoy asked if everyone was present. When Mason nodded in assent, McCoy shouted, "Then arrest them!" Secretly, his men had surrounded the cabin. Now, they moved in. Mason, his sons, and the rest were put in chains and transported to New Madrid, where on the morning of January 17 they stood trial.

The trial was under the jurisdiction of a Spanish court, a frontier tribunal trying as hard as it could to give the defendants a fair trial without really knowing the dictates of the American democracy. Nor did they need to apply them since this was Spanish territory. Who cared what the Americans wanted? But by then, there were more Americans in the Spanish territory than there were Spaniards. Like it or not, Spain had to at least put up the facade of a fair, democratic trial.

Each witness swore "on the cross of his sword and by the Holy Scriptures" to tell the truth. There was a semblance of modern courtroom ethic in that each witness was thoroughly questioned, though who was the defense attorney and who was the prosecutor was decidedly unclear, especially considering the testimony was, bizarrely, taken in French. Mason was his own star witness.

The big man's defense was one of the most sorrowful stories that could be imagined. He claimed to have been persecuted into the territories for the crimes of others. He had come across the border to escape those lies. It was a conspiracy, plain and simple, by small, evil men to besmirch his reputation. It was not the first or last time that a criminal would use "the other guy" defense.

Asked why he had lived a hunted man, never showing his face, even to declare his innocence, Mason shot back that he knew his enemies had mastered the courts and had helped prosecutors build as strong a case as possible against him. What possible good could come if he exposed himself to such danger?

On the other hand, Mason was duly aware that the Spanish authorities would offer leniency if the accused helped to expose an even greater threat to the state than his poor, miserable self. The commandant offered that this would be looked upon favorably upon sentencing, at which Mason testified that John Taylor was one of the guilty parties they were seeking.

"And he sometimes goes by other names which I cannot recall," Mason concluded.

That brought John Taylor to the stand. An observer said that Taylor "was always downcast and fierce, his hair red, his face meager and his stature below that of the average man."

Taylor's story was that he wasn't really Taylor. His name was John Setton. He was an Irishman who immigrated to America's shores in 1797. He enlisted in the army and subsequently left it when he deserted "near the high coast." That was when John Setton became John Taylor.

After that, Setton/Taylor rambled through the western settlements. Honest and forthcoming, he had worked at various times as a skilled carpenter and unskilled workingman. Once, at Nogales, his employer had been His Majesty, the King of Spain. Later, he hunted with the Choctaw Indians. That adventure came to an end when a former officer recognized him as John Setton, army deserter, and had him arrested and jailed.

While in jail, he met a fellow soldier named Wiggins and together, they set about successfully escaping. Once free, Wiggins made introductions to Samuel Mason. At this point in his testimony, the commandant stopped Taylor and asked him again if his name was Setton. Taylor replied that yes, he was indeed Setton.

The commandant then inquired if he knew the name "of the man Harp?"

The silenced courtroom waited for the answer. "Setton took a few moments to compose himself, then answered that he had heard the name," said a contemporary account. Without missing a beat, he continued his story.

Mason and his sons had essentially taken Setton prisoner and forced him to accompany them in their criminal transactions. Under threat of death, he signed confessions to various robberies on the trace and on the river, including the attack on Baker on the trace and the robbery of Anthony Glass, "though it was known that Glass was Mason's man at Nachez." Apparently, there was no honor among thieves.

Mason took the stand to dispute Setton's testimony. He admitted to holding him captive, but only because he knew him to be guilty of many felonious crimes. He kept him, hoping to eventually trick him into publicly confessing to the very crimes Mason had been accused of.

On January 31, 1803, the judges ruled,

[T]he proceedings of this trial, originally set down in writing on 91 sheets of paper written on both sides, as well as the pieces of evidence tending to conviction, together with seven thousand piasters in United States banknotes, be forwarded to Honourable Governor General Don Robert McCoy, Captain of the Militia, whom we have charged to conduct the prisoners, Mason and consorts, to New Orleans with the view of their trial being continued and finished, if it so please the Honorable Governor General.

It took two weeks to sail from New Madrid to New Orleans. All the while, Mason, Setton, Mason's sons, children, and one wife, were kept under armed guard by Captain McCoy and four of his militia. Once in New Orleans, the High Court looked over the case and decided that since most of the crimes the defendants had committed were on American soil, it was only right and customary that they be turned over to the courts of the Mississippi Territory for trial. That led Mason, Setton, and company to their second voyage of discovery, this time upriver on a small sailing sloop to Natchez.

It was March 26, 1803, and a great storm gripped the Mississippi. Thunder, lightning, gale force winds and dangerous currents challenged the sloop. They had been on the river then for a month and were about 100 miles south of Natchez. The storm had thrown them toward the far bank, near the small town of Pointe Coupee, Mississippi.

Suddenly, a gale force wind splintered the mast. It fell into the roiling waters. The ship's captain managed to get the vessel to shore, where most of the men, including the guards, were sent to make a new mast. Seeing an opportunity, Mason, Setton, and the rest made a break for it.

Captain McCoy, who was still on board, ran out when he heard the prisoners escaping. He instantly confronted Mason, who brought up a rifle he had stolen and fired. The ball went through McCoy's breast. As McCoy faltered and went down, he fired his own gun, striking Mason's head.

Residents of Pointe Coupee spotted the floundering boat.

Before the antagonists could continue their bloody duel to the death, the townspeople, who had seen what was happening, had advanced on the sailboat in a series of rickety boats. Mason, who had only been grazed by the bullet, led his party through the dense undergrowth to the trails he knew so well and vanished for three months.

In June a group of men traveling on the trace spotted him in the dense underbrush. There was an exchange of shots and then Mason vanished once again.

In July the same Samuel Mays who had fled when Henry Havard, one of Mason's former companions, had been killed, arrived in Natchez. He claimed that Mason had held him up on the trace. Quickly, he reprovisioned and set back out to get the highwayman.

For three more months, there were no more Mason sightings. Then one day in October, Mays came back into Natchez, accompanied by Mason's old nemesis/companion/friend, John Setton. They apparently had made some sort of bargain, because Setton agreed to help Mays capture Mason and collect the reward on his head.

By late October, they were back, accompanied by a strange object wrapped in clay. They told the authorities that they had found Mason hiding in the swamp near Lake Concordia, west of Natchez. Joining his party, they waited until the right moment and then pounced upon him and, using a tomahawk, cut off his head.

Brought before the Natchez magistrates, they cracked open the clay ball and produced Mason's head. There was no doubt it was he. Only Mason had that oddly protruding front tooth. Setton and Mays demanded the reward. They had produced the man's head. Where was the bounty on it?

While the magistrates tried to figure out what to do, a man came forward. He said that he had recognized amongst the horses that Setton and Mays came in on two of his that had been stolen. It certainly would not have been surprising if two unsavory characters like Setton and Mays were horse thieves. Then, another man came forward, Captain Stump from Kentucky. He looked closely at Setton and proclaimed, "Why, that man's Wiley Harp." Natchez's magistrates had not yet received the report of the trial at New Madrid and were unaware of Mason's testimony alluding to Setton's true identity.

Setton kept to his story and denied he was Harp. The magistrates, using good common sense, put Setton into jail under armed guard and then asked any townsfolk who knew Little Harp to come forward and help verify his identity. Several men came forward to say he was Harp and to all, Setton offered denial. The matter was finally settled when a man from Tennessee named John Bowman told the magistrates, "If he's Little Harp, he'll have a scar under the left nipple of his breasts, because I cut him there in a difficulty we had, one night at Knoxville."

John Setton blustered and fumed that he was not Harp and resisted when men came forward to tear off his shirt but in the end, it ripped anyway and exposed the scar, as Bowman had said, under his left breast. But luck was, again, with Little Harp.

He and his partner Mays escaped, only to be quickly recaptured in Greenville, a town 20 miles north of Natchez. It was there that they finally stood trial for various murders and were convicted on all charges. The sentence, of course, was death.

On February 8, 1804, they were taken from jail, out through town, to the gallows field to be executed. They walked, hands tied behind their backs. At the gallows field, two nooses had been thrown over a beam that hung between two forked trees. Under each noose was a braced ladder. The prisoners were made to mount it until their necks went through the nooses.

They stood on the topmost rung, necks snugly encased. Little Harp said nothing. Mays whined that fate had dealt him a cruel blow, claimed to never have murdered, and stated that he had done society a favor by helping to kill Mason. Then the ladders were knocked from beneath their feet and they swung out into eternity. Their necks snapped. By the time they were cut down, their hearts had stopped beating.

The townspeople proceeded to behead both. Harp's head was put on a pole along the trace north of the town. Mays was put on a pole along the trace south of the town. It was a message to all those who would conspire to transgress.

Many American serial killers would come and go in the years to come. Some would have more bizarre personal stories but none quite like the Harps. Their murdering ways became the stuff of legend, right into the 20th century.

Walt Disney's *Davy Crockett and the River Pirates* dramatized the frontier legend that it was Davy Crockett who brought Mason and the Harps to ground. Later, writer Eudora Welty used Little Harp's head as a comic device in her story "The Robber Bridegroom." When it became a play in the mid-1970s on Broadway starring Barry Bostwick, Little Harp's "head" was displayed in a box that would be opened sporadically throughout the play for comic effect. It is doubtful anyone in the audience including this writer, knew "the head's" true history.

The elimination of the Harps had taken the first great criminal "dragnet" in United States history. The relentless pursuit of the murdering cousins had forced all those criminal elements in the posse's wake to be driven westward. Thieves, cutthroats, robbers, highwaymen, killers, prostitutes, and con men had all been chased west and north. Many settled along the lower Ohio River where it joins the Mississippi. From Red Bank to Fort Massac, the area became a den of thieves. Red Bank had become populated by outlaws to be contended with by a future generation of lawmen. As for Mason, his criminal legacy remains. In the annals of crime, he is the only Revolutionary War hero who became an even more famous outlaw.

See also CAVE-IN-ROCK, ILLINOIS; THE WESTERN FRONTIER.

Harper's Ferry, Virginia (1794) America's first arsenal established

In 1794 President George Washington selected Springfield, Massachusetts, and Harper's Ferry, Virginia, as the sites of the new national armories. President Washington noted that by choosing the latter in particular, the country would be getting the benefit of the great waterpower provided by both the Potomac and Shenandoah Rivers which could be used to manufacture weapons in the Harper's Ferry weapons production facility.

No thought was given to Harper's Ferry's defense in case of insurrection. And why should it be? America was a new country. The idea that after such a hard-won victory anyone would want to undermine the Constitution was unthinkable.

John Brown was 62 years in the future.

See also JOHN BROWN, A.K.A. OSAWATOMIE BROWN.

Morgantown, Pennsylvania (1797) first execution of a schizophrenic

The life and confession of Charles O'Donnel, who was executed at Morgantown, June 19, 1797, for the wilful murder of his son, though he had murdered a woman about 27 years before that time. . . .

Charles O'Donnel is the first known schizophrenic to be executed in America. O'Donnel's story says as much about the time he was born into as the crimes he committed. Today, O'Donnel would be diagnosed, hospitalized, and treated for his illness. In 1797, he was simply executed for his crimes.

O'Donnel was an Irish immigrant who married and had many children but was incapable of sustaining his family life. He often disappeared on drinking binges that soothed the strange voices in his head. His wife could not live with his erratic behavior and so left him with the children.

O'Donnel subsequently killed a woman who "offended" him and later stood "mute while the woman's husband, an old wretch of a man, was brought before the bar and charged with her murder."

"I grew very angry and struck my wife on the head with a water pail," confessed the old man, who was so senile that he thought he had done the despicable act.

O'Donnel knew he would be hanged if he confessed and so he remained silent. What cared the authorities if he felt no control over the things he did? It was only after the murder of his son, when he gave his confession to that act, that he admitted killing the woman 20 years before.

"Oh the distressing scene that opened to my view at that time," said O'Donnel, recalling the old man's trial.

I thought I was of all men the most miserable. My wife had sworn the peace against me and gone off; my child whom I had begotten had turned disobedient, abused me to my face, attempting to take my life and left me; my eldest son, some time before that had beaten me very severely. (Upon my attempting to whip him, he threw the falling axe at me and was very near hitting me on the head. He then ran off cursing me bitterly.)

O'Donnel had become convinced his children were plotting to kill him and resolved "even to murder my own son William [Billy] whom I had begotten and raised to the age of fifteen." He prepared a rope, hung it over William's bed, and decided to murder him the next night.

Sometime after midnight, O'Donnel rose and went to the bedside where his son lay sleeping in order to take his life but his resolve faltered and he withdrew. A short time later he made a second attempt, but again lost his nerve in a swell of fatherly affection.

O'Donnel's third attempt held the course. He lay down on the bed, put the rope around his son's neck, made it fast, and gave a sudden pull. His son snapped awake and leaped over his father pulling him out of the bed and onto the floor. William was now tethered to a leash that his father held in his hands.

"Daddy, for the Lord's sake, do not kill me," O'Donnel remembered his son saying.

"Daddy, I will be obedient and work for as long as I live," adding he would go and personally ask his mother to come home if I would spare his life. "O Daddy, think of Charles," a son of mine who died about two years before at whose death I was much grieved.

Still, the father refused to spare his son's life.

He then in floods of tears and many bitter cries asked me where I would bury him. I told him I would open a heap of stones, which was near the house and put him in it.
"Daddy, bury me under the apple tree in the garden."
I promised him that I would wrap him in [white] linen and bury him where he requested.

Why William did not resist is unknown. Maybe he thought his father would resist the compelling urge to murder at the last minute. At the very least, William must have been in shock. Even today, psychologists can only speculate why some children resist, successfully, when a parent attempts to murder them, while others acquiesce.

After he had prayed about 20 minutes, resting on his knees, with his back to me, he arose and as he got up, I jerked the rope. Being strangled, he fell on the floor. I then put my knees against his shoulders and drew the rope around the bedpost with all my strength and held about 10 minutes in which time he expired.

O'Donnel concealed the body in some elder bushes, determined to hide his crime with a story that his son ran away. By that lone action, he made it difficult for a jury to believe him out of his mind and extend him mercy, for if he was insane, why did he intend to cover up his crime? That, on the surface, appears to be a rational act.

Some time in the night, I awoke to find myself on the same bed on which I had laid my murdered son, horror again seized my mind. I jumped out of bed as if pursued by thousands of enemies, ran to the door and looking toward the stone heap, immediately saw my dear son in his natural appearance who looked full in my face and stood near the apple tree where he requested to be buried.

The next morning, O'Donnel's daughter asked after Billy who failed to appear at his mother.

O'Donnel lied, but when informed by the daughter that Billy was missing, O'Donnel's wife knew in her heart what he had done and "dreamed" of the murder. The next day, she confronted O'Donnel, and refused to go home unless he would tell her what he did with the body.

O'Donnel kept up his denials and his wife cried and called him "Murderer!" O'Donnel attempted to assuage his guilty conscience with drink. Meanwhile, a search was made for the body. It wasn't found, but still, the sheriff suspected O'Donnel and arrested him on suspicion of murder.

The county sheriff who investigated acted much as a contemporary forensic investigator. If the boy had indeed been murdered by his father, then the body had to be back at the farm. And without the body, conviction would be difficult.

The sheriff searched the O'Donnel farm again and on the fifth day after the murder, the corpse was taken out of the stone heap. O'Donnel, who was present, recounted his reaction: "Oh my God, what guilt and horror seized my mind! I could no longer conceal the crime; but ran and fell upon him and embraced and kissed him. Knowing myself guilty, I confessed the murder and was straight-away conveyed to Morgantown jail where I was bound in heavy chains and left to mourn my wretched fate."

There was no such thing as an insanity defense. A person was either committed to jail for punishment or executed.

"I now commit my body to the gallows and my soul to him who gave it. I humbly believe that he will receive it to a mansion in glory where I hope to rest," O'Donnel said to complete his confession, which is signed: "Charles O'Donnel, Witness, The Reverend Simon Cochran, who took it from his own mouth 2 days before his execution."

And so, O'Donnel was executed.

PART THREE

WESTWARD EXPANSION AND THE CIVIL WAR

FIVE
1800-1850

Introduction

By 1800, second-, third-, and fourth-generation Americans were being born. The American character was forming. Americans imagined on a grand scale because they had to—the majority of the continent was unexplored. From the settlement of St. Louis west, the country remained a mystery, and more than anyone else Thomas Jefferson wanted to know what was there.

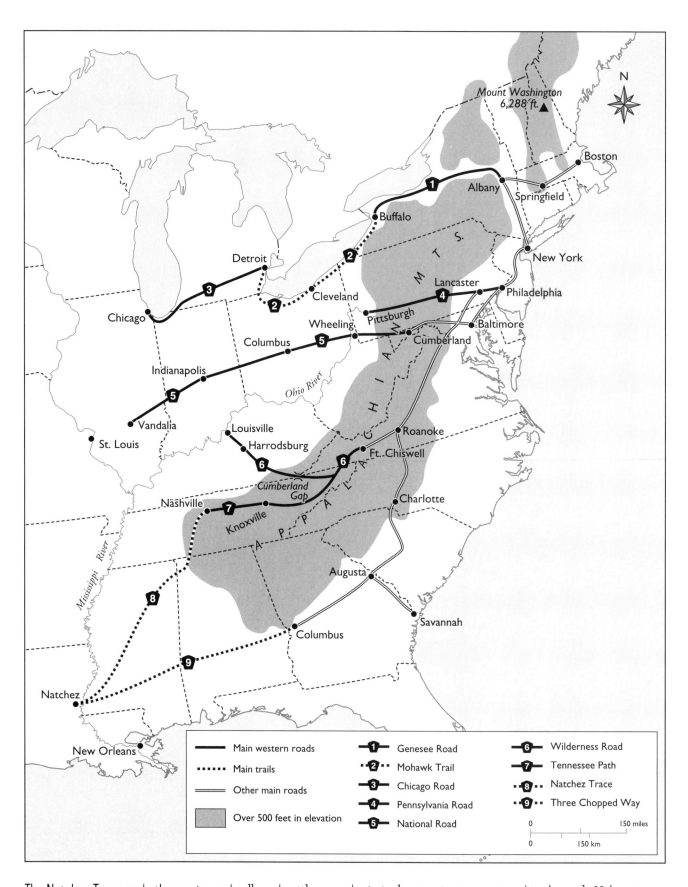

The Natchez Trace and other main roads allowed settlers—and criminals—to migrate westward in the early 19th century.

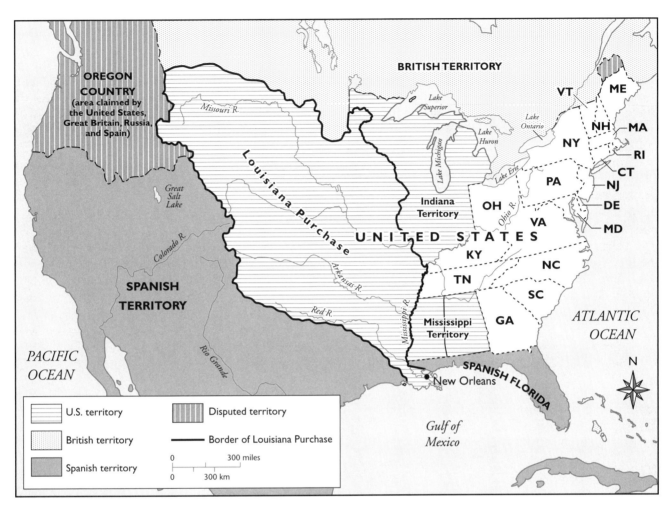

The Louisiana Purchase, in 1803, doubled the size of the United States.

Louisiana Purchase (1803)

When the United States approached France in April 1803 with the intention of buying the French-owned territory of Louisiana, the French demanded hard cash. On April 20, 1803, in Paris, France, U.S. envoys James Madison and Robert R. Livingston agreed to pay 80 million francs, about $15 million, including 20 million francs for discharging claims of American citizens against France. As a result Napoleon, the emperor of France, received a lot of money to finance his empire, and the United States got 828,000 square miles, doubling the size of the country.

Unexplored West (1803–1806) the Lewis and Clark expedition

It was Thomas Jefferson's idea to outfit a federal expedition to find the fabled Northwest Passage, a direct way to get from the interior of the country to the West Coast.

In 1803 Jefferson was an old revolutionary in his early 60s at a time when few men lived past the age of 50. He was physically not up to such a trek, though he was ready and able to train someone else to do it. To achieve his goal, Jefferson enlisted the aid of his protégé, Meriwether Lewis. In 1802 Lewis was a 28-year-old man of heroic stature, a fellow Virginian who served as the president's personal secretary.

Jefferson believed that Lewis's unique talents as frontiersman, soldier, and well-educated gentleman would translate well into a commission to lead the western expedition that Jefferson envisioned. When presented with the opportunity, Lewis jumped at the chance—with one proviso. He wanted his old friend William Clark along as cocommander. Jefferson readily assented and the Lewis and Clark expedition to explore the western frontier of the United States was actively conceived.

But by opening up the West to discovery and of course subsequent settlement, Jefferson was also opening it up to crime. The president could never have envisioned the human carnage that would follow in the next two centuries as criminals of all sorts found their way into the newly explored territories.

HARPER'S FERRY, VIRGINIA (1803): MERIWETHER LEWIS ARMS THE LEWIS AND CLARK EXPEDITION

On March 16, 1803, Meriwether Lewis arrived at the Harper's Ferry Arsenal in western Virginia. In hand was a letter from the secretary of war, Henry Dearborn to Joseph Perkins, the armory superintendent. It began:

Sir:

You will be pleased to make such arms and iron work as requested by the Bearer Captain Meriwether

Lewis and to have them completed with the least possible delay.

Lewis needed firepower to shoot game and repel attackers. He found what he needed at the armory. He loaded up with 15 rifles, 15 powder horns, 30 bullet molds, 30 ball screws, extra rifle and musket locks, gunsmithing tools, tomahawks, and 24 knives. On April 18, 1803, Lewis left Harper's Ferry with his weaponry and went west on his now famous expedition.

During the next three years, the Lewis and Clark expedition made its way west of Pittsburgh, down the Ohio River, then up north on the Missouri River through Illinois, Missouri, and Iowa, and into the unexplored lands of South Dakota, North Dakota, Montana, Idaho, and Oregon, all the way to Fort Clatsop, south of Puget Sound on the Pacific. Lewis had one violent encounter with Indians during which he and his men were forced to shoot.

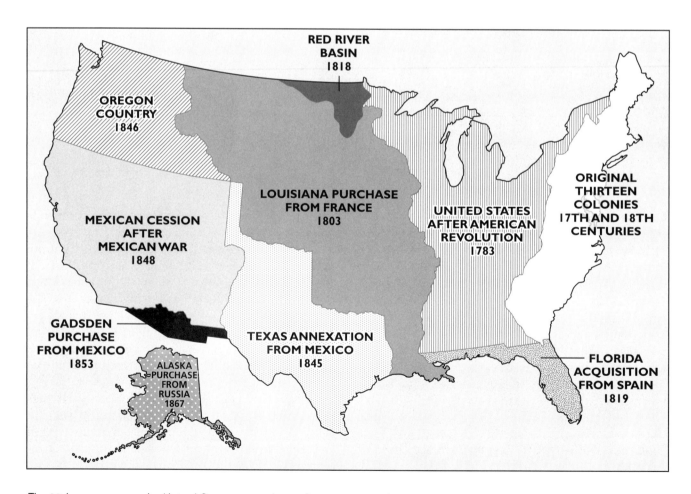

The 19th century saw the United States expand greatly as it acquired western territories.

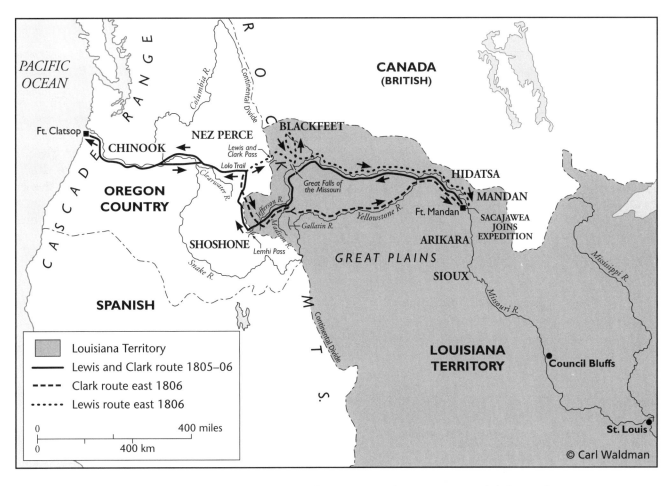

Sacajawea and the Lewis and Clark Expedition, 1804-6. Serving as guide, interpreter, and diplomat, Sacajawea was crucial to the success of the expedition.

Taking essentially the same route back east, Lewis arrived in Washington in 1806 and personally reported to the president between September 23 and December 31, 1806. Much of what Lewis had to say about exploiting the continent's resources had to do with the fur trade. In his report to the president, Lewis wrote:

The Missouri and all its branches from the Cheyenne upwards abound more in beaver and Common Otter, than any other streams on earth, particularly that proportion of them lying within the Rocky Mountains.

When made public, Lewis's report began a westward expansion that would define the country for the next century.

In subsequent years, men of all types came to exploit the fur trade. This included traders aiming to con the Indians out of their furs in return for trinkets; gamblers who hoped to cheat the trappers, fur traders, and settlers out of their money (and if necessary, kill them to get it); and prostitutes working to entertain the men who came to the new country. At the top of the criminal chain were the murderers, men and sometimes women who killed out of passion, profit, and occasionally, because they liked it.

NATCHEZ TRACE, TENNESSEE (1809): FIRST SUICIDE OF AN AMERICAN HERO

As America developed, the canons of the Catholic Church and the Protestant movement influenced the passage of laws governing criminal behavior. Both Catholics and Protestants denounced suicide and Catholics considered it a mortal sin. Consequently, it was common in a state's criminal code to include a prohibition against suicide, making it a criminal act.

Of course, there was the obvious difficulty of enforcing the law against someone who was successful in killing himself or herself. But having the law on the books was thought to discourage the act and allowed survivors to be prosecuted. The law made the moral statement that a person has no more of a right to murder himself or herself than anyone else does since it was accepted belief that God gives life and only God can take it away.

None of this weighed on Meriwether Lewis's mind. What did was a severe depression. He had been subject to depression his whole life. Intense activity of the type he experienced during the expedition helped him cope with it, but he knew he could

only hold the demons at bay for so long. His promotion had not helped.

The president had rewarded his former personal secretary's heroism by making him governor of the Louisiana Territory. Lewis had taken up his post in St. Louis, but problems with the financial affairs of his office caused him to travel to Washington in fall 1809 to set things in order.

His depression deepening, Lewis wrote his last will and testament on September 11. He was drinking heavily, taking pills, and using snuff to conquer the heaviness that lay over his soul like a damp woolen blanket. Some friends traveling with him realized he was suicidal, and they kept a close watch

The inn along the Natchez Trace where Meriwether Lewis committed suicide in 1809 (Library of Congress)

on him. But problems with straying horses kept Lewis's friends out on the trail, and that left Lewis alone, finally, for one night. Late in the afternoon of October 6, Lewis arrived at Grinder's Inn on the Natchez Trace, 72 miles south of Nashville. He acted erratically, pacing around the place, and when he took to his room after nightfall, the owner heard him muttering to himself.

Inside his room, Lewis had two loaded pistols. Lewis placed the first against his skull and pulled the trigger. The ball exploded out of the muzzle in a cloud of smoke and sparks, but it only grazed his skull. Lewis did not hesitate, and with the second pistol aimed downward, he shot himself in the chest. He was still not successful. After trying and failing to kill himself not once but twice, he lingered for hours. But Lewis was, to the end, a man of action, and he grabbed his razor and used it to cut himself until he was restrained by a fellow traveler who responded to the pistol shots. Finally, he collapsed. He died from his wounds as the sun came up.

Meriwether Lewis was buried adjacent to the inn, the spot marked by a broken shaft that was put in as a marker for his gravesite in 1849. As for the scene of the crime, Grinder's Inn on the Natchez Trace survived into the 1940s when it finally faded into wind and history.

See also DANIEL BOONE; JOHN BROWN, A.K.A. OSAWATOMIE BROWN; CAVE-IN-ROCK, ILLINOIS (1729); JOSEPH HARE; THE WESTERN FRONTIER (1790–1800).

Jean Lafitte (c. 1780–c. 1826) hero and criminal ruler of the port of New Orleans

In the early days of the 19th century, piracy was common off the shores of the United States. Anyone caught doing it could be hanged, and some were. The motive for such a severe penalty was that pirates tended to be ruthless, cold-blooded, depraved individuals. They would just as soon murder a merchant for his goods as pick a traveler's pocket. For the most part, pirates were uneducated sorts who made their living at the business end of a cutlass and a gun.

Jean Lafitte was none of that. He was probably the cleverest criminal to operate in the United States during the first half of the 19th century because he figured out a way to exploit the geography of the country to make lots of money.

Lafitte always described himself as a "corsair" or "privateer." He plundered no American ships, earned a presidential pardon for his criminal activities, became a criminal again, and then, best of all, had

the good grace to absent himself from the American criminal stage before his final ruin. Lafitte was a true buccaneer, a pirate at once handsome, cultured, and deadly. He would attack the ships of any nation to make a buck, but he loved the United States, and if one of his men attacked an American ship, Lafitte hanged him. Lafitte was so patriotic that he risked his life for his love of country, the same country that allowed him to amass criminal wealth and remain unprosecuted for many of his crimes.

Lafitte's early family life is shrouded in mystery. Lafitte's family may have hailed from Haiti, Spain, France, or any number of Caribbean islands. Lafitte lied so much about his origins that it was impossible to really know where he came from. At various times, he wrote that he hailed from Brest, Marseille, and St.-Malo, in France; Orduna, in Spain; and Westchester, New York. While he worked hard to build up his "man of mystery" mystique, Lafitte left enough clues to place his birth date between 1778 and 1780.

Lafitte was known as one of the most knowledgeable navigators of the intricate Louisiana bayou transportation system. These were channels, both natural and artificial, cut through the marsh and swamp of the southern Mississippi Delta region. Such knowledge could be acquired only after years of traversing these waterways. It therefore seems probable that Lafitte's family immigrated to the United States when he was a boy and that he probably grew up in southern Louisiana.

Lafitte first showed up in New Orleans as a young man in his early 20s in 1803, when he and his brother Pierre opened a blacksmith's shop on the Rue de St. Phillippe. The handsome Lafitte cut a dashing figure and hobnobbed with the city's French and Spanish aristocracy. Lafitte was better educated than most of the latter—he spoke English, French, Italian, and Spanish fluently, and he could converse on a variety of topics from arts to science. He was well read and respected.

Lafitte was among New Orleans's most prominent businessmen. He was a primary supplier of goods to the city. The smithy that he and brother Pierre had opened was just a front for the Lafittes' real business—they were pirates who used the smithy as a cover from which to distribute their pirated goods. What Lafitte had done to create his criminal enterprise smacked of genius.

BARATARIA

The island of Grand Terre had always been a hideout for criminals. It was one of three that stood in

Jean Lafitte's blacksmith shop in New Orleans, the front for Lafitte's privateering business (Library of Congress)

Barataria Bay, the site where the Mississippi River spills out into the Gulf of Mexico. Blackbeard the Pirate had used the place to hide from the British navy as early as 1718. But it was Lafitte who first capitalized on the island's location for criminal profit.

Lafitte was paying a fortune in customs taxes even on his pirated goods; high government taxes on slaves made plantation owners so angry, they were determined to avoid paying the taxes at all costs. Lafitte clearly had a legitimate constituency that he was not serving well. But he was a pirate visionary and he saw the potential in Barataria.

Lafitte organized his criminal enterprise with himself at the top. He demanded that his men treat him as boss and they did or found themselves either dead or banished, depending on the boss's mood. They could stay on Barataria as long as they wanted as long as they gave Lafitte respect—and his share of their plunder.

Lafitte saw the three islands as a way of creating an impregnable criminal enterprise. He mounted artillery facing the only entrance, the inlet that led to the gulf, so if anyone attacked Barataria, they would be confronted by cannonballs. With his defenses established, Lafitte turned back to business.

The pirate figured out that if his fleet of 50 pirate ships landed outside the coast, they would not have to pay government tariffs. Lafitte's buccaneers preyed primarily on Spanish ships that they waylaid in the Gulf of Mexico. Wines, cheese, medicines, slaves—Lafitte's men seized every imaginable manner of good both inanimate and human. After attacking and retreating with their ill-gotten gains, the pirates sailed back to Barataria.

The success of Lafitte's operation was dependent upon his childhood knowledge of the bayous. In order to get his shipments of illegal contraband into the city for distribution, he needed his barges to navigate the bayous. He mapped them out for his captains and then proceeded on "public works" projects of widening waterways and digging much-needed canals.

Below the city of New Orleans, Lafitte's spoils-laden barges were off-loaded into pirogues, small canoe-like boats. To avoid paying tariffs, they went up the Bayou St. John, tiny lakes and open waterways beyond the site of the U.S. customs stations. When the pirogues finally made land, his men off-loaded their goods, did a quick inventory, and placed them on flatbed wagons, which were covered with tarpaulin and then driven into the city to the waiting shop owners. In this way, proceeding in the dead of night, Lafitte was able to avoid paying tariffs and therefore could heavily discount his merchandise.

In the wake of the Louisiana Purchase, Louisiana and the Mississippi Delta region were largely overlooked by the North. For many years into the 19th century, little was done to improve the transportation system and thus encourage the flow of goods and commerce into the South. Lafitte's machinations became a necessity to the economically challenged region.

Lafitte strove to please his clients. He reasoned that since the system he had devised still entailed the use of a middleman, the shop owner, to reach the ultimate buyer, the citizens of the city, he would sell directly to the public.

Within the bayous forests of dense oak trees encased islands. The largest of these was easily reachable from New Orleans, lying halfway out in the harbor. It was called "The Temple," and it was there that Lafitte established a bazaar. "Come One! Come All! To Jean Lafitte's Bazaar & Slave Auction," the pirate advertised on handbills he distributed throughout the city. "Tomorrow at the Temple, For Your Delight, Clothing, Gems and knick-knacks From the Seven Seas."

And the public came. At the Temple they could get the best of goods cheaper than in the shops, and have the experience of mixing with Lafitte and his pirates. "The most respectable inhabitants of the state purchase goods from J. Lafitte of Barataria," one customer wrote in a letter to a friend.

Jean Lafitte enjoyed the spoils success. On the island of Grand Terre, he constructed a large brick two-story house facing the sea. When he was not in the city attending to his business, he could be found there, enjoying himself amid luxurious furnishings. An invitation to Lafitte's home was prized; everyone from businessmen to courtesans vied to be entertained by Lafitte at Grand Terre.

Lafitte had a wonderful office with wide arched French doors. In it, he conducted regular meetings with his captains, in which they plotted what ships the pirates were going to attack next. Lafitte had a standing order that no U.S. ship was ever to be fired upon by his men, under penalty of death, but ships of any other nation were fair game.

Lafitte stole many slaves from the ships he plundered. Lafitte supplied slaves to anyone who wanted them, including clergy, who used the Africans to work the Louisiana monastery grounds and the vegetable gardens next to Ursuline Convent in New Orleans. In addition to stealing them, he also bought them from traders in Cuba for $300 each, then sold them for $1200 in New Orleans. Despite his $900 profit on every slave trade, he was still delivering his goods at well below market price.

Not everyone in New Orleans was happy about the discounts Lafitte provided on Grand Terre. Governor Claiborne tried time and again to stop Lafitte's criminal machinations with little or no effect. Lafitte was just too popular and his prices too low. No matter what harassment Claiborne devised, Lafitte always trumped him.

Claiborne put a price on Lafitte's head. Handbills were plastered all over the city, announcing "$500 FOR THE CAPTURE OF JEAN LAFITTE"

Lafitte tore them down and replaced them with his own, declaring "$1500 REWARD FOR THE CAPTURE OF GOVERNOR CLAIBORNE TO BE DELIVERED TO THE ISLAND OF BARATARIA. Signed, JEAN LAFITTE"

This kind of cat-and-mouse game went on for a few years until Lafitte got fed up after he and his brother were finally arrested and spent a night in jail. Out on bail the next morning, Lafitte sought the best lawyer he could find, who happened to be otherwise engaged.

Lafitte had always had a good relationship with John Randolph Grymes, New Orleans's district attorney. The two men respected each other and kept out of each other's way. Lafitte needed an advocate who understood the law and had the respect of the legal establishment. Grymes thereby agreed to resign his post, for a handsome fee, and represent Lafitte. He would argue before the U.S. government that Lafitte had sworn undying loyalty to the U.S. and should be left alone, and that he was not breaking any laws. Before Grymes could get his hearing, the British intervened.

THE WAR OF 1812 (1814): AMERICA'S PATRIOT PIRATE
Connections are what a criminal lives for. Good connections can get you out of trouble, and bad ones can get you killed. Lafitte had both.

The government had looked the other way for a long time while he prosecuted his business, but times were changing. Being a "corsair," as Lafitte liked to put it, was no longer considered a criminal profession that, like prostitution, served the public. The territorial governor was determined to contain piracy in the territory, even if it meant putting the popular Lafitte out of business. But events were at work that would effect both Lafitte and the country he cherished.

Most wars stem out of some sort of economic disagreement, and the War of 1812 was no exception. The United States and Britain disagreed over who owned the rights of way in shipping channels. So acrimonious did the dispute become that each blockaded commercial lanes, severely limiting world trade for both nations. England followed up by attacking American ships and impressing American seamen into the British navy as galley slaves. Making matters more convoluted, both nations claimed control over the trading routes through the Great Lakes.

Fighting developed along the U.S./Canadian border, where British Tories rallied the Indians to their cause. When Congress learned that Indians in the employ of the British were attacking settlers and shippers, war resulted. On June 18, 1812, President James Madison declared war on England. British soldiers moved swiftly to invade the Michigan and Illinois territories, and U.S. forces in these areas took

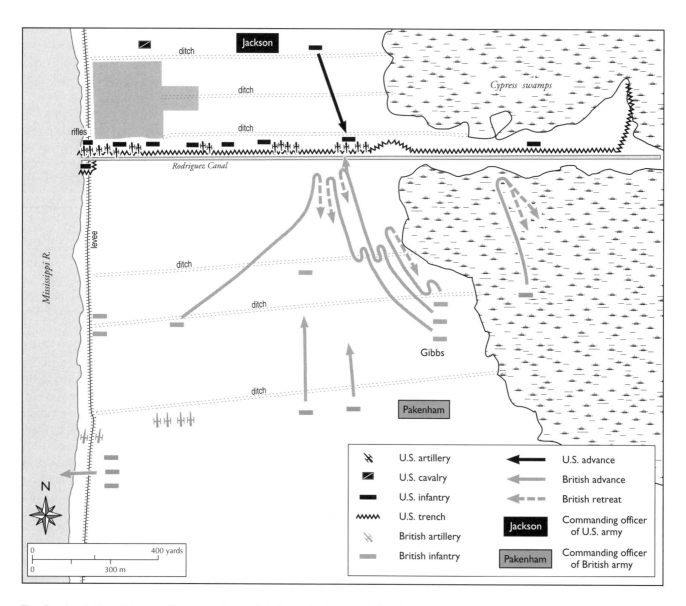

The Battle of New Orleans. Alongside General Andrew Jackson and the American forces, Jean Lafitte and 1,000 of his pirates fought and defeated the British.

heavy losses. Throughout the Great Lakes region, cannon fire signaled an unceasing battle between the two combatants.

Down south, the people of New Orleans were not very concerned with what was happening. They were thousands of miles away and seemingly impervious to such politics. Louisiana was a state, but it still had a stronger French than American presence in its culture, and sympathy for the U.S. war effort was limited.

Things might have remained so if the British had not gotten greedy. They marched on the Upper Mississippi Valley in an effort to control the river and the western frontier and effectively cut the burgeoning nation in half. To succeed, it was necessary to conquer the lower half of the river. The British therefore planned to invade New Orleans through the Gulf of Mexico.

The president dispatched General Andrew "Old Hickory" Jackson to defend New Orleans. Jackson was expecting the invasion to begin by the middle of December 1814. When he summoned his commanders for a meeting at his headquarters to finalize battle plans, everyone, with the exception of Jackson, was surprised to see Jean Lafitte stroll in. The pirate was dressed gallantly in a leather cape and sheathed rapier. He was there to help the general defend the country he loved, and Jackson readily sought advice from the man who knew every corner of every New Orleans swamp, the only man who knew the southern shipping lanes backward, forward, and frontward.

Kentucky militia arrived to fortify the defenses. Intelligence told the Americans that they were sorely outnumbered and outgunned. The British were ready to land with their crack troops, The Royal North Britain Fusiliers, the Fighting Third, and the Royal Highlanders. Those units had given Napoleon a run for his money at Waterloo.

Jackson sent recruiters across the state. He needed troops badly and immediately got 1,000 when Lafitte pledged his pirates in support of the American cause. The corsair also armed his men from his stores and presented Jackson with as many guns and flints and as much gunpowder as needed to arm the rest of his ragtag army.

Throughout the next month, the Americans fought the British in a series of skirmishes. Lafitte himself led an army of sharpshooters who engaged in guerrilla warfare behind enemy lines. Jackson was surprised to discover that the pirates were fearless fighting men.

PLAINS OF CHALMETTE, LOUISIANA (1815): LAFITTE THE HERO

The Battle of New Orleans took place on the evening of January 7, 1815, on the Plains of Chalmette, outside New Orleans. General Packenham, commanding the British forces, had an army of 7,000 against Jackson's 4,000, and that included 1,000 of Lafitte's pirates. Fully 25 percent of the American forces that stood up against the British on that day were murderers, robbers, thieves, burglars, and pickpockets and they all knew how to fight. They were armed with extra muskets and powder from Lafitte's pirate stores, giving them the firepower of 8,000 soldiers.

During the battle, rockets burst through the fog, landing at the feet of the Americans.

"They're only rockets!" Jackson shouted to his men. "Keep your heads low and they don't part your hair!"

The Baratarians needed no such warning. Not only did they follow that advice, but did so with unceasing bravery under fire, standing their position coolly with cups of coffee in their hands. Lafitte, though, was not around to partake. He had gone into the woods, behind enemy lines, with a detachment of marksmen. The men at the line could hear their rifle fire as the pirate and his command held back a regiment of British redcoats.

Then the bagpipes started, the mournful sound meant to unnerve the Americans. The fog began to lift, and through it Jackson and his men could see the British advancing. They came within 1,250 yards of the American position, then 100 yards and Jackson fought to hold his men steady. When the British were 50 yards away, Jackson gave the order to fire, and the Americans opened up with all they had. When the gunsmoke cleared, thousands of the British lay dead or dying. The Americans reloaded and fired again, downing another line of advancing troops. Behind the lines, Lafitte and his men played havoc with the British, who thought they were being fired on from all directions.

The Americans opened up with their artillery. The pirates had towed cannons that had once defended Barataria from sea attack to the city where they joined in the fusillade.

General Packenham tried to rally his troops, but it didn't work. Broken in spirit and body, the British were forced to retreat. The Americans, aided valiantly by Lafitte and his pirates, had won. By the end of the day, the fog had burned off and the Americans could see the result of the battle. Next to the battle of the Little Bighorn, it was probably the most lopsided defeat in American military history. Some 2,600 British corpses littered the battlefield, compared to 13 Americans. Thanks to Lafitte, Jackson had gained the greatest victory of his career, a victory that would eventually catapult him into the White House. That the battle had unknowingly been fought after the war was over made no difference.

The two sides had signed an armistice in Britain the previous month. Word had just not gotten as far south yet as New Orleans. That required a rider carrying dispatches, with the word passing by hand, starting with a messenger at the Hudson River docks. When the ship containing the American negotiators docked in New York Harbor, communication with the rest of the continent began. The message that the war was over was sent by rider after rider, south from New York to Philadelphia, to Baltimore, to Washington, down through Virginia, and then to the Deep South before it finally got to New Orleans.

Finally, weeks after the actual event, the participants in the battle found out the war was over. They had fought for nothing. But if Jackson had lost, there would have been nothing to stop the British from continuing the war. The British had already burned the White House and the District of Columbia. Many historians believe the British would have torched New Orleans if they had won the battle.

In typical New Orleans southern fashion, a ball was held on January 23 to celebrate victory. The pirates mixed with the patriots on the dance floor. Lafitte charmed the ladies. Later that evening, he met with Governor Claiborne and they laughed about their differences.

In respect of their contribution to winning the battle, General Jackson absolved Lafitte and his men of any pending criminal charges.

Jackson wrote to Lafitte before he left the city,

I do an act of justice and at the same time one very agreeable to my feelings to state the services you have rendered during the late invasion of your country. . . . Sir, to one of those to whom the country is most indebted, I feel great pleasure in giving this testimant of your worth, and to add ther sincere promise of my private friendship and high esteem.

President Madison issued a proclamation granting a full pardon to Lafitte and his men, restoring to them the citizenship, which they had forfeited when they became pirates. Never before or since has a criminal been labeled a national hero by a sitting and a future president at the same time. It proved to be Lafitte's undoing. He was now forced to act the part and that meant no piracy.

What makes Lafitte such a compelling figure is that he then petitioned the government to return his

An original sketch of the battle of New Orleans by General Jackson's engineer (National Archives)

ships and supplies that had been confiscated at the start of the war. He wanted them restored so he could go the privateer route again. The government replied that Lafitte's "possessions" were illegal contraband. They were not going to return ill-gotten gains. Lafitte was either hero or criminal. Lafitte's reply was to bitterly buy back eight of his ships at auction from the government he had helped in time of need.

Next, the government decided to auction some of the goods it had confiscated from Lafitte's warehouse on Grand Terre. Among the booty was found a unique set of jewelry that had belonged to a wealthy Creole woman who had taken a trip to France years before but had never returned. Rumor spread that the jewelry had wound up in Lafitte's hands because he had attacked the ship the Creole woman was on, an American ship.

Lafitte was outraged. He had acted as a true patriot and now his own country was turning against him. And then, he remembered. Years before, one of his captains had disobeyed his standing order and attacked an American ship. Lafitte himself had hanged the malefactor when he got back to Barataria. But Lafitte made the mistake of keeping the evidence of the crime, including the Creole woman's unique jewelry.

Lafitte knew he was defeated. The government now had a way to act against him. He knew that he would be exiled and forced to quit Barataria. Then, on September 2, 1814, the British threw him a life preserver. Five emissaries from the Royal Army and Royal Navy went to see Lafitte at Barataria.

The British had finally figured out that to win a war in America, frontal assaults did not work. Guerrilla tactics did. The British presented Lafitte a commission in the Royal Navy—and the spoils of war—in return for the assistance of him and his men in navigating the Louisiana bayous in a rearguard action against the Americans. The pirate would also gain citizenship and permanent legitimacy as a British subject.

It was the best offer anyone had ever made to Jean Lafitte. Turning it down meant banishment by his own country. Accepting the offer guaranteed him what he craved more than anything—legitimacy.

Lafitte turned the British down and thereby sealed his own doom. He wrote Governor Claiborne:

This point of Louisiana which I occupy is of great importance in the present crisis. I tender my services to defend it; the only regard I ask is that a stop be put to the proscription against me and my adherents. . . . If you were thoroughly acquainted with the nature of my offenses, I should appear to you much less guilty and still worthy to discharge the duties of a good citizen.

Lafitte also promised to leave should the governor not accept his proposal. In a second letter, he wrote to a friend, John Blanque, a Creole member of the Louisiana state legislature in which he revealed the secret British effort to get him to renounce the U.S. and his refusal to do so, while once again swearing his undying allegiance to the Stars and Stripes.

Claiborne's response came in the form of six gunboats, the warship *Carolina*, and three barges laden with extra men and ammunition. They all sailed into Barataria Bay and without even requesting Lafitte's surrender, opened fire. Lafitte could not believe that the American government was shelling him. Even had his men wanted to mount a defense, Lafitte would not let them. He would not fire on a fellow American.

The remnants of Lafitte's pirate crews, including Lafitte himself, fled through the marshes. As for the federal troops, they looted Grand Terre for days after the place was leveled. Claiborne's men later estimated Lafitte's treasure to be valued in excess of $50,000, a fortune at the time.

In April 1817 Lafitte took the eight ships he had purchased back from the government, ships he had, luckily kept out of harm's way, and sailed them out of Barataria Bay for the last time. Their first port of call was Santo Domingo, where the Spanish were not happy to receive the man who had formerly preyed on their shipping. They, too, kicked him out.

Lafitte sailed for Galveston Island, off the coast of Texas in the Gulf of Mexico, and there he established his new headquarters. Although owned by Spain, Galveston was part of Texas, which was a province of Mexico. Lafitte made a mutually beneficial deal with the Mexicans who were anxious to gain their independence from Spain.

In return for allowing him to continue his pirating activities, Lafitte agreed to the Mexicans' request that he concentrate his efforts on Spanish ships. He was back in business as boss. Once again, Lafitte built a big, fine house for his family. This time, he placed cannons in the upper windows of the house, their sights trained on the water through which his enemies might choose to attack him.

Lafitte's new venture did not last long. His ranks of experienced pirates decimated, he was forced to rely on the depraved jetsam and flotsam that found its way to his little village on the island. Most of these men were cutthroats without a vestige of honor or a sense of responsibility in serving the boss for the good of the greater whole. Even the boss could not control some of them when they went out drinking and whoring. Soon, both the Mexicans as well as the Americans turned on him once again as the depredations of Lafitte's "pirates" added up.

In late 1820 the USS *Enterprise* docked in Campeche Bay adjacent to Galveston Island. Aboard was a naval diplomat, Lieutenant Larry Kearney, who had been dispatched by President Madison himself. Kearney ordered Lafitte off Galveston Island. Lafitte stalled but eventually was forced to give in. He did not want the slaughter of Barataria to be repeated.

In May 1821 the American fleet landed on Galveston Island. They found Lafitte's village in ruins, burned to the ground. This time, Lafitte had made sure he was not going to be looted. As for the pirate, he was nowhere to be found.

At that moment, Jean Lafitte disappeared into history. No one knows where he went; no one knows when he died or where he is buried. The only thing that is known for certain is that without the pirate's assistance, Britain would have won at the Battle of New Orleans.

See also JIM BOWIE; WASHINGTON, D.C. (1835).

Jim Bowie (1796–1836) slave trader, adventurer, Alamo hero

Living on the frontier meant living with danger as a companion. Aberrations of character were not uncommon. Bowie's place in American criminal history is as the first of a modern form of criminal, someone who embodied the continent's conflicting impulses. Jim Bowie was neither criminal nor lawman, but a seemingly queer combination of both that was uniquely American.

In 1817, at the age of 21, Jim Bowie arrived on Galveston Island with his brothers Rezin and John. The importation of slaves to the United States had finally been outlawed; slavery had not. The Bowie brothers illegally bought slaves from Jean Lafitte and then resold them at tremendous profit to the Louisiana sugar planters through present-day Beaumont, Louisiana, or via the Sabine and Calcasieu Rivers. They kept this up for a few years, but after awhile, Bowie found it boring.

Slaving was considered an honorable profession, and everyone who knew Bowie knew him as a man of good character, though he did have a notorious temper. Bowie engaged in countless knife duels, once disemboweling a man with the Bowie knife he had been given by his brother, Rezin Bowie, the weapon's creator. Jim's use of the knife so effectively in duels popularized the weapon and made it legendary.

More than one murderer would subsequently turn to the Bowie knife as a means of killing and even cutting up the corpse for disposal. Jim Bowie, however, went on to become a defender of the Alamo, where he died when Santa Ana stormed the fort in 1836. Upon his death, Jim Bowie became an American hero. Over the years, Bowie's criminal past as an illegal slave trader has been overshadowed by his status as an American hero.

See also JEAN LAFITTE.

Joseph Hare (?–1817) king of the highwaymen

Joseph Hare was the most famous highwayman of his time. He was a real professional, smooth and charming, but never hesitating to pull the trigger. People knew Hare would shoot if they did not "stand and deliver." That's why, in his whole life as a highwayman, Hare reportedly never killed.

Circumstance had taken Hare from the Natchez Trace where he had made his reputation back to the east of his youth. He told the minister who visited him the day of his execution that he had been born in Chester County, Pennsylvania. Like many of the century's future desperadoes, he was an easterner. Robert Coates has a much less succinct description of his childhood that goes toward explaining his adult actions.

He was a hoodlum at heart, and the hard, sharp crowded life of the cities sharpened and pinched him. New York, Philadelphia, Baltimore.

As a boy, he had been apprenticed to a tailor, and the love of fine fabrics and flashy raiment remained with him to the end. A handsome lad, he loved a well cut coat and a snug fitting pair of breeches.

At 21 Hare went to Philadelphia and sailed with an old friend of his father's a sea captain, to New Orleans. He was in town for just one day before he stopped a Spaniard and took his watch and $17. The Spaniard seemed poor, and Hare left him his watch and part of the money.

Hare saw that New Orleans was a city bursting at the seams with money from the flatboatmen and planters who had come to town to sell their wares.

He would pick their pockets, trip them up in the dark and bludgeon them free of their cash, and commit burglaries on the unsuspecting. But he had a greater idea in mind.

Hare knew that the businessmen sold their goods, then traveled laden with cash up the Natchez Trace toward their homes. He put together a gang of criminals and then set out on the trace to help himself to some of this booty. The trace was particularly dangerous in the "three hundred mile strip of canebrake, swamp and desolation ruled by the Chickasaws and Choctaws," but the danger to travelers was not from the Indians. In fact, the "Chickasaws always boasted that they had never shed the blood of a white man in anger," and the Choctaws were known as "the happiest and best people" around. No, the danger came from men like Hare, who marched through the canebrake like they owned it and levied their own tax against any man who crossed their path.

Hare and his gang went northward. Just beyond Natchez, they came upon a group of men entering the Indian Territory. Using berry juice to stain their skins, they posed as Indians.

I spoke to them in the Creek tongue of which I knew a few words. It was as if I had been an Indian. I told them we were Indians that did not think it any harm to take money from white People and if they raised one of their arms to fire on us, we would send them to eternity, every man of them. Then I had heard one of the men say when I took his goods out of the saddlebags. "Lord bless my soul" and gave a very heavy sigh. I remember I thought he was frightened for his life and I told him, "I have never asked any man for his life."

One of the men looked very blank at seeing all his money taken from him and swore he'd be damned if he didn't deserve better luck "for he had got it after an hour and a half's hard fighting!" He told me he had been on board a privateer, and seen some danger, but he could not fight without a noise and this damned place [the wilderness] was so quiet and mournful. He felt as if he were going to the devil every moment.

I told him I would stand his friend, and gave him his watch and several gold pieces and he looked as thankful as if I had done him a favor instead of robbing him. We took three hundred doubloons, 74 pieces of different sizes and a large quantity of gold bars, six inches in length and eight square—thirty weight of it. With the others, I found 700 doubloons and five silver dollars and four hundred French guineas and 67 pieces the value of which I could not tell until I weighed them. I got twelve or thirteen thousand dollars altogether from

THE LIFE AND ADVENTURES
OF
JOSEPH T. HARE,
THE BOLD ROBBER AND HIGHWAYMAN,
With 16 Elegant and Spirited Engravings.
BY THE AUTHOR OF
THE LIFE OF JOHN A. MURRELL.

H. LONG & BROTHER, 32 ANN STREET, NEW YORK.

The history of the above extraordinary criminal is well deserving a niche in the felon pyramid next beside the great marauder Murrell, whose wonderful career has become a part of the history of the West. Though widely different in character from the renowned land pirate, and though the scourge of an earlier generation, Hare possessed qualities scarcely less remarkable than his satanic prototype, and his exploits may claim even a stronger interest, from the fact that he figured as the first great freebooter of the Republic. If Murrell may be called the "MASSA RONI of the West," Hare may be designated as the "RINALDO RINALDINI of America."
Police Gazette.

PRICE TWENTY-FIVE CENTS.

Joseph Hare's widespread fame led to the publication of an account of his life and adventures. (Courtesy of Carl Sifakis)

the company, all of it in gold. The whole that I had to my share from that robbery came to 7,000 dollars.

After that, Hare and his men holed up for a while, waiting for the right time to strike again. Hare was looking for a hideout in the canebrake and he found it near the northern border of the Chickasaw country, a bit south of the Tennessee state line.

We came across a spot that seemed a very good retreat, and a very comfortable home too. It was one side of a canebrake, where the cane grew very thick and tall, and would have concealed us from the best eyes. These cane breaks are very much frequented by wild animals of all sorts, especially wildcats, and are kept clear of generally.

Our habitation was in a cleft rock, where one rock jutted very much over another, and made sort of a cave, that we could easily make safe from every savage that walked the wild wilderness. We had a good feather bed in our cave.

Coates points out that Hare's biggest enemy was not the Indian, but the wilderness itself. He was a city boy first and foremost who must have found the wilderness a desert for his soul. A diarist, his words carry great emotion and description of the deprivations he was forced to endure in the silence and danger of the wilderness.

"As for me, I could not sleep," he writes of one night, "but lay looking, sometimes in the fire which I had kindled, and sometimes at the stars, and listening to the wind in among the cane break, which made such a mournful rustling sound . . ."

Hare only gave himself so much time for existential questions. He was a highwayman who enjoyed practicing his chosen profession.

We came across a company of four men. I had hard work to save their lives. We stopped them: we had hid all the horses from the sight of the road. I stepped up to the one that had holsters before him and told him that I had twelve highway robbers under my command and the first man that moved should be blown to hell. The dry cane made great crackling; it was so thick in that spot that a man could not be seen ten feet from the road.

It was a cloudy day, and everything looked black and gloomy, and the sound of the cane, though it did not frighten me, made me feel very strange and out of the way . . .

Nothing happened. There was Hare, alone on the trail, and the men he had stopped, trying to gauge whether he was telling the truth. If Hare was not bluffing, reaching for their guns could cost them their lives.

Hare's men called from their hiding place that they did not have disguises on. If he let the men live, they could all be arrested and recognized later. The victims, the fight leaching out of them now that they knew men in the undergrowth had them covered, begged for their lives.

Whether they could have won or not is conjecture. The pistols at the time were not accurate and frequently blew up on the person firing them. But at point blank range they could blow a hole in a man's belly the size of a fist. It was not a pleasant fate to contemplate.

Hare was not a murderer. He would not fire unless fired upon. He recalled, "It was well thought of [the lack of disguise] and further that if there should but one man move till I gave the signal, they would all be landed in eternity; and with this I called to one of my companions to come up and take their money."

Their total take was $7,000. Hare's wilderness venture was making himself rich, but the wilderness was taking its toll. He grew restless and sometimes rode out on his own.

"I was by myself," he wrote, "and had left the men at the cave. I had one pistol with me and felt a desire to do something by myself."

A slave trader from Natchez had just completed a sale in the New Orleans slave market and was bound up the trace for home. Hare saw him.

I rode up on his left side and told him to deliver his money, for I was the devil, and would take him to hell in a second if he did not drop that gun off his shoulder and his pistols too, if he had any.

Hare had not drawn his weapon. Maybe he thought his arch tongue and sartorial splendor would cause his victim to deliver the goods without a struggle. The trader, meanwhile, looked around and saw no one but Hare. The trader dropped his gun from his shoulder, as if to proffer it. As it came level with Hare's stomach, he raised the muzzle slightly and pulled the trigger. The muzzle fire swept out in Hare's face. His hat was blown off and his horse reared. The highwayman pulled at the reins to control his mount, then jerked his pistol out from his belt.

The smoke from the musket so obscured the scene that Hare could not see his intended victim. He fired anyway and, not hearing a cry of pain, assumed he had hit no one. Then, behind on the trace, he heard men on horseback approaching. Hare turned and saw that at least one was armed with a rifle. He turned back. The smoke had cleared.

"I had not hurt the trader in the least but he looked frightened and I told him to clear himself as fast as he could or I would give him another fire."

The trader galloped off, and Hare recovered his hat and reloaded, waiting for the two strangers to approach. The strangers and Hare actually exchanged silly pleasantries, though all present knew what had happened. Hare was not stupid; he was not about to try two hold-ups in one day by himself. Hare and the men rode off in opposite directions.

After that, Hare decided to get out of the wilderness. He and his men headed north for Nashville,

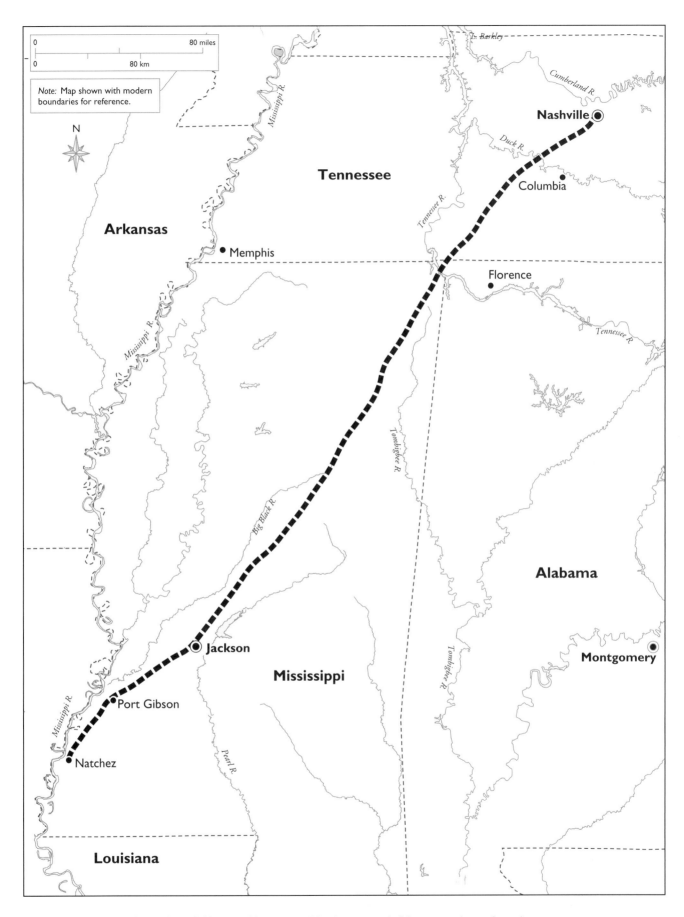

The Natchez Trace, where Joseph Hare and his gang of highwaymen held sway in the early 19th century

where they took rooms at a nice hotel and lived the good life as men about town. They stayed there for a month, then bought passage in a flatboat to Natchez and thence to New Orleans. They roistered about in the gay city until their money was down to nothing, and then it was time to get back to business.

They got Spanish passports to escape from their American brethren should the need arise. Armed with the papers, guns, and provisions, they set off into the wilderness again. It was during this second expedition that Hare began keeping his diary in earnest. Coates points out that among the first words he wrote were these:

Let not any one be induced to turn highwayman by reading this book and seeing the great sums of money I have robbed for it is a desperate life, full of danger, and sooner or later it ends at the gallows.

Hare was beginning to develop a religious conscience about his thievery. He knew it to be wrong and felt guilty. When one of his gang, who made a profession of marrying and leaving women after absconding with their dowry, tried the scam on a "little Spanish girl fresh from a nunnery in Baton Rouge," Hare preached to the man of the error of his ways. He then tried to get him to return the girl to her parents. His friend reciprocated by leaving the next morning with the girl and Hare's wallet, which contained $700. A few days later, Hare found him.

I met him at a tavern where he was boasting of being able to whip any man in town. I thought this was a good opportunity to take my satisfaction out of him.

They fought.

Every time I caught hold of him he bellowed for help. He was like a wolf caught in a sharp trap. I whipt him until he hollowed, "Enough!" I gave him as handsome a dressing as any man ever got.

Hare beat the man so badly he thought he was dead. He and his men rode down to Pensacola, Florida, Spanish soil, in case the constables came looking for him. There, he took refuge in a boardinghouse.

"One day one of the boarders asked me if I had heard the news. I was alarmed." Hare thought he had been discovered. "It was only that I and my companions were picked to give the next ball that week." As was general custom, the gentlemen of the town alternated in sponsoring a cotillion.

After leaving Pensacola, he was arrested as an American spy at the border and later released. Hare was now reading the Bible in earnest and found its power transformative. He became the only evangelical highwayman extant and preached the error of their ways to his criminal companions. Unfortunately, he was not very successful, probably because he never led by example.

One afternoon, he robbed a drover. He later recalled,

About nine-o'clock, the night I robbed the drover, I was riding along very rapidly to get out of the reach of pursuit. I saw standing right across the road, a beautiful white horse, as white as snow, his ears stood straight forward and his figure was very beautiful.

When I approached him and got within six feet of him, he disappeared in an instant, which made me very uneasy. It made me stop and stay at a house near there, all night.

The drover went to the authorities in New Orleans and came back with a posse looking for Hare. They found him in bed. His trial and conviction were swift. He served five years in jail, where he continually read the Bible. When he was released, he rode back up the trace and wrote, "I think this white horse was Christ and that he came to warn me of my sins and to make me fear and repent."

Hare rode all the way to Baltimore, where he tried to go straight. He got a job with a tailor, where he worked for 6 months at his old trade. But the old yearning for the road came over him. He left Baltimore for Albany to make a big score. He robbed a few men on the road, spent the money quickly and, broke again, rode up to Canada where he robbed Canadians, and holed up in Ballston Springs. He continued,

Then I made a robbery on the road that leads from Chester to Lancaster. I married a young girl. I was almost broke, I needed robbery again. In Princeton, New Jersey, I robbed the trunk of a merchant. I got 30,000 and was caught the next day. I got five years in prison and served two years and was pardoned. After leaving jail, I went to Philadelphia and at last the idea occurred to me of robbing the U.S. mail.

Until then the most Hare had been guilty of were state crimes, but robbing the mails was a federal offense. Yet Hare, always daring the consequences, gathered two companions and, arming themselves with pistols and dirks (daggers), set out to rob the night mail coach from Baltimore to Havre de Grace, Maryland, on March 12, 1818:

These two new robbers, I did not place much confidence in. They had never seen any such robbery and one was so young, I was afraid his resolution would fail. On Wednesday night two or three miles open this side of Havre de Grace, I made them help me to put a fence across the road before the mail passed that way on its way to Philadelphia and Baltimore.

As the coach approached through the dark night, "I saw the lamp burning and the stage and two men in the stage." The stage stopped at the roadblock Hare and his men had set up. He ran up very quickly so that they would not have time to get out their weapons, and told the driver that they were six highway robbers all armed with double-barrel pistols and dirks. He warned them not to fire, and said all he wanted was the South Carolina mail and their money. Hare searched the mail for money and got all he could. One of his victims was left tied to a wagon wheel. This man begged for the return of his watch, which he claimed was a family heirloom. Hare held his lantern high to look for the timepiece and as he did, the light revealed his undisguised features.

He gave the man back his watch. Leaving, Hare retreated to Baltimore and split from his companions, and the first thing he did was get some new clothes made. A customer in the shop where Hare was looking at coats identified him as the man who had robbed the stage he was on. The police were secretly summoned.

The victim had seen Hare's face when he had raised the lamplight to identify and return the pocket watch. How ironic that such a selfless act should have caused his ultimate undoing. Hare was taken into custody on suspicion of mail robbery, a crime punishable by death.

At trial, he was identified again and conviction seemed inevitable, but Hare's attorney, Charles Mitchell, had a brilliant legal mind. Mitchell looked through his law books and found a little-known fact in Maryland law.

At his client's arraignment, he told Hare not to answer the charges against him. Hare obeyed. Hare was being charged with a federal crime, and under a previously passed act of Congress, if a prisoner stood mute at the bar, his plea was to be entered as guilty. However, this act was only enforceable in cases involving treason and other capital crimes against the government.

When the act passed, robbing the mail was not a capital crime. It was a later congressional act that made it so. Mitchell argued that since the second act had not been retroactive and the provisions of the first act did not apply, then no plea could be taken if his client stood mute.

It was a brilliant move. The court did not know what to do. Mitchell's argument was persuasive. Months went by as the court tried to figure out what to do. Finally, the federal court came down with its opinion that if a prisoner stood mute at the bar, his recalcitrance amounted to a constructive confession, implying guilt. Under state law, in grave offenses such as Hare had been charged with, a lack of a plea meant the court had to proceed as if the defendant had pleaded not guilty.

There were two pleas now, guilty and not guilty for the same alleged crime of robbing the US mail. Regardless of plea, a trial took place and Hare was convicted after four days of testimony and deliberation. Mitchell's attempt at making new law had failed.

"For the last 14 years of my life, I have been a highway robber and I have robbed on a larger scale and gotten more success than any robber in Europe or in the country that I have ever heard of; but I have the consolation of reflection. That I never killed nor wounded any man and that no man's blood is on my hands," said Hare in his dying confession.

On the morning of September 10, 1818, the most successful and most humane highwayman in U.S. history was led from his cell into the yard of the Baltimore prison. There was a problem with the trapdoor in the gallows that delayed the hanging for an hour. To pass the time, Hare read his Bible calmly.

Shortly before 10 A.M., he was led up the gallows steps and the noose was placed around his neck. There were no last words. At a few minutes after 10:00, the hangman pulled the lever, the trapdoor shot open, and Hare was flung out into the eternity with which he had threatened so many of his victims. The great highwayman's neck snapped. He died instantly.

See also SAMUEL "BLOODY SAM" MASON; THE WESTERN FRONTIER.

Harper's Ferry, Virginia (1817) manufacturing patented rifles

In 1817 John H. Hall received permission from the federal government to manufacture his patented rifles at Harper's Ferry. The armory cranked up into full production mode as weapons were stockpiled over the next 42 years, until 1859.

Even with its importance to the nation's defense having thus been increased, the government did nothing to improve the security of the facility. Any group of armed men sufficient to overpower the facility's few guards could take over the place easily. Various areas within the facility, especially the attached firehouse, would serve as excellent defensive positions for such a determined band.

The thought just never occurred that someone might actually raid the armory and use the weapons against the United States. Insurrection was as remote a possibility as Missouri becoming a free state.

See also JOHN BROWN, A.K.A. OSAWATOMIE BROWN.

Missouri Compromise (1820–1821) crime expands west
The Missouri Compromise was an attempt by the Congress to keep peace in the ever-growing United States. Just like every compromise the government had made starting in 1776, when Adams had to strike the antislavery section of the Declaration of Independence that Jefferson wrote in order to appease southern opposition, the Missouri Compromise was doomed to failure. It was a simple matter of adding and subtracting. As new states were added to the original 13, a tally was kept of which ones allowed slavery and which ones did not. By 1818 Missouri had enough people within its territorial borders to be granted admission into the Union. The population consisted largely of southern settlers who had brought their proslavery ways with them. The citizens of the prospective state figured they would be admitted as a slave state. James Tallmadge saw it differently.

A congressman from New York, Tallmadge proposed and then helped pass an amendment to the Missouri statehood bill that called for the emancipation

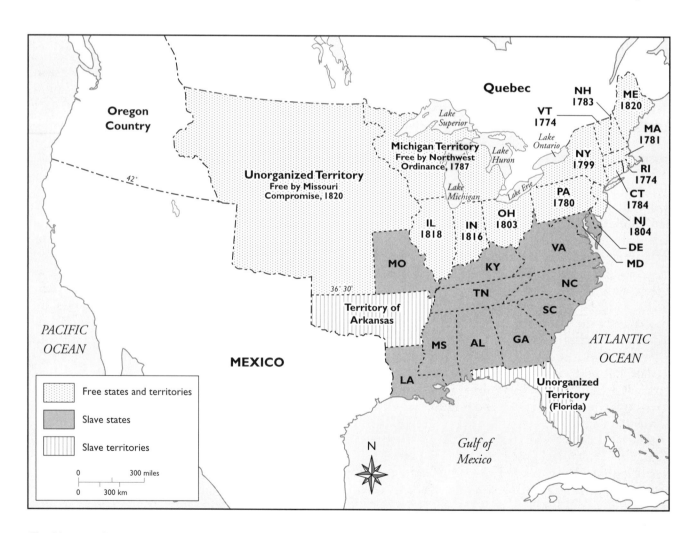

The Missouri Compromise of 1820 permitted Missouri to enter the Union as a slave state but made all other parts of the Louisiana Territory north of the 36°30' line.

of all slaves born in Missouri and banned the importation of new ones. The amendment assured that at some time in the future, slavery would be eliminated in Missouri, but the battle over the amendment was so contentious that it died in the Senate and Missouri was left stateless.

In 1819 Alabama was admitted to the Union as a slave state. That gave the slave and free states equal representation in the Senate. The next year Maine joined the Union as an antislavery state.

With Maine a "free" state, the northerners gained an edge their southern brethren could not tolerate. Once again, Missouri was brought up in Congress. Southern politicians pushed for admittance of the territory as a slave state to equal out the balance of power that had existed since colonial days.

In the Senate the two bills providing for separate admission of Maine and Missouri were joined into one. It contained a clause forbidding slavery in the remainder of the Louisiana Purchase north of the present-day southern boundary of Missouri. This compromise was meant to allow northerners to vote for it while appeasing the south, but the House rejected the combined bill. A conference committee from both houses of Congress convened to consider the issue, and decided to make the bills separate once again.

In March 1820 Maine was made a state and Missouri was authorized to pass a state constitution that had no restrictions on slavery. The Northerners would have gone along in order to keep the peace, except they noticed that the Missouri constitution contained a provision that barred free Negroes from immigrating to the state. That meant that free Negroes from the northern states, who held the same citizenship rights as the whites in their states, would be outlawed from even setting foot in Missouri's borders. Anxious for statehood, the Missouri legislature responded by pledging that nothing in its constitution would ever be interpreted to mean that the state was trying to usurp the rights of U.S. citizens. If a free black could prove he was free (which meant he was a citizen) he could stay. If he could not, out he went.

Both houses of Congress finally passed the Missouri Compromise in 1821. Missouri officially became a state on August 1, 1821. And that is how the seeds of further villainy were sown, seeds that would blossom into full-blown insurrection. One man was already planning that revolt and needed just a few short years to make his vision a reality.

See also JOHN BROWN, A.K.A. OSAWATOMIE BROWN; WASHINGTON, D.C. (1854).

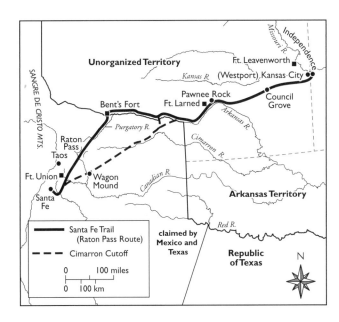

The Santa Fe Trail (ca. 1821–72) opened the Southwest to settlers and criminals alike.

Santa Fe Trail (1821) crime enters the Southwest

Opened by William Bucknell, the Santa Fe trail became the great commercial route between Franklin, Missouri and Santa Fe, New Mexico. It was a critical roadway in the expansion of the country across the west and into the southwest, the area romantically referred to as the Old West. Wagon trains, composed of settlers, prospectors, criminals and ordinary people out for adventure, traveled the Santa Fe Trail. In Kansas, the trail cut through the southwestern part of the state, where Plains Indians, including the Kiowa and Cheyenne, did not especially like the settlers coming in to take their land. The wagon trains needed protection as did the U.S. Mail Service, whose carriers also traveled the trail.

The danger would grow so bad that a fort would later be built and a permanent military presence established to protect those traveling along the trail.

John A. Murrel (1804–?) the Napoleon of American crime

Sir Arthur Conan Doyle, creator of Sherlock Holmes, described Holmes's arch nemesis Professor Moriarty as "the Napoleon of crime." In the Sherlock Holmes stories, Moriarty is the architect of a vast criminal conspiracy that, at the end of the 19th century, had spread across London and beyond. John A. Murrel may have been the model for Moriarty.

Murrel was, indeed, the Napoleon of American crime, and Conan Doyle was an avid reader of American crime literature.

For most of his career, Murrel was unknown to law enforcement authorities. He organized his criminal network throughout the west without a line in newspapers, magazines, or pamphlets. He used the Natchez Trace in particular and the subsidiary transportation systems of plantation roads, newly developed state roads, and, of course, the river to spread his vast criminal empire. It is a testament to his criminal brilliance that few in his own time knew who he was.

Yet Murrel remains the single most brilliant architect of a criminal conspiracy bigger than any modern mob could imagine. Murrel was as ruthless as Harry Tracy, as deadly as Dillinger, and as smart as Nathan Leopold.

The task of exposing him fell to a young man named Virgil Stewart, who would prove to be the greatest undercover agent up to that point in American history.

On June 1, 1833, Virgil Stewart left the town of Jackson, Tennessee. It was hard to leave, because Parson John Henning and his wife had taken in the rootless Stewart like one of their own, going so far as to lend him money to start a farm. But Stewart was a wandering sort.

Virgil hailed from Georgia, where his father died when he was a youngster. His mother deserted him to fend for himself, and the boy drifted westward, working on plantations until he made his way to Jackson, where the Hennings took him in. Now he was selling his farm and drifting south to seek his fortune. Stewart headed into the newly opened Choctaw Territory.

The Choctaw Territory was a region of swamp and canebrake that stretched across the northern half of Mississippi, encompassing the lower and more dangerous portion of the Natchez Trace. The purchase of the Choctaw land by the U.S. government meant that the area could finally be "civilized," government parlance for clearing the land of Indians and outlaws. Getting rid of the former was actually easy because the Choctaws had left after the sale and gone further west. Getting rid of the latter was another matter. The death of the outlaws would only come as civilization spread.

In fall 1833, at the town of Chocchuma, a land sale was held. Stewart wanted to buy and figured to get down there early. Making his way south by mule and flatboat, he arrived in the town of Tuscahoma, where he decided to spend the summer.

He was now in the area defined by the Choctaw Purchase, not too far from Chocchuma, and he planned to wait in Tuscahoma until the fall and then ride on to buy his land.

Stewart had been traveling with "civilized goods," including cloth and bullet molds, cutlery and tinware, and was looking for a sales outlet. He found it in Edward Clanton's store. Clanton was the town's storekeeper and ready to do business. He gave Stewart store credit for his goods and also a job tending the store in return for room and board. Clanton frequently traveled on business trips through the territory, leaving Stewart in full charge of the store. The man's travels never raised suspicion, nor should they have, considering they were no one's business but Clanton's.

On one of his frequent visits home, Clanton introduced Stewart to William Vess and his wife. The Vesses and Stewart hit it off, and soon Stewart had arranged to board at the Vesses spacious home. Through the two families, the Vesses and the Clantons, Stewart soon became a familiar figure in the town.

Vess was a carpenter, though he did not seem to work much. He would vanish for days at a time on some sort of mysterious projects then reappear again. It was difficult to figure out where his money came from, but he had money. The Vesses served coffee with every meal, and in those days, coffee was an expensive luxury.

By fall and the time of the land sale, Stewart had established himself so well in the town that he decided not to go. He was then a partner in Clanton's business and, with the explosion of homesteaders, there was much money to be made. Stewart stayed in town through the early winter of 1833–34, but he grew restless and decided to go visit his friends the Hennings up in Jackson.

On January 18, 1834, Stewart rode north again along the Natchez Trace into Tennessee. It took a week, but when he arrived in Jackson at the Hennings homestead on January 25, bad news awaited him. Parson Henning told him that someone was stealing his slaves. The Constitution classified slaves as property. State law made stealing them a capital crime. For Parson John Henning, the loss was a devastating blow because his slaves did much of the heavy work around his homestead, and he did not have the money to replace them.

The Hennings's predicament bothered Stewart immensely. This couple had been the only parents he had ever had, and Stewart's anger toward the

Murrel's portrait was done while he served time at the Tennessee State Prison at Nashville. (James E. Medler Collection, Clements Library, University of Michigan)

thief grew in proportion to the love he had for the Hennings. He asked the parson if he knew the thief's identity. Henning answered that he did not know for sure and that he would rather lose the slaves than accuse an innocent man. Mrs. Henning, though, interrupted. She knew who it was.

She told Stewart that the man who had stolen the slaves was John A. Murrel. There was no clear-cut evidence against him, but they were certain he was the culprit.

Mr. Henning explained that Murrel was a recent settler to the area. He had arrived from Memphis with a wife and kid brother. He bought land, opened a large farm, and lived high on the hog with no evident means of support. He was clearly not a farmer himself. Yet he rode the finest horses, dressed in New Orleans's finest raiment, had boots and hats from the east, and was always riding out on mysterious missions for days at a time.

Murrel had developed a reputation in the community as a wealthy man to be reckoned with, yet there was something about him that people seemed to abhor. Maybe it was that he was too well dressed, too courtly, too handsome, like someone waiting to prey on those less fortunate. With his mysterious comings and goings, he was the Hennings's logical suspect, but, again, nothing could be proven. The Hennings just had a hunch.

Stewart wanted to help his benefactors, yet how could he? He and the Hennings decided he would gain Murrel's confidence and see where it would lead. Thus was born the plan that would make Virgil Stewart the great undercover detective. What happened next Stewart would later chronicle in a pamphlet published throughout the United States.

On the morning of January 25, 1834, Stewart rode out from the Hennings farm and reached the settlement of Estanula. Here, there was a toll bridge across the Big Hatchee River. He asked the toll taker if knew a man named Murrel from Jackson. The toll taker said that he did and that the man often passed that way. Stewart asked him to point him out.

Stewart waited. It happened that the bridge had very little traffic that day but in the afternoon a handsome man wearing a Bolivar coat came riding by. He had two silver-handled pistols in saddle holsters for easy access. He quickly paid the toll and moved on. The toll taker turned to Stewart and said, "That's Murrel." Stewart rode out after him and within a mile had drawn abreast of the prosperous-looking fellow.

To gain his confidence, Stewart immediately made up a story: "The times is that hard and it's such a tight squeak for a fellow to make his living that if he sees a prime piece of horseflesh and is sharp enough to seize on it, why I say he deserves it. Always excepting when the horse happens to be mine," and he slapped his thigh and laughed.

Murrel relaxed his initial misgivings and gave Stewart a once-over.

"There are some slick ones about," Murrel said. "Right here in Tennessee there is a company of rogues so sharp that nothing can be done about them. But let a man learn the use of the law and nothing can touch him."

They would be riding for a while now, Stewart knew, for he was getting the villain to trust him. As Murrel talked, at convenient moments along the way, Stewart would secretly take out a pin and scratch names and dates on his saddle skirts. In that way, he carved into his saddle all that Murrel told him of his criminal shenanigans.

Riding through the densely thicketed country, Stewart wrote, "The weather was very cold and the road much cut up and then hard frozen and covered with sleet. It was bad traveling."

"Now there is that company," Murrel said in the sleet, "that I spoke of, sharp rogues." They were two brothers. The first was "one of the best judges of law in the United States." The other was a "keen shrewd fellow" at the head of a criminal conspiracy. "They [their gang] work under him [the rogue] robbing, stealing and he paves the way for them so that the law can never reach him."

Stewart could see that Murrel liked men to admire him, so he flattered the gentleman and bid him to continue. Murrel suddenly turned the tables and asked Stewart his name. Thinking quickly, Stewart came up with the pseudonym Adam Hues. He claimed to hail "from the Yalo Busha River country in the Purchase."

Stewart convinced him that he was a young man out for a good time, whatever it took, on this side or the law or not, it made no difference. Murrel liked

that, perhaps thinking he might have a willing convert here. He had still not revealed his true criminal identity, so Stewart probed further.

"What age is this wondrous man you speak of?"

"He is about thirty," replied Murrel, who was 30 at the time. He then proceeded to rattle off the adventures of this mysterious man. "He persuaded slaves to run off. He would hide them, then wait until the owner advertised in the local paper and then collect the reward."

But Murrel had bigger money in mind than simply accepting one reward.

Now sir, that advertisement amounts to the same as a power of attorney, to take his property, the nigger, and hold it for him. And if a man chooses to make a breach of trust in this case, and instead of carrying the nigger to the owner, converts him to his own use property,

A dramatization by a contemporary artist of the highwayman Murrel accosting a traveler (James E. Medler Collection, Clements Library, University of Michigan)

why that is not stealing and the only way the owner can get at him is in a civil action.

And who do you think owns the bank where he [the slave stealer] keeps his cash? Why one of his [the criminal's] own clan that would stand with him no matter what happens.

The criminal would then sell these same slaves time and again, each time convincing them to escape, thus he could sell them three or four times, until the whole valley would be looking for him.

Murrel then went on to describe how this criminal had once taken one such slave, who was long past his usefulness out on the bank of a secluded creek which ran by the farm of a friend, where he shot the slave through the head. He disposed of the body by cutting open the belly, removing the innards, filling it with sand and throwing it in the river to sink. It was the same method of disposal the Harp brothers and Sam Mason had used, except Murrel had refined it.

They stayed that night at the home of one of Murrel's confederates. The next day, Murrel rose early, and they were off again by daylight. The talk on that second day turned away from robbery to murder.

Murrel explained how the "older brother" was a dangerous man to cross. He had friends everywhere, and his men robbed on the river and the trace and he took a share of their booty. He had friends on the right side of the law who could even protect him if he was captured. What Murrel was describing was the biggest criminal conspiracy on the North American continent.

Murrel asked Stewart to go to Arkansas with him, but Stewart demurred at first. He was getting in deeper than he had ever thought he would. He knew if he stayed with Murrel, he was risking his life: If Murrel discovered his deception, he had no doubt he would wind up dead, his body cavity filled with sand, at the bottom of the Mississippi. The stakes, though, had gone up.

No longer was it a simple matter of proving Murrel had stolen the Hennings's slaves. The man, if he was not bragging, seemed to have criminal designs on the very fabric of the republic itself. Stewart made up his mind: He was committed to see Murrel in jail or dead. He agreed to go with him.

Robert Coats in *The Outlaw Years* recounts what happened next.

Murrel led him to a clearing, well hidden from the trail. Here they dismounted. He pulled a slab of jerked beef from his saddlebag; they sat side by side on a fallen log, hacking at the meat with their case knives, chewing huge mouthfuls. Murrel took a swig at the bottle and looked with a grinning eye at his companion.

Murrel then confessed his identity. He had been born in middle Tennessee, he told Stewart. His parents had little property, but they were intelligent people. His father was an honest man, though Murrel thought none the better of him for it. His mother taught all her children to steal as soon as they could walk and covered for them whenever she could. Murrel's first good haul came from a peddler who lodged at his father's house one night. Murrel took a bolt of linen and several other things from the man's trunks.

Murrel then worked his way up the criminal ladder, going from such petty thefts to highway robbery. For the latter, he had as teacher one Harry Crenshaw, an evil fellow who had once been part of Jean Lafitte's pirate crew. Crenshaw and the young Murrel went out on Boone's Wilderness Road, where they took up conversation with a young trader named Woods. At an isolated point on the trail, Crenshaw gave a sign to Murrel, who handed him a whip that he used to strike the skull of the unsuspecting Wood. The hilt of the whip was filled with lead, and Wood fell from the saddle instantly, unconscious.

They turned the man's pockets inside out and got $1,262. But Woods was not dead, only stunned. They meant to finish him but they needed to do it quickly before someone else came along. They pulled him, one by the heels, the other by the head, to the top of a nearby ravine and pushed him down, watching as the man's body broke on the tree branches on the way down. It was Murrel's first killing but not his last.

Crenshaw and Murrel rode on down to New Orleans and separated there. Murrel, who liked the ladies, visited a whore, but she robbed him while he slept. Broke, he rode back out on the trace to get money. After four days, he finally spied a well-set-up traveler.

As the man approached, Murrel pulled his pistol and leapt in front of him. The man stopped and held his hands up. Murrel told him to dismount and then walked him off the trace down to a pebbly creek bottom. Murrel ordered him to strip off all his clothes and turn his back. The traveler asked if Murrel was going to shoot him, but the highwayman made no answer. The victim begged for time to pray before he died, but Murrel was a busy man and wouldn't give him time to make his peace. As the man turned again, Murrel shot him through the head. He disposed of the body in his usual manner.

He took the man's money, horse, supplies, and clothes and rode into Natchez a wealthier man. It was there that Murrel realized that the days of highwaymen like Mason, the Harps, and Hare were over.

Travel was too swift now. News got around quicker about who to avoid and where there were problems along the trail. Communities seemed in closer touch. In order for outlaws to prosper in such an environment, they needed organization. There was strength in numbers.

Murrel deduced that in order to succeed in such a great criminal enterprise as he anticipated he needed a front for his criminal activities that no one would ever think to look behind. Therefore, he married and built a house. He became a friend to people of importance in his community. He became an expert on the law so that when he was charged, which he expected, he could defend himself and use the law to his advantage.

For criminal headquarters, he established a hideout near the Shawnee Village. It was there that the men he recruited to rob and steal on the river and the trace, met to make their plans and divide up their ill-gotten gains. Over the next few years, Murrel's criminal organization grew. Robberies on the river and the trace abounded, and Murrel got his share of every one. Exploiting the institution of slavery was at the heart of his criminal conspiracy.

Slaves in the Choctaw Territory disappeared constantly and in increasing numbers. On the rare occasion when the thieves were tracked down and imprisoned, those making the accusations were "coerced" by friends of the accused to shut up. If that did not work, accommodating judges and juries would deliver acquittals.

On the trail, Murrel described to Stewart the extent of his criminal network and how it was organized. He called his conspiracy the Clan.

The Clan is not of the same grit; there are two classes. The first has all their designs and the extent of their plans to themselves. For this reason, all who would be willing to join us are not capable of managing our designs; and there would be danger of their making disclosures, which would lead to the destruction of our designs before they are perfected. This class is what we call the Grand Council.

The second class, those which we trust with not only that which they are immediately concerned with. We have them to do what we are not willing to do

ourselves. They always stand between us and danger. They are called the Strykers.

It was obvious, Stewart realized, that this latter group did not hesitate to kill in pursuit of the Clan's goal, which Murrel now revealed to be the instigation of a rebellion among the slaves throughout the slaveholding states.

Such an uprising would leave cities like Memphis and Natchez defenseless and their expensive shops and businesses would be ripe for the picking. Appealing to the man's ego, Stewart convinced Murrel to write down a list of his Clan. And then came a gilt-edged invitation. Murrel invited Stewart to join him at the head of the company that would attack Memphis. Apparently Murrel felt "an ambition to demolish the city which was defended from the ravages of the British Army by the great General Jackson."

Murrel was organized and controlled crime in three states—Tennessee, Alabama, and Kentucky. But it was an overlooked detail, the theft of a horse that had belonged to a widow in Williamson County, that tripped him up. Murrel had been caught red-handed, and none of his political contacts could come to his rescue.

"The verdict and judgement was that Murrel should serve twelve months imprisonment; be given thirty lashes on his bare back at the public whipping post; that he should sit two hours in the pillory on each of three successive days; be branded on the left thumb with the letters H.T. in the presence of the Court; and he rendered infamous," Coates wrote.

The entire sentence was carried out, and when Murrel next found freedom in one year's time, he was prepared to kill all but his own family in pursuit of his criminal endeavors.

The next day, Stewart and Murrel crossed the Arkansas River and rode deeper into the forest. Stewart knew that he was beyond "hope of resistance or escape; he knew that if by the merest chance or error he were betrayed it would mean his certain end and worse, no word of his ending would ever, perhaps, be heard." He would become like most of Murrel's victims.

That night, they lodged at an inn and the next morning set out for what Murrel said was the Clan's headquarters. About a mile down the trail, Stewart suddenly announced that he had left his gloves back at the inn and rode back to retrieve them. When he got there, he told the innkeeper an almost incoherent tale of Murrel's theft of slaves and his other exploits. The innkeeper asked him what he could do to help and Stewart asked only that if he didn't come back, some word of his going would be sent on to Parson John Henning. He took a pistol from the innkeeper, and then returned to Murrel with the weapon concealed on his person.

After riding for a few more hours, they came out in a tiny clearing where a Parson Hargus had constructed a small cabin. He had an old rowboat, which they clambered into and rowed across the river. Upon making the far bank, Murrel went to the plantation of a Mr. Irvin. He told Irvin he was a slave trader. Irvin said he could use three field hands and Murrel promised to deliver them within a fortnight. Murrel and Stewart rowed back across the river, got on their horses, and set off again down the trail.

They came upon a lake and a hut on the bank. A couple of men were lounging by the doorway. Stewart noticed they were unshaven, unkempt, and heavily armed. They saluted Murrel and then one of them led the way down to a landing and ferried them over the lake. On the other side, they slogged through the swamp until Murrel put his hand on Stewart's arm and pointed out the headquarters of the Clan. Their hideout "was a large low building of fresh cut logs, built like an Indian council-house with one long room and a number of smaller chambers opening, alcove fashion, along the side."

There were chairs and rough-hewn furniture.

Pegs had been driven between the logs in the wall and here were hung the belongings of the present occupants, their saddle bags and holsters, shot pouches, leather shirts. Some ten or eleven men were grouped about the fireplace where a huge log was burning. Murrel made for it. The others made way for Murrel and saluted their chief; later, a dozen more men drifted in as the news spread that Murrel had arrived.

Stewart was subsequently introduced and made a member of the Clan by swearing allegiance during a secret oath. The men drank whiskey and told stories. Murrel got drunk and began to boast of what he would do to Stewart's friend, Parson Henning. He said that he would give anything to have him across the Arkansas, and once he had him across, he would torture him.

Stewart had had enough. He needed to get out. He was afraid that if he drank too much and lowered his guard he would say something to reveal his true identity. He and Murrel agreed to meet back across the river at the inn they had stopped at.

Stewart left, relieved to spend some time alone. The following day, when Murrel arrived they set off for home together. Murrel and Stewart soon arrived at Wesley. Each attended to personal business before getting back together the following day to depart. As he left, Murrel wrote out for Stewart, who had made up a story about going down to the Yalo Busha country, a list of approximately 100 Clansmen he might encounter along the way.

Stewart quickly made for Parson Hennings's house, arriving after midnight. He acquainted his old friend with his adventures and Murrel's criminal conspiracy, paying particular attention to the dangers of a slave rebellion. Settlers who had slaves were always afraid they would run away or, worse, rebel. The last thing they wanted to do was destroy the very property that enabled them to work their land.

Parson Henning collected some of the county's most upright citizens to assist in arresting Murrel. Stewart made sure that when Henning and his men sprung the trap, he was to be addressed by his assumed name of Hues. Stewart wanted Murrel to think he was still sympathetic to him, so none of Murrel's criminal confederates would come after him.

When Murrel rode into his plantation, a dozen armed men greeted him. Murrel did not even break a sweat; he had been arrested before. He could handle them. The men questioned him about his comings and goings. The officers in charge asked him who went with him to Arkansas. Murrel's replied it was a young man named Hues.

The officer then called for Hues, and when Hues presented himself before him, Murrel appeared to lose his spirits and fortitude. He looked like he would faint, and they gave him water several times before he recovered. As he was being escorted under heavy guard to the county jail at Jackson, Murrel miraculously recovered his nerve and asked his guards about Hues.

Having been told to keep Stewart's identity a secret, the guards replied that he was a stranger.

Murrel was committed to prison in February 1834, and his trial scheduled for the following July. He was charged with "Negro stealing," a hanging offense. Despite the authorities' best intentions to hide Stewart's involvement, Stewart was going to be the star witness at Murrel's trial.

During the discovery phase, when each side in a court case has to release the information it intends to submit at trial, Stewart's name was discovered on the prosecution's witness list. It then became obvious what Stewart's intentions were. In response, Murrel dispatched an assassin to take care of the star witness against him. Robert Coates recounts an assassination attempt against Stewart:

> Stewart carried a pistol that he had taken from his portmanteau. When the lead assassin on his right leveled his weapon, Stewart fired at his face. The ball struck him on the corner of his forehead. He fell back, apparently lifeless and as he fell his gun fired. The bullet passed under the belly of Stewart's horse.

Stewart received a bullet wound fighting the other two assassins, who escaped. He went back to the Hennings, who nursed him to health. But the experience made him even more determined.

Before trial, Murrel tried another tactic. Using his vast criminal network, he conspired to discredit Stewart's character. Prominent businessmen, judges, and officers of the law made disparaging remarks about Stewart in the newspapers. They were men of the Clan. But the more they pushed, the more stubborn Stewart got. As long as he could walk, he would testify against his tormentor.

At Murrel's trial in July 1834, the Tennessee courthouse was crowded to overflowing. Stewart was called to the stand. He was sworn in as the first prosecution witness and he began his narrative of his adventures. Testimony stopped at dark and started up again the next morning at nine. By the end of that day, he had finished answering the prosecution's questions, only to be confronted by Milton Brown his third day on the stand.

As a Congressman a few years in the future, Milton Brown would attain greater fame when he introduced in Congress the bill by which Texas was annexed to the United States. For now, he would have to subsist on the fame engendered by being Murrel's lawyer. Brown tried to use the tactic of putting the witness on trial instead of the defendant, attacking Stewart's character during his testimony. The strategy failed. John A. Murrel was found guilty of "Negro stealing" and sent to the state penitentiary in Nashville for 10 years at hard labor. He showed no emotion upon his sentencing.

After his conviction, Murrel soon found he had no friends left. Law enforcement officers went after the Clan members on the list he had given Stewart and drove them out of the state. Murrel's wife deserted him and moved out of Tennessee. But still Stewart worried.

The Clan was large, he knew, larger than anything Murrel had committed to paper. They would

still be looking for him. To set the record straight, and especially to counteract the rumors that Murrel had spread that he was a man of little character, Stewart drew up a digest of his testimony at trial. The document contained his description of the trip he took with Murrel, his conversations with the murderer and thief, his experiences at Clan headquarters and the incomplete list of Clan members that Murrel had given him. He had it published in pamphlet form and distributed throughout the territory.

Almost immediately, penny dreadful writers sensationalized the entire account. The most sensational of all was done by the famous *Police Gazette,* which called its story the "pictorial life" of the "Great Western Land Pirate John A. Murrel." Stewart had hoped his pamphlet would vindicate his character and provide a warning against Murrel's plans. Unfortunately, it failed. Murrel seemed harmless behind bars. His conspiracy of the Clan seemed like the product of an outrageous mind. Worse, the very people Stewart had sought to protect the people of Tennessee, judged him a double-crosser for informing on his friend the way he did. As for the Clansmen, they proved to be daunting.

There were many more than those on Murrel's list. Even with their leader in jail, some of them fomented a slave rebellion that ultimately failed. Vigilante committees were formed throughout the state to take care of those identified as Clansmen or their confederates.

Perhaps the real price Tennessee paid for allowing John A. Murrel within its borders was that it would never again have that sense of serenity that its forests and lakes engendered. People may not have believed Stewart's story but it sure made them anxious. As for Murrel, he served out his sentence working at "shoemaking, lathing, tailoring, coopering, and carding," like the other 80 prisoners of the state penitentiary. He studied law and the Bible, but the fight had been beaten out of him.

Released in 1844, he seemed an invalid, his mind gone. He disappeared. But it is not beyond reason that Murrel may have used his "condition" to cover some criminal scheme. No one knows. John A. Murrel's place of death and burial is unknown. As for the man who brought him down, Virgil Stewart eventually married, had children, and became a prosperous businessman.

But he never did any more sleuthing.

See also JEAN LAFITTE; JEFFERSON RANDOLPH "SOAPY" SMITH.

Washington, D.C. (1835) the first assassination attempt on a U.S. president

On January 30, 1835, President Andrew Jackson went to the Capitol to attend a funeral. After the service, the president emerged from the building where Richard Lawrence was waiting for him. An unemployed house painter with a deranged mind, Lawrence believed Jackson had conspired to keep the poor out of work, and he decided to do something about it. He pointed a pistol at the president's breast and pulled the trigger. The percussion cap exploded. There was a small explosion, an exhalation of smoke, then . . . nothing. It was a misfire; the bullet did not discharge.

Years earlier, with the aid of Davy Crockett, Jackson had successfully fought the Seminoles in Florida's swamps. Later, in a duel, he killed a man who had insulted his wife. In 1815 he successfully defended New Orleans from to the British at the battle of New Orleans. Despite being 67 in 1835,

Andrew Jackson circa 1840, the first president to be a victim of an assassination attempt. This is one of the first photographs taken of an American president. (Library of Congress)

Jackson was still a soldier. He was not about to let some ruffian shoot at him or even attempt to without retaliation. Jackson flew into a rage and raised his cane to beat his presumptive assassin.

Lawrence produced another pistol from his belt, took careful aim at Jackson's chest, and fired. Jackson's luck held, and Lawrence's pistol misfired for the second time that day. He did not have another chance, as policemen and bystanders wrestled him to the ground.

Robert Lawrence was subsequently tried and convicted of the attempted assassination of the president, and he never again saw a day as a free man. He spent the rest of his miserable life going between asylums and prisons, dying a forgotten man.

As for Jackson, he was convinced that Lawrence was in the employ of his political enemies, the Whigs, who wanted him dead because of his plan to destroy the Bank of the United States. Whether Jackson's theory was misguided is up for conjecture, but Lawrence's contribution to U.S. criminal history is not.

Robert Lawrence was the first person to attempt the assassination of a U.S. president, an office previously held sacrosanct, even by the criminal class. No longer would the presidency be held in such high esteem in the underworld. Future killers could now view the president as a target like anyone else, and just as mortal.

See also JEAN LAFITTE.

Paterson, New Jersey (1836) Colt invents the revolver

Up until 1836 handguns could fire only one shot at a time. Percussion pistols, the standard of the time, required that the pistol be loaded with cap and ball each time it was fired. That meant a lengthy wait during reloading.

Criminals never knew when they would have to discharge a pistol and, like everyone else, they never knew when a pistol would misfire. For these reasons, highwayman like Joseph Hare carried a few pistols at a time. Hare knew that any delay in firing was deadly because it gave the victim time to retaliate.

Sam Colt's invention of the first revolver in 1836 gave criminals a weapon they could use to kill more than one person at a time without reloading. No longer would they have to be weighted down with one-shot guns. The new one, model 1836, fired six bullets by cocking the hammer and pulling the trigger. Colt's revolving breech pistol would sweep the country.

See also CHICAGO (1886); HAYMARKET SQUARE, CHICAGO (1886); NEW HAVEN, CONNECTICUT (1873); WASHINGTON, D.C. (JULY–SEPTEMBER 1881).

Baltimore, Maryland (1844) Morse demonstrates the telegraph

Until 1844 all communication in the United States was done through newspapers, magazines, pamphlets, and word of mouth. That all changed with the demonstration of the telegraph by Samuel F. B. Morse.

Morse was a famous American painter, a true Renaissance man who also had an inveterate interest in electricity. A Yale graduate, Morse turned his energies from painting in 1832 to André-Marie Ampère's idea for the electric telegraph. During the next 10 years, Morse incorporated ideas from scientists in other countries who were working on the same idea.

In 1844 Morse demonstrated to the U.S. Congress the results of his 12 years of research: the first practical telegraph. He transmitted the message, "What hath God wrought?" from a telegraph in Washington, D.C., to a similar one in Baltimore, Maryland.

Now sheriffs and marshals could telegraph down the line to their colleagues when they had information on outlaws who were at large. Boston, for example, could contact New York and tell them, by telegraph if a confidence artist was working the area.

Being a criminal would never be a safe occupation again. Fifteen years hence, one of the country's greatest criminals, John Brown, would be undone by a telegraphic message sent from Washington to Baltimore.

See also BOSTON, MARYLAND (1876); BUFFALO, NEW YORK (1901); HAYMARKET SQUARE, CHICAGO (1886).

Lansing, Michigan (1846) first state to outlaw capital punishment

Following English law, every state in the Union had capital punishment, but that all changed in 1846. Legislators in Lansing, the capital of Michigan, made history when, in 1846, they voted to outlaw capital punishment in the state. It is a law that still exists today.

New York, New York (1846) a new wave of immigration

With the country continuing its westward expansion, people abroad began to see America's shores as a chance for a new start. Things were particularly bad in Ireland where the Great Potato Famine of 1845 had caused families to starve to death. Not wanting to endure another terrible year, Catherine McCarty immigrated to America on the ship *Devonshire*.

The *Devonshire* sailed into New York Harbor on April 10, 1846, passing two deserted islands, Bedloe, which would become the site of the Statue of Liberty and Ellis, which would become the great immigration processing depot. But in 1846 immigrants like Catherine disembarked at one of the many Hudson River wharves where immigration officials checked their papers before allowing them to enter the city.

Catherine settled in the Irish section of the Bowery slums. In 1854 she gave birth to her first son, Joseph. Her second son, William Henry, was born in 1860. He would later be better known by his aliases William Bonney and Billy the Kid.

See also INDIANA AND KANSAS (1868–1874); NEW MEXICO (1877).

SIX
1850-1900

Introduction

The mid-19th century is the most volatile period in American history. The 50-year span would see incredible advances in technology, including the invention of the electric light, the automobile, the telephone, and the first metal detector, the latter two inventions by Dr. Alexander Graham Bell, who would figure prominently in the events surrounding a presidential assassination.

The United States moved west and with it the criminal. Crime pushed westward ahead of civilization, crime that before had festered in the Eastern cities. Crime breathed some of that western air and spit it back with bullets.

Along with the creation of some of history's greatest inventions, this time period also saw the emergence of new forms of crime: The rise of the railroads laid the track for history's first train robbery. Bank robbery became a common crime after the Civil War.

If there is any one event in American history that brought out the worst in the country's criminal element, it was the Civil War. In 1861 the United States was really two lands, North and South, and Americans were about to fight and die in record numbers to settle the dispute. The actual conduct of the Union army in the Civil War was a direct enforcement of constitutional law that prohibits states from seceding from the Union. As far as the Union army saw it, they were confronting the greatest single criminal act in the country's history—secession.

Like any war, the Civil War inflamed passions on both sides that led frequently to murder. William Quantrill, the Confederate guerrilla leader, is a prime example of the type of sociopathic personality that flourished amidst the violence. John Brown was close behind.

Bitterness at the war's outcome led to the rise of outlaw gangs throughout the Midwest and Southwest, right into the 20th century. The James-Younger Gang, all former Confederate guerrillas, was of course the best-known. It is no accident that many of the Old West "badmen," including Georgia's famed Doc Holliday, were Southerners born, bred, and embittered by the war.

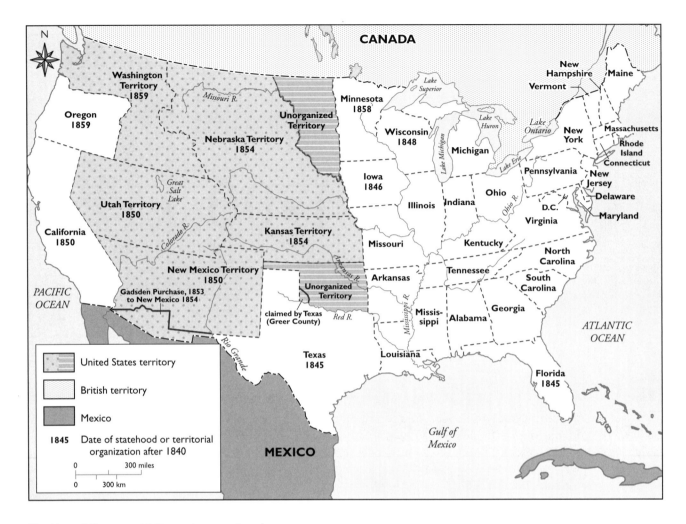

The United States in 1860, on the eve of civil war

The time period is as much about the men who stood up to the criminals. Never before in American history had the country seen such a dedicated group of peace officers willing to sacrifice their lives to bring law and order to the West. Lawmen like Bat Masterson, Wyatt Earp, and Bill Tilghman became American legends in such fabled towns as Wichita, Dodge City, Abilene, and of course, Tombstone. By surviving and prospering into the 20th century, these men actually helped spread their fame as living legends. But the truth about their lives, turning away from a century-old distortion, shows they were much more complicated than anyone has ever realized.

One crime stands alone during this period: the assassination of President Abraham Lincoln by John Wilkes Booth. His plot was not simply to kill the president but to actually wipe out the entire leadership of the executive branch of government. If he had succeeded, the Union might indeed have fallen as Booth, and the South, had hoped.

N
CANADA
Washington Territory
Oregon
Idaho Territory 1863
Montana Territory 1864
Missouri R.
Dakota Territory 1864
Minnesota
Lake Superior
Wisconsin
Lake Michigan
Michigan
Lake Huron
Lake Ontario
Lake Erie
New Hampshire
Vermont
Maine
New York
Massachusetts
Rhode Island
Connecticut
Pennsylvania
New Jersey
Delaware
Maryland
D.C.
Great Salt Lake
Nevada 1864
Utah Territory
California
Colorado R.
Colorado Territory 1861
Nebraska Territory 1864
Iowa
Illinois
Indiana
Ohio
Ohio R.
West Virginia 1863
Virginia
Kansas 1861
Arkansas R.
Missouri
Kentucky
North Carolina
Tennessee
Arizona Territory 1863
New Mexico Territory
Unorganized Territory
Arkansas
South Carolina
PACIFIC OCEAN
Greer County (claimed by Texas)
Red R.
Mississippi R.
Missis-sippi
Alabama
Georgia
ATLANTIC OCEAN
Texas
Louisiana
Rio Grande
Florida
MEXICO
Gulf of Mexico
U.S. states
U.S. territory
Confederate states
1863 Date of statehood or territorial organization after 1860
0 300 miles
0 300 km

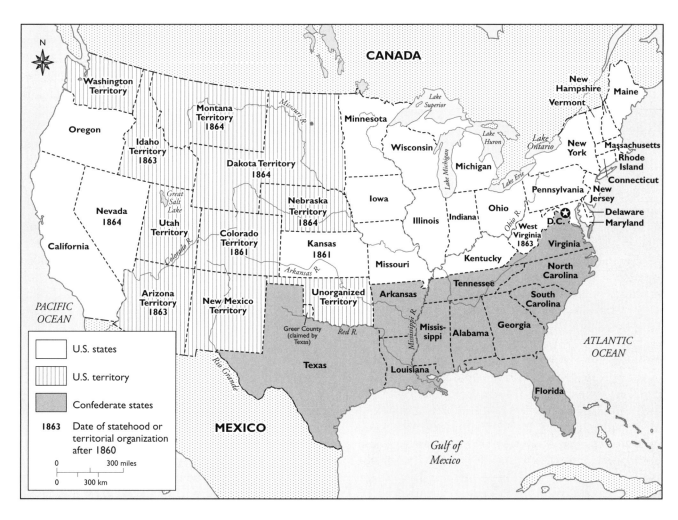

The United States in 1864

Washington, D.C. (1854) the Kansas-Nebraska Act

Modern sociologists, psychologists, psychiatrists, and anthropologists may be torn over whether social conditions, genetic traits, environmental factors, or some combination of them all caused the criminal personality to form. Yet, they would be hard pressed to find any single moment in U.S. history when the social conditions were more ripe to form a criminal personality than the years surrounding the passage of the Kansas-Nebraska Act.

No single piece of legislation did more to promote the development of horrific crime than the Kansas-Nebraska Act, which became law on May 30, 1864. The ways of Hare, Mason, and the Harps appear genteel compared with the truly evil men about to emerge in a social environment that would let their psychopathic tendencies flourish.

By 1850 the land west of Iowa and Missouri was long overdue for territorial organization by the federal government. Since the river counties of the Platt and Kansas Rivers that ran through these areas already existed, organization shouldn't have been a problem, except for one thing. Everyone in the Senate, northern abolitionists and southern slaveholders alike, had an interest in whether this new area would officially become a slave state or a free state. Congress only admitted states to the Union after decreeing whether slavery would be allowed in the new state or not. In this way, the Union maintained roughly the same number of slave states as free states.

There had already been four failed attempts in Congress to organize the west. Representatives of the South continued to derail the proposal out of bitterness over the Missouri Compromise. In order to finally pass legislation that settled the territorial organization of the West, Senator Stephen A. Douglas, chairman of the Senate Committee on Territories, decided to offer the South a concession.

In 1854 Douglas proposed a bill that contained a unique provision—instead of Congress deciding the issue of slavery, the future state would. When the new territory applied for statehood, the settlers would vote on whether they became a free state or a slave state. Douglas called this principal popular sovereignty, or squatter sovereignty. The final version of Douglas's bill, presented for full Senate approval, called for the creation of not one but two new territories, to be called Kansas and Nebraska. The western boundary of the Kansas Territory included Pike's Peak, perhaps the only time in Kansas's history that a real mountain interrupted its flat plains. Kansas would later cede this portion to Colorado. But it was the Nebraska Terri-

tory that would prove the real prize. It stretched from northern Kansas to the Canadian border and included the present-day states of North and South Dakota.

Douglas's bill mentioned nothing about which territory would allow slavery and which would not, though it was assumed that Kansas would, since it bordered Missouri, and that Nebraska, being in the north, and stretching to the Canadian border, would not. What Douglas had forgotten was that the Missouri Compromise expressly forbid slavery beyond the present-day northern boundary of Missouri. If either territory voted for slavery, it would be illegal.

To remedy the matter, an amendment was quickly crafted that repealed this section of the Missouri Compromise. The outraged abolitionists lobbied their representatives in Congress to strike the amendment. But Douglas and the Democrats, including President Franklin Pierce, held firm. On May 30, 1854, the Kansas-Nebraska Act with its squatter sovereignty provision was passed into law and the amendment to the Missouri compromise stood.

Squatter sovereignty set the stage for armed conflict between the proslavery and antislavery forces that already existed in the new territories. Abolitionists were not about to let the proslavery forces dominate Kansas's politics without a fight. What complicated the matter even further was a disagreement between north and south over where the proposed transcontinental railroad would run. Southern expansionists, led by Secretary of War Jefferson Davis, wanted a southern route; northerners wanted the right of way in their states. The railroad would have to acquire land wherever it went. Whoever controlled the right of way would make tremendous money.

See also "BLOODY KANSAS" (1856–1861); MISSOURI COMPROMISE (1820–1821).

"Bloody Kansas" (1856–1861) breeding ground for crime

To understand crime in the second half of the 19th century is to understand Kansas. In the 12-year period prior to the Civil War, the territory was known as "Bloody Kansas." Kansas's decision on popular sovereignty was in some ways a referendum on whether the Union would continue to tolerate slavery because within Kansas's borders resided men and women whose souls were at war with a question of conscience for every American who voted prior to the Civil War: Should people be enslaved because their skin was black? Looked at on a present-day map, Kansas is in the direct center of the country, but

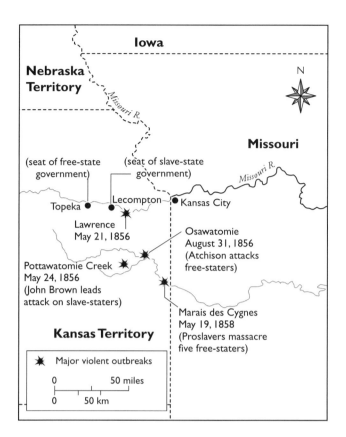

The question of slave state or free led to bloodshed in Kansas, as proslavery and antislavery groups attacked one another. John Brown and his radical abolitionist followers killed two proslavery families in Pottawatomie Creek in May 1856; they fought to defend Oswatomie, a free settlement, from proslavery forces in August 1856.

a century and a half ago, the states north and east of its borders did not exist. The discord that characterized Kansas was a perfect breeding ground for deviant personalities. Such individuals existed on both sides of the controversy. In the abolitionist movement, for example, were those members who would stop at nothing, including murder and sedition, to see slavery ended. Chief among this small group was John Brown.

See also JESSE JAMES (1847–1882); WILLIAM CLARKE QUANTRILL (1837–1864).

John Brown, a.k.a. Osawatomie Brown
(1800–1859) insurrectionist and criminal conspirator

The abbreviation "a.k.a." stands for "also known as" and is usually reserved for criminals who use something other than their legal name in their criminal

activities. John Brown was such a man. He is also the only convicted seditionist in U.S. history to be looked at by many decent and honorable people as a genuine hero. That he was guilty of cold-blooded murder on two occasions often remains overlooked, and how a man of such dichotomy could exist in one body is a curious story.

John Brown was born in Torrington, Connecticut, on May 9, 1800. When he was about five years old, his father moved the family to Hudson, Ohio, where his Calvinist parents taught him to worship the Bible and hate slavery.

As a child, Brown began to take special note of the maltreatment of black slaves. He absorbed the sentiments of the antislavery movement that dominated the area. By the time he was a man, John Brown was a dedicated abolitionist. Needing to make a living, he went to work as foreman of his family's tannery.

In 1820, at age 20, he married a local Hudson girl, Dianthe Luske. Before she died during childbirth in

John Brown (National Archives)

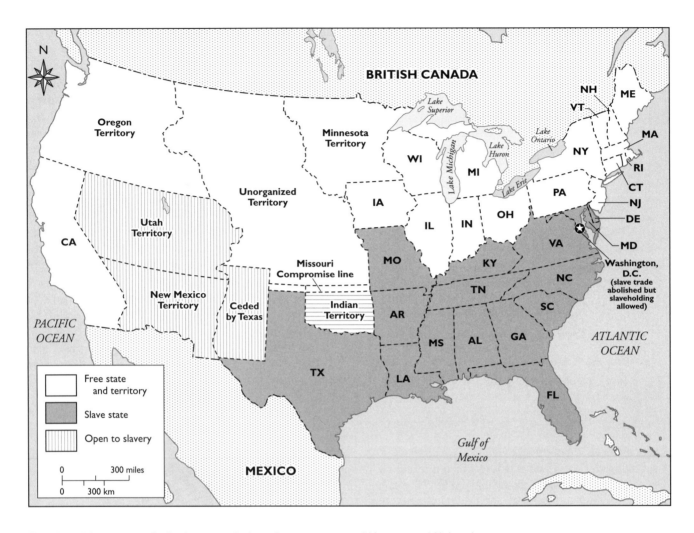

The United States as it looked in 1850, before the partitioning of Kansas and Nebraska

1831, their marriage produced seven children. Besides working at the family tannery, during the years of his first marriage Brown supported his family by working as a farmer and a surveyor.

Within a year after Dianthe's death, Brown, then 32, wed 16-year-old Mary Anne Day of Meadsville, Pennsylvania. Brown's second marriage produced 13 more children, only six of whom lived to adulthood. All together, of John Brown's 20 children, only half survived their childhood, which even in the 19th century, was an alarming rate of mortality in one family.

During the next two and a half decades, Brown went in and out of many businesses. He built and sold several tanneries, was a land sale speculator, sheep man, and a broker for wool growers. He was a failure in each endeavor. He felt himself more of a visionary than a businessman.

Brown's family suffered through financial hardship because of his inability to make money. In 1842 he filed for bankruptcy. He became depressed, but not over his financial conditions. Instead, his depression centered on slavery, and despite his financial setbacks, Brown always found a way to support the abolitionist cause. Brown participated in the Underground Railroad. He founded an organization called the League of Gileadites whose goal it was to protect escaped slaves from slave catchers.

In 1847, Frederick Douglass met Brown for the first time in Springfield, Massachusetts. It was at this meeting that Brown first outlined to Douglass a plan that he had been thinking about to lead a war to free the slaves. His idea was to use force to accomplish his goal and to kill anyone that stood in his way. Douglass could not help but admire the man's zeal.

"Though a white gentleman, [Brown] is in sympathy a black man, and as deeply interested in our cause, as though his own soul had been pierced with the iron of slavery," Douglass would later write.

In 1848 Gerrit Smith, a wealthy abolitionist, donated 120,000 acres of his property in the Adirondacks to black families who were willing to clear and farm the land. Soon, free blacks were living there in a colony called Timbucto. Knowing that many of the families were finding life in this isolated area difficult, Brown offered to establish his own home there and teach his neighbors how to farm the rocky soil.

In 1849 John and Mary Ann Brown moved with their children to North Elba in northern New York State, near Lake Placid. While living in North Elba, Brown began associating with blacks in this community. For a white man to be doing that in the middle of the 19th century was astonishing. Most abolitionists, while touting freedom, frowned on the notion of racial equality. Once again, though, Brown was a failure. He had always been a lousy farmer. His attempt to show the free Blacks how to farm the tough Adirondack soil was doomed from the start.

John Brown turned 50 at the century's half-way point. That was an old age then, but Brown did not feel his years. Still feeling far from the sense of God-given purpose, he began having frequent visions of slave uprisings, during which racists paid horribly for their sins. Brown came to believe that God had sought him out to make these visions a reality. Brown went wherever he felt God wanted him to in service of the abolitionist cause.

For the rest of her husband's life, Mary Brown sustained the family by planting rye, carrots, turnips,

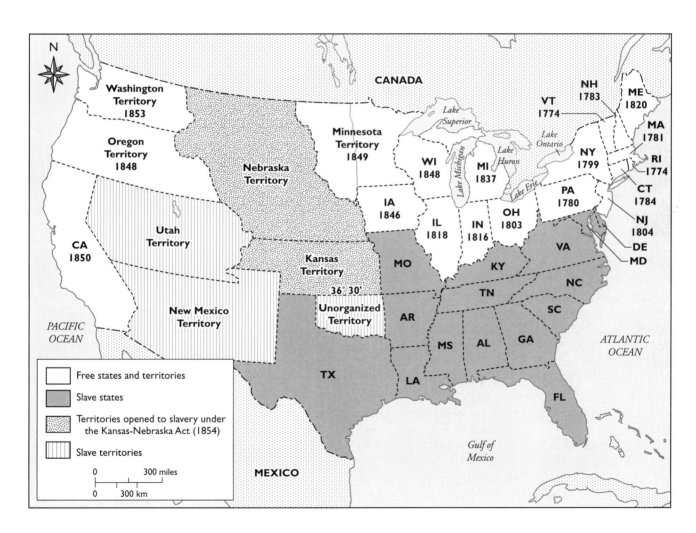

The United States as it looked in 1854, following passage of the Kansas-Nebraska Act, which allowed slavery in the Kansas and Nebraska Territories by virtue of popular sovereignty

and other hardy crops suited to the short Adirondack spring and summer. The family was willing to make any sacrifices necessary to further the abolitionist cause. As for Brown, he would never again live at North Elba permanently due to his antislavery campaigns, but he returned intermittently to check on his family.

In August 1855 John Brown rode out from North Elba going west. He was on his way to Kansas, where five of his sons had already taken up residence. He joined them in the Osawatomie River colony, a small free settlement of fewer than 100 men, women, and children. Their goal was to make the state a haven for antislavery settlers so that when the time came to vote on statehood, Kansas would go "free."

In 1856 proslavery forces attacked Lawrence, the abolitionist town in the eastern part of the state. The pressures that had been building in John Brown's head to see something finally done against slavery burst from his subconscious. It was now time for him to act as God's messenger on a mission of revenge.

Brown organized a militia unit. Appointing himself captain, Brown led his militia down Pottawatomie Creek on an evening in May 1856. With him were six men—four of his sons and two radical abolitionists. Arriving at the cabins of two proslavery families along the creek, Brown and his men dragged them out of their sleep into a living nightmare.

That the proslavers were unarmed and had done nothing to provoke the use of lethal force made no difference to Brown. Using sabers and swords that glinted dull red in the moonlight, he had his militia hack them to pieces. Standing out there on the Kansas prairie, with pieces of freshly carved flesh at his feet, the blood of the innocent mixing with the rich earth, Brown finally found the star that had eluded him his whole life. Previously abolitionists looked to the government to outlaw slavery. Brown had abandoned this nonviolent tenet of the abolitionist creed, and he had targeted well. The eastern newspapers hailed him as a hero of the abolitionist cause.

Brown was now certain of his mission. God had put him on earth to use violence to free the slaves. Slavers, knowing such an action would devastate them financially, decided that Brown had to be eliminated. In August 1856, proslavery forces numbering 250 men attacked the Osawatomie River colony. Brown defended the abolitionist settlement with a force of 30 men. It was the stuff of legend, and once again, the eastern abolitionist papers lined up on Brown's side. No one paid any attention to

the fact that Brown lost and was forced to retreat or that the settlement was burned by the proslavery forces.

The papers began calling him "Osawatomie Brown," and soon, a play by that name opened on Broadway. Show business and news had blended together to make John Brown into a living legend. The man who had failed at everything he had ever done achieved his greatest success as a spree murderer, but John Brown paid a heavy price for his notoriety.

His son Frederick was killed defending Osawatomie. But not only was Brown willing to die for his principles, he was also willing to have his children die for the same reason. And they were only too willing. Brown had done a good job inculcating them with his beliefs. Brown's fervor continued to build with visions of slaves rising up and killing their white oppressors.

BOSTON, MASSACHUSETTS (1857–1859): THE SECRET SIX

After his son's death, Brown headed east and spent the next few years in New England fund-raising for the abolitionist cause. While he was doing that, he continued to plot murder.

One day in 1857 Brown wandered into the offices of the Massachusetts State Kansas Committee, where he met Franklin Sanborn. Brown had come to the committee searching for money and guns to continue his work in Kansas. He found a ready conspirator in Sanborn. Sanborn was an idealistic 26-year-old Harvard graduate, a schoolteacher from Concord, New Hampshire, who was friends with the philosopher/poets Ralph Waldo Emerson and Henry David Thoreau. He believed fervently in the abolitionist cause and functioned as the Kansas Committee's acting secretary.

Brown exploited his reputation. He held Sanborn spellbound with stories of his revenge killings at Osawatomie and his defense of Pottawatomie. By meeting's end, Sanborn agreed to get Brown whatever he needed. Thus began the conspiracy of the "Secret Six" to attack the U.S. government.

Sanborn was socially connected. He introduced Brown to many of the elite members of Boston society whose allegiance lay with the abolitionists. Of course, they knew of Osawatomie Brown and stood fascinated in his presence, likening him with his stern countenance to some character out of the Bible. But unlike Brown, these were essentially dilettantes who would provide the funding for others who would commit the actual violence.

It did not take long for Brown to gather six of these influential and propertied men to funnel money to his cause during 1857 to 1858. Besides Sanborn, the conspiracy pulled in:

1. Thomas Wentworth Higginson, an amateur boxer and minister who hailed from one of New England's oldest families
2. Reverend Theodore Parker, a controversial Unitarian minister who delivered eloquent diatribes against slavery from the pulpit
3. Gerrit Smith, who donated the North Elba land in the Adirondacks to the free blacks and Brown
4. Dr. Samuel Gridley Howe, a pioneer in educational reforms for the blind, insane, and retarded
5. George Luther Stearns, one of the chief financiers of Emigrant Aid Company, which facilitated the settlement of Kansas by antislavery homesteaders

In May 1858 John Brown arrived back in Boston, where Sanborn called for a meeting of the Secret Six at the American House Hotel. It was at that meeting that Brown told the Secret Six that he was going to attack and capture the U.S. Armory at Harper's Ferry, Virginia, and from there, launch his slave rebellion into Virginia.

"[It was] an amazing proposition," Sanborn would later write, "desperate in its character, seemingly inadequate in its provision of means, and of very uncertain results."

For these reasons and others—Brown had upped the stakes and wholesale death could result—Sanborn argued against it: "But no argument could prevail against his settled purpose, with many or with few—and he left us only the alternatives of betrayal, desertion, or support. We chose the last."

They may have been against the plan at the outset, but the Secret Six were soon excited. Finally there would be violent action against the sin of slavery. The members proceeded to raise money to buy guns, bullets, and supplies for Brown's holy army.

The problem with most criminal conspiracies is that they don't last very long. The more who know about it, the bigger the chance someone will talk. More often than not, this happens and the conspiracy is exposed. Unfortunately, Brown had a big mouth.

Franklin Sanborn was surprised one day to get a letter from an inmate at the Kansas State Penitentiary who had served with Brown in Kansas. He claimed the Massachusetts State Kansas Committee owed him money for his work with Brown. If he was not paid, he would expose the plot to attack Harper's Ferry. He even claimed to know the identities of the Secret Six.

Gerrit Smith called a meeting. He proposed to immediately cut off all aid and connections with Brown. "I never was convinced of the wisdom of this scheme," he later said. "It seems to me it would be madness to attempt to execute it."

Most of the others tried to convince Smith that the idea had merit but maybe the raid itself should be postponed. Higginson, though, vehemently opposed a delay, and accused Smith of being a coward.

The group voted to delay the raid and, more important, to insulate themselves from any legal responsibility. They would continue to funnel money to Brown, provided he kept the Secret Six in the dark about his plans. If legal authorities subsequently asked them if they knew anything, they could honestly say they did not. It was one of the first examples in American criminal history of plausible deniability.

The group knew the raid was coming. They knew the target. They just did not know when.

HARPER'S FERRY, VIRGINIA (1859): JOHN BROWN'S RAID

In summer 1859, a tall, fierce-looking man with dark, ominous features rented a farm near Harper's Ferry, Virginia, in nearby Maryland. The man's name was Isaac Smith.

Smith trained his close-knit group of 22 men in military-style maneuvers. Among the 22 were three of John Brown's sons—Oliver, Owen, and Watson. When Smith was satisfied they knew their roles, on Sunday night, October 16, 1859, they marched into Harper's Ferry. Smith rode point, but once again he was going by his real name, John Brown.

Brown cut the telegraph lines so word of the raid could not reach Washington. That done, Brown and his men proceeded with his plan to take over the armory, arm the slaves, and foment a slave rebellion against their white oppressors.

On Sunday evening, October 16, Charles White had just finished preaching his regular biweekly sermon in Harper's Ferry. In the early morning hours of October 17 he was awakened by his host, A. H. Herr, and informed of a disturbance in the town. He went out to investigate and thus became an eyewitness to history. Several weeks later, he wrote to his brother-in-law John Felt, of Salem, Massachusetts, on what he had observed.

Berryville Nov 10th 1859.

Dear John

Brown and his men must have been in town as accurately as we can discover about Eleven o'clock Sunday night—as the watchman in the bridge who was taken by them a prisoner had stuck his last peg at half past ten. As you know I preached there that night.

We knew nothing until daylight when the gentleman with whom we were staying came into our room and notified us. After breakfast we went out to reconnoiter—and found we were guarded on both sides by Sharps rifles—revolvers and pikes—and not a single available gun or other weapon of defense in all our part of the town which was isolated from all the other part there being a mountain in front—the river behind—and on each side these bands of men at Rifle works and Armory. And we had no idea how many there were.

These men were passing two or three at a time all the morning just in front of us. They could have been easily killed if we had had guns. All we could do was to wait. About one o'clock, the men of Bolivar (the part of the town over hill) got guns from an isolated building of the Armory works. It was the stock house.

A few weeks before, a number of guns had been removed from their usual place in front of the armory yard to this stock house which was the last house back of the yard. The insurgents supposed these had all the guns—but the men of Bolivar who are mostly armorers knew of the stock house guns. When they succeeded in getting them towards the middle of the day they came down the hill or over it rather and fired so heavily upon the insurgents at the Rifle factory that they had to run.

When the villains ran they crossed the Winchester Rail-road and made for the river. One ran towards us with his pike and beckoned us to come to him. We ran immediately toward the whole of them—the Bolivar men pressing on them from the mountain—we on one side. One or two of our men had by this time procured guns.

One negro was drowned—a slave—the only one of whom we have doubts as to his complicity with them & that because he ran with them. When Alstadts man who ran towards us came up—I asked him how came he there & what he was doing with the pike—he said they

At Harper's Ferry, Virginia, John Brown and his raiders crossed the Baltimore & Ohio (B&O) Railroad bridge that spans the Potomac River. They overpowered the bridge watchmen and proceeded to gain access to the arsenal. Photo circa 1905. (Author's collection)

had taken him and his master the night before—brot them down & told him if he didn't keep guard at Rifle factory they would kill him. I believe he was innocent.

While talking a reckless fellow came up—levelled his musket at the negro's head within an inch or so—and was about to pull the trigger. I asked him not to fire, as did others. He swore he'd kill him & that he had orders from the Captain of Charlestown Company. I told him no matter what the Captain said we had the man prisoner—perhaps he was innocent—he was ours—and stepping between the two, I ordered him not to fire. Several then took hold of his gun & saved the negro.

Perhaps you laugh at my orders. Of course I had no delegated authority but so enraged were the multitude that it was with difficulty they were restrained from hanging & shooting several on the spot. I did all I could to prevent it.

What Reverend White did not write was that when Brown and his men swooped down on the town, there were only two guards protecting the armory and arsenal. Before they could be subdued, a black railroad baggage handler named Hayward Shepherd confronted them. He demanded to know what they were there for and was shot to death for his effrontery. John Brown never saw the irony that the first casualty of his great raid was a member of the race he professed so much sympathy for.

Brown and the raiders overpowered the watchmen. Several other prisoners were captured, including Lewis Washington, the great-grand-nephew of George Washington. Brown now had control of the complex. With the telegraph lines cut, he figured he could proceed to loot the place, take the weapons, and arm the slaves for their rebellion against their white masters. But like most criminals, Brown made a mistake.

After gaining control of Harper's Ferry, Brown and his men had detained a Baltimore and Ohio train that was passing through. After five hours of figuring out what to do with it, Brown inexplicably let it go. The train chugged east and arrived in Baltimore the next day at noon. No sooner was the conductor off the train than he used Morse's invention and wired Washington of the insurrection. Those early reports did not contain many details. Even Brown's name as the leader of the insurrectionists was initially omitted. All that the army had to act upon was that one word, "insurrection." It was the worst federal crime of all.

Back at Harper's Ferry, Brown was waiting for local slaves to rise up against their owners and join the raid, but that did not happen. The Reverend White wrote in a letter:

During the affair the negroes about H. F. were terribly alarmed and clung as closely as they could to master & mistress. One negro hid under a water wheel in the armory canal and didn't come out till Tuesday—and then was afraid Brown might catch him. One slave has since died of fright—whom Brown had prisoner.

It appears that the local slaves thought Brown a lunatic.

With the town rising up against him, much of Brown's plan was already dashed. Things continued to get worse the following morning. From inside, Brown watched as local militia companies surrounded the armory, cutting off all of his escape routes. Brown had no choice now—he had to make his stand. He and his men barricaded themselves in.

As the long day wore on, the raiders began shooting at the townsmen and militia. Three Harper's Ferry citizens were killed. The townspeople convened to the local saloons to decide their next move.

Inside the armory, Brown selected nine prisoners and moved them to the armory's small fire engine house, which later became known as John Brown's Fort. From here, he would mount what he envisioned as his last stand against slavery. But before he could do that, his own men panicked. William H. Leeman tried to escape by swimming across the Potomac River. This was what the townspeople had been waiting for. Drunk and angry, they used Leeman for target practice. Afterward, his bullet-riddled corpse lay motionless in the river.

At 3:30 on Monday afternoon, October 18, 1859, military authorities in Washington telegraphed an order down the line to Baltimore. The dispatch ordered a certain colonel in the Army Corps of Engineers, to immediately take a detachment of marines to Harper's Ferry and quell the rebellion.

If that colonel was not successful in quickly putting down Brown, others might seek to do the same. In the south, firebrands like Jefferson Davis were calling for secession. If that happened, there would be full-scale civil war. And if the Union did not fall in such a conflict, it would surely teeter. But success could be no better. Stopping Brown by killing him could only make him into a martyr, making war even more inevitable. No one could foresee what would happen until the colonel whom the army had selected to quell the rebellion arrived on the scene and assessed the situation.

What happened next is best described by Israel Green, the commanding member of the party of marines eventually detailed to storm the armory and stop Brown. This account originally appeared in *The North American Review*, December 1885.

At noon of Monday, October 18, 1859, Chief Clerk Walsh, of the Navy Department, drove rapidly into the Washington Navy-yard, and, meeting me, asked me how many marines we had stationed at the barracks available for immediate duty. I happened to be the senior officer present and in command that day. I instantly replied to Mr. Walsh that we had ninety men available, and then asked him what was the trouble. He told me that Osawatomie Brown, of Kansas, with a number of men, had taken the arsenal at Harper's Ferry, and was then besieged there by the Virginia State troops.

Mr. Walsh returned speedily to the Navy Department building, and, in the course of an hour, orders came to me from Secretary Tousey to proceed at once to Harper's Ferry and report to the senior officer; and, if there should be no such officer at the Ferry, to take charge and protect the government property.

With a detachment of ninety marines, I started for Harper's Ferry that afternoon on the 3:30 train, taking with me two howitzers. It was a beautiful, clear autumn day, and the men, exhilarated by the excitement of the occasion, which came after a long, dull season of confinement in the barracks, enjoyed the trip exceedingly. At Frederick Junction, I received a dispatch from Colonel Robert E. Lee, who turned out to be the army officer to whom I was to report. Colonel Lee directed me to proceed to Sandy Hook, a small place about a mile this side of the Ferry, and there await his arrival.

It was a classic confrontation. Robert E. Lee, the man who would become the symbol of the Confederate States of America was being asked by the federal government to defend the Constitution at Harper's Ferry. An aristocrat from the wealthiest and most respected of southern families, the Lees of Old Virginia, Robert E. Lee was a dashing, elegant man with the mind of an intellectual and the compassion of a poet. A scion of the south, he abhorred slavery. Lee was most famous in the military as the only man to ever graduate from West Point without a demerit to his name. Lee had seen action during the Mexican War. Later, he was reassigned to the Army Corps of Engineers.

At ten o'clock in the evening, his [Lee's] first order was to form the marines out of the car, and march from the bridge to Harper's Ferry. This we did, entering the enclosure of the arsenal grounds through a back gate.

Colonel Robert E. Lee, who attempted to negotiate the surrender of John Brown and company and ultimately ordered their capture (Library of Congress)

At eleven o'clock Colonel Lee ordered the volunteers to march out of the grounds, and gave the control inside to the marines, with instructions to see that none of the insurgents escaped during the night. There had been hard fighting all the preceding day, and Brown and his men kept quiet during the night.

At half-past six in the morning Colonel Lee gave me orders to select a detail of twelve men for a storming party, and place them near the engine-house in which Brown and his men had entrenched themselves. I selected twelve of my best men, and a second twelve to be employed as a reserve.

The engine-house was a strong stone [actually brick] building perhaps thirty feet by thirty-five. In the front were two large double doors, between which was a stone abutment. Within were two old-fashioned, heavy fire engines, with a hose-cart and reel standing between them, and just back of the abutment between the doors. They were double-battened doors, very strongly made, with heavy wrought-iron nails.

Lieutenant J.E.B. Stewart [Stuart] accompanied Colonel Lee as a volunteer aid. He was ordered to go with a part of the troops to the front of the engine-house and demand the surrender of the insurgent party.

On the way to the engine-house, Stewart and myself agreed upon a signal for attack in the event that Brown should refuse to surrender. It was simply that Lieutenant Stewart would wave his hat, which was then, I believe, one very similar to the famous chapeau which he wore throughout the war. I had my storming party ranged alongside of the engine-house, and a number of men were provided with sledgehammers with which to batter in the doors. I stood in front of the abutment between the doors.

J. E. B. Stuart, later to become famous as one of Lee's Confederate generals, knocked on the door of the engine house. Brown himself answered it and was handed a letter that Lee had just penned. Written in clear script, it said:

Harpers Ferry
18 Oct. 1859

Colonel Lee, U.S.A., comm, the troops sent by the President of the U.S.A. to suppress the insurrection at this place demands the surrender of the persons in the Armory buildings.

If they will peaceably surrender themselves from the pillaged property, they shall be kept in safety to await the order of the President.

Col. Lee represents to them in all frankness that it is impossible for them to escape, that the armory is surrounded on all sides by troops, and that if he is compelled to take them by force, he cannot guarantee their safety.

(Signed) Col. Lee,
Col. Comm.

After Brown read the letter, "He at once began to make a proposition that he and his men should be allowed to come out of the engine-house and be

Sketched by an artist on the scene for *Frank Leslie's Illustrated Newspapers*, the marines storm the building where John Brown and other insurgents made their last stand at Harper's Ferry. (Library of Congress)

given the length of the bridge start, so that they might escape. Suddenly Lieutenant Stewart waved his hat, and I gave the order to my men to batter in the door," said Green.

The hammers were taken to the doors; they weren't even dented. Green noticed a ladder lying a few feet from the engine-house in the yard. Green ordered his men to use as a battering ram.

He continues,

The second blow broke it in. This entrance was a ragged hole low down in the right-hand door, the door being splintered and cracked some distance upward. I instantly stepped from my position in front of the stone abutment, and entered the opening made by the ladder. At the time I did not stop to think of it, but upon reflection I should say that Brown had just emptied his carbine at the point broken by the ladder, and so I passed in safely.

Getting to my feet, I ran to the right of the engine which stood behind the door, passed quickly to the rear, and came up between the two engines. The first person I saw was Colonel Lewis Washington. He was standing near the hose-cart, at the front of the engine-house. On one knee, a few feet to the left knelt a man with a carbine in his hand, just pulling the lever to reload.

"Hello, Green," said Colonel Washington, and he reached out his hand to me. I grasped it with my left hand, having my saber uplifted in my right, and he said, pointing to the kneeling figure, "This is Osawatomie."

Washington's delivery of the stunning news was calm, almost deadpan.

As he said this, Brown turned his head to see who it was to whom Colonel Washington was speaking. Quicker than thought, I brought my saber down with all my strength upon his head. He was moving as the blow fell, and I suppose I did not strike him where I intended, for he received a deep saber cut in the back of the neck. He fell senseless on his side, then rolled over on his back.

He had in his hand a short Sharpe's cavalry carbine. I think he had just fired as I reached Colonel Washington, for the marine that followed me into the aperture made by the ladder received a bullet in the abdomen, from which he died in a few minutes.

By that time three or four of my men came rushing in like tigers. . . . They bayoneted one man skulking under the engine, and pinned another fellow up against the rear wall, both being instantly killed. I ordered the

men to spill no more blood. The other insurgents were at once taken under arrest, and the contest ended.

I saw very little of the situation within until the fight was over. Then I observed that the engine-house was thick with smoke, and it was with difficulty that a person could be seen across the room. In the rear, behind the left-hand engine, were huddled the prisoners whom Brown had captured and held as hostages for the safety of himself and his men.

The prisoners were the sorriest lot of people I ever saw. They had been without food for over sixty hours, in constant dread of being shot, and were huddled up in the corner where lay the body of Brown's son and one or two others of the insurgents who had been killed.

Green's comments about Lee seem like a snapshot of time.

I can see Colonel Lee now, as he stood on a slight elevation about forty feet from the engine-house, during the assault. He was in civilian dress, and looked then very little as he did during the war. He wore no beard, except a dark mustache, and his hair was slightly gray. He had no arms upon his person, and treated the affair as one of no very great consequence, which would be speedily settled by the marines.

Immediately after the fight, Brown was carried out of the engine-house, and recovered consciousness while lying on the ground in front. On the following day, Wednesday, with an escort, I removed him to Charleston [Charles Town], and turned him over to the civil authorities. No handcuffs were placed upon him, and he supported himself with a self-reliance and independence which were characteristic of the man.

JEFFERSON COUNTY, VIRGINIA (OCTOBER–NOVEMBER, 1859): THE TRIAL OF JOHN BROWN

John H. Kagi, Jeremiah G. Anderson, William Thompson, Dauphin Thompson, Brown's sons Oliver and Watson, Stewart Taylor, and the free black men Lewis S. Leary and Dangerfield Newby were all killed fighting with Brown. One marine, Luke Quinn, was killed during the storming of the engine house. He was the man whom Green suspected Brown shot in the abdomen.

Two slaves who were Washington's property and another prisoner, John Allstadt, were also killed. Whether or not the slaves voluntarily took up arms with Brown is unknown. One drowned while trying to escape and the other died in the Charles Town prison following the raid.

Of the rest, John E. Cook and Albert Hazlett escaped into Pennsylvania, but were captured and brought back to Charlestown. Aaron D. Stevens, Edwin Coppoc, and free African Americans John A. Copeland and Shields Green were all captured and imprisoned. Five raiders escaped and were never captured: Brown's son Owen, Charles P. Tidd, Barclay Coppoc, Francis J. Merriam, and free African American Osborne P. Anderson.

Virginia formerly requested to President Buchanan that Brown be turned over to and tried in the state of Virginia. The president readily acquiesced to Virginia's request. He ceded primary prosecution of the case from the federal to a state government.

Colonel Lee turned Brown, Stevens, Coppoc, Copeland, and Green over to the U.S. marshal, who then turned them over to the sheriff of Jefferson County, Virginia for trial in state criminal court.

On October 20, 1859, on the first day of the fall term of the Virginia circuit court, a grand jury was convened in Charleston. Its first act was to indict John Brown on charges of treason and murder committed in the state of Virginia. The penalty for conviction on either charge was death.

Brown pleaded not guilty. Assigned to the case was Judge Andrew Parker of the Circuit Court of Virginia. Almost immediately, a problem with Brown's prosecution developed.

The charge of treason against the state of Virginia was specious, considering that Brown had not attacked a Virginia military installation but rather one run by and under the control of the federal government. Still, Virginia believed it had jurisdiction since he had come into the state for the purpose of committing treason.

In ceding the Brown case to a state, President Buchanan set an extremely important legal precedent in U.S. history. Sixteen months later, when South Carolina extended its state sovereignty by firing on U.S. land at Fort Sumter, the decision to try Brown in state court was cited as precedent. Buchanan's acquiescence in *Commonwealth of Virginia v. John Brown* gave the South precedent for seceding from the Union, which began the Civil War.

For now, however, what Virginia and particularly Judge Hunter wanted was to make sure Brown had a fair trial. Immediately, lawyers financed by the Secret Six showed up to defend Brown. They were also there to make sure Brown kept his mouth shut and didn't inform on his patrons. John Brown knew that if he were to inform on the Secret Six, the state might give him leniency. If he didn't, he knew he

would be convicted and hanged. He believed most of all that his martyrdom would hasten the abolishment of slavery.

Brown never named anyone in the conspiracy as an accomplice. He never testified against the Secret Six or any of his surviving men. During the month-long trial, Brown did not cooperate with his counsel, preferring instead to represent himself. But the judge made sure that his lawyers sat with him at all times. In the end, Brown admitted that he had been given a fair and impartial hearing.

When the time came for a verdict, the jury didn't hesitate—they found Brown guilty of murder and treason charges against the state of Virginia. The judge asked if he had anything to say before sentence was pronounced.

John Brown rose to address the court.

"I have, may it please the court, a few words to say," Brown began in a strong, clear voice.

In the first place, I deny everything but what I have all along admitted—the design on my part to free the slaves. I intended certainly to have made a clean thing of that matter . . . I never did intend murder, or treason, or the destruction of property, or to excite or incite slaves to rebellion, or to make insurrection.

This court acknowledges, as I suppose, the validity of the law of God. I see a book kissed here which I suppose to be the Bible, or at least the New Testament. That teaches me that all things whatsoever I would that men should do to me, I should do even so to them. It teaches me, further, to remember them that are in bonds, as bound with them. I endeavored to act up to that instruction. Now, if it is deemed necessary that I should forfeit my life for the furtherance of the ends of justice, and mingle my blood further with the blood of my children and with the blood of millions in this slave country whose rights are disregarded by wicked, cruel, and unjust enactments—I submit; so let it be done!

Brown concluded with a few more thoughts and sat down.

The judge didn't buy any of it. Brown was convicted of insurrection against the state of Virginia. For his crime, he was condemned to be executed on December 2. His counsel asked the Virginia court of appeals for a stay of execution, but their request was refused. Brown and the others were removed to the Charleston jail to await execution.

When federal authorities searched the farmhouse Brown had used as a hideout prior to the raid, they found letters of correspondence between Brown and his Boston backers. The Secret Six weren't so secret any more. The six conspirators waited and sweated, expecting any minute to be extradited to Virginia and tried for murder and treason like Brown. They had to decide whether to stay or run. Howe and Sterns high-tailed it to Canada, deciding to remain there until after the execution. On two separate occasions, Sanborn also fled to the great white North but returned.

Gerrit Smith was not well enough to make the trip. He had a nervous breakdown and was carted off to an insane asylum. As he was led away, he waved his arms frantically and shouted that he was going to Virginia to suffer with John Brown.

Higginson was the steadiest of the bunch. He wouldn't run and in fact thought up a last-ditch attempt to save Brown's life by kidnapping Virginia's Governor Wise. Failing to undertake such a fool-hardy quest, he become despondent over his guilt in the affair.

"I should have realized the need to protect John Brown from himself," he later said.

The Reverend Theodore Parker was worse off than any of the others. He was in Rome, dying from tuberculosis. He made a public statement that hailed Brown as an American saint. If that were true, Brown would be the only American saint ever to kill a U.S. Marine who was lawfully discharging his duty.

JEFFERSON COUNTY, VIRGINIA (DECEMBER 2, 1859): JOHN BROWN EXECUTED

Newspapers in the North began to publish reports that threats had been made by northern sympathizers to rescue Brown. Governor Wise ordered Virginia troops to Charlestown to guard the prisoners until after their execution. By late November about 1,000 troops, including cadets of the Virginia Military Institute was standing guard outside the jail.

Colonel J. T. L. Preston, of the Military College of Lexington, Virginia, wrote the following letter a few hours after the execution of John Brown. He had been there on duty, as an officer of the corps of cadets.

CHARLESTOWN, December, 2, 1859.

The weather was very favorable; the sky was a little overcast, with a gentle haze in the atmosphere that softened, without obscuring, the magnificent prospect afforded here. Before nine o'clock the troops began to put themselves in motion to occupy the positions assigned to them on the field. To Colonel Smith had

been assigned the superintendence of the execution, and he and his staff were the only mounted officers on the ground until the Major General and his staff appeared.

By 10 o'clock all was arrayed, the general effect was most imposing, and at the same time picturesque. The cadets were immediately in rear of the gallows, with a howitzer on the right and left, a little behind, so as to sweep the field. They were uniformed in red flannel shirts, which gave them a dashing, Zouave look, and were exceedingly becoming, especially at the battery. They were flanked obliquely by two corps, the Richmond Grays and the Company F, which, if inferior in appearance to the cadets, were superior to any other company I ever saw outside of the regular army. Other companies were distributed over the field, in all amounting to perhaps eight hundred men. The military force was about fifteen hundred.

Shortly before eleven o'clock the prisoner was taken from jail, and the funeral cortege was put in motion. First came three companies, then the criminal's wagon, drawn by two large white horses. John Brown was seated on his coffin, accompanied by the sheriff and two other persons. The wagon drove to the foot of the gallows, and Brown descended with alacrity and without assistance and then ascended the steep steps to the platform. His demeanor was intrepid, without being braggart. He made no speech.

John Brown's manner gave no evidence of timidity, but his countenance was not free from concern, and it seemed to me to have a little cast of wildness. He stood upon the scaffld but a short time, giving brief adieus to those about him, when he was properly pinioned, the white cap drawn over his face, the noose adjusted and attached to the hook above, and he was moved, blindfolded, a few steps forward. It was curious to note how the instincts of nature operated to make him careful in putting out his feet, as if afraid he would walk off the scaffold. The man, who stood on the brink of eternity, was afraid of falling a few feet to the ground!

The sheriff asked the prisoner if he should give him a private signal before the fatal moment. He replied, in a voice that sounded to me unnaturally natural that "it did' not matter to him, if only they would not keep him too long waiting."

Brown had to wait, standing on the trapdoor for 15 torturous minutes until the troops were put in the "ready" position.

He stood . . . upright as a soldier, motionless. I was . . . watched him . . . to see if I could detect any signs of shrinking or trembling in his person, but there was none. Once I thought I saw his knees tremble, but it was only the wind blowing his loose trousers.

Finally, Colonel Smith announced to the sheriff, "We are all ready, Mr. Campbell." The culprit still stood steady, until the sheriff descending the flight of steps, with a well-directed blow of a sharp hatchet, severed the rope that held up the trap-door, which instantly sank sheer beneath him. He fell about three feet and the man of strong and bloody hand, of fierce passions, of iron will, of wonderful vicissitudes, the terrible partisan of Kansas, the capturer of the United States Arsenal at Harper's Ferry, the would-be Catiline of the South, the demigod of the Abolitionists, the man execrated and lauded, damned and prayed for, the man who, in his motives, his means, his plans, and his successes, must ever be a wonder, a puzzle and a mystery, John Brown, was hanging between heaven and earth.

There was profoundest stillness during the time his struggles continued, growing feebler and feebler at each abortive attempt to breathe. His knees were scarcely bent, his arms were drawn up to a right angle at the elbow, with the hands clenched; but there was no writhing of the body, no violent heaving of the chest.

At each feebler effort at respiration his arms sank lower and his legs hung more relaxed, until at last, straight and lank, he dangled, swayed slightly to and fro by the wind.

And here the gray-haired man of violence meets his fate, after he had seen his two sons cut down before him earlier in the same career of violence into which he had introduced them. So perish all such enemies of Virginia! All such enemies of the Union!

Brown stayed upon the gallows for nearly forty minutes and, after being examined by a whole staff of surgeons, was deposited in a neat coffin to be delivered to his friends, and transported to Harper's Ferry, where his wife waited it.

J. T. L. Preston

Preston's account is perhaps the most eloquent of its kind. No one had ever described an American execution in such vivid detail and with such deep sadness. But in his eloquence, Preston had missed one vital detail.

John Brown riding to his execution, sketched by an artist on the scene (Library of Congress)

Brown's death sentence was that he be hanged, and the sentence was not carried out to the letter of the law. Death by hanging involves breaking the neck instantly when the trapdoor is opened and the body drops, so there is little or no pain. But sometimes, when the hangman is not adept at fixing the noose, the neck doesn't break on the drop. In that case, the noose just tightens around the neck and restricts breathing. The victim struggles as the noose continues to tighten. After a few minutes of painful struggling, he finally dies from asphyxiation. That is exactly what happened to Brown.

In Rome, Reverend Parker of the Secret Six was on his deathbed. When informed of Brown's death, he said, "The road to heaven is as short from the gallows as from the throne."

Among the Virginia militia in attendance that day was a future murderer. He was a handsome man of 21 who in civilian life was an actor who made his stage debut at the age of 17 in Baltimore. He had interrupted his acting career to serve in the Virginia militia that was present at Brown's execution. The militiaman's name was John Wilkes Booth.

Knowing he would be denied a last opportunity to speak his mind on the gallows, Brown made a statement before he was led out to ride his coffin. He said: "I, John Brown, am now quite certain that the crimes of this guilty land will never be purged away but with blood."

It was as rueful an epitaph as it was for the future of the United States. In many places in the North, church bells tolled and small arms were fired into the sky to mark the time of Brown's execution. Churches held prayer vigils for him and public meetings were convened to glorify his deeds and sanctify his cause.

No church bells were rung to commemorate the lives of his victims.

Following additional trials, convicted seditionists Shields Green, John A. Copeland, John E. Cook, and Edwin Coppoc were executed on December 16. Aaron D. Stevens and Albert Hazel were hanged on March 16, 1860.

As for Brown, his wife Mary had his body returned to the Adirondacks to be interred on the Brown farm, according to his wishes. Later, the bodies of his sons and the bodies of 10 of his associates who were killed at Harper's Ferry were also brought to the farm for burial.

On April 3, 1860, federal marshals attempted to capture the ringleader of the Secret Six, Franklin Sanborn, who was back in Concord teaching school. The brave citizens of Concord, who had quite a history of rallying to the side of the underdog, collectively decided that enough blood had been shed on the whole Brown affair. They wouldn't let the federal troops have Sanborn. Rather than shed anymore innocent blood, the federals wisely left.

Mary Brown and her children remained at the farm for a few years after John's death. However, the farm eventually failed, and in 1863 the remaining members of the Brown family moved to California. By that time, a mere four years later, the Civil War was in full bloom and Brown had become a Union hero. John Brown's name became the slogan under which, as a battle hymn, the northern troops invaded and overran the South. No one seemed to find it odd that this hero was a convicted seditionist.

See also "BLOODY KANSAS"; JOHN WILKES BOOTH; HARPER'S FERRY, VIRGINIA.

Dakota Territory (1861) the country opens up

Brown and the slaves had fought over the soul of the nation in the center of the country. War might be inevitable, but so was expansion.

In 1861 a treaty with the Sioux Nation opened up the country that comprised Nebraska. In present-day boundaries, this area includes the present states of North and South Dakota, eastern Wyoming and eastern Montana. The area was named Dakota Territory.

Eyeing virgin land settlers began to come. So did criminals, and thus the "Thieves Road" opened.

See also MONTANA; FORT LARAMIE, WYOMING.

William Clarke Quantrill (1837–1864) soldier and murderer

John Brown's death coupled with the continual violence in "Bloody Kansas" made civil war inevitable. As is always the case, the threat of war brings out murderous personalities that flourish in times of killing. One of the worst was William Clarke Quantrill.

Quantrill was born at Canal Dover, Ohio, on July 31, 1837, to Thomas Henry Quantrill and the former Caroline Cornelia Clarke. As a young man, he taught school briefly in Ohio and Illinois.

Quantrill traveled west with some friends in 1857, but they had a falling out by spring 1858, when one of them accused him of horse stealing, a hanging offense. Quantrill quickly found a job as a freighter (mule and horse handler) on a wagon train traveling west to Salt Lake City. Most of the other freighters were Missourians with southern sympathies. As they slogged their way through to Salt Lake City, Quantrill and the Missourians discussed slavery, and eventually his mind shifted toward the southern view of things. He agreed that Negroes were property and should be treated as slaves.

At Fort Bridger, Salt Lake City, and elsewhere in the territory, Quantrill took part in a number of murders and thefts. He fled an arrest warrant in Utah in 1860 and returned to Kansas, where he took up residence in Lawrence. Soon he joined a group of abolitionists who were going across the border to Missouri to free some slaves, and on the sly, let his proslavery brethren know they were coming. When they got to the Missouri farm to free those slaves, the southerners were ready. The abolitionists were ambushed; three were killed. Quantrill, of course, survived.

Quantrill watched as Fort Sumter was attacked in 1861 and the Civil War began. With it came raids by the Kansas-based Jayhawkers, a guerrilla band that rode into Missouri to punish slave owners by killing them. Quantrill admired their tactics and decided to emulate them.

By early 1862 Quantrill had assembled a group of guerrillas that consisted of every kind of murderer, thief, and scoundrel he could find. In the minority were embittered farmers, who wanted to retaliate for the Jayhawker attacks on their property and other deprivations that they blamed on the Union. Quantrill and his men fought side by side with Confederate forces at the battle of Wilson's Creek in Oakhills, Missouri, in August 1861. After that, they operated as a unit of irregulars, attacking Union camps, patrols, and settlements. In November 1862 Quantrill and his men showed their true colors when they murdered 12 unarmed teamsters. Such conduct was unfit for any civilized military commander or unit. The Union authorities immediately declared them to be outlaws. The south remained neutral on whether Quantrill was one of their own.

In 1863 Quantrill captured Independence, Missouri, and a force of Union troops. In appreciation of his efforts, the Confederate States of America swore in Quantrill and his band as a legitimate wartime fighting unit. Quantrill was given the rank of captain; it was not enough. Quantrill wanted his own regular command. He petitioned the Confederacy for exactly that, but his reputation for brutality preceded him. His request was denied, and the Confederacy sought to appease him with a promotion to the rank of brevet (wartime) colonel.

After he became a full-fledged officer in the army of the Confederate States of America, Quantrill began to plan his attack on Lawrence, Kansas. Prior to this the proslavery farmers of Missouri had been continuously antagonized by the Jayhawkers, the pro-abolitionist guerrillas led by Jim Lane and Doc Jennison. The Jayhawkers would proceed across the border from Kansas into Missouri, burn and loot the homes of Confederate sympathizers, sometimes killing them, then flee back across the border to Kansas. Because Lawrence was abolitionist headquarters in Kansas, the town's citizens worried continuously about a similar attack from Missouri. Yet, the townspeople had little or no security and no contingency for dealing with an attack.

Early on the morning on August 21, the town awoke to the sound of thundering hooves and gunshots. Citizens opened their eyes to see Quantrill's guerrillas whooping and hollering as 400 invaded the town, blasting away with guns, hacking away with sabers. Once the guerrillas secured Lawrence, they eagerly proceeded to loot and burn as many houses as they could. They cleaned out all the banks and stores, then drained the taverns and saloons of every last bit of whiskey. Quantrill could have stopped there, having inflicted a vicious reprisal on the Jayhawkers, but Quantrill and his men were killers at heart. They proved it that day by killing every man they saw. They slaughtered 180. In the space of 90 minutes, the streets of Lawrence went from the reek of horse manure to burning human flesh.

Yet Quantrill failed to achieve his military objective. The Jayhawker leaders escaped. What made the event that much more perverse was that federal troops stationed in Missouri had unofficially sanctioned it. As far as the federals were concerned, the Jayhawkers were no better than Quantrill. They operated without federal mandate and therefore needed to be stopped. Why should they take the Jayhawkers down, the federals reasoned, when Quantrill would do the job for them?

The federal troops stationed on the Missouri-Kansas border knew Quantrill was taking more than 400 men into Kansas, and they allowed it to happen. When Quantrill returned to Missouri after the pillage of Lawrence, they let him ride off rather than engage him in a full-blown battle.

Many of the survivors of Quantrill's raid wrote of their experiences in letters and reminiscences. These are just a few:

O. W. McAlaster: "It being very warm, I was up about 5 o'clock on the morning of August 21, 1863. A noise attracted my attention, and I looked south and saw between 300 and 400 horsemen . . . in an instant they spread out . . . shooting every person they saw. . . . They reached a camp of thirty-two unarmed recruits . . . I saw them shooting down these men, who ran in every direction, some crawling under sidewalks and into bushes, only about five escaping with their lives. Then I realized that Quantrill and his guerrillas were upon us."

Sophia L. Bissell: ". . . about ½ mile away were ever so many men on horseback, coming along very quickly, strung out, oh, I should think there must have been three or four hundred of them. In a few minutes . . . we heard them say, 'Halt!' and then . . . they all separated into bands and went yelling and shooting as fast as they would ride, a band for each street . . ."

Brigetta Dix Flintom: "I saw men jumping from windows and fleeing for their lives. Several were killed as they ran."

Hiram Towne: "Almost everyone was abed and they were all over the city in ten minutes and shot down every one that showed his head, so that they had no chance to get together to defend the town . . ."

Mary Carpenter Rankin: "We . . . had been married ten months. When two of the raiders called at our house and saw my husband, they fired a shot at him and after his race through the yard they fired a second shot. Of what passed around us I know and remember nothing, until I sat beside the body of my husband and saw him in a rude coffin and laid away in a corner of our yard."

W. H. Simpson: "When Quantrill raided Lawrence I was five and one half years young. My father, Henry M. Simpson, then lived in West Lawrence. Back of our house was a large field of corn, growing as Kansas corn is in the habit of doing, lustily tall and thick. That field, with its 'walls of corn' saved our lives. I well remember being hurriedly dragged into the maze of maize just as the rebels came up the front steps looking for abolitionists. The day was hot. It dawned that way. We had no water, no breakfast, and nothing to satisfy hunger except ears of half-green corn. The necessity for keeping quiet was impressed on my mind; but probably I was too badly scared to make a noise, anyway. The flames from our burning house scarcely had died down when we came out of our hiding place and were taken care of by kind neighbors—glad just to be alive."

Mrs. J. B. Sutliff: "My husband was not killed, he being away on business and our home was not burned. I saw Mr. Griffith and told him to run to the ravine. He reached it and saved his life. I had to warn Mrs. Griffith to keep away from him. I can hear the pounding of nails yet, for Ira Brown and Hiram Towne made coffins for two nights in their shop just across the alley from my home."

Mat Shaw: "The church was used as a morgue. I put men to work, making rough coffins and used 250 feet of walnut lumber and fifty pounds of nails that I happened to have in the shop."

Priscilla Jones: "They were digging graves all night Friday, begun burying just at daylight Saturday morning and worked till dark . . . there was one hundred and twenty-three bodies found, some burnt so you couldn't tell what it was."

Richard Cordley: "The walls of the brick and stone buildings were still standing, black, gloomy and threatening. The smoke was still rising from the ruins and in the deep cellars the fires were still glowing."

While on their way to Texas, Quantrill and his guerrillas came upon the 100-man headquarters escort of Union general James G. Blunt. They attacked on October 6, 1863, and killed 80 men and wounded 18 in the Barter Springs Massacre. It was called a massacre because many of the Union soldiers were murdered after having surrendered.

On October 26 Quantrill reported at Bonham to General Henry E. McCulloch of the Confederate Army. One of McCulloch's officers later described Quantrill as standing about five feet, 10 inches, weighing about 150 pounds, with fair hair, blue eyes, and a florid complexion.

Lieutenant General Edmund Kirby Smith, commander of the Trans-Mississippi Confederacy, liked Quantrill and ordered McCulloch to use Quantrill and his men to help capture the increasing number of deserters and conscription-dodgers in North Texas. Quantrill's men were consistent in their demeanor—they captured few and killed several. Realizing his mistake, McCulloch pulled them off this duty and sent them to track down retreating Comanches from a recent raid on the northwest frontier. Again, they failed.

During this winter, Quantrill's lieutenant, William "Bloody Bill" Anderson, took some of the men and organized his own guerrilla band. Now there were two marauding groups in the area. Settlers in the north Texas counties of Grayson and Fannin became targets for raids. Quantrill's guerrillas murdered and robbed. Regular Confederate forces had to be assigned to protect residents from the activities of the irregulars.

Finally, General McCulloch had enough of the undisciplined and murderous Quantrill and his band. He summoned the raider for a meeting. On March 28, 1864, when Quantrill appeared at Bonham as ordered, McCulloch had him arrested on the charge of ordering the murder of a Confederate major.

On the same day he was captured, Quantrill added to his legend. He escaped and returned to his camp near Sherman, pursued by more than 300 state and Confederate troops. Linking up with his men, he led them across the Red River into Indian Territory (Oklahoma), where they resupplied from Confederate stores.

Quantrill had escaped the Confederate brotherhood but his own brotherhood had had enough of him. His men had grown disenchanted with his leadership in Texas. They were murderers and pillagers, not Indian trackers. How were they to slake their blood lust or make money with such activities? His authority over his followers disintegrated completely when they elected George Todd, one of Quantrill's former lieutenants, to lead them.

Quantrill determined to win them back. He concocted a cockeyed plan to lead a company of men to Washington where they would assassinate President Abraham Lincoln. He was so ill thought of by the Confederacy by then that he had no knowledge that a Confederate agent named John Wilkes Booth was already plotting to do exactly that.

The force Quantrill raised for his attack against the president assembled in Lafayette County, Missouri, in November and December 1864. Ironically, he and his former archenemy, John Brown, had in common that both had plotted sedition—only Brown had the nerve to carry his plan out.

Informed of the strength of Union troops east of the Mississippi River, Quantrill decided he would not be able to march as far east as Washington, let alone St. Louis. He abandoned his plan and returned to raiding.

From a high of 400 men at Lawrence, the dissolute Quantrill now had a group of 33 followers. With them, he entered Kentucky early in 1865. In May or early June of that year, a Union irregular force surprised his group near Taylorsville, Kentucky. Quantrill and his men fled, and Quantrill was later trapped in a barn at the Wakefield Farm, about one mile from Smiley, Kentucky. Captain Edward Terrell of the Union army and his cavalry detachment quickly arrived on the scene and opened fire.

Trying to escape, Quantrill was struck by two balls from a Spencer rifle. The first hit his hand, but the second hit him in the spine, instantly paralyzing him from the waist down. The Union soldiers could have killed him right there and no one would have uttered a word, such was Quantrill's bloody reputation. But the last thing Union generals wanted was a martyr to the southern cause.

Quantrill was taken by stretcher to a military hospital and then transferred to a military prison at Louisville, Kentucky. He died there on June 6, 1865, and was buried in the Old Portland Catholic Cemetery at Louisville.

Quantrill's story should have ended there with his physical presence remaining in the 19th century. It did not. In 1887 his mother had his bones disinterred and brought back to his home state of Ohio for reinterment. Unfortunately, the man she paid to do the job was an entrepreneur. He stole some of Quantrill's skeleton. Years later, parts of it showed up in a Kansas collector's home. In 1993 those same bones were moved to Higginsville, Missouri, and reinterred in the Confederate cemetery located in the city.

QUANTRILL'S GUERRILLAS

Most of Quantrill's guerrillas were no more than psychopathic killers and amoral criminals who found a home looting, sacking, and killing with Quantrill's band. It was wartime and they could disguise their actions as patriotic by siding with the southern cause. The kinds of individuals Quantrill actively recruited to his band can best be seen in William "Bloody Bill" Anderson and Archie Clement.

WILLIAM "BLOODY BILL" ANDERSON

Hailing from Huntsville, in Randolph County, Missouri, Anderson moved with his family to Council Grove, Kansas, in his teenage years, where his father was killed during the border wars. This kind of loss, which became only too common in the pre–Civil War years, only served to stoke the embers of hate in Anderson's soul. Joining Quantrill, he eventually led his own regiment.

Anderson quickly developed a reputation as a butcher. Within the Union army, he was known as a brutal murderer who shot his prisoners. Some doubted his humanity. Always ready to do some butchering, he carried four rifles on his horse, four Colt Navy pistols in his waistband, a saber, a hatchet, and a bag of pistols wrapped around his saddle horn.

In September 1864 Anderson truly lived up to his name. During a raid on Centralia, Kansas, Quantrill surprised 26 Union soldiers who were in transit to St.

Joseph. The guerrillas lined them up single file. Then, one at a time, Bloody Bill shot each through the head.

The Centralia massacre inflamed the northern troops. They set out to find and kill Anderson. One mile north of Orrick, Missouri, he and his men were located by a Union force of 150 men commanded by Majors Samuel Cox and John Grimes. Cornering Anderson in a barn, Cox and Grimes led their men in storming it. A few moments later, the mass murderer Anderson lay dead, the blood from two dozen bullet holes mixing with the straw on the barn's floor.

The Union soldiers buried Anderson. They had such disdain for him that they did not see fit to mark his grave.

ARCHIE CLEMENT

Seventeen-year-old Archie Clement was a kid by anyone's definition of the word—except when it came to killing. As a killer, he was a true professional who made his more famous contemporary, Billy the Kid, seem like a choirboy in comparison.

Hailing from Kingsville, Johnson County, Missouri, Archie was slight of build, small, blond and grey-eyed. His stature belied his abilities. Archie had the unique distinction of being Bloody Bill Anderson's lieutenant, executioner, and scalper. When Anderson ordered Archie to kill, Archie did, without hesitation. Wearing a perpetual smile, he would scalp and mutilate his victims because it gave him pleasure to see them suffer.

Archie took over Anderson's command after his death. He survived the war, only to be killed by Bacon Montgomery in Lexington, Missouri on December 13, 1866.

See also "BLOODY KANSAS" (1856–1861); JESSE JAMES (1847–1882); JAMES-YOUNGER GANG (1866–1881).

Henry Wirz (1822–1865) mass murderer and war criminal
Henry Wirz stands as the greatest convicted mass murderer in United States history. His explanation for his actions as the commandant of the Andersonville prisoner of war camp in Georgia, where 13,000 Union army soldiers died over a period of 18 months, was, "I was only following orders." It was the first time a war criminal ever used such a defense.

Many view Wirz as a scapegoat to the southern cause. He is, after all, the only Confederate ever to be tried and convicted of crimes against the United States of America. While his ultimate responsibility for the obscenity that was Andersonville may be sub-ject to conjecture, the facts of his life, and the crimes he was convicted for, are not.

Henry Wirz was born in Zurich, Switzerland, in 1822. After graduating from the University of Zurich, he went to medical colleges in Paris and Berlin. Graduating with a medical degree, he practiced for a few years in Europe, then immigrated to the United States in 1849.

Wirz arrived in Kentucky a mere 60 years after Daniel Boone first blazed a trail into the place. By that time, Kentucky was already a state with a thriving agrarian economy supported by slave labor. Wirz established a medical practice and five years later, in 1854, he married a widow who had two young daughters. That is when Wirz fell victim to that most American of diseases—wanderlust.

In 1855 he took his family down the Natchez Trace, by that time a thriving two-lane highway. The Wirz family went as far south as they could on the trace, into Louisiana. It was the same place of wild canebrake that was once terrorized by men like Murrel, Mason, the Harps, and Joseph Hare. But they were all dead now and their like could only be found in the penny dreadfuls.

Louisiana had entered the Union as a slave state. It was a place of opportunity that Wirz intended to mine. He established a thriving practice. Doris gave birth to a third daughter, Cora. By 1861 Wirz seemed set to live out his life as just another immigrant success story. But with the attack on Fort Sumter, the Wirzes lives changed as much as any southerner's.

Like many immigrants, Wirz was passionately patriotic about his adopted country, only his was the Confederate States of America (CSA). He enlisted in Company A, Fourth Battalion, Louisiana Volunteers, and was given the rank of sergeant. The Confederacy was so desperate for fighting men that it was willing to sacrifice a man of Wirz's education and abilities and put him in a front-line unit.

During May 1862 Henry Wirz fought honorably against the Union army at the battle of Seven Pines. It was a dramatic fight in which General Joseph Johnston, commanding the Confederates, surprised two companies of Union soldiers. On the second day of fierce fighting, Sergeant Wirz took a minie ball through his right arm. The bullet did enough damage that the arm was permanently paralyzed.

Clearly, Wirz's practice of medicine would be severely curtailed. Surgery would be impossible for him to perform. Subsequently, Wirz was promoted to captain "for bravery on the field of battle." However, his paralysis meant he could no longer serve in combat.

The CSA still did not know what do with one of its most educated soldiers. It solved the problem by making Wirz a clerk at Libby Prison in Richmond, Virginia. His commanding officer was Brigadier General John Henry Winder, the provost marshal in charge of Confederate prisoner-of-war camps. He took a liking to the doctor/soldier/clerk. Seeing Wirz's talent, he gave him a promotion to major with responsibilities as his adjutant general.

Overseas, meanwhile, the CSA was attempting to gain diplomatic recognition from England and France. To do so would legitimize their struggle internationally and invite foreign governments to lend financial support. The Confederates were, as usual, desperate for a few good men, this time those that were well educated and could work with the British and other governments whose recognition they sought. On the advice of General Winder, CSA president Jefferson Davis enlisted the aid of Henry Wirz.

Davis concurred with Wender that the cultured, multilingual Wirz, who spoke fluent German and Dutch, was an ideal candidate to aid the southern cause. President Davis sent him on a secret mission to England while back home changes were occurring in the status of prisoners of war (POWs).

Prior to 1863 both sides adhered to an agreement by which prisoners of war were regularly exchanged. Ulysses Grant, the hard-drinking, cigar-chomping maverick general that Lincoln had chosen to lead the Union army, noticed that the Union, which had more resources, generally kept its Confederate prisoners in fine fettle. But when they were traded, the Confederates gave up malnourished Union soldiers. With everything the South had, including food, being directed toward the war effort, Union POWs were starving. Many had scurvy. Some died from starvation, others from ill-treated wounds and infection. Medicine, too, was scarce in the South. Grant knew that the repatriated, well-fed Confederate POWs were sent back to the front lines while their Union counterparts were just lucky to be alive. It was an uneven exchange that in Grant's view was prolonging the war.

Andersonville Prison. Note the "deadline," the fence that cuts across the picture. Prisoners were shot if they approached it. (Library of Congress)

For its part, the South found itself using old forts, warehouses, and jails to house its Union prisoners. General Robert E. Lee, John Brown's conqueror, was now the commander of the Confederate Army. He had done his job so well that all of these antiquated facilities were overflowing with Union POWs. There was a real need to construct a prison deep in the Confederacy to house the overflow. A site in the Georgia backcountry between Macon and Columbus, in Sumter County was chosen. Initially, the prison was called Camp Sumter. Later, the name was changed to Andersonville.

It was an ideal location, away from populated areas, so far south that even if a prisoner escaped, he would have to ride hundreds of miles just to get back to Union lines. The prison had a nearby railhead serviced by the Georgia Southwestern Railway from which soldiers could be off-loaded from the boxcars that had shipped them from battlefields all across the South and West.

What the first prisoners found when they got to Andersonville for its opening on February 24, 1864, really was not a prison at all but rather a heavily armed stockade. There were no bars. Giant, 20-foot pine stakes stuck into the ground made a rectangular pen $16\frac{1}{2}$ acres square. Intended to house a maximum of 10,000 prisoners, the barracks were half finished lean-tos and whatever the Confederates could scrounge.

A slow-moving stream that ran right through the compound was used for everything—water supply, bathing, and cooking. Upstream, outside the camp, guards used it for urinating, defecating, and dumping garbage and animal waste. In Andersonville, there was no such thing as potable water. Prisoners developed dysentery from drinking it. Wounds washed with this poison turned gangrenous.

Henry Wirz returned to the Confederate States of America in January 1864. Rejoining General Winder, who was now in charge of all Confederate prisons,

Union soldiers in Andersonville lived under deplorable conditions. (National Archives)

A rare photograph shows a long trench being dug by slaves and others at Andersonville Prison. The Confederates needed space to bury the 10,000 Union soldiers who died in the POW camp. (National Archives)

Those who tried to escape found themselves facing the "deadline," a rail of pine logs, set back 25 feet from the prison's pine log walls. The guards had orders to shoot on sight any prisoner who crossed it.

In April 1865, when Lee surrendered to Grant at Appomattox, Andersonville was part of that surrender. Accompanied by his family, Wirz left the army and went to Indiana. His biggest problem, he expected, was how to be a doctor with only one good arm.

Back at Andersonville, the Union army was assessing the depths of the tragedy. A total of 13,000 Union POWs died in Andersonville during the 14 months the prison was in operation. Wirz had been the commandant for all of those months. One of three prisoners who went to Andersonville died. Upon the discovery of the abominable conditions at the prison, poet Walt Whitman wrote: "the dead there are not to be pitied as much as some of the living that have come from there—if they can be called living." The public clamored for somebody to pay.

See also WASHINGTON, D.C. (1865).

Wirz served at prisons in Richmond and Tuscaloosa. In April 1864 Winder appointed Wirz the commandant of Andersonville Prison. Three months later, General Grant decided he had had enough.

In June 1864 General Grant stopped all prisoner exchanges. The population at Andersonville swelled to more than 26,000. To make matters worse, Union general Sherman was marching to the sea, cutting the Confederacy in half and burning everything in the Union army's path. Prisoner rations that had been meager at best became next to nothing.

Every day hundreds died from malnutrition, disease, and other causes. Prisoners were never given clothing and some died from exposure. Bodies were piled alongside the "deadhouse" outside the prison because the deadhouse itself was already full of rotting corpses. But Lee was still doing his job. By August the prison population on Andersonville's 16 1/2 acres was 33,000; by October, 45,000. In population alone, it was the fifth-largest of all cities in the Confederacy.

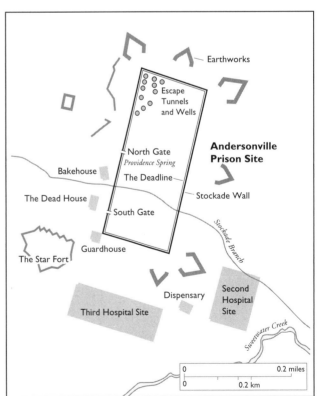

The Confederate Army's prisoner-of-war camp Andersonville, where thousands of Union soldiers died of starvation, disease, and other causes

"Matt Sanders," a.k.a. Martha Sanders
(1861–1871) Confederate spy and bigamist

Martha Sanders was a rather precocious young woman who hailed from Bloomfield, Kentucky. She married Richard Maddox in Missouri in 1861. The happy couple was honeymooning just as the Civil War began.

Calling herself "Matt," Martha became a notorious Confederate spy. Shortly after the war, her husband died and she married George Shepherd, who had served as a lieutenant under William Quantrill. Shepherd then tried to hold up the bank at Russellville, Kentucky, in 1868, but he was captured and sentenced to prison for three years. Martha wasted no time in leaving him and marrying Alexander McMakin, a wealthy neighbor of her father.

When Shepherd came home in 1871, she refused to go back to him, so Shepherd had her charged with bigamy. Martha had neglected to divorce him before marrying McMakin. Saving the court time and money, Martha obtained a divorce before her case came to trial, and the charge was dropped.

Now known as Martha McMakin, she lived out her days as a wealthy Southern belle. Many of those who surreptitiously supported the Confederate cause were not so lucky.

See also JOHN WILKES BOOTH (1838–1865).

John Wilkes Booth (1838–1865) first presidential assassin

Like Dillinger, who would come after him, and Hare before him, John Wilkes Booth was the best-known and most daring criminal of his time. And as with all presidential assassins, his active involvement on the criminal scene was brief. Booth was the first, the most intelligent, the most politically motivated; he really believed killing Lincoln was an act of war, not murder. Booth was born to play the role of the first presidential assassin. He came from an acting family. Though British born, his father Junius Booth, Sr. was America's most respected actor. He had passed on his talent and love for the theater to three of his male heirs—Junius Jr., Edwin, and John Wilkes.

John was born on May 10, 1838, on a farm near Bel Air, Maryland, about 25 miles from Baltimore. He was born into a family with a history of schizophrenia, debauchery, and slavery. The ninth of 10 children, John grew up taking for granted the slaves who worked the family farm. That was the way it was supposed to be—black slaves did all the menial labor.

During the colder winter months, the family repaired to a home that Junius Sr. owned on North Exeter Street in Baltimore. There Junius Sr. drank too much and had spells of madness. Today, he would probably be diagnosed as an alcoholic and a schizophrenic. This sick man was John's father and greatest influence.

As a teenager, John attended St. Timothy's Hall, an Episcopal military academy in Catonsville, Maryland. There Booth was attracted to the teachings of the Know-Nothing Party. The Know-Nothings, forerunners of today's white supremacists, believed that the country should be preserved for the "native-born Caucasian citizens."

After his father died in 1852, Booth left school to help work the farm. His sister Asia Booth Clarke would later write about Booth's delusions of grandeur. "I must have fame! fame!" Always cognizant, even at a young age, that he would toil in his father's shadow, Booth's goal was to become a more famous actor than his father had been.

John Wilkes Booth began his stage career when he was 17 in 1855 at the Charles Street Theater in Baltimore. He did not play another role until two years later, when he worked at Weatley's Arch Theater in Philadelphia. During his run there, he showed his inexperience, frequently forgetting cues. Booth moved on to Richmond, Virginia, in 1858 for a season at the Marshall Theater.

While at the Marshall he became more confident of his acting abilities and became widely popular with audiences, who flocked to see him. Booth fell in love with what he perceived as the genteel life of a southerner and that helped define his political views. He hated abolitionists

By 1859 Booth had had his head filled with proslavery, pro-South dogma and decided to act on his beliefs. He joined the Richmond Grays, a unit in the Virginia Militia, for the sole purpose of witnessing John Brown's execution. After Brown's death, he resigned. Once back in civilian life, Booth the actor was constantly in demand throughout America. He was making $20,000 a year acting, a fortune in those days. Newspapers and magazines hailed him as the handsomest man in America. Booth was a lean, athletic five foot, eight inches tall, with piercing black eyes, jet black hair, and ivory skin. The ladies loved him, and he loved them back. But when the time came to defend his beloved South, he demurred. Booth promised his mother, Mary, that he would not join the Confederate Army.

John Wilkes Booth (National Archives)

Booth spent the war years romancing many women, including actress Henrietta Irving, who had a stormy relationship with the mercurial actor. Irving slashed Booth in the face with a knife when she learned that Booth had no intentions of marrying her.

In between romances, he acted. In spring 1862 Booth was arrested in St. Louis for making antigovernment remarks. The charges, in light of the First Amendment, were dropped. John told his sister Asia, "So help me holy God! My soul, life, and possessions are for the South."

In 1863, at Ford's Theatre, President Lincoln sat in the very same box he would occupy two years hence and watched Booth perform the role of Raphael in the play *The Marble Heart*. That same year, Booth formed an oil company. He had an idea to make money in the burgeoning business and make it his life's work.

He retired from the stage at the ripe old age of 26 in 1864 to manage this investment. But the oil busi-

ness never panned out, and he gave it up the same year. In between, he allegedly found time to smuggle much-needed medical supplies to Confederate forces. In November he wrote to his brother-in-law: "This country was formed for the white not for the black man. And looking upon African slavery from the same stand-point, as held by those noble framers of our Constitution, I for one, have ever considered it, one of the greatest blessings (both for themselves and us) that God ever bestowed upon a favored nation."

At this point in Booth's life, nothing seemed to be working out well. People compared him unfavorably to his father. His business investments failed. Even lovers like Irving turned against him. As if that was not enough, the Union was winning the war and would soon defeat the Confederates.

By late summer 1864, Booth was conspiring to kidnap President Lincoln. He planned to seize the president in Washington and spirit him south to Richmond. He would exchange Lincoln for Confederate soldiers in Union prison camps, who would be repatriated to the South and immediately be taken to the frontlines to replace the worn, ragged Confederate troops.

Booth used his charisma and talent to attract a core group of conspirators with similar political ideals. They were Michael O'Laughlen, Samuel Arnold, Lewis Powell, a.k.a. "Lewis Paine," John Surratt, David Herold, and George Atzerodt. Surratt, a secret dispatch rider for the Confederates, had introduced Booth to the rest of the conspirators. They chose to discuss their plans at an inn in Surrattsville owned by Mary Surratt, John's mother.

On March 15, 1865, Booth decided to change the venue. He met with the entire group at Gautier's Restaurant on Pennsylvania Avenue, about three blocks from Ford's Theatre, to discuss the kidnapping of Lincoln. All that was needed was the right moment, which soon came when Booth learned that the president was to attend a play at the Campbell Hospital, just outside Washington, on March 17, 1865.

At the last minute Lincoln decided not to attend the performance. Some of the conspirators were so downhearted by this turn of events that they abandoned the group. John Surratt, for one, fled immediately. He was soon followed by Samuel Arnold, who later commented that Booth "became a monomaniac on the success of the Confederate arms, a condition that generally follows when a man's thoughts are constantly centered upon one subject alone," according

President Abraham Lincoln (National Archives)

Two days later, on April 11, the president delivered a speech at the White House to a large group of former slaves and ordinary citizens celebrating the Union victory. Booth was there. During the speech, the president suggested conferring voting rights "on the very intelligent [blacks], and on those who serve our cause as soldiers."

The speech pushed Booth over the edge, and he conceived a plot so devastating, he believed, the Union would never recover from it. It would be the last act of a defiant Confederacy. Here is what John Wilkes Booth, Confederate Agent, had figured out:

Under the constitutional line of succession, after the president was the vice president, president pro tempore of the Senate and finally, secretary of state. By eliminating Vice President Andrew Johnson and Secretary of State William H. Seward, the only one left that could assume power was the president pro tempore of the Senate, Lafayette LaSabine.

Seward and Johnson were men of real vision, courage, and talent who, Booth knew, could lead upon Lincoln's death. LaSabine got into the Senate because he had been a faithful local politician beholden to the Whig Party. Nothing in his background showed any capacity to act as president or to lead a wounded country coming out of a great civil war.

to the *Baltimore American* in 1902. Such were the actor's social contacts that even while conspiring murder, he was still socially active.

Sometime in the winter of 1864–65, Booth took up with Lucy Herbert Hale, daughter of John Parker Hale, a former abolitionist senator from New Hampshire. By March they were secretly engaged. On March 4, 1865, John Wilkes Booth attended Lincoln's second inauguration as the invited guest of Lucy Herbert Hale. The future assassin sat so close to the president that he later told his friend Samuel Knapp Chester in confidence, "What an excellent chance I had to kill the President, if I had wished, on inauguration day!"

Booth fooled around with some other kidnapping plans; all fell through. On April 9, 1865, Robert E. Lee surrendered to Ulysses S. Grant at Appomattox Court House, Virginia. The war was over. The Union had won. Booth was furious and wanted Lincoln dead.

The box at Ford's Theatre where Lincoln was assassinated (National Archives)

With LaSabine as president, the Union could fall.

In late March Secretary of State Seward had suffered major injuries in a carriage accident. His jaw had been broken, for which he wore a protective collar around his face. He also had a dislocated shoulder.

By April 7 Booth had dispatched Paine to Seward's house, where the handsome Paine flirted with Seward's parlor maid Margaret Coleman. While he was doing that, he noticed the routine of the house and planned how he would gain admittance when they were ready.

Washington, D.C. (April 14, 1865) assassination of Abraham Lincoln

The reason Booth had not been able to kill Lincoln earlier was that he had never had the opportunity. On the morning of April 14, 1865, when he dashed into Ford's Theatre to pick up his mail, he got exactly that. Henry Clay Ford, a young lad who worked at the theater, informed Booth that the president would be attending that evening's performance of Our American Cousin. Booth knew the theater well, having played it many times. Here was his opportunity.

Booth now knew for certain where the president was going to be at a certain place and time. Booth had performed in Our American Cousin many times and knew every line. He also knew that the line that elicited the most laughs would be delivered at approximately 10:15 at the evening's performance. What better place for the foremost actor of his generation to commit the crime of the century than on the stage of the theater where he had had some of his greatest theatrical triumphs?

The key to the murder, and his escape, he soon realized, was the exploitation of the road system into and out of Washington. By 1865 the city had settled into its present urban outline. Major roads into and out of the city had already been built, and Booth could pick which ones to use in his escape.

Booth was not a martyr; he was too egotistical for that. He saw himself as serving the southern cause, which meant that as soon as he shot the president, he would be on his horse and out of there, hightailing it for the south where he expected to be hailed as a hero.

After Booth left Ford's, he walked down to a stable at C Street where he rented a fast roan mare. He told James W. Pumphrey, the stable operator, that he would pick the horse up at 4:30 that afternoon. He then returned to his room at the National Hotel.

Police detectives investigating the Lincoln homicide would later piece together Booth's hour-to-hour meetings with his coconspirators. The detectives never realized that those meetings were part of a plan much greater than simply assassinating the president.

At 2 P.M., Booth went to the Herndon House and met with fellow conspirator Lewis Paine. Booth told Paine what he was going to do that night and what he expected Paine to do. At 2:30 P.M., Booth was at the Surratt boardinghouse. He gave Mary Surratt a package containing a pair of field glasses. He told her to take them to her tavern in Surrattsville. At 3 P.M., Booth was at the Kirkwood House to tell fellow conspirator George Atzerodt that his job that night was to assassinate Vice President Andrew Johnson, but Atzerodt was not present to receive Booth's instructions. Booth inexplicably left a note for Vice President Johnson saying that he had called. Perhaps it was a casual acknowledgment that if he were not successful in implementing his plan, he had come pretty close.

At 4 P.M., Booth picked up his rented horse. He spent the next hour having a drink at a local tavern and writing a letter to the National Intelligencer, a Washington newspaper. In it, he explained that his plans had changed, from the kidnapping to the murder of the president.

Walking down Fourteenth Street at 5 P.M., Booth met a fellow actor named John Mathews. He gave Mathews the letter and asked him to deliver it to the National Intelligencer the next day. Booth mounted his horse and rode off, passing by Ulysses S. Grant's carriage. On a side street, fate intervened when he almost rode right into Atzerodt, who was on foot. Booth dismounted and told Atzerodt of his deadly assignment that night to assassinate the vice president.

Once and for all, John Wilkes Booth was certain he could bring down the Union. What he had not counted on was that he had picked the wrong man to commit the Johnson murder. While Paine was an able assassin, Atzerodt was a weak criminal. He did not fancy having to shoot anyone, let alone the vice president. Nevertheless, Booth told him to kill Johnson as close to 10:15 as possible.

Employees at Ford's Theatre, including Ned Spangler, were happy to look up at 6:00 as John Wilkes Booth strolled in. He invited several of them out for a drink at Taltavul's Star Saloon. Afterward, Booth went back to the theater and did a dry run: He walked the route he would travel during the assassination. Inside the door of the president's box, he secreted a severed piano leg.

After he killed Lincoln, he planned to leap the 10 feet from the president's box down to the stage, then make a quick exit stage right, out the door to his waiting horse. From there he would flee Washington and head to the safety of Virginia.

Back at his hotel room. Booth put on calf-length boots, new spurs—he would, after all, be riding hard that night—and black clothes. He wore a black hat. In his pockets he placed his diary, a compass, and a derringer. Though small enough to conceal easily, the weapon took a large, .44-caliber lead ball. It was a single-shot pistol that was deadly at extremely close range.

Around 9:30, Booth arrived at Ford's Theatre. He asked Ned Spangler to hold his horse in the alley in back of Ford's. Spangler, who was busy changing sets for the play, inquired if another employee, Joseph C. Burroughs, could accommodate Mr. Booth. Burroughs agreed to hold the mare until Booth returned.

For a rational man, planning a murder is one thing, doing it is entirely another. Shooting a man is hard enough, but shooting a man who also happens to be president in the back of the head, might provoke some hesitation. Maybe that is why Booth did not proceed directly to Lincoln's box. Instead, he went to the tavern next to the theater and asked for a bottle of whiskey and water.

It was the last chance for Booth to fade into the pages of history as a well-known actor instead of the first presidential assassin. As Booth made his final decision another customer walked over to Booth and said, "You'll never be the actor your father was."

Booth replied, "When I leave the stage, I will be the most famous man in America."

WASHINGTON, D.C. (APRIL 14, 1865): ATTEMPTED ASSASSINATION OF SECRETARY OF STATE WILLIAM SEWARD

On the evening of April 14, Paine and David Herold rode to Seward's residence in Lafayette Square. The plan was for Paine to do the job while Herold held the horses for the getaway.

Paine knocked on the door of the secretary's house. When it was opened by William Bell, the secretary's houseboy, Paine claimed to be delivering medicine from Seward's doctor and proceeded up to the second floor landing, off of which was Seward's bedroom.

At the top of the stairs, he was greeted by Seward's son Frederick, who served as his father's assistant secretary of state. Paine could not talk his way into the sickroom; Frederick would not let him

Lewis Payne, the Confederate agent who tried to assassinate Secretary of State Seward the night Booth killed Lincoln (National Archives)

in. Paine turned to go downstairs, then whirled, a Whitney revolver having materialized in his hand. He pointed it at Frederick's temple. He pulled the trigger, but the gun did not go off—it misfired. Before Frederick could react, Paine used the barrel to pistol-whip him a few times across the head until he fell.

Paine pulled his backup weapon, a Bowie knife, from his belt. He smashed through the door of Seward's sickroom and leaped onto the sick man. Paine slashed at the neck of the secretary repeatedly with the Bowie knife, but all that happened was that Seward's leather brace set off sparks when the blade struck it on an angle. Undaunted, Paine slashed out again, this time across the secretary's face, producing a deep wound.

Other people in the house heard the commotion and rushed to Seward's aid. Seward's nurse, his son Augustus, and the secretary himself managed to fight off the would-be assassin, who, seeing he would not be able to complete his task, broke free of the men and fled down the stairs. Going out, he ran into a State Department messenger whom he stabbed in the back.

Outside, Paine discovered that Herold had deserted him. His horse was tied to a tree. Paine mounted, and he was off into the night.

At about 10:07, Booth entered the theater lobby. Just as he had practiced earlier that day, he went up the stairs to the dress circle. Spying the president's box, he noted there was no guard. In front of the box sat Charles Forbes, the president's footman, and no one else.

Booth was across the hallway and handing Forbes his card in a second. Recognizing the famous actor, Forbes let him pass. Booth entered the box quietly, propping it open with the severed piano leg he had hidden during his earlier run-through.

Booth found himself in a small anteroom. He opened the inside door. There was the president. He was sitting in his box with his back to Booth. Next to him were his wife, Mary, and Major Henry Rathbone and his wife. Booth stole up behind the president and pointed his derringer behind Lincoln's head, near the left ear. Booth had timed well. At 10:15, just as the theater exploded in laughter in response to a line delivered onstage, he pulled the trigger. The bullet blew out the side of the president's neck, lodging deep inside his body.

"Sic semper tyrannis!" Booth shouted, Latin for "Thus always to tyrants."

A smart military man, Major Rathbone knew that Booth had used a one-shot derringer. He had no fear when he grabbed for the assassin. They began to wrestle. Rathbone might have gotten the better of him and ended Booth's flight there and then, but the assassin knew he was engaged in a fight for his life. Booth pulled his knife and stabbed Rathbone in the arm, down to the bone.

Booth had succeeded in besting Rathbone. That should have been his only obstacle to escape, but now fate truly struck him hard. Booth was certainly athletic enough to drop the 10 feet to the stage unharmed, but one of his spurs caught on the flag that draped the president's box. He lost his balance for a moment, and when he landed, he landed hard. His fibula bone snapped just above the ankle. It made no difference. Booth was finally surpassing his father. He ran across the stage and disappeared out the back of the theater. Some would later swear he had bowed at center stage.

Joseph Burroughs still held the horse outside. Booth thanked him for his efforts, got on the horse, and galloped out of town. Before 11 P.M., he had crossed the Navy Yard Bridge. David Herrold caught up with Booth near Soper's Hill. The two then rode together to the tavern in Surrattsville. There they picked up the package that Booth had sent ahead, which contained field glasses and ammunition. They also picked up a Spencer rifle. They had a drink of whiskey, which failed to quell the pain in Booth's leg. Booth needed medical help immediately.

The fugitives rode off into the dark Maryland countryside. At about four A.M., they stopped at the home of Dr. Samuel Mudd. Mudd set Booth's leg. Booth and Herold stayed hours afterward, eating a warm meal and warming themselves by the fire. After that, they were off again.

Gideon Welles was Lincoln's secretary of the navy. After the president was shot, he was awakened with the grim news. Together with Secretary of War Edwin Stanton, they rushed to Ford's Theatre, only to find confusion in the assassin's wake. Quickly discovering that the president had been taken to a house directly across from the theater owned by a Mr. Petersen, Welles left Stanton and flew across the street and up the steps of the brownstone.

Welles passed through a long hall to the rear, where the president lay on a bed, breathing heavily. Welles found a physician, Dr. Hall, whom he knew and asked how the president was. Hall responded that the president was dead to all intents, although he might live three hours or perhaps longer. Today, the diagnosis would be brain death. Welles recounted,

The giant sufferer lay extended diagonally across the bed, which was not long enough for him. He had been stripped of his clothes. His large arms, which were occasionally exposed, were of a size, which one would scarce have expected from his spare appearance. His slow, full respiration lifted the clothes with each breath that he took. His features were calm and striking. I had never seen them appear to better advantage than for the first hour, perhaps, that I was there. After that his right eye began to swell and that part of his face became discolored.

This was from the internal hemorrhaging caused by the bullet lodged in the president's head. Government

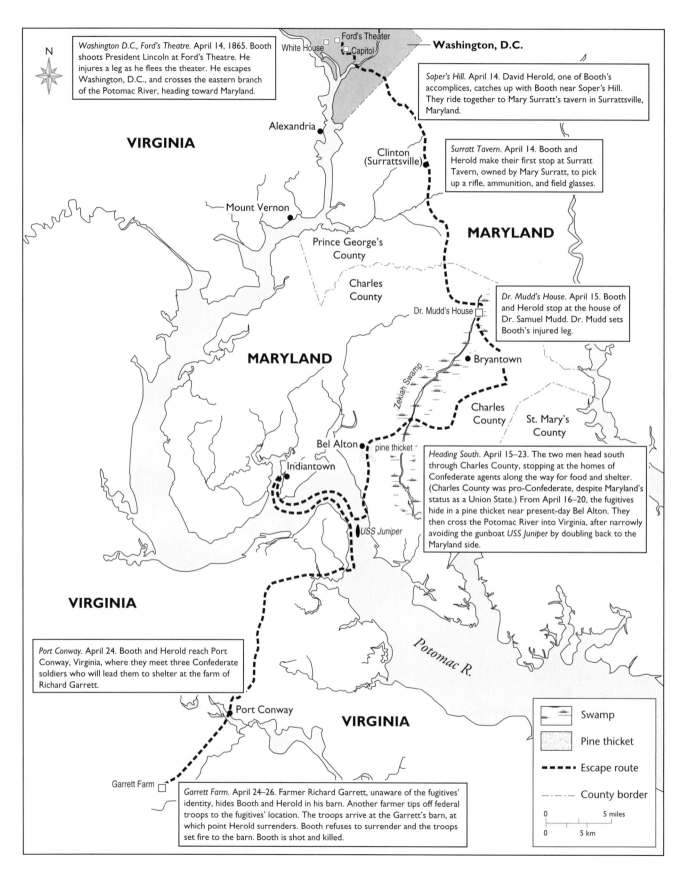

N

Washington D.C., Ford's Theatre. April 14, 1865. Booth shoots President Lincoln at Ford's Theatre. He injures a leg as he flees the theater. He escapes Washington, D.C., and crosses the eastern branch of the Potomac River, heading toward Maryland.

Ford's Theater

White House Capitol

Washington, D.C.

Soper's Hill. April 14. David Herold, one of Booth's accomplices, catches up with Booth near Soper's Hill. They ride together to Mary Surratt's tavern in Surrattsville, Maryland.

● Alexandria

VIRGINIA

Clinton (Surrattsville)

Surratt Tavern. April 14. Booth and Herold make their first stop at Surratt Tavern, owned by Mary Surratt, to pick up a rifle, ammunition, and field glasses.

● Mount Vernon

MARYLAND

Prince George's County

Charles County

Dr. Mudd's House

Dr. Mudd's House. April 15. Booth and Herold stop at the house of Dr. Samuel Mudd. Dr. Mudd sets Booth's injured leg.

MARYLAND

● Bryantown

Zekiah Swamp

Charles County

St. Mary's County

Bel Alton pine thicket

Indiantown

Heading South. April 15–23. The two men head south through Charles County, stopping at the homes of Confederate agents along the way for food and shelter. (Charles County was pro-Confederate, despite Maryland's status as a Union State.) From April 16–20, the fugitives hide in a pine thicket near present-day Bel Alton. They then cross the Potomac River into Virginia, after narrowly avoiding the gunboat *USS Juniper* by doubling back to the Maryland side.

USS Juniper

VIRGINIA

Port Conway. April 24. Booth and Herold reach Port Conway, Virginia, where they meet three Confederate soldiers who will lead them to shelter at the farm of Richard Garrett.

Potomac R.

● Port Conway

VIRGINIA

Garrett Farm

Garrett Farm. April 24–26. Farmer Richard Garrett, unaware of the fugitives' identity, hides Booth and Herold in his barn. Another farmer tips off federal troops to the fugitives' location. The troops arrive at the Garrett's barn, at which point Herold surrenders. Booth refuses to surrender and the troops set fire to the barn. Booth is shot and killed.

Swamp

Pine thicket

Escape route

County border

0 ——— 5 miles
0 ——— 5 km

John Wilkes Booth's escape route, following the assassination of President Lincoln

officials began to arrive, including Senator Sumner, Speaker of the House of Representatives Colfax, Secretary McCulloch, and other members of the president's cabinet. Notably absent was Secretary of State Seward, who had been wounded earlier in the evening by Paine and was himself in bad circumstances. He would, however, survive his wounds.

Welles continued,

About once an hour Mrs. Lincoln would repair to the bedside of her dying husband and with lamentation and tears remain until overcome by emotion. A door which opened upon a porch or gallery, and also the windows, were kept open for fresh air. The night was dark, cloudy, and damp, and about six it began to rain. I remained in the room until then without sitting or leaving it, when, there being a vacant chair which some one left at the foot of the bed, I occupied it for nearly two hours, listening to the heavy groans and witnessing the wasting life of the good and great man who was expiring before me.

About 6 A.M. Welles went out for some fresh air. Large groups of people gathered to inquire about the president's condition, and he was forced to tell them there was no hope. They were grief-stricken at his reply. Welles also noted how African Americans were reacting to the dire news.

"The colored people especially and there were at this time more of them, perhaps, than of whites, were overwhelmed with grief."

At a little before seven, Welles returned to the side of the dying president.

His wife soon after made her last visit to him. The death struggle had begun. Robert, his son, stood with several others at the head of the bed. He bore himself well but on two occasions gave way to overpowering grief and sobbed aloud, turning his head and leaning on the shoulder of Senator Sumner. The respiration of the President became suspended at intervals and at last entirely ceased at twenty-two minutes past seven.

Soon after, Andrew Johnson was sworn in as the 17th president of the United States.

It took detectives working for the District of Columbia police two days before they fully put together the composition of the Confederate assassination ring. Then, on April 17, soldiers from Washington finally picked up Booth and Herold's trail out of Washington and followed it to Mary Surratt's inn. They were just beginning their questioning of Surratt when someone knocked on the door.

Two nights before, after Lewis Paine had attempted his assassination of Secretary of State Seward and fled the city on horseback, he had quickly gotten lost. Paine was not familiar with the capital's streets. Eventually, he panicked. Abandoning his horse, Paine escaped into the woods, where he wandered around for two nights with nothing to eat and sparse clothing for the chilly weather. By the third night, he had grown so weary that he took the chance of discovery by going back on foot to Surratt's boardinghouse at 541 H Street, NW. Paine arrived there at about 11 P.M. The detectives who were there to question Mary Surratt were as surprised as anybody else when a man fitting Lewis Paine's description walked in the front door. They arrested him on the spot. Confronted with his similarities to the suspected coconspirator, he claimed to be a simple laborer. Overhearing this conversation, Mary Surratt chimed in that she had never hired him. The detectives decided to arrest everybody—Mary Surratt, Lewis Paine, and even, Surratt's boarders. Later in the day, another group of investigators found a letter in Booth's hotel room addressed to someone named Sam. Authorities figured out that the Sam in question was Samuel Arnold. They arrested him and also Michael O'Laughlin, a man whose only crime appears to be that he was Booth's boyhood friend.

THE DEATH OF JOHN WILKES BOOTH

On April 20, 1865, George Atzerodt looked up from his bed to see the front door of his hotel room burst in by armed federal troops. After searching his room, they discovered weapons and property that belonged to Booth. Atzerodt was immediately arrested.

On April 24 Dr. Samuel A. Mudd was arrested for setting Booth's leg. Authorities did not believe Mudd's story that Booth's features remained in shadow the entire time he was there, well over eight hours. They think Mudd knew him and was a Confederate sympathizer. With five conspirators, including Lewis Paine, who had been positively identified, in custody, Secretary Stanton ordered that the heads of the alleged conspirators be covered with hoods.

Meanwhile, Booth and Herold crossed into Virginia. Booth was confident that they would get a hero's welcome. Instead, they were treated like pariahs. Booth's miscalculation was thinking that southerners wanted more fighting. They were worn out and had surrendered. The last thing they wanted to engage in was further armed conflict. They managed to get a farmer named Richard Garrett to hide them in his barn. Far from a hero's welcome, the assassin of Lincoln was instead given a bed of hay, starvation rations, and no further medical treatment for his leg.

Back in Washington, Secretary of War Stanton wanted the assassins captured. He put more troops into the field to get them. On April 24, 1865, 10 days after the president had been assassinated, Lieutenant Edward Doherty was put into the same position as Robert E. Lee not five years before—his would be the duty to defend the Union's honor.

Doherty sat on a bench opposite the White House talking with another officer when suddenly a messenger interrupted their conversation. The messenger handed Doherty a written set of orders from his superior officer that directed Doherty to put into the field immediately a squad of cavalry to act as a posse. Their goal was to cross the Potomac and search the Virginia countryside for Booth and Herold.

Moving into the field with his squad, Doherty centered their search around the Rappahannock River, where the fugitives had last been seen. Doherty found a farmer who told him that the two fugitives were at a farm owned by Richard Garrett. Doherty and his men galloped to the farm, arriving in the early morning hours of April 26.

Doherty dismounted, and knocked at the front door, seizing Garrett when he came out. While Doherty interrogated Garrett, some of the men entered the house to search it. Soon one of the soldiers found Garrett's son hiding in the corncrib. When confronted he revealed that the fugitives were in the barn. Doherty's men surrounded the barn. He kicked the door several times without receiving a reply. The barn was secured with a padlock, but young Garrett supplied the key. Doherty unlocked the door and called out again. This time Booth responded.

"For whom do you take me?" Booth said.

Doherty replied, "It doesn't make any difference. Come out."

Booth said, "I am a cripple and alone."

"I know who is with you, and you had better surrender," answered Doherty.

Booth refused. "I may be taken by my friends but not by my foes."

Doherty threatened to burn the barn and directed a corporal to pile up some hay in a crack in the wall

of the barn and set it alight. Booth threatened to shoot the man, and so Doherty called him off.

But Booth's partner had had enough and decided to surrender. Doherty tried to no avail to coax Booth out as well. Herold then emerged unarmed from the barn, leaving Booth inside with all their weapons. Doherty eased forward.

Doherty wrote,

I said to Herold, "Let me see your hands." He put them through the partly opened door and I seized him by the wrists. I handed him over to a non-commissioned officer. Just at this moment I heard a shot, and thought Booth had shot himself. Throwing open the door, I saw that the straw and hay behind Booth were on fire. He was half-turning towards it.

He had a crutch, and he held a carbine in his hand. I rushed into the burning barn, followed by my men, and as he was falling caught him under the arms and pulled him out of the barn. The burning building becoming too hot, I had him carried to the veranda of Garrett's house.

While I was taking Herold out of the barn, one of the detectives went to the rear and pulling out some protruding straw, set fire to it. I had placed Sergeant Boston Corbett at a large crack in the side of the barn, and he, seeing by the igniting hay that Booth was leveling his carbine at either Herold or myself, fired, to disable him in the arm; but Booth making a sudden move, the aim erred, and the bullet struck Booth in the back of the head, about an inch below the spot where his shot had entered the head of Mr. Lincoln.

Afterward, on the veranda where he lay, Booth asked me by signs to raise his hands. I lifted them up and he gasped, 'Useless, useless!' We gave him brandy and water, but he could not swallow it. I sent to Port Royal for a physician, who could do nothing when he came and at seven o'clock Booth breathed his last. He had on his person a diary, a large bowie knife, two pistols, a compass and a draft on Canada for 60 pounds.

AUTOPSY AND IDENTIFICATION OF THE ASSASSIN

The identification of Booth's body and his autopsy are models of forensic excellence. Even today's technology could not make it any better.

Federal authorities brought in at least a dozen people who knew Booth to identify the body. Along with Dr. Joseph Woodward, Surgeon General Joseph K. Barnes performed the autopsy. On April 27, 1865, Barnes wrote of the results in a letter to Secretary of War Edwin Stanton:

Sir,

I have the honor to report that in compliance with your orders, assisted by Dr. Woodward, USA, I made at 2 P.M. this day, a postmortem examination of the body of J. Wilkes Booth, lying on board the Monitor Montauk off the Navy Yard.

The left leg and foot were encased in an appliance of splints and bandages, upon the removal of which, a fracture of the fibula (small bone of the leg) 3 inches above the ankle joint, accompanied by considerable ecchymosis, was discovered.

The cause of death was a gun shot wound in the neck—the ball entering just behind the sterno-cleido muscle—2 1/2 inches above the clavicle—passing through the bony bridge of fourth and fifth cervical vertebrae—severing the spinal chord and passing out through the body of the sterno-cleido of right side, 3 inches above the clavicle.

Paralysis of the entire body was immediate, and all the horrors of consciousness of suffering and death must have been present to the assassin during the two hours he lingered.

Booth's third, fourth, and fifth cervical vertebrae were removed during his autopsy. They are currently displayed at the National Museum of Health and Medicine at the Walter Reed Army Medical Center. Also, a fragment from his thorax is in a bottle in the Mütter Medical Museum at the College of Physicians of Philadelphia.

Stanton ordered that Booth's body be buried in the Old Penitentiary on the Washington Arsenal grounds in what is now Fort Lesley J. McNair. It was carried to a cell in the prison. A grave was dug. Wrapped in an army blanket, the body was lowered into the hole, then covered by a stone slab.

After Booth's death, the country thirsted for revenge. Secretary of War Stanton convened a special military tribunal to try the rest of the conspirators. There was no precedent for trying civilians before a military tribunal. Some legal scholars believe this was nothing more than a kangaroo court.

The military tribunal's first action was to indict Booth's coconspirators, including former CSA president Jefferson Davis and other Confederate leaders, in a general plot to kill Lincoln. Entries in Booth's diary actually refuted this charge but Stanton suppressed the diary to allow the government to make its case.

On May 1, 1865, George Atzerodt gave a recorded confession to a detective on the staff of Maryland's Provost Marshal. It is particularly important because during it, Atzerodt said, "I am certain Dr. Mudd knew all about it, [the assassination] as Booth sent (as he told me) liquors & provisions for the trip . . . about two weeks before the murder to Dr. Mudd's."

The prosecution never established that Mary Surratt was anything but an unwitting pawn in Booth's deadly game. Allegedly, she knew nothing of what was being plotted under her roof. In the end, it made no difference. The country was hungry for blood and the special military tribunal delivered. Paine, Herold, Atzerodt and Surratt were all convicted of conspiring to assassinate the president and sentenced to death.

McLaughlin got life in prison. The court even charged Edward Spangler, the man who held Booth's horse, with abetting Booth's escape and sentenced him to six years. The doctor who set Booth's leg, Samuel Mudd, was sentenced to life imprisonment in Florida's Dry Tortugas prison. The court felt he was also a conspirator.

On July 5, President Johnson approved the verdicts and sentences of the military tribunal. On July 6, Major General Hartrafant met with the four condemned prisoners to inform them they would be hanged the next day. But on July 7 Judge Wylie of the Supreme Court of the District of Columbia issued a writ of habeas corpus that had been requested by Mary Surratt's lawyers. That meant that the government had to say exactly what Mrs. Surratt was guilty of and what evidence they had to show her guilt. In this case, it also meant that the government would have to show justification for hanging her.

Upon being told of the writ, President Johnson signed an executive order that said: "I hereby declare that the writ of habeas corpus is suspended in cases such as this."

Not only was the president saying that by executive order he could suspend the constitutional right of habeas corpus, he was doing exactly that without legislative approval. That became the prisoner's death warrant.

At 1:30 P.M. on July 7, almost three months after President Lincoln's assassination, David Herold, Lewis Paine, and Mary Surratt were led up the gallows steps in back of the Old Arsenal building. At the top, black hoods were fitted over their heads. The nooses were tied around their necks and tightened. The death warrant was read and the prisoners were asked if they had any last words.

"May we meet in another world," said George Atzerodt.

He was the only one of the four to speak. The trap doors were thrown open by the executioner; the prisoners dropped.

By 1869 the blood hysteria attending the president's assassination had died down. Mudd, Spangler, and McLaughlin were all pardoned. For McLaughlin, it was too late: He had died of yellow fever in the Dry Tortugas.

As for Booth, in 1867 the government exhumed his corpse and reburied it in a pine box in a locked storeroom in Warehouse I at the prison. Two more years would pass before the assassin's remains were finally released to his family. The corpse was again positively identified as Booth. By that time, the corpse was so decayed that extra care had to be taken because the skull had become detached from the body.

Booth's corpse was transported to Baltimore and buried in the Booth family plot in Green Mount Cemetery. Subsequent legal efforts in 1994 to exhume the body for another "conclusive" identification were rejected by the courts.

All subsequent speculation that Booth somehow survived Corbett's shot and that he escaped from the burning farmhouse to live out his life is false. To this day, the Federal Bureau of Investigation (FBI) has a file on Booth, including the evidence of its investigations that Booth somehow, miraculously, survived. It concludes that he did not.

See also ASSASSINATION OF PRESIDENT GARFIELD (JULY–SEPTEMBER 1881); JOHN BROWN, A.K.A. OSAWATOMIE BROWN; BUFFALO, NEW YORK (1901); DALLAS, TEXAS (1963); MIAMI, FLORIDA (1933); "MATT SANDERS," A.K.A. MARTHA SANDERS; WASHINGTON, D.C. (1881–1882); WASHINGTON, D.C. (1982).

Washington, D.C. (1865) war crimes trial of Henry Wirz

The North was angry. In the four years of the war, this section of the country had formed a stronger identity than it ever had. The North looked at Lincoln's assassination as a Confederate plot; the North was looking for revenge.

Not more than two weeks after Booth was shot, Henry Wirz was taken into custody by Union forces and taken to Macon, Georgia, for questioning by army investigators. Afterward, he was briefly released, then officially arrested by Union soldiers and taken by rail to Washington. There, he was placed in the Old Capitol Prison on May 10, 1865, to await trial on charges of war crimes.

Late that summer, Clara Barton, a nurse who would go on to found the American Red Cross, arrived at Andersonville to assist in the identification and processing of bodies. The Andersonville National Cemetery was dedicated on July 26, 1865.

The army appointed a special military tribunal to try Major Henry Wirz. It was headed by General Lew Wallace, who later wrote the celebrated novel *Ben-Hur*. Some of the charges and specifications against Wirz contained in the National Archives include the following:

CHARGE I: Maliciously, willfully, and traitorously, and in aid of the then existing armed rebellion against the United States of America, on or before the 1st day of March, A.D. 1864, and on divers other days between that day and the 10th day of April, 1865, combining, confederating, and conspiring, together with John H. Winder, Richard B. Winder, Joseph [Isaiah H.] White, W. S. Winder, R. R. Stevenson, and others unknown, to injure the health and destroy the lives of soldiers in the military service of the United States, then held and being prisoners of war within the lines of the so-called Confederate States, and in the military prisons thereof, to the end that the armies of the United States might be weakened and impaired, in violation of the laws and customs of war.

Clara Barton, founder of the American Red Cross, reported on the abhorrent conditions at Andersonville, which helped prompt the war crimes trial of Captain Wirz. (National Archives)

The lone specification in the charge listed the hideous conditions at Andersonville, calling Wirz to task for his responsibility in the matter, which included

. . . subjecting to torture and great suffering; by confining in unhealthy and unwholesome quarters; by exposing to the inclemency of winter and to the dews and burning sun of summer; by compelling the use of impure water; and by furnishing insufficient and unwholesome food— of large numbers of Federal prisoners, to wit, the number of 30,000 soldiers in the military service of the United States of America, held as prisoners of war at Andersonville, in the State of Georgia, within the lines of the so-called Confederate States, on or before the 1st day of March, A.D. 1864, and at divers times between that day and the 10th day of April, A.D. 1865, to the end that the armies of the United States might be weakened and impaired and the insurgents engaged in armed rebellion against the United States might be aided and comforted.

So far, the government was still making general charges. That soon ended as the specification continued:

And the said Wirz, still pursuing his evil purpose, did keep and use ferocious and bloodthirsty beasts, dangerous to human life, called bloodhounds, to hunt down prisoners of war aforesaid who made their escape from his custody, and did then and there willfully and maliciously suffer, incite, and encourage the said beasts to seize, tear, mangle, and maim the bodies and limbs of said fugitive prisoners of war, which the said beasts, incited as aforesaid, then and there did, whereby a large number of said prisoners of war, who, during the time aforesaid, made their escape and were recaptured, and were, by the said beasts then and there cruelly and inhumanly injured, insomuch that many of said prisoners, to wit, the number of about fifty died.

If the government was to be believed, Wirz had been a sadistic, murdering animal. Further allegations claimed that Wirz used "for the pretended purposes of vaccination, impure and poisonous vaccine matter, which said impure and poisonous matter was then and there, by the direction and order of said Wirz, maliciously, cruelly, and wickedly deposited in the arms of many of said prisoners, by reason of which large numbers of them, to wit, 100, lost the use of their arms, and many of them, to wit, about the number of 200, were so injured that they soon thereafter died."

Again if the government was to be believed, Wirz was taking out his bitterness about his own arm hav-

ing been shot up by the Union soldiers by doing exactly the same to them, only his shot was a needle in the arm with deadly toxins. If true, it presaged similar actions by the Nazis less than 100 years later.

Additional charges included multiple counts that Wirz cold-bloodedly executed prisoners by shooting them in the head; beating and jumping on a prisoner with "the heels of his boots"; torturing a prisoner by putting him in the stocks; "binding the necks and feet of said prisoners closely together, and compelling them to carry great burdens, to wit, large iron balls chained to their feet" as a result of which one prisoner died; and perhaps worst, "did cause, incite, and urge certain ferocious and bloodthirsty animals, called bloodhounds, to pursue, attack, wound, and tear in pieces a soldier belonging to the Army of the United States."

Lewis Schade, Wirz's attorney, felt that the prosecution of his client was nothing more than scapegoating. Writing later of the trial, Schade intimated what he felt the real goals of the Union were in prosecuting Wirz.

To increase the excitement and give eclat to the proceeding and to influence still more the public mind, the trial took place under the very dome of the Capitol of the nation. A military commission, presided over by a despotic general, was formed, and the paroled prisoner of war, his wounds still open, was so feeble that he had to recline during the trial on a sofa. How that trial was conducted the whole world knows!

Schade failed to note that during the trial, when asked by prosecutors to account for his responsibility in the deaths of the union prisoners at Andersonville, Wirz testified, "I was only following orders." It was the first time such a defense was offered in what would later be called the first war crimes trial in history.

The finding of the court was that Wirz was guilty of nearly all the charges. Judgment was swift:

And the court does therefore sentence him, Henry Wirz, to be hanged by the neck till he be dead at such time and place as the President of the United States may direct, two-thirds of the members of the court concurring herein.

The proceedings, finding, and sentence in the foregoing case having been submitted to the President of the United States, the following are his orders:

EXECUTIVE MANSION, November 3, 1865.

The proceedings, finding, and sentence of the court in the within case are approved, and it is ordered that the sentence be carried into execution by the officer commanding the Department of Washington on Friday the 10th day of November, 1865, between the hours of 6 o'clock a.m. and 12 o'clock noon.

ANDREW JOHNSON

Wirz's only hope now was to appeal directly to Johnson to commute his sentence. He wrote President Johnson asking exactly that on November 6, 1865:

To the President of the United States. Mr. President: With a trembling hand, with a heart filled with the most conflicting emotions, and with a spirit hopeful one moment and despairing the next, I have taken the liberty of addressing you. When I consider your exalted position; when I think for a moment that in your hands rests the weal and woe of millions—yea, the peace of the world—well may I pause to call to my aid courage enough to lay before you my humble petition.

Wirz had no remorse. He even had the gall to state before Johnson that "It is not my desire to enter into an argument as to the merits of my case." Rather, he pleaded for freedom on the basis of the ordeal he had so far suffered and his own belief in his innocence:

The pangs of death are short, and therefore I humbly pray that you will pass your sentence without delay. Give me death or liberty. The one I do not fear; the other I crave. If you believe me guilty of the terrible charges that have been heaped upon me, deliver me to the executioner. If not guilty, in your estimation, restore me to liberty and life. A life such as I am now living is no life. I breathe, sleep, eat, but it is only the mechanical functions I perform, and nothing more. Whatever you decide I shall accept. If restored to liberty, I will thank and bless you for it.

Johnson was not going to be conned. He turned him down. What happened next particularly irked Schade.

"On the night before the execution of the prisoner (November 9, 1865)," Schade would later write, "a telegram was sent to the Northern press from this city, stating that Wirz had made important disclosures to General L. C. Baker, the well-known detective, implicating Jefferson Davis, and that the confession would probably be given to the public." The press had leaked the story of a deal Wirz had been offered. A high Cabinet official had assured Wirz through Schade that if he would implicate Jefferson Davis in the atrocities committed at Andersonville, his sentence would be commuted.

The execution of Captain Wirz (National Archives)

"The Captain simply and quietly replied, 'Mr. Schade, you know that I have always told you that I do not know anything about Jefferson Davis. He had no connection with me as to what was done at Andersonville. If I knew anything about him, I would not become a traitor against him or anybody else even to save my life.'

Thus ended the attempt to suborn Captain Wirz against Jefferson Davis. That alone shows what a man he was. How many of his defamers would have done the same?"

On the day of his execution, November 10, 1865, Wirz wrote to Schade:

Mr. Louis Schade. Dear Sir: It is no doubt the last time that I address myself to you. Please help my poor family—my dear wife and children. War, cruelest, has swept everything from me, and today my wife and children are beggars. My life is demanded as atonement. I am willing to give it, and hope that after a while, I will be judged differently from what I am now. If any one ought to come to the relief of my family, it is the people of the South, for whose sake I have sacrificed all.

Yours thankfully,
H. Wirz.

With his wounded arm in a sling, Wirz mounted the scaffold two hours later. His last words were that he died innocent.

Schade described what happened next.

But who is responsible for the many lives that were lost at Andersonville and in the Southern prisons? It was certainly not the fault of poor Wirz.

Not even Christian burial of the remains of Captain Wirz has been allowed by Secretary Stanton. They still lie side by side with those of another and acknowledged victim of military commissions, the unfortunate Mrs. Surratt, in the yard of the former jail of this city.

Henry Wirz's trial set historic precedent for future war crimes trials. It was cited as justification for the war crimes trials following both World War I and World War II.

"I was simply following orders" was no longer acceptable as a defense when soldiers committed crimes against humanity. The Wirz trial clearly provided that there are limitations of the extent that military orders violating the rules of war or common laws of humanity, may be followed. It established

that military personnel will be held personally accountable for following such orders.

Fort Dodge, Kansas (1865) law and order comes to Kansas

Amid all the controversy surrounding Wirz's trial and execution, little public attention was fixed on one of the nation's more violent places—southwestern Kansas. Indians, despondent at the continual encroachment on their land, were raiding settlements and farms. Hold-up men had come into the territory and were preying on stagecoaches. Law and order was needed, and the army finally established Fort Dodge, on the Santa Fe Trail near the present site of Dodge City, Kansas.

See also WYATT EARP (1853–1928); WILLIAM BARCLAY "BAT" MASTERSON (1853–1921); WILLIAM MATTHEW "BILL" TILGHMAN (1853–1923).

United States purchases Alaska (1867) Seward's folly

Even would-be assassin Lewis Paine's knife across his face had not stopped William Seward. He recovered from his wounds and went on to serve in Andrew Johnson's cabinet, once again as secretary of state. Seward would, ironically, become the catalyst for crime spreading to Alaska and the Yukon.

It was Seward who saw the potential of the Alaskan wilderness. It was an area of great mass that contained a bounty of natural resources. Though much of Alaska was frozen tundra, the Alaskan seacoast had a relatively mild climate where it rarely went below zero degrees Fahrenheit in the winter. There are sections of the Dakotas that cannot claim that distinction.

Russia had established a presence in Alaska in the early 18th century when Vitus Jonassen Bering explored the land that would become the 49th state. It was Bering who lent his name to the strait of water that separated the United States from Russia. And it was Russia that decided to approach the United States to buy the frozen region.

Overtures were made during President James Buchanan's administration (1857–61) but negotiations stalled during the Civil War. Afterward, Seward entered into secret negotiations with Russia. On March 30, 1867, Russia agreed to sell Alaska to the United States for $7 million. Critics called the deal "Seward's folly" and the new territory, "Andrew Johnson's polar bear garden." Johnson, though, was an expansionist and was happy to make the deal.

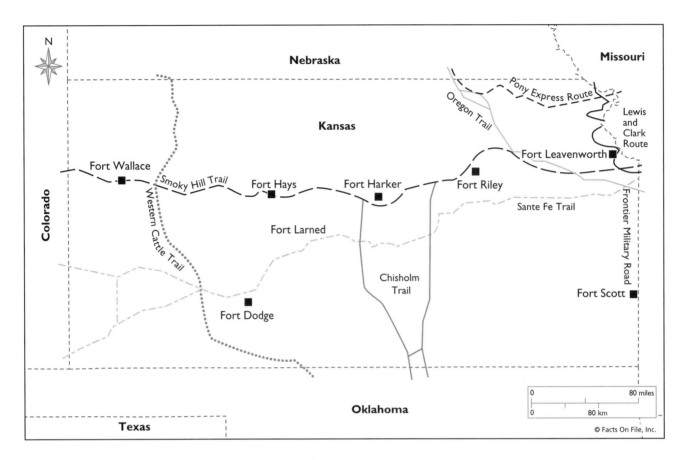

The army forts on the Kansas frontier were crucial to the expansion of the United States, as they protected the settlers from highwaymen and hostile Native Americans. Fort Dodge was established along the Santa Fe Trail near the present site of Dodge City.

Congress, however, did not feel the same way. By only one vote, the Senate ratified the treaty that bought Alaska. Many years would pass before the potential of the Alaskan wilderness was clear.

Not until the Yukon gold rush at the century's end did criminals flock to the area to take advantage of the prospectors and settlers. When they did, it would lead to one of the last gunfights in U.S. history, between a town marshal and Soapy Smith, the badman who controlled Alaska's rackets.

See also JEFFERSON RANDOLPH "SOAPY" SMITH.

Washington, D.C. (1867) the court-martial of George Armstrong Custer

In 1867 a brash, up-and-coming cavalry officer, Lieutenant Colonel George Armstrong Custer was court-martialed on the following charges: shooting deserters without a trial; failing to support troops under fire; and failure to retrieve the bodies of killed soldiers.

Custer had been a daring soldier, leading many charges during the Civil War. He had risen to the rank of brevet major general. After the war, he was awarded the rank of lieutenant colonel. But as an Indian fighter out west, his record was spotty. In the battle of the Washita that year, from which the charges stemmed, Custer had led a cavalry charge against a Cheyenne village. When the smoke cleared, Custer claimed in his report to his superiors that he had killed 103 warriors.

He lied.

Custer had killed only 11 people, and most were old men. The other 92 mortal casualties were women and children. A later generation would characterize such an atrocity as a "war crime," since Custer's men were not in danger when they killed.

Even as he prepared to leave the battlefield, Custer was reminded that a detachment of 128 men under the command of Major Joel Elliot had fled down the Washita River from a superior force of Cheyenne

George Armstrong Custer, the youngest brevet major general in the history of the United States (Library of Congress)

warriors. Elliot and his men had failed to report in. Rather than dispatch troops or even scouts to find out what had happened to Elliot, he ordered his men to quit the battlefield because, "As it was now lacking but an hour of night, we had to make an effort to get rid of the Indians, who still loitered in strong force on the hills," Custer later wrote in his autobiography, *My Life.*

In the following spring came the thaw and the discovery of the bodies of Elliot and his men. Charges were leveled at Custer and a military court quickly found him guilty. He was given a year's suspension of rank to be served without pay.

See also MONTANA (1876).

Fort Laramie, Wyoming (1868) Treaty of 1868
Meeting at Fort Laramie, Wyoming, representatives of the United States and the Sioux Nation signed what came to be known as the Treaty of 1868.

The treaty's provisions established the Great Sioux Reservation in Dakota Territory while reaffirming the Sioux hunting rights. The Sioux agreed to be provisioned by the U.S. Bureau of Indian Affairs, which took over meeting their wants and needs. Serious violations of the treaty would be viewed by the U.S. government as a federal crime. The U.S. Army would enforce the treaty's provisions against hostile Indians. The government was laying the legal foundation for branding the Indians as criminals, who would then, legally, be brought to ground by force, or exterminated.

See also MONTANA (1876); WASHINGTON, D.C. (1867).

Union Pacific Railroad (1850–1869) east and west united
By the 1850s the building of a transcontinental railroad had become a pressing issue. The east continued to expand toward the west. There had to be a better way of getting there than by horse. Thus the railroad was conceived as the chief means of transportation into the country's interior.

By 1865, because of the Civil War, little construction had been done to make the transcontinental railroad a reality. Seeking to move things along, the Republicans, who controlled Congress, gave a charter to the Union Pacific Railroad Company. The charter allowed for the construction of a line from Omaha, Nebraska, to the California/Nevada border. There, it would connect with the Central Pacific Railroad, whose track would be laid simultaneously from Sacramento. After some delays, construction finally began in 1865.

The jumping-off point was Omaha, but the right of way chosen for the Union Pacific track soon encroached on Indian land. The Indians responded with occasional outbursts of violence. Coupled with construction problems, the path west was a difficult one. General William Tecumseh Sherman testified before Congress, saying, "This railroad is a national enterprise, and we are forced to protect the men during its survey and construction, through, probably, the most warlike nation of Indians on this continent, who will fight for every foot of the line."

The Union Pacific persevered. Finally, on May 10, 1869, northwest of Ogden, Utah, the Union Pacific joined up with the Central Pacific. The dream to connect the continent was finally realized. The transcontinental railroad was a reality.

Indiana and Kansas (1868–1874) Catherine McCarty moves west

Like many easterners after the Civil War, Irish immigrant Catherine McCarty decided to move her family west. Catherine took her sons Joseph and William Henry to Anderson, Indiana in 1868.

They stayed there all of a year and still Catherine was not satisfied, so they packed up again and moved farther west, this time on the frontier at Wichita,

Kansas, where Catherine operated a laundry service. William Henry was 13 years old in 1870 when his mother took up with a man named William Antrim. He moved the family to Coffeyville, a little settlement south of Wichita. Years later, the Dalton Gang would make the town famous when they attempted to hold up two banks in Coffeyville at the same time.

In 1870 Coffeyville was little more than a few stores and a main street. Nevertheless, 13-year-old

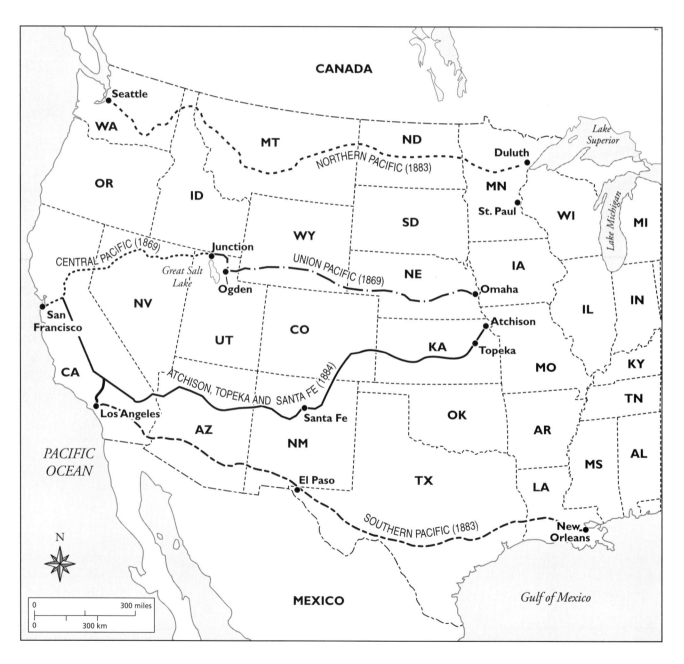

Early Pacific railroad lines, 1865–84. The growth of railroads, including the Union Pacific, established the connection between the East and West coasts and bred a new crime: train robbery.

William Henry found something worth robbing. A city constable's log in 1873 notes that William Henry McCarty and an associate "huckleberry" (or idiot) were arrested for petty theft. There was no jail time, only a paddling by the sheriff.

When Catherine was diagnosed with consumption (tuberculosis), the family decided to seek a drier climate. With Antrim, they moved to New Mexico, where, in 1873, Catherine and Antrim formally married. They opened a boardinghouse in Silver City, a mining boomtown. But on September 16, 1874, Catherine McCarty Antrim died from consumption.

William Henry adored his mother and took her death hard. A week later, on September 23, William Henry committed his second crime—stealing laundry. Upon his capture, someone remarked that he was "just a kid." The name stuck. Forever more, William Henry McCarty would be hailed by his better-known alias, "Billy the Kid."

See also LINCOLN COUNTY, NEW MEXICO (1878–1879); NEW MEXICO (1877); NEW MEXICO (1881); NEW YORK, NEW YORK (1846).

Washington, D.C. (1871) acting commissioner reports of the Bureau of Indian Affairs

On November 15, 1871 the Acting Commissioner of the Bureau of Indian Affairs, R. Klum, made the following report to Congress about the Sioux of the Dakotas:

Those upon the reservation selected for the whole nation are quiet; many of them are friendly-disposed, and evince a willingness to abandon the hunter-life and become tillers of the soil. While the Government continues to provide for the wants of the Sioux, feeding and clothing them—means by which they are kept in a better humor than they otherwise would be—no outbreak or disorder of any extent need be apprehended. Some trouble is anticipated on account of the suspicion with which some of them look upon the projected Northern Pacific Railway being run through what they claim to be their country; but as yet no decided demonstration of opposition has been made by them. The Sioux of the band under the noted chief Red Cloud have for the time being a temporary location north of the Platte River, about thirty miles south of Fort Laramie, Wyoming Territory.

There would be trouble. Not all the Sioux had taken to the reservation. Some still roamed free. As far as they were concerned, the railroad did not have the right of way through their ancestral lands.

See also MONTANA (1876); FORT LARAMIE, WYOMING (1868).

Kansas (1871–1873) the bloody Benders

"Bender Hotel Horror in the Western Prairies" was how a contemporary pamphlet reported on the case.

The Benders were a family of four: the patriarch, 55-year-old John Bender, his wife, son, and his beauteous daughter Kate. She was the key to the homicides that happened in Cherry Vale, a small town by the railroad.

Dr. William H. York had been traced there. York had gotten off the train in Cherry Vale and then disappeared. Concerned friends tracked him down to the little inn run by the Bender family.

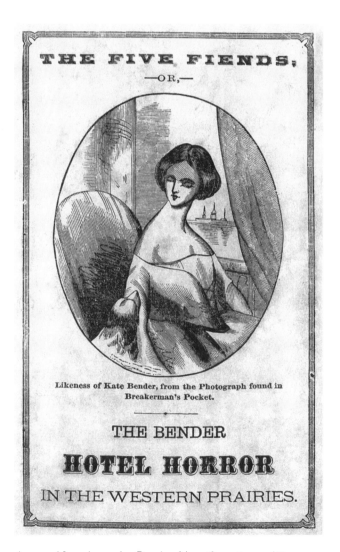

A pamphlet about the Benders' horrific crimes (Clements Library, University of Michigan)

An illustration from the pamphlet pictured on the preceding page (Clements Library, University of Michigan)

The Benders had come to Cherry Vale in 1871 and built a small house. Inside, the searchers discovered, it was partitioned into two rooms separated by a canvas cloth. On one side was a table, stove, and shelves for groceries. In the back were beds, a sledge-hammer and a trapdoor above a pit-like cellar. Lifting the trapdoor, the searchers discovered the cellar was full of dried blood.

Searching outside a short time later, the men found a mound, under which was buried Dr. York. The autopsy would later show the cause of death to be blows to the base of the skull. "Some deadly weapon had been used to drive in the parietal bones," the autopsy report stated. York's skull had been crushed, a painful way to die. But the murderer, or murderers, had been very thorough. They had to be sure the victim was dead. A later account of the crime described it as follows: "With no other motive than a tiger-like desire to revel in blood, the brutal

murderers had cut York's throat so completely as nearly to sever the head from the body."

But York was only the beginning. The next grave the searchers discovered outside the house contained the bodies of George W. Longcor and his little daughter. Longcor had been killed in the same manner as York. "The pretty innocent girl with long soft brown hair had been thrown down alive upon the corpse of her father, while the Bender fiends hurriedly shoveled the earth and clods upon her till they had smothered out her life with her last gasping cry for mercy."

Eventually, seven bodies of men who had had the misfortune to visit the Bender establishment, plus the young child, were dug up. That made the body count eight. They were identified by acquaintances, relatives, and friends. All had been killed in precisely the same manner. Yet, "[o]ne peculiarity struck all the spectators. Each corpse had the left arm crossed upon the breast before being buried."

Posing the corpse was part of the Benders' signature behavior. One of the 21st century's most successful and respected criminal profilers, Dr. Maurice Godwin, in his classic book *Criminal Psychology and Forensic Technology,* views signature behavior as "types of extraordinary violence similarities. For example, the victim was beaten beyond the point needed to kill her. Or, the killer seemed preoccupied with the victim's clothing or took some time to pose the victim's body."

Law enforcement officials quickly discovered what the Benders' modus operandi was. The murders happened this way:

The traveler would enter the store and while he was making his purchase, 55-year-old John Bender would eagerly scan him. If Bender thought the man worth killing, the old scoundrel would give a signal by dropping an old cowbell on the floor. As soon as Kate heard this in back, she would exit in the rear, come in again, and convince the customer to stay for dinner.

Afterward, Kate would challenge the guest to a trial of mesmerism, which she had taught herself in preparation. She would place the victim in a chair then force his head back into a cloth partition, indenting the cloth. This signaled her father or brother, waiting on the other side with a hammer. They struck and then moved the unconscious victim to the trapdoor pit where they crushed their prey's parietal bones and stripped his clothing. Then they severed the throat and stored the body in the pit until it could be buried.

The Benders had managed to commit these killings right under the town's collective nose. What's more, their victims' corpses were discovered three weeks after the last murder had been committed and by that time the Benders had fled. That meant the killers had a three-week head start on any posse, but it made no difference. The Benders vanished into the wilderness, never to be seen again.

Black Hills, Dakota Territory (1874) the Thieves' Road

Rumors had begun emerging that gold was found in the Black Hills of the Dakotas. If the rumors were true, there could be a problem because the Sioux still claimed that they owned that land. It was not included in the terms of the 1868 treaty.

To substantiate the rumors, and in the process to establish military outposts on Sioux land, the U.S. Army dispatched into the Black Hills the redoubtable Colonel Custer and 1,000 troops under his command. It was also a commercial venture: Riding with the troops were geologists. During the expedition, they found gold. Returning to civilization, they publicized their research, and the result was a sudden influx of prospectors to the area. To the Sioux, the path the white men took to steal the Black Hills became known as "the Thieves' Road."

By the end of 1875 there were 15,000 men mining illegally in the Black Hills. In the spring, President Grant requested the presence of chiefs Red Cloud, Spotted Tail, and others in Washington for a meeting to discuss the status of the Black Hills. Eventually, the Indians turned down a $6 million offer for the Black Hills. By November President Grant had abandoned his policy of at least tacitly keeping the miners out and called for the army to actively protect the miners and settlers.

See also MONTANA (1876); FORT LARAMIE, WYOMING (1868); WASHINGTON, D.C. (1867).

Washington, D.C. (1875) Indians given "hostile federal criminal" identity

In 1875 the U.S. Senate convened a committee to look into corruption in the Bureau of Indian Affairs. Among other charges was that agents did not give the Indians all the provisions they were entitled to—they kept a good portion for themselves and sold it on the side, exacerbating the situation.

The hearings were public, and the star witness was Lieutenant Colonel George Armstrong Custer. Testifying before the committee, Custer implicated President Grant's brother Orvill in a series of schemes to defraud the government. The president, who did not particularly like his brother, still prized loyalty and Custer clearly did not exhibit that trait in his testimony. As punishment, Grant had Custer removed for a full year from command of the Seventh Cavalry.

On December 6, 1875, Commissioner Klum ordered a renegade band of Lakota Sioux back onto the reservation by January 31, 1876. Those who refused would be treated as hostile, meaning they would be restrained on sight and arrested on criminal charges. If they resisted, they would be shot dead as criminals.

Many Sioux who were off the reservation did not hear about the order until the spring thaw. By that time, it was too late to come in, and the army labeled them as hostile, forcing them to go on the run as federal criminals.

On February 1 the secretary of the interior relinquished jurisdiction over the hostile Indians to the War Department. It then became the job of the

Department of the Army to bring them in. By spring the army planned to put three companies of soldiers into the field to capture the Sioux and some Cheyenne who had not reported to the reservation. Custer was desperate to be put back in command of the Seventh Cavalry so he could join this mission.

Custer's mentor was General Philip Sheridan, one of Grant's favorites. Sheridan lobbied Grant on Custer's behalf. Eventually, Grant relented and restored Custer's command of the Seventh Cavalry in time for its departure in May 1876 from Fort Lincoln.

See also FORT LARAMIE, WYOMING (1868); WASHINGTON, D.C. (1867).

Boston, Massachusetts (1876) first great crime-fighting tool invented

Alexander Graham Bell's telephone revolutionized law enforcement in the United States.

Until the phone's invention, law enforcement relied on the telegraph for transmission of information about criminal suspects. If the James Gang, for example, was spotted by a farmer on the road to Bodie, the farmer would then have to saddle up, ride into town, and get the marshal to compose a telegram that would then be transmitted down the line to Bodie. Because of the delay, Bodie would have already been raided by the time they received the telegram.

The telephone meant that any two points connected by wire could hear a voice transmission instantaneously. Not only could law enforcement use the phone for warning, they could use it to share information on criminal suspects and check out alibis. And yet, the revolution took time. Bell had to patent his invention, create a company to market it, and get the public to accept and pay for it. But by the 1890s, a place as isolated as New Mexico already had some of its major towns wired.

See also BALTIMORE, MARYLAND (1844).

Montana (1876) the Battle of Little Bighorn

Officially, the government of the United States would come to view the Battle of Little Bighorn as a crime of the greatest magnitude: some 272 American soldiers killed in less than a half-hour by 5,000 hostile Cheyenne and Sioux. Yet, no one in the group of survivors of the battle of Little Bighorn ever stepped forward to accept responsibility for

the disaster. Contrary to popular myth, not all of Colonel Custer's men died with him at his last stand.

Custer and the Seventh Cavalry had been following the trail of hostile Indians for days. On the morning of June 25, 1876, they finally found them encamped in what the Indians called the Valley of the Greasy Grass. The white man called it the Little Bighorn Valley, a gently sloping fertile plain that bordered the Little Bighorn River. The hostiles had encamped on the far side of the river.

Looking out from a mountaintop called the Crow's Nest many miles away, Custer's Indian scouts spotted the village, but could not make out the village's size. It was obscured by a forest within which the hostiles had camped. From the smoke rising from their campfires, it looked to be an incredibly large force.

Warned that he was facing a force much bigger than he had first anticipated, Custer did not hesitate. He could not afford to lose. He rode down into the valley with his men, forming a plan in his mind as he went along. At the midpoint of the valley floor, still not certain of the village's size, he divided his men into three groups.

The first, under the command of Captain Frederick Benteen, was to scout for hostiles to the east, in the foothills of the Wolf Mountains. The second, under the command of Major Marcus Reno, would cross the Little Bighorn River and mount a charge into the Indian village from the south. The third group, consisting of the 272 men under Custer's direct command, would attack the village from the north.

If things had gone as planned, Custer would have crushed the Indians between two forces, with a third out in the field for reinforcements. It would have been the greatest victory the army had ever seen over the hostiles and maybe propelled him to the presidency. It did not quite work out that way.

George Herendon served as a scout for the Seventh Cavalry. He was a civilian contractor to the army, attached to Major Reno's command. As part of Reno's command, he charged across the Little Bighorn River with the major and met an overwhelming force of Sioux surprised by the white man's incursion in the late afternoon.

"Reno took a steady gallop down the creek bottom three miles where it emptied into the Little Horn, and found a natural ford across the Little Horn River," Herendon told a reporter for the *New York Tribune* after the battle.

He started to cross, when the scouts came back and called out to him to hold on, that the Sioux were coming in large numbers to meet him. He crossed over, however, formed his companies on the prairie in line of battle, and moved forward at a trot but soon took a gallop.

After scattering shots were fired from the hills and a few from the river bottom and Reno's skirmishers returned the shots, he advanced about a mile from the ford to a line of timber on the right and dismounted his men to fight on foot. The horses were sent into the timber and the men forward on the prairie and advanced toward the Indians.

The Indians, came across the prairie and opened a heavy fire on the soldiers. After skirmishing for a few minutes, Reno fell back to his horses in the timber. The Indians moved to his left and rear, evidently with the intention of cutting him off from the ford.

There seemed to be firing all around him; Reno got confused. He ordered his men to mount, then changed his mind seconds later. Reno was standing next to one of his scouts when suddenly the man's head was blown apart, scattering blood and brain matter into Reno's face. Panicking Major Reno had the bugler sound retreat.

The command headed for the ford, pressed closely by Indians in large numbers, and at every moment the rate of speed was increased, until it became a dead run for the ford. The Sioux, mounted on their swift ponies, dashed up by the side of the soldiers and fired at them, killing both men and horses. Little resistance was offered, and it was complete rout to the ford. I did not see the men at the ford, and do not know what took place further than a good many were killed when the command left the timber.

At about this time, Reno, who was doing everything he could to hold his command together against the onslaught of approximately 5,000 warriors, looked up on the bluff that overlooked the river. There he saw Custer waving his hat and riding down toward the north end of the village as planned. To Herendon, who was trapped, this meant nothing. "Two soldiers were wounded so badly they could not use their arms," Herendon recalled.

The soldiers wanted to go out, but I said no, we can't get to the ford, and besides, we have wounded men and must stand by them. The soldiers still wanted to go, but I told them I was an old frontiersman, understood the Indians, and if they would do as I said I would get them

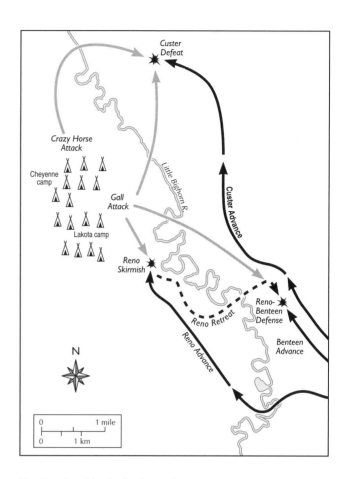

The Battle of Little Bighorn, June 25, 1876, showing troop and Indian movements

out of the scrape which was no worse than scrapes I had been in before. About half of the men were mounted, and they wanted to keep their horses with them, but I told them to let the horses go and fight on foot.

They stayed in the bush about three hours, and could hear heavy firing below in the river, about two miles distant. I did not know who it was, but knew the Indians were fighting soldiers, and learned afterward it was Custer's command. Nearly all the Indians in the upper part of the valley drew off down the river, to fight Custer. It lasted about one hour, until the heavy firing ceased.

When the shooting below began to die away I said to the boys "come, now is the time to get out." I told them the Indians would come back and we had better be off at once. Eleven of the thirteen said they would go, but two stayed behind.

I deployed the men as skirmishers and we moved forward on foot toward the river. When we had got nearly to the river we met five Indians on ponies, and they fired on us. I returned the fire and the Indians broke and we then forded the river, the water being heart deep. We finally got over, wounded men and all, and headed for Reno's command, which I could see drawn up on the bluffs along the river about a mile off. We reached Reno in safety.

We had not been with Reno more than fifteen minutes when I saw the Indians coming up the valley from Custer's fight. Reno was then moving his whole command down the ridge toward Custer. The Indians crossed the river below Reno and swarmed up the bluff on all sides. After skirmishing with them, Reno went back to his old position which was on one of the highest fronts along the bluffs. It was now about five o'clock, and the fight lasted until it was too dark to see to shoot.

Men cried out in the darkness from their wounds. Reno took the packs and saddles off the mules and horses and made breastworks. He also dragged the dead horses and mules into a line and sheltered his men behind them. Some dug rifle pits with their butcher knives which are still there today. All slept on their arms.

At dawn, the Indians opened heavy fire and a desperate fight ensued until 10 A.M. The Indians charged Reno three or four times, coming up close enough to hit soldiers with stones. Captain Benteen, who had joined Reno with his command the previous night, saw a large mass of Indians gathered on his front to charge. He ordered his men to charge on foot and scatter them.

For once during the battle of the Little Bighorn, Benteen led the charge and was upon the Indians before they knew. The Indians, surprised that Benteen had taken the offensive, were forced to retreat, taking heavy losses. Herendon recalled:

Benteen is one of the bravest men I ever saw in a fight. All the time he was going about through the bullets, encouraging the soldiers to stand up to their work and not let the Indians whip them; he went among the horses and pack mules and drove out the men who were skulking there, compelling them to go into the line and do their duty. He never sheltered his own person once during the battle, and I do not see how he escaped being killed. The desperate charging and fighting was over at about one o'clock, but firing was kept up on both sides until late in the afternoon.

Reno and Benteen's command remained on the bluff above the river until the next day, when General Alfred Terry and his command rescued them. It was then that Terry's scouts discovered Custer's Last Stand.

Custer's position two miles directly north of Reno and Benteen's had been overrun by Indians. Scattered about him on what would come to be known as Custer's Hill were the last 42 men of his command who died with him. All told, the nearly 300 men under Custer's direct command were dead and slaughtered, many horribly mutilated. Except for the fact that he had been shot to death, Custer's body was left intact.

It had been the worst military defeat for the U.S. Cavalry in history. To ascribe it to superior Indian forces or tactics would be to give the hostiles credit, which the government would not do.

See also ROANOKE COLONY (1857); FORT LARAMIE, WYOMING (1868); WASHINGTON, D.C. (1867).

James Butler "Wild Bill" Hickok (1837–1876)
gunfighter

In the second part of the 19th century in America, the country had changed to the point that criminals were not always criminals. Their murderous talents began to be recruited by the very people they used to prey upon. James Butler "Wild Bill" Hickok was the prototype for this kind of criminal.

Born in 1837 near Ottawa, Illinois, Hickok had a long nose and protruding lip and quickly acquired the nickname of "Duck Bill." That changed quickly to Wild Bill after word of his proficiency with a pistol spread through the frontier settlements. He met future U.S. marshal Bill Tilghman when the latter was a boy and influenced him to become a lawman.

During the late 1850s, Hickok went to Kansas and became a stagecoach driver for the Butterfield line. By 1861 he found himself in a dispute with a man named McCanles, whom he shot in the back. Somehow, this became a heroic showdown with the "McCanles Gang" when he described the incident to a reporter for a *Harper's Weekly* magazine article.

During the Civil War, he added to his legend when he became a scout for the Union army. After the war Hickok drifted west and ended up getting elected sheriff of Ellis County, where he killed two men in the performance of his duty. "One of these killings was a remarkable performance," writes Carl Sifakis in his two-volume book, *The Encyclopedia of American Crime*. Hickok "had his back turned on a troublemaker named Sam Strawan when the latter started to draw. Hickok whirled, drew, and shot first, killing Strawan."

How good was Hickok? In *Wyatt Earp—Frontier Marshal,* by Stuart N. Lake, Wyatt Earp is quoted as saying that "It may surprise some to know that a man of Hickok's skill could make a six-gun effective up to four hundred yards." That is a tremendous distance to fire from with a weapon known to be inaccurate at 100 yards.

Two years later, Hickok showed up in Abilene, Kansas, a rip-roaring cowtown where he was promptly hired as city marshal with the order to clean the place up. As for many frontier peace officers, part of the process involved graft taken from the gambling and prostitution businesses that serviced the town and its visitors.

Hickok's record as Abilene town marshal was spotty. Always quick on the draw, he accidentally killed his own deputy Mike Williams, thinking Williams a bandit trying to sneak up on him. Despite the fact that the town fathers eventually dismissed Hickok in ignominy, the shootist's ability with his cap and ball pistols remained legendary.

Buffalo Bill Cody subsequently hired Hickok for his wild west show. Hickok tired quickly of the vaudevillian turn but by then, his legend had spread in the exaggerated dime novels of the period. He was the most celebrated gunfighter in America.

During the early summer of 1876, Hickok drifted into Deadwood, Dakota Territory. This was a mining town that serviced the prospectors seeking their fortune in the Black Hills. Hickok decided to try his hand at gambling, an occupation with which he had limited success from time to time.

At Mann's Saloon Number 10, on August 2, 1876, 39-year-old Wild Bill Hickok was engaged in a poker game. Hickok's back was not against the wall. Instead, he was seated in the middle of the table, making things easy for Jack "Broken Nose" McCall.

Secretively, McCall came up behind Hickok. The famous gunman never knew what hit him when a bullet from McCall's gun found its way into the back of his brain. Hickok collapsed to the table, instantly dead. His hand opened up, and the cards fell on the table—two pair, aces and eights, and a queen. It would forevermore be known as "the dead man's hand."

McCall would later claim at the inquest that the reason for the killing was that Hickok had shot his brother, and he was just taking revenge. When asked why he had not challenged Hickok to a duel, McCall replied, "I didn't want to commit suicide."

See also WILLIAM MATTHEW "BILL" TILGHMAN (1853–1923).

New Mexico (1877) the Kid kills his first man

After his mother died, Billy the Kid's stepfather William Antrim refused to take him in. Billy was placed in a number of foster homes but by age 15, he had gone out on his own.

He killed his first man, Frank "Windy" Cahill, on August 18, 1877, after the two men had a disagreement. Billy escaped Arizona and headed back to New Mexico where he joined up with Jesse Evans.

Evans was the leader of a gang of rustlers and killers called "the Boys." In October 1877 the Boys rode into Lincoln County, where Billy had a disagreement with Evans and decided to leave. Rancher John Tunstall immediately hired him. Tunstall, an Englishman, and his attorney and partner Alex McSween were in a business dispute that had escalated into a feud with rancher John Dolan. Dolan and his partner John Rilex controlled the House, a business combine that in turn controlled the law and everything else in Lincoln County.

On February 18 Tunstall and his men, including Billy the Kid, were driving a herd of horses to Lincoln. Men in the employ of Dolan and county sheriff Brady ambushed the group. Tunstall was killed, but the Kid and the others escaped.

Billy had formed a strong friendship with Tunstall. He felt that Tunstall had taken him in when no one else would, so he decided to avenge his friend's death. Ironically, he turned to the law and got a friend to appoint him a deputy constable. On February 18, 1878, the Kid, Fred Waite, and Constable Atanacio Martínez attempted to serve warrants on the men who murdered Tunstall. Instead, Brady's men disarmed them and took them prisoner. A few days later, they were all released from jail. In the interim, Tunstall had been buried; the Kid had missed the funeral.

Billy was angry. He had also taken on a new alias, William Bonney. His friends still called him "the Kid."

See also INDIANA AND KANSAS (1868–1874); LINCOLN COUNTY, NEW MEXICO (1878–1879); NEW MEXICO (1877); NEW MEXICO (1881); NEW YORK, NEW YORK (1846).

Lincoln County, New Mexico (1878–1879) the Regulators

On March 1, 1878, Lincoln County appointed John Tunstall's foreman, Dick Brewer, as constable charged with the responsibility to bring in Tunstall's murderers. The Kid was one of those deputized for

Brewer's posse, whose members took to calling themselves "the Regulators."

After arresting Bill Morton and Frank Baker, two of the men believed responsible for Tunstall's death, the Regulators decided to execute them instead of bringing them in for trial. For good measure, they also killed one of their own, William McCloskey, whom they believed to be a traitor.

On April Fool's Day 1878, the Regulators ambushed the sheriff and his deputies who Billy suspected were in cahoots with Dolan. Sheriff William Brady and Deputy George Hindman were killed. Billy and company were subsequently indicted on murder charges. Instead of turning themselves in, they hid out at the Chisum Ranch, where they remained for the winter.

The Regulators' revenge had escalated the situation. Now they were outlaws, and warrants were put out for their arrest. To make matters worse, the Dolan faction decided to strike back.

Dolan's gunfighters and his newly appointed sheriff, George Peppin, surrounded the house of Alex McSween, Tunstall's partner. It happened that many of the Regulators, including Billy, were visiting and trapped inside. Desiring more firepower, Dolan sent for Colonel Dudley at Fort Stanton for assistance.

Dudley arrived with troops and a howitzer, a type of Gatling gun. They laid siege to the house, waiting for the men to come out; they would not. On the fifth day, Dolan got impatient. He ordered his men to set the house on fire. By nightfall, the house was completely ablaze. Inside, the heat from the flames was overwhelming. The Regulators began to panic. Only 17 years old, Billy the Kid took charge.

The Kid divided the men into two groups. He led the first group out the door, running in one direction to draw the line of fire toward them. McSween's party made a run for it in the other direction. Dolan and his men, of course, were firing the entire time. McSween and three of his men were killed, while one Dolan gunman bit the dust. The Kid and the rest escaped into the encroaching darkness.

With McSween's death, the Lincoln County War was over. The Regulators disbanded, but in their wake the Kid was now a fugitive. For the next few years, he would make his living cattle rustling and robbing. Sometimes, he would murder.

The legend of Billy the Kid says that he killed a man for every year he was alive. While that appears to be an exaggerated claim, he certainly had a kill total in the double digits, making him enough of a

pest that Lincoln County would eventually have to do something about his murderous ways.

See also INDIANA AND KANSAS (1868–1874); NEW MEXICO (1877); NEW MEXICO (1881); NEW YORK, NEW YORK (1846).

Chicago, Illinois (1879) the Reno court of inquiry

After Custer's Last Stand, Major Marcus Reno, Custer's second in command, became the most reviled man in America. All through the military his name was whispered with the word *coward* attached to it, and many papers labeled his behavior at the Little Big Horn as cowardly.

The argument was that had Reno held the line south of the village, Custer's plan would have worked. He would have subdued the Indians in the north. With Reno doing his part, it would have been a great victory. Somehow, no one factored in the sheer number of hostiles against which the army was pitted.

Reno himself resented all the innuendo. Finally, he asked President Rutherford B. Hayes for a hearing at which to clear his name. Hayes appointed a military review board to look into the charges against Reno. If the board cleared him, no further action would be taken. If it did not, formal charges would be brought against him.

The penalty for cowardice under fire was death.

The Reno Court of Inquiry convened at Chicago's Palmer House on January 13, 1879. The hearing took a month and included 1,300 pages of recorded testimony. Much of it, by soldiers who fought alongside Reno in the village and later on the hilltop, backed up his story that the Indian force was so great, there was no way he could have held the line.

In his wonderful biography of Custer, *Son of the Morning Star*, historian and novelist Evan McConnell points out that "[d]uring a recess in this trial, Captain Frederick Benteen was asked by a *Chicago Times* reporter why there seemed to be so much trouble with Indians. Benteen answered that larceny by agents of the Indian Bureau was responsible. There had been, he said, 'enormous pilfering and stealing.' Agents whose annual salary was $1,500 were saving as much as $15,000 annually. Treat the Indians honestly and there should be no problem."

As for Reno, with no direct evidence to prove otherwise, the court was forced to conclude that he had not acted with cowardice. But they made it clear in their ruling that some of his subordinates did more for the safety of his command than he did. Among the men who fought alongside him on the bluff over the river were soldiers who, for their heroic actions against the hostiles, were awarded the Congressional Medal of Honor.

Reno's neck had slipped through the noose. The army was not about to let it happen twice. By the end of 1879 Reno was dishonorably discharged for being a peeping Tom. For Reno the legacy of the battle was his descent into criminal behavior. He died from tongue cancer, probably the result of chewing tobacco.

See also FORT LARAMIE, WYOMING (1868); WASHINGTON, D.C. (1867).

Dodge City, Kansas (1871–1885) buffalo, bullets, and badmen

By 1871 Fort Dodge was established, and the surrounding area began to be looked at as safe to settle in. A settler named Henry L. Sitler built a three-room sod house to oversee his cattle ranch. Over the next few years, Sitler's place became a rest stop for buffalo hunters and traders.

The next year, 1872, Dodge City was officially incorporated as a town. Sitler's cabin was the town's first building. The area itself quickly became a hotbed of commercial activity fueled by the eastern desire for buffalo skins. Outside the town, vast herds of buffalo thundered across the Plains, just waiting for the hunters to pick them off one by one with their long, accurate Sharps rifles.

Eastern businesses paid a fortune for these skins. The brisk trade in skins centered on Dodge City, where the Atchison, Topeka and Santa Fe railroad laid rails. Now, instead of a mule train back east bearing the skins, they could be shipped cheaply and conveniently on the railroad.

South of the railroad tracks on Front Street, stacks of fresh, flea-laden buffalo hides lay baking in the noonday sun. Buffalo hunters patronized the town's saloons, brothels, hotels and stores. After the hunters left some of these places, the proprietors noticed they could not get the odor out that these buffalo men carried with them. Someone began to call these men "stinkers" and the name stuck.

Two "stinkers" were Wyatt Earp and William Barclay "Bat" Masterson.

Both men were in their early 20s. Earp was pensive, long, and lean, with an upturned dark mustache. He had a taciturn demeanor that belied his deadly ability with a revolver, though Earp was not a fast draw. His talent lay in his courage: He could coolly and accurately shoot a pistol under fire.

His young friend Masterson was not yet the well-dressed dandy of legend. When he and Earp met on the trail, Masterson was just a sawed-off, tough-looking kid from back east, who was always a little vague about his origins. Sometimes he said he hailed from Illinois, sometimes he said he was a French Canadian by birth. It was almost like he was inventing himself as he went along.

On their short forays into Dodge for supplies, Masterson and Earp found a place bursting at the seams. During the next 10 years it would expand tenfold. Already, south of the tracks on Front Street, rickety wood frame buildings and tents had been erected. Grocery stores, general stores, a barbershop, a blacksmith shop, and a saloon were all erected. It became local legend that the term *red light district* was coined because trainmasters who patronized the Front Street brothels brought along their red lanterns, assuring that the area would be known as the "red light district." The district, along with the rest of Dodge, continued to prosper.

As the capital of the buffalo trade, Dodge City shipped approximately 850,000 buffalo skins around the country during the next three years. During those early years, no local law enforcement existed. That was when the town was indelibly stamped with its reputation of lawlessness. Men openly carried revolvers in holsters and just as easily used them on anyone they found offensive. Buffalo hunters fought gamblers, railroad workers fought drifters, and everyone fought the soldiers.

Sometimes these disagreements led to gunfights, which led to men being shot down in their boots. Thus emerged the legend of "dying with your boots on." As with any town, Dodge needed a place to bury its dead. The city set up an area outside town on a hillside in which to inter the bodies of the unfortunate gunshot victims. And because the unfortunates had died with their boots on, the place was christened Boot Hill.

By 1875 the wholesale slaughter of the buffalo had taken its toll. The animals were being hunted into extinction. No longer would vast herds roam across the plains. Dodge needed another way to make its living. It found it in the beef business.

At just about the time the buffalo trade in Dodge was dying off, Texas cattlemen figured out that the best and fastest way to get their cattle to market was to drive them up through the Texas Panhandle and then through Oklahoma into Kansas. The Chisolm Trail ended in Dodge City, which was how Dodge became the nation's beef lifeline.

Dodge's stockyards overflowed with Texas cows. The city prospered, and so did the cowboys who had driven the cattle to market. The problem was that being a cowboy was an itinerant trade that often attracted shiftless characters with criminal dispositions. The cowboy ways were raw and violent. Many carried guns in holsters on hips and rifles in saddle-mounted scabbards. When coming in off the trail, they were susceptible to fancy women and alcohol. Passions aroused and gunplay resulted.

Along with the cowboy money came crime. Every kind of criminal opportunist drifted into Dodge, from murderers to con men, thieves to hold-up men. The townspeople knew that their town could not survive if crime was allowed simply because the Texans brought money into town. No one would want to settle in a lawless place.

There were two types of law enforcement jobs available in Dodge: marshal of the town, charged with keeping law and order in the city's environs, and sheriff of Dodge County, of which Dodge City was the county seat. As for enforcing the law, it could be stretched a little in Kansas due to the violent times. If law officers had to go a little bit further than the eastern "coppers"—so named because of their copper badges—so be it, as long as whatever extra legal measures they employed brought peace and stability to the community.

The city passed an ordinance that guns could no longer be worn or carried north of the "dead line." The dead line was defined as the railroad tracks. North of the tracks was the area where the "good" people of the town had settled. South of the tracks, along Front Street, anything was acceptable. Anyone who defied the law was forcibly disarmed.

More than 5 million head of cattle found their way to Dodge City over the next 10 years. During this time, Wyatt Earp, Bat Masterson, and Bill Tilghman were among the select group of lawmen who stood their ground and enforced the law in Dodge. But by 1882 the threat of hostile Indians had been quelled by the army and Fort Dodge was closed.

By 1886 the railroad had spread to Texas, and Texans no longer needed to drive their cattle along the Chisolm Trail to market in Dodge. The cattle drives ended and with it, Dodge's prosperity. It had become what it is today—a law-abiding town with a rich history of criminal justice.

See also WYATT EARP (1853–1928); WILLIAM BARCLAY "BAT" MASTERSON (1853–1921); WILLIAM MATTHEW "BILL" TILGHMAN (1853–1923).

John Henry Holliday, D.D.S., a.k.a. "Doc" Holliday (1852–1887) homicidal dentist

There are many killer doctors in American criminal history but only one homicidal dentist of reknown: Doc Holliday.

In 1849 in Georgia, druggist Henry Burroughs Holliday married Alice James McKay. Their first child, Martha Eleanora Holliday, was born on August 14, 1850. Infant mortality was high at that time, and Martha was one such victim, passing away just six months later. Henry and Alice had another baby soon, as shown in an item in the local church records in Griffin, Georgia:

John Henry, infant son of Henry B. and Alice J. Holliday, received ordinance of baptism on Sunday, March 21, 1852 at the first Presbyterian Church in Griffin.

In 1854 Henry Holliday was given some land in Valdosta, Georgia, where he moved his family. Growing up, John Henry was very close to his mother, whom he adored. Tragedy struck in 1866. When he was just 15 years old, John Henry's mother died. He was completely devastated. His father barely perceived his son's grief, choosing to mask his own by marrying again three months later.

John Henry was an extremely bright young boy. As a man, he showed a keen intelligence and desire to succeed. Taking up the family mantle in medicine, he decided to study dentistry and in 1870, enrolled in the Pennsylvania College of Dental Surgery. He studied there for two years and graduated with his doctor of dental surgery (D.D.S.) degree in 1872.

John Henry went home to Georgia. He went to Atlanta, where he bought into the practice of Dr. Arthur C. Ford. He had the full intention of making dentistry his life's profession. He would marry and have children. It all made sense until he began coughing.

At first, it was just a little cough that he was sure would go away. But it stayed. Finally, he went to his physician, who promptly diagnosed him with tuberculosis. He visited various specialists in Atlanta, who all told him the same thing: He had just a few months to live, but he might extend his time on earth if he moved to a drier climate.

As a medical man, Doc Holliday knew it was a dire diagnosis. With no other means of combating the lung disease, doctors tried to extend life by convincing the patient to move to a drier climate. Drier climates were then thought to prolong the lives of tubercular patients.

Depressed that his life was over just as he was ready to start it, John Henry packed his bags and took the Southern Pacific railroad west, to the end of the line. In October 1873, finding himself in Dallas, Texas, with enough money to keep him going briefly but without future means of support, he hired on with a local dentist. He soon discovered that nobody wanted a tubercular dentist. Patients refused to see him. Dr. John Henry Holliday had to give up dentistry for good.

Throughout his short stay in Dallas, John Henry began patronizing the town's gambling halls, where he found that he had ability at cards. He was an excellent gambler, especially when it came to bluffing. His brooding dark eyes gave nothing away. He decided to try his hand at gambling full time since he had nothing else to fall back on. Holliday soon noticed that being a gambler was a violent profession; it brought you into contact with many unsavory characters. He needed a means of defending himself.

Since a knife was easier to conceal than a gun, John Henry bought a few blades at the local hardware store and practiced secreting them in his clothing and then flipping them out, blade pointed outward, at a moment's notice. When he was not doing that, he would go out of town with a new Colt .45 that he had purchased and take target practice at bottles he had brought along for the occasion.

It was during this time when he sat gambling at the Dallas tables that people began addressing him regularly as "Doc." The nickname stuck. Forevermore, he would be introduced as Doc Holliday. He cemented his reputation by an armed confrontation in Dallas with a saloonkeeper. Neither man was hurt, though both were arrested for disorderly conduct.

What was interesting about the experience is that Doc liked it. He liked the excitement of fighting. What made him deadly was his ability to attack without fear of consequence. He was going to die anyway. What did he care if he got killed in a duel? It seemed to get something out of his system. A few months later, Doc got into a gunfight with a local citizen, killing him. Doc left Dallas quickly, the sheriff and town marshal in hot pursuit. Doc gave them the "slip."

There was always money to be made from the army, Doc realized, and so he found himself dealing faro in the town of Jackson, Texas, not far from the army base at Fort Richardson. Once again Doc got into trouble, this time with a soldier. After shooting the man dead—an action Holliday enjoyed since he was still a Confederate at heart—he left Jackson even more quickly than he had left Dallas—and for good reason. Killing a soldier was a federal crime. He not only had local law enforcement to contend with, but the deputy U.S. marshal for the area was after him.

Doc holed up in the mountains of Colorado. He spent time gambling in Leadville, Georgetown, Pueblo, and Central City. During this period, he killed his third man and had to leave yet another state as a fugitive. The peripatetic, homicidal gambler/dentist wound up back in Texas at Fort Griffin.

Doc got a job dealing cards at the saloon run by John Shanssey. He became friendly with a local prostitute named "Big Nose" Kate Elder. Soon, they were a couple. One day in the saloon, a tall lean man came in to talk to Shanssey. He was an old friend from Shanssey's buffalo hunting days. The man's name was Wyatt Earp.

Earp was searching for a train robber, and Shanssey thought Doc might have some information that could help him. Earp and Holliday began to chat, and they had instant respect for one another. They would become lifelong friends.

After Earp left, Doc got into an argument with a man named Ed Bailey. He became the fourth victim of the homicidal dentist. Unfortunately for Doc, people liked Bailey.

The town would not have it. They dispatched a posse to get Holliday at his hotel. Big Nose Kate set a fire around the front of the building that drew the lynch mob away, while she and Doc sneaked out the back way to some horses that she had waiting. They hightailed it out of town and fled to Dodge City, where, in 1877, Wyatt Earp was the town marshal. His brothers Virgil and Morgan were his deputies.

Seeking to mend his ways, Doc once again took up dentistry but to no avail. People still did not want a consumptive dentist coughing in their face, and they feared his reputation as a killer.

Holliday had promised Earp that he would do nothing in the town to embarrass his friend. He had too much respect for Wyatt Earp to do anything, even a killing in self-defense, that would hurt him. Then one day, a group of Texans came into Dodge fresh off the trail and headed south of the deadline to party on Front Street. They failed to check their revolvers, and Earp went after them to enforce the law.

Wyatt came into the Long Branch saloon where he confronted the men, who closed in around him. There was a gun rack at the side where the men were supposed to park their weapons. Doc Holliday strolled nonchalantly up to the rack, took his Colt out of the holster, cocked the trigger, and shot one of the cowboys in the shoulder. In the confusion, Earp drew his gun, and the two men forced the cowboys out into the street where they dispersed without any more gunplay. Wyatt never forgot the favor.

From 1878 until 1881, Doc Holliday wandered through the Colorado mining camps. In Trinidad he had a gunfight with a local, Kid Colton, in which Colton found himself on the wrong end of a Colt .45 bullet. After he was dead, Doc left town before a "necktie party" could form to throw a noose around his neck. That was Doc, always one step away from his own death.

Making his way into New Mexico Territory on the railroad, he wound up in the town of Las Vegas. Tired of the gambler's life, Doc hung out his shingle. This time, the third, was not the charm. The results were the same. So he took his gambler's "poke" and invested it in a saloon.

A few weeks later, a gunman named Mike Gordon got into an argument with Doc, who promptly killed him. Doc hit the trail once again, with the law in hot pursuit. He went back to Dodge City, where he could be around a man he trusted, Wyatt Earp. But when he got there, he found that the Earps had left for Tombstone, Arizona. There had been a silver strike in a mine near the town. Tombstone was growing by leaps and bounds. There was much money to be made in Tombstone and the Earps had determined to be part of the moneyed class.

That was all right with Doc. He took up with Big Nose Kate again, and together, they took the Southern Pacific train south into Arizona and then went by stage to Bisbee and the last stop on the stage line, Tombstone. The town stood less than 100 miles from the Mexican border in southeastern Arizona. Kate set up her own whorehouse while Doc tried his luck at the tables.

The gunfight at the OK Corral that soon followed Holliday's arrival is the most-written-about episode in the annals of American criminal violence.

By 1887 Doc Holliday had grown tired of the sporting life. He moved to Glenwood Springs, Colorodo in May, hoping that the vapors of the sulfur springs might do him some good. Instead he quickly grew weaker, the tuberculosis finally taking over his body. He took to bed, where he remained for the last two months of his life. On the day of his death, Doc awoke from a coma and drank a glass of whiskey. Looking down at his bootless feet, he said, "This is funny." Then he lay back on the pillows and died.

See also DODGE CITY, KANSAS (1871–1885); WYATT EARP (1853–1928); WILLIAM BARCLAY "BAT" MASTERSON (1853–1921).

Wyatt Earp (1853–1928) businessman, murderer, lawman

Wyatt Earp is as ruthless a killer as any in American history. He is also the most famous lawman in American history. That dichotomy is what makes him so compelling. The absolute fact that in all the gunfights he was in he never received so much as a scratch made him a legend. Earp's brilliance was his ability to work both sides of the law, sometimes simultaneously, to the point that even when he committed cold-blooded murder, he got away with it. The secret of Wyatt's success was that he always thought of himself as a businessman. If he happened to kill to protect his interests, that was perfectly acceptable as the price of doing business in the violent towns he happened to find himself in.

Born in Monmouth, Illinois, on March 19, 1848, Wyatt Earp was the third son of Nicholas Earp and Victoria Ann Cooksey. After Wyatt's birth, his family spent the next few years moving back and forth between Illinois and Iowa, until finally, in 1864, they moved to California for five years, then back east to Lamar, Missouri in 1869, when Nicholas Earp became the constable for Lamar and then justice of the peace.

On the same day the father became a judge, his son Wyatt, who was only 21 years old, was appointed as Lamar's new town constable. Wyatt swore the following oath upon taking his first position as a peace officer in 1869:

I, Wyatt S. Earp do solemnly swear that I will to the best of my ability, diligently and faithfully without partiality or prejudice discharge the duties of Constable, within and for Lamar Township Barton County Missouri. [signed] Wyatt S. Earp

On January 10, 1870, Wyatt Earp married Urilla Southerland. Wyatt had married well. His new in-laws were well respected in Lamar. They also happened to own the Lamar Hotel, where the Earps lived for a short while until Wyatt bought a house and lot for $50 in August 1870.

Wyatt was all set to begin his new life when tragedy struck: Urilla died suddenly in 1870. Some accounts say it was from typhus, others claim she died in childbirth. Then things got worse for Wyatt.

On March 14, 1871, Barton County filed a suit against Wyatt Earp for $200. It was alleged that while constable for Lamar, Wyatt had collected licensing fees that should have been turned over to the town for use in building and maintaining schools. Instead, the suit alleged, Earp pocketed the money. The charges were eventually dropped after Earp and his father, Nicholas, left the state.

Charles Morgan, in an affidavit filed with the lawsuit, commented: ". . . he has good reason to believe that Wyatt S. Earp deft. is not a resident of this state, that Wyatt S. Earp has absconded or absented himself from his usual place and abode in this state so that the ordinary process of law cannot be served against him."

Morgan was right. Two weeks later on March 31, 1871, a fellow named James Cromwell filed a second lawsuit against Wyatt Earp. Cromwell alleged in his suit that Earp had falsified court documents referring to the amount of money that he had collected from Cromwell to satisfy a judgment. Allegedly, Earp had pocketed the difference, leaving Cromwell to make it up. If it were true, it was a slick a scheme as a con man could devise.

With Cromwell holding the bag, the current Lamar constable seized Cromwell's mowing machine and sold it for $38 to satisfy the judgment. In his suit, Cromwell claimed that the machine had a value of $75 and that Earp owed him this amount because Earp had falsified the court documents about the amount he had paid to satisfy the judgment against him. A summons was issued to get Earp before the court to answer the charges, but it went unserved.

On April 21, 1871, the case went forward. Earp lost. The court issued an execution for costs. It ordered the Barton County sheriff to seize the "Goods, Chattels and Real Estate" of Wyatt S. Earp.

April 1, 1871, Bill Of Information. U.S. vs Wyatt S. Earp, Ed Kennedy, John Shown, white men and not Indians or members of any tribe of Indians by birth or marriage or adoption on the 28th day of March A.D. 1871 in the Indian Country in said District did feloniously willfully steal, take away, carry away two horses each of the value of one hundred dollars, the property goods and chattels of one William Keys and prey a writ [signed] J. G. Owens.

But there was nothing to seize, Wyatt was long gone.

Wyatt Earp had graduated from petty crime to serious federal charges. On April 6, 1871, Wyatt Earp was taken into federal custody on the horse theft charge. He was arraigned on August 14 and bond was set at $500.

Indicted formally on the charge on May 15, Wyatt Earp was nowhere to be seen. A warrant was issued for his arrest. Federal marshals proceeded to look for and fail to find him. The warrant was ultimately returned unserved on November 21, 1871, and Earp was never tried on the charge. His codefendant Edward Kennedy was later acquitted.

In a sworn statement she later gave to authorities, Anna Shown, wife of John Shown, accused Earp and Kennedy of forcing her husband to help steal the animals. Mrs. Shown also claimed that Earp and Kennedy threatened to kill her husband if he testified against them.

Whether Earp was a horse stealer and strong-arm thug early in his career is unclear, but he was definitely a serious man not to be trifled with.

In the early 1870s Earp drifted out to the Kansas frontier, where he became a buffalo hunter for a time. It was in those days, hunting on the plains, that he made the acquaintance of Bat Masterson. They would become lifelong friends and colleagues.

By 1874 Wyatt Earp was in Wichita, Kansas, working as "muscle" in collecting debts for a local businessman. One year later, on April 21, 1875, Wyatt Earp was appointed to the Wichita police force at a salary of $60 a month. In Wichita, Earp began to build his reputation as an intrepid frontier lawman. Local newspapers commented on how well he did his job as peace officer in containing the rowdy element, but he also had his misadventures. On January 12, 1876, the *Wichita Beacon* reported that Earp had let his pistol slip from his holster, fall to the ground, and discharge. Luckily, the errant bullet hurt no one.

As the Wichita town election of 1875 approached, Earp got into a fight with the Democrat who was running against his boss, Republican Mike Meagher. Earp was fined $30. When the time came for reappointment, Earp was denied.

On May 12, 1876, Wichita's police committee filed a report against Earp, accusing him of pocketing city monies collected from licenses and fines. As usual, he was not around to answer the charges. He had moved on to Dodge City, where later that month he became a deputy city marshal. Until the end of the decade, with some time off for prospecting in the Black Hills, he was on the city police force.

In July 1878 a Texas cowboy named George Hoy became rowdy in the town and started shooting his pistol. Earp and another deputy marshal, Jim Masterson (Bat's brother), turned and saw Hoy firing from horseback. Hoy turned his horse about to leave town, still firing wildly. Earp and Jim Masterson took aim and fired. One of the two bullets hit Hoy, who fell from his horse and later died from his wound.

Earp finally quit the Dodge City police force around September 1879. By November he was in Tombstone, Arizona. He left behind a considerable legacy. He may have had his hand in the till, but Wyatt Earp was well liked and respected in the towns in which he marshaled. Throughout his career as a Kansas lawman, Earp displayed both courage and a wily ability to survive physically and politically.

See also DODGE CITY, KANSAS (1871–1885); DR. JOHN HENRY "DOC" HOLLIDAY (1852–1887); WILLIAM BARCLAY "BAT" MASTERSON (1853–1921); TOMBSTONE, ARIZONA (1881).

New Haven, Connecticut (1873) Winchester '73 model rifle

The Winchester Repeating Arms Company of New Haven, Connecticut, was a major innovator in the manufacture of rifles. Bandits and lawmen alike prized the weapons.

In 1873 Winchester began manufacture of its most famous rifle, the Winchester '73. Its lever action enabled a bullet to be loaded into the chamber for firing by simply pulling the lever down and up. It would become fabled in the Old West and such a popular item across the country that it would be manufactured in the same design until 1919.

Besides the quick lever action, the other reason for the rifle's popularity was its versatility. The weapon came in .32, .38, and .44 caliber models. At the same time, Colt began producing single action army revolvers in the same calibers. This was a tremendous breakthrough.

Carrying a rifle and revolver, which could fire interchangeable cartridges, was invaluable on the frontier, where ammunition resupply was always a problem. One could not just go to a general store out on the frontier. Whatever ammo was stocked was all that was available. Carrying a revolver and rifle that used the same bullets meant both weapons could be used as long as the bullets held out.

Criminals now had one more piece to add to their arsenal of firepower.

See also PATERSON, NEW JERSEY (1936).

Assassination of President Garfield (July–September 1881) Alexander Graham Bell races to save the president's life

On July 2, 1881, Charles Guiteau shot President Garfield in the back as the president was about to depart for a vacation from the Baltimore and Potomac Railroad Station. Guiteau was promptly arrested and remanded to the District of Columbia jail near the Anacostia River.

President Garfield was removed to the White House, where doctors ministered to his wounds. The bullet had lodged deep inside the president's body, and surgeons could not operate because they were not certain where it was. Yet they had to do something to save his life.

The president's men turned to the one man who might be able to invent a machine to detect the bullet and thus allow the surgeons to safely and effectively

President James A. Garfield (Library of Congress)

132

operate. Dr. Alexander Graham Bell, Ph.D., was a Scottish immigrant who had made a name for himself as the inventor of the telephone. He later wrote about his participation in the effort to save the president's life in a paper that he read before the American Association for the Advancement of Science in 1882: "I was called in to try and locate the bullet without probing through sensitive tissues," he wrote. "While brooding upon the problem of the detection of the bullet in the body of President Garfield, these (induction) experiments made in England returned vividly to my mind."

Bell conceived of an invention that could detect metal in the body, using one invention that had already been proven: the telephone. The idea was that two metal coils could be brought over the seat of the bullet and the telephone would announce the presence of the bullet by the audible sound [of the phone's bell]."

To test his invention, on July 22, "the new explorer instrument" detected an old bullet in the body of a human subject, Lieutenant Simpson. It was a feeble sound but a true one, nevertheless, Bell believed. It was time to test his invention on the president.

In the three weeks since President Garfield had been shot, surgeons continued unsuccessful probes for the bullet while the president grew weaker. Convinced that his machine might work, Bell raced to the president's side. He recalled,

On the evening of July 26th, our apparatus was carried to the Executive Mansion and an experiment made upon the person of the President. It produced uncertain and indefinite results.

The invention failed to detect the bullet. Bell was convinced it had something to do with "connecting the condenser." He tried experimenting again on three Civil War veterans who still had lead in their bodies from battle. This time the results were perfect. The invention had worked on all three.

Alexander Graham Bell had invented the world's first metal detector.

I therefore dispatched a messenger to the Executive Mansion (Sunday morning, July 31st) with a note for Dr. Bliss [Garfield's physician] to let him know that the instrument was in a condition to be used should any necessity arise for an immediate experiment. I was requested to make another trial upon the person of the President at the evening dressing of the wound.

Bell sent a telegram to his wife on July 31, 1881, the night before his second attempt to find the bullet in Garfield's body. (Library of Congress)

On Monday morning, August 1, 1881, Bell was summoned to the White House.

During the July 26th experiment, a sudden sonorous effect had been observed on passing a point near the spot where the surgeon suspected the bullet to be lodged, but I had been unable to verify by a second observation passing over the same place. When the new explorer [Bell's name for his invention] was passed over the suspected spot, nothing was heard.

Bell did hear a slight pulsating sound as the instrument was moved about.

With the view of eliminating any error of observation caused by the pulsations due to simply the movement of

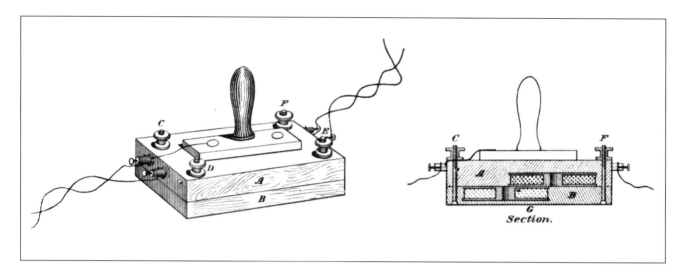

Apparatus used in the second experiment upon President Garfield, August 1, 1881 (Clements Library, University of Michigan)

the instrument, I lifted the latter to a height of about 50 percent above the body of the President and moved it to and fro.

Bell brought in a colleague. They conferred.

It seemed reasonably certain that the area of feeble sound was due to some external cause and was not simply an effect of expectancy. In the absence of any other applicable cause for the phenomenon, I was forced to agree in the conclusion that it was due to the presence of the bullet and I so stated in my report to the surgeons.

Still, Bell was unsatisfied. In other experiments he had made, the sound was louder, so he went back to the White House to make sure all the metal had been removed from the president's bed. Sure enough, he discovered that underneath the president's horsehair mattress was another mattress made of steel wire.

But Garfield died before Bell could pass the invention over his body again. Had the president not been lying on a mattress of steel wire, it is probable Bell would have detected the bullet and an operation would have been performed to remove it.

Bell continued his work and finally demonstrated his invention publicly on October 7, clearly locating a Confederate bullet in the cheek of Calvin E. Pratt of Brooklyn, who had been shot in the battle of Gaines Mills, June 1867.

Bell had invented the first method of probing the body with an electric field, foreshadowing such 20th-century inventions as the sonogram, cardiogram, magnetic resonance imaging (MRI). Yet despite his achievement, the president had died. That elevated the charge against Charles Guiteau to murder of the president of the United States.

TRIAL AND EXECUTION OF CHARLES GUITEAU, 1881–1882

For the first time in American history, a presidential assassin was being tried for his crime. John Wilkes Booth had perished before he could stand trial.

The trial of Charles Guiteau began on November 14, 1881, and did not end until May 22, 1882. Since there was little doubt about Guiteau's guilt—eyewitnesses put him at the scene—Guiteau's counsel probed his background, eventually deciding to use insanity as their defense. Such a defense was as revolutionary in law as Bell's invention was to medicine. During the trial, the facts of Guiteau's life were laid out for the jury.

Born on September 8, 1841, in Freeport, Illinois, Guiteau was the fourth of six children. His mother died when he was five years old, and his father was a dedicated follower of the religious theology of John Humphrey Noyes, founder of the Oneida Community in New York State in the 1840s. Noyes's doctrine was a form of self-described "millennial communism," a strange mixture of biblical prophecy and Karl Marx.

In 1859 an inheritance from his maternal grandfather provided Charles with the income to attend the University of Michigan in Ann Arbor. He hoped he would enjoy life there but it was not to be; he grew increasingly despondent. He turned to Noyes's teachings, as his father had, for solace. By 1860 Charles Guiteau had joined the Oneida Community in New York.

He stayed for five years but was still not happy. On April 3, 1865, the future assassin conceived of the notion that he had been chosen by God to spread Noyes's "millennial communism" by founding a daily newspaper. Guiteau went to Hoboken, New Jersey, and attempted to start a paper called the *Daily Theocrat*. He failed.

On July 20, 1865, he applied to reenter the Oneida Community. He did, but quit on November 1, 1866. By August 1867 Guiteau had spent his inheritance and he went for assistance to his brother-in-law, George Scoville, husband of his sister Frances. (After the death of their mother, Frances had practically raised her younger brother. She would provide Guiteau with both moral and financial support throughout his life.) He offered Guiteau a job in his law office in Chicago, as well as a place to live. Guiteau accepted, but his unhappiness overwhelmed him again. A few months later, he quit and returned to New York, ostensibly to work for Henry Ward Beecher's newspaper, the *Independent*. Unfortunately, the famous abolitionist had no editorial positions available. Guiteau wound up selling subscriptions and advertisements on commission.

As his life spiraled downward, Guiteau decided to sue the Oneida Community on a trumped-up charge of withholding compensation for the work he said he had performed for them previously. After a series of threatening letters to Noyes that amounted to blackmail, Guiteau was forced to stop when Oneida's lawyers threatened to prosecute him for extortion.

In 1868 Guiteau returned to Chicago, got a job as a law clerk, studied for and passed the Illinois bar, and set up a small private practice. In 1869 he married Annie Bunn, a librarian at a local YMCA. Guiteau abused his wife, going so far as to lock her in a closet for nights on end.

After the Chicago Fire of 1874, Guiteau and his wife moved back to New York, where she finally divorced him that same year. He tried and failed to start another newspaper, then went back to his sister Frances and moved in with her and his brother-in-law. After a few months there, Guiteau suffered a psychotic break. One day, his sister Annie went out back, where Guiteau was chopping wood. She passed close to him, and Guiteau suddenly raised the axe toward her in a threatening manner. A local

doctor was summoned. The doctor recommended having Guiteau institutionalized.

Knowing what was in store for him if he stayed with his sister, Guiteau fled and disappeared. Two years later, in 1876, he reappeared as an evangelical convert at Dwight Moody's revivalist meetings. From 1877 to 1879, Guiteau became an itinerant preacher, writing and publishing his own sermons. In 1880 Guiteau, a Republican, became involved in the Republicans' intraparty conflict between the "Stalwart" faction, led by Roscoe Conkling, and the "Half-Breeds," led by James G. Blaine. The Stalwarts attempted to nominate Ulysses S. Grant for a third term, while the Half-Breeds supported James Abram Garfield.

At first, Guiteau had sided with the Stalwarts. But when Garfield gained the nomination, Guiteau changed sides. After Garfield's election in 1881, Guiteau moved to Washington, D.C., in the hope of being rewarded by the party with a political sinecure. He lobbied Secretary of State James G. Blaine for an appointment. It is unclear whether he was rebuffed or received no response at all. Whatever happened, Guiteau changed sides again, rejoining the Stalwarts.

In the middle of May 1881, he decided that the president needed to be "removed." On June 16, 1881, he delivered the first of several explanations for his action, an "Address to the American People." He also wrote a letter to the White House and a similar one to General William T. Sherman to be delivered after he killed the president. It said: "I have just shot the President . . . His death was a political necessity. I am a lawyer, theologian and politician. I am a Stalwart of the Stalwarts . . ."

The jury at his trial chose to ignore Guiteau's obvious mental illness. They found him responsible for his actions at the time he shot Garfield. The jury also chose to ignore the autopsy report, which showed medical malfeasance. Dr. Bliss's probing for the bullet did more damage than leaving it alone would have. Guiteau was convicted, and a writ of execution was issued.

Appeals were filed, supported by testimony of neurologists who had examined Guiteau. The assassin's family appealed directly to President Chester A. Arthur to intercede but to no avail. The president denied Guiteau's appeal.

On June 30, 1882, Charles Guiteau was hanged at the District of Columbia jail. Within the decade, medical experts reviewing his case would pronounce it a miscarriage of justice, claiming that Guiteau had clearly not been responsible for his actions for years.

See also JOHN WILKES BOOTH (1838–1865); BUFFALO, NEW YORK (1901); DALLAS, TEXAS (1963); MIAMI, FLORIDA (1933); WASHINGTON, D.C. (1982).

Tombstone, Arizona (November 1881) the gunfight at the OK Corral

Reaching the mining boomtown of Tombstone, Arizona, in 1880, the Earp brothers quickly set up shop to take advantage of the money flowing through the town. They had a set method of doing it in every town in which they worked, a way that one family could work both sides of the law at the same time.

James and his wife would establish drinking, gambling, and whoring establishments. In later years, the vice squad of any big city police force would have investigated their activities, but then, it was tolerated as the price of business.

Wyatt had the reputation as a killer. As long as he backed up his brothers, it made no difference if he had an official post or not. Once one Earp brother was employed as marshal or sheriff, the others came along in the bargain. It was no surprise then that phase two of the Earp business plan always called for one or more brothers to be employed as peace officers.

Phase 3 was enforcement. Having the Earps as partners in any gaming or drinking establishment meant, in effect, buying protection. The Earps would keep out the riffraff. On the legal side, the Earps as lawmen were rigorous enforcers of the law. Putting themselves up against murdering cowboys and the like was not altruism; it served the Earp business interests.

Wyatt, Virgil, Morgan, and James Earp arrived in Tombstone on November 29, 1879. Virgil was the sole lawman in the bunch, having previously been appointed a deputy U.S. marshal in Tucson. Because Virgil's appointment did not come with a salary, he was still behind the eight ball financially. He got a job as deputy city marshal to Fred White.

Wyatt muscled his way into the Oriental Saloon, and without one shred of capital he became a part owner. James took a job as the Oriental's bartender. Wyatt also worked on the side as an armed guard for Wells Fargo, a job Morgan later replaced him at when Wyatt decided to devote himself full time to the Oriental.

Whether Wyatt had any police power at the time of the gunfight in Tombstone remains open to conjecture. Various unsubstantiated accounts say that he was a deputy U.S. marshal. But no official document

appointing Wyatt to the federal post has been found. More likely, he simply assisted his brother Virgil in the discharge of his duties.

In 1880 Wyatt served for awhile as deputy sheriff of Pima County. Prior to the gunfight, Virgil tried to take care of the legal niceties by appointing Wyatt a "special officer" for Tombstone. What is clear is that the Earps, upon arriving in Tombstone, incurred the enmity of the Clanton-McLaury Gang.

What happened was that six army mules were stolen from Fort Rucker, Arizona. To track down the missing animals, the army asked for and got the assistance of Deputy Sheriff Wyatt Earp, Deputy Marshal Virgil Earp and Wells Fargo agent Marshal Williams. They followed the trail to the McLaury ranch, which was run by the McLaury brothers.

At the ranch Wyatt and party discovered tools that could have been used to change the brands of the animals in question. But the mules still being missing, there was no direct evidence trying the McLaury's to the affair. Then, on July 30, 1880, an army lieutenant published a notice in the *Tombstone Epitaph* newspaper. It implicated Frank McLaury and offered a reward for anyone who could provide evidence to convict him.

McLaury, of course, was furious. He gave the paper a printed response in which he vigorously denied the allegation. As far as he was concerned, the Earps were behind the original notice in the paper and he would get them for spoiling his good name.

Things started to heat up when, on October 28, William "Curly Bill" Brocius, and a few of his friends were shooting up the town in a drunken stupor. Brocius worked for McLaury. City Marshal Fred White tried to disarm him but was shot by Brocius for his efforts. At the sound of the gunshot, Wyatt had come running.

Before Brocius could shoot again, Wyatt hit him twice on the head with the barrel of his six-shooter and dragged him off to jail. White, who was still living, was carried to the doctor's office. The rest of Brocius's cowboy friends were arrested by Virgil and Wyatt and hauled off to jail.

Next morning, all were taken before the magistrate. Reliable witnesses testified that Marshal White's last statement before he lapsed into unconsciousness was that he fired Brocius's gun himself while in the process of grabbing for it. The judge had no choice but to free Brocius. In the eyes of the law at the time, the shooting was therefore an accident. Two days later, White died from his wounds.

Soon, word came into Tombstone that Pima County, of which Tombstone was a part, would be partitioned off to make a second county, Cochise, which would contain Tombstone. Wyatt quit his job as Pima's deputy to run for the position of sheriff of the new county. At that time, the sheriff's position was by appointment of the territorial governor.

Johnny Behan took Wyatt's place as deputy. Being that Wyatt was a Republican and so was Governor John Fremont, and Behan was a Democrat, it looked like Wyatt was a shoo-in. Behan made a deal with Wyatt—if Wyatt pulled out, Behan would make him his under-sheriff. Wyatt would do the fieldwork, and Behan the administrative chores. Between them, they would split the money from the $40,000-a-year position.

Wyatt agreed to the deal. But when Behan was appointed sheriff, he never followed through on his end of the bargain. Wyatt wound up with nothing. To a businessman like Wyatt, that was unacceptable, and he planned to get his revenge when the time was right.

The Earps next fell afoul of the Clantons. Ike Clanton and his brothers Billy and Phineas ran a ranch. The Clantons had allied themselves with the McLaurys and were referred to in the newspapers as the Cowboy Faction. When Wyatt's horse was reported missing and later found in the possession of Billy Clanton, Wyatt was ready to execute the man for horse-stealing, but thought better of it and let the matter go.

On March 15, 1881, the Benson stage was robbed, and masked gunmen murdered driver Bud Philpot, a likable man. A posse, including the Earps, was sent out to apprehend the badmen. They tracked down a fellow named Luther King. The Earps questioned him and King named Bill Leonard, Harry Meade, and Jim Crane as the murderers of Philpot. All were associates of the Cowboy Faction. King was taken in as an accessory to the robbery and murder.

A few weeks later on June 5, Big Nose Kate, who had an argument with Doc Holliday, named her lover as having been involved in the stage holdup. Doc was indicted by a grand jury on murder, stage robbery, and also federal charges of interfering with the mail. The district attorney would subsequently drop the charges before trial, stating, ". . . (I am) satisfied there was not the slightest evidence to show guilt of the defendant." It seemed that Kate just had it in for Doc because he had hit her one too many times.

Sides were forming rapidly. Besides the Clantons and McLaurys on the cowboy side were Brocius, Pete Spence, Frank Stilwell, and the legendary quick-draw artist Johnny Ringo. The Earps also believed that Behan was in the employ of the cowboys.

On the side of the law were the Earps, Doc Holliday, John Clum, the publisher of the *Tombstone Epitaph* and a few influential townspeople.

Because Tombstone was close to the Mexican border, the Clantons and McLaurys rode across the border and rustled Mexican cattle. They drove the cattle across the border and sold them in the United States for top dollar. The Earps' continual encroachment on their turf was depriving them of this and other illegal activities. The Clantons and McLaurys were not above rustling cattle from U.S. ranchers and did so on many occasions.

And then Josie Marcus, a San Francisco showgirl from a good Jewish family, came to Tombstone. She was playing one of the music halls when she took up with Johnny Behan. They lived together, but despite this, Wyatt began openly courting her. Under Behan's baleful eye, Josie fell for the businessman/lawman hard and fast.

In June 1881 Wyatt determined once and for all to bring in Philpot's killer. If he could do that, he knew he could win the next election for Cochise County sheriff. Wyatt struck a deal with Ike Clanton. In return for Ike setting up the three stage robbers, Wyatt would give him the reward money under the table. Ike agreed but then got scared. He was afraid the other members of his gang would hear about the deal and cut his throat. The deal fell through.

In June Virgil finally got the job he coveted when he was appointed city marshal. In September the Bisbee stage was robbed, but his time there was a positive identification. The stage driver fingered Pete Spence and Frank Stilwell. The latter was working as Johnny Behan's deputy.

Virgil arrested them both. That was the straw that broke the camel's back. The Earps began receiving anonymous death threats on a regular basis. The *Tombstone Epitaph* would report ". . . that since the arrest of Spence and Stilwell, veiled threats [are] being made that the friends of the accused will 'get the Earps.'"

On the evening of October 25, Ike Clanton was drinking in Tombstone's Alhambra Saloon when he began making threats against the Earps and Doc Holliday. When Doc found out, he stormed into the Alhambra and challenged Ike to a showdown.

Morgan Earp, appointed deputy marshal by his brother Virgil, happened to be in the saloon and broke up the fight before a shot could be fired.

Later that night Ike, roaring drunk, confronted Wyatt on the street, and warned him that he would get his tomorrow. Wyatt said, "Go home, Ike, you talk too much for a fighting man." Showing that business came above all, Ike spent the night gambling and drinking with Virgil and Johnny Behan. Next morning, Ike started the day with more threats on Holliday's life.

"Doc has got to fight!" he told Virgil.

Late that morning, Virgil was woken out of a sound sleep by his deputy. Ike, it seemed, was running around town, drunk, yelling at everyone that he was going to kill the first Earp he saw. Most important, he was carrying a rifle with which to commit the murders he so frequently talked about. Not wasting time, Virgil came up on him fast and knocked him down with his pistol then dragged him off to court.

Once in court, Ike, who couldn't seem to keep his mouth shut, told Wyatt that the biggest fight in his life was coming. The Earps and the Clantons were going to have it out. Wyatt's response: "If you are anxious to make a fight, I will go anywhere on the Earth to make a fight with you."

Tom McLaury then made some more threats to Wyatt when they met on the street. Wyatt's response was to pistol-whip him and leave him bleeding in the dust. When Frank McLaury and Billy Clanton came into town later, they met up with Billy Claiborne, Ike Clanton, and Tom McLaury in the lot next to Fly's Photography Studio. All the men were armed. Someone overheard them threatening the Earps and relayed those threats to town marshal Virgil Earp.

Virgil was having a drink in the Oriental with Johnny Behan when a town gadfly came running in to say he overheard the Clantons and McLaurys making threats on the lives of the Earps. Virgil then asked Behan to accompany him to Fly's to disarm the cowboys. Behan instead offered to "go down there and try to get the cowboys to give up their revolvers." But Virgil's mind was made up.

Walking out on the street, he ran into Morgan, Wyatt and Doc. He asked them all to accompany him down to Fly's to disarm the cowboys.

Virgil handed his shotgun to Doc and told him to hide it under his long coat. He did not want to cause any excitement on the way over the Fly's. In return, he took the cane Doc had been carrying. With Virgil and Wyatt in front and Doc and Morgan in back,

they begin walking down Front Street. As they approached Fly's, Johnny Behan suddenly ran out from where the cowboys were bunched together in an alley next to the OK Corral. Behan tried to convince Virgil not to continue.

"They will murder you," Behan told Virgil.

Virgil told him he was just going to disarm them. Behan said that he has already done that, but Virgil didn't believe him and the party of four brushed by him.

In the alley between the OK Corral and Fly's, the cowboys had gathered: the two Clantons and two McLaurys, Billy Claiborne, Frank Spence, and Frank Stilwell. Virgil calmly asked them to throw up their hands and turn over their guns.

"You sons of bitches have been looking for a fight, now you can have one," Doc reportedly said.

Virgil heard the distinctive click of a hammer being drawn back. At that moment, Billy Claiborne managed to slink away without anyone noticing.

The moment dragged on, each group staring the other down until Wyatt and Frank McLaury jerked leather together. McLaury's shot went wild. During the next 30 seconds, the life and legend of Wyatt Earp truly blended. The way he stood up that day with bullets pinging around him, the way he coolly and calmly took aim at his enemies and fired, fixed in the public's mind the image of the courageous frontier marshal battling the forces of evil. Nothing, of course, could be further from the truth: Wyatt was simply protecting his and his brother's business interests.

After those first two shots, the intense firing went on for 30 seconds. During that time, Ike turned tail. He ran up to Wyatt and grabbed his arm, trying to make him stop firing. "This fight has commenced," Wyatt told Ike. "Go to fighting or get away."

Ike took refuge in Fly's while the fighting continued. Thirty seconds later, when the gunsmoke cleared, Frank and Tom McLaury were dead and Billy Clanton was mortally wounded. Virgil had been shot through the hip, Morgan in the back, and Doc took a graze to the hip. Only Wyatt stood tall. Bullet holes pockmarked the edges of his coat and trousers but none had hit home. Wyatt was completely unharmed.

As they were taking Billy Clanton away on a stretcher, he yelled, "The son of a bitch [Doc Holliday] has shot me, and I mean to kill him." Doc had to be restrained from shooting him, though he need not have bothered. Billy Clanton died a short time later.

TOMBSTONE, ARIZONA (1882): THE WELLS SPICER HEARING

Even Wyatt Earp could not kill three men and get away with it without the law taking a closer look. There is no question that Wyatt had enough political clout in the town to fix the verdict. But there is also no evidence that the verdict was anything less than the result of a magistrate doing his job.

Justice's Court, Township No. 1, Cochise County, A.T.—Before Wells Spicer, J.P., Territory of Arizona vs. Morgan Earp et al.

The case has now been on hearing for the past thirty days, during which time a volume of testimony has been taken, and eminent legal talent employed by both sides. The great importance of the case, as well as the general interest taken in it by the entire community, demand that I should be full and explicit in my findings and conclusions, and should give ample reasons for what I do.

Spicer said that his decision was based on proven fact during the hearing, not circumstantial evidence. He said that what had been established beyond reasonable doubt was that "On the morning of the 26th day of October, 1881, and up to noon of that day, Isaac [Ike] Clanton, the prosecuting witness in this case, was about the streets and in several saloons of Tombstone, armed with revolver and Winchester rifle, declaring publicly that the Earp brothers and Holliday had insulted him the night before when he was unarmed, and now he was armed and intended to shoot them on site. These threats were communicated to defendants Virgil Earp and Wyatt Earp."

Spicer pointed out that Virgil Earp was chief of police of the city of Tombstone, and charged as such by the city ordinances with the duty of preserving the peace, and "of arresting, with or without warrant, all persons engaged in any disorderly act whereby a breach of the peace might be occasioned, and to arrest and disarm all persons violating the city ordinances which declare it to be unlawful to carry on the person any deadly weapon within the city limits without first obtaining a permit, in writing."

Now came the legal rationale for justifiable homicide. Virgil Earp, as chief of police, assisted by Morgan Earp, who was also at the time a special policeman in the pay of the city and wearing his badge, arrested and disarmed Ike Clanton, and inflicted upon the side of his head a blow from a pistol.

Spicer summed up the events leading to what newspapers were calling "the gunfight at the OK Corral." Spicer concluded:

In view of these controversies between Wyatt Earp and Isaac Clanton and Thos. McLaury, and in further view of the quarrel the night before between Isaac Clanton and J. H. Holliday, I am of the opinion that the defendant Virgil Earp, as chief of police by subsequently calling upon Wyatt Earp and J. H. Holliday to assist him in arresting and disarming the Clantons and McLaurys, committed an injudicious and censurable act; and although in this he acted incautiously and without proper circumspection. Yet, when we consider the condition of affairs incident to a frontier country; the lawlessness and disregard for human life; the existence of a law-defying element in our midst; the fear of feeling of insecurity that has existed; the supposed prevalence of bad desperate and reckless men who have been a terror to the country and kept away capital and enterprise, and considering the many threats that had been made against the Earps, I can attach no criminality to his [Virgil's] unwise act. In fact, as the result plainly proves, he needed the assistance and support of staunch and true friends, upon whose courage, coolness and fidelity he could depend in case of an emergency.

"Capital" and "enterprise" won the day.

The Earps and Doc Holliday were exonerated for their actions at the OK Corral. The gunfight would pass into history but the feud between the cowboys and the Earps had just begun.

Shortly after the Wells Spicer hearing, Morgan Earp was shot in the back while playing pool in a town saloon. His assassins, believed to be part of the Cowboy Faction, escaped unidentified into the night. Morgan died in his brother Wyatt's arms.

Morgan's assassination pushed Wyatt over the edge. Without a badge to protect him, Wyatt embarked on a killing spree that made his reputation as one of the most lethal and feared murderers in U.S. criminal history. Within the next few months, he would head up a posse that at times included Doc Holliday and Texas Jack Vermillion, a well-known gunfighter and another loyal Earp friend. Seeking out the members of the cowboy faction, Earp killed them one by one. But the result was wanton killing, too much for the territorial government to tolerate. A warrant was issued for Wyatt's arrest. As usual, he was not around to receive it. Knowing it was coming, he had fled Arizona.

Wyatt Earp was only 34 years old, but he had already done the deeds that would create his myth. Despite the many blemishes to his record, he later managed to convince reporters to write about him as the town tamer of the Old West. His entertaining though historically whitewashed autobiography, 1934's *Wyatt Earp—Frontier Marshal,* by Stuart N. Lake, was in print as recently as the middle 1990s.

Like Emmett Dalton and Bill Tilghman, both of whom had yet to make their reputations, Wyatt Earp went to Hollywood in the 20th century to cash in on his celebrity. Earp died at the age of 81 on January 13, 1929. He is buried in the Jewish section of the Hills of Eternity cemetery in Colma, near San Francisco, his wife Josie's hometown.

New Mexico (1881) Pat Garrett kills Billy the Kid

From 1879 to 1881, Billy the Kid was on the run. During that time, he retreated to a deserted fort about 140 miles west of Lincoln. It was there that he made the acquaintance of a hunter named Pat Garrett. The hunter and the outlaw became friends.

In 1880 Garrett was elected sheriff of Lincoln County. Running on the reform ticket, he promised to capture Billy. Garrett eventually tracked the Kid down and brought him back for trial. Billy was imprisoned in the town's makeshift jail.

On the night of April 28, 1881, Billy, escorted by a guard, had gone to the outhouse. Afterward, they walked back. Billy was just climbing the steps back up to the jail when he broke away from his guard. He grabbed the guard's revolver and shot him with it. Responding to the shots, a second guard ran down the street to see what he could do. Billy was still at the top of the stairs leading back to his cell. He took careful aim and dropped the second guard. Mounting a horse, he galloped out of town.

Pat Garrett was away from Lincoln when Billy made his break. When he got back, he did a curious thing. Instead of forming a posse and going after Billy immediately, he decided to wait. His idea was to let the Kid think he was not coming after him. Then he would slip and make a mistake.

In July Garrett received word that the Kid was at his old hideout, Fort Sumner, 140 miles west of Lincoln. Taking two deputies, Poe and McKinney, Garrett rode the long, dusty trail to Fort Sumner. Garrett knew that Billy the Kid had become a folk hero to many of the people in the settlement. Garrett and his deputies rode into Fort Sumner, a strange collection of old, ramshackle buildings, in the middle of nowhere. Garrett unsaddled there, got some coffee, and entered an orchard, which ran down to a row of old buildings, some of which were occupied

Pat Garrett cashed in on his celebrity after killing Billy the Kid by lending his name to a "penny dreadful" about how he killed the Kid. (Library of Congress)

by Mexicans, about 60 yards from the house of Peter Maxwell, an old friend of his.

We approached these houses cautiously, and when within earshot, heard the sound of voices conversing in Spanish. We concealed ourselves quickly and listened; but the distance was too great to hear words, or even distinguish voices. Soon a man arose from the ground, in full view, but too far away to recognize. He wore a broad-brimmed hat, a dark vest and pants, and was in his shirtsleeves. With a few words, which fell like a

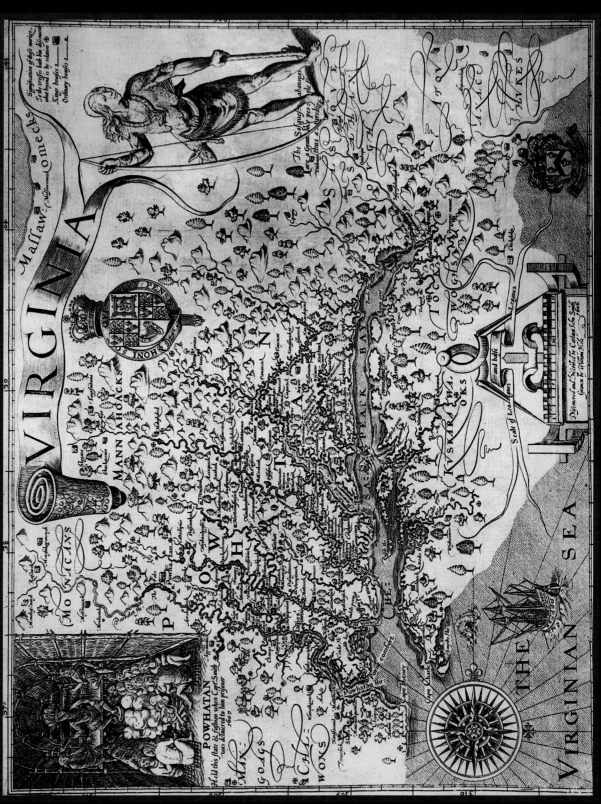

A map of
Virginia drawn
in 1606 by
Capt. John
Smith,
Pocahontas's
first love.
It was not
published
until 1624.

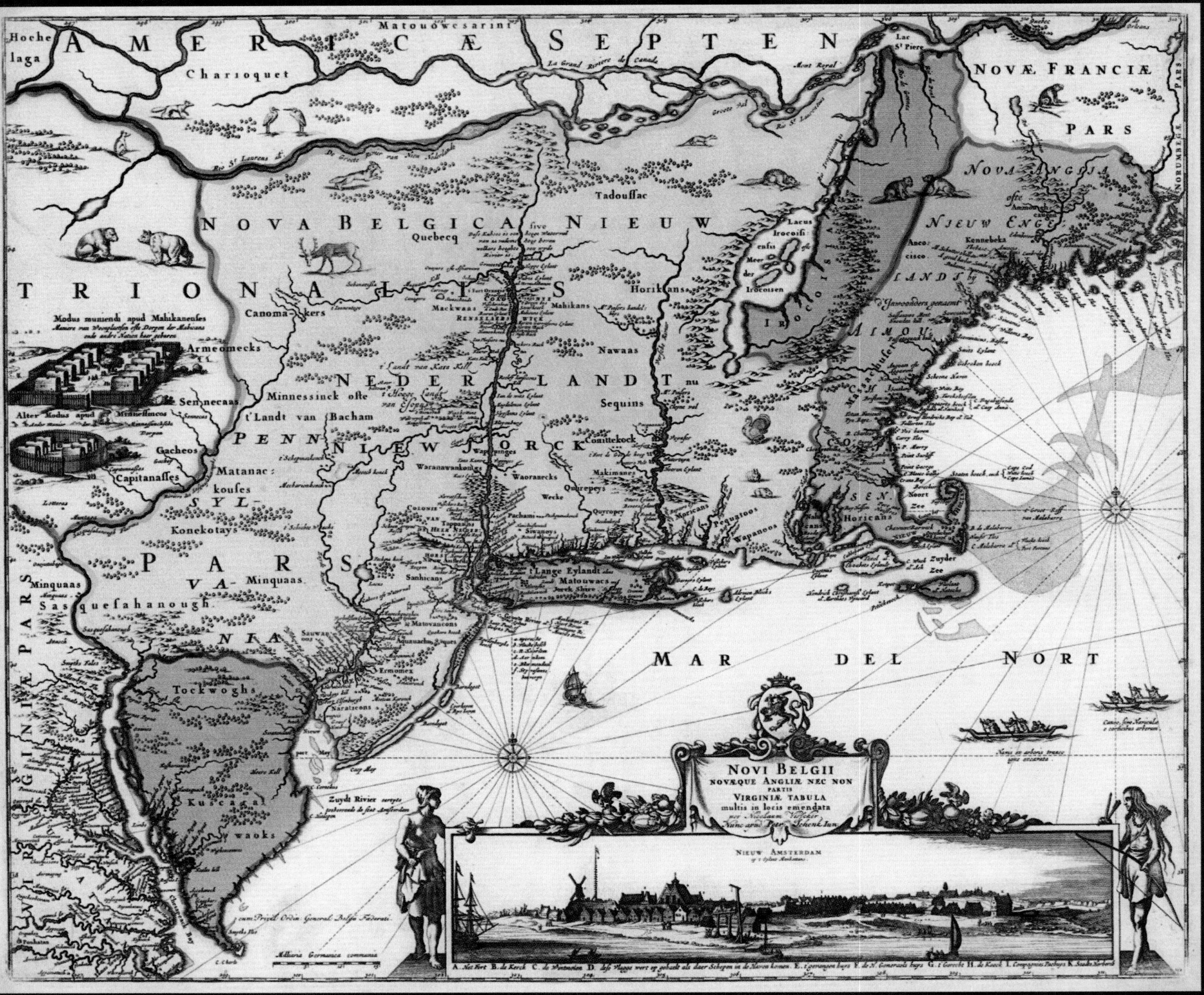
AMERICÆ SEPTENTRIONALIS
NOVÆ FRANCIÆ PARS
NOVA BELGICA sive NIEUW NEDERLANDT
NOVA ANGLIA
NIEUW ENGELANDT
PENNSYLVANIA
NIEW JORCK
MAR DEL NORT
Hoche laga
Matouowesarini
Charioquet
Tadoussac
Quebecq
Canomakers
Armeomecks
Sennecaas
Minnessinck ofte t'Landt van Bacham
Gacheos
Capitanasses
Matanackouses
Konekotays
Minquaas
Sasquesahanough
Tockwoghs
Kuscarawaoks
Mackwaas
Mahikans
Nawaas
Sequins
Horikans
Conittekock
Waoranecks
Wecke
Makimanes
Quirepeys
Quyropey
Pachami
Siwanoys
Pequatoos
Wapanoos
Horicans
Kennebeka
Ancocisco
Lacus Irocoisiensis
Irocoisen
Sanhicans
Matovancons
Ermomex
Waranawankongs
t'Lange Eylandt alias Matouwacs
Noort Zee
Zuyder Zee
Zuydt Rivier
Chesapeack Bay
Modus muniendi apud Mahikanenses
Alter Modus apud Minnessincos
NOVI BELGII NOVÆQUE ANGLIÆ NEC NON PARTIS VIRGINIÆ TABULA multis in locis emendata
NIEUW AMSTERDAM

New England the Middle Atlantic region, including Nieuw Amsterdam (later Manhattan) and Virginia, drawn by Nicolaes Visscher in 1685.

New Jersey,
Pennsilvania
[sic], New
York, and
New England,
1747

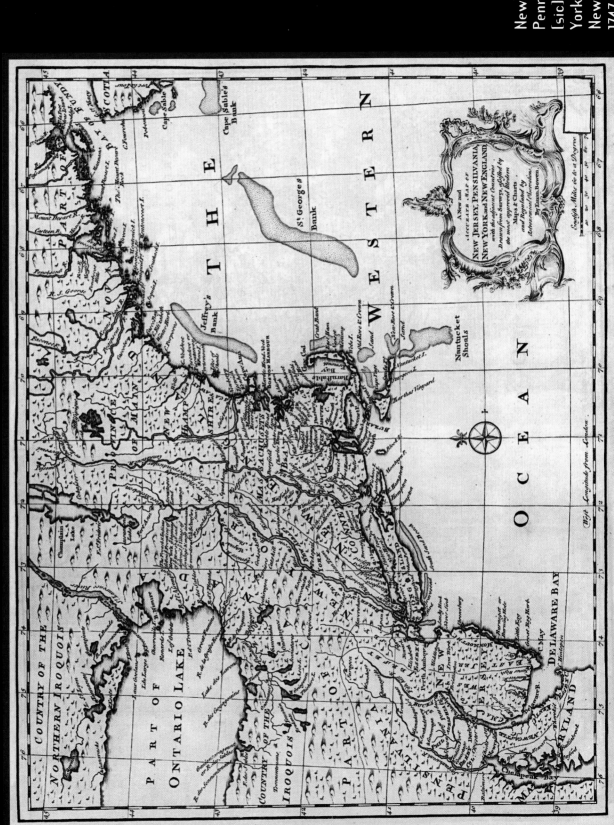

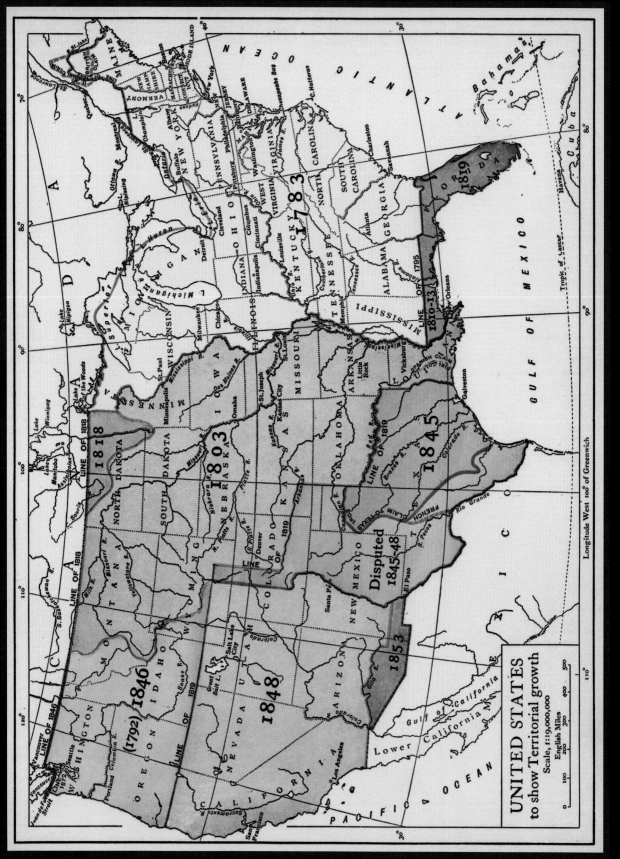

UNITED STATES
to show Territorial growth
Scale, 1:19,000,000
English Miles
0   100 200 300 400 500

This rare map of the United States shows territorial growth in 1783, 1803, 1810, 1818, 1819, 1845, etc.

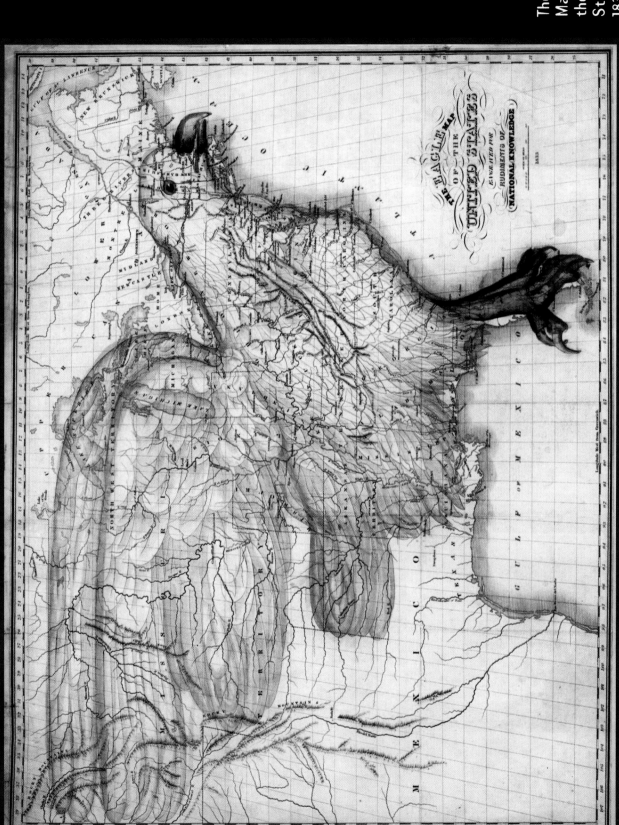

THE EAGLE MAP
OF THE
UNITED STATES
ENGRAVED FOR
RUDIMENTS OF
NATIONAL KNOWLEDGE

It was on the Capitol steps in the foreground that President Jackson was almost assassinated by Richard Lawrence in 1835. This kind of panoramic map was popular during the period.

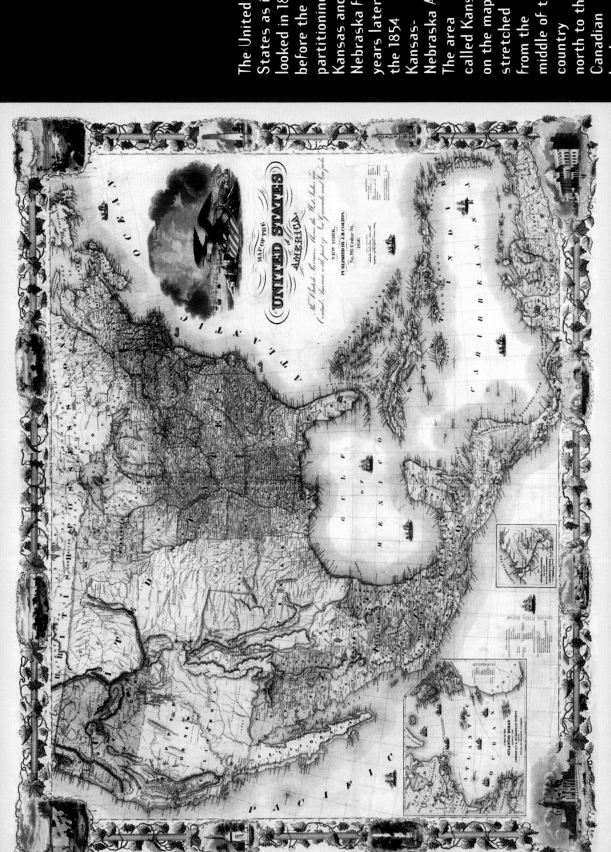

The United States as it looked in 1850, before the partitioning of Kansas and Nebraska four years later by the 1854 Kansas-Nebraska Act. The area called Kansas on the map stretched from the middle of the country north to the Canadian border.

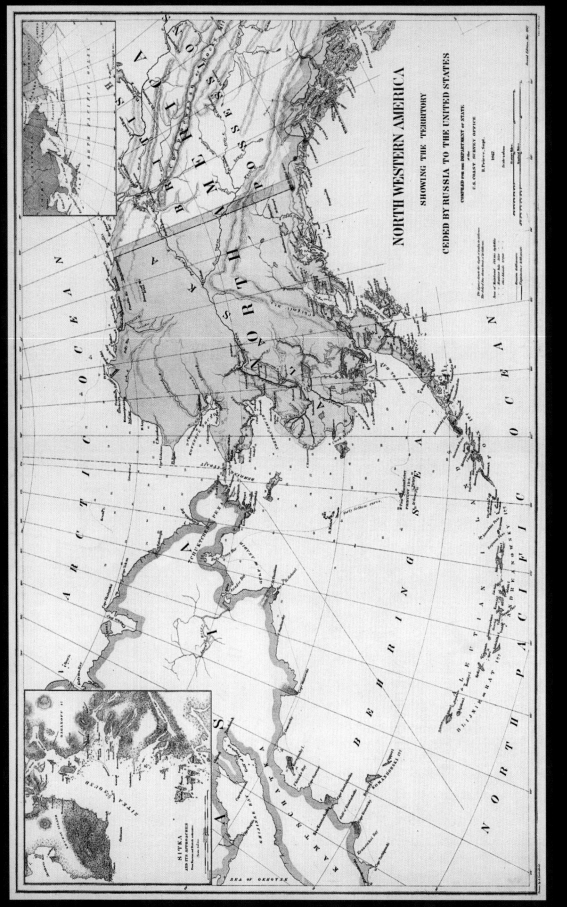

"Seward's Folly," the territory called "Alaska"; the Russians ceded it to the United States in 1867.

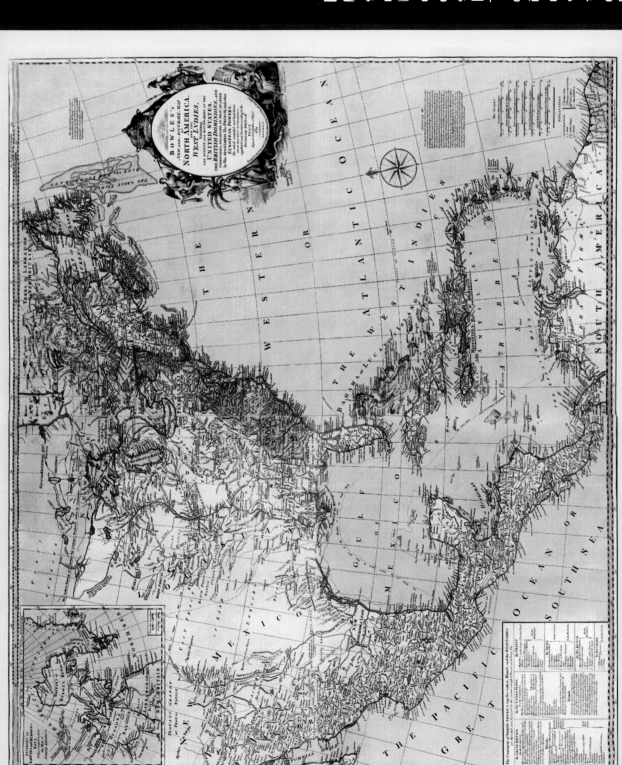

Bowles's map from 1783 shows the newly formed United States clutching the eastern seaboard of North America. The area west of the states is largely unexplored which is why there are no divisional boundaries.

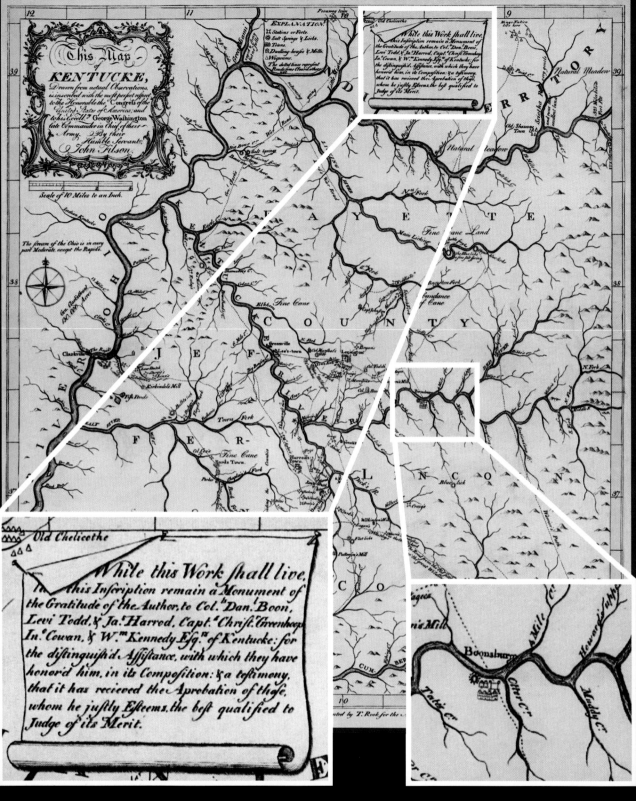

Detail

Detail

Kentucky, 1784, after Daniel Boone had explored its environs. The inscription in the upper right corner by cartographer John Filson gives a special thanks to Col. "Dan" Boon; Boone's settlement, Boonsboro can be found alongside the Kentucky River.

A
Map of
LEWIS AND CLARK'S TRACK,
Across the Western Portion of
North America
from the
MISSISSIPPI to the PACIFIC OCEAN;
By Order of the Executive
of the
UNITED STATES,
in 1804,5&6

The western track taken through the unexplored country by Captains Meriwether Lewis, William Clark and their Corps of Discovery.

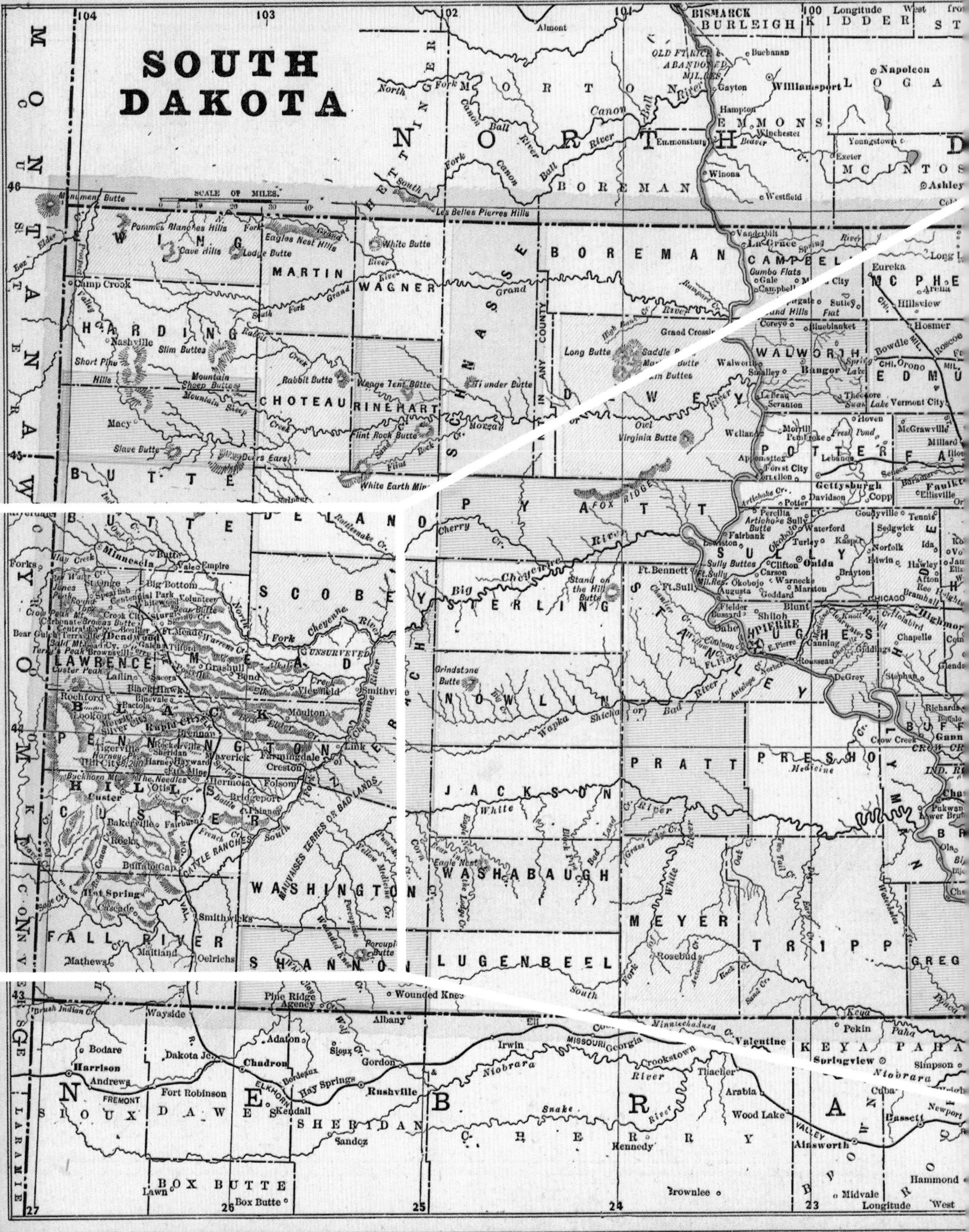

SOUTH DAKOTA
SCALE OF MILES.
BISMARCK
BURLEIGH
KIDDER
Longitude West from
Almont
MORTON
NORTH
EMMONS
LOGAN
MCINTOSH
BOREMAN
Napoleon
Williamsport
Gayton
Hampton
Emmonsburg
Winchester
Youngstown
Exeter
Ashley
Winona
Westfield
Buchanan
HETTINGER
Canon Ball River
Monument Butte
Les Belles Pierres Hills
WING
Pommes Blanches Hills
Cave Hills
Lodge Butte
Eagles Nest Hills
White Butte
MARTIN
WAGNER
SCHNASSE
BOREMAN
CAMPBELL
Vanderbilt
La Grace
Gumbo Flats
Gale
Campbell
Eureka
MCPHERSON
Hillsview
Hosmer
Bowdle
Roscoe
Camp Crook
HARDING
Nashville
Slim Buttes
Short Pine Hills
Mountain Sheep Butte
Rabbit Butte
Wedge Tent Butte
Thunder Butte
Long Butte
Saddle Butte
Grand Crossing
WALWORTH
Walworth
Smalley
Bangor
EDMUNDS
Theodore
Vermont City
CHOTEAU
RINEHART
Flint Rock Butte
DEWEY
Virginia Butte
Scranton
Hoven
McGrawville
Macy
Slave Butte
Deers Ears
White Earth Mine
POTTER
Appomattox
Forest City
Lebanon
Gettysburgh
Faulkton
BUTTE
DELANO
FOX RIDGE
PYATT
Potter
Davidson
Cherry Cr.
Artichoke Butte
Sully Buttes
SULLY
Waterford
Turley
Onida
Clifton
Carson
Warnecke
Marston
Brayton
Forks
Minnesela
Butte
Vale
Empire
SCOBEY
Big Cheyenne
STERLING
Stand on the Hill Butte
Ft. Bennett
Ft. Sully
Fort Sully Mil. Res.
Okobojo
Augusta
Goddard
Blunt
Big Bottom
Spearfish
Centennial Park
Whitewood
Sturgis
Crook City
Deadwood
Ft. Meade
Bear Butte
Bear Gulch
Galena
Tilford
LAWRENCE
MEADE
UNSURVEYED
Custer Peak
Laflin
Grashull
Bend
Black Hawk
Rochford
Pactola
Rapid City
Brennan
Moulton
Lookout
Sheridan
Tigerville
Harney Pk.
Hill City
Maverick
Farmingdale
Creston
PENNINGTON
Smithville
Link
Fielder
Bussard
Oahe
PIERRE
E. Pierre
HUGHES
Canning
Rousseau
Ft. Pierre
Coulson
DeGrey
STANLEY
NOWLIN
Grindstone Butte
Wapka Shicha or Bad River
Buckhorn Mt.
The Needles
Hermosa
Folsom
CUSTER
Custer
Bridgeport
Fairburn
Bakerville
Rocks
PRATT
PRESHO
LYMAN
JACKSON
White River
CATTLE RANCHES
MAUVAISES TERRES OR BAD LANDS
Buffalo Gap
Hot Springs
Cascade
WASHINGTON
WASHABAUGH
Eagle Nest
MEYER
Rosebud
TRIPP
Smithwicks
FALL RIVER
Maitland
Oelrichs
Mathews
SHANNON
Porcupine Butte
LUGENBEEL
Pine Ridge Agency
Wounded Knee
Wayside
Albany
Keya Paha
Pekin
Valentine
KEYA PAHA
Springview
Simpson
Adaton
Bodare
Harrison
Andrews
Dakota Jc.
Chadron
Gordon
Irwin
Georgia
Crookstown
Thacher
Niobrara River
Hay Springs
Rushville
Bordeaux
ELKHORN
FREMONT
Fort Robinson
NEBRASKA
SIOUX
DAWES
SHERIDAN
CHERRY
Kendall
Sandoz
Snake River
Kennedy
Arabia
Wood Lake
Cuba
Bassett
Newport
Ainsworth
VALLEY
BROWN
ROCK
Hammond
BOX BUTTE
Box Butte
Lawn
Brownlee
Midvale
Longitude West
MONTANA
WYOMING
CROOK
WESTON
CONVERSE
LARAMIE
104
103
102
101
100
46
45
44
43
27
26
25
24
23

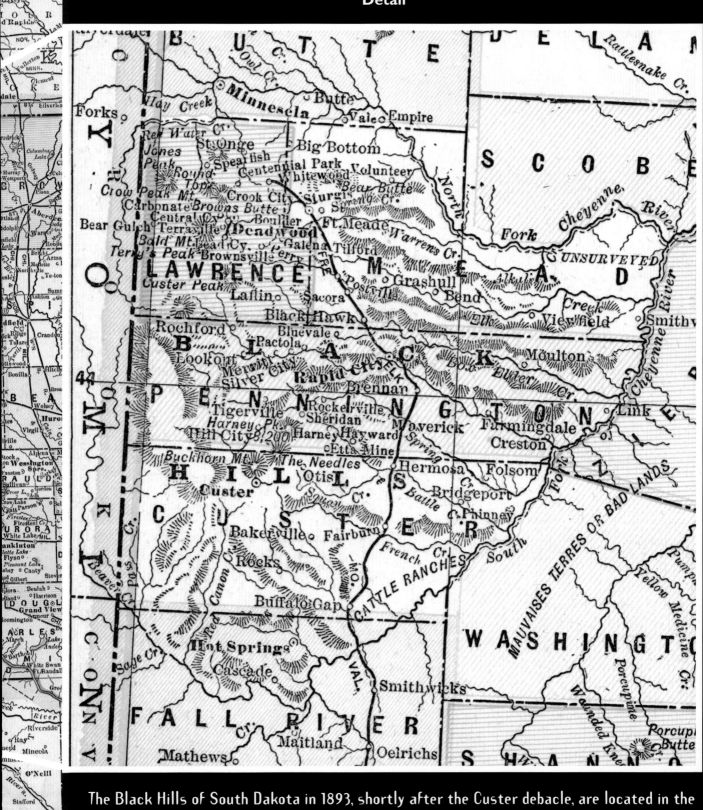

The Black Hills of South Dakota in 1893, shortly after the Custer debacle, are located in the far western portion of the state, not far from the Wyoming border. Note "Deadwood" in Lawrence County, where Wild Bill Hickok was assassinated by "Broken Nose" Jack McCall.

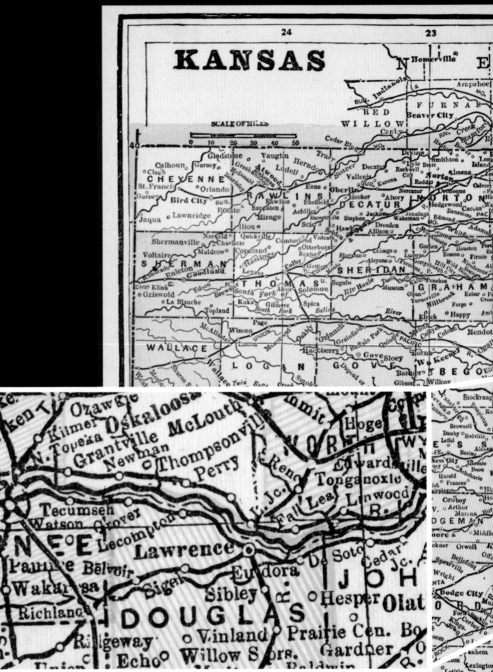

Detail

Kansas, in 1893. Note Lawrence, in the far
northeastern corner of the state next to
Missouri. It was here that Quantrill
staged his famous raid.

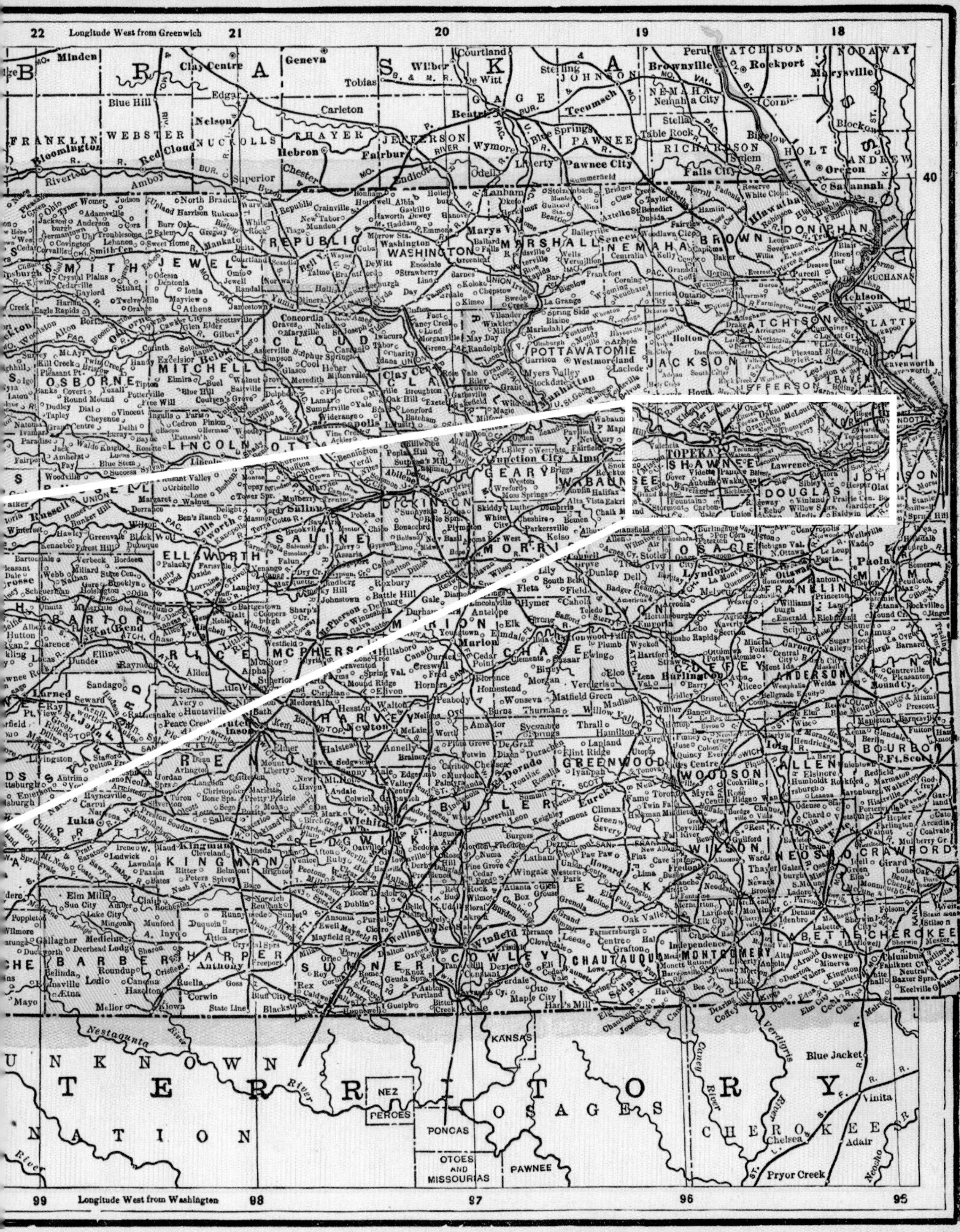

Longitude West from Greenwich
22
21
20
19
18
40
B R A S K A
NODAWAY
GAGE
JOHNSON
NEMAHA
PAWNEE
RICHARDSON
FRANKLIN
WEBSTER
NUCKOLLS
THAYER
JEFFERSON
HOLT
ANDREW
REPUBLIC
WASHINGTON
MARSHALL
NEMAHA
BROWN
DONIPHAN
SMITH
JEWEL
CLOUD
POTTAWATOMIE
JACKSON
ATCHISON
MITCHELL
OSBORNE
CLAY
LINCOLN
GEARY
WABAUNSEE
SHAWNEE
DOUGLAS
JOHNSON
TOPEKA
RUSSELL
ELLSWORTH
SALINE
DICKINSON
MORRIS
OSAGE
FRANKLIN
MIAMI
BARTON
RICE
McPHERSON
MARION
CHASE
LYON
COFFEY
ANDERSON
LINN
STAFFORD
RENO
HARVEY
BUTLER
GREENWOOD
WOODSON
ALLEN
BOURBON
PRATT
KINGMAN
SEDGWICK
WILSON
NEOSHO
CRAWFORD
BARBER
HARPER
SUMNER
COWLEY
CHAUTAUQUA
MONTGOMERY
LABETTE
CHEROKEE
KANSAS
UNKNOWN
TERRITORY
NATION
NEZ PERCES
OSAGES
PONCAS
OTOES AND MISSOURIAS
PAWNEE
CHEROKEE
Longitude West from Washington
99
98
97
96
95

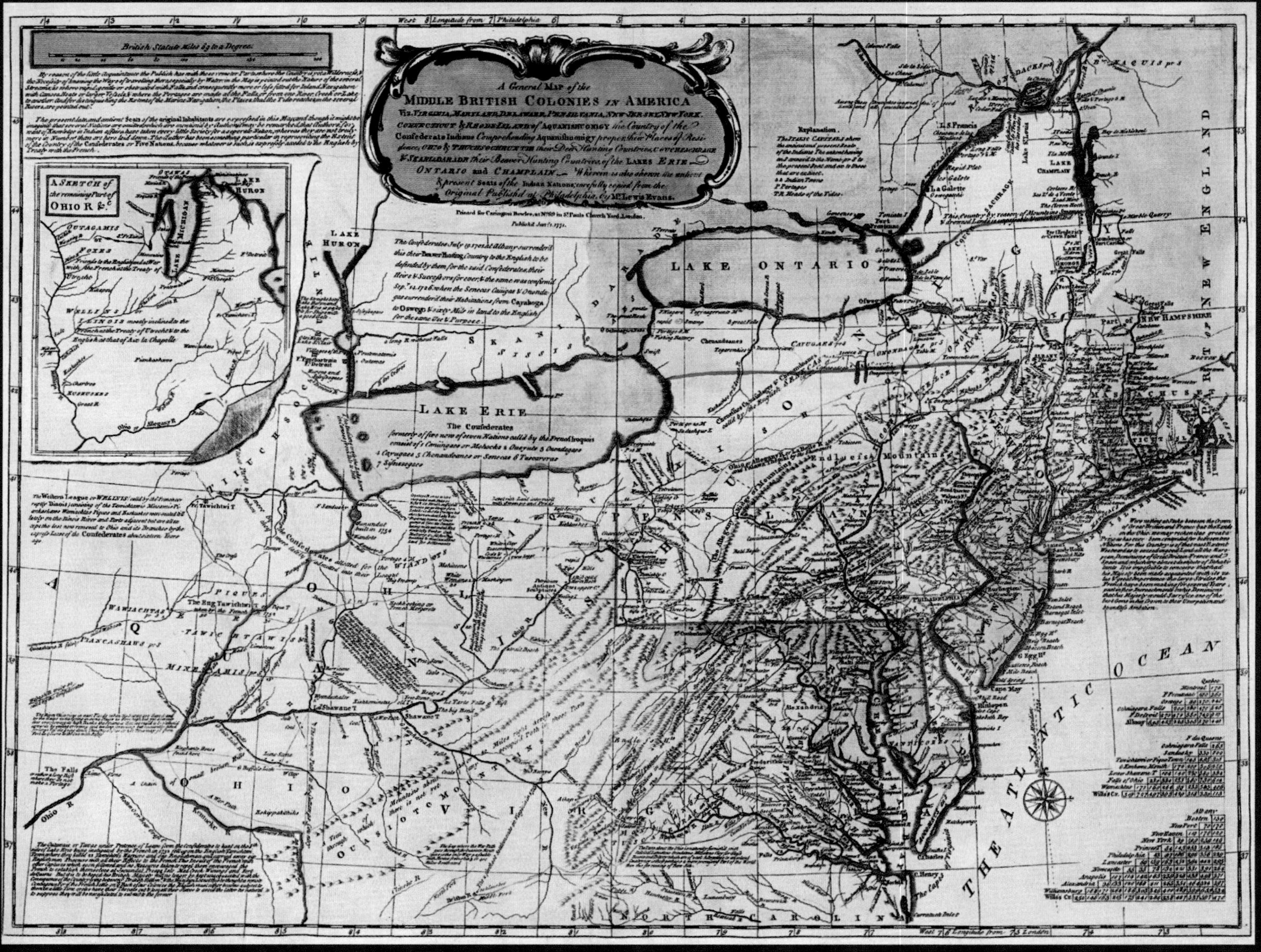
A General Map of the MIDDLE BRITISH COLONIES in AMERICA
LAKE ONTARIO
LAKE ERIE
LAKE HURON
NEW ENGLAND
THE ATLANTIC OCEAN
A SKETCH of the remaining Part of OHIO R &c.
British Statute Miles 69 to a Degree.
Explanation.
NORTH CAROLINA
Philadelphia

The Middle British Colonies of America, 177

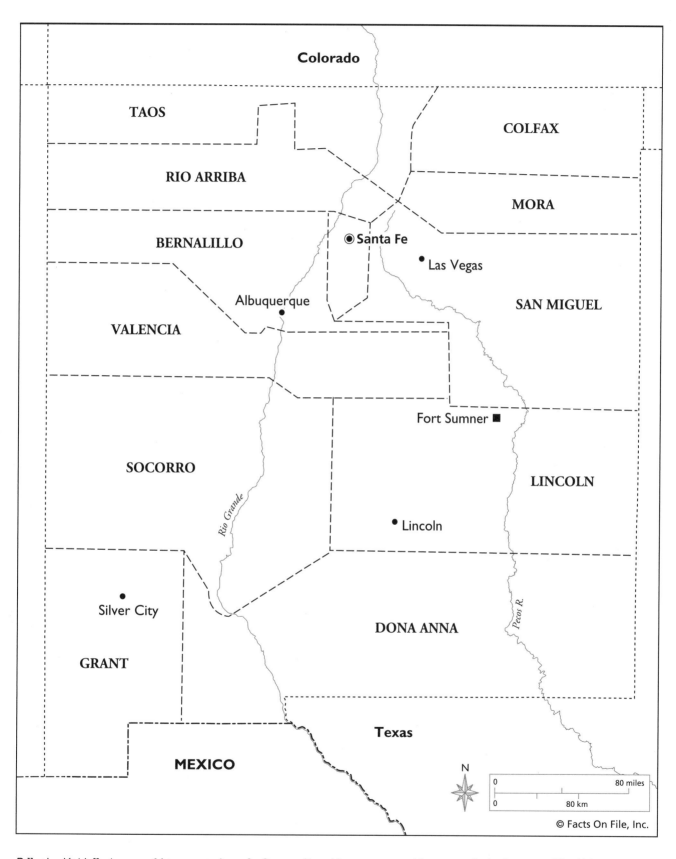

Billy the Kid killed most of his men in Lincoln County, New Mexico, pictured here as it looked in 1883. The Kid was killed in 1881 in Fort Sumner, New Mexico, by Pat Garrett.

murmur on our ears, he went to the fence, jumped it, and walked down towards Maxwell's house. Little as we then suspected it, this man was the Kid.

He had actually gone over to Garrett's friend Maxwell to get some fresh meat from the hunter.

When the Kid, by me unrecognized, left the orchard, I motioned to my companions, and we cautiously retreated a short distance. When we reached the porch in front of the building, I left Poe and McKinney at the end of the porch, about twenty feet from the door of Pete's room, and went in. It was near midnight and Pete was in bed. I walked to the head of the bed and sat down on it, beside him, near the pillow. I asked him as to the whereabouts of the Kid. He said that the Kid had certainly been about, but he did not know whether he had left or not. At that moment a man sprang quickly into the door, looking back, and called twice in Spanish, "Who comes there?" No one replied and he came on it.

Garrett, according to his account, hid near Maxwell's bed. He saw Billy in stocking feet, holding a revolver in his right hand and a butcher knife in his left. He came directly toward Garrett. Before he reached the bed, Garrett whispered, "Who is it, Pete?" but received no reply. It struck Garrett that it might be Pete's brother-in-law, Manuel Abreu, who had seen Poe and McKinney and wanted to know their business. The intruder came close to him, leaned both hands on the bed, his right hand almost touching Garrett's knee, and asked, in a low tone, "Who are they, Pete?" At the same instant, Maxwell whispered to Garrett, "That's him!"

Simultaneously the Kid must have seen, or felt, the presence of a third person at the head of the bed. He raised quickly his pistol, a self-cocker, within a foot of my breast. Retreating rapidly across the room he cried: "Quién es? Quién es?" ["Who's that? Who's that?"] All this occurred in a moment. Quickly as possible I drew my revolver and fired, threw my body aside, and fired again. The Kid fell dead. He never spoke. A struggle or two, a little strangling sound as he gasped for breath, and the Kid was with his many victims.

Garrett's account of the Kid's last moments has been questioned because anyone who knew the Kid knew he would never hesitate to fire at an intruder. As an outlaw, any stranger had to be dealt with as a potential lawman, which meant quickly and with deadly force. Despite this obvious hole in his account, it has never been officially questioned.

See also JOHN DILLINGER (1903–1934); CHARLES ARTHUR FLOYD, A.K.A. "PRETTY BOY" FLOYD (1906–1934); JESSE JAMES (1847–1882); LINCOLN COUNTY, NEW MEXICO (1878–1879); LESTER M. GILLIS, A.K.A. "BABYFACE" NELSON (1908–1935); NEW MEXICO (1877).

Jesse James (1847–1882) bank and train robber

Jesse James was by far the most famous guerrilla who fought with William Quantrill, not because of what he did while he was in the violent man's service but because of what he did later.

Jesse James has never been easy to quantify. Some historians look at him as a murderer, others as a disgruntled former rebel. To his fellow Missourians, he was a hero; to the railroad, a malignant threat. James was actually a criminal innovator, the first American to actually rob a moving train.

The triple accidents of birth, environment, and social conditions had united to produce a highwayman with the élan of Hare, the genius of Murrel, and the psychopathy of the Harps. That James was able to lead the gang that bore his name for a full 16 years while he remained the most hunted man in America is tribute to his criminal abilities. No outlaw before or since has been so successful for such a long period of time.

To understand Jesse is to understand that he would stop at nothing to achieve his goals. His goals were to rob and to inflict pain, the latter on the Yankees that had tried to kill him when he rode with Quantrill and now threatened the very livelihood of his state. With the ever-expanding railroad pushing out Missouri farmers and not always giving them fair price for their land, Jesse used these social conditions as the rationale for his criminal activities.

That rationale might have worked in the beginning, but as Jesse and the James-Younger Gang kept racking up murders, it became clear that any pretense they had as southerners shedding the Yankee Civil War yoke was just garbage they encouraged in the press. Jesse was a master at manipulating the press into believing whatever he said because whenever possible, he gave them full access. Even on his honeymoon in Galveston, Texas, he gave a newspaper interview to a reporter who had tracked him down.

Here was a gang leader that not only had class, but also went out of his way to address his adoring public. Jesse knew that people loved to hear his exciting stories, and he encouraged that by talking out publicly. It was Jesse who began identifying the gang during robberies. He did that by introducing himself.

Jesse loved putting himself in danger. He had been shot twice in the chest, and one of the wounds had never healed properly. It still ached, particularly in cool, damp weather. No matter. How long could he live anyway? He did not worry about it.

When the Civil War began, Jesse's older brother Frank James and his friends, the Younger brothers—Cole and Jim—joined up with Quantrill. Cole and Jim hated northern soldiers because a northern cavalryman had killed their father in a barroom brawl. As for Jesse, he was barely in his teens. He stayed home to tend the farm.

Anyone in Missouri who served with Quantrill was considered an outlaw whose home could be burned down by Union troops in retaliation. In 1863 a Union army detachment invaded the Samuels farm looking for Frank. In response to repeated questions about Frank's whereabouts, young Jesse sassed the northerners, going so far as to attack one of the soldiers. Their response was to beat him and burn the family's farm to the ground.

When he recovered, Jesse sought out Quantrill. At age 17, in 1864 he joined up and was assigned to Bloody Bill Anderson's detachment. His first engagement took place in September 1864 in Centralia, Kansas. Anderson's detachment, which included the James and Younger Brothers, swooped down on the small town.

In a replay of Lawrence, men were dragged from their shops and shot, but Anderson lacked Quantrill's restraint—he allowed his men to rape women in the street. Jesse, whose reputation was that of a gentleman, supposedly did not engage in the latter practice, but he was there when Anderson shot the 26 Union soldiers and did nothing to stop the massacre.

After Anderson was killed, Jesse served directly under Quantrill and developed a reputation as a tough fighting man. During one battle, witnesses saw him riding right into the Union ranks, holding the reins in his teeth and firing pistols from both hands. He shot six northern soldiers and was credited with killing three of them.

Jesse was well liked by Quantrill's men, having an affable personality and dry wit. Once, when cleaning his Remington revolver, he shot off the tip of a finger by accident. "Now ain't that the most dingus-dangest

thing you ever seen?" he asked. After that, Cole Younger nicknamed him "Dingus."

After the death of Quantrill and the surrender of the remainder of his army to northern troops in Kentucky, Jesse and Frank returned home, only to find that the Union forces had struck again. Dr. Samuels, their stepfather, had rebuilt the family homestead after the first attack, but the Union had come back, this time for Jesse and Frank, and once again they had burned the place down.

Before Frank and Jesse could join their family, who had fled for safety to Nebraska, they took to the Missouri hills. On their heels were Union troops searching for any remnants of Quantrill's band. Still considered outlaws, the brothers would be hanged if they were found.

Jesse had some business with a former member of Quantrill's band named Ike Flannery. Ike had inherited several thousand dollars after the war and Jesse killed him for the money. Ike's uncle, George W. Shepard, swore to avenge his nephew's death and did years later, when he killed James Anderson, Bloody Bill Anderson's brother, on the statehouse steps in Austin, Texas.

In April 1865, with the war finally at an end, President Lincoln offered blanket amnesty to all who had fought for the southern cause. In Missouri that meant traveling to the city of Liberty to take a formal oath to the Republic. The James boys decided to do exactly that. Accompanied by Cole Younger, Frank and Jesse set out for Liberty to swear allegiance to the Union, but they never made it.

In Washington John Wilkes Booth had assassinated the president. This made Union troops stationed around the nation vow revenge. In Missouri Union soldiers ambushed the former rebels outside Liberty. In the ensuing gunfight, Jesse took a .36-caliber slug in the rib cage, close to his heart.

Frank and Cole Younger were able to get Jesse to the safety of his family in Nebraska. Thinking he was going to die, Jesse convinced his mother to let him die on southern soil. The family secretly transported him across the border to Harlem, Missouri, to the home of his mother Zerelda's brother, John Mimms.

Dr. Samuels operated on his stepson and saved his life. While convalescing in Mimm's home, Jesse was cared for by his first cousin, 19-year-old Zerelda Mimms, who had been named after her Aunt Zee. Jesse credited his recovery to her care. They fell in love and, despite the fact that they were first cousins, decided that they would eventually marry. First,

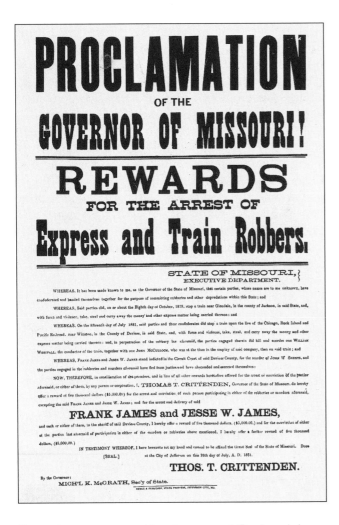

PROCLAMATION

OF THE

GOVERNOR OF MISSOURI!

REWARDS

FOR THE ARREST OF

Express and Train Robbers.

STATE OF MISSOURI, EXECUTIVE DEPARTMENT.

WHEREAS, It has been made known to me, as the Governor of the State of Missouri, that certain parties, whose names are to me unknown, have confederated and banded themselves together for the purpose of committing robberies and other depredations within this State; and

WHEREAS, Said parties did, on or about the Eighth day of October, 1879, stop a train near Glendale, in the county of Jackson, in said State, and, with force and violence, take, steal and carry away the money and other express matter being carried thereon; and

WHEREAS, On the fifteenth day of July 1881, said parties and their confederates did stop a train upon the line of the Chicago, Rock Island and Pacific Railroad, near Winston, in the County of Daviess, in said State, and, with force and violence, take, steal, and carry away the money and other express matter being carried thereon; and, in perpetration of the robbery last aforesaid, the parties engaged therein did kill and murder one WILLIAM WESTFALL, the conductor of the train, together with one JOHN McCULLOCH, who was at the time in the employ of said company, then on said train; and

WHEREAS, FRANK JAMES and JESSE W. JAMES stand indicted in the Circuit Court of said Daviess County, for the murder of JOHN W. SHEETS, and the parties engaged in the robberies and murders aforesaid have fled from justice and have absconded and secreted themselves;

NOW, THEREFORE, in consideration of the premises, and in lieu of all other rewards heretofore offered for the arrest or conviction of the parties aforesaid, or either of them, by any person or corporation, I, THOMAS T. CRITTENDEN, Governor of the State of Missouri, do hereby offer a reward of five thousand dollars ($5,000.00) for the arrest and conviction of each person participating in either of the robberies or murders aforesaid, excepting the said FRANK JAMES and JESSE W. JAMES; and for the arrest and delivery of said

FRANK JAMES and JESSE W. JAMES,

and each or either of them, to the sheriff of said Daviess County, I hereby offer a reward of five thousand dollars, ($5,000.00,) and for the conviction of either of the parties last aforesaid of participation in either of the murders or robberies above mentioned, I hereby offer a further reward of five thousand dollars, ($5,000.00.)

IN TESTIMONY WHEREOF, I have hereunto set my hand and caused to be affixed the Great Seal of the State of Missouri. Done [SEAL.] at the City of Jefferson on this 28th day of July, A. D. 1881.

THOS. T. CRITTENDEN.

By the Governor:
MICH'L K. McGRATH, Sec'y of State.

Rewards were promised for the arrest of Frank and Jesse James. (Author's collection)

though, Jesse had some unfinished business with the North.

For the next 16 years, Jesse led a gang composed of former guerrillas and other murderers in attacking banks, stagecoaches, and trains. While he was making his legend, Jesse made sure to thoroughly separate his personal from his professional life.

In his personal life he used various aliases, the best-known being Tom Howard, which he was using at the time of his death. His wife Zee knew what he did, but it never mattered; like a true outlaw's wife, she loved him for the loving husband and gentle father he was. And Jesse was all that. He had three children, and some of Jesse James's great-grandchildren are still alive today.

After the disastrous Northfield, Minnesota, raid in 1876, Jesse's criminal star began to wane. There

were a few more robberies. By 1881 the remainder of the gang was working at their criminal trade infrequently. Frank had married and was living in Tennessee under an assumed name and Jesse and Zee had moved to St. Joseph, Missouri, where he hid in plain sight as the businessman Tom Howard.

Jesse began to grow restless for the old life. Into the gang's decimated ranks he enlisted Bob and Charlie Ford, two untried distant cousins. Unknown to Jesse, the Ford brothers made a deal with Missouri governor Crittenden to collect the $10,000 bounty on the outlaws' heads.

On April 3, 1882, Bob and Charlie Ford came to Jesse's house to discuss an impending robbery. After going over some of the particulars, Jesse noticed that a framed picture on the wall that said "Home Sweet Home" was crooked. Jesse turned his back to the Fords, put a chair against the wall, and mounted it to right the picture. The time was about 8:27 A.M.

That was Bob Ford's chance.

The bullet from Bob Ford's gun entered Jesse's head below the right ear and lodged in the frontal bone near the left ear. The bullet knocked him back into the wall. He fell to the floor with a bounce that laid him on his back. By that time, he was already dead.

Hearing the commotion, Zee ran in from the next room and shouted, "What have you done?" The Fords did not wait to reply, but fled.

In the wake of Jesse's death, many stories circulated that it was a fake and that the great outlaw was really still alive. But the man who identified Jesse's body in the town mortuary was Captain Harrison B. Trow, who had fought with Jesse under Quantrill. A later disinterment in 1995 also confirmed Jesse's identity.

Contrary to legend, Frank James did not swear vengeance. Instead, he surrendered his weapons personally to Governor Crittenden. He would subsequently be tried on any number of criminal charges and in each case was fully acquitted.

As for the Fords, they were tried and convicted for Jesse's murder and sentenced to hang. Governor Crittenden intervened with a full pardon and the reward money.

Charlie could not live with the guilt. A few years later, he committed suicide. After going back east to star in a vaudeville melodrama, *How I Shot Jesse James,* Bob Ford drifted out to Colorado, where he had the misfortune to make the acquaintance of Jefferson "Soapy" Smith, who had him killed over a disagreement.

See also CLYDE CHAMPION BARROW AND BONNIE PARKER; "BLOODY KANSAS"; JOHN BROWN; JOHN

DILLINGER; CHARLES ARTHUR FLOYD, A.K.A. "PRETTY BOY" FLOYD; LESTER M. GILLIS, A.K.A. "BABY FACE NELSON"; INDIANA AND KANSAS (1868–1874); JAMES-YOUNGER GANG; LINCOLN COUNTY, NEW MEXICO (1877); NEW MEXICO (1878–1879); WILLIAM QUANTRILL; SALEM, OREGON (1902).

James-Younger Gang (1866–1881)

The James-Younger Gang became the prototype for the depression-era gangsters of the 1930s. They were even more efficient in their ability to rob with impunity and success. The James-Younger Gang Homepage on the Web credits the gang with the "jobs" listed in the table to the right.

The total take from all those robberies amounts to $262,200 in Union dollars, a fortune in those days, millions by today's standards. That easily qualifies the gang as the most successful in criminal history. Jesse James's robbery of the Chicago, Rock Island and Pacific Railroad near Adair, Iowa, on July 21, 1873, is credited with the first train robbery.

Rumors had spread through the frontier that a large gold shipment in the amount of $75,000 was aboard the train. Jesse sent Frank James and Cole Younger to Omaha to learn when the gold shipment was to reach Adair, an isolated spot Jesse had singled out for the robbery. He stayed behind, camped in the hills above Adair, with four other members of the gang—Jim and Tom Younger, Clell Miller, and Bill Chadwell. The latter two had also murdered with Quantrill.

When Frank James and Cole Younger got their tip that the gold shipment was on its way east, they rode back to Adair and told Jesse, who laid the plans for the train robbery. The afternoon of the robbery, July 21, 1873, the James-Younger Gang called at the railroad section maintenance house. Splitting up, some of them distracted Mrs. Robert Grant, wife of the section foreman. They posed as workmen, and she gave them some pies and other food while in the back, the rest of the robbers broke into a handcar house and stole a spike bar and hammer.

Down at the railroad bed, Jesse picked out a secluded spot between Council Bluffs and Des Moines. There was not a house for miles. The prairie was broken up into ravines and sloughs that were almost impassable except to expert horsemen like the James-Younger Gang.

Using the stolen spike bar and hammer, they pried off a fishplate connecting two rails and pulled out the spikes. This was on a curve of the railroad track

west of Adair, near the Turkey Creek bridge on old U.S. Highway No. 6 (now County Road G30). A rope was tied on the west end of the disconnected north rail. The rope was passed under the south rail and led to a hole they had cut in the bank in which to hide.

It was barely dark, around 8 P.M. when the train came around the bend. The rail was jerked out of place and the engine plunged into the ditch and toppled over on its side. Engineer John Rafferty of Des Moines was crushed when he fell out and the train landed on top of him. Fireman Dennis Foley was also injured in the wreck and later died of his injuries. Several other passengers were injured as well.

Jesse and Frank James climbed into the express car. Pulling their guns, they forced John Burgess, the guard, to open the safe. Anticipating the biggest payday of their young careers, they pushed Burgess aside. Inside the safe, they found only $2,000 in currency. It turned out that their information was wrong. The gold shipment was on the next train down the line. So it was not total loss, the gang went through the

Date	Location	Event	Amount
February 13, 1866	Liberty, Mo.	Clay County Savings Association	$62,000
October 30, 1866	Lexington, Mo.	Alexander Mitchell and Co. Bank	$2,000
March 20, 1868	Russellville, Ky.	Nimrod Long Banking Co.	$14,000
December 7, 1869	Gallatin, Mo.	Daviess County Savings Bank	$700
June 3, 1871	Corydon, Iowa	Ocobock Brothers' Bank	$6,000
April 29, 1872	Columbia, Ky.	Bank of Columbia	$600
September 26, 1872	Kansas City	Kansas City Exposition Ticket Office	$10,000
May 27, 1873	St. Genevieve, Mo.	Ste. Genevieve Savings Bank	$4,100
July 21, 1873	Adair, Iowa	Chicago, Rock Island and Pacific Railroad	$6,000
January 15, 1874	Hot Springs, Ark.	Stagecoach	$3,000
January 31, 1874	Gad's Hill, Mo.	Iron Mountain Railroad	$12,000
April 1874	Austin, Tx.	Stagecoach	$3,000
December 8, 1874	Muncie, Ks.	Kansas Pacific Railroad	$55,000
September 5, 1875	Huntington, W. Va.	Bank	$10,000
July 7, 1876	Rockey Cut, Mo.	Missouri Pacific Railroad	$15,000
September 7, 1876	Northfield, Minn.	First National Bank	
October 8, 1879	Glendale, Mo.	Chicago and Alton Railroad	$40,000
September 3, 1880	Mammoth Cave, Ky.	Stagecoach	$1,800
March 11, 1881	Muscle Shoals, Ala.	Government Paymaster	
July 15, 1881	Winston, Mo.	Chicago, Rock Island and Pacific Railroad	$2,000
September 7, 1881	Glendale, Mo.	Chicago and Alton Railroad	$15,000

A LIST OF THE PEOPLE INJURED OR KILLED BY THE JAMES-YOUNGER GANG

ASKEW, DAN
Found dead April 12, 1875. A neighbor of the James family, he was believed to have hidden Pinkerton spy Jack Ladd. This is believed to be a revenge killing for the January Pinkerton bombing of the James farm.

BUNKER, A. E.
Assistant Cashier at Northfield, Minnesota. Shot in shoulder, recovered.

DANIELS, EDWIN/EDWARD
Pinkerton agent shot and killed while trying to apprehend the Youngers.

GRIFFEN, B. G., SR.
Killed May 22, 1867, at Richmond, Missouri. The father of Frank Griffen, he was shot twice while trying to come to his son's assistance.

GRIFFEN, FRANK S.
Killed May 22, 1867, at Richmond, Missouri. He was shot in the head.

GUSTAVSON, NICHOLAS
Killed September 7, 1876, Northfield, Minnesota. A Swedish immigrant who could not speak English, he was shot in the street during the Northfield robbery.

HEYWOOD, JOSEPH L.
Killed September 7, 1876, Northfield, Minnesota. Frank allegedly shot him after Jesse threatened to cut his throat.

LADD, JACK
He was believed to be a Pinkerton spy who worked for Dan Askew. His murder is commonly believed to be a revenge killing for the January Pinkerton bombing of the James farm.

LONG, NIMROD
Scalp wound March 20, 1868, Russellville, Kentucky. Recovered.

LULL, CAPTAIN LOUIS J.
Also known as W. J. Allen, he was a Chicago Pinkerton agent who was shot and killed trying to catch the Youngers.

MARTIN, R. A. C.
Killed April 29, 1872. He was a cashier at a Columbia, Kentucky, bank that the gang robbed.

McCLAIN, JUDGE JOHN
Shot in the arm March 2, 1867, during the attempted Savannah, Missouri, robbery. He eventually recovered.

RAFFERTY, JOHN
Killed July 21, 1873. Engineer of the train during the Adair robbery, he was crushed when the engine derailed and overturned.

SHAW, JOHN B.
Killed May 2, 1867. Shot in the chest during the Richmond bank robbery.

SHEETS, JOHN W.
Killed December 7, 1869. Shot in head during the bank robbery at Gallatin, Missouri. It is believed he was shot because he was mistaken for Major S. P. Cox, the man who killed one of Jesse's mentors, Captain Bill Anderson.

SMALL GIRL
Shot in the leg September 26, 1872, at the Kansas City Exposition. She recovered, but her name is not recorded.

WESTFALL, WILLIAM
Killed July 15, 1881. He was the conductor of the train held up by the gang at Winston, Missouri, shot twice. It was alleged that he brought the Pinkertons to the James farm for the assault on January 25, 1875.

WHICHER, JOHN W.
Killed in 1874. He was a Pinkerton detective, and no one was ever charged with his murder, though it was widely suspected that the James Gang was responsible.

WYMORE, GEORGE "JOLLY"
Killed February 13, 1866. He was shot in front of the Green Hotel after the Clay County Savings Association bank robbery in Liberty, Missouri. His family later reported that it received a letter of apology from Jesse James.

wrecked passenger cars and collected about $3,000 in currency and loot from the passengers.

The robbery had actually been a failure, but the newspapers had a field day. The *Daily Iowa State Register* edition of Tuesday, July 22, 1873, gave it extensive coverage:

The C. R. I. & P. R.R. train, due here in Des Moines from the west last night at 10:30 o'clock did not arrive on time, and about 11 o'clock the news spread over the city that it had been attacked, ditched and sacked by a masked gang of robbers, half-way between Anita and Adair, 61 miles west of Des Moines. The first dispatch received was about 10:30 o'clock, from superintendent.

The account went on to describe the robbery's particulars. The way the robbery was finally reported, Levy Clay, a railroad employee on the train,

walked to Casey [a nearby town] where the alarm was sent by a telegrapher to Des Moines and Omaha, and soon the news was spread all over the nation. A train loaded with armed men left Council Bluffs for Adair and dropped small detachments of men along the route where saddled horses were waiting. The trail of the outlaws was traced into Missouri where they split up and were sheltered by friends.

None of the train robbers announced their identity, but Jesse James's identity was established quite early in the investigation. From the *Council Bluffs Nonpareil*, July 25, 1873:

The man that seemed to be the leader is described as follows: He is about five feet seven or eight inches high, has light hair, blue eyes, heavy sandy whiskers, broad shoulders, straight and tolerably short nose, a little turned up, tolerably high broad forehead, intelligent looking, and looked like a tolerable well educated man, and did not look like a working man, from 36 to 40 years old.

This was Jesse James.

The second man was tall and slender, light complected, rather delicate looking, had a high forehead, not very broad, light brown hair, very long, and light whiskers, inclined to be sandy, he was near six feet high, long slender hands, and did not look as though he had ever done any work in his life, his nose is a little Roman, he had blue eyes, he looked like a man who was well educated, was very polite, and not inclined to talk much, he was from 36 to 40 years old, he was dressed in light clothes.

This was Frank James. Accurate descriptions followed of Cole Younger, Jim Younger, and Tom Younger.

The same newspaper reported on July 29, 1873:

From a detective who had been in pursuit of the robbers of Chicago, Rock Island and Pacific road, the St. Joseph Herald, *gets these statements:*

Two of the gang are the James boys, of Clay County, Mo., the same party which robbed the Chariton and Clarendon banks; one of them is of the Rambo party which attempted to rob the Chillicothe bank, and the other two are supposed to belong to Pattonsburg, or Chillicothe.

The article then tracked the gang's escape across the country.

This Jesse James is known to be the chief of the gang of robbers which is a terror from their headquarters in Clay County to Sherman, Tex. Indeed, when it is known that they have committed any depredations, everyone gives up further effort to capture them.

The gang was never captured after the Adair robbery and charges were never brought. Interestingly, during their earlier robberies, the gang did not identify itself. Law enforcement was left to do that. From the *St. Louis Times*, July 25, 1873, reprinted in the *Carthage Banner*, Carthage, Missouri, Thursday, August 7, 1873:

Information was received yesterday at the police headquarters which taken with facts before known, leave not the shadow of doubt but that several members of the party who robbed the train on the Chicago, Rock Island and Pacific Railroad near Adair, Iowa, on Monday night, were the gang who robbed the Ste. Genevieve Bank last May and have been connected with other villainies of a similar character, perpetrated during the past three or four years.

The members of the band were almost without exception engaged on one side or the other in the Southwest during the civil contest, and know the wilds . . . of Osage country, and all Missouri, foot by foot. Osage township, Jackson county, is the rendezvous for several of them, and when not on the war path they range around in the east part of Jackson, the west of Clay, and the wilder portion of Ray and Lafayette counties. They have homes there where their families live and cultivate small farms. All about them are relatives and friends who, although they would not

Jesse James was a lad that killed a many a man,
He robbed the Glendale train;
But that dirty little coward that shot Mister Howard,
Has laid poor Jesse in his grave.

CHORUS:
Poor Jesse had a wife to mourn for his life,
Three children, they were brave,
But that dirty little coward that shot Mister Howard,
Has laid poor Jesse in his grave.

It was Robert Ford, that dirty little coward,
I wonder how does he feel?
For he ate of Jesse's bread and he slept in Jesse's bed
And laid poor Jesse in his grave.

It was his brother Frank who robbed the Gallatin bank
And carried the money from the town;
It was in this very place that they had a little race
For they shot Captain Sheets to the ground.

They went to the crossing not very far from there
And there they did the same;
With the agent on his knees, he delivered up the keys
To the outlaws Frank and Jesse James.

It was on a Wednesday night, the moon was shining bright,
They robbed the Glendale train;
The people they did say for many miles away,
It was robbed by Frank and Jesse James.

He robbed from the rich and was a friend to the poor;
He had a heart and a hand and a brain.
With his brother Frank, he robbed the Northfield bank
And stopped the Glendale train.

It was on a Saturday night, Jesse was at home,
Talking to his family brave,
Robert Ford came along like a thief in the night
And laid poor Jesse in his grave.

The people held their breath, when they heard of Jesse's death
and wondered how he ever came to die;
It was one of the gang, called little Robert Ford,
He shot poor Jesse on the sly.

Jesse went to his rest with his hand on his breast;
The devil will be upon his face.

be guilty of such deeds, with shield the perpetrators of them to the last.

Whoever the reporter was, he got it right on the money. Not only was the James Gang responsible for the robbery alluded to in the article, but Jesse made sure to regularly share some of the spoils from the gang's robberies with his neighbors, essentially as a bribe for them to keep their mouths shut. In that way, he could continue to live in his hometown, Kearney, and his home county, Clay, with impunity.

The *Daily Iowa State Register* concluded of the Adair robbery:

The robbers had calculated that there would be an extra large expressage, not knowing that the Sunday expressage had passed over the road Sunday night. The robbers held their guns to John Burgess' head while they went through the safe. Frank Cox, the road master, who is at the wreck, has organized, ready to start at daylight this morning, on the track of the robbers, a mounted troop of forty men. SS. Stevens, agent of the C. R. I. & P. R.R. at Council Bluffs, sends out this morning an engine on the Northwestern and one over the B & M road, carrying posses of men, hoping to interrupt robbers. He will also send men on the regular trains in all directions.

Coverage both laudatory and critical would follow the gang throughout their careers. The next big event in the gang's life came in 1876.

THE GREAT NORTHFIELD, MINNESOTA, RAID (1876)

Charley Miller, a recently inducted gang member, came up with the idea of robbing the bank in his hometown of Northfield, Minnesota. The plan Miller proposed was essentially a replay of a robbery the gang had committed in Kentucky a few years before when they held up a rather flush bank. Miller argued that a similar job could be done in Northfield with equal or even better success. The gang could get in and out before the townspeople had a chance to react.

Things did not work out as Miller predicted. On September 7, 1876, the James-Younger Gang attempted to rob the First National Bank of Northfield. The townsfolk, realizing what was happening, armed themselves and opened fire on the bandits as they attempted to flee. Gang members Charley Pitts and Bill Chadwell were killed. Cole, Jim, and Bob Younger were literally shot to pieces. Jesse and Frank escaped unscathed.

Outside the town, the robbers split up, with the Jameses returning safely to Missouri. The Youngers, though, were not so lucky. Captured two weeks later, they were tried and sentenced to prison. While Jesse and Frank would continue to lead a reconstituted gang, they were never as successful after Northfield and effectively ceased operations with Jesse's death in 1882.

Both Jim and Cole Younger were paroled from prison in 1902. Cole would go on to become an evangelist and died at Lee's Summit, Missouri, in 1916. But Jim had a hard time on the outside. He couldn't cope with it. Jim Younger was found dead of a bullet wound to the head on October 19, 1902. It was officially ruled a suicide. Even to the end, Jim Younger was a lawbreaker.

Frank James would be tried for robbery and murder on the Chicago, Rock Island and Pacific Railroad at Winston, Missouri, in 1881. Acquitted, he never served a day in jail and died on February 18, 1915.

See also CLYDE CHAMPION BARROW AND BONNIE PARKER; "BLOODY KANSAS"; JOHN DILLINGER; CHARLES ARTHUR FLOYD, A.K.A. "PRETTY BOY" FLOYD; LESTER M. GILLIS, A.K.A. "BABY FACE NELSON"; INDIANA AND KANSAS (1868–1879); JESSE JAMES; LINCOLN COUNTY, NEW MEXICO (1877); NEW MEXICO (1878–1879); WILLIAM QUANTRILL; SALEM, OREGON (1902).

Frisco, New Mexico (1884) Elfego Baca and the battle in the plaza

Elfego Baca stands alone at the summit of American crime. He was a man who actually killed in the name of the law when he was not, in fact, a peace officer. What happened after those killings would make Baca a legend in the Old West of the 19th century.

Legend has it that Elfego Baca's mother was playing in a baseball game in 1865 when she leaped up to spear a line drive. When she came down, the story goes, "Elfego entered the ball game!" What is indisputable is that Baca was born in 1865 in Socorro, New Mexico, when it was a sleepy little southwestern town that served the army post at Fort Craig.

Shortly after Elfego's birth, his father moved the family to Kansas, where he lived until his early teens, when the Baca family moved back to Socorro. Since Baca's last visit, it had become a center of trade and all the criminal vices that go with that—drinking, gambling, prostitution, and, of course, murder.

In the interim, silver had been discovered in the nearby Magadalena Mountains. Mining interests had moved in from the East and Midwest. What had once been a distant outpost of civilization was now a mining town with up to 3,000 miners based there at any one time.

The nearest big town was Frisco, 125 miles away from Socorro, where the cowboys from the local ranches came to burn off steam. Whenever they came to Frisco, the town's citizens stayed out of their way. They knew that whiskey and guns just did not mix. Between both Socorro and Frisco, there were scores of murders, drug dealings, crooked card games, claim jumping, robbery, thievery, every conceivable kind of criminal behavior. It was an explosive situation.

In October 1884 a group of cowboys from the Slaughter Ranch came to Frisco to tie one on. Relations between the Hispanics and whites were always tense, with the whites treating the Hispanics as second-class citizens. The cowboys took it to the next level, brutalizing the Hispanics because of their skin color and heritage.

The deputy sheriff, Pedro Sarracino, was overmatched. He was one against many. Not knowing what to do, he got on his horse and rode the 125 miles to Socorro to appeal to Baca for help. Baca was a cocky 19-year-old, an expert with a Colt .45 who styled himself as a champion of his people. He wanted to be a lawman and had fashioned himself a crude badge that he planned to pin on when the time was right.

Baca rode back to Frisco with Sarracino and the two talked to the justice of peace. The judge felt that the cowboys, who numbered as many as 150, could not be stopped. It was just too dangerous. They had too many guns. Nevertheless, Baca promptly arrested one of the cowboys. His friends demanded his release. Instead, Baca told them he would count to three before he shot. When he fired they ran, but one man and his horse were hit. The next morning about 80 cowboys returned.

ALBUQUERQUE, NEW MEXICO (1936): BACA SPEAKS

Interviews with Old West gunfighters by 20th-century journalists are rare. Most were dead by the time American journalism came of age in the 1920s. Those who survived, like Wyatt Earp, tended to excise those parts of their lives that were criminal. Bat Masterson told the truth, but no one believed him.

In 1936 journalist Janet Smith interviewed Elfego Baca as part of the Works Progress Administration's (WPA) Federal Writers Project, an attempt by the presidential administration of Franklin Delano Roosevelt to make sure that such eyewitnesses to history as Baca had their stories taken down accurately. Janet Smith interviewed Baca in his office in 1936. At the time, Elfego was 71.

"I never wanted to kill anybody," said Elfego Baca. "But if a man had it in his mind to kill me, I made it my business to get him first."

That day in 1884 when the cowboys from the Slaughter Ranch came to get their buddy whom Baca had arrested, they fired first. Baca claimed he took refuge in a log house and returned fire through the large open chinks in the structure.

The cowboys attempted to burn the place, but the roof refused to ignite. They tried dynamiting the building, but it held tough and Baca kept on shooting. Because the floor of the cabin was below the ground, he was able to duck down and let the bullets fly uselessly over his head. Occasionally, he would lift his head up, take careful aim, and fire.

After 33 hours of battle, Baca had killed four and wounded eight. Eventually, a group of townspeople he trusted convinced him to surrender to civil authorities.

"I surrendered only on condition that I keep my guns. They placed six guards over me but they rode 25 steps ahead of me to Socorro," Baca recalled.

But before the party left for Socorro, where Baca had agreed to let the courts try him for murder, he ate dinner with some men, including Jim Cook.

"Jim Cook was one that was shooting at me. He was a pretty tough man but he came near getting it."

At Socorro, he was tried twice for murder and both times acquitted. The star piece of evidence for the defense was the door of the log cabin, which contained more than 400 bullet holes. Years later, as an old man, Cook would send Baca a picture of himself that he inscribed: "To Elfego Baca in memory of that day in Frisco."

See also NEW MEXICO (1894).

Haymarket Square, Chicago (1886) the first dynamite bomb

No revolver of the period had more than six cylinders, which meant only six bullets could be fired at a time. But what if you were a criminal who was not a dead shot and you wanted to kill more than six people at a time? The criminal's ability to kill en masse did not exist until 1866, when Alfred Nobel invented dynamite in Helenborg, Sweden.

The historic record is not clear on who was the first thief to use dynamite in the United States to blast into a safe or vault. However, the use of the first dynamite bomb to kill people in America is well documented. That distinction belongs to what has become known as the Haymarket Affair.

It began on May 3, 1886, with the strike of workers at the McCormick Reaper Works in Chicago. Attempting to break up the strike, police officers fired into a crowd of striking workers. Several were killed and wounded. The next evening, socialist and anarchist labor leaders held a meeting of the workingmen near Haymarket Square. The meeting's speakers incited the crowd to action, denouncing the police shootings. They implored the workers to continue their struggle for an eight-hour workday and other improvements in working conditions.

The meeting was breaking up when police, under the command of Captain William Ward and Inspector John Bonfield, arrived on the scene. Trying to disperse the crowd with force rather than words, the police aroused the workers' anger. Someone, threw a dynamite bomb into the crowd of police. One cop was killed and many others injured. The story was front page news across the country.

Public opinion leapt against the radical left, resulting in, according to the Library of Congress, "the first 'Red Scare' in America." Eight prominent Chicago anarchists were arrested and charged with conspiracy to murder. Although there was no evidence to tie any of them to the bombing, they were convicted after the jury deliberated only three hours. One defendant got 15 years in prison, the rest, death.

On November 11, 1887, four were hanged. One escaped the hangman's noose by committing suicide. The remaining two had their sentences commuted by the governor to life in prison. But one fact had been lost: For the first recorded time in America, dynamite had been used in furtherance of a criminal act—it had been used to kill. The criminal precedent had been irretrievably established. Now, criminals had a state-of-the-art weapon in their arsenal.

See also ASSASSINATION OF PRESIDENT GARFIELD (JULY–SEPTEMBER 1881); BALTIMORE, MARYLAND (1844): JOHN BROWNING; HENRY FORD; PATERSON, NEW JERSEY (1836).

Kansas's Dalton Gang (1890–1892) train and bank robbers

No matter how much the frontier pushed westward, Kansas, even as the 20th century drew to a close, remained a hotbed of criminal activity. It was the state that bred the Dalton Brothers.

Raised in Coffeyville, Kansas, in the southwestern portion of the state, the Dalton Brothers—Frank, Grat, Bill, Bob, and the baby of the bunch, Emmett—did not start out as outlaws. The oldest brother, Frank, was a federal deputy marshal, killed in a gun battle with the Smith-Dixon Gang in 1887. Upon their brother's death, Grat and Bob came home from California and assumed the family mantle.

In 1889 Grat was commissioned a deputy town marshal for the Muskogee (Oklahoma Territory) court. Bob Dalton was appointed a deputy marshal for the federal court in Wichita, Kansas, working in the Osage Indian Nation. Emmett occasionally worked as a lawman and helped his brothers out by joining their posses, but he made his main living as a cowboy hiring out to the highest bidder.

Emmett got a job at the X Bar Ranch near the Pawnee Indian Agency, where he met up with two cowboys who would become gang members: Bill Doolin and William St. Power, who also used the aliases "Bill Powers" and "Tom Evans." A friendly sort, Emmett also made the acquaintance of cowboys who worked on nearby ranches, including Charlie Pierce, George "Bitter Creek" Newcombe, Charlie Bryant, and Richard (Dick) Broadwell, alias "Texas Jack" or "John Moore." All would eventually become members of the Dalton Gang.

The Dalton family luck began to change in the late 1880s when Bob Dalton, at that time head of the Osage police, was accused of selling whiskey to the Indians. Grat Dalton also had his troubles, and was fired for conduct unbecoming a federal officer. The brothers were at a loss. It did not take long for them to see which side of the law, at that moment, presented the most economic opportunity. Unlike the Earps, they had been committed to the law and they felt betrayed by it.

In July 1890 Bob, Grat, and Emmett were accused of horse stealing in Idaho Territory. The Dalton Brothers fled the law and escaped to California, where they rendezvoused with brother Bill.

Ever since the James Gang had invented railroad robbery, it had become a popular method of increasing one's "poke," or take. On the night of February 6, 1891, the Southern Pacific Railroad was robbed at Alila, California. The Daltons stood accused of the crime. The peripatetic brothers fled once again. Emmett and Bob made it to safety; Grat and Bill were arrested.

Federal marshals tracked Bob and Emmett back to Indian Territory. They hid in the Indian nations, where they met up with Emmett's old cowboy friends, Charlie Bryant and Bitter Creek Newcombe. That was the official beginning of the Dalton Gang. Soon they were identified while robbing a train in Wharton, Oklahoma Territory. They netted $1,800, but Charlie Bryant was captured and killed about a month after the robbery, leaving the Dalton Gang short one man.

Once again Emmett's cowboy buddies came to his assistance. Bob and Emmett, accompanied by Bitter Creek Newcombe, Bill Powers, Dick Broadwell, Charlie Pierce, and Bill Doolin, stopped, boarded, and robbed the Katy train at Leliaetta, Indian Territory (later Oklahoma). Their take that night, September 15, 1891, was $2,500.

Back in California, on July 3, 1891, Grat Dalton was found guilty of the Alila train robbery. Before he could be sentenced, he escaped from jail on September 18 and fled back to Indian Territory, where he joined his brothers' gang.

On July 14, 1892, the Dalton Gang struck again near Adair, Iowa Territory, the site 19 years earlier of the first train robbery committed by the James Gang. The Daltons stopped, boarded, and robbed the train before the deputies on board were even aware that anything was happening. The outlaws managed to escape unharmed, but not before one civilian was killed and another injured.

Now the Dalton brothers were intent on one big score.

On October 5, 1892, the Dalton Gang rode into their hometown of Coffeyville, Kansas. Disguised with phony wigs and beards were Grat Dalton, Emmett Dalton, Bob Dalton, Bill Powers, and Dick Broadwell.

The goal that day was to rob two banks at the same time—the First National Bank and the C. Condon Bank. No one had ever done that before. If they were successful, they would steal enough money on which to retire from robbery. They would also make history.

The original plan was to tie up their horses outside the banks. That did not work because the hitching rail they intended to use had been removed for civic improvements. Instead, they parked their horses in a nearby alley.

Crossing the town's plaza, the gang split up. Three went in one bank, two into the other. David Elliot, editor of the local newspaper and an eyewitness to the unfolding events, described what happened next.

Realizing what was happening, the townspeople armed themselves and were ready for a showdown with the bank robbers. While this was going on outside, the Condon Bank Powers, Broadwell, and Grat Dalton forced three employees at gunpoint to fill a sack with money. Deciding that was not enough, the gang demanded that the safe be opened. A teller lied to the robbers, telling them it was on a time lock and could not be opened for another 10 minutes. Dalton decided they would wait.

The townspeople opened fire from outside the Condon Bank. Bill Powers and Dick Broadwell replied from the inside. Grat Dalton tried using hostages to get out the front door, only to be met by a fusillade of shots.

In the First National Bank, Bob and Emmett Dalton had forced the bank employees to fill their sack with money from the teller trays. Hearing the shots from the townspeople outside, Bob made the decision to use some of the bank employees as human shields. He ordered three bankers to walk out from behind the counter in front of him and stand at the front door.

As soon as Grat Dalton, Dick Broadwell, and Bill Powers left the Condon Bank, they came under fire. Grat Dalton and Bill Powers each received mortal wounds before retreating 20 steps. Dick Broadwell was shot and killed as he attempted to run.

Bob and Emmett Dalton successfully escaped the First National Bank, only to be fired upon moments later. Bob was shot and killed by a Coffeyville resident. Emmett, though also seriously wounded, would survive his wounds and be sentenced to state prison. He would next be heard from in 1907. As for the remainder of the Dalton Gang, they were just getting started.

See also DOOLIN GANG; JAMES-YOUNGER GANG.

Detroit, Michigan (1892) Ford invents the automobile

Born in 1863, Henry Ford had the dream of designing a horseless carriage. As early as age 16, working on his father's Dearborn, Michigan, farm, he showed extraordinary mechanical aptitude. By 1890 he was working as a machinist and engineer for the Edison Company in Detroit. Ford continued working on his own as well until finally, in 1892, he completed his first automobile.

Not until the 20th century did mass production by Ford and his eventual competitors cause the invention to become the revolutionary means of locomotion that it did. But that day in 1892 Ford was also laying the groundwork for a unique innovation in criminal enterprise.

The ability to fire a weapon from a moving vehicle would revolutionize the way criminals did business. By the 1930s the image of the gangster firing a Tommy gun from a moving auto would become indelibly imposed on the national psyche as an example of American crime at its worst.

But that was all in the future. For now, horses would have to suffice as a means of transportation.

See also JOHN BROWN; PATERSON, NEW JERSEY (1836).

H. H. Holmes (1861–1896) Philadelphia's serial killer

Philadelphia's H. H. Holmes was the most efficient serial killer of his time. After his capture, when a newspaper paid him money for a confession, he claimed to have killed 27 people. Some would say he was a monumental liar, but considering the evidence of his crimes found at his residence, it is a figure that is hard to dispute.

H. H. Holmes was described in the pamphlet that laid out his crimes "as a man of ordinary height and full beard. He dressed in the latest of fashions, had flawless manners, and continually wore a smile that showed his teeth and gave his face a revolting expression. His eyes seemed lit with a dark Satanic light that occasionally changed slightly in color."

The crime scene for all of Holmes's murders, was his home, which newspapers called "the Castle." It was located at 701 63rd Street, in the middle of the City of Brotherly Love. Holmes had designed it himself and selected workmen to do the construction who could keep their mouths shut, because what he was really building was a place to commit murder after murder.

The Castle was three stories high. From Holmes's third-floor bedroom, a secret stairway reached the street and the basement. The bedroom also had a trapdoor. Underneath was a chute running from the roof to the cellar—he never knew where he might want to kill someone, so he made it efficient.

There was a blind wall between the stairs and the chute, essentially a secret passageway. The third floor also had a grouping of trapdoors but the pièce de resistance was on the first floor, which had secret, airtight vaults where Holmes could store the bodies of the victims that he had lured to the Castle and then killed. Still, the greatest discovery that policemen would make upon their examination of the Castle was the basement.

H. H. Holmes (Clements Library, University of Michigan)

Holmes had had his workmen install two sheet iron tanks that covered the entire cellar floor. A writer recounted, "When the police searched the tanks, in one they found in the bottom a white fluid which gave forth an overpowering odor. In the other they found bones, that were late identified as human."

Holmes filled the tanks with acid to dissolve his victims. The bones were all that was left.

Holmes was arrested on September 28, 1894. He had romanced a woman named Carrie Pietzal and then killed her and her five children: Alice, Nellie, Howard, Desire, and the baby, Wharton. He was tried and convicted of their murders and sentenced to death.

At Philadelphia's Mommensing Prison, at 10:12 A.M. on May 7, 1896, the Commonwealth of Pennsylvania hanged Holmes until he was dead.

See also KANSAS TERRITORY (1871–1873); THE WESTERN FRONTIER (1790–1800).

New Mexico (1894) forensics solves murders

After the shootout in Frisco, Elfego Baca became the self-appointed sheriff of Socorro County. One of the most famous cases he worked on during his term in office was that of the Manzano Gang.

As Baca told Janet Smith of the WPA:

There were ten of them. They used to go to a place near Belen and empty the freight cars of grain and one thing and another. Finally they killed a man at La Jolla. Contreros was his name. A very rich man with lots of money in his house, all gold.

After Contreros got shot, they called me up at my office in Socorro and told me that he was dying. I promised to get the murderers in forty-eight hours. That was my rule. Never any longer than forty-eight hours.

Baca suspected certain men of being the killers. A phone call from Albuquerque, the state capital, soon told him that the suspects had alibis. He turned his thoughts to the Manzano Gang. Accompanied by two men, he started out on horseback in the direction of La Jolla.

Just as the sun was rising, they came to the ranch of Lazaro Cordova. They rode into the stable and found Cordova's son-in-law Prancasio Saiz already busy with his horse.

Baca would later recall the conversation this way.

"'Good morning,' I said to him. 'What are you doing with your horse so early in the morning?'"

Saiz replied that he was merely brushing him down a little. Baca walked over and placed his hand on the saddle. It was wet inside. The saddle blanket was steaming. He looked more closely at the horse. At first sight, it had appeared to be a pinto, white with brown spots. Baca thought he remembered that Saiz rode a white horse.

"'What happened to that horse?' I asked. He said that the boys had had the horse out the day before and had painted the spots on him with a kind of berry that makes reddish-brown spots."

Baca kept questioning Saiz, establishing that his father-in-law had gone the day before to a fiesta at La Jolla and had not returned. "I told him that I had heard he was a pretty good shot, that he'd better come along and help me round up the men I was after for the killing of Contreros in La Jolla."

Saiz tried to beg off. He said that he had work to do on the ranch, but Baca insisted to the point of intimidation. Saiz saddled his horse and rode out with Baca and his other two posse men. They tracked the outlaws to a graveyard where the gang had camped and where Baca found the remnants of a meal. "Then I found where one of them had had a call to nature." Baca examined the feces, which contained undigested beans and chili seeds.

I told one of my men to put it in a can. Saiz didn't know about this, and in a little while he went over behind some mesquite bushes and had a call to nature. After he came back I sent my man over, and by God it was the same stuff—the same beans and red chili seeds! So I put Saiz under arrest and sent him back to the jail at Socorro with one of my deputies, although he kept saying he couldn't see what I was arresting him for.

Baca and his other deputy proceeded in the direction of La Jolla. Before long they saw a man on horseback coming toward them. They stopped to chat. Baca eyeballed the man as a criminal and never told him he was a lawman. The man said he was from Texas.

The Texan remarked that Baca was pretty heavily armed. Baca replied "I generally arm myself this way when I go for a trip in the country."

The Texan told him that if he wanted fresh horses, he could get them at his ranch, just down the road. Baca figured that this was an attempt to throw him off the trail, so as soon as the Texan was out of sight, he struck out east over the mountains for Manzano. Just as he was entering the village he saw two of the gang coming down the hill on foot, leading their horses. He placed them under arrest and sent them back to Socorro with his other deputy.

It was about 2 A.M. when Baca passed the Cordova ranch again on his way back. He roused Lazaro Cordova, who had returned from La Jolla by that time, and told him to dress and come with him to Socorro. Baca remembered,

The old man didn't want to come, and kept asking "What you want with me anyhow?" I told him that he was under arrest, and on the way to Socorro, I told him that unless he and his son-in-law came across with a complete statement about the whole gang, I would hang both of them. . . . I had the goods on them and knew . . . they were both in on the killing of Contreros. I put him in the same cell with his son-in-law, and told him it was up to him to bring Saiz around. The two men confessed and Baca eventually captured the whole gang.

Setting the trend for the many police officers who would come after him, Elfego Baca went on to study law. He was elected Socorro County Clerk in 1893 and served in this capacity until 1896. During his tenure as county clerk, Baca was admitted to the bar.

Between 1896 to 1898 he was mayor of the city of Socorro. In 1900–01 he was the school superintendent of Socorro County. He returned to the law in 1905, when Governor Otero appointed him district attorney for Socorro and Sierra Counties. But just one year later, in 1906 Baca had made himself so unpopular that he was asked to resign and did. He last held elected office as the sheriff of Socorro County, this time from 1919 to 1920.

Baca practiced law in Albuquerque for the rest of his life. He died at his home there on August 27, 1945.

Doolin Gang, a.k.a. the Wild Bunch (1892–1895)

The Doolin-Dalton Gang was the immediate forerunner of the depression-era gangs of the 1930s. In fact, modern gangs owe much to the Doolin-Dalton Gang's contribution to the criminal profession of robbery.

First and foremost, they were successful. In all the banks they robbed, they made a lot of money. But that was because unlike the James Gang and the Dalton Gang, they were professionals. Robbing was their profession. They were not guerrillas turned robbers like the James brothers or lawmen turned robbers like the Daltons—they were *pros*.

In the wake of the Dalton Gang's Armageddon at Coffeyville, three members of the gang were still at large—Bittercreek Newcombe, Charley Pierce, and Bill Doolin. Doolin was a shrewd cowboy who had learned the value of manipulation and intimidation in his line of work.

Seven days after the raid, John J. Kloehr of Coffeyville got a letter in the mail. Kloehr had killed three of the four outlaws. The letter said that three members of the gang were still alive and they were coming to get him. Coffeyville went into a panic. These were farmers and businessmen, not professional gunfighters. They had beaten the robbers once, but that did not mean they could do it again.

While the citizens of Coffeyville tried to decide what to do about the ominous threat, 18 miles west of Coffeyville, four masked men robbed the train at Caney. The police suspected Bill Doolin of masterminding both the robbery and the threat on Kloehr's life.

What the police did not know was that Doolin needed reinforcements. Four men were not enough for a gang, because not all could necessarily participate in every action. He needed more, so Doolin recruited. The first to join up was Oliver "Ol" Yontis. On November 1, 1892, Yontis joined Doolin and Newcomb to rob the Ford County Bank at Aspearville, Kansas. Yontis's tenure, however was short-lived. The marshals caught up with him at his sister's farm where he had hid out after the robbery. He barely had time to draw his gun before the lawmen shot him dead.

No matter. Doolin had a reputation now as a successful bank robber. Outlaws flocked to be part of what the press would label as Bill Doolin's "Wild Bunch." Tulsa Jack, Dan Clifton (also known as "Dynamite Dick"), George "Red Buck" Waightman, Roy Daugherty (also known as "Arkansas Tom Jones"), and William "Bill" Dalton all joined. Bill was the last of the Dalton brothers still at large and was still interested in engaging in the family profession.

The Doolin-Dalton Gang robbed bank after bank. The U.S. marshals pursued them doggedly. Finally, in June 1893 the marshals received word that the gang was in the town of Ingalls, Oklahoma Territory, for the summer. On September 1, 1893, two wagons loaded with 13 marshals hiding under canvas rumbled into the town. The marshals emerged from their hiding place and took up strategic positions around town.

When the robbers showed themselves during the course of the day, the lawmen opened fire. After a blazing gun battle, Arkansas Tom was wounded. He would later be sentenced to 50 years in prison for his crimes. But the gang had exacted its toll. Three deputies were dead, as were two townspeople caught in the deadly crossfire.

The Wild Bunch continued. In 1894 it took on two new recruits: William F. Raidler, also known as "Little Bill," and Richard West, also known as "Little Dick." The gang then proceeded to rob the Farmers and Citizen's Bank in Pawnee, Oklahoma Territory, on January 23, 1894. Less than two months later, two men robbed the railroad station at Woodwin. Doolin and Dalton were the prime suspects.

On May 10 seven members of the Wild Bunch pulled off a bank robbery in Southwest City, Missouri. During that job, the gang had to shoot its way out of town. The town saw one of its citizens killed by the gang and three more wounded. The gang escaped with just one robber wounded, but not seriously.

The Doolin-Dalton Gang became a victim of its own success. Before 1894 ended, Bill Dalton had decided to go out on his own. Along with Big Asa Knight, Jim Knight, George Bennett, and Jim Wallace, Dalton robbed the First National Bank in Longview, Texas, on May 23, 1894. Bennett was killed and three of the gang wounded during the getaway.

On June 8, 1894, federal marshals found Bill Dalton at his hideout near Ardmore, Iowa Territory. They had been trailing him for weeks. Surprised by the lawmen, Dalton resisted arrest and was shot dead. The gang decided to disperse.

EUREKA SPRINGS, ARKANSAS (1896): THE CAPTURE OF BILL DOOLIN

During his years as a desperado, Bill Doolin had married. Devoted to his wife, Edith, he realized that the marshals were closing in; his time as an outlaw was numbered. Doolin had been wounded years before in a shootout, which gave him painful rheumatism. He decided to go to Eureka Springs to partake of the healthful waters there, then return home and move his family west to California.

Marshal Bill Tilghman was hot on his trail. Using a modern method of policing, Tilghman had received word from informants that the leader of the famed Doolin-Dalton Gang had gone to the springs to take the waters. Tilghman arrived in town disguised as an itinerant preacher. When he moved in to arrest Doolin, at first the outlaw did not know who he was.

When Doolin recognized him, he was looking down the barrel of Tilghman's Colt .45. Despite the threat of a loaded gun in the hands of a crack shot, Doolin reached for the revolver in his shoulder holster. They struggled until Tilghman calmly informed Doolin that unless he gave up immediately, he would fire. Doolin gave in, and Tilghman had his prize. Doolin later told a newspaper reporter, "If it had been anyone else I would have pulled my gun."

What was significant about the encounter was not that Tilghman got his man but that he chose not to kill when the opportunity to do so was afforded him. Tilghman brought his quarry alive to the jail in Guthrie, Oklahoma. Then the marshals turned to hunting down the rest of the gang.

Red Buck Waightman got into a gun battle with deputies near Arapaho, Oklahoma Territory, and died on March 4, 1896. Dynamite Dick was arrested on an unrelated charge in Texas and extradited back to Oklahoma on murder charges. Then on July 5, 1896, Doolin, Dynamite Dick, and 12 other prisoners

escaped. Doolin made it back home to Lawson, Oklahoma Territory, where his wife, Edith, was staying with her family.

Doolin made plans to move with Edith farther west, but before he got a chance to implement his plan he was on the dodge again. On August 24 Deputy Marshal Heck Thomas and his posse surprised Doolin, who decided, unfortunately, to fight it out. Thomas and his posse fired, and Doolin fell dead in a hail of bullets.

With Bill Doolin's death, the last of the great post–Civil War gangs came to an end.

See also KANSAS'S DALTON GANG (1890–1892); WILLIAM MATTHEW "BILL" TILGHMAN (1853–1923).

Jefferson Randolph "Soapy" Smith (1860–1898)
America's first gangster

By 1898 every conceivable kind of crime had occurred as far west as California. With no place to go except a new territory, the frontier moved north and so did the criminal.

Gold was discovered in Alaska in 1897. The Alaskan Gold Rush was on, and it would lead to the last "showdown" of the American West, not in Tombstone or Dodge or Abilene, but in Skagway, Alaska, in 1898.

Jefferson Randolph Smith was born in Georgia in 1860. His father, a lawyer, headed his slave-owning family. Financially devastated by the Civil War, the family moved to Texas and what they hoped were greener pastures. They made every effort to give young Jeff a good education, but when he came of age, he preferred the cowboy life.

In 1876 16-year-old Smith went on his first trail drive, up to Abilene, Kansas. It was on the town's streets that he first was attracted to a shell game being played by a con man. The con man would bet spectators that they couldn't find a pea hidden under one of three walnut shells, then move them around so fast that the sucker had no idea where it was.

The greatest thing that ever happened to Jeff was losing his cowboy wages, all of it, to the con man on that Abilene street. Jeff realized that he could make a lot more money as a professional gambler more easily than he could as a cowboy. He switched occupations instantly.

For the next decade Smith traveled through the frontier towns, learning the tricks of his trade. No con was beneath him, whether it was gambling with marked cards, running a crooked faro game, or the shell game. Smith was also not above conning a drunken man into an alley, knocking him out, and stealing his cash.

Smith might have remained a petty hustler were it not for Old Man Taylor. Taylor was known throughout the West as king of the shell game. Smith ran into him running the game in Leadville, a Colorado mining boomtown, in 1885. Smith soon talked himself into a partnership with Taylor who, one day, showed him the "soap trick."

Taylor would wrap bars of soap in paper. One wrapped bar would have a $100 bill inside. He then put all the soap on sale for $5 a bar. Smith, the shill, would buy the first bar, open it, and discover a crisp new $100 bill. The luckless miners then bought up the rest of the bars. Of course, there were no $100 bills in any of them, but by the time the miners realized they had been conned, Smith and Taylor were already out of town with the profits of their illegal venture.

Smith moved to Denver. His modus operandi was to set up a little folding table on a street corner near the train station where there was lots of passenger traffic. He did not want local law enforcement to roust him, so he generally left the local suckers alone, preferring to ply his trade on unsuspecting out-of-towners. An ebullient sort, Smith told jokes to the crowds that inevitably assembled around him, then brought out the soap bars.

What the crowd did not know was that when he arrived in Denver, Smith took most of the city's con men and organized them in a loose confederation with him at the head. Inevitably it was one of Smith's men that picked the $100 bar; huge sales always followed.

One fleeced customer decided to file a complaint with the Denver Police Department. Smith was hauled in for booking. The arresting officer could not remember his first name. Recalling that the swindle involved soap, he wrote "Soapy Smith" as the name of the suspect and it stuck.

It was in Denver that Soapy realized how important it was to a criminal operation to have close ties with the police. He began to pay them off so he could operate in peace. If one of his men were arrested, it was easy to fix his release.

Knowing how important it was to neutralize the platform of the reformers who would put him out of business, Soapy set up a meals-for-the-needy program, including free Thanksgiving turkeys. Soapy gave heavily to local churches. He was a real humanitarian.

If someone deserved killing, Soapy and his men would surround the miscreant and shoot him simultaneously. This way, no one could rat because everyone was responsible.

Soapy Smith saved his money and eventually opened the Tivoli Saloon and Gambling Hall in the heart of downtown Denver. Always mindful of his civic duty, Soapy allowed local ministers to hold Sunday prayer services in his saloon.

When gold was discovered in Creede, Colorado in 1890, Soapy moved his criminal operations to take advantage of this new source of cash. Using muscle and charm, he became the town's rackets boss. No one operated a crooked gambling operation without Soapy taking a "taste."

To enforce his edicts, Soapy established the Orleans Club on Creede Avenue. It was the place where all the thieves, murderers, pimps, strongarm men and every kind of miscreant gathered to hear their boss tell them what to do. Soapy organized a quasi government for his underworld, with him as the head and final arbiter. Soapy used his criminal clout to provide protection to the town's businesses, his friends, and anyone that would pay him.

Eventually, government was organized in Creede. The town fathers gave Soapy an ultimatum—leave or be hanged. Soapy chose the former and went back to Denver where he opened a phony railroad ticket office. Soapy's newest scam called for him to advertise $5 tickets to Chicago. This was a bargain price.

When travelers flocked to Soapy's "station" to buy them, the buyers were told that the tickets were not sold every day. With nothing to do right then and time on their hands, the marks were admitted to the station's back room, where Soapy had set up crooked games of chance.

By 1897 Colorado's governor, Davis "Blood Bridles" Waite, decided that enough was enough. Denver was too corrupt and needed to be cleaned up. He ordered the city fathers to do the job or he would have the state militia do it for them. When the city fathers did not heed his warning, he dispatched the state militia to Denver.

Soapy's response was brilliant. He instantly appropriated the title of "Colonel." Riding on a white charger like something out of a Dumas story, Colonel Soapy Smith raised an army and surrounded city hall. They would fend off the governor's troops or die trying. Soapy positioned himself in the cupola of the city hall, holding a dynamite bomb, ready to throw it at the militia if fired upon. Some 20,000 people showed up to see the confrontation.

Soapy's patriotism, of course, was a con to protect his life and his business interests in Denver. The U.S.

Army, realizing a deadly confrontation was imminent, dispatched troops from Fort Logan to keep the peace.

Rather than take to bloodletting, Governor Waite agreed to withdraw his militia and let the federals handle the matter. He also agreed to let the Colorado Supreme Court rule on whether he could dispatch militia to a town that was not obeying the rule of law.

Soon after the troops' withdrawal, the Colorado Supreme Court issued its verdict. The court said that Waite did indeed have the power to remove Denver's commissioners (the town council) but that Waite had not given the town a chance to comply with his edict and had acted too quickly. Waite was allowed to remove the present corrupt commissioners, and new

ones were elected. As reformers, the first thing they did was run Soapy Smith out of town.

Soapy drifted south to Mexico, where he tried to convince embattled Mexican president Porfirio Díaz that he needed a foreign legion of U.S. mercenaries. Díaz let him actually begin to recruit men before he realized what a mistake it was and gave Soapy his walking papers.

It was through the newspapers that Soapy found out what was happening in Alaska. Gold had been discovered. Miners were flocking to the North to make their fortunes. That meant a lot of easy money flowing around, some of which Soapy was determined to have.

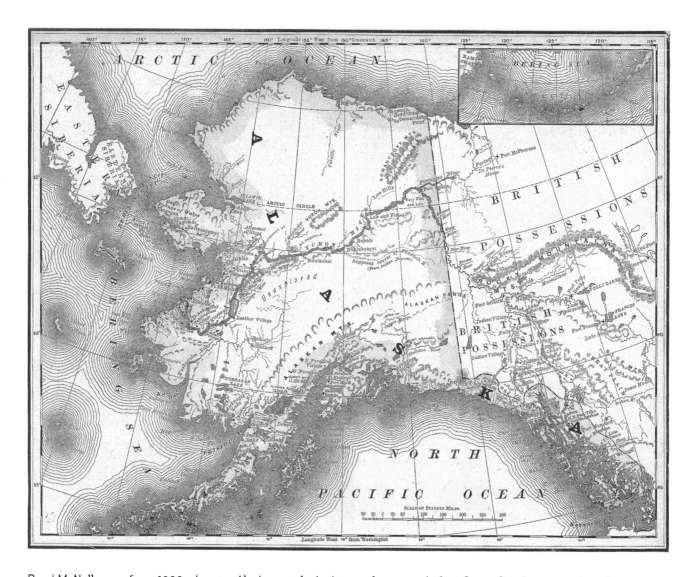

Rand McNally map from 1892, showing Alaska as it looked just a few years before Soapy Smith migrated north. Soapy would have taken a ship north from San Francisco through the North Pacific Ocean, docking at the future city of Skagway. (Author's collection)

In 1897, when Soapy arrived, Alaska was a wild and woolly place with the same degree of decadence as Dodge and Tombstone in their day. There were also the same kinds of criminal characters. And like Dodge in the early days, there was no law enforcement. Criminals were free to do as they pleased while honest folk went about their business and tried to ignore them—unless, of course, they happened to get caught in the crossfire of an armed dispute, which happened many times.

Skagway was the embarkation point for the Yukon gold country. It was said that gold dust oozed through the floorboards of the town's saloons. Seeing the opportunity, Soapy settled in Skagway.

He organized the town's criminals, roughly 100 of them, along the same lines he had in Denver. Soapy ran the rackets—crooked gambling houses, phony telegraph offices, and a phony army enlistment tent where the victim's clothes and possessions were stolen while a "doctor" gave him the "once over."

Soapy's con men would meet newcomers at the docks. Disguised as anything from newspapermen to clergymen, they would size up the marks. Those with a fat wad of cash would be marked for later robbery or sent immediately to one of Soapy's crooked "fronts."

Soapy ruled the place with an iron fist. He was so powerful that the Canadian government would not ship payrolls along the roads Soapy controlled. Soapy, though, had gotten too greedy and turned stupid. He did not do any of his public works projects. Eventually, the citizens tired of his criminal rule.

In 1898 Soapy fleeced a miner out of $2,500. Rather than fade into the night as most of his marks did, the miner decided to do something about it. He rallied Skagway citizens behind him. Forming a vigilance committee, Frank Reid, a civil engineer, was appointed as town marshal to stand up to Soapy.

There is no evidence that Reid had any law enforcement background. but that day, he might have been Wyatt Earp. All alone, Reid and Smith faced each other with holstered guns on Skagway's docks. Both men slapped leather at the same time. The bullet from Reid's Colt .45 entered Soapy's chest, penetrating to the heart, killing him instantly. But by that time, Soapy had also gotten off a shot that wounded Reid, who later died. Reid's heroic action saved Skagway from Soapy's criminal rule, but it signified much more.

Their gunfight signified the end of 19th-century crime. In the 20th century, criminals would no longer have a chivalrous code of honor that they at least pretended to try to uphold. In the 20th century, criminals would no longer hold back.

See also ALEXANDRIA, VIRGINIA (1992); JOHN A. MURREL (1804–?).

PART FOUR

THE TWENTIETH CENTURY

SEVEN
1900–1950

Introduction

America had made it to the 20th century. No matter what criminal enterprise had been thrown against it, be it Booth and his plot to destroy the government or Murrel's criminal conspiracy, the country had survived and was prospering.

The agrarian nation of the 17th through the 19th centuries was slowly and in some places reluctantly becoming an industrialized society. In the West, the frontier was no more, but horses had yet to be supplanted by automobiles as the dominant method of transportation. In the South, the Civil War was still a raw wound. Anger toward the North, for releasing the slaves and for the arrival of the carpetbaggers (the northern economic opportunists who came south after the war to make a buck), had reached its zenith.

Crime through the first decade of the new century was as vibrant and original as ever. Train robbery was still in vogue in certain sections of the country, while in others, a socioeconomic conundrum was developing.

There had always been a lower and upper class in America. Now a new middle class was forming. As people got a taste of a better life, they wanted more; they wanted to move up in class. Some were willing to murder to get there. Greed had always been a reason for murder, but now social acceptance could be added to the list of reasons to commit homicide.

As the century dawned, pamphlets, once the primary means of communicating news and ideas, were passé. Newspapers and magazines were now the most popular mode of communicating with the public. Competition for readership was fierce. This fueled tabloid sensationalism. "Crime of the century" and "trial of the century" became common labels—the latter right up to the millennium.

Racism was predominant. Black people were hanged by the Ku Klux Klan and other white supremacists simply because of their color. But blacks were not the only victims. America as a whole was tolerant of religious differences, but many Americans did not trust Catholics or Jews. Anti-Semitism reared its ugly head, and Jews were also hanged by white supremacists because of their religious beliefs.

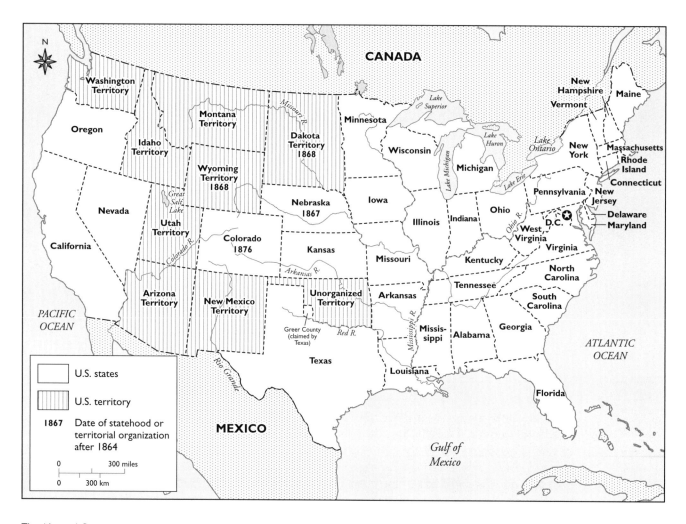

The United States in 1888

As for the Old West, it may have been dying, but it was going out kicking and screaming. Weaving through all of it was a pervasive feeling among law enforcement that a new kind of crime was coming.

The technology of killing was developing more rapidly than society's ability to harness it. As the weapons of killing got more sophisticated, the manifest destiny of the United States ended at the Pacific Ocean. With all that criminal energy reaching its geographic limits, there had to be some place to channel it. The 20th century saw crime implode in the United States. Having gone to the limits of the country's geographic borders, crime returned with modern fire-power and modern methods. Criminals would eventually employ machine guns, hand grenades, automatic weapons, rocket launchers, and every conceivable type of hand-held weapon.

What made all of these weapons so dangerous? In a word, roads. As the new century dawned, America's few roads were usually not much more than trails, muddy in the rain, dusty the remainder of the time. While Ford's automobiles could be produced affordably, there were no roads on which they could safely be driven. Spare parts and tires, tire patches, tools, emergency food, and gasoline, all had to be carried by turn-of-the-century automobile

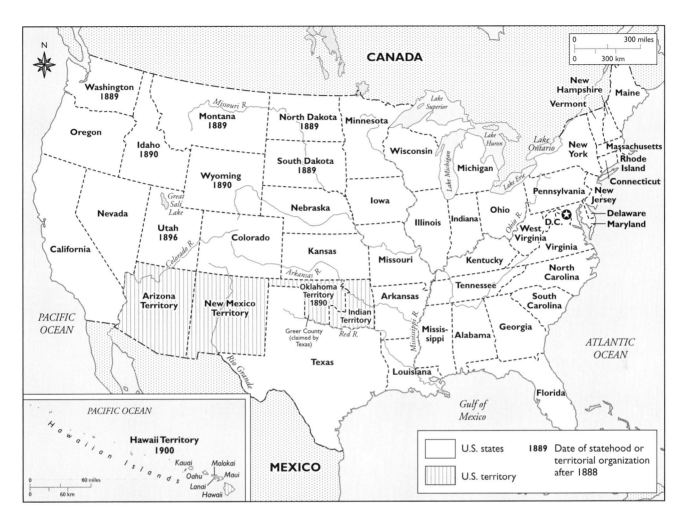

The United States in 1900

travelers because the roads were so bad that they could literally shake a car to pieces.

The problem was that the local, state, and federal governments were not in agreement about fiscal responsibility. Since the middle of the 19th century, the responsibility for road building and maintenance had fallen on the states and localities. If a state or locality did not do its share, the roads were impassable. Frequently, this was the case.

Such decisions had national import. How could a traveler go by automobile, for example, from the east to the west coast? One couldn't, since the roads were not kept up. That, plus the country's reliance on the railroad as the dominant method of interstate travel and commerce, made federal intervention unlikely.

What changed things, strangely enough, was the bicycle. In the 1890s bicycles revived interest in roads. In 1891 the state of New Jersey became the first to pass a "state-aid" road-building plan that called for state appropriations to be made available to counties for road improvements. Seeing the deep public interest in the problem, the federal government created the Office of Road Inquiry in 1883, under General Roy Stone.

Early in the 20th century, Stone's successor, Martin Dodge, began to advocate the concept of a federal aid bill, the substance of which was that federal monies would be appropriated for distribution to states especially for the purpose of building roads. Progress, however, came slowly.

Senators wondered if they had the constitutional authority to authorize such monies. That and other doubts led to the bill's defeat before even one vote was cast. Over the course of the next 10 years, road bills would be introduced and withdrawn as they were consistently defeated by opponents. Yet, progress was being made.

Many farmers joined the "good roads" movement. They had just been exposed to Rural Free Delivery, a system whereby for the first time, the U.S. Postal Service delivered mail to houses out in the country. Before this, people had to pick up their mail in town. But the price of convenience was building the roads on which the postal trucks could travel safely. That meant expenditures. Suddenly, farmers who had previously fought progress embraced it.

Still, in 1900, few had cars. They needed to become more popular before there was real impetus for Congress to act. Perhaps most important, there had to be a resolution to the constitutional question of whether the federal government had the power to dispense road-building money to the states.

But before any of these peaceful questions could be answered, crime once more came back to the front pages.

Buffalo, New York (1901) Leon F. Czolgosz and the assassination of William McKinley

The century started with a bang.

On September 6, 1901, 28-year-old Detroit native Leon F. Czolgosz shot President William McKinley twice with a .32-caliber revolver. History books identify the assassin of McKinley as an anarchist, but no mention is made that medical experts examined him in an attempt to ascertain whether he was insane.

Since Garfield's assassination 20 years before and the subsequent reexamination of the guilt of his assassin, Charles Guiteau, both science and the law had moved forward with the idea that insanity was a legitimate medical condition that could mitigate guilt at trial. Knowing this, as soon as McKinley was shot and his alleged assassin taken into custody, the government moved hastily to form a panel of medical experts to examine the man who had killed the president.

This blue-ribbon panel of local experts was given the difficult charge of interviewing Czolgosz. He was the man captured with the smoking gun at the Pan American Exposition in Buffalo, New York, and held in jail while McKinley, mortally wounded, lay dying at a nearby hotel. The results of the panel would subsequently be reported in the *Philadelphia Medical Journal* of 1901, which began:

> *Official Report of the Experts of the People in the case of the People v. Leon F. Czolgosz*
>   *Joseph Fowler, M.D., Buffalo*
>   *Floyd S. Crego, M.D., Prof. of Insanity and Brian Diseases in the University of Buffalo*
>   *James V. Putnam, M.D., Prof. of Nervous Diseases in the University of Buffalo*

The examiners, all medical men, began with a physical examination:

> *Leon is 28 years old, born of Polish parents at Detroit. He is 5 ft. 7⁵/₈ inches, 136 pounds, with fair complexion. His pulse and temperature are normal, his skin moist.*
>   *Czolgosz claimed to have never had any serious illnesses.*
>   *He had a common school education, reads and writes well. He doesn't drink to excess although he drinks beer every day and uses tobacco moderately. He eats well, moves his bowels regularly.*
>   *His face is symmetrical, one eyebrow elevated as it had been cut some years ago by a wire while he was working in a wire factory. He has a small scar on his left cheek due to a slight work injury.*

With the physical examination showing nothing out of the ordinary, the doctors began to question Czolgosz about his political beliefs. Czolgosz did not have enough sense to keep his mouth shut and let the government build its case without his help.

> *I don't believe in the Republican form of government and I don't believe we should have any rulers. It is right to kill them. I had that idea when I shot the President and that is why I was there. I planned to kill the President 3 or 4 days ago after I came to Buffalo. Something I read in* The Free Society *suggested the idea. I thought it would be a good thing for the country to kill the President.*

Then he detailed how he went about stalking McKinley.

> *When I got to the grounds, I waited for the President to go into the Temple. I did not see him go in but someone told me he had gone in. My gun was in my right pocket with a hand over it. I put my hand in my pocket after I got in the door, took out my gun and wrapped the handle over my hand. I carried it that way, until I got to the President. No one saw me do it. I did not shake hands with him.*

Responding to questions about why he chose that place to commit the crime, Czolgosz explained,

> *I didn't want to shoot him at the falls [Niagara]; Temple instead was planned from the beginning.*
>   *I know other men who believe what I do, that it would be a good thing to kill the President and have no rulers. I have heard that at the meetings in public halls. I have heard quite a lot of people talk like that. Emma Goldman [the great anarchist] was last one I heard. She said she did not believe in government or rulers.*

Asked what his family believed, Czolgosz responded,

> *My family does not believe as I do. I paid $45.50 for my gun. After I shot him twice, they knocked me down and trampled on me. Somebody hit me in the face. I said to the officer that brought me down, "I done my duty."*
>   *I don't believe in voting. It is against my principle. I am an Anarchist. I don't believe in marriage. I believe in Free Love. I fully understand what I was doing when I shot the President. I realized that I was sacrificing my life. I am willing to take the consequences. I know what will happen to me. If the President dies, I will be hung.*

When asked what message he was trying to convey by his actions, Czolgosz replied, "I want to say to the public—'I killed President McKinley because I done my duty.' I don't believe in one man having so much service and another man should have none."

On the second day of the examination, much of the same ground was covered, but new information about his planning began to emerge.

For many months Czolgosz had been an ardent student of anarchy. He heard lectures by an exponent of that doctrine. He had left the church five years before, as he said, because "he didn't like their style." He had attended an anarchists meeting six weeks before the assassination and also in July.

On the Friday before the crime, he was in Cleveland. Prior to that, he had been in Buffalo for three weeks. He had no visible means of support, so it was surprising that he could travel, but Czolgosz explained, "I saved 3 or 400 dollars in 5 or 6 years" to finance his plot.

The examiners were curious. Did he have some partners in his conspiracy, perhaps in Cleveland? Czolgosz shook his head.

"I just went there to look around and buy a paper," he answered, in the most normal tone of voice.

What the examiners should have questioned was the ease with which this presidential assassin not only managed to travel the country in pursuit of his plot, but the failure of the president's own men, the Secret Service, to effectively guard him from any stranger with a gun.

"During the second examination," the doctors collectively wrote,

Leon became very indignant because his clothing was soiled at the time of his arrest and he had not had an opportunity to care for his clothing and person as he wished. He refused to show how he covered his weapon until he had a clean hand.

His desperation to keep himself tidy, demonstrates that he was not careless in dress and appearance as most insane persons. He required clean clothing and as he had a small amount of money, a shirt and handkerchiefs were purchased for him.

The doctors noted that at no time during their examination did he feel any remorse for his actions. By September 9 the doctors noted a marked change in his readiness to answer questions. He began to refuse answers and to change his story.

Suddenly, Czolgosz denied that he had killed the president or meant to kill him. He seemed to be newly on guard. At the close of the interview, he was told that it was too late to deny statements already made. He then said, "I am glad I did it."

In subsequent interviews he declined to discuss the crimes in any detail. He told his guards he would not talk with his lawyers because he did not believe in them and did not want them. The experts concluded their report:

In conclusion, we concur that he was sane at the time he planned the murder, when he shot the President and when he was on trial. We come to this conclusion from the history of his life as it came from him. He had been a sober and law abiding individual till he was 21 years of age. After he cast his first vote, he made the acquaintance of Anarchist leaders who invited him to their meetings. In a short time, he adopted their theories.

We come to the conclusion that in the holding of these views, Czolgosz was sane because these opinions were formed gradually under the influence of the Anarchist leaders.

The report goes on to say that Leon did not suffer from hallucinations, nor did he have any visions of grandiosity; he did not believe he was specially chosen to do the deed. He always referred to the anarchist belief that the killing of rulers was a "duty." The examiners continued:

He did it alone. His is not a case of paranoia, because he has no systematized delusions and because he is in exceptionally good condition and has an unbroken record of good health. He has false beliefs the result of false teaching and not the result of disease.

Physically, he has not a hint of cruelty or of perverted tastes and habits. He is the product of Anarchy, sane and responsible. Signed, Joseph Fowler, M.D., Buffalo, Floyd S. Crego, M.D., Prof. of Insanity and Brian Diseases in the University of Buffalo, James V. Putnam, M.D., Prof. Of Nervous Diseases in the University of Buffalo.

With no defense, Leon F. Czolgosz was found guilty of the assassination of President McKinley and hanged. Except for his anarchist beliefs, no one has ever given any other reason for his actions.

See also ASSASSINATION OF PRESIDENT GARFIELD (JULY–SEPTEMBER 1881); BALTIMORE, MARYLAND (1844); JOHN WILKES BOOTH (1838–1865); DALLAS, TEXAS

(1963); MIAMI, FLORIDA (1933); WASHINGTON, D.C. (1835); WASHINGTON, D.C. (1982).

Salem, Oregon (1902) in pursuit of Harry Tracy

Harry Tracy is the most famous escaped convict in U.S. history. Never before or since has a murderer who was a crack shot with a Winchester or Colt escaped custody to kill again and again and again and yet have the U.S. public on his side.

The latter is not too surprising considering that early in his criminal career, Tracy was a member of Butch and Sundance's Hole in the Wall Gang.

Even John Dillinger, who would come after him and whose exploits Tracy rivaled, did not exploit the emerging transportation system as Tracy did in not only his escapes but also his crimes. Tracy may have been the first 20th-century criminal to rob a moving streetcar.

In his escape from prison, still talked about by people in Oregon, Tracy used almost every conceivable method of transportation known at the time—foot, horse, boat, and probably train. Like Dillinger, he conducted his most famous criminal exploits in a brief period of time, and finally, also like Dillinger, the man made headlines and died young.

Arrested and tried on burglary charges in Utah in 1897, Tracy was convicted and sentenced to time in the Utah State Penitentiary. His stay behind bars was brief. Disguised as an armed guard, Tracy soon made his escape and drifted into Colorado, where he killed a rancher. Arrested, he escaped again from custody.

Tracy wound up in Portland, Oregon, where he made the reacquaintance of an old partner in crime, David Merrill. Together they did something unique: They began robbing the streetcars that crisscrossed the city. In between trips, they burglarized the homes of Seattle's wealthy citizens.

In 1898 the law caught up with them. Arrested, tried, and convicted of highway robbery and burglary, they were both sentenced to serve time in the Oregon State Prison in Salem in 1899. Merrill got a lighter sentence. Tracy wondered why.

THE ESCAPE

Tracy had people working for him on the outside. Just as they had in the break from the Utah prison, he had his confederates smuggled him not one revolver but two, as well as two rifles and ammunition. On the morning of June 9, 1902, Tracy and Merrill grabbed their weapons from hiding, determined to shoot their way out.

Tracy fired a shot that entered the back of guard F. B. Ferrell, killing him. For some reason, inmate Frank Ingraham tried to assist guard Frank Gerard. For his efforts, Merrill rewarded him with a bullet through the kneecap. (Ingraham's leg later had to be amputated because of the wound, but he wound up being pardoned by the governor for his heroic effort. The leg apparently was worth his freedom.)

In the prison's foundry, Tracy and Merrill rushed through the corridor and out into the prison yard. At the sight of the heavily armed convicts, guard S. R. Jones came running. Just as he was reaching for his gun, Tracy stopped and fired, hitting Jones from a full 150 yards away and killing him.

Tracy and Merrill climbed an interior wall, grabbing two other guards as shields. As they ran through a second interior courtyard, another guard came upon them and fired. Tracy's response was to ram the barrel of his pistol over the heart of hostage B. F. Tiffany. He pulled the trigger, putting a bullet through two chambers of Tiffany's heart. Merrill's hostage also fell, and he played dead, though he had not been shot.

With the guards reluctant to approach Tracy because of his deadly aim and willingness to kill, the two convicts made it over the wall and into the surrounding countryside. In the wake of their escape, the warden called out the local police. Through wire and phone, word spread throughout the northwest that once again, Harry Tracy was on the loose. This time, he had nothing to lose.

For the next two weeks, the escaped cons headed north. They stole clothes, food, money, and horses. Posses sent out after them never seemed to be fast enough or smart enough to catch them.

Crossing into Canada, Tracy and Merrill ingratiated themselves with a farmer near Vancouver who invited them into his cabin for a meal. On a table inside was a copy of the *Oregonian*, the state's premier newspaper. Delighted to see their pictures in the paper, the convicts cut them out.

Reading the article, Tracy finally learned why Merrill had gotten a shorter sentence than he had: his old friend's mother was the one who ratted Tracy out in return for a reduced sentence for her boy. Tracy, of course, was furious. He confronted Merrill with this information and challenged him to a shootout. Merrill agreed that they would turn, count out 10 paces, turn again, and fire. But Tracy did not wait. He turned after eight paces and shot Merrill in the back. The shot caused Merrill to spin around. He brought his revolver up to fire, whereupon Tracy shot him on the left side.

Still, the man was alive. Tracy solved that problem with a shot into his skull. With Merrill out of the way, Harry Tracy continued on alone.

Around 5 A.M. the next day, Harry Tracy found himself at the Capital City Oyster Company near Olympia, Washington. Entering the building, Tracy introduced himself to owner Horacio Alling and his cook William Adair. They knew who he was from the front-page coverage of Tracy's escape and subsequent adventures.

They prepared a meal for the killer, who held the two men at gunpoint while he ate. Two more men, John Messegge and Frank Scott, came into Alling's office for something. Tracy invited them to sit on the floor with the others while he finished his meal.

A true con man who was always figuring the angles, Tracy noticed a launch called the *N&S* moored in the bay. He figured it would make a good escape vehicle and noticed there were only two men aboard. He ordered Adair to invite Captain A. J. Clark, the *N&S*'s master, and his 15-year-old son Edward to come on shore for breakfast.

Clark and his son came on shore and sat down to a well-cooked breakfast, curious, though, as to why the man in the corner was holding a gun on them. Reportedly, they believed it some sort of joke until after the meal, when the gunman identified himself as Harry Tracy and told them he was going to steal their boat.

Under duress, Messegge tied up and gagged Alling and Adair. Then Tracy did the same to Messegge. With those three taken care of, Tracy went out to the boat with Frank Scott and the Clarks as hostages. They headed north to Seattle. The hostages would later tell the papers that during the trip up to the Queen City of the North, Tracy bragged about the men he had murdered.

They made Meadow Point, north of Ballard, where they anchored. Captain Clark would later recall that upon disembarking, Tracy said, "I'll send you a lot of money for kidnapping you and the launch, for I will have a lot of dough pretty soon now. You have acted pretty decent by me."

Taking Frank Scott and Edwin Clark as the last remaining hostages, the three set out for Seattle. Tracy was not stupid enough to arrive directly in the city. He had deliberately docked the boat on the outskirts so he could slip in unobtrusively.

During their long walk, they came across a man who Tracy wanted to hold up. Scott talked him out of it by appealing to the killer's sense of decency. He told Tracy that if they held the man up, he, Scott,

would be implicated. Tracy agreed and since he did not want to get Scott in trouble, resisted his criminal impulse for probably the only time in his life.

A few hours later, Tracy let them go. Scott asked him what he intended to do. Tracy replied that he was going to hold up a policeman for his revolver. Tracy was angry that he was now armed only with a Winchester rifle. After taking a gun off a cop, he would go down to Clancy's Saloon on Pike Street and hold it up, Tracy continued telling Scott. Clancy's was known to be a "flush" business. Tracy left and Scott ran back to Meadow Point.

Out on the boat, the prisoners had gotten free. They reached Seattle after midnight. Immediately, they told the police that Tracy was in town and what he intended to do. A posse left town to try and catch him before he entered the city. As for the men who were kidnapped, they were led to a restaurant by newspapermen anxious to take down their story. Before long, the story of Harry Tracy's latest escapades, and the desperate situation of the people of Seattle, went out over the national wires.

THE CON

Seattle detectives descended on Clancy's Saloon, but Harry Tracy was nowhere to be found. He had deliberately led them off the trail. When Tracy told Scott where he was going, he knew Scott would tell the police. Tracy was actually in the nearby town of Bothell.

After a railroad watchmen spotted him walking along the train tracks with a shouldered rifle, a posse set out to stop Tracy. They tracked him down to his hiding place, a gulch outside Wayne. Tracy knew they were coming and decided to meet them head on. The posse was approaching the end of the gulch when he came out from behind a tree stump not 30 feet away from them. To a crack shot like Tracy, this was like a shooting arcade.

He shot newspaperman Karl Anderson in the face, but luckily he was only wounded. Not so Sheriff Charles Raymond, who died from so many of Tracy's bullets that his chest was a bloody pulp and his left arm practically shot off. Tracy instantly turned his fire on newspaperman Louie B. Sefrit, who became the second newspaperman to survive a Tracy wound.

Tracy whirled to face Deputy Sheriff Jack Williams of Snohomish County who was attempting to outflank him. Tracy's bullets shattered the barrel of Williams's revolver, sending shrapnel into his chest and left wrist. As the rest of the posse began helping the wounded, Tracy stole off into the woods.

He fled the forest, determined to make his way back to Seattle. Before he got there, he reached the farm of Louis Johnson near Green Lakes, "Hi, I'm Tracy," he told Johnson, who quickly followed the armed man's order to hitch his horses to a wagon, which they rode toward Seattle.

On the way, they stopped in Woodland Park. Choosing randomly, Tracy invaded the home of Mrs. R. H. Van Horn, where he stole some clothing. He got Mrs. Van Horn to make him dinner, while he searched the house for anything of value. He found a revolver. While eating his meal, Tracy chatted with Mrs. Van Horn as if they were neighbors. She later told the papers that Tracy said, "I have never held up a woman before. And I don't like to bind you, but if you will promise me not to give it out, I will not leave you abound."

Mrs. Van Horn asked him if he had killed David Merrill the way the papers said he had. Tracy proceeded to detail the deal that Merrill had made. Yes, he shot him in the back, but given the opportunity to do the same, Merrill would have taken it. Their conversation was interrupted when a delivery boy arrived with her groceries. Promising Tracy she would tell the boy nothing, she took the boy into the kitchen, where she told him everything. When the boy got back to town he informed the police.

Sheriff Edward Cudihee of King County, Patrolman E. E. Breece of the Seattle Police Department, and a hastily deputized miner named Neil Rawley arrived at the Van Horn House and hid outside. As soon as Tracy left, they planned to cut him to pieces.

Tracy walked out of the Van Horn house accompanied by Johnson as a human shield. The lawmen had the element of surprise, but they quickly lost it when Breece came out from hiding and strode purposedly up to Tracy, telling him to give it up.

Tracy responded by firing his Winchester point-blank into Breece's chest, killing him. Gunfire erupted all around him, but Tracy was long gone by the time Cudihee sorted out the mess. In the end, Breece was dead and Rawley lay wounded. He died the next day. Tracy meanwhile, was terrorizing another family.

Forcing his way into the Ravenna home of farmer August Fisher, he ordered the man's wife to cook him breakfast. He told the Fishers stories of his adventures and then left with a brown paper bag lunch and some new clothes he had stolen from them. This time, he did not bother tying up his victims because the Fishers had a baby that needed to be taken care of.

For the next few days, Tracy repeated this pattern of barging into innocent people's homes to get food

and clothing, all the while covering his captives with his trusty Winchester. He always asked to see the local papers, pleased to see how much ink his escape was generating, disappointed when his picture did not make the front page.

While Tracy rested, Sheriff Cudihee was in hot pursuit again with a new posse. He tracked Tracy to Bainbridge Island, but by the time he got there, Tracy had escaped, once again by boat. He landed for a second time in King County, where he made his way across the Cascade Mountains into eastern Washington.

END OF THE LINE

In early August Tracy was seen aboard a ferry crossing the Columbia River. Another sighting followed, in Coulee City. Authorities assumed he was headed for Spokane.

On August 3, near the town of Creston, 18-year-old George E. Goldfinch was stopped by a dark stranger on horseback. Goldfinch would later remember the man said, "I'm Tracy, the convict. Who are you?"

Goldfinch told him his name and said, "Pleased to meet you—I think."

Tracy asked him for directions to the nearest ranch. Goldfinch complied with directions to the nearby Eddy ranch, run by two unmarried brothers. Accompanied by Goldfinch, Tracy went to the Eddy spread where Goldfinch introduced him to Lou and Eugene Eddy. Needing rest, Tracy stayed at the Eddy ranch for a few days. He let Goldfinch go with a warning: If Goldfinch told the cops where he was, the Eddys were dead.

Over the next few days, Tracy ate, slept, bathed, shaved, and generally had a comfortable time. He showed off his markmanship to the Eddys, shooting out a knothole in a pine board from 60 yards away. What Tracy had not counted on was young Goldfinch's heroism. The 15-year-old disobeyed Tracy's orders and used a telephone to call the sheriff in nearby Creston. The sheriff got a posse together, and on the morning of August 6, it approached the Eddy ranch on foot.

Mowing hay in a pasture, Lou Eddy discovered the concealed lawmen. Looking up, they saw a man come out of the barn that Eddy identified as Tracy. As the lawmen approached the barn, Tracy shouted out to them, asking who they were. C. C. Straub, a member of the posse, answered back, "We are constables of the law!"

Tracy ran back into the barn and came out with his rifle blazing. The posse shot back. Tracy managed to reach cover behind a boulder. The posse hid behind nearby rocks and jockeyed for position, firing as they went. For some reason, Tracy ran toward a wheat field, and then his luck expired. Not one but two bullets hit him in the leg, and he fell.

The first bullet caused a minor flesh wound in the back of his thigh. But the second hit mid-calf, shattering both bones. Tracy crawled into a waist-high wheat field and was obscured from view.

Back at the ranch, reinforcements had arrived. No one, though, was brave enough to go out into the wheat field to capture the escaped convict. He was just too deadly with a rifle to take a chance. Instead, they surrounded the field and decided to wait him out.

By that time, Tracy was in intense pain and bleeding profusely. He did not know it, but the second bullet had severed an artery in his leg. If he did not stop the blood flow, he would be dead in minutes. To save his life, he would have had to press on the artery midpoint, at the groin. Instead, he pushed a handkerchief down into the wound. Of course, it did not work, and the blood kept flowing out as Tracy got weaker and weaker.

Tracy, who had vowed not to be taken alive, probably knew he had reached his end. He put his Colt under his right eye and squeezed the trigger. The lawmen heard the shot, but decided to wait until morning before entering the field. When they did, they found Tracy, dead from a bullet that entered below the right eye.

His body was brought back to Creston, where the townsfolk viewed it. When people starting ripping at Tracy's clothes and cutting locks of his hair for souvenirs, his corpse was returned for burial to Salem, Oregon. In Salem, the embalmer put chemicals in the casket that would eventually destroy the corpse. The authorities did not want anyone digging it up and selling off parts of Tracy's body for souvenirs.

See also JESSE JAMES (1847–1882); JAMES-YOUNGER GANG (1866–1881).

Kitty Hawk, North Carolina (1903) the Wright brothers invent the airplane

On December 12, 1903, the idea that an airplane could be used in a criminal plot, that it could be held for ransom or skyjacked, simply did not exist. Neither did the concept that criminals could hop onto jets in order to kill or consummate their business deals. On December 12, 1903, none of those things were possible because the airplane did not exist. But the next day, things changed. Out on a lonely,

windswept North Carolina beach came two brothers, Orville and Wilbur Wright, to see if their seven years of work would finally pay off.

The Wrights ran a bicycle shop in Dayton, Ohio. In 1896, when they started, gliders had already been invented. But the Wrights were visionaries who dreamed that one day humans would fly through the air under their own power. To realize their dream, they knew they would first have to become expert glider pilots.

Kitty Hawk, the Wrights realized, was the best place to achieve their dream. The beach's winds would provide constant lift to the wings of their craft. In 1902 they came with a glider of their own design and made 700 successful flights. One year later they came back, ready to make history.

Their plane was powered by an engine of their own design. Every strut, every nut, every bolt, the wings, the fuselage—everything was hand made by the Wrights. With Orville Wright at the controls and his brother Wilbur on the beach urging him on, the plane raced down the beach. Suddenly, the speed of the plane, coupled with the lift from the ever-present winds, lifted the plane into the air.

Wilbur clocked the plane's flight as 12 seconds aloft, 20 feet above the ground. Before the plane came back down and skidded to a stop, Orville had flown a full 120 feet. That was not much of a distance but it was in the air, under the plane's own power. The airplane had been invented. Eventually, planes would be used as state-of-the-art transportation, enabling criminals to move not only from one end of the continent to the other unimpeded, but from one continent to another.

New York (1903–1904) fingerprints used to identify criminals

It was back in 1892 that Britain's Sir Francis Galton, Charles Darwin's anthropologist cousin, published his groundbreaking book *Fingerprints*. The result of many years of careful study, the book scientifically established that each person's fingerprints are unique and unchanging. No two fingerprints are exactly the same. Galton figured that the odds of two individual fingerprints being the same were 1 in 64 billion.

That same year, Juan Vucetich, an Argentine policeman, used Galton's pattern types to establish the world's first fingerprints file. Vucetich made history when he used fingerprints to positively identify a criminal for the first time. It took another 10 years before England began to use fingerprints to identify criminals.

America had been slow in catching on but did in 1903 when the New York State prison system began the first systematic use of fingerprints to identify criminals. The following year, 1904, fingerprint identification began to be used in Leavenworth Federal Penitentiary in Kansas. That same year St. Louis, the Gateway City, garnered honors for being the first city in the United States to use fingerprints as a means of identifying active criminals. Not surprisingly, the pioneering British detectives from Scotland Yard assisted the Americans in learning how to use 20th-century technology to stop 20th-century crime.

Washington, D.C. (1905–1919) origins of the interstate highway system

Logan Waller Page was a scientist who believed that science could make the life of the average citizen better. That included taking the United States's greatest scientific minds and asking them to figure out scientifically, unemotionally, and most importantly not beholden to any political machine, how best to pave the United States. Through his tenure at the Office of Public Roads, Page would lobby Congress for road-building funds and eventually put his plans into action to begin building a highway system for the 20th century.

In December 1914 the American Association of State Highway Officials was founded. This lobbying organization gave the states a strong voice in Congress for federal assistance in road building. But it would take a general rather than a bureaucrat to take the next step forward.

During World War I General John Pershing was assigned to command the U.S. Expeditionary Force that went to Europe in 1917. While in Europe, Pershing became fascinated by the European highway system. By the time he was back in the United States after the war, he had begun thinking about the movement of troops across the continent in the event of war on the American mainland.

To figure out how well equipped the United States was in moving troops for such a war, Pershing assigned a junior officer, Dwight D. "Ike" Eisenhower, to find out. Ike left Fort Mead, outside Washington, D.C.—the same place where the Lincoln conspirators were hanged 54 years before—with 81 vehicles. Their destination was the Presidio army base in San Francisco.

Most of the 3,000-mile route was over unpaved, rough roads. The trip was an unmitigated disaster. It took Ike and his trucks 62 days to get to the West Coast. When he finally returned to Washington and

reported his findings to Pershing, the general drew up a plan for an ambitious 8,000-mile interstate highway system. It was released in 1922.

Pershing's plan to unite all the states in one ribbon of highway was a brilliant one. Unfortunately, it fell on deaf ears. President Woodrow Wilson was not interested, and neither was Congress.

The railroad industry had been lobbying in Washington for sometime to improve and expand the country's railroad infrastructure. The idea was to make railroads the principal and primary means of interstate transportation. Congress and the president acquiesced. Pershing's plan would have to wait for another presidential administration to become a reality.

Upstate New York (1906) "An American Tragedy"

With the publication of his book *Sister Carrie* in 1900, journalist Theodore Dreiser began to make a name for himself as a novelist who was fascinated by the conflict between human needs and the demands

Chester Gillette (Clements Library, University of Michigan)

GRACE BROWN'S

LOVE LETTERS

Grace Brown (Clements Library, University of Michigan)

Brown and Gillette dated sporadically throughout 1905 and 1906. To Gillette, it was never anything more than a dalliance with a member of the lower class. For Brown, it was more serious, especially when she became pregnant with Gillette's child.

Brown went home to her parents and began an impassioned correspondence with Gillette. Those letters would later be used at trial to prove motive. Two are reprinted in this book for the first time in almost 100 years.

In a subsequent letter that the prosecution presented at trial, Brown happened to mention that she could not swim. She also assumed Gillette would marry her, though Gillette never wrote that. Nevertheless, responding sympathetically, Gillette promised a trip to the Adirondack Mountains. Brown took that to mean they were going on a wedding trip.

Gillette met Brown in Deruyter, New York, on July 9, 1906, and they began their holiday together. They spent the first night in Utica. The next morning, they took the train to Tupper Lake, where they spent their second night. On the morning of July 11, they decided to stop at Big Moose Lake in Herkimer County and go boating. Strangely, Grace left her trunk in the train station and her hat in the hotel. Chester took his suitcase, with a tennis racket tied to the front, onto the rowboat that they rented together. They spent the afternoon boating on the lake.

That night, Gillette arrived alone at the Arrowhead Hotel in Inlet. He stayed there until his arrest three days later. Grace's body had been found in the lake, and he was the logical suspect. Later, he was charged with her murder.

During his trial in November and December 1906, Gillette testified that Grace Brown had jumped into the lake and committed suicide because of her pregnancy. He panicked, left her there, and checked into the hotel, where the police found him. The district attorney, though, had a different version of events.

The district attorney said Chester hit Grace over the head with the tennis racket that had been attached to his suitcase. He wanted to get rid of her so that he, a child of privilege, would not be burdened with a woman of the lower class and her baby.

Describing the proceedings, a contemporary account of the crime contained in the Medler Collection states,

Her dead body had been found in Big Moose Lake July 11. Attorney George W. Word for the prosecution offered into evidence the letters which Grace Brown "the little factory girl," had written to her recreant lover and then read them to the jury.

of society. Six years later, the murder of Grace Brown by Chester Gillette and the ensuing "trial of the century" provided the source material for Dreiser's *An American Tragedy,* the first American "true crime novel."

Dreiser dramatized events, of course. The real story was much more interesting.

Beginning in 1905, Gillette and Brown worked together at a skirt factory owned by Chester's uncle in Cortland, New York. Gillette's family was well-off enough to send him to the prestigious Oberlin Academy prep school. Brown, a farmer's daughter, came from more modest circumstances.

South Otselic
July 3, '06

My dear Chester—

I shall be alone all day. Don't you wish you were going to be here? Won't you forgive me? I do so wish I could die. Is it wicked to want to die? My head aches and I am so blue. Oh dear, if you were only here and would kiss me and tell me not to worry anymore, I would not mind all this but with no one to talk to and ill all the time, I really believe I will be crazy. I will never be cross again dear and I will try so hard to please you.

Darling. I am crying so I can't see my lines and will stop. You have never known clearly how badly I need you, how much I want you this very minute. With love and kisses

"The Kid"

PS: Chester, won't you please write and post in the morning. Take the letter down to the office.

South Otselic
July 6, 1906

My Dear Chester—
4th of July firework.

Oh dear, you don't realize what all of this is to me, I know I shall never see any of them again and mamma! I don't know what I shall do without her. . . . She has trouble enough as it is and I couldn't break her heart like that. If I come back dead, perhaps if she does know, she won't be angry with me. I will never be happy again dear. I wish I could die. You will never know what you have made me suffer dear. I want to see you but I wish I could die.

Please think dear that I had to give up a whole summer's pleasure and you will surely be brave enough to give up one even for me. Bless you till then. Lovingly, and with kisses, "The Kid."

I will go right to the Tabor House and you come for me there. Please come up Sunday night dear.

The District Attorney, a strong man not given to sentiment, paused repeatedly in the reading to regain his self control while over the crowded courtroom there fell a tense silence as the great crowd listened with streaming eyes and suppressed sobs to the saddest story that ever a judge and jury listened to. These letters so sweetly pathetic, so unconsciously dramatic, tell the old sad story with a vividness and power that the greatest writers of all ages have failed to reach. And we read them with dim eyes and with but one feeling and that of unutterable pity.

The jury found Chester Gillette guilty of first-degree murder and sentenced him to die in the electric chair. Newspapers reviled Gillette's cowardly behavior. The public clamored for his execution. Maintaining his innocence to the end, Gillette was executed at Auburn Prison on March 30, 1908.

See also WILLIAM BARCLAY "BAT" MASTERSON (1853–1921).

New York, New York (1906) Harry K. Thaw murders Stanford White

The murder of Stanford White in 1906 is the first in history to be labeled "the crime of the century" by newspapers. From coast to coast, the papers raced to get every licentious detail in print. The coverage was fueled by the sexually duplicitous, jealous, and murderous behavior of the participants: world-renowned architect Stanford White; his killer, the warped multimillionaire Harry K. Thaw; and their mutual love interest, beautiful showgirl Evelyn Nesbit.

In the end, the story was really about three things: the lives of men of privilege, an actress whose greatest role was herself, and the first of a long line of millionaire killers that got away with it. Controversy over the death penalty notwithstanding, in the history of American crime, not one millionaire who ever stood trial for murder has been sentenced to death. Thaw was among the first whom the state tried to execute.

Stanford White was a contemporary and rival of Frank Lloyd Wright and just as renowned. Where Wright's influence was heavy in the Midwest, White's sphere was the Northeast. Preeminent in New York City and its environs, White built his reputation designing ostentatious palaces for America's moneyed class.

Before 1906 White had designed about 40 opulent Long Island structures, including the old Garden City Hotel and the Harbor Hill mansion in Roslyn. In his designs White set the standard for the architects of the Gilded Age—an opulent beauty that staggered the eye. By the late 1880s White had become the favorite of the nouveaux riches. The latter made parts of Long Island, once fishing villages, into upper-class bastions where the rich amused themselves with yachts, polo playing, and fox hunting.

"They wanted to live like the nobility of Europe, with huge estates secluded behind gates," Suzannah Lessard wrote in her 1996 book, *The Architect of Desire: Beauty and Terror in the Stanford White Family.* "He [White] partied with them, did favors for them and ultimately fulfilled their desires by creating aristocratic 'cottages' for them." But White also had a destructive side.

Stanford White was the son of Richard Grant White, a noted writer, editor, music critic, and Shakespearean scholar. Born in New York City on November 9, 1853, White as a child showed artistic talent that his family encouraged. His painted emotionally moving pictures and wanted to be a professional painter.

At the time, most American painters were self-taught. White, though, wanted lessons. A friend of his father's, painter John La Farge, offered White the best advice he ever got: forget painting and try architecture.

When he was 16, White made the acquaintance of Henry Hobson Richardson, one of the first Americans to study at Paris's École de Beaux-Arts. Richardson was impressed with White's candor and enthusiasm. Three years later, he gave White a job as a student draftsman. White developed his design skills and quickly moved up the ladder to become one of Richardson's chief assistants.

Working for Richardson at the time was Charles McKim, who had also attended the École de Beaux-Arts. In 1872 McKim left to start his own architectural firm. He took as partners William Rutherford Mead and William Bigelow. Six years later, White met up with Richardson in France. Traveling together through France and Spain, the two became friends. When they returned to the United States in 1880, White discovered that Bigelow had retired and there was a partnership open at McKim's firm. McKim asked him to join and White agreed. McKim, Mead, and White would go on to become one of the most successful architectural firms in history.

In 1884 White married Bessie Springs, whose father Richard Bull had helped found Smithtown on Long Island. Three years later, they had a son, Lawrence Grant White, who later went on to become

an architect. He joined his father's firm in 1914, and in 1920 became a partner.

White designed Madison Square Garden as a showplace and there, on top of the building, he built himself a loft. He told his family, he would stay there to design some of his great works on the nights that he did not come home. His wife bought this and seemingly never questioned him. Though he may have used the space to design buildings, the loft became better known for its red velvet swing. White would throw lavish parties and invite teenage showgirls from Broadway, and inevitably, some wound up swinging from the red velvet swing to White's delight. Often, White had affairs with these women.

White wined and dined them, bought them presents and paid to fix their teeth at a time when dentistry was still a luxury. Most of the showgirls came from the lower class, and White's generous support helped pay the expenses of his young protégées.

White's lifestyle included attending the theater regularly. In 1901 the hit Broadway show *Floradora* featured a chorus of six young girls. These famous girls were dressed prettily and danced simply. The male chorus sang:

> *Tell me, pretty maiden,*
> *Are there any more at home like you?*

The girls replied:

> *There are few, kind, sir,*
> *But simple girls and proper, too.*

Among the six chorines, White took a special liking to a fresh-faced, innocent-looking brunette from Pittsburgh named Evelyn Nesbit.

Evelyn Nesbit was born in Pittsburgh, Pennsylvania, in 1885. She had a younger brother named Howard. Her father was an attorney who died prematurely, leaving the family destitute. Her mother tried making money by running boardinghouses, but they all failed, and she took in washing and sewing to survive. The family was always moving to wherever their mother found work. Evelyn found escape through the romance of dime novels. When she saw pictures in magazines of beautiful women, she imagined herself one of them. Howard tried getting a job when he was 12 to help support the family, but his weak constitution got the better of him and he had to quit.

By the time she reached puberty, Evelyn knew she was beautiful. She had a thick, luxurious mane of copper-colored hair, clear, delicate features, and olive skin. Evelyn knew what she wanted—escape from poverty. The only means at her disposal to help her escape was her looks. Introduced to a well-known Philadelphia artist named John Storm, she became his model. That led to jobs with other artists.

Artists and photographers thought she looked virginal and portrayed her that way. Soon, the 15-year-old Evelyn had the family move to New York so she could pursue her career. Evelyn immediately found work as an artist's model, but soon discovered, like many women who would come after her, that the real money was in modeling fashions for photographers.

Nesbit was smart enough to know the career of a model was short. But notoriety might gain her stage parts. Sure enough, when a theatrical magazine published her photo, an offer came to join the chorus of *Floradora*. It was there that she caught Stanford White's eye. What happened the evening they met was later recounted by Nesbit at her husband's murder trial.

Evelyn Nesbit (Library of Congress)

Nesbit testified that the affair with White began when she visited him at his Madison Square Garden rooftop apartment, where White had taken her after a show. They drank champagne. Something about the stuff had a strange effect on Evelyn. After one glass, she collapsed into unconsciousness that was apparently caused by a doctored drink.

She awoke a few hours later on White's satin bedcovers, and White told her that now she was his. White had raped her while she was unconscious.

They began an affair that lasted for some time, during which White saw that Evelyn's teeth were fixed and she and her family taken care of financially. However, White eventually grew tired of the affair and drifted away to other girls. The parting was amicable. Then one night, a "stage door Johnny" named Henry "Harry" Kendall Thaw came backstage after a performance. Evelyn knew him by reputation as the mercurial multimillionaire heir to a railroad and ore fortune from Pittsburgh.

Harry was a sadist who liked inflicting pain, favoring a dog whip on his women. Defenseless animals were also a favorite target when women weren't around. Thaw had an unusually close relationship with his mother. Whenever Harry got in trouble, which was most of the time, Mother Thaw bought him out of it. It was this man that Evelyn Nesbit chose to marry.

On their honeymoon, Thaw used his dog whip on Evelyn until she revealed the truth of her relationship with White. Though she bore White no ill will, she was forced to confess under Thaw's torture that they had carried on an affair for a few years and that, at least initially, she had been taken by force. The thought that White had defiled his wife troubled Thaw deeply.

As for Nesbit, she accepted Thaw's beatings and debasement for the privilege of having married into society's upper crust. If she could hold out long enough, eventually she could divorce Thaw and get a good settlement.

On June 25, 1906, the Thaws arrived at the supper club theater on the roof of Madison Square Garden. "Mam'zelle Champagne," a musical revue, was playing. Red-haired, ruddy-cheeked, and laughing, Stanford White was in the first row. Thaw, entering with Evelyn, spotted White across the room. Excusing himself for a moment, Thaw made his way through the crowded theater. Reaching inside his pocket, he pulled out a small-caliber pistol that he held at his side, ready to fire.

Thaw came abreast of White's table and fired from only a few feet away. He got off three shots directly into White's face before the architect slumped dead to the floor. Showing little emotion, Thaw opened the pistol and removed the last three bullets. Holding the empty gun over his head to show that he had finished shooting, he made for the exit.

The crowd had frozen at the sound of the shots. Seconds passed as people realized this was not part of the show. Someone had just shot and killed Stanford White.

"What have you done this time Harry?" Evelyn is reported to have said.

Thaw was later taken into police custody and placed in the Tombs, a windowless prison located near the Brooklyn Bridge. Even in those isolated surroundings, Mother Thaw managed to take care of him. While he was in the Tombs for nine months awaiting trial, Mother Thaw sent him catered meals every day from Delmonico's, a famous restaurant of the rich.

Muckraking journalists dug up all kinds of stories about White's carousing with young women. New York City's tabloids competed amongst themselves to publish the accounts of young girls that White had "kept." Anthony Comstock, a famous moralist of the day, thought Thaw had done right. Comstock was just expressing a widely held view that more men like Thaw, who insisted on good morals, made the country a better place to live. President Roosevelt, no stranger to the law—he had been New York City's police commissioner before becoming governor—followed the case carefully from the White House.

During the months leading up to Thaw's trial, newspapers coast to coast did everything they could to keep the White/Thaw/Nesbit case on the front page. Publishers had found out that murder sold papers. And then, to add a new wrinkle, on the eve of the trial, Evelyn's mother, Mrs. Charles Holman, announced that she would clear White's good name.

In the first example of a victim's family member manipulating the press, Mrs. Holman had her spokesperson release a statement criticizing Thaw for his murderous actions, while praising White as a valued contributor to the human race. As for her daughter, she claimed Evelyn was "head-strong, self-willed and beautiful and that led to all her trouble." In response, Mother Thaw sent one of her attorneys to see Mrs. Holman. When the prosecutor later contacted her to testify at the trial, she was suddenly too sick to testify. Meanwhile, the press begged Evelyn for a statement.

Evelyn wanted out. In private, she made a deal with Mother Thaw to stand by Harry during his time

of trouble. Afterward, she was to get a divorce and money to set her up for life.

With the deal consummated, Evelyn called a press conference and told the assembled throng that she was confident her husband would be found not guilty. Leading up to the trial, Evelyn rarely left her hotel suite except to visit Harry at the Tombs.

With her deal with Evelyn in place, Mother Thaw hired the best legal talent available for her son. Lead defense counsel Delphin Delmas was a nationally known criminal defense attorney. Representing the state and county of New York was prosecutor William Travers Jerome. He was politically savvy and knew a victory here would propel his career, but like most good prosecutors, he focused on the state's position: Thaw had committed premeditated murder and needed to be punished for it.

In New York State, that punishment was electrocution.

Delmas's strategy was clear from the beginning. He could not argue against the facts—Thaw had killed White in front of hundreds of witnesses. What could be argued was Thaw's mental condition at the time. Thaw was known to have serious mental problems, and Delmas held that when Thaw pulled the trigger, he was temporarily insane and did not know the difference between right and wrong. Therefore, Delmas entered Thaw's plea as "not guilty by reason of temporary insanity" and then set out to prove it to a jury. If he succeeded, it would be a first because no one in the history of American jurisprudence had ever been found not guilty by reason of insanity in a capital crime.

Six months after the murder, Thaw's trial began, and though the century was only six years old, newspapers labeled it "the Trial of the Century." After the opening arguments, in which the two lawyers staked out their territory, Jerome called witnesses who testified as to Thaw's sentiments regarding White; he had made threats against him on numerous occasions. But the charge of murder in the first degree requires a higher degree of proof than mere threats. Jerome knew it was necessary to prove premeditation, that Thaw talked about it specifically sometime prior to the murder. He got what he needed when Walter Paxton, Madison Square Garden's engineer, testified.

Paxton had been near the elevators that Thaw and Evelyn rode that night. He testified that when the couple came into the theater and saw White, Thaw made comments about wanting the man dead. The prosecution rested, and the defense began their case.

A parade of doctors and friends were called to the stand to testify to Thaw's aberrant behavior. Others testified to White's decadent reputation. This was a clever tactic by defense attorney Delmas to put the dead White and his amorous ways on trial. If the jury could be made to believe that what Thaw did was morally right, they might not even have to prove insanity to win an acquittal.

After these witnesses, it was time for the star attraction: Evelyn Nesbit Thaw. Evelyn had been to the trial every day in support of her husband. Now, it was her turn to testify in his defense.

Under Delmas's patient questioning, Evelyn recounted her relationship with White. She told how it had started innocently, between a paternal older man and his young protégée. She told about their lunches at "Stanny's" rooftop apartment and her delight in the red velvet swing. Then Evelyn launched into the sad tale of how Stanny had given her drugged champagne and raped her. The courtroom was silent as she testified. As Evelyn revealed detail upon detail of White's nefarious character, some jurors could be seen getting angry. Delmas then made Evelyn admit that she had told Thaw the story. His response was to break down and cry at his wife's defiling. But Harry K. Thaw was a real man—despite the fact that she had lost her virginity to White, he chose to marry her, for which she was eternally grateful.

When it was the prosecutor's turn, Jerome brought out Evelyn's showgirl past. Through his questioning, Jerome tried to imply that she knew exactly what White's intentions were and she went along anyway because of the good an affair could do for her. Jerome even tried to plant doubt that the champagne had been drugged at all.

Evelyn claimed to have hated White, but if she did, Jerome wanted to know, why did she continue to keep company with him?

Evelyn said that she had resisted his advances, but had to finally give in because she was the sole support of her family. Jerome kept up the pressure, hoping Evelyn would waver and admit her affection for White, but it never happened. Instead, the public felt sorry for her. Jerome began to worry about getting a conviction.

When the case went to the jury, it turned out that Jerome's worrying was for naught. The jury deadlocked 7-5 to convict. Delmas could take heart that five jurors had bought his insanity defense. The judge officially ruled it a hung jury. Nine months later, the second trial of Harry K. Thaw began, and the same witnesses delivered the same salacious testimony amid the same public clamor for any bit of titillating news. This time, though, the jury reached a verdict, finding that Thaw was temporarily insane at the time he killed White. As such, the judge ruled, he needed confinement and treatment in an asylum.

To many in America, Harry K. Thaw was a folk hero, the defender of a young damsel's morals, a man who put his money where his gun was. With his money and influence, no one expected Thaw's confinement to be long, least of all Thaw. It was no surprise, then, that his journey in a private railroad car to the Mattawan asylum was more a cause for celebration than remorse.

Thaw had filled his private railroad car with all of his partying friends and a supply of whiskey, champagne, and food. When the train pulled into Manhattan, crowds cheered Thaw's arrival. Thaw did not expect to be on the inside for long. He expected his family to get him out immediately, and when they did not, he jumped ship.

Thaw escaped to Canada. Prosecutor Jerome, livid upon being told of Thaw's escape, immediately phoned Canadian authorities and asked them to locate and return Thaw to New York State for justice. Since Thaw made no secret of his identity or location, he was swiftly extradited to America. The court reviewed his case, and instead of finding that there was ample evidence to charge him with prison escape, decided to reexamine his sentence.

The public wanted Thaw free and made no secret of its feelings. So did Mother Thaw, who was continuing to pull strings behind the scenes. Thus, it was not a complete surprise when the court ruled that Thaw was now sane, his mind evidently jarred back to reality by his escape to Canada.

Once freed, Thaw's first act was to file for divorce from Evelyn, who by then, had given birth to a child conceived during one of the times she had visited Thaw in the Tombs, when the guards had left them alone. Thaw denied paternity, and there was no blood test at the time to establish that fact. Evelyn demanded that Mother Thaw pay her the $1 million for standing by her husband. Mother Thaw demurred. Evelyn was enraged. Not only did she not get the lump sum, but the alimony from her subsequent divorce settlement did not pay all her bills. With a child to support, she had to return to show business.

Evelyn made a triumphant comeback in vaudeville and on Broadway and soon married her partner in a song-and-dance act, Jack Clifford. They lasted longer as partners than spouses. After divorcing Clifford,

Evelyn's celebrity began to fade and, eventually, so did her looks, until the jobs dwindled down to nothing. She drifted into drug addiction, alcoholism, and poverty and lived anyplace that was cheap. Occasionally, Thaw slipped her some money to pay bills.

Evelyn Nesbit Thaw died in 1966. She was 81 years old. She had survived White by 50 years and her husband by 19.

After he got his freedom, Harry K. Thaw lived his life as he always had until the end. He died in 1947 at age 76. In 1975, novelist E. L. Doctorow published his version of the White/Nesbit/Thaw saga in his novel *Ragtime*. But what no one really looked at was the devastating effects of White's murder on his family.

His wife had loved him and so did his kids, but in the Victorian age, they had to live with tremendous humiliation over White's decadent behavior. Suzannah Lessard, White's great-granddaughter, wrote that White's name was spoken only in whispers in his family, even 50 years after his death. Lessard, born 40 years after her great-grandfather's death, says that Stanford White's murder still haunts his family.

Today, White is remembered for being one of the 20th century's most celebrated murder victims, his architecture forgotten by most, except for aficionados.

Washington, D.C. (1907) the first and only criminal trial before the Supreme Court

The trial of Sheriff Joseph F. Shipp before the Supreme Court in 1907 is the only criminal trial to be held before the Supreme Court in U.S. history.

On January 23, 1906, a 21-year-old white woman named Nevada Taylor was on her way home from her bookkeeping job in downtown Chattanooga, Tennessee. She claimed she was raped by a black man in a local cemetery. Her only description of the rapist was that he had "a soft, kind voice."

Upon hearing the girl's story, Sheriff Joseph Shipp of Hamilton County searched for the rapist, witnesses, and any evidence he could find. All he came up with was a black leather strap used in the rape. After offering a $50 reward, which grew with public contributions to $375, Shipp got a break.

On January 25 Will Hixon, a white man who worked near the scene of the rape, came forward. He told Shipp that he saw a black man "twirling a leather strap around his finger," shortly before the rape. This mysterious figure became the chief suspect, and eventually police settled on Ed Johnson, a

black man arrested after being found riding on an ice truck. Despite being subjected to the third degree for three hours, Johnson denied any knowledge about the rape.

Meanwhile, more than 1,500 people gathered in the courtyard in front of the county jail, shouting and holding guns and ropes aloft. Tennessee governor Cox ordered the National Guard out, but by the time troops arrived, the jail had been heavily damaged. The lynch mob discovered that Johnson was not in residence. Earlier in the day, he had been moved to Nashville for his own protection.

On January 27 Taylor went to Nashville to provide a positive ID of her attacker. The line-up consisted of Johnson and a second black man. Standing in front of Taylor, the two were asked to say several sentences so Taylor could hear their voices. Taylor, having a 50-50 chance, identified Johnson, "like the man I remember [with] the same soft, kind voice." Losing no time, Shipp telegraphed Judge S. S. McReynolds to empanel a grand jury. That afternoon, Hamilton County District Attorney Matt Whitaker presented evidence against Johnson. The grand jury promptly issued a rape indictment. Trying to make sure that the trial was fair, Judge McReynolds appointed Lewis Shepherd, W. G. M. Thomas, and Robert Cameron to represent Ed Johnson.

In a *Nashville Banner* article published on February 2, 1906, Johnson publicly declared his innocence. Four days later, on February 6 the trial began in Chattanooga. Taylor was the star witness. She identified Johnson as her rapist, and soon after, Will Hixon testified that Johnson was the man he had seen with a strap in his hand.

Johnson's lawyers used the "other guy" defense. Their witnesses testified that at the time of the rape, approximately 6 P.M., Johnson was drinking across town at the Last Chance Saloon. Therefore, he could not have been the man who raped Taylor. To support his claim, Johnson took the witness chair and vociferously denied the charges against him.

On rebuttal, the prosecution again called Taylor. A juror was allowed to ask Taylor whether she "can state positively that this is the Negro?" She replied, "I will not swear that he is the man, but I believe he is the Negro who assaulted me."

Without Taylor's testimony, the prosecution had no other evidence. There was nothing else to tie Taylor to the girl or the crime scene. Yet, upon hearing Taylor say she could not positively identify Johnson as the man who raped her, a member of the jury yelled out, "If I could get at him, I'd tear his heart out right now."

Judge McReynolds already had more than adequate reason to declare a mistrial. Jurors are not supposed to question witnesses during a trial, let alone pronounce verdict publicly before they are given the case. Nevertheless, McReynolds allowed the case to go to the jury. After deliberating for seven hours, the jury came back with a unanimous verdict of guilty.

Thinking that the lynch mob would be satisfied if Johnson waived his right to appeal, which would probably result in the court having mercy and giving him a life sentence, Johnson's lawyers convinced him to do exactly that. Apparently not aware of this "plea bargain," Judge McReynolds sentenced Johnson to be hanged on March 13.

Facing death, Johnson got Noah Parden, an African-American attorney, to handle his appeal. Parden then told the judge he wanted to file his appeal immediately. Judge McReynolds, in turn, told Parden to wait a day and then file. When Parden came back the next day, McReynolds denied the motion, holding that it was filed one day too late.

Realizing that his client was being railroaded, Parden filed a writ of error with the Tennessee Supreme Court. That court unanimously declined to postpone Johnson's execution or consider any other aspects of the case. Running out of options and time, Parden went to the federal courts. He filed a petition for writ of habeas corpus in federal district court in Knoxville.

In his brief, Parden alleged that Johnson was denied due process of law, a fair and impartial trial, and equal protection of the law in violation of the U.S. Constitution. In response, District Judge Charles Clark issued an order temporarily preventing Sheriff Shipp from taking Johnson from Knoxville, where he was imprisoned, to Chattanooga for execution.

On March 10, 1906, each side presented its case before Judge Clark at federal district court in Knoxville. At 12:47 A.M., Judge Clark issued his ruling: The Sixth Amendment's guarantee of an impartial trial does not apply to state trials. He did, however, stay Johnson's execution until March 23 to allow time for an appeal to the U.S. Supreme Court.

In the wake of the decision, Sheriff Shipp and other officials publicly questioned whether a federal judge had the power to postpone the execution. Governor Cox agreed and overruled the federal court. He set an earlier execution date of March 20.

On March 15 someone set fire to the building in which Parden rented offices. The fire was put out before there was major damage. But the message was clear—anyone who supported Johnson faced retribution from an unseen enemy. Undaunted, Parden boarded a train for Washington, D.C., to argue his case before the Supreme Court. On March 17, 1906, Parden pleaded Johnson's case for a writ of habeas corpus before Supreme Court justice John Marshall Harlan. Harlan said he would consider before ruling. Parden went home to wait for news.

Back in Washington, Harlan met with the other Supreme Court justices at the home of Chief Justice Fuller. In an unprecedented move, the Court decided to issue an order granting Johnson's appeal and staying his execution.

On March 19, 1906, at about 8 P.M., a group of armed men approached the jail where Ed Johnson was being held. Sheriff Shipp was not at the jail, and the lynch mob had no problem getting into Johnson's cell. Confronted by men who were there to lynch him, Johnson closed his eyes and recited the Twenty-third Psalm. Before he could finish, the lynch mob threw a rope around Johnson's and, cheering, marched him out of the jail and down six blocks to the Walnut Street Bridge.

Johnson's last words were,

I am ready to die. But I never done it. I am going to tell the truth. I am not guilty. I have said all the time that I did not do it, and it is true. I was not there. I know I am going to die and I have no fear to die and I have no fear at all. . . . God bless you all. I am innocent.

And then Ed Johnson was swung out from a limb over the Tennessee River.

The effects of Johnson's lynching were profound. For the first time, African Americans publicly protested the lynching of one of their own by hurting the white establishment financially. On March 20 the entire black population of Chattanooga protested the lynching of Ed Johnson by staying home from work. To keep order the mayor ordered all the town's saloons closed and 200 men deputized.

In Washington, the justices of the Supreme Court had been watching what was happening in Chattanooga. In a meeting to discuss what might be done about the lynching, Justice Harlan said, "The mandate of the Supreme Court has for the first time in the history of the country been openly defied by a community."

Justice Oliver Wendell Holmes told reporters, "In all likelihood, this was a case of an innocent man improperly branded a guilty brute and condemned to die from the start."

On March 21 President Roosevelt, who also condemned the lynching, met with Attorney General William Moody to discuss what action, if any, the federal government might take in the matter. The president then ordered the Secret Service to look into the lynching.

Back in Chattanooga, there were some who openly criticized the lynchers and their sympathizers, but when it came time to vote, Sheriff Shipp got reelected in a landslide. Quietly, though, the Secret Service was conducting its investigation. They reported back to the president on April 20 that they had evidence implicating 21 members of the mob and five officials, including Sheriff Shipp, in Johnson's murder.

On May 17, 1906, Attorney General Moody met with Chief Justice Fuller and Justice Harlan to plan the federal government's response to the lynching. Moody decided to charge those involved with criminal contempt of the Supreme Court, an unprecedented charge. At the formal indictment on October 15, 1906, the defendants and their lawyers appeared in Washington before the justices of the Supreme Court and entered their pleas. All members of the lynch mob pleaded not guilty and claimed to either have alibis for the time of the lynching or that they had been mistaken for someone else.

On December 4, 1906, oral arguments were held for two days on the question of whether the Court had jurisdiction to consider the contempt charges against the 26 defendants. The highlight was when Justice Holmes asked a defense lawyer, "But you would agree that this Court has the authority to determine that the Sixth Amendment [guarantee of a fair trial] is binding on the state courts, do you not?"

The Supreme Court's unanimous opinion, delivered by Justice Holmes on Christmas Eve, December 24, 1906, said that the Court did indeed have jurisdiction to try the 26 defendants. That cleared the way for the first and only criminal trial in Supreme Court history.

On February 12, 1907, James Maher, deputy clerk of the Supreme Court, began taking evidence in the U.S. Customs House in Chattanooga in the trial of Shipp and the other defendants. Thirty-one government witnesses testified for five days. Then, citing other business, the Supreme Court recessed the trial until June.

When the trial resumed on June 15, it took the defense only five days to present its case, which was based on demonstrating that the wrong men had

been charged. The justices dismissed charges against 17 of the defendants based on the evidence presented. The court then scheduled closing arguments in March before rendering the final verdict on Shipp and the remaining nine defendants.

On March 2, 1909, the attorney general closed the government's case. The next day, defense attorneys countered with their arguments for the nine defendants. Unlike a regular criminal trial, in which the court renders its verdict immediately, the Supreme Court stuck to its tradition of taking months to weigh the evidence. Finally, on May 24, Chief Justice Fuller announced the court's decision in *United States v. Shipp et al.*

Fuller wrote that "it is absurd to contend" that Shipp "did not know a lynching would probably be attempted on the 19th," that he "acquiesced" in the lynching, and that he demonstrated "utter disregard for this court's mandate." Shipp, the jailer, and four members of the lynch mob were found guilty. The other three defendants were found not guilty.

Under Supreme Court order, U.S. marshals arrested Shipp and the others who had been back home awaiting the verdict. They were taken to Washington for sentencing. On November 15 Chief Justice Fuller asked Shipp and the other convicted men to rise before the bench of the assembled justices of the Supreme Court.

Shipp and two men from the lynch mob were sentenced to the limit of the law: 90 days' imprisonment in the U.S. Jail in the District of Columbia. The other three defendants received 60-day sentences. While the sentences were paltry, the message spoke volumes. Anyone who defied an edict of the federal government would be prosecuted to the fullest extent of the law.

In a sense, the Johnson lynching can be viewed as the first civil rights prosecution in American history. Certainly it was a forerunner of later civil rights criminal investigations and court cases in the 1960s. But at the time, Chattanooga thought it had bested the federal government.

On January 30, 1910, Shipp arrived home in Chattanooga to a hero's welcome. His sentence completed, he had come home to see 10,000 like-minded Chattanooga citizens greet him at Terminal Station. Shipp died on September 18, 1925, and is buried in Forest Hills Cemetery, the same one in which Nevada Taylor claimed she was raped.

As for Ed Johnson, it would take a long time before the state of Tennessee reexamined his case. In 1999 Leroy Phillips coauthored a book called *Contempt of Court: The Turn-of-the-Century Lynching*

That Launched a Hundred Years of Federalism. Convinced of Johnson's innocence and the need to rectify this past wrong, he filed a petition with Criminal Court Judge Doug Meyer to have Johnson's 94-year-old conviction overturned. The judge agreed, and the state of Tennessee officially overturned the conviction. One more ghost in the struggle for civil rights was laid to rest.

Washington, D.C. (1907) *Wilson v. Shaw*

In this landmark case, the plaintiff argued that the U.S. government did not have the right to buy Panamanian land to build the Panama Canal.

Justice David Brewer of the Supreme Court wrote in the majority opinion that Congress not only had that power but also the power to construct interstate highways. The rationale was the provision of the Constitution that allows the government to regulate interstate commerce. While the legal hurdle had now been cleared to pave U.S. roads, it was still up to Congress to allocate the monies to do exactly that.

Washington, D.C. (1908) the origin of the FBI

Under federal law, the chief examiner for the Department of Justice was authorized by the attorney general to administer all the department's investigative matters. That meant that whenever a federal crime was suspected, the chief examiner's organization would investigate. In 1909 the attorney general made it official when he renamed the chief examiner's organization the Bureau of Investigation.

Dearborn, Michigan (1908) Ford introduces the Model T

Henry Ford, who invented the automobile a decade before, continued his innovations and in 1908, introduced a low-priced car that the average person could afford.

Before the Model T, only the wealthy could pay for a custom-made automobile. But the Model T was mass-produced on an assembly line, lowering the price and making the invention available to the masses. Americans flocked to their local Ford dealers. Led by the American Automobile Association (AAA), motorists soon became an impassioned lobby in Congress for federal intervention in road building.

One main problem needed to be resolved before Congress would appropriate monies and begin construction. Motorist groups and the burgeoning auto industry wanted hard-surfaced interstate roads. They were less interested in servicing the infrastructure than they were in getting themselves from point A to point B. In contrast, farmers wanted weatherproof farm-to-market roads which, by necessity, would be concentrated in rural areas.

While the two sides debated, criminals still relied on the horse and the locomotive to do their dastardly work.

See also DETROIT, MICHIGAN (1892).

Robert Leroy Parker, a.k.a. "Butch Cassidy" (1866–1908), and Harry Longabaugh, a.k.a. the Sundance Kid (1864–1908)

The deaths of Robert Leroy Parker, also known as "Butch Cassidy," and his partner Harry Longabaugh, also known as "the Sundance Kid," stand as a turning point in the annals of American crime.

Original badge of the Bureau of Investigation, forerunner of the FBI (National Archives)

The crime of train robbery, invented by the James Gang and taken to its highest and most profitable level by Butch and Sundance, would be no more. Also, the ability of American criminals like Butch and Sundance, to seek solace in South America would never be as easy again because the United States was cooperating with foreign governments in pursuit of fugitives.

Butch and Sundance's Bolivian demise meant the end of an almost chivalrous form of banditry that began with Joseph Hare in the early 19th century. They were its final practitioners and the best. In all the trains and banks they robbed in the United States, Butch Cassidy and the Sundance Kid never killed anyone.

That is a record.

Butch Cassidy was born Robert Leroy Parker on April 15, 1866, in Beaver, Utah. Despite being raised by pioneering Mormon parents on a ranch near Circleville, Utah, Parker reached his teens full of vim and vigor. He was befriended by an old rustler named Mike Cassidy, whom he idolized. In his late teens Parker left home for good to seek his place in the world.

Many teenagers of the time were like him, skirting that fine line between being an outlaw and an itinerant cowboy. The latter were relied on for cheap labor on ranches throughout the West. When the jobs stopped coming, the cowboy, who never made much money in the first place, had no savings. His only choice was to turn to banditry. Parker was particularly adept at riding that line.

Parker worked as a cowboy on several ranches. On the side, he rustled cattle to supplement his wages. He also took a job as a butcher in Rock Springs, Wyoming. What he took away from that experience was his new nickname, Butch, short for butcher. Realizing that he was doing some things that his parents might not be proud of, he changed his last name to Cassidy, in honor of his old mentor.

The name-changing turned out to be fortuitous. In 1896 Butch Cassidy was arrested for cattle rustling. He served 18 months behind bars, after which he petitioned Wyoming's governor for early release. The governor believed that Butch had served enough time and offered him a deal: If paroled, Butch had to promise to go straight.

Butch was an honest man. He told the governor he could not promise that; he was set in his criminal ways. But what he could promise was that if he were released, he would never again do anything illegal in Wyoming. Considering Butch's record and criminal potential, the governor knew a good deal when he saw one. Butch was released. For the rest of his life, he never committed a crime in Wyoming.

By 1896 Butch's genius for organization and planning were becoming apparent. He became friends with Harry Longabaugh—the Sundance Kid. Their partnership would make history.

Harry Longabaugh was born in Lancaster County, Pennsylvania, in 1867. When he came of age, Longabaugh drifted west. In 1887 he stole a horse from the VVV Ranch in northeastern Crook Country, Wyoming. Sheriff Ryan of Crook County caught him near Miles City, Montana. For the next 18 months, Longabaugh served time in Sundance, the county seat of Crook County. After he got out, Longabaugh began calling himself the Sundance Kid.

Making friends with Butch Cassidy, he was recruited into a gang that Cassidy was forming. Along with the other outlaws that Cassidy got to join up—Harvey Logan ("Kid Curry"); Ben Kilpatrick ("the Tall Texan"); Elzy Lay; and "News" Carver—they became famous when they named themselves the Wild Bunch, not to be confused with the gang Bill Doolin led.

From the late 1890s through the first years of the 20th century, Cassidy's Wild Bunch robbed more banks and trains successfully than any other gang before or since. Throughout the western United States, their fame preceded them. And in all the trains and banks they robbed, they never killed anyone, which made the gang popular with the public.

In early summer 1899 Butch Cassidy decided that the Wild Bunch would hit the Union Pacific Flyer near Wilcox, Wyoming. They pulled the job on June 2, 1899. In the mail car that day was Robert Lawson. A mail clerk for the Union Pacific Railroad, Lawson recounted his experience in the June 8, 1899, issue of the *Buffalo Bulletin*. Lawson recalled how the train stopped in the middle of nowhere because there was a large log blocking the track.

As soon as we came to a standstill, Conductor Storey went forward to see what was the matter and saw several men with guns, one of whom shouted that they were going to blow up the train with dynamite. The conductor understood the situation at once and, before meeting the bandits, turned and started back to warn the second section.

The robbers mounted the engine and at the point of their guns forced the engineer and fireman to dismount, after beating the engineer over the head with their guns, claiming that he didn't move fast enough, and marched them back over to our car.

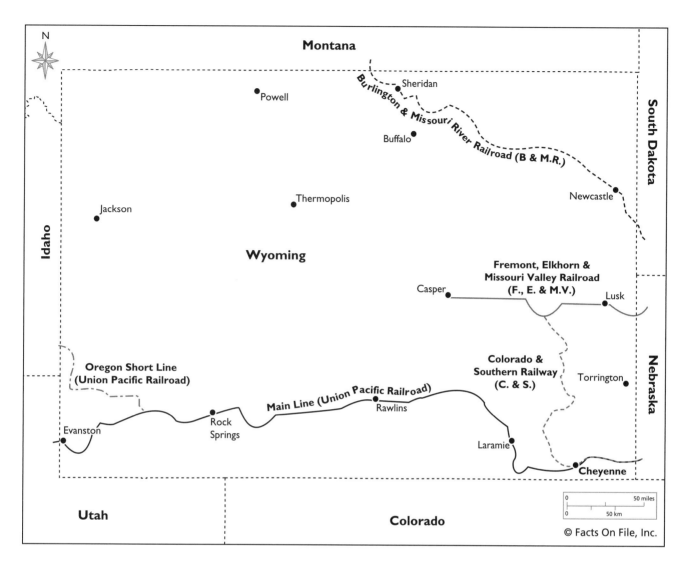

Butch Cassidy and the Sundance Kid committed their hold-ups along the rail routes of Wyoming.

In a few moments, we heard voices outside our car calling for Sherman and looking out saw Engineer Jones and his fireman accompanied by three masked men with guns. Burt Bruce, clerk in charge, refused to open the door, and ordered all lights extinguished. There was much loud talk and threats to blow up the car were made, but the doors were kept shut. In about 15 minutes, two shots were fired into the car, one of the balls passing through the water tank and on through the stanchions.

Following close behind the shooting came a terrific explosion, and one of the doors was completely wrecked and most of the car windows broken. The bandits then threatened to blow up the whole car if we didn't get out, so Bruce gave the word and we jumped down, and were immediately lined up and searched for weapons.

They said it would not do us no good to make trouble, that they didn't want the mail, that they wanted what was in the express car and was going to have it, and that they had powder enough to blow the whole train off the track. After searching us, they started us back and we saw up the track the headlight of the second section.

They asked what was on the train, and somebody said there were two cars of soldiers on the train. This scared them and they hastened back to the engine, driving us ahead. They forced us on the engine, and as Dietrick moved too slowly they assisted him with a few kicks.

While on the engine, Dietrick, in the act of closing the furnace door, brushed a mask off one of the men, endeavoring to catch a glimpse of his face. The man quickly grasped his mask and threatened to "plug" Dietrick. They then ran the train ahead across a gully and stopped. There were two extra cars on the train. They were uncoupled. Others of the gang went to the bridge, attempting to destroy it with their giant powder, or dynamite, which they placed on the timbers.

After the explosion at the bridge they boarded the engine with the baggage, express, and mail cars and went for about two miles. Upon arriving at the stopping place, they proceeded to business again and went to the express car and ordered the messenger, E. C. Woodcock, to open. He refused, and the outlaws proceeded to batter down the doors and blew a big hole in the side of the car. The explosion was so terrific that the messenger was stunned and had to be taken from the car.

They then proceeded to the other mail car, occupied by clerks O'Brian and Skidmore and threatened to blow it up, but the boys were advised to come out which they did. The robbers then went after the safes in the express car with dynamite and soon succeeded in getting into them, but not before the care were torn to pieces by the force of the charges. They took everything from the safes and what they didn't carry away they destroyed. After finishing their work they started out in a northerly direction on foot.

Lawson would later tell lawmen that the robbers, the tallest of whom was about six feet, all wore masks reaching below their necks. The leader appeared to be about 35 years old and spoke "with a squeaky voice, pitched very high." That was Cassidy.

Time was running out for the Wild Bunch. The Pinkerton National Detective Agency had been hired by the railroads to bring Butch and the gang to ground. They did the next best thing: they secured their clients' trains well, guarding them with cars full of heavily armed and provisioned mercenaries. Butch realized that if the gang continued its work in the United States, they would wind up dead.

Butch Cassidy, his friend the Sundance Kid, and Sundance's paramour, Etta Place, fled to South America, where they purchased a ranch in Argentina. But after a few years of going the straight and narrow, they took up stealing again.

Butch Cassidy and the Sundance Kid took to robbing banks in several South American countries until they wound up trying to do the same thing in Bolivia. The Bolivian army, which had other ideas, cornered

the duo, and what happened after that point is open to conjecture.

There is some strong evidence to show that Butch and Sundance died in a shootout with the Bolivians. At least one attempt has been made by forensic anthropologists to find Sundance's remains and identify them. In an alternate theory, Butch's sister would later claim that they eluded death and that Butch came back to America to live a normal life until he died. In this version, the sister never confirms her story by revealing Butch's gravesite despite making these claims on the nationally Syndicated *Mike Douglas Show* in the 1970s.

Did Butch and Sundance die in a hail of bullets in South America, or did they return to America unscathed? No one really knows.

William Barclay "Bat" Masterson (1853–1921) New York City marshal and crusading reporter

Bat Masterson was a has-been gunfighter, gambler, and fight promoter when, in 1902, he found himself at a bar in Denver with the barrel of a Colt .45 poking into his back. The man on the other end of the gun was Jim Marshal, himself a famous Western lawman.

Bat had gotten into a dispute with one of the town's politicos and had beaten him up with his cane. Hired by the town's mayor to kick Bat out before there was real bloodshed, Marshal knew the safest way to approach Bat was from behind with a loaded gun. Marshal gave Bat until sundown to get out of town.

Bat always knew when he held a losing hand. Leaving his wife Emma behind, and promising to send for her when he got work, he boarded the eastbound train, figuring that New York City gave him the best chance to make a new life. He figured to exploit his celebrity in the Big Town. Bat had no sooner disembarked in New York in fall 1902, when he was arrested for grand larceny.

An elder of the Mormon church, George Snow, claimed that he and Bat had been on the train together, during which time Bat had fleeced him in a card game. Theatrical magnate John Considine, Sr., put up Bat's bail and the charges were later dropped when Snow recanted his story. Still, Bat's brush with the law was not over.

He was arrested again, this time for violation of the state Sullivan Law: carrying a concealed weapon without a permit. Bat complained to the *New York World*, "Why, there's 40,000 fakers in New York carrying guns bigger than mine and not a word about it." Realizing that it was the famous western

Bat Masterson (National Archives)

that the position of U.S. marshal for Oklahoma was his for the asking.

"It wouldn't do," Bat later wrote in a letter to the president, adding,

A man of my peculiar reputation couldn't hold such a place without trouble. If I were to go out to the Indian Territory [Oklahoma] as Marshal I can see what would happen. I'd have some drunken boy to kill once a year. Some kid who was born after I took my guns off would get drunk and look me over; and the longer he looked the less he'd be able to see where my reputation came from. In the end, he'd crawl round to a gun play and I'd have to send him over the jump.

So Mr. President, with all thanks to you, I believe I won't take the place. I've finally got out of that zone of fire and I hope never to go back to it.

It was then that T.R. did the next best thing and offered Bat a political sinecure, an appointment as deputy marshal of the city of New York. Bat accepted.

DEPUTY MARSHAL OF NEW YORK
On March 28, 1905, one of the most famous gunfighters in the history of the West took his oath of office. New York's newest deputy marshal had flashbulbs popping in his face from the cameras of a half-dozen photographers who wanted to show their readers the slightly round, pudgy, middle-aged form of the sheriff of Dodge City.

Bat told the press that he wanted to vehemently deny that he was a "badman." When a tabloid reporter asked him how many men he had killed, Bat said "All that talk was Tommy rot. This tale about notches—that's what gets next to me," Bat continued. "Who ever heard of a pistol having notches on it? I've seen a pistol once or twice myself—though not so often as some folks believe—and I've yet to see the first notch on the handle to one. I'm going to be a Marshal here just like any other one, I suppose. There won't be any occasion for trouble."

It was not hard to imagine him gunning down the two men in Dodge City who had killed his brother Ed, or Sergeant Ralph King in Texas, who looked unkindly on Bat's ministrations to a saloon girl named Molly. Those three killings, all ruled justifiable homicides by coroner's inquests and grand juries, were actually the extent of Bat's gunplay.

Such was the lack of communication in the Old West that by the time the stories of those deaths were repeated, Bat's reputation as a killer had grown to legendary proportions. This was only added to by

marshal they had in custody, the New York police quickly dropped the charges.

At 47, Bat was broke and out of prospects. Desperate for work, he called on friends to approach President Theodore Roosevelt, "T.R.", for a political appointment. T.R. who had spent time out West grieving after his wife and mother died on the same day, knew of Masterson but only by reputation.

T.R.'s previous appointment to federal posts of other gunfighters such as Pat Garrett, the man who shot Billy the Kid, were not well received. With an election approaching, the president did not want to give any more ammunition to his political opponents.

T.R. asked Bat's confidant, Alfred Henry Lewis (whose brother owned the *Morning Telegraph*) if Bat could read and write. He did not want the westerner causing him embarrassment by proving to be illiterate. After receiving assurances that he indeed could, T.R., being the shrewd politician that he was, waited until he won election on November 8, 1904. One of his first acts after being sworn in was to secure Bat a federal appointment.

Bat took the train down to Washington and met with T.R. in the White House. T.R. informed him

the exciting and authentic tales of Bat's days as a buffalo hunter, army scout, Indian fighter, and frontier gambler.

During his tenure as deputy marshal in New York, Bat spent most of his time hobnobbing with the president at the White House and with the New York gentry. Bat sent for his wife and he and Emma took up residence at 300 West 49th Street, an ornate apartment building that still stands.

During his time as marshal, Bat renewed his acquaintance with the two Lewis brothers, Alfred and William. William, editor and publisher of the *Morning Telegraph*, was aware of Bat's background as a boxing promoter in Denver and his skill with a pen. Bat had written many an article for western papers, what would be known today as op-ed pieces. In 1907 Masterson authored a series of well-received articles on the deadly art of gunfighting for *Human Life* magazine. His literary talent, coupled with his boxing acumen, seemed like a sure fire winner to Lewis.

FIGHTING CORRUPTION

After he left the Federal Marshals Service, Lewis gave Bat a column in the *Morning Telegraph* called "Masterson's Views on Timely Topics." More often than not, he wrote about the fight game, of which he had intimate knowledge.

Aided by his reputation as a legendary lawman, Bat soon became one of the country's foremost sports authorities, widely quoted in the newspapers from coast to coast. Having been a referee, promoter, second to many fighters, and a gambler, he was one of the few writers with a direct and intimate knowledge of the pugilistic art.

In his columns Bat Masterson campaigned against the corruption that flourished in the boxing business. There was no greater scam going on than the betting on professional prizefights. Every gambler knew that any championship fight could be fixed and yet, they bet anyway, figuring they might hit it big.

Masterson exposed the crooked fight promoters and suspect fights. As a sportswriter, he was the direct antecedent of such opinionated and legendary sports columnists as Red Smith, Dave Anderson, and Dick Young. Also, because he was a celebrity in his own right, he was allowed to write on any topic that interested him.

BAT MASTERSON AND CHESTER GILLETTE

Only one journalist came to the defense of Chester Gillette: William Barclay "Bat" Masterson. It took an Old West lawman to buck the popular sentiment.

Near the end of the trial, Bat wrote a *Morning Telegraph* piece with the bannered headline:

> ## NEW STYLE LYNCH LAW IN UPSTATE NEW YORK

"This trial is a flagrant travesty of justice," Bat wrote. "It's an inexcusable insult to the intelligence and civilization of New York." Referring to the court's willingness to get the defendant into the electric chair as soon as possible, Bat declared, "The entire proceedings are a subversive of law and order and a disgraceful mockery of justice."

The authorities of the upstate New York county where the trial took place found Bat and his editor guilty of criminal contempt for, respectively, writing the article and publishing it. They were taken into custody. While awaiting the bail bondsman, Bat told a reporter for the *New York Sun*:

I've been through a great deal out west, lived in Dodge City when it was the toughest town on the cattle trail, ran a vaudeville house, enlisted as a scout under General Miles against the Comanches. And here in my sober fifty-second year, I get into trouble for writing something in the paper. If that isn't a funny trick of fate, I don't know what is.

Bat supported Gillette right up to the moment he was put in the electric chair and the executioner threw the switch.

DODGE CITY, KANSAS (1910): MASTERSON RETURNS TO DODGE

In 1910 Bat went out west again to Reno, Nevada, to cover the title fight between Jack Johnson and Jim Jeffries. Jeffries was a retired former heavyweight champion. He willingly allowed himself to be cast as the first "Great White Hope," the man who would wrest the heavyweight crown from the champion, a black man named Jack Johnson.

During the week leading up to the fight, some of the greatest gamblers in the country came to Denver to see what kind of action they could get on the fight. On July 4 Bat reported on the fight itself, during which Johnson hammered Jeffries back into retirement. After the fight, Bat hopped the first eastbound train headed back to New York.

It turned out to be the Santa Fe Line, which he took from Colorado into Kansas. He had traveled these very same tracks countless times in his younger years as a lawman, gambler, and ladies' man. Upon his return to New York, he wrote in his column in the *Morning Telegraph* on July 31, 1910:

In coming down the Arkansas Valley from Pueblo to Dodge . . . I could not help wondering at the marvelous change that had come over the country in the last twenty years. As I looked from the car window after reaching the Kansas line at Coolidge, I saw in all directions groves of trees, orchards and fields bearing abundant crops of corn, wheat and alfalfa. . . . The idea that the plains of Western Kansas could ever be made fertile was something I had never dreamed of.

At 8 A.M. the train got into Dodge and stopped for a 30-minute breakfast break. Twirling his cane, Bat looked around. He saw the roadbed that he and his long-dead brother Ed had graded, near where he and Wyatt Earp placed their buffalo hides for sale and shipment when they were "stinkers."

The city jail was still there, and so was the wooden sidewalk where his brother Ed was shot. The street where Bat cradled his dead brother's head in his arms was now graded and paved.

"But why dwell further on the subject. They are now but memories. Dodge City is now a thriving little country village, surrounded by a thrifty farming community. There are many of the old-timers still living there and it is doubtful if they would care to live elsewhere. They are well-to-do and happy. And may they live long and continue to prosper, is my sincere wish," Bat Masterson finished his July 31, 1910, column in the *Morning Telegraph*.

THE GREAT WHITE HOPE

Masterson had the extreme good fortune to be writing during the period 1907 to 1915. In sports history, it has been described as the "White Hope" era.

This was the period of time when history in sports was being made. Only 42 years after the Civil War ended, an African-American fighter, the son of slaves, held the greatest of all sports honors. Jack Johnson, became the heavyweight champion of the world. This did not sit well with the Ku Klux Klan or even in the more liberal parts of the eastern United States. Jackson, with his deliberately provocative manner, was like a cocksure gunfighter luring some young kid to challenge him.

One white fighter after another was summoned to take on Johnson, who knocked them all out. Bat heaped contempt on these attempts, not because he

was a champion of racial equality but because the White Hope craze produced such a crop of bums. Bat's patience was finally worn to the quick by Carl Morris, an inept white fighter, who for one year in 1911 was made to believe by his manager, Frank Ufer, that he could beat Johnson.

Known as the Sapulpa (Oklahoma) Giant, Morris knocked out a series of opponents carefully selected by Ufer, who kept building his fighter up in the press. In summer 1911 Ufer brought Morris to New York for the final phase of his drive to the championship when Morris was to fight "Fireman" Jim Flynn.

Bat was in the minority of fighting experts who refused to be impressed by Morris or his manager's claims that he was the legitimate Great White Hope. "A big lumbering slob with nothing to recommend him but his courage," Bat called him in his column. Then he really gained Ufer's ire by continuing that the Morris-Flynn bout was "financed, as to both sides of the contention, by the same man," namely Ufer, who was paying the training expenses of Flynn as well as his own fighter. In other words, the fight was fixed.

Ufer fired back, "Bat is an alleged bad man and gunfighter who made his reputation by shooting drunken Mexicans and Indians in the back."

The *New York Globe* immediately printed Ufer's charges. After the Sapulpa Giant became the Sapulpa Sap when Flynn knocked him out, Bat sued Ufer in New York State Supreme Court for $10,000 in damages ($200,000 in today's money), charging slander; the *Globe* was named as codefendant.

THE TRIAL OF BAT MASTERSON

From out of the West came a procession of character witnesses not seen before or since during civil litigation.

During the period between being a buffalo hunter and lawman, Masterson had served as a scout for the army. Bat's first character witness was Lieutenant General Nelson A. Miles, Commanding General of the Army. It was Miles who confronted Sitting Bull after Custer's Last Stand and drove the Hunkpapa medicine man and his acolytes to flee into Canada. Miles was the conqueror of the great Apache chief Geronimo and the leader of the U.S. forces in the liberation of Puerto Rico. He placed his prestige as the foremost American soldier of his time on Bat's word that his reputation was made on far worthier grounds than those claimed by Ufer.

Then called to the stand by the plaintiff was a dark-eyed, intense-looking man. Mustachioed and middle-aged, he was sworn in as a witness upon being asked by the plaintiff's attorney to state his name he said, "Wyatt Earp." Earp had been prospecting for gold out west when he got the telegram from Bat's attorney asking him to come to New York and be a character witness.

By all contemporary accounts, if you were a friend of Wyatt Earp's, he would do anything for you. When Wyatt heard that his old undersheriff was in trouble, he took the first train east. Earp testified to Bat's courage and his ability to cope with dangerous situations.

Earp's knowledge of the law helped him present cogent testimony. While his fame might not have preceded him just yet, he bore an uncanny resemblance to the gunman in the 1902 seminal motion picture, *The Great Train Robbery,* that everyone had seen. In fact, the lead character was patterned after Earp.

In the end, the court saw things Bat's way and awarded him $3,500 in damages. Bat Masterson went on to cover the most famous boxing match in history, the "Great White Hope Fight" in Cuba in 1915, when Jack Johnson, who could no longer quell the pressures on him to relinquish his title, finally gave in and took a dive in the 20th round, making the awkward Jess Willard heavyweight champion of the world. In fact, not only did Bat cover the fight, he was the timekeeper for all 20 rounds. Williard then signed on to fight the number-one contender.

At the time, Luella Parsons, who would later become famous as one of Hollywood's most powerful gossip columnists, was a reporter for the *Morning Telegraph.* She came to Bat and told him she had had a dream in which the challenger beat Willard.

"I went to Bat with $50, all the money I had in the world and asked him to place the bet for me—on the challenger. 'He hasn't got a prayer,' Bat told me. 'Keep that money in your purse.'" Parsons would later tell a reporter.

The challenger's name was Jack Dempsey. He knocked Willard out.

"For days after Dempsey landed the surprise blow that made him heavyweight champion of the world, Bat Masterson, the big, bold sheriff of Dodge City, couldn't look me in the eye without cringing," Parsons recalled.

Despite occasional lapses of judgment, Bat was usually right about the boxing game.

"Bat was more feared than loved in the boxing world. His opinions were sometimes colored by prejudice that none could shake, but there was never any doubt about his honesty," James P. Sinnott, a *Morning Telegraph* columnist, would later write of him.

Bat did much of his reporting at night and got to visit the city's prime watering holes, such as the Metropole bar at Seventh Avenue and 47th Street. He drank and chatted with such luminaries as Stanford White and his future assassin Harry K. Thaw; Arnold Rothstein, the infamous gambler who fixed the 1919 World Series that led to the Black Sox scandal; Giants baseball manager John J. McGraw; Buffalo Bill Cody, who frequently brought his Wild West Show to New York; and *New York American* columnist Damon Runyon, who would later become famous for creating the musical *Guys and Dolls.*

Bat died on October 27, 1921, slumped over his desk with the next day's column in his typewriter. It hit Damon Runyon particularly hard.

"His death was a strangely quiet closing to a strangely active career," he wrote in his column. "It was the loss of a personal friend, and of one of the most indomitable characters this land has ever seen. He was a 100 percent, 24 karat real man. He was always stretching out a helping hand to some down and outer. He had a great sense of humor and a marvelous fund of reminiscence and was one of the most entertaining companions we have ever known. There are only too few men in the world like Bat Masterson and his death is a genuine loss."

Bat's death was big news. *The New York Tribune* reported, "He died at his desk gripping his pen with the tenacity of which he formerly clung to the hilt of his six-shooter." William Lewis's eulogy in the *Morning Telegraph* was simple and heartfelt. "William Barclay Masterson was one of the whitest, squarest men that ever lived." And the *New York Times* headlined its obituary with a reference to the siege of Adobe Walls. It was the time when Bat, as a youth, held off a marauding band of Indians for three days with little ammunition, food, or water.

Even in death, Bat Masterson was bigger than life. He was buried in Woodlawn Cemetery in the Bronx. The epitaph on his headstone reads "Loved by Everyone."

See also WYATT EARP (1853–1928); FORT DODGE, KANSAS (1865); CORTLAND, NEW YORK (1906).

Washington, D.C. (1914) founding of the AASHO

In December 1914 the American Association of State Highway Officials was founded. This lobbying organization would give the states a strong voice in Congress for federal assistance in road building.

Spring Green, Wisconsin (1914) the Frank Lloyd Wright murder case

Since Stanford White's murder, Frank Lloyd Wright had assumed the mantle as America's most famous and feted architect.

Taliesin, Welsh for "shining brow," was the name of the magnificent home Wright built on a hill in the Wisconsin countryside to celebrate his love for his soul mate, Mamah Borthwick Cheney. On August 15, 1914, Wright was at Chicago's Midway Gardens, a project he was designing on the South Side. He was in the field office, staring intensely at blueprints, when the phone rang. He plucked the receiver off the cradle, placed it at his ear, picked up the microphone and spoke into it. The *Chicago Tribune* the next day reported the conversation this way:

"Wright here."

"This is Frank Roth at Madison," said a voice over the wire. "Be prepared for a shock. Carlton has killed your wife—that is, Mrs. Cheney—the two children and one of your draftsmen. Carlton set fire to the bungalow and got away. He must have gone crazy. A posse is chasing him. You'd better get to Taliesin right away."

In a panic, Wright hung up and made several unsuccessful attempts to get a telephone wire to Taliesin. It was then late afternoon. Wright ran out into the warm summer air. He hailed a taxi that took him to Union Station. Boarding the first train north, he arrived in Spring Green, Wisconsin, hours later. A waiting motor car whisked him off into the countryside. He smelled the smoke before they topped the hill.

Taliesin, the place Wright described as their "spiritual hegira," was a charred ruin. Mamah's body was laid out in the parlor of his cousin's house nearby. Strangely, she had died not from fire but an ax blow to the head. So had all the others who escaped Taliesin during the blaze. From coast to coast, newspapers described Borthwick's murder as "the crime of the century."

In 1911 Wright had designed a home for Chicago financier Edwin Cheney and his wife Mamah Borthwick. During construction, Frank and Mamah fell in love. They were soul mates married to the wrong people. They left their respective spouses and children to "live in sin." Traveling the world, they were the first "jet setters" when air flight was still in its infancy. Back home, newspapers vilified them for their "indecent" actions. Eventually, they returned to the United States.

After divorcing their respective spouses, Wright and Mamah settled in the Wisconsin valley that had been home to Wright's family for generations. There, Wright built Taliesin in 1914. That summer, World War I began in Europe. Wright gave it no mind; he had more pressing concerns.

An intense egotist, Wright knew he would be spending much of the summer of 1914 in Chicago, working on the construction of the Midway Gardens. He needed a butler to help Mamah. On the advice of a friend, he hired Julian Carlton, a native of Barbados.

On Saturday, August 15, 1914, the staff and residents of Taliesin, nine in all, sat down to lunch. Included in the group were Mamah, at 47 the same age as Wright; her two children, nine-year-old Martha and 12-year-old John; two of Wright's draftsmen; and three other employees.

Julian Carlton appeared in his white jacket and asked permission to clean some carpets with gasoline. Given the go-ahead, he went outside, but instead of pouring the liquid on the carpets, he began to pour it around the outside of the house.

As the inhabitants continued to eat lunch, Carlton quietly bolted the doors and windows. Suddenly, someone smelled the gas. They looked down and saw the flammable liquid dribbling in under the door. A moment later, Carlton set off the liquid with a match and the room became an inferno.

The occupants ran to the exits but found the doors locked. There was only one way out—the windows. They were all locked, save one, which had been deliberately left open. According to the story in the next day's edition of the *Chicago Tribune*:

"As fire raced through the house, the Negro stood guarding a window. With his hand ax, he cut his victims down one by one as they leaped from the burning structure."

Afterward, Carlton hid in the basement but was soon captured by Sheriff John T. Williams. In a running gun battle with vigilantes determined to lynch Carlton, Williams held them off until his prisoner was safely in jail at the county seat.

Despite the fact that the coroner's jury (headed up by Wright's uncle) found Carlton insane, Williams was equally certain Carlton was not. A courageous, experienced peace officer, Williams felt there was a logical reason for the crime. He gained Carlton's confidence and the killer promised to tell Williams his motive. But before he did, Carlton committed suicide. Historians have since speculated on, but never discovered, the motive for the crime.

Wright would never again have the personal or professional serenity that characterized his years with Borthwick. Even on his death, April 9, 1959, he asked his then wife Olga to bury him next to Borthwick, who had died more than a half century earlier. His acolytes loaded his coffin into a pickup truck and drove back to Wisconsin, where he was buried within yards of Borthwick's grave.

Cobb County, Georgia (1914) the lynching of Leo Frank

The lynching of Leo Frank is one of the first great hate crimes of the 20th century. It was a murder case in which the conspirators had the gall to pose for pictures beside the freshly lynched body of their victim, knowing full well that even if such a picture were published, which it was, they would never be indicted, which they were not.

By birth Leo Frank was a Jew and a Southerner. He was born in Cuero, Texas, in 1884, and his family moved when he was a child to the great Jewish community that existed in Brooklyn, one of the five boroughs that comprise New York City. He attended Brooklyn public schools all the way through high school. In 1906 Frank graduated from Cornell University with a bachelor's degree in mechanical engineering.

After picking up a few jobs in Massachusetts and Brooklyn, Frank moved to Atlanta, Georgia, in 1907. His uncle owned the National Pencil Company and had hired him as the factory's new supervisor. Over the next three years, Frank became a much-liked employer, respected for his fairness. In his personal life Frank was an active and respected member of Atlanta's Jewish community, the largest in the South.

In 1910 Frank married Lucille Selig, daughter of a prominent Jewish family. In 1912 he became president of his local B'nai B'rith chapter. In 1913 Mary Phagan turned up dead.

Mary Phagan was a 13-year-old child. In Georgia at the time, a 13-year-old was allowed under state law to hold a full-time job, which Mary did at the National Pencil Factory. Mary's job was placing metal tips on pencils. Mary had been temporarily laid off in April, because a shipment of metal tips was late. She was due $1.20 in back wages and went to the factory to collect on Confederate Memorial Day, April 26. She met with Leo Frank, who gave her the money, and she left.

Newt Lee, a black night watchman at the factory, discovered the blood-soaked body of Mary Phagan on April 27. Two notes were found nearby that would take on great significance as the case pro-

gressed. Atlanta detectives immediately arrested Lee and Arthur Mullinax, a former streetcar driver who used to drive Phagan to work. They were charged with suspicion of murder. The next day, April 28, two more men were arrested on the same charges. They were John Gantt, the factory's former bookkeeper who openly showed affection for Phagan. The second was an unnamed black man.

The official records of the case would later show the second man to be Jim Conley. A sweeper at the pencil factory, he had an extensive record of petty theft and disorderly conduct. Conley was arrested on suspicion of murder charges because he had been discovered attempting to rinse out a shirt in one of the factory's sinks. The police later determined that the stains on the shirt were blood.

On May 8, 1913, a coroner's jury ordered Newt Lee and Leo Frank to be charged with murder in the first degree. It was a death penalty offense. In the aftermath of the indictment, the case went national. The telegraph wires burned up as newspapers covered every aspect of the case from coast to coast. Not one but two national detective agencies, the Pinkertons and the Burns Detective Agency, vied for the opportunity to investigate the case.

Atlanta's police chief released a statement that he had factual evidence which would convict the girl's murderer. Upon being pressed to produce it, he demurred. Everyone was vying for the honor of solving Mary Phagan's murder.

On May 18 the *Atlanta Constitution* reported that the police had Jim Conley in custody. Since his arrest on May 1, Conley had been talking to the prosecutor, Hugh Dorsey. The prosecution's entire case would eventually rest on Conley's shoulders.

Short and squat, the 27-year-old Conley would go on to give police three different depositions. Key details varied in each. In Conley's first deposition, given on May 24, he said that the day before the murder, Frank had called him into his office. Frank proceeded to dictate letters to Conley, during which Conley alleged that Frank muttered something like, "Why should I hang?"

This contradicted Conley's earlier verbal statements to police. In those statements, Conley claimed he was illiterate. If he was, how could he take down Frank's letters? Despite this inconsistency, the police were convinced that Conley was telling the truth, and that, therefore, Frank was guilty of Phagan's murder.

In a second sworn statement given four days later, Conley contradicted himself yet again when he stated that the letters had been dictated to him on the day of the murder. Then on May 29, Conley offered new information: Conley claimed that he helped Frank carry Mary Phagan's body to the basement.

In this account, Frank called him into his office. The girl was already dead. Frank claimed she had fallen against a lathe in the machine shop and died. It took some convincing, but Conley eventually agreed to help Frank dump the body. Afterward, the two men went back to Frank's office where he dictated the letters like nothing had happened.

That same day, prosecutor Hugh Dorsey entered the grand jury room in Cobb County. He had told reporters beforehand that he was going to press for an indictment of Leo Frank and no one else. In fact, it took the Cobb County grand jury only 10 minutes to indict Leo Frank on the charge of first-degree murder. If convicted, Frank faced death. Newt Lee was set free.

The state of Georgia made Jim Conley a material witness against Leo Frank. He was placed in jail until the trial, in virtual isolation from anyone other than the police or Dorsey and unavailable to questioning by the defense lawyers. As for the grand jury's other findings, the undertaker who embalmed the girl claimed there was evidence of sexual assault, but the county's own physician said there was insufficient evidence to come to that conclusion.

By May 28, handwriting samples from Frank, Lee, and Conley had been released, along with a portion of the notes found near Phagan's body. The only handwriting that matched the notes was Conley's, who promptly changed his story yet again.

Now, he said that he wrote the notes on the day of the murder on Frank's orders. He had fallen asleep while guarding Frank in his office. When he heard Frank's whistle, he came running up the stairs to his boss's office, where Frank latched onto Conley's stocky frame for support. That is when Frank asked Conley to write the notes and muttered the words, "Why should I hang?"

Conley then volunteered the one piece of information that would have broken the case open and seen the right man indicted: Before meeting with Frank, he had defecated into the elevator shaft. The official record of the case shows that the detectives took note.

Dorsey then had Conley well-prepared for his appearance as the prosecution's star witness at trial. On May 30, 1913, he had police take him back to the scene of the crime. Conley went over every detail—how he helped Frank load the girl's dead body into the elevator and how he took the elevator to the basement where he dumped it.

Looking down into the elevator shaft, detectives saw the feces Conley had previously deposited there. That made Conley a liar.

Conley had sworn to police that he had defecated in the shaft earlier in the evening. Later, at Frank's request, he had taken the elevator down to the basement, where he got off, dumped the body, then shot back up again to meet with Frank in his office. If that were true, the elevator would have mashed the feces when it hit bottom, releasing its foul odor.

In fact, the human waste was still fresh and unmashed. Police and prosecutor either noticed this error and failed to report it or just never noticed it. The defense failed to note this inconsistency at trial.

During the first two months of summer 1913, Luther Z. Rosser, one of Frank's defense attorneys, publicly accused the police chief of "bank[ing] his sense and reputation as both a man and politician on Frank's guilt." If the police had proceeded with an open mind in their investigation, Jim Conley would be charged with murder, not Leo Frank, Rosser asserted.

On July 23 Jim Conley was brought in by Hugh Dorsey to go over his trial testimony one more time. Five days later, the trial began.

Leo Frank's murder trial took place between July 28 and August 26, 1913. There was no direct testimony by prosecution witnesses that tied Frank to the crime. The best Hugh Dorsey could do was have character assassination witnesses testify who implied, without evidence, that Frank was some sort of sexual deviant. The star witness, Jim Conley, testified on August 4 to yet another version of his oft-told tale.

This time, Conley claimed that Frank told him that he had killed the girl after she refused his sexual advances. Conley then helped Frank dispose of the body in the basement. Then they returned to Frank's office, where Frank said he would pay off Conley if he kept his mouth shut. That is when Frank, Conley claimed, uttered the ominous phrase, "Why should I hang?" Frank then had Conley write the notes found near the body.

On cross-examination by the defense, Conley admitted giving police several statements after he was discovered washing out the bloody shirt in the factory. He also admitted he had a police record. Despite being confused on some details, Conley stuck to the crux of story. The prosecution soon rested.

When it was the defense's turn, they brought numerous character witnesses to the stand to testify to Frank's good character. Throughout the trial, thinly veiled anti-Semitic comments were elicited and published from various officials. The hope was that the character witnesses would show Frank to be incapable of committing the crime of which he had been accused.

On August 18, the 19th day of the trial, Leo Frank took the stand in his own defense. Testifying for four hours, he firmly told the jury that Jim Conley's story was nothing more than a tall tale. Frank claimed to have been in his office during the time the coroner fixed for the murder. He stuck to his story when Dorsey cross-examined him.

The summations brought the case's anti-Semitism to the forefront. Defense attorney Reuben Arnold stated during his closing statement that if Frank had not been a Jew, there would never have been any prosecution against him.

Arnold claimed that the Leo Frank case was like the Dreyfus affair in France, where a man was tried, convicted, and sentenced simply because he was a Jew. Hugh Dorsey countered that it was the defense who introduced the issue of Frank's being a Jew.

"The word Jew never escaped our lips," Dorsey told the jury, "the Jews rise to heights sublime, but they also sink to the lowest depths of degradation!"

Dorsey portrayed Frank as a Jekyll/Hyde character. Without a trace of physical evidence to support it, he charged that Frank was a deviant who masked these tendencies from his family and friends with a placid exterior. The defense countered that Conley was the murderer and was testifying against Frank to save his own neck.

Outside the courthouse, the crowd was getting ugly. They wanted to see the northern Jew convicted. The newspapers encouraged Judge Roan to postpone giving the case to the jury until Monday. They were afraid that deliberating on Saturday would lead to a weekend of rioting and violence.

The judge agreed. In the jury's presence, Roan met with the chief of police and the army commander of the local military barracks. Roan wanted to know about their ability to quell an uprising. The defense later pointed out in its appeals that at that moment, the jury was clearly led to believe that a verdict of not guilty would result in a riot.

His back against the wall, defense attorney Reuben Arnold came back Monday and told the jury that Frank was the latest in a long line of Jews persecuted for their religious beliefs. Again he exhorted the jury that Jim Conley was the true murderer.

Conley was not alone among prosecution witnesses to have an unsavory character. But if the truth came down to whom the jury believed, Jim Conley

or Leo Frank, the answer was obvious. They came in four hours later, finding Leo Frank guilty of murder in the first degree. But Frank and his lawyers were not in the courtroom when the verdict was published. Fearing mob violence if the verdict went Frank's way, Judge Roan had put them in protective custody.

When Frank and his lawyers were finally told of the verdict, they were, surprisingly, shocked. They thought that they had at least proven reasonable doubt. They had not counted on the fear, bigotry and anti-Semitism of the post-Reconstruction South.

The next day, August 26, Judge Roan sentenced Leo Frank to hang for the murder of Mary Phagan. He set October 10 as the date of execution. That date would subsequently be changed many times as Frank's appeal wound its way through the bureaucracy.

Frank appealed the verdict and sentence to the Georgia Supreme Court. He lost. Shortly after the court's ruling, the state's biologist released the information that the hair discovered on the lathe at the "murder scene" was not Mary Phagan's. Dorsey discounted the scientific analysis of his own expert. Dorsey said that if other witnesses said it was Mary Phagan's hair, then it must have been her hair.

Frank's appeal was turned down by the U.S. District Court. That left the matter to the U.S. Supreme Court. Suddenly, Frank had a very unlikely ally—the man who had sentenced him to death.

Judge Roan felt that Frank did not deserve death and that the death sentence should be commuted to life in prison. Also supporting Frank was Jim Conley's own lawyer, William M. Smith. He made the unusual public announcement that he believed his client, Conley, to be the murderer. Smith claimed that he had looked at all the evidence again and that it showed Conley's guilt, not Frank's. But as a matter of law, he had nothing new to offer.

During the time the Frank case was prosecuted, newspapers and magazines experienced a surge of investigative reporting. Frank's case was taken up by several prominent journalists on the national level who wrote a series of articles that concluded Frank was innocent. It was those series of articles that made Leo Frank into a national story. But where it really counted, in Georgia, the local press did not place much value in Smith's statement or the stories published about Frank in the newspapers and magazines coming out of the North.

Finally, Leo Frank got his day with the U.S. Supreme Court. Based upon his review of the facts of the case, Associate Justice Oliver Wendell Holmes would later write that Frank had been denied due process. During the trial, the judge and the defense lawyers and possibly members of the jury were threatened with lynching if Frank were found not guilty. Shouts of "Hang the Jew!" had been heard over the courthouse grounds. Georgia governor John Slaton had the National Guard prepared for possible rioting if Frank were found innocent.

But Holmes and Justice Charles Evans Hughes were dissenting justices. The other seven, the majority, refused Frank's appeal. Leo Frank's date of execution was set for June 22, 1915.

On May 31 Frank's attorneys filed a clemency appeal with the Georgia Prison Commission in the hope of having his death sentence commuted. They denied the condemned man's appeal. That left the matter to one man: Governor John Slaton. Governor Slaton had 20 days left in his term before he had to step down. A highly popular governor and before that state legislator, he was a leading candidate for the U.S. Senate.

Tom Watson, a powerful Georgia Populist politician and publisher, offered to support Slaton for the Senate on the condition that he deny Frank clemency. The easy way out would be to leave the Frank problem to his successor, who would take office at midnight June 20, two full days before Frank's execution. But John Slaton was a man of honor.

Carefully, he reviewed the police reports, case files, and court record of the case. He took into account the dissenting votes of the U.S. Supreme Court and especially the recommendation for clemency from the trial judge. After reviewing the case fully, John Slaton believed Leo Frank was innocent. He believed that in time, his innocence would be proven.

What was more important than clearing him at the moment was saving his life. Slaton signed an executive order commuting the death sentence to life in prison. He ordered Frank transported immediately to Milledgeville Prison.

Relieved that he had been spared from death and fully expecting to be cleared, Leo Frank was transferred to Milledgeville. During the next two months, Tom Watson in his magazines *Watson's Magazine* and *The Jeffersonian* published openly anti-Semitic editorials that urged Georgia's citizens to take the law into their own hands and inflict frontier justice on Leo Frank because the governor would not.

On July 18 a prisoner slashed Leo Frank's throat. Two other prisoners, by coincidence doctors, rushed to Frank's aid. They stopped the blood flow and stitched him up. A month later, just before midnight

on August 16, 1915, 25 men from the Atlanta area, driving in eight automobiles, pulled in at the Milledgeville Prison gates.

Overpowering the two guards on duty, they handcuffed the warden and the superintendent. They carried a rope. Some would later claim that the lynch mob consisted of some of Marietta's finest citizens, including a clergyman and an ex-sheriff.

Confronted in his cell, Frank calmly started to dress, and was told that he need not bother. Dressed only in prison shirt and pants, he was rushed out to a car and driven seven hours across the state. It took all night, but as dawn broke, the lynch mob stopped at an oak grove outside of Marietta.

The leaders tried to get Frank to confess to the murder of Mary Phagan. He calmly declined. Those in the group who were later interviewed said that his denials were convincing; many in the group decided he should not be lynched. The leaders, though, prevailed. When asked if he had a last request, Frank asked to have his wedding ring returned to his wife.

Once more he was asked to confess. He said nothing. A table was set up under a tree. His hands shackled in front, he was led up onto the table. They threw a rope over a stout limb, and then tied a hangman's noose around his neck. They kicked the table out from under him, and Leo Frank was left hanging. The lynch mob quickly dispersed as Frank struggled against the rope until it strangled him to death.

News of the hanging quickly spread. A crowd gathered at the lynching site. Photographers photographed the festive group gathered around the body. Included in the pictures were members of the lynch mob who had come back to view their handiwork. The photographs were available as postcards in Marietta for many years afterward.

Men, women, and children all came to view the northern Jew hanging from the old oak tree. Some of them tore strips of cloth from Frank's clothes. Other snipped strands from the rope, making sure not to go too deep with their knives, lest the rope unwind and the corpse drop. Eventually, after some in the crowd made attempts to mutilate the body, it was cut down and taken into Atlanta.

Even in death, Frank's rights were violated. Without family consent, officials decided to put the body on public view. With the police supervising the crowds, Georgia citizens came to view Frank's body. Later that night, against Talmudic law, the undertaker embalmed him.

Leo Frank's body was transported back to Brooklyn by his wife Lucille. He was buried at Mount

Leo Frank after he was lynched (Atlanta History Center)

more than 70 years after his lynching by the prominent citizens of Marietta, Georgia.

See also TIMOTHY MCVEIGH (1968–2001); MIDWESTERN BANK BANDITS (1994–1997); STONE MOUNTAIN, GEORGIA (1915).

Stone Mountain, Georgia (1915) the rebirth of the Ku Klux Klan

On November 15, 1905, a group of masked men met on top of Stone Mountain in Georgia. They called themselves the Knights of Mary Phagan. Burning a cross that lit up the dark sky, they initiated the new invisible order of the Ku Klux Klan (KKK).

A terrorist organization that advocated white supremacy, the Klan had been founded in Pulaski, Tennessee, in 1866 by six former Confederate officers. The six believed that Lincoln's great mistake was freeing the slaves. They were going to do something about it. Their leader, a former Confederate general named Nathan Bedford Forrest, became the first Imperial Wizard of the KKK.

Thousands of lynchings and others were perpetrated by the Klan and its adherents in the years after the Civil War. But as the 19th century wound down, so did the Klan's popularity. The Phagan murder reawakened the monster from its slumber. Respond-

Carmel Cemetery on August 18, 1915. But the case was not over. Jim Conley was convicted of burglary in 1919. He served only one year of a 20-year sentence, the result of his "cooperation" in the Frank case. A gambling arrest followed in 1941 and then an arrest for being drunk and disorderly in 1947. After that, Jim Conley vanished from view until he died in his 70s in 1962. He never recanted his testimony. To his grave, he claimed Leo Frank had killed Mary Phagan and ordered him to dispose of the body in the elevator shaft.

In 1982 an old man, Alonzo Mann, came forth with the information that he had seen Jim Conley dragging Mary Phagan's body. Mann, then a 13-year-old office boy at the pencil factory, was told by Conley not to tell what he had seen, or Conley would kill him.

Encouraged by Alonzo Mann's testimony, the Anti-Defamation League of B'nai Brith asked the Georgia Board of Pardons to grant Leo Frank a posthumous pardon. After first rejecting the application, they pardoned Leo Frank on March 11, 1986,

---

"The Ballad of Mary Phagan"

Little Mary Phagan
She left her home one day;
She went to the pencil-factory
To see the big parade.

She left her home at eleven
She kissed her mother good-by;
Not one time did the poor child think
That she was a-going to die.

Leo Frank he met her
With a brutish heart, we know;
He smiled, and said, "Little Mary,
You won't go home no more."

—as reproduced by F. B. Snyder in
The Journal of American Folk-Lore, 1918

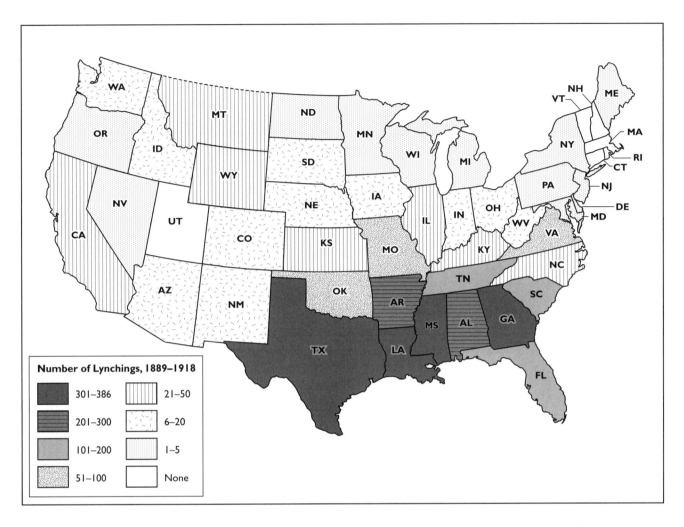

Lynching rates by state, between 1889 and 1918. The Ku Klux Klan perpetrated thousands of lynchings in the years after the Civil War.

Number of Lynchings, 1889–1918

�damask	301–386	‖‖	21–50
▬	201–300	∴	6–20
▨	101–200	░	1–5
∷	51–100	☐	None

ing quickly to this threat, the Anti-Defamation League of B'nai Brith was founded.

There was one more casualty yet to go in the Frank case, however. It was former Governor John Slaton who had pardoned Leo Frank. The voters of Georgia never forgave him his heroism. They refused to elect him to office again.

See also COBB COUNTY, GEORGIA (1914); TIMOTHY MCVEIGH (1968–2001); MIDWESTERN BANK BANDITS (1994–1997).

Chicago, Illinois/Cincinnati, Ohio (1919) the Black Sox scandal

Baseball was America's game. American boys and girls looked up to ballplayers as heroes, and people really believed the mythology that had been built up by press and owners alike that these athletes embodied the noblest of virtues. The reality, of course, was much different.

Ballplayers were underpaid working stiffs just trying to support their families. They all had off-season jobs to make ends meet. The owners took all the gate money, and there was no revenue sharing as there is today. After a lifetime of major league service, ballplayers had nothing to show for their efforts but broken-down bodies. Financially, they were no better off than when they started. It was a system that made players financially open to corruption.

While it is still debatable who approached who first, it was Chicago White Sox first baseman Chick Gandil and professional gamblers "Sport" Sullivan and "Sleepy Bill" Burns who initially conspired to fix the 1919 World Series. Later, Arnold "the

Brain" Rothstein, the country's foremost professional gambler, and Abe Attell, former featherweight champion of the world, would get involved.

Joseph "Sport" Sullivan of Boston and William "Sleepy Bill" Burns of New York were professional gamblers. It was their "scouting" of the Sox that convinced them that the players could be bribed to lose the series. According to their later testimony at trial, to pull it off they needed certain key players to throw the games. Their entry to the team was first baseman Chick Gandil.

By 1919 Gandil was a 32-year-old major leaguer with nine years of service. He had a lifetime batting average of .277, quite ordinary for the time, and was ready to retire. He had no moral compunctions about meeting with Sullivan and Burns, agreeing to accept a bribe and helping to arrange the fix. Gandil first recruited Eddie Cicotte, the team's star pitcher.

By the end of the 1920 season, Cicotte had a lifetime record of 208 victories and 149 losses, with an earned run average of 2.37. In later years, it would have easily earned him election to the National Baseball Hall of Fame in Cooperstown, New York.

Yet with those numbers, he had no monetary prospects when his arm gave out. Cicotte would later admit he decided to throw the games he was involved with and then helped convince Claude "Lefty" Williams to do the same.

Williams was the team's number-two pitcher. He ended the 1919 season with a 23-and-11 record and 2.64 ERA. With the experimental nine-game World Series that the two teams were playing, Williams was guaranteed three if not four starts. Like Cicotte, he was a player the gamblers needed in their pocket if they were to succeed.

With the team's two key pitchers in tow, Gandil next turned to the infield. He recruited starting shortstop Charles "Swede" Risberg. Risberg brought along his roommate, utility man Fred McMullin, who really was not necessary for the fix, but without him, Risberg would not cooperate.

As for the rest of the infield, Gandil would not even approach second baseman Eddie Collins and catcher Ray Chalk, knowing full well that the hard-nosed veterans would never do anything to damage the game. He did, however, approach third baseman George "Buck" Weaver, who turned him down cold.

Gandil turned next to the outfield. He recruited centerfielder Oscar "Happy" Felsch, who had knocked in 86 RBIs and batted .275 in 1919. Gandil needed one more outfielder to make sure the plot worked. "Shoeless" Joe Jackson was the eighth man

Gandil chose for his plot. Jackson was an illiterate man who happened to be a genius when it came to hitting a baseball. Jackson's lifetime batting average of .356 would later place him third for all time, behind only Ty Cobb and Rogers Hornsby. Ted Williams, Willie Mays, Barry Bonds—none could get close to Jackson's lifetime batting average.

What is known for certain about Jackson's participation in the conspiracy is that he took money from the gamblers. Jackson would later claim that he took the money under duress, that Gandil had clearly implied a physical threat if he did not. Gandil was certainly associating with professional gamblers who didn't hesitate to use force.

Gandil reported back to Burns and Sullivan that he had arranged things. All that left was to arrange the price and place their bets. But Burns, Sullivan, and Gandil were small-timers when it came to gambling on a national level. Between them they just did not have enough money to really make a killing. They turned to Arnold "the Brain" Rothstein to bankroll the operation.

Arnold "the Brain" Rothstein was the country's foremost professional gambler. Unlike other professional gamblers before him, like Doc Holliday, for example, Rothstein preferred hired guns to handle any muscle that was needed in his racket. He was also smart enough to insulate himself from the people perpetrating the crime.

To fix the World Series, Rothstein came up with the cash, which was then given to an associate, Abe Attell, a former featherweight boxing champion. Attell gave the money to Sullivan and Burns, who made the payoff to Gandil. Gandil distributed the money among the players. According to later testimony, each of the players got $5,000, except for Gandil, an ornery sort, who kept $35,000 for himself.

All was ready. Now it was time to execute the fix.

After a 140-game season, the 1919 World Series began in Cincinnati on October 1, 1919. It was a best-seven-of-nine series. Eddie Cicotte started for the White Sox. The score was tied 1-1 going into the fourth inning when Cicotte went into his act. He quickly gave up five runs, effectively burying his team before the game was half over. The Sox lost game one, 9-1.

The gamblers raked it in. Not only did they have bets on the final results of the Series, they bet on each game. They bet again on the Sox to lose the second game because Lefty Williams was starting for the Sox. That night, Charlie Comiskey, the owner of the Chicago White Sox, and his manager "Kid" Gleason, met to discuss the game. Among other things, they discussed rumors that someone had fixed the series.

Williams started the second game. He did not even attempt to make it look good. A control specialist, Williams walked three and gave up three runs in the fourth inning. Final score: Cincinnati 4, Chicago 2. Again, the gamblers raked it in.

For the third game, the gamblers did not bet as heavily. While they still had Gandil and his boys, pitcher Dickie Kerr was not in on it. Dickie did not know he was supposed to throw the game. Instead, he went out and threw strikes. From the first baseman's bag, Gandil saw how unhittable Kerr was. Manager Kid Gleason was certain to leave him in as long as he kept pitching well. In the fifth inning, Gandil strode to the plate. With Felsch and Jackson on base, Gandil stroked a double. Felsch and Jackson scored. Kerr went on to pitch a nine-inning shutout that the Sox won, 3-0.

After Kerr's brilliant effort, Cicotte came back in game four to do something no pitcher has ever done before or since: make two errors on the same play in the same inning in a World Series game. It happened in the fifth inning. Cicotte's "misplays" enabled the Reds to score twice on their way to a 2-0 shutout.

The next day, Lefty Williams came back for game five. In the fifth inning, with the score tied 1-1, Williams gave up four runs and the Sox went on to lose 5-0. By then, baseball writers were openly speculating that the vaunted White Sox were throwing the series.

Rothstein's genius as a gambler was his ability to manipulate the inside of the event to his own advantage and to make it look good. He was no fool. He knew that the more things looked phony, the more the cops would investigate. He was not eager for the trail to lead back to him.

Game five opened in Cincinnati on October 7. Once again, Dickie Kerr gave another gritty performance. And once again, Chick Gandil had to give in on a game. With the score tied 4-4 in the 10th inning, Gandil singled Weaver home with the go-ahead run. Kerr pitched a scoreless 10th, for a brilliant 10-inning victory. But the game's real achievement was Gandil's hit in the clutch.

With Cincinnati leading 4 games to 2, Cicotte started the sixth game. Cicotte could have thrown that one, too, but something happened that day. Maybe it was the gamblers telling him to win so the series was prolonged, thereby increasing the gamblers' take, or maybe his competitive urges just overwhelmed his shame. Cicotte went out and pitched a nine-inning 4-1 victory. The deciding run was driven in by "Shoeless" Joe Jackson.

That left only two games to play, with Lefty Williams starting the eighth game. That evening Williams and his wife were visited by a thug. Who he was working for is unknown. He threatened Williams and his family with physical harm if Williams made it past the first inning in tomorrow's game.

The next day, October 9, 1919, Williams gave up four consecutive hits and four runs in the first inning and was quickly given the hook. His team went on to lose 10-5. Jackson hit a home run in support of the losing cause. Despite the fact that they were the heavy favorites going into the series, the Sox lost, 5 games to 3, in the first best of nine World Series.

The final statistical tally for the series told the story of how well the fix worked. According to *The Baseball Encyclopedia,* the final line on Cicotte was 1-2 with a 2.95 ERA, while Williams was 0-3 with a 6.62 ERA. Risberg batted .080, Felsch .192, and Gandil .233. Curiously, Jackson, who was supposed to be in on it, batted .375, the highest of any regular for either team.

Conspiracies are hard to keep secret. The more people involved, the more they talk, especially if there is a monetary incentive.

On October 15 Charlie Comiskey gave a statement to the press offering a $20,000 reward to anyone who came forward with verifiable information that the 1919 World Series was fixed. Two months later, on December 15, journalist Hugh Fullerton, a syndicated Chicago sports writer, published an article in the *New York World.* The headline made his argument clear: "IS BIG LEAGUE BASEBALL BEING RUN FOR GAMBLERS, WITH BALLPLAYERS IN THE DEAL?" Fullerton demanded that baseball confront its gambling problem. It was he who first suggested that federal judge Kenesaw Mountain Landis be appointed to head a special investigation into gambling's influence on the national pastime.

Through the winter and spring of 1920, the question of whether the Sox had thrown the series seemed to lie dormant. Behind the scenes, law enforcement and politicians in Chicago discussed what to do. On September 7, 1920, with the baseball season still going on, a Cook County grand jury was finally convened to look into whether or not a game between the Chicago Cubs and Cincinnati Reds had been fixed the week before. The action provided the impetus to get the investigative ball rolling. Two weeks later on September 24, the grand jury finally turned its attention to the White Sox.

New York Giants pitcher Rube Benton testified that he knew for a fact that the series was fixed. He named Gandil, Felsch, Williams, and Cicotte as being in on it. Three days later, the story of the grand jury's investigation finally broke publicly when details appeared in newspaper articles across the country. Suddenly, the White Sox were labeled "the Black Sox" by the press; the name stuck.

Exactly what the authorities promised Eddie Cicotte is unclear. Or maybe it was just conscience. Then again, Cicotte, like the other players, was interrogated rather harshly by the Chicago police. He may have just been scared.

On September 28, Cicotte confessed before the grand jury. He named seven other players including Jackson and Weaver, despite the fact that Weaver had turned Gandil down and did not take a dime.

"I don't know why I did it," Cicotte told the grand jury. "I must have been crazy. Risberg, Gandil, and McMullin were at me for a week before the Series began. They wanted me to go crooked. I don't know. I needed the money. I had the wife and the kids. They know about this. I don't know what they'll think.

"Now I've lost everything. Job. Reputation, everything. My friends all bet on the Sox. I knew, but I couldn't tell them."

The anguish in Cicotte's statement was balanced by Jackson's. He gave a voluntary statement before the grand jury the following day, in which he said that he was threatened with death unless he accepted the bribe.

"I did tell them once, 'I am not going to be in it,' I will just get out of it altogether," Jackson testified.

Gandil's response:

"He said I was into it already and I might as well stay in. I said, 'I can go to the boss and have every damn one of you pulled out of the limelight.'"

Gandil said:

"He said, 'It wouldn't be well for me if I did that.'"

Jackson was clearly afraid that if he didn't do what Gandil requested, he might be murdered.

When Jackson left the grand jury room that day, he was confronted outside by a young boy who, like many of the era, idolized him. The boy allegedly said to him, "Say it isn't so, Joe."

Jackson's response was cryptic and yet, if taken at face value, implies more players besides Gandil were team "enforcers" for the gamblers. Jackson allegedly replied to the boy, "The Swede is a hard man." By "Swede," of course, he meant the shortstop Risberg.

On February 12, 1921, Weaver and Jackson filed a joint petition to the court arguing their innocence based on the fact that neither man threw any game and, in fact, they had between them the highest batting averages and best fielding percentages of any players in the series. The court denied their petition and the case moved steadily forward.

It would take another eight months of grand jury investigation, but on July 5, 1921, all eight "Black Sox," as well as Burns, Sullivan, and Attell were indicted by the Cook County grand jury on charges that they had perpetrated a fraud. The indictment read:

"Shoeless" Joe Jackson at bat. Jackson was one of the "eight men out" who were banned from baseball for conspiring to fix the 1919 World Series. (Author's collection)

That the defendants participating in said games as players, conspired, confederated and agreed together with the defendants not participating therein to so conduct themselves throughout the said games and each of said games and so manipulate their playing in each of said games as to make certain in advance of the playing of said games the outcome thereof and the winner thereof, and so as to make certain in advance of the playing of all of the games of said series the outcome of the majority of the games of said series and the winner of the majority of said series of games.

The trial took place in a packed Chicago courtroom in 1921. One of the prosecution's star witnesses was "Sleepy Bill" Burns, who outlined the plot in detail. When it was time for cross-examination, defense attorney James "Ropes" O'Brien tried to smear Burns by showing that he had previously accepted illicit money from American League president Ban Johnson, but Burns denied the allegation.

At the end of the trial, Judge Hugo Friend charged the jury. He explained that to deliver a guilty verdict, the jury must find that the players conspired "to defraud the public and others, and not merely throw ballgames."

The jury was out a mere two hours. When it came back, the chief clerk read the verdict. Lefty Williams was the first one found not guilty. The courtroom erupted in glee. As the string of "not guiltys" continued, the cheers got louder and louder. When the "Black Sox" had been found not guilty, hats and confetti began flying around the courtroom. Some of the jurors lifted players to their shoulders and paraded them around the courtroom.

To one group at least, the verdicts were not a surprise. Anticipating that the hometown crowd would find for the home team, baseball's owners had unanimously named Judge Kenesaw Mountain Landis to the newly created office of commissioner of baseball to restore the game's damaged integrity. Landis's first action came swiftly. Less than 24 hours after the verdicts, Landis issued a verdict of his own.

Regardless of the verdict of juries, no player who throws a ballgame, no player that undertakes or promises to throw a ballgame, no player that sits in conference with a bunch of crooked players and gamblers where the ways and means of throwing a game are discussed and does not promptly tell his club about it, will ever play professional baseball,"

And then, he banned the "Black Sox" for life.

Despite the fact that Weaver took no money, despite the fact that Jackson was allegedly threatened by Gandil if he did not accept the money, and despite the fact that both men led both teams in the series with their batting averages and sparkling play in the field, they, too, could no longer play baseball.

For years afterward, Weaver maintained his innocence and every year petitioned for reinstatement. Jackson, too, applied for reinstatement, but his case was weaker since he had taken the money. They would be on baseball's inactive list until the days they died. The banned "Black Sox" players would come to be known by a later generation as the "eight men out."

Second baseman Eddie Collins and catcher Ray Schalk, two of the players who did not participate in the conspiracy, were later enshrined in the National Baseball Hall of Fame in Cooperstown, New York.

New York, New York (1919–1928) the invention of the "tommy gun"

Like all the inventions that brought massive firepower to the criminal arsenal, the Tommy gun was not intended to be a criminal's weapon. Rather, its inventor, George Thompson, looked at it as a weapon that could be used by U.S. soldiers in future wars. Thompson's idea was to automate the firing of pistol bullets but with a longer barrel that allowed for greater trajectory. In the "tommy gun," as it was nicknamed, Thompson created the first automatic hand-held weapon.

Thompson had actually retired from active military duty in 1914 at the age of 54 to go to work in private industry. After he was called to active duty again during World War I, the Allied victory gave him the opportunity once and for all to retire from the service and turn his attention to his primary interest. Thompson was convinced that an intermediate weapon between a pistol and a rifle would be a requirement in all future wars.

The inventor had noticed how the large firearms companies owned numerous patents on current weapons. Any modification to them, which was the cornerstone of Thompson's idea, meant vast royalty payments to these controlling companies. Thompson wanted to create his own patent so he could control his financial destiny.

The key to implementing Thompson's vision was finding a way to get through the technical challenges he had set himself to create an intermediate type of weapon. It would have to be one with little recoil, yet powerful enough in its continued firing action of a large-caliber slug, the kind that could do lethal damage to a human being.

The solution to both of Thompson's problems, design and business, lay with an invention by one John Blish. A U.S. Navy commander, Blish had patented a delayed blowback breech system in 1915. Thompson believed that this invention, engineered properly, would make what he envisioned as a handheld automatic weapon a reality.

Thompson offered Blish shares in the company he was organizing in exchange for the patent on his delayed blowback mechanism. Blish accepted and George Thompson's Auto-Ordnance Company was founded in 1916.

Between 1919 and 1928, George Thompson worked to perfect his invention. With his Model 1928, Thompson's many years of hard work had finally perfected what Thompson called his "submachine gun." Navy personnel throughout the 1930s were issued the weapon. To criminals, of course, that meant nothing.

Not a criminal alive would put patriotism before making a buck. Criminals quickly latched onto the fact that the Thompson submachine gun would allow them to fire bullets more quickly than ever before. That meant not just isolated shots at pursuing lawmen but the ability to actually mow them down with continuous fire. It also meant that much more firepower to use in assaults, bank robbery, kidnapping, and the top of the criminal ladder, murder.

See also JOHN BROWNING (1855–1926).

Prohibition (1920–1933) bootlegging and the rise of organized crime

Article XVIII of the Constitution of the United States

Section 1. After one year from the ratification of this article the manufacture, sale, or transportation of intoxicating liquors within, the importation thereof into, or the exportation thereof from the United States and all territory subject to the jurisdiction thereof for beverage purposes is hereby prohibited.

Section. 2. The Congress and the several States shall have concurrent power to enforce this article by appropriate legislation.

Section. 3. This article shall be inoperative unless it shall have been ratified as an amendment to the Constitution by the legislatures of the several States, as provided in the Constitution, within seven years from the date of the submission hereof to the States by the Congress.

In 1919 the Eighteenth Amendment was ratified, and Prohibition became law in January 1920. Almost immediately the public debated its legitimacy. People were not willing to suddenly stop drinking, even if it was illegal. They were determined to get alcohol somewhere and bootleggers were only too happy to supply the now illegal brew. Speakeasies replaced saloons, and many Americans consumed bootleg liquor in the privacy of their own homes.

Throughout the 1920s, bootlegging and rumrunning were big business and made millionaires out of such characters as Al Capone and Joseph Kennedy. Liquor was smuggled in across the Mexican and Canadian borders or by boat along the Atlantic coast, and gangs set up distilleries and

Joseph "Old Joe" Kennedy (Photo №KFC2144P, John F. Kennedy Library)

The U.S. Coast Guard stopped this rumrunner, but many other boats carrying bootleg liquor made it through. (Library of Congress)

breweries that operated under the noses of corrupt police and politicians. These were not so much the sophisticated criminal machinations of the Mafia's Five Families—who came into being during the following decade—but rather a loose criminal conglomeration of gangs operating for the same purpose: to corner the market on illegal booze and make money from countless willing buyers. The internal competition among bootleggers led to innumerable killings.

Capone's gang in Chicago is perhaps the best-known of the Prohibition-era bootleggers, but Detroit's Purple Gang and New York's Owney Madden ring were also very successful in the bootlegging business. Al Capone himself summed up the service he provided: "I'm just a businessman, I provide what people need."

In 1933, with the support of President Franklin D. Roosevelt, Congress adopted the Twenty-first Amendment and repealed Prohibition, freeing Americans from the yoke of an unenforceable law. It was clear that not only had the legislation of public morality been a failure, but it had also cost the government millions of dollars in fighting bootlegging while fostering widespread corruption of government and law enforcement figures alike. After Prohibition, organized crime would turn to gambling, labor racketeering, and the drug trade for profits. But it was the money these criminals made as bootleggers that essentially financed the creation of the modern mob.

More important, bootlegging inspired criminals to get organized in gangs in a way they hadn't

Al Capone (National Archives)

before and planted the roots of modern international crime.

San Francisco, California (1920) Roscoe "Fatty" Arbuckle

By 1920, when he was accused of murder, Roscoe "Fatty" Arbuckle was the most popular comedian in American cinema. He is also the first celebrity in American criminal history accused of rape and murder and the first celebrity subsequently blacklisted from working in films despite the fact he was not guilty on all charges.

It had been an exhausting 18 months, during which Roscoe, as he preferred to be called by his friends, had made six films for Adolph Zukor's Paramount Pictures. Seeking a respite, he took off for three days in San Francisco. Accompanying him was his friend Fred Fischbach.

When they got to San Francisco, they checked into the St. Francis Hotel. On September 5, 1921, Fischbach decided to hold a party in the 12th-floor suite

that he and Arbuckle occupied. He did not consult with Arbuckle when he put his guest list together. One of the party guests was an aspiring actress in her 20s named Virginia Rappé. Rappé had reportedly had five abortions before age 16 and had been thrown off the Keystone movie lot because she had a known problem with venereal disease.

Accompanying Rappé was Maude "Bambina" Delmont. By the time she arrived at the party, California police had already filed at least 50 counts of extortion, bigamy, fraud, and racketeering against her. When Arbuckle saw that both Rappé and Delmont, women of dubious reputation, were at the party, he voiced his concern to Fischbach. He feared that their reputation might bring a police raid.

At 3 P.M., Arbuckle went into his bedroom to change clothes. Entering the adjoining bathroom, he found Virginia Rappé passed out on the floor. Arbuckle lifted Rappé and placed her on the bed. She asked for water; he gave it to her. At 3:10 P.M. by Arbuckle's later estimation, he left, fully clothed, to get help. Soon, he returned with some of the other party guests. There was Virginia Rappé, fully clothed, screaming in pain.

The front desk was then called for help with Rappé, who Arbuckle carried into nearby Room 1227. Delmont followed, passing out drunk on a nearby bed. Arbuckle had had enough. With hotel management in charge, he left to go sightseeing with a friend.

Four days later, the coroner concluded, Rappé died of peritonitis, brought on by a rupture of her Fallopian tubes and further complicated by a gonorrhea infection. Delmont, ever on the lookout for an angle, had another one. She went to the police and filed charges that Arbuckle had raped Rappé and in the process caused her death.

Roscoe "Fatty" Arbuckle, America's most beloved comedian, was arrested for murder.

"Yellow" journalism was a common enough journalistic technique during this era. Journalists would sensationalize a case with few facts and a lot of innuendo. No one did a better job of it than William Randolph Hearst, the newspaper magnate whose life would later become the basis for Orson Welles's 1941 film *Citizen Kane*.

Hearst had his national string of papers play up the Arbuckle case. In headline after headline, the Hearst papers cast innuendo on Arbuckle's sexual activities and sexual lifestyle. Hearst himself once bragged in front of Buster Keaton, the great silent screen comedian and filmmaker who was best friends

Film star Roscoe "Fatty" Arbuckle puts up a war bonds poster in New York in 1917. Three years later he was arrested for the murder of a young actress, of which he was acquitted. (National Archives)

with Arbuckle, that the Arbuckle story sold him more papers than the sinking of the *Lusitania.*

Other papers hopped on the bandwagon to nail Arbuckle before the case got to trial. Even the "great gray lady" of papers, the *New York Times,* printed articles that made it seem that Arbuckle was guilty.

With such publicity, readers tended to believe in Arbuckle's guilt. No one presented Arbuckle's side. Women in particular, once part of his great movie audience, turned against the actor, believing he was responsible for Rappé's death. It was almost as if the more salacious the reported details, the more it must be true.

With the case winding down closer to trial, San Francisco district attorney Mathew Brady was perturbed that his key witness, Maude Delmont, kept changing her story. Brady then pressured another

woman, Zey Prevon, with perjury unless she agreed to corroborate the statement Virginia Rappé allegedly made to Delmont: "Roscoe hurt me."

Brady had a weak case, and the trial judge, Sylvanin Lazarus, realized it. He reduced the charges against Arbuckle to manslaughter. As for Arbuckle, he could not believe that the state was prosecuting him or that his audience had left him flat.

"I don't understand it," Arbuckle said. "One minute I'm the guy everybody loves, the next I'm the guy everybody loves to hate."

Fatty Arbuckle's trial began on November 14, 1921. On Monday, November 28, 1921, Arbuckle took the stand in his own defense and testified. Arbuckle stated what had happened, offering the same account he gave police and anyone else who asked him: It was not his party, the girl collapsed, he had nothing to do with it and, in fact, tried to help her.

There was medical testimony from both sides that established that the victim died of a ruptured bladder and acute peritonitis. It was established that Rappé had to have been in pain from her condition before the party. Most important, the medical testimony made it clear that the ruptured bladder was not caused by someone heavy lying down on her or by intercourse. That seemed to, finally, let Arbuckle off the hook.

During his closing Arbuckle's attorney Gavin McNab accused the San Francisco Police Department of "A deliberate conspiracy against Arbuckle. It was the shame of San Francisco. Perjured wretches tried, from the stand, to deprive this defendant, this stranger within our gates, of his liberty."

It made no difference. The trial ended with a hung jury voting 10-2 for acquittal. Brady decided to try Arbuckle again. The second trial again resulted in a hung jury, with the same vote, 10-2—only this time, they voted to convict. During the second trial, Arbuckle did not testify, and his lawyers took this to mean that his silence was an admission of guilt, accounting for the guilty votes by the jury. They determined to learn from this error.

During the third trial, Arbuckle once again testified, and very persuasively. McNab again accused the prosecution of a conspiracy to railroad Arbuckle. This time, on April 12, 1922, the result was different—12 votes for acquittal, plus an additional two for acquittal voted by the alternates. Arbuckle was freed, but not before the jury offered what is the most unusual apology in the history of U.S. criminal jurisprudence:

Acquittal is not enough for Roscoe Arbuckle. We feel that a great injustice has been done him. We feel also that it was only our plain duty to give him this exoneration, under the evidence, for there was not the slightest proof adduced to connect him in any way with the commission of a crime.

He was manly throughout the case, and told a straightforward story on the witness stand, which we all believed. The happening at the hotel was an unfortunate affair for which Arbuckle, so the evidence shows, was in no way responsible.

We wish him success and hope that the American people will take the judgment of fourteen men and women who have sat listening for thirty-one days to the evidence, that Roscoe Arbuckle is entirely innocent and free of all blame.

Yet, despite the jury's recommendation, Hollywood turned a deaf ear. Will Hays, chairman of the Hays Office, Hollywood's film industry censorship organization, issued the following statement:

After consulting at length with Mr. Nicholas Schenck, representing Mr. Joseph Schenck, the producers, and Mr. Adolph Zukor and Mr. Jesse Lasky of the Famous Players–Lasky Corporation, the distributors, I will state that at my request they have cancelled all showings and all bookings of the Arbuckle films.

Paramount let him go. No one wanted to employ him. Roscoe Arbuckle became the first actor to be blacklisted from the very industry he had helped create. It would not be until 1932 that his name was finally taken off the blacklist and Arbuckle could work again. Jack Warner signed him to do six two-reel comedies for Warner Brothers. Arbuckle finished them all in one year. Upon release, they were successful and Warner signed Arbuckle to do a feature.

Just as he was getting his due, Arbuckle died from a heart attack on June 29, 1933 at the age of 46. Buster Keaton said that his friend died from a broken heart.

John Browning (1855–1926) inventor of the Browning Automatic Rifle (B.A.R.)

It is doubtful that criminals around the country mourned when John Browning died. But they should have, especially the depression-era bank robbers who would come to rely on his weapons. The innovations he brought to firearms, making them more powerful, more accurate, and more

A machine shop in 1914 where Browning automatic rifles were manufactured (Library of Congress)

portable, made him the most innovative firearms inventor since Sam Colt.

Browning's genius began to show itself when he made his first gun, a single-shot rifle, when he was 14 years old. He would go on to a 47-year career in the gun-making business. During those years, his company manufactured 50 million sport and military weapons.

It was Browning who, in 1902, automated the manual shotgun. He used a mechanism that allowed for loading multiple shells and then injecting them into the breech for firing using a pump action on the lower part of the weapon. It became popularly known as the pump action shotgun and is still manufactured today. Any criminal who uses one owes a debt to Browning.

But it was the Browning Automatic Rifle, commonly known as the B.A.R., that brought him his greatest fame. Until Browning's invention, rifles had to be manually fired, that is, the trigger had to be pulled once for each round fired. Browning changed all that.

The B.A.R., while weighing only 18.5 pounds, was capable of firing 550 rounds accurately in the space of 60 seconds. It became a popular weapon in World War I and the popular choice of many depression-era gangs and outlaws. Browning would also go on to modify the famous Colt .45 Peacemaker, designing the .45 automatic that became the standard sidearm for officers during World War II.

See also NEW YORK, NEW YORK (1919–1928).

Washington, D.C. (1923–1935) Federal Bureau of Investigation formed

In 1923 the Bureau of Investigation within the Justice Department took over the functions of the Federal Bureau of Criminal Identification. Ten years

Stanley Finch, the first director of the Bureau of Investigation (National Archives)

J. Edgar Hoover became director of the Bureau of Investigation in 1925 and led it for over 40 years. (National Archives)

later, in 1933, things were changed yet again when the Bureau of Investigation absorbed the Bureau of Prohibition to form the Division of Investigation by an executive order on June 10, 1933.

The division was designated the Federal Bureau of Investigation (FBI) by an act of Congress on March 22, 1935. By federal law, the FBI was charged to investigate federal law violations; operate a technical laboratory and national police academy; and gather, classify, preserve, and exchange criminal identification records. In 1934 the FBI was given the jurisdiction to investigate violations of federal laws. These included kidnapping and bank robbery, and the cases they were involved in thrust the bureau and its director J. Edgar Hoover into national prominence.

Most of all, Federal law allowed the FBI to use deadly force to bring criminals to ground.

William Matthew "Bill" Tilghman (1853–1923)
leader of the guard

Bill Tilghman was the greatest of the Old West lawmen. Single-handedly or in tandem with two other marshals, Heck Thomas and Chris Madsen, he was responsible for the capture and deaths of more desperados than anyone else. In sheer numbers of badmen bested, Tilghman puts Wyatt Earp, Bat Masterson, and Pat Garrett to shame. With Garrett, he shares a dubious distinction.

Out of this group, he and Garrett are the only ones who were murdered.

As a child, the Kansas-raised Tilghman met the famous lawman Wild Bill Hickok, who was his idol. It was an indelible experience Tilghman promised himself that one day he would grow up to be a lawman just like Hickok.

In his late teens Tilghman left the Kansas farm that had been his home to hunt on the western frontier. In the space of just one year, from 1871 to 1872, he killed 3,000 buffalo using his father's .40-caliber Sharps rifle. Tilghman's own notebooks show that he killed a total of 11,000 buffalo. According to records at the time, his more famous contemporary, Buffalo Bill Cody, never claimed more than 4,280 buffalo kills.

When the vast buffalo herds dwindled, Tilghman began running with outlaws Hurricane Bill Smith and Mart Childers. They stole horses from the very Indians Tilghman purported to respect. For a few years, Tilghman drifted in and out of trouble, always one step ahead of the law, but he could see

the handwriting on the wall: Unless he mended his ways, he would wind up at the end of a rope. When Bat Masterson offered him an opportunity, he grabbed at it.

In 1877, Masterson was the sheriff of Ford County, whose county seat was Dodge City. Masterson hired Tilghman as his undersheriff. Realizing that a frontier lawman, on his pitiful salary, was susceptible to bribes no matter how lofty his ideals, Tilghman pursued a second career as a rancher. He established a ranch outside Dodge, where he settled with his first wife, Flora Robinson. Throughout his career, that ranch and later another in Oklahoma where he raised and bred racehorses, gave him the independent income that helped him remain incorruptible.

Tilghman's greatest success as a lawman came in the 1890s, when he, Chris Madsen, and Heck Thomas became known as "The Three Guardsmen." "The Three Guardsmen" were deputy federal marshals charged with tracking down the outlaws that had begun to run in gangs that spread terror throughout the Oklahoma Territory. Bill Tilghman was the leader of the Guardsmen. After a four-year pursuit, he single-handedly captured Bill Doolin in Eureka Springs, Arkansas, on January 12, 1896.

After leaving the federal marshals service, Tilghman settled down on his ranch. For his wife, Flora, who had endured the lonely, anxious nights of a policeman's wife, it was too late. She died from tuberculosis and Tilghman was left to raise his three children, William, Jr., Dorothy, and Vonia, alone.

Tilghman sold the property and moved to a horse ranch in Chandler, Oklahoma, in 1899. He married his second wife, Zoe Stratton, in 1903. A graduate of the University of Oklahoma, a high accomplishment for a woman of her day, Zoe was 23 years old. Tilghman was 49. A year later, their idyll was shattered by a presidential summons. President Theodore Roosevelt wanted Tilghman to go to Mexico to track down the paymaster of the San Francisco Railroad who had absconded with the railroad's payroll. Tilghman, of course, took the job.

Tilghman spent days in Mexico City's railroad terminal, talking with the locals, gaining their confidence, looking for leads, until he discovered that the paymaster was working as a conductor on a train coming out of Aguascalientes, a town about 300 miles northwest of Mexico City. Tilghman took the first train out. Tilghman was not in Aguascalientes more than a few hours before he sighted his quarry, surprised him in his hotel room, and escorted him to the train station and out of town, all without firing a shot.

In 1913 the outlaw-turned-evangelist Al Jennings produced a silent movie called *Beating Back*. Upon its release, the film, which glorified the Oklahoma outlaws while portraying the deputy marshals as stupid and sadistic, became a nationwide hit. In response, Tilghman agreed to direct and act in a movie that would set the record straight. Because he wanted authenticity, Tilghman took more than a year to do *The Passing of the Oklahoma Outlaws*, which traced the bloody career of the members of the Doolin Gang. Appearing as themselves before the camera were Tilghman, Chris Madsen, and Arkansas Tom, the lone survivor of the Doolin Gang.

While Tilghman was filming on the Oklahoma prairie, in the nearby town of Stroud history was taking place. A gang led by the notorious bank robber Henry Starr was attempting to do what the Daltons had failed to do: successfully hold up two banks in one town on the same day. Starr had done it, and was ready to enjoy the spoils, when he was wounded during his getaway. Leg shattered by a bullet, left for dead by his compadres, Starr was quickly captured.

The townsfolk wanted to lynch him. Hearing of the outlaw's predicament, Tilghman left his movie set and arrived in time to stop the lynching. Art imitated life when Tilghman concluded his movie with the scene of Starr being shot, and his success at protecting him.

Unfortunately, the completed film bombed at the box office. Nevertheless, Tilghman was proud and toured the country with the film, providing live commentary. Eventually, the film made a modest profit.

In 1923, before his ascendancy to the sheriff's job in Cromwell, Tilghman took on one last job that he was able to see through to completion. Along with his old friend Chris Madsen and Major Allan Herskowitz, the commander of the Oklahoma National Guard, the reconstituted Three Guardsmen supplanted a plot by the Ku Klux Klan to take over the Oklahoma town of Okmulgee. Then came Tilghman's last assignment.

At the request of Oklahoma's governor, Tilghman had come out of retirement at the age of 70. His job was to go into the oil boomtown of Cromwell and crush the murdering bunch of gangsters that controlled it. A 70-year-old man with flowing white mustache and erect bearing, Tilghman seemed a relic as he rode into Cromwell at the wheel of his Model T Ford. The dichotomy could not have been greater: a 19th-century lawman with old-fashioned values doing battle with a new breed of 20th-century gangsters that did not hold to the chivalrous code of conduct of the Old West, gangsters like prohibition agent Wiley Lynn. Lynn controlled Cromwell's drug trade, and he hated Tilghman. But after a few skirmishes, Tilghman still did not have enough on Lynn to charge him.

On November 1, 1924, Lynn got into a drunken brawl. Tilghman came running at the commotion and asked Lynn for his gun. Lynn handed the marshal his gun, butt first. In Tilghman's day, if an outlaw offered you his gun, he meant it. It was a matter of honor, even to a so-called badman. But to a modern gangster like Lynn, honor meant nothing.

As Tilghman reached for it, Lynn flipped the revolver back around and pulled the trigger, pumping three shots into Tilghman's stomach. The local newspaper described Tilghman's dying expression as "surprised."

In the wake of Bill Tilghman's death, Cromwell purged itself of its criminal element. Inside of six months, the drug trade and all the other rackets that had flourished in the town were kicked out. Most gave credit for the transformation to Tilghman, who cleaned the town up from his grave.

As for Lynn, he was charged with Tilghman's murder. During his trial, Lynn testified that he shot at Tilghman in evident fear of his life, which was all his lawyer had to prove for a "justifiable homicide." The jury found him not guilty.

A few years later, Wiley Lynn was killed during a fight with a state policeman.

See also WYATT EARP (1853–1928); WILLIAM BARCLAY "BAT" MASTERSON (1853–1921); KANSAS'S DALTON GANG (1890–1892); DOOLIN GANG, A.K.A. THE WILD BUNCH (1892–1895).

Chicago, Illinois (1924) thrill killers Leopold and Loeb

It had been 18 years since America's first trial of the century. Back in 1906, it had been Harry K. Thaw whose fate hung in the balance, and in 1924, it was a pair of murderers who have come to be known as one: Leopold and Loeb.

The case started in Chicago in 1924, within the fractured mind of wealthy 18-year-old Richard Loeb. The youngest graduate ever from the University of Chicago, Loeb had an obsession with crime. He read detective stories constantly, and they gave him ideas. Richard loved planning crimes. When he stepped over the line and started committing petty ones, it gave him a thrill. But he never did anything more than steal, and after a while, the newness wore off.

Loeb needed more.

As a criminal, Loeb had one great advantage over many others: Richard Loeb was a true psychopath. He had no conscience or sense of guilt. To him, crime was just an intellectual exercise, a game. His real goal was to commit the perfect crime just to show that he could do it, and Loeb decided he needed a partner to help him achieve it. He selected a friend, 19-year-old amateur ornithologist Nathan Leopold.

Of ordinary looks, Nathan Leopold was also from wealth, the son of a millionaire box manufacturer. He had already achieved national recognition as the country's leading authority on the Kirtland warbler, an endangered songbird. But it was as a philosophy student that Leopold showed his character. Leopold was intensely attracted to the work of Friedrich Nietzsche.

In his books, Nietzsche criticized moral codes. He believed that legal obligations did not apply to those who approached the "superman" ideal. His influence on early 20th-century academics was so strong that the relative merits of those ideas had been intensely discussed at the University of Chicago. It was there that Leopold had come to the conclusion that Nietzsche was right.

Leopold's idea of Nietzsche's superman was his friend Richard Loeb. The two also had a physical relationship, which made Leopold vulnerable to Loeb's criminal charm. Loeb became the driving force to commit murder, to see if they could indeed commit the perfect crime. Leopold would later write, "Loeb's friendship was necessary to me—terribly necessary."

His motive in committing murder? "To the extent that I had one, [it] was to please Dick." Their lawyer, Clarence Darrow, later characterized their relationship as being "weird and almost impossible." Leopold and Loeb planned their murder carefully and spent hours discussing and refining a plan.

The victim would be chosen at random, someone seized without a struggle. That called for the kidnapping of an easy person to handle—a child. The child should be wealthy, like they were. Their demand for ransom was to establish the motive of greed for the crime, thus sending the police off in another direction. This was their brilliant plan.

On May 21, 1924, the pair was cruising around a wealthy Chicago suburb in a rented Winton auto. About five in the afternoon, they spotted 12-year-old Bobby Franks walking home from school. Loeb pulled to the curb and hailed Franks by name. He knew him because their families socialized. Loeb knew Bobby liked tennis and asked him to get into the car to discuss tennis rackets.

Who killed young Bobby Franks is still a mystery. Leopold said Loeb did it; Loeb said Leopold did it. The consensus of investigators was that it was Loeb who used a chisel to hammer away at the boy's skull until he was dead. What is clear is that afterward Loeb drove the rented Winton to a marshland near the Indiana line. He and Leopold stripped the body naked, poured hydrochloric acid over the corpse to hinder identification, and stuffed the body in a concrete drainage culvert. Satisfied with their nocturnal activities, Leopold and Loeb returned to Loeb's home where they proceeded to burn Franks's clothing in a basement fire.

As far as Leopold and Loeb were concerned, they had erased all traces of their crime. Now all they had to do was go ahead with the ransom plot to establish the phony motive and throw police off the scent. That same night, Mrs. Franks received a phone call from a man who identified himself as "George Johnson." It was really Leopold, who told Mrs. Franks that her boy had been kidnapped. He was unharmed, he told her, and the ransom demand was coming shortly. The next morning, the Franks family got a special delivery letter. Inside was the ransom demand. The kidnapper was asking for $10,000 in old, unmarked bills. The note said to expect further instructions that afternoon.

Leopold ("George Johnson") called Jacob Franks, Bobby's father, at three o'clock to tell him a taxi was about to arrive at his home and that he should take it to a specified drugstore in South Chicago. Just as Franks headed out to the yellow cab, a second call came, this one from the police. The body of Bobby Franks had been found by a laborer who happened to see a flash of what turned out to be a foot through the shrubbery covering the open culvert where the body was dumped. Bobby was identified through his description and clothing.

The police did not find blood nor any signs of a struggle near the body. The natural conclusion was that the boy had been killed someplace else and his body dumped in the culvert. An examination of his head wounds made it evident he had been bludgeoned to death. A pair of hornrimmed glasses was discovered near the body, and police theorized that the murderer had dropped them while disposing of the corpse.

Acting on that theory, police fanned out across Chicago, to every optometrist in the city. The frames turned out to have a unique hinge dispensed by a single

Chicago optometrist. That optometrist, police later learned, had written only three such prescriptions. One was to Nathan Leopold. Leopold was brought in for questioning.

Leopold proceeded to confirm that the glasses were indeed his. He claimed that he must have lost them on one of his frequent birding expeditions. A detective asked him how the glasses might have fallen out of his pocket. Could Leopold demonstrate? Leopold tried, but after a few attempts at bending and turning in various ways, he could not dislodge the glasses from his coat. Police then ratcheted up the questioning. They asked him what he had been doing on May 21, the day Bobby Franks was murdered. Leopold said that he and his friend Richard Loeb had driven out to College Park in Leopold's car and spent the day trying to pick up girls.

Loeb was brought in for questioning. He confirmed Leopold's alibi. Despite the glasses, prosecutors did not have enough to charge them. They were ready to

Richard Loeb (left) and Nathan Leopold at their trial in 1924 (Courtesy of Carl Sifakis)

release Leopold and Loeb when two additional pieces of evidence surfaced.

An earlier search of the Leopold home had turned up a typewriter that did not match the ransom note's typeface. But typewritten notes taken from a member of Leopold's law school study group were found to match the type from the ransom note. Now they had a positive match on the notes that they could trace back circumstantially to Leopold.

The second piece of evidence was a statement from the Leopold family chauffeur. The chauffeur had made it in the hope of establishing Nathan's innocence. He figured that Leopold had told police the truth, that his car never left the garage the day of the murder, so that was what he told the cops, who then knew that Leopold was lying. Confronted with this inconsistency in his story, Leopold held fast. Not so Loeb.

Intimidated by the police, and perhaps not really caring what happened, Richard Loeb confessed first. As soon as Loeb confessed, Leopold, the acolyte, acquiesced. Their confessions differed only on the point of who did the actual killing, with each pointing the finger at the other. Leopold later claimed that he pleaded with Loeb to admit to killing Franks. Instead, Loeb replied, "Mompsie [his mother] feels less terrible than she might, thinking you did it and I'm not going to take that shred of comfort away from her."

If ever two killers seemed bound for the electric chair, it was Leopold and Loeb. There was such a public outpouring of sympathy toward the Franks family and a corresponding flow of bile toward Leopold and Loeb that a fair jury would be hard to come by.

Unlike in the first "trial of the century," when Harry K. Thaw was found not guilty of murder by reason of insanity, the defense lawyer would not be able to put the victim's lifestyle on trial. Bobby Franks was not the bon vivant Stanford White was. Bobby Franks was an innocent boy.

The man who showed up in Chicago to try and save the accused killers' lives had unruly hair, a rumpled jacket, egg-splattered shirt, suspenders, and tie askew. He combed his thin gray hair across his forehead, but a cowlick always drooped over one eye. His name was Clarence Darrow.

Since the 1890s, Clarence Darrow had been the country's most prominent defense attorney. He was distinguished not just by his acknowledged legal brilliance but his impassioned defense of things he believed in, including unions, free speech, and civil liberties. It had been Darrow for the underdog since the 19th century, and here he was in the 20th, entering his 67th year, still defending those no one else would touch.

Leopold, who had a conscience and would come to deeply regret the killing, later described his attorney as a great, simple, unaffected man, with a "deep-seated, all-embracing kindliness." In his book *Life Plus Ninety-nine Years,* Leopold wrote that if asked to name the two men who "came closest to preaching the pure essence of love," he would say Jesus Christ and Clarence Darrow.

Darrow was as clever as he was compassionate. After considering the evidence against his clients, Darrow formed a plan of attack. He changed their plea from not guilty to guilty. Suddenly, Leopold and Loeb had copped to the prosecution's charges. The boys admitted to kidnapping and murder, felony offenses punishable by death. Darrow made the decision to change the plea to prevent the state from getting two opportunities to get a death sentence.

Leopold and Loeb had been charged with kidnapping and murder, both death offenses in Illinois. The state had planned to try the boys on one charge at a time. If they failed to get a conviction on the first charge, they would get a second bite of the apple with the second. Darrow decided not to give the state that chance.

Once the plea was entered the case moved automatically to the sentencing phase. Under Illinois law, the death penalty could be imposed only by the presiding judge, John A. Caverly. Darrow felt Caverly was a "kindly and discerning" man. Caverly alone could impose the death sentence on the accused men. Darrow would not let him forget that when he argued for his clients.

Darrow decided to base his defense of Leopold and Loeb's actions by not offering a defense at all, but rather an explanation to show their insanity. If he could show that the boys, because of their insanity, were not responsible for their actions, the judge might have mercy.

The prosecution argued that was nonsense. Psychiatric testimony was admissible only if the defendants claimed insanity during trial. They had offered no such evidence, since they chose to plead guilty. The defense could not then introduce insanity evidence after the fact.

Darrow argued strenuously that evidence of mental disease should be considered as a mitigating factor in consideration of the sentence. In the most critical ruling of the case, Judge Caverly decided for the defense and allowed the psychiatric evidence to be introduced.

Darrow sent a telegram to Sigmund Freud in Vienna, asking if the father of psychoanalysis would come to Chicago to testify for the boys. Poor health prevented Freud's involvement in the case. Darrow instead decided to build his case on the backs of four respected psychiatrists who would testify that Leopold and Loeb were not culpable for various psychological reasons and should thus not be held accountable for their actions.

During the month-long hearing, the state presented more than 100 witnesses proving—needlessly, in the opinion of many—every element of the crime. The defense presented extensive psychiatric evidence describing the defendants' emotional immaturity, obsessions with crime and Nietzschean philosophy, alcohol abuse, glandular abnormalities, and sexual longings and insecurities.

Lay witnesses, classmates, and associates of Loeb testified as to his belligerence, inappropriate laughter, and lack of judgment, childishness, egocentricity, and argumentative nature. In rebuttal, the state offered psychiatrists who saw normal emotional responses in the boys and no physical basis for a finding of mental abnormality.

On August 22, 1924, Clarence Darrow began his summation for the defense in a "courtroom jammed to suffocation, with hundreds of men and women rioting in the corridors outside," as a newspaper reporter wrote. The environs underscored Darrow's argument "that the court was the only thing standing between the boys and a bloodthirsty mob.

"Where responsibility is divided by twelve, it is easy to say 'away with him'; but, your honor, if these boys are to hang, you must do it by your cool, premeditated act, without a chance to shift responsibility," Darrow told Judge Caverly.

For more than 12 hours, Darrow reminded Judge Caverly of the defendants' youth, the seeming genetic inheritance of violent and perverted tendencies, their sexual needs—homosexuality was considered a mental illness at the time—and the many environmental influences that had led them to the commission of their crime. Darrow argued that life was "a series of infinite chances." Why should the boys' wealthy background be held against them, any more than their genetic murderous impulses should bring about their deaths at the hands of the executioner?

Nature is strong and she is pitiless. She works in mysterious ways, and we are her victims. We have not much to do with it ourselves. Nature takes this job in hand, and we only play our parts. In the words of old Omar Khayam, we are only impotent pieces in the game.

What had this boy [Loeb] had to do with it? He was not his own father; he was not his own mother. All of this was handed to him. He did not surround himself with governesses and wealth. He did not make himself. And yet he is to be compelled to pay. Tell me that you can visit the wrath of fate and chance and life and eternity upon a nineteen-year-old boy!

Darrow had long been an opponent of the death penalty. Once again he attacked it, declaring it "roots back to the beast and the jungle." Time and again Darrow challenged the notion of "an eye for an eye. If the state in which I live is not kinder, more humane, and more considerate than the mad act of these two boys, I am sorry I have lived so long."

A life sentence was punishment severe enough for the crime, the attorney argued passionately. He reminded the judge how little Leopold and Loeb would have to look forward to in the long days, months, and years ahead: "In all the endless road you tread there's nothing but the night."

It was an appeal to the inherent value in human life. Even Leopold and Loeb had some value to their lives, Darrow insisted. When Darrow finally ended his appeal, tears were streaming down the face of Judge Caverly and many courtroom spectators. One reporter wrote, "There was scarcely any telling where his voice had finished and where silence had begun. It lasted for a minute, two minutes."

State's Attorney Robert Crowe closed for the prosecution. Noting Darrow's reputation, he sarcastically characterized him as "the distinguished gentlemen whose profession it is to protect murder in Cook County, and concerning whose health thieves inquire before they go out and commit a crime."

Crowe ridiculed Darrow's attempt to excuse the crime in light of the boys' background and genetics. "My God, if one of them had a harelip I suppose Darrow would want me to apologize for having them indicted." The "real defense" in the case, Crowe said, was "Clarence Darrow and his peculiar philosophy of life."

The prosecutor characterized the defense psychiatrists as "three wise men from the East." He accused one of them of being "in his second childhood" and "prostituting his profession." For Crowe, the Franks murder was a premeditated crime committed by two remorseless defendants, whom he referred to as "cowardly perverts," "snakes," "atheists," "spoiled smart alecs," and "mad dogs." They needed to be punished appropriately, with death.

I wonder now, Nathan, whether you think there is a God or not. I wonder whether you think it is pure accident that this disciple of Nietzsche's philosophy dropped his glasses or whether it was an act of Divine Providence to visit upon your miserable carcasses the wrath of God.

At a later date, Leopold admitted to wondering the same thing. Crowe closed by imploring Judge Caverly to "execute justice and righteousness in the land."

It would be a full two weeks of agonizing over the evidence before Caverly reconvened the court to announce his decision.

"A crime of singular atrocity," was how the judge characterized the murder of Bobby Franks. Yet Caverly cautioned that his "judgment cannot be affected" by the causes of crime. It was beyond the province of the court to "predicate ultimate responsibility for human acts."

At that point it was still unclear which way the judge was leaning. Then he pointed out that "the consideration of the age of the defendants," and the possible benefits to criminology that might come about by studying their psyches ultimately persuaded him to spare their lives. The judge had decided that life, not death, was the better punishment. He cautioned that sparing the boys' lives was really no favor.

"To the offenders, particularly of the type they are, the prolonged years of confinement may well be the severest form of retribution and expiation."

Whether Caverly was referring to the defendants' crime or sexual preference was never made clear. To Darrow it made no difference—he had won his victory and saved the boys' lives.

Shortly after the verdict, Leopold and Loeb were transferred to the Illinois state penitentiary in Joliet where they were supposed to spend the rest of their lives behind bars.

Richard Loeb was killed in 1936 by a fellow inmate toward whom Loeb had made repeated sexual advances. James Day told authorities that Richard Loeb had been pressuring him to have sex and he had consistently refused him. But Loeb would not take no for an answer. Day used a concealed razor to slash Loeb's throat. Nathan Leopold rushed to the prison hospital to be at his old friend and lover's bedside. He stayed with him until he died.

James Day was charged with the premeditated murder of Richard Loeb. The state claimed at trial that it was a deliberate and unprovoked attack. Day's defense was that he was in the act of resisting Loeb's advances when he killed him. If there was a jury extant that would convict Day of killing one of the country's most infamous killers, it was not the one that sat in his judgment. Day's jury found him not guilty of premeditated murder, and he was sent back to Joliet to finish out his previous term of imprisonment.

During his time inside, Leopold kept his intellectual activity as acute as he could to stave off boredom. He taught in the prison school and designed a new system of prison education while reorganizing the prison library. In between, he taught himself to write and speak 27 foreign languages.

Later on, during World War II, he volunteered to be tested with an experimental malaria vaccine. He also worked as an X-ray technician in the prison hospital. In fact, Leopold led such an exemplary life behind bars that Robert Crowe, the man who had prosecuted him, championed Leopold for parole. In the 1950s Crowe was a retired, elderly man, a far cry from the firebrand who had demanded Nathan

Leopold die in the electric chair for his crimes. Reportedly, Crowe offered to write a letter to the Illinois Parole Board urging Leopold's release.

In 1958, after 34 years of confinement, Leopold was released from prison. To escape the publicity accompanying the release of *Compulsion,* a movie based on the 1924 crime (and which Leopold and his lawyer, Elmer Gertz, challenged in a lawsuit as an invasion of privacy), Leopold moved to Puerto Rico. There Leopold resumed his formal studies and earned a master's degree. He taught mathematics and worked in hospitals and church missions. He resumed his interest in birding and wrote a well-received reference book, *A Checklist of the Birds of Puerto Rico.*

In a 1960 interview Leopold said that he was still in love with Richard Loeb. Nevertheless, he married. During his subsequent years in Puerto Rico, Leopold wondered on more than one occasion whether his 34 years in prison could in some way be balanced by his years of freedom.

Following 10 days of hospitalization, Nathan Leopold died in obscurity on August 30, 1971. He was 65 years old and had spent the last 13 years of his life free. According to all accounts, he was completely rehabilitated. He had long given up Nietzsche's superman ideal. In fact, he seemed to spend his entire life in atonement for Bobby Franks. The morning after his death, his corneas were removed for transplantation. One was given to a man, the other to a woman.

New York, New York (1927) Ruth Brown: America's most famous murderess

Were it not the competition among New York tabloids of the Roaring Twenties to see who could top whom with sensational front-page photographs, Ruth Brown might not have been just the most sensational murder case of the time. Instead, Brown became America's most famous murderess of the first half of the 20th century.

Brown was 13 years old when she took her first full-time job as a telephone operator working for Alexander Graham Bell's company, AT&T. Working the night shift, she studied shorthand and bookkeeping during the day. She told friends that her ultimate goal was to switch positions, then marry her boss, who would be a wealthy executive, not some phone company guy.

A few years later, Ruth managed to procure employment at *Motor Boating* magazine as a secretary. She got very friendly with her boss, editor

Nathan Leopold in July 1957, several months before he was paroled (Courtesy of Carl Sifakis)

Albert Snyder. In 1915, when she was 20 years old, she and Snyder married. But Snyder was not a great catch. He came loaded with problems.

The biggest was that he had been engaged to another woman, Jessie Guishard, for 10 years and was still stuck on her. When he and Ruth began to live together after they were married, it was his ex-fiancée's picture he first hung up on the wall of their new home. Ruth objected.

"She's the finest woman I have ever known," he told Brown, who later included that information in her statement to police.

The marriage started out on this rocky slope and went downhill from there. Albert was older than his wife by 13 years. He did not like dancing or parties as Ruth did. She bobbed her hair in the style of the day, loved to dance the Charleston, played bridge, and loved to go to nightclubs. While Brown cavorted, Albert stayed home and looked after their daughter Lorraine, who was born in 1918.

Columnist Damon Runyon, whose short stories would later become the basis for the musical *Guys and Dolls,* described Brown as "a chilly-looking blonde with frosty eyes and one of those marble you-bet-you-will chins."

Dissatisfied with her life, Brown met Judd Gray in June 1925 on a blind date. A 33-year-old salesman for the Bien Jolie Corset Company, Gray fell instantly in love with Brown and she with him. They began an affair that lasted two years. It so consumed Brown that she compromised her daughter's safety.

One of the pair's favorite rendezvous was the Waldorf Astoria on Park Avenue and East 51st Street. On more than one occasion, Brown would later admit, she left Lorraine in the hotel's lobby while she went upstairs and had relations with Gray in a rented room.

As for Albert, he suddenly became accident prone, and throughout 1926, mishaps kept befalling him. Judd Gray would later admit that Ruth tried to kill him through drowning, poisoning, and gassing. Each attempt failed, either through some mistake on Ruth's part or Snyder's incredible constitution.

On March 20, 1927, Ruth called the cops to report that her husband had been murdered. She told police that she and Albert had returned from a party at 2:30 A.M. After putting Lorraine to bed, Albert went to bed too. Ruth, who was not tired, stayed downstairs in the living room.

Ruth said she was reading a book when a burglar suddenly entered. Sporting an "Italian-style" mustache, the burglar hit her on the head. Ruth woke up five

hours later. Her hands were tied. Struggling to her feet, she trod the short distance to her daughter's room and woke Lorraine up. Lorraine ran to neighbors. Ruth would not allow the responding neighbors to untie her until police arrived.

When the police did arrive, detectives discovered Albert's body in the bedroom. It smelled of chloroform. He was tied hand and foot, and his head had been bashed in. Picture wire was tied so tightly around his neck that it cut into the skin. Three bullets were on the floor. A revolver had been placed on the bed next to Albert.

Ruth told the cops that money was missing from her husband's wallet. Also, she had discovered that some of her jewels were missing. Detectives theorized that someone had used chloroform to knock out Albert, and then did him in by bludgeoning and strangling. Bludgeoning or strangulation would have done the job alone, but police theorized to do both someone must have been awfully angry.

In murder cases, cops always look to the closest relative first. In this case, that was Brown. A search of the crime scene soon located the money she said was missing. Someone had hid it under their mattress. Police immediately theorized that the whole thing was a set-up and that Snyder had been done in by his wife, who tried to stage it to look like a burglary.

In Ruth's desk police found a $200 check made out to H. Judd Gray. There was also a tie clip with Judd's initials on it and Ruth's little black book, listing names of men with whom she evidently did some sort of business. Twenty-eight names were in the book.

Police checked the dead man's safe deposit box. Inside they found a life insurance policy in his name, with a double indemnity clause: If he was murdered, the policy paid double. The beneficiary was Ruth Brown Snyder.

Things were looking bad for Brown. For Gray, it was no better. Gray had been spotted shortly after the time fixed for Snyder's murder at a bus stop nearby, asking a cop how long it took before the next bus would show up. That established that he was physically close to the crime scene when the murder happened.

Police tracked Gray on the city's bus line to Jamaica, Queens, where he changed to a taxi into Manhattan that traversed the 59th Street Bridge. The cabbie remembered Gray because he gave him only a lousy five-cent tip. Damon Runyon wrote that Gray was "an inert, scared drunk fellow that you couldn't miss among any hundred men as a dead set-up for a blonde, or the shell game, or maybe a gold brick—on trial for what might be called for want of a better name: the Dumb-bell Murder. It was so dumb!"

Gray and Brown were brought in for questioning. Confronted with the strong circumstantial material that the police had managed to gather, they confessed, and each blamed the other. Gray claimed that Brown tied the wire around her husband's throat. As for Ruth, her story was that Judd went into the bedroom and when he came out, said, "I guess that's it."

It took the jury only one hour and 30 minutes to convict both defendants of murder in the first degree. The judge immediately sentenced them both to death in the electric chair. After numerous appeals, the execution date was finally set for January 22, 1928. Every newspaper was vying for a photo of the convicted murderers, but the *New York Daily News* went a step further.

They dispatched photographer Thomas Howard to the execution with a camera secretly strapped to his leg. If he could manage to get a shot of Brown when the executioner pulled the lever, he would have history's first picture of a woman dying in the electric chair.

That is exactly what happened.

The picture of Brown strapped into the electric chair with a black hood over her head, as the electricity shot into her body, ran on the front page of the *New York Daily News* on January 12, 1928. It remains the tabloid picture against which all crime photographs are measured. The significance of the case is how the 20th-century press made it more than it was, presaging similar cases, including the O. J. Simpson case in the 1990s.

Miami, Florida (1933) attempted assassination of President-elect Franklin Delano Roosevelt

Giuseppe Zangara is the first and only man in American criminal history to attempt to assassinate a president-elect. Zangara was born in Ferruzzano, Italy, on September 7, 1900. His mother died when he was two years old. His father remarried and forced Zangara to quit school when he was six to help support the family. Along with an uncle, he immigrated to the United States in 1923. He drifted from job to job, until settling in Miami, Florida, where he worked as a bricklayer.

Zangara, like many others, found it difficult to survive during the Great Depression, which he blamed on President Herbert Hoover. When Franklin

Delano Roosevelt defeated Hoover in November 1932 to win the presidency, Zangara transferred his hate from one man to the other and decided to do something about it.

The would-be assassin read in a paper that Roosevelt was making a pre-inaugural trip to Miami's Bayfront Park. Zangara bought a .32 caliber pistol and was so determined to use it that he would not let his height—he stood five feet tall on his tiptoes—stop him from doing so. On February 15, when the president-elect appeared at the park, Zangara was in the crowd. Having difficulty seeing Roosevelt through the throng, Zangara mounted a chair and, spotting his victim, he opened fire. But he was a poor marksman.

Not one shot hit Roosevelt. Instead, Zangara accidentally shot the man by Roosevelt's side, Chicago mayor Anton Cermak. Four people in the crowd were also wounded. Roosevelt accompanied Cermak to the hospital, and Cermak said, "I'm glad it was me and not you, Mr. President."

Zangara was quickly put on trial, convicted of attempted murder of Cermak and the bystanders, and sentenced to a total of 84 years in prison. When Cermak died from his abdominal wound on March 3, the charges were upped to murder. Tried and found guilty, the diminutive immigrant was sentenced to death. Zangara replied with contempt and defiance, calling the judge a capitalist and a crook, and claiming he was unafraid of the electric chair. On March 20, 1933, Zangara was executed at Florida State Penitentiary.

See also ASSASSINATION OF PRESIDENT GARFIELD (JULY–SEPTEMBER 1881); JOHN WILKES BOOTH; BUFFALO, NEW YORK (1901); DALLAS, TEXAS (1963); WASHINGTON, D.C. (1835); WASHINGTON, D.C. (1982).

Prohibition Repealed (1933)

In 1933 the Nineteenth Amendment was finally repealed and Americans were lifted from the yoke of Prohibition. It was clear that not only had the legislation of public morality been a failure, it had cost the government millions of dollars in fighting bootlegging. As for the criminals, whole empires were built on the illegal brews.

It was the money from bootlegging that financed the building of the modern mob. For bootlegger Joseph "Old Joe" Kennedy, the millions he made from bootlegging enabled him to buy political connections for himself and his family. By the late 1930s, as the world headed to war, President Franklin D. Roosevelt appointed "Old Joe" ambassador to Great Britain. As for his bootlegger buddies, they turned their attention to other illegal business which when organized became The Five Families, aka the modern mob.

See also WASHINGTON, D.C. (1920).

United States (1930–1941) the Great Depression

Throughout the 1920s, the stock market boomed. Things started to go wrong in 1928 and 1929 when the newly created Federal Reserve attempted raising interest rates to discourage stock speculation. That brought about a recession.

As for the stock market, the decade had seen it grow on borrowed money. People bought stocks with borrowed money and used those stocks as collateral for buying more stocks. It was a house of cards that finally fell when the stock market crashed on October 29, 1929, "Black Tuesday."

The unstable economy continued to wither until the United States, and the rest of the world, was plunged into the Great Depression. Throughout the 1930s, unemployment rose to a high of 25 percent in 1933, averaging close to the 20 percent mark for the rest of the decade. The human toll was staggering. People went hungry and homeless. The Midwest was hit particularly hard.

Farmers who could not pay their bills lost their farms when banks foreclosed. Merchants were forced to fold their tents because no one had money to buy goods and services. Amid such poverty, it was not surprising that a new era in crime was born.

The men and women who would come to be known as the Depression-era outlaws were a direct product of their times. They all came from poor families of the lower classes. It is easy to see why they chose crime, considering the desperate nature of the times.

Clyde Champion Barrow (1909–1934) and Bonnie Parker (1911–1934), a.k.a. "Bonnie and Clyde"

Not before or since have any criminals used the emerging road system to commit crime and then elude the law better than Bonnie and Clyde. Both were expert drivers, with Clyde a master of the getaway. But as good as he was a driver, Clyde was an even better gunsmith.

Clyde Barrow invented the sawed-off weapon. He did it by sawing off the barrel of a Browning Automatic Rifle, making it more concealable though no less deadly. Clyde also made sure that the gang was always armed with at least one Browning, which Bonnie carried on occasion. As for handguns, Clyde was no fool. He preferred automatics capable of delivering the most bullets in the least amount of time.

Clyde found his criminal match in Bonnie, a woman who had more panache in her pen than Clyde had in his gun. Her letters to the press describing their criminal exploits became legendary. They met down in Texas, deep in the Panhandle, where jobs were hard to come by. Bonnie Parker was 19 years old in 1930 when she met Clyde Barrow. At the time, Bonnie was married to an imprisoned murderer. Clyde was 21 and unmarried.

Soon after their first meeting, Clyde was arrested for burglary and sent to county jail. Bonnie went to visit him and smuggled in a gun that Clyde used to escape. Soon recaptured, he was sent back to prison and paroled in February 1932. What happened next was possible only due to the rapid advancement of the motor car.

The invention itself was still in its infancy in 1932. Not everyone had a car. It was a true luxury item. Most people used buses and trains to get from point A to point B, but that required being on someone else's schedule. In rural areas like the Texas Panhandle, some still relied on horses for transportation. But gradually, people had gotten cars, and as a result, even in the backwoods sections of the country, there were rough highways now for motor cars to traverse.

For someone like Clyde Barrow, who never had two nickels to rub together, the only way he could afford a car was to steal one. He did that on numerous occasions, including after his jailbreak. Traveling in a stolen car, he and Bonnie immediately enlisted a young gunman named William Daniel Jones. With Jones, he and Bonnie began robbing groceries and filling stations. They did not come under the FBI's radar until they stole a car in Illinois and transported it across state lines. That made it a federal offense.

On May 20, 1933, the U.S. government issued a warrant against Clyde Barrow and Bonnie Parker for interstate transportation of stolen property. The chase was on. Over the next year and a half, Bonnie and Clyde—accompanied by Jones and, later, Clyde's brother Buck and his wife Blanche—"committed 13 murders and several robberies and burglaries," according to their FBI file.

Barrow, for example, was suspected of murdering two police officers at Joplin, Missouri, and kidnapping a man at Hillsboro, Texas; committed robberies at Lufkin and Dallas, Texas; murdered one sheriff and wounded another at Stringtown, Oklahoma; kidnapped a deputy at Carlsbad, New Mexico; stole an automobile at Victoria, Texas; another murder at Dallas, Texas; abducted a sheriff and the chief of police at Wellington, Texas; and committed a murder at Joplin, Missouri, and a murder at Columbia, Missouri.

During their brief reign as America's criminal sweethearts, Bonnie kept up a regular correspondence with the press. She loved sending them joke photographs. She loved to be photographed smoking a cigar and holding up a Thompson submachine gun. Another time, she had a shot taken in which she was pointing a B.A.R. at Clyde, a sneering smile creasing her lips.

The press loved the couple and plastered their exploits across the front pages of America's newspapers. Bonnie and Clyde were nationally famous. And yet, most of their robberies were of small businesses. They were not bank robbers like Dillinger, with huge hauls worth killing over. Bonnie and Clyde would just as soon shoot people over $50 as $5,000. They were amoral. That made them lethal murderers and the authorities knew it.

Counting the FBI, state, and local police in half a dozen states, there were thousands of police officers camped out on America's roads just waiting to spot them. The gang's downfall finally began on July 29, 1933, in Iowa. During a shootout with police, Buck Barrow was fatally wounded and his wife Blanche captured. Five months later, in November, William Daniel Jones, who bore an uncanny resemblance to "Pretty Boy" Floyd and was frequently mistaken for him, was captured in Houston, Texas.

On November 22, 1933, a trap was set by Ted Hinton, deputy sheriff of Dallas, Texas. Acting on a tip, Hinton and other lawmen set up on a roadblock near Grand Prairie, Texas. Just as Bonnie and Clyde came abreast in a stolen car, the lawmen opened fire. But they had waited too long.

Clyde managed to pull the car off the road, firing as he went, and then back onto the highway. Stomping the gas pedal, he sped away. It was about this time that Bonnie sent her famous poem, "The Ballad of Bonnie and Clyde," to newspapers. It was picked up by the wire services and distributed nationally:

The road gets dimmer and dimmer
Sometimes you can hardly see,
Still it's fight man to man,
And do all you can,
For they know they can never be free.

If they try to act like citizens,
And rent them a nice little flat,
About the third night they are invited to fight,
By a submachine gun rat-a-tat

They don't think they are tough or desperate,
They know the law always wins,
They have been shot at before
But they do not ignore
That death is the wages of sin

From heartbreaks some people have suffered,
From weariness some people have died,
But take it all and all,
Our troubles are small,
Till we get like Bonnie and Clyde.

Some day they will go down together,
And they will bury them side by side,
To a few it means grief,
To the law it's relief
But it's death to Bonnie and Clyde.

On January 16, 1934, Bonnie and Clyde determined to break five prisoners out of Eastham State Prison Farm at Waldo, Texas, including an old gang member, Raymond Hamilton, who was serving sentences totaling more than 200 years. The pair concealed guns in a ditch and got word to the inmates. When the five came out on a work party, they retrieved the weapons and fired on the guards, killing two.

As the remaining guards fired back, Clyde Barrow barreled up in a stolen car, firing his Tommy gun. Besides Hamilton, Henry Methvin of Louisiana was among the escapes. On April 1, 1934, Bonnie and Clyde were on the outskirts of Grapevine, Texas, when they literally ran into two young highway patrolmen out looking for them. Before the cops could fire on the outlaws, Bonnie and Clyde dropped them with machine gun and B.A.R fire. Five days later, on April 6, Bonnie killed a cop at Miami, Oklahoma. During that same incident, they kidnapped the town's police chief, who was shot and wounded.

Back in Washington, the FBI was anything but idle. The file reads,

The FBI had jurisdiction solely on the charge of transporting a stolen automobile [across state lines] although the activities of the Bureau Agents were vigorous and ceaseless. Every clue was followed. "Wanted"

notices were distributed to all officers, furnishing fin- gerprints photograph, description, criminal record and other data.

The agents followed the trail through many states and into various haunts of the Barrow gang, particularly Louisiana. The association with Henry Methvin and the Methvin family of Louisiana was discovered by agents, and they found that Bonnie and Clyde had been driving a car stolen in New Orleans.

The FBI now determined to share its information with state officials in the hope that the killers could be brought to ground. FBI field agents learned that Bonnie and Clyde had been sighted in a remote section of Louisiana southwest of Ruston. The Methvin family home was not far away. The agents discovered that Bonnie and Clyde frequently visited them.

The FBI informed local law enforcement in Louisiana and Texas of their findings. Before anyone could react, new information came in to the bureau. Bonnie and Clyde had "staged a party at Black Lake, Louisiana on the night of May 21, 1934. Bonnie and Clyde were due to return to the area two days later."

Louisiana may have long since been settled, but only residents could safely negotiate the dense and lush growth in the warm, moist climate. Bonnie and Clyde did not have the knowledge of the bayous that Lafitte had or of the Natchez Trace and its surrounding areas that Hare, the Harps, and Mason knew like the back of their hands. The police would never have a better opportunity to draw the killers into a trap.

Jurisdiction was given to a combined posse of lawmen from Louisiana and Texas. Calling the shots was Texas Ranger Frank Hamer. Hamer had his men conceal themselves along the highway near Sailes, Louisiana, before dawn on May 23, 1934. As dawn broke in the eastern sky, Bonnie and Clyde appeared in an automobile. Before the police fired, Clyde realized he had driven into a trap. Hitting the brakes, he attempted to back up and out of trouble as he had so many times in the past.

The bullets tore into Bonnie and Clyde. Even after death, their bodies still jerked spasmodically as the cops kept shooting. When they finally stopped moving, they had already been dead over a minute.

Bonnie had been right.

See also JOHN DILLINGER (1903–1934); CHARLES ARTHUR FLOYD, A.K.A. "PRETTY BOY" FLOYD (1906– 1934); LESTER M. GILLIS, A.K.A. "BABYFACE" NELSON (1908–1935); JESSE JAMES (1847–1882); JAMES- YOUNGER GANG (1866–1881).

Charles Arthur Floyd, a.k.a. "Choc" Floyd, a.k.a. "Pretty Boy" Floyd (1904–1934)

"Pretty Boy" Floyd was born Charles Arthur Floyd on February 3, 1904, in Georgia. He was the fourth of eight children born to Walter Lee Floyd and his wife Minnie Echols.

As a boy, Charley was well liked by his brothers and sisters. He was easygoing, with a good sense of humor, and liked to play pranks on his siblings. His parents were Baptists who took their brood to church every Sunday. Charley grew up in a God-fearing, hard-working family.

In 1911 Walter Floyd packed up his family and moved to Sequoia County at the southern foothills of the Cookson Hills in Oklahoma. There he became a tenant farmer. The area had changed little since it was Indian Territory patrolled by federal marshals. It was still lush and overgrown, a perfect place to hide out if the law happened to be after you.

People in the Cookson Hills watched out for each other. Many families brewed moonshine or corn liquor. It was just something to help the family pay the bills; no one looked at it as anything illegal. Charley and his brothers peddled their father's home- made brew to make some extra money for the family.

In 1915 the Floyd family moved to Akins, where Walter opened a general store. By that time Charley was almost finished with his schooling. It was common practice at the time for children to drop out of school after the sixth grade to help their family in whatever business they happened to be in.

Charley helped his father in his store and on their farm. As a teenager, he formed a liking for a popular local brew called Choctaw Beer. From that came his first nickname. Everyone began calling him "Choc."

Choc Floyd became fascinated with the adventures of a local named Henry Starr, the sometime bandit and murderer who was gallant with the ladies and never robbed a workingman. In 1913 Starr had been captured and was in the lockup in Stroud, Indian territory, when some local residents came by to hang him. Bill Tilghman, who was filming his movie nearby, came over to the jail and stopped the lynching. Starr later served 4 years in jail of a 25-year sentence, but his call to justice did not serve as a warning to Choc.

Choc's most serious crime before he was 15 was stealing a box of cookies from J. H. Harkrider's store in Sallislaw. He was caught and immediately con- fessed, for which he was let off with a warning.

At age 19 Choc joined a crew of migrant farm- workers that worked their way through Oklahoma and Kansas. Many of them were drifters who joined up for the season. Some were on the lam from the law. Choc found he was comfortable with these men, who bragged about their criminal experiences. To an impressionable teenager, they made crime seem like an easy, fun-filled life.

These men had a certain ruthlessness about them. In a fight, they would do anything to win. Kicking, stomping, made no difference as long as they won and the other guy slinked off bloodied and battered. Choc liked that. His older sister Ruth would later claim that these men "changed his way of thinking and doing."

Returning to the Cookson Hills after the harvesting season, Choc became a bum, frequenting the town's billiard and music halls. In May 1922 Choc and his friend Harold Franks decided to hold up the Akins post office. Breaking in, they discovered all of $3.50 in dimes. In his first professional act as a felony offender, Choc took the coins. He and Franks were soon arrested on a federal warrant. Choc had made the mistake of "knocking over" federal property.

Akins was a close community where everyone knew everybody, so it did not come as a surprise when witnesses to the robbery failed to show in court. They were giving Choc a break. Without eyewitnesses, the case was weak and the judge dismissed the charges.

After his acquittal, Choc trod the straight and narrow for a few years. He grew into a handsome young man with dark brown wavy hair, dimples, and a flashing smile. Aggressive, intelligent, and nervy, he had the perfect attributes of either a successful businessman or a successful criminal.

In early 1924 Choc married a local girl from Bixby named Ruby Hargraves. He was 20, and she was 16. They bought a small house in Akins and soon had a son that they named Charles Dempsey Floyd, the middle name after the heavyweight champion who knocked out Jess Willard. Choc was a good father and husband who worked in the cotton fields to make a living. But the work was hard, and he knew from the roustabouts in his migrant farming days that there were easier ways to make money.

Along with a 19-year-old petty thief named John Hilderbrand, Choc left wife, child, and home in 1925 and headed for St. Louis. Within a month, they had held up half a dozen groceries and service stations. Their total take was paltry—$565. But the work was easy and, for Choc, absolutely thrilling.

In September a friend of Hilderbrand named Joe Hlavatry called Hilderbrand with a tip. A large payroll

Charles Arthur Floyd, a.k.a. "Pretty Boy" Floyd (National Archives)

delivery was expected at Kroger's Food Store during the late morning of Friday, September 11, 1925. That morning, Choc, Hilderbrand, and the fellow who had given them the tip, stole a Cadillac and parked it in the alley next to the Kroger building.

At a few minutes before 1 P.M., an armored truck drove up alongside the store's loading dock. A guard began unloading satchels of money. When everything was finally off the truck, the robbers entered the office building and went straight to the cashier's office. The robbers drew revolvers from long trench coats.

Keeping the guards and other personnel covered, Choc and Hlavatry grabbed the money sacks and left quickly. A few days later, the thieves showed that their moment of professionalism during the robbery—no one was hurt or maimed—was just that, a moment.

Rather than maintaining secrecy, the thieves bought a shiny new Studebaker and proceeded to drive it around Fort Smith, Arkansas. Suspicious of the bums and their new vehicle, police detained them. After questioning, Hilderbrand and Hlavatry confessed to the robbery and named Choc Floyd as an accomplice. All three were charged with highway robbery on September 16, 1925.

Newspapermen found something interesting about the three holdup men. Their apparent naiveté in spending money that they should have kept hidden, and the way they nevertheless professionally went about the robbery, attracted headlines. The payroll master at Kroger's, interviewed for an article, referred to Choc as "a mere boy—a pretty boy with apple cheeks."

The name stuck. Choc became "Pretty Boy" Floyd. To a depression-ridden country eager for a hero, he would become a legend. But Choc himself hated the moniker.

Pleading guilty, Choc served four years in the Jefferson City State Penitentiary. He was released in 1929. Afterward, he spent the next two years making a name for himself as a modern highwayman.

Choc was arrested twice on suspicion of highway robbery, a crime that still existed in the books. He had actually stopped cars and proceeded to rob the occupants. On May 20, 1930, Choc was arrested by the Toledo, Ohio, police department on a bank robbery charge. This time the charge stuck. Convicted, he was sentenced to a maximum of 15 years.

The state penitentiary was in Columbus, Ohio. Choc boarded a train from Toledo that would take him there. During the train ride, Choc talked his guards into taking off the handcuffs so he could go to the bathroom. One of them, packing a Colt automatic, followed him. He waited outside while Floyd did his business.

Inside, Choc broke the window in the bathroom and jumped for it. When the guard finally realized what was happening and busted in the door, all he saw was a broken window. Choc was long gone. The train was finally stopped but there was nothing anyone could do unless they wanted to go racing across the rolling hills after Floyd in the gathering darkness.

Choc made headlines for days after his dramatic escape:

"PRETTY BOY" ESCAPES TRAIN TO PRISON
FLOYD ESCAPES INTO NIGHT
GUARDS SURPRISED WHEN "PRETTY BOY"
ESCAPES

THE KANSAS CITY MASSACRE

On the morning of June 17, 1933, there occurred in front of the Union Railway Station in Kansas City, Missouri one of the most brutal, premeditated mass murders recorded in the annals of American law enforcement. The killings, which took the lives of four

peace officers and their prisoner, are now known as the "Kansas City Massacre."

So begins the FBI file on the "Kansas City Massacre," allegedly "Pretty Boy" Floyd's greatest criminal escapade. Acting in concert with Vernon Miller and Adam Richetti, the trio, according to the FBI, attempted to free Frank Nash, a gangster and federal prisoner who was being transported to the U.S. Penitentiary in Leavenworth, Kansas.

Nash had originally been sentenced on March 1, 1924, at Oklahoma City for assaulting a mailman. He escaped in 1930, and the FBI immediately began searching for Nash throughout the entire United States and parts of Canada. After an intensive investigation that showed that Nash had assisted other prisoners in escaping from Leavenworth, he was tracked down by federal agents.

Like outlaw Bill Doolin before him, he had gone to Eureka Springs, Arkansas, to partake of the therapeutic waters. There, on June 16, 1933, federal agents recaptured him. Nash had learned a little bit more, though, than Doolin about organizing a gang.

"During the course of the FBI's investigation for Nash, it was learned that he had closely associated

Frank Nash was the man two other gangsters were trying to free from police when their escape escalated into the "Kansas City Massacre." (National Archives)

with known gunmen who had participated in a number of bank robberies throughout the middle west," the FBI file continued. It was these underworld contacts that provided protection for him in Eureka Springs and were not very happy when he was recaptured. Several began scheming to free him.

Gunman Vernon Miller was at the Horseshoe Tavern in Kansas City when he heard of Nash's fate. He "made a number of telephone calls to several of his criminal associates for assistance in carrying out this scheme." Always loyal to his friends, Floyd immediately took off to help Miller and took with him another holdup artist, Adam Richetti. The two wound up "detained in Bolivar, Missouri, when their car became disabled." Waiting for it to be repaired at a local garage, "Sheriff Jack Killingsworth entered the garage unexpectedly and was immediately recognized by Richetti, who seized a machine gun and held the sheriff and garage attendant against the wall in a defenseless position. Floyd assisted in this when the two drew .45 automatic pistols and ordered all of the parties to remain motionless while they effected their escape."

Not wanting to wait for their car to be fixed, they hijacked another, loading all their weapons inside, along with a hostage, Sheriff Killingsworth. They drove

Vernon C. "Vern" Miller was one of the suspects the FBI identified in the "Kansas City Massacre." (National Archives)

out of town, and then hijacked the car of a Walter Griffith. After releasing the sheriff, they finally arrived in Kansas City "about ten p.m. on June 16, 1933, when after driving around the streets for some time, they abandoned this automobile and stole another car in that city," and then drove to Miller's house.

When they got there, Miller filled them in on what was happening. Nash was going to be taken back to Leavenworth. He would arrive by train in Kansas City tomorrow morning to be transferred back to prison by automobile. The idea was to snatch him before he got into the auto.

On the morning of June 17, 1933, according to the FBI, Miller, Floyd and Richetti drove to the Union Railway Station in a Chevy sedan. They selected places in the street in front of the train station and waited. When Nash arrived, he was escorted by FBI agents, including Special Agent Raymond J. Caffrey; Otto Reed, chief of police of McAlester, Oklahoma; Kansas City police officers W. J. Grooms and Frank Hermanson; and two other FBI agents.

Upon being removed from the train, Nash, in manacles, was immediately taken to Caffrey's waiting automobile. Nash was placed in the front seat of the car. In the rear were the two FBI agents and Otto Reed. Grooms and Hermanson took up positions around the car, just as Agent McCaffrey approached the left door of his automobile from the front. He looked up when he heard someone shout, "Up! Up!"

Three assassins had sneaked up on the cops' blind side. Witnesses later confirmed they were carrying machine guns and automatic pistols.

From the FBI file:

An instant later, the voice of one of the gunmen was heard to say "Let 'em have it." Immediately a fusillade of gunfire came from the weapons of the attackers. Shots were fired from the front and from all sides of Agent Caffrey's car.

Grooms and Hermanson were instantly killed in the deadly crossfire. Inside the car, Otto Reed fell dead from extensive bullet wounds. "One of the FBI agents was severely wounded by bullets which entered his back and was [subsequently] confined to bed for several months."

Caffrey was also killed by a bullet that passed directly through his head as he stood beside the car. As for Frank Nash, "a misdirected gunshot entered his skull, thereby defeating the very purposes of the conspiracy to gain his freedom." Nash fell dead from the gunshot.

Floyd, Richetti, and Miller escaped unharmed. The papers called it "the Kansas City Massacre." Coverage was extensive from coast to coast. The FBI made sure to play up Floyd's part in the massacre. But there really was no evidence that Floyd was involved, and in fact, he probably was not.

Up to the time of the massacre, Choc had never killed anyone the authorities knew about. Choc was a modern-day Hare, a highwayman who robbed for money and no other reason. He was not a cold-blooded killer. Based upon this, his modus operandi in every single robbery he was accused and/or convicted of, it is doubtful he would have deliberately committed murder to free a man he hardly knew.

During the last decade of the 20th century, researchers cast serious doubt on the FBI account.

". . . the FBI account is based more on speculation, perhaps even perjury. Survivors could not initially identify Floyd or Richetti to give the Bureau the excuse it needed to go after Floyd, the first bandit to make national news . . ." wrote William Helmer with Rick Mattix in their 1998 book, *Public Enemies*.

What is clear is that a short time after the massacre, Miller's body was discovered outside Detroit. It was presumed that his fellow criminals killed him for reasons unknown though understandable: Miller had made lots of enemies in the criminal underclass. No suspect was ever charged.

Whether he was involved or not, Floyd now had FBI agents gunning for him. Director J. Edgar Hoover wanted him dead or alive. Choc knew that the best thing he could do was escape the Midwest for his own safety, so he went to Buffalo, New York. Using assumed names, Floyd and Richetti and their wives moved into an apartment building in Buffalo in 1934 and kept a very low profile.

Back in Washington, Hoover was still hot for their capture. He used the Kansas City Massacre as the rationale to lobby for increased FBI involvement in what had, until then, been only state-related crimes and therefore state charges. Hoover lobbied for passage of the 1934 Fugitive Felons Act that made it a federal crime to avoid prosecution by stepping across state lines. That meant that the capture of fugitives like Floyd came under the bureau's aegis.

Hoover got the legislation he wanted. As a result, he created the bureau's "Public Enemies" list that would go on to become legendary. Choc hit number one on that first list, followed by the bank-robbing Hoosier John Dillinger.

After seven months of isolation in a Buffalo winter, Choc had had enough. He and Richetti went back to the Cookson Hills. While visiting his family, Choc read of Bonnie and Clyde's bloody demise by cops armed with Browning Automatic Rifles. He learned that the Justice Department was targeting him next, yet he did not seem to care.

Instead of getting out of the crime racket with his life, Choc kept going. Some accounts claim that he met his mother during his time in the Cookson hills at a secret location because the agents were shadowing her. During this meeting, Choc allegedly told her goodbye, as if he had had a portent of his own doom. In a segment of the A&E TV series *Biography*, Glendon Floyd, Choc's nephew, recalled his last visit with "Uncle Charley."

"The last time I saw my uncle he was coming down an old dirt road, and I was probably about 8 years old. I got close to him and I was looking at him. He was grinning. He was in an old straw hat and overalls and a silk undershirt. That was my uncle."

Soon after this last meeting, Choc joined Dillinger's gang and took part in the holdup of the Merchants National Bank in South Bend, Indiana, on June 30, 1934. Returning to Buffalo, he realized that this robbery had been the last straw. The heat from the government was too intense.

Choc decided that to stay in the United States with all those federal agents hunting him was foolhardy. He would do what Butch and Sundance did—get out of the country. He decided to go south too, to Mexico, but first he would return to the Cookson Hills to give his family a chance to move with him south of the border.

On the way there, he and Richetti got into a car accident in Ohio when their car hit a telephone pole in fog at the junction of Interstate 7 and the Pennsylvania Railroad tracks. No one was hurt but the accident caught the eye of the law, who came to investigate the accident and found themselves facing a hail of gunfire from the two outlaws.

Richetti took off into the brush, chased by lawmen who eventually captured and disarmed him. Choc shot his way out, injuring one lawman in the foot, and took off into the forest. Under interrogation Richetti gave a false name, but he and Choc were identified anyway. Word went out to the FBI in Washington that Richetti was captured and Floyd was nearby. Hoover responded by sending his agent Melvin Purvis, to Ohio to get Choc.

Purvis arrived in East Liverpool, Ohio where he set up his Headquarter and put together his posse, which included federal and local lawmen. It took two days of fruitless searching before Purvis developed a lead. A man fitting Choc's description, wearing a pin-striped suit, was seen near the Bell schoolhouse, 10 miles from East Liverpool. Purvis found a farmer who admitted that he fed a man matching Choc's description who came begging for food at his door. The farmer identified Choc from a mug shot.

OCTOBER 22, 1934

The last time Choc had eaten was the previous day, when the farmer had taken pity on him. Choc knew the cops were closing in; their pursuit had run him to ground. Trapped in the county, he had no place to go. He was wet from a heavy rain, tired, and, most of all, hungry. One meal in 24 hours was not enough to sustain him in such conditions.

Choc found a farmhouse on the edge of a cornfield down a path that a sign identified as "Spruceville Road." A middle-aged woman answered his knock. Wearing a striped housedress and white apron, she introduced herself as the Widow Conkle. Choc told her he was hungry and lost and asked if she could give him something to eat. Conkle invited him in. Conkle would later tell the police, Choc washed up at the pump outside.

Conkle fried pork chops and cooked rice and potatoes, which Choc ate voraciously. He claimed that while hunting, he had gotten drunk and been separated from his party. About 4 P.M. Widow Conkle's brother arrived and Choc asked him for a lift in his motor car to any bus line close by. The brother agreed to take him to Clarkson, the next town up the line.

Choc had just gotten into the brother's car when he spotted two official-looking cars coming down Spruceville Road. Choc did not know that Purvis and his men were inside, but he sensed trouble. Choc jumped out of the car and ran for the cover of the woods, about 200 yards in front of him through an open field. In his hand was a .45 automatic.

The G-men got out and ran after him. According to the FBI, the lawmen shouted at Choc to surrender but the outlaw kept running. Chester Smith, a World War I sharpshooter who was one of the local men under Purvis's command, fired one bullet from his rifle that was meant to wound. It found its target in Choc's right arm. The impact of the slug forced him to the ground. He got up quickly and ran again, looking at the forest like it was his deliverance.

Purvis called to him to surrender. When he did not, Purvis then had his advancing men halt, aim, and fire. Choc went down in the fusillade of bullets. Purvis was the first to reach him. He reportedly asked, "Were you at Kansas City?" and Choc replied, "My name is Charles Arthur Floyd," before he died.

In this version of the story, the FBI keeps its heroic image by giving Choc a fair chance to surrender and then killing him only when they had no choice. But this account has been questioned by no less a personage than the one man whom no one questions shot Floyd fairly—Chester Smith.

In Helmer and Mattix's *Public Enemies*, they quote Smith's 1974 account of Floyd's death, which is far different from the official FBI version. According to the two authors, after Smith wounded Choc and the outlaw got up to run again, Smith wounded him a second time, not fatally. Choc fell in the cornfield, still alive. Smith had picked up his pistols so he figured he was disarmed.

The federal agents and local lawmen surrounded Choc. Purvis exchanged a few words with Choc, asking him of his involvement in the Kansas City Massacre. Choc answered, "I wouldn't tell you son of a bitch nothing!"

Smith's account has Purvis turning to an agent holding a machine gun and telling him, "Shoot into him." The agent set his weapon to "single shot" and fired into Choc. Purvis then left to make a call. Smith thought he was going to call an ambulance. Instead, he called Hoover in Washington to tell him Floyd was dead.

While Purvis made his call, Smith helped carry Choc to the roadside, where he soon died. The body was put into one of the two cars and taken to a funeral home in East Liverpool. Smith claimed that he waited so long to tell his story because he was reluctant to challenge the FBI's word. But by 1974, most of the men involved in Floyd's death were dead themselves. He saw no further point in maintaining his silence.

If Smith's account is true, it means that the FBI never gave Choc a chance. They just executed him. It is possible that the truth might someday be known by using modern forensic methods of comparing the autopsy record, if it has not been compromised, plus a reexamination of the bullet entry wounds.

See also CLYDE CHAMPION BARROW (1909–1934) AND BONNIE PARKER (1911–1934), A.K.A. "BONNIE AND CLYDE"; JOHN DILLINGER (1903–1934); LESTER M. GILLIS, A.K.A. "BABY FACE" NELSON (1908–1935); JAMES-YOUNGER GANG (1866– 1881); JESSE JAMES (1847–1882).

John Dillinger (1903–1934) America's most famous criminal

In the history of American crime, there is no criminal more infamous or brilliant than John Dillinger. While many in modern times have forgotten about Jesse James, just the name "Dillinger" is enough to provoke images of violent shootouts and dramatic prison escapes. Dillinger's escape from the heavily guarded Crown Point, Indiana, jail using a wooden gun is not only legendary but also fact.

John Dillinger had the chivalry of Joseph Hare, the charisma of Jesse James, the success of Butch and Sundance, and the deadly aim of Harry Tracy. But like most criminals, he was not born this way—he was made.

John Herbert Dillinger was born on June 22, 1903, in Indianapolis, Indiana. His father Wilson was a fairly prosperous man who owned a grocery store and four houses.

Tragedy struck the Dillinger home when little Johnnie was three years old. His mother Mollie died. His sister Audrey, 14 years his senior, took care of him for one year, then married and left home. Five years later, in 1911, when Johnnie was eight, Wilson remarried. Neighbors would later recall Johnnie as a likable boy, ever cheerful, neatly dressed, not much different from any boy of the period. At home, though, Johnnie was being abused by his father.

Like many fathers, Wilson had problems with discipline. On one hand, he liked spoiling his son, but on the other, the boy never seemed to listen. On those occasions, he beat his son with a barrel stave, or he might lock Johnnie in the house for the entire day. Not surprisingly, Johnnie was always getting into trouble.

Johnnie had a gang he called "The Dirty Dozen" that stole coal from railroad cars. When he was 16, Johnnie dropped out of high school. Because he was good with his hands, Johnnie got a job at a machine shop. Despite the fact that he was bringing money into the household, he faced his father's wrath whenever he happened to arrive home later than expected.

In 1920 Wilson sold his Indianapolis property, bought a farm outside the city, and retired. He figured the change would be good for his son, who seemed to be keeping company with some shady characters. Unfortunately, Johnnie liked the city too much and drove the 10 miles into Indianapolis on his motorcycle.

Besides his job, Johnnie was developing quite a life in the city. He visited prostitutes regularly and drank and fought his way through many of the city's bars. He got into trouble and the easiest way out was service to his country; Johnnie joined the navy. He was a sailor for all of five months. When he could no longer take the discipline and boredom, he went absent without leave. Soon after, Johnnie met and

John Dillinger rivaled Jesse James for sheer popularity. (National Archives)

225

married Beryl Hovious on April 12, 1924. The groom was 20, the bride 16.

On September 6, 1924, Dillinger committed his first felony. Using a cloth-wrapped iron bolt as a blackjack, he beat a grocer, Frank Morgan, who was carrying home the week's receipts. Dillinger took the money but was swiftly captured by police.

Wilson Dillinger was embarrassed and ashamed. He wanted the stain on his family name to go away, and the best way to do that was to have Johnnie plead guilty and pay for his crime. Wilson convinced his son that the court would go easier on him if he did, and Johnnie agreed. Despite the fact it was his first adult offense, and he therefore had no record, the judge gave him 10 to 20 years in state prison for simple assault. Dillinger was all of 21 when the bailiff carted him off to begin serving his sentence.

Dillinger could not believe it. He had done what his father said, and he had been betrayed.

He was sent to the Indiana State Reformatory in Pendleton, where he was assigned to the shirt factory as a sewing machine operator. The dexterous Dillinger was so good with his hands that he not only completed his work in record time but also took on the work of some of his fellow convicts, which made him extremely popular and respected. Among the convicts he helped out were Homer van Meter and Harry Pierpont.

Dillinger was not a psychopath. In letters to family and friends, he wrote with great feeling about his love for family and his yearning to be free. In a 1928 letter, Dillinger wrote to his wife:

Dearest we will be so happy when I can come home to you and chase your sorrows away[. . .] For sweetheart I love you so all I want is to just be with you and make you happy.[. . .] Write soon and come sooner.

Beryl did not bother. On June 20, 1929, Beryl was granted a divorce. Dillinger wrote, "I began to know how you feel when your heart is breaking. For four years I had looked forward to going back home, and now there wasn't going to be any home to go back to."

Despite being a model prisoner and an integral part of the prison baseball team, one month later Dillinger was denied parole. He requested a transfer to Indiana State Prison in Michigan City. The reason he gave was that they had a better ball team. The real reason was that Pierpont and van Meter had been transferred there, and he wanted to join them to discuss some things.

Dillinger was always photographed with that killer sneer. (National Archives)

Going to Michigan City turned out to be a mistake. The place had a much harsher level of discipline and many older prisoners, which depressed Johnnie. Dillinger decided that since he was incarcerated, he might as well learn something. He determined to learn everything he could about the criminal trade from the best teachers in the business, the cons at Michigan City.

Probably his key meeting during this time was with Walter Dietrich, an associate of Herman K. Lamm. Lamm had been a German army officer during World War I, and he became a successful bank robber by applying his military training to the "trade." Lamm would always find out about a bank's layout before robbing it, and then assign each member of the gang a job. For example, the driver of the getaway car would plan the escape route and practice driving it several times. Dillinger determined to put that kind of experience into practice when he got out.

On May 22, 1933, Dillinger was finally paroled. Embittered because of his long stay behind bars, he was raring to go. Inside of four months, he smuggled guns back into the prison. His friends Harry Pierpont, Charles Makley, John Hamilton, Walter Dietrich, and Russell Clark used the guns to escape on September 27, 1933.

A few days before the breakout, Dillinger was arrested in Dayton, Ohio, on September 22 on bank robbery charges. His newly escaped friends proceeded to break Dillinger out of jail in Dayton, and in the process they killed the sheriff.

With the members of his newly created gang, Dillinger broke into police stations where he stole guns and ammunition. Then it was time to use the "Lamm method" to rob banks. Pat Cherrington, girlfriend of Dillinger Gang member John Hamilton, later said that the way Dillinger and van Meter—who had been released on parole—cased a bank was to "identify themselves as being officials of the NRA [National Recovery Administration, a Federal agency]. They advised the bank president that they were calling on all banks throughout the state in a survey, and they were very much interested in how the various codes were operating."

While Dillinger and van Meter cased the bank on the inside, other gang members meticulously drove the escape route, noting any problems. Maps were drawn and gasoline hidden along the way at various points in case it was needed. Using the "Lamm Method," the Dillinger Gang robbed bank after bank, cutting a wide swath across the Midwest. According to the FBI, they killed 10 men and wounded 11 others.

Newspapers reported their every crime; Dillinger became a folk hero. In fact, the gang was so popular that even while vacationing in Florida in December 1933, they were accused of bank robberies in the Midwest that they did not commit. Dillinger said, "Hell! This is going too far. How could I shoot a dog in Chicago from down here in Florida?"

On January 15, 1934, Dillinger killed a cop named O'Malley during a bank robbery. He would later tell his lawyer, "I've always felt bad about O'Malley getting killed, but only because of his wife and kids. . . . He stood right in the way and kept throwing slugs at me. What else could I do?"

On January 25, 1934, Dillinger and most of the members of his gang were arrested in Tucson, Arizona. While his compadres were sent back by rail to Lima, Ohio, to stand trial on bank robbery charges, Dillinger was transported alone back to Indiana by plane for the murder of the cop O'Malley. Plane travel was still rare and to transport a felon that way was almost unheard of, but Dillinger was a special catch. Dillinger, though, did not want to fly. "Hell, I don't jump out of these things" he said. Dillinger put up such a struggle getting into the plane that he was

shackled and chained to a post inside the flying machine.

After his plane landed, Dillinger was escorted under armed guard to the Crown Point, Indiana, jail. It was a jail that authorities guaranteed was "escape proof." Dillinger was interned there on January 30. Five days later, he made his escape by threatening guards with a very realistic gun, that was actually a piece of wood blackened with shoe polish that had been smuggled in to Dillinger. He fooled the guards, drove off in the sheriff's car, and promptly made his way back to his old Chicago stomping grounds.

In Washington, J. Edgar Hoover was delighted. He had wanted to get a crack at Dillinger, but he needed him to commit a federal crime. When Dillinger transported his car across state lines, Hoover had his opportunity. He assigned "Pretty Boy" Floyd's executioner, Melvin Purvis to get the outlaw.

Dillinger spent part of the month of April visiting with his girlfriend Billie Frechette's family. Dillinger was never anything but a gentleman to Frechette and he really loved her. Shortly after this visit, they returned to Chicago, where Frechette got arrested for helping her boyfriend. Dillinger, though, slipped through the police dragnet.

Because his face was so recognizable from wanted posters and newspaper pictures, Dillinger could not go out in public. His buddy Homer van Meter suffered from the same "identity crisis." Together, they had plastic surgery to alter their appearance on May 27, 1934, at the home of Jimmy Probasco, a bar owner with mob ties. Until late June, the two men recuperated from the surgery at Probasco's home.

During that time, Louis Piquett, Dillinger's lawyer, and Arthur O'Leary, Piquett's investigator, visited the house frequently to confer with their client. The two men found Dillinger to be friendly and good-natured; he rarely cursed. He dressed conservatively like the bankers whose money he coveted and had manicured fingernails. He was a voracious reader and loved talking about current events and his other great love, baseball.

Considering his occupation, Dillinger had no illusions. "I'm traveling a one-way road, and I'm not fooling myself as to what the end will be. If I surrender, I know it means the electric chair. If I go on, it's just a question of how much time I have left," he told O'Leary.

On one point, Piquett and O'Leary agreed passionately—Dillinger was not a "nut case." He disliked killing and did everything he could not to shoot. That is consistent with his profile as a professional criminal rather than a psychopathic killer.

May 27, 1934, was a special day for the bank robber. On that day, he turned 31 years old and, simultaneously, Hoover made him "Public Enemy Number One." The government offered a $10,000 reward for his capture. Because there are always bottom feeders in the criminal underworld who will betray their "friends" for a price, Dillinger had to be particularly careful. But sometimes, no matter how careful you are, you don't see it coming.

After Frechette's capture, Dillinger took shelter with a Romanian woman named Anna Sage. Sage

ran some whorehouses and had been arrested for pimping the girls. In order not to be deported, she made a secret arrangement with Purvis. In return for being allowed to stay in the United States, she would deliver Dillinger. To make absolutely certain the FBI identified Dillinger, she told Purvis she would wear a red dress. The man standing next to her would be Dillinger. Forevermore Sage would be known as the legendary "woman in red."

On July 22, 1934, Dillinger decided to go to the movies. He invited along Sage and Polly Hamilton, another girl with which he kept company. They went to see *Manhattan Melodrama*, starring Clark Gable,

The Biograph Theater, in front of which Dillinger was gunned down, showed a film of the outlaw's death. (National Archives)

at the Biograph Theater in downtown Chicago. After the movie, Dillinger strolled outside, arm in arm with the women. Sage was wearing a red dress. Sensing that something was wrong, Dillinger broke away from the women. Trying to run, he was felled by two shots, one of them from Melvin Purvis's gun. He died instantly.

He was taken to a Chicago morgue and laid out on a table where a death mask was taken of his face. After identification was absolute and an autopsy performed, the body was released to his family. Three weeks later, on July 25, 1934, Dillinger was buried in the family plot in Crown Hill Cemetery in Indianapolis.

Strangely enough, Dillinger committed all of his crimes during a 14-month period, between the time he was released from prison until he was killed. Yet because his star shone so brightly on the criminal stage and because he proved in the planning and execution of his robberies that his intelligence was greater than that of his contemporaries, his popularity has remained undiminished with time.

See also CHARLES ARTHUR FLOYD, A.K.A. "CHOC" FLOYD, A.K.A. "PRETTY BOY" FLOYD (1906–1934); JESSE JAMES (1847–1882); LESLIE M. GILLIS, A.K.A. "BABYFACE" NELSON (1908–1935).

Livingston, New Jersey (1934) the Lindbergh baby kidnapping

Children were rarely kidnapped from their home in the middle of the night, until that night in 1934 when Bruno Richard Hauptmann crept up a ladder and into Charles Lindbergh Jr.'s room. The toddler was fast asleep when Hauptmann snatched him and fled down the ladder.

Charles Jr. was the son of Anne Morrow Lindbergh and her husband Charles. To understand Charles Lindbergh's place in U.S. history, in the 1920s and 1930s, it helps to know he was more popular than Babe Ruth, Franklin Delano Roosevelt, and Clark Gable combined. His solo flight across the Atlantic in 1926, the first ever, had made him an icon.

Charles Lindbergh had everything—fame, fortune, a beautiful, intelligent wife, and a wonderful child. Then, in one moment, the idol of millions turned human with his grief and he became even more popular. Lost in it all was the fact that a homicide had been committed, if not the absolute first of its kind, certainly the most widely publicized.

The Lindbergh Baby Kidnapping Case began on a cold, rainy March night in 1932. Police would

later estimate that the Lindbergh's 20-month-old child, Charles Jr., was kidnapped from the family estate in Hopewell, New Jersey, sometime between 8 and 10 P.M.

Near the open nursery window was a small white envelope. Lindbergh opened it. It was a ransom note that said:

> *Dear Sir!*
>
> *Have 50,000$ redy 2500$ in 20$ bills 1500$ in 10$ bills and 1000$ in 5$ bills. After 2-2 days we will inform you were to deliver the Mony. We warn you for making anyding public or for notify the polise the child is in gute [sic] care. Indication for all letters are singnature [sic] and 3 holes.*

Outside the house, police found a homemade extension ladder propped against the side of the house under the child's bedroom. The side rails of the middle section were split. Police deduced that must have happened by the increased weight the kidnapper had to handle when he descended carrying the child in his arms.

Nearby, detectives also found a chisel and what seemed like the best clue of all: large footprints leading away from the house toward the southeast. Investigators never explained why the footprints were not measured.

Next morning word of the kidnapping made news coast to coast. The Lindbergh estate became a carnival of news gawkers and hawkers. It was the biggest story going, and the press was determined to report everything about it to a public that sympathized intensely with the Lindberghs and lusted for the blood of the kidnapper.

Inside his home, Lindbergh was conversing with Colonel H. Norman Schwartzkopf, the newly appointed head of the New Jersey State Police. Lindbergh told Schwartzkopf in unequivocal terms that he would be negotiating with the kidnappers. He would brook no official interference. He requested that no one be arrested until the ransom was paid and the baby was back in the bosom of his family. The Lindberghs then went live on NBC radio and told the kidnapper they would keep quiet on any arrangements made—read paying ransom—that would bring their toddler back safely.

On March 4, two days after the baby was snatched, Lindbergh received the first note from the kidnapper. It said, "Don't by afraid about the baby. Two ladys keeping care of it day and night." The Lindberghs were warned to keep the cops "out of the cace." A later note would tell Lindbergh where to deliver the money.

The focus of the case soon shifted to the Bronx, New York, where a retired principal, 72-year-old John Condon, wrote a letter to the *Bronx Home News* newspaper. In it, he offered the kidnappers $1,000 of his own money and promised "to go anywhere, alone, to give the kidnappers the extra money and promise never to utter his name to any person."

The following day, Condon found in his mailbox a letter from the kidnapper asking him to "get mony from Mr. Lindbergh" and telling him to await further instructions. Condon called Lindbergh and told him of the letter. Lindbergh told Condon to come out to his estate in Hopewell to discuss the letter. At the meeting that followed, Lindbergh gave Condon things to help identify the baby, including his favorite toys. He then told Condon to place a "Money is ready" note in the *New York American*.

On March 12 the doorbell at Condon's Bronx apartment rang. Answering the door, Condon was confronted with a man who handed him a letter. The man said that another man in a brown topcoat and brown felt hat had stopped the taxi he was driving and asked him to deliver the letter to a Decatur Avenue address.

The letter, from the kidnapper, demanded that Condon take a car to a place near an empty hot dog stand, near which might be found a note explaining where to go next. He was to be at that location in "³/₄ of a houer."

Condon went to the location and found the next note. It told him to "follow the fence from the cemetery direction to 233rd Street. I will meet you." Condon walked toward the cemetery gate when he saw a figure inside the cemetery, deep in shadows, signaling him. The man had a handkerchief over his nose and mouth.

"Did you [get] my note?" the man asked in a German accent. Did Condon have the money? Condon replied that he could not bring the money until he saw the baby. Then, spotting another man outside the cemetery, the shadowy figure said "It's too dangerous!" He turned and ran.

Condon chased the man, and they sat down together on a bench. Condon told the man, who called himself John, that he had nothing to fear; no one would hurt him. But the man feared retribution. "What if the baby is dead?" he asked. "Would I burn if the baby is dead?"

Condon countered by requesting why he was asked to deliver a ransom if the baby was dead.

"The baby is not dead," John asserted. "Tell the Colonel not to worry. The baby is all right. Tell Colonel Lindbergh the baby is on a boat." John said he would soon send Condon the baby's sleeping suit for positive identification.

A few days later Condon received a package. Inside was the sleeping suit worn by Charles Jr. on the night of his kidnapping. Worried that the kidnappers would kill his child, Lindbergh was all set to pay the ransom.

On Tuesday, March 31, Condon got a new note from John demanding that the ransom be ready by Saturday evening. Internal Revenue Service (IRS) officers helped put the ransom together with marked gold notes. If anyone tried to pass them, they would be a dead giveaway.

On Saturday evening, a note was delivered to Condon telling him where to drop the ransom. Accompanied by a gun-toting Lindbergh, Condon drove to a florist shop. Under a table outside, he found another note that directed them to a cemetery across the street. Lindbergh decided to stay at the florist shop and see what happened.

Across the street in the cemetery, Condon met John again. After some negotiation, John handed over a note with the baby's location: Charles Jr. was on board a ship called the *Nelly*. The note said: "You will find the Boad [boat] between Horseneck Beach and gay Head near Elizabeth Island." Condon handed over the ransom and left. The next morning at dawn, Lindbergh was flying along the Atlantic Coast, searching for a boat called *Nelly*.

At a little after 3 P.M. on May 12, 1932, a truck driver named William Allen stopped just north of the small village of Mount Rose, New Jersey, to relieve himself in the woods along the roadside. As he walked off the road to find a private place, he happened to look down. By then he was about 75 feet from the road. There, amid the leaves and earth of a shallow grave, he saw a baby's head and foot sticking up out of the ground.

Shortly thereafter, Schwartzkopf confirmed that it was indeed the Lindbergh baby. Subsequent autopsy results strongly suggested the child died from a blow to the head. It was unclear how the blow was inflicted. Investigators surmised that the kidnapper's foot slipped on the ladder on the way down and, in the process of trying to right himself, he dropped Charles Jr., who died when his head struck the ground. The kidnapper then carried the baby off for burial and went through with the whole kidnapping hoax to collect the ransom. Clearly this was not the work of a professional criminal.

Police made little progress on the case. Their best lead was the marked gold notes which began appearing in 1932 and 1933 in circulation. At first, the notes were spent all over New York City. Then, a concentration was passed in Yorkville, a neighborhood of German immigrants on the Upper East Side of Manhattan. The first big break came in November 27, 1933, when a cashier at a movie house recalled taking a gold note for a movie from a guy who matched Condon's description of John.

The next break came nine months later, in September, when the head teller of a Bronx bank saw a gold note with "4U-13-14-N.Y." penciled in the margin. The letter surmised the notation was for a license plate, penciled in by a gas station attendant. After further investigation, police tracked down a gas station attendant at an upper Manhattan service station. The attendant remembered the note came from an average-sized man with a German accent, driving a blue Dodge. The gas station attendant said that he told the man, "You don't see many of those anymore."

"No, I have only about one hundred left," the man replied and drove off. Suspicious of the man and the note, the attendant wrote down the license plate number, which police ran through the files of the New York State Motor Vehicle Bureau. The license plate matched a car belonging to a 35-year-old Bronx carpenter and German immigrant. His named was Bruno Richard Hauptmann.

The next morning Hauptmann was arrested as he was leaving his home in his blue Dodge. He had a $20 gold note on him, and a search of Hauptmann's garage uncovered more than $13,000 in gold notes. Hauptmann claimed the money belonged to Isidor Fitsch, a German friend who had gone back to Germany and then died a few months later of tuberculosis. Fitsch left some of his belongings with Hauptmann. Upon discovering the notes among Fitsch's stuff, Hauptmann decided to spend some of it. He kept the discovery from his wife, Anna.

In the weeks that followed, Hauptmann became the prime suspect. He was interrogated intensely—"the third degree"—fingerprinted, and put in line-ups. He also gave handwriting samples. Detectives investigating the Fitsch story found no validity to it. But in Hauptmann's attic, investigators found a sawed-off board that they guessed Hauptmann used to repair the ladder found at the Lindbergh home on the night of the kidnapping. As for Hauptmann himself, neighbors said he was a withdrawn, hard-working man. Hauptmann himself denied all knowledge of the matter.

On September 24, 1934, Hauptmann was charged in federal court with extorting $50,000 from Charles Lindbergh and was held without bail. Two weeks later, in the Hunterdon County Courthouse in Flemington, New Jersey, the 23-member grand jury unanimously voted to indict Hauptmann on first-degree murder charges. The federal government agreed to step aside and let New Jersey try him on the more serious charge. The trial was set for January 2, 1935.

Newspapers, with their short memories, labeled it "the trial of the century," though it was actually the third, after Harry K. Thaw and Leopold and Loeb.

Flemington, the Hunterdon County seat, became a circus. Always looking to make a buck, vendors hawked miniature kidnap ladders and supposed locks of Charles Jr.'s hair.

Almost 1,000 reporters, thousands of spectators and others, including celebrities Walter Winchell and Jack Benny, descended on Flemington to attend the trial. Bat Masterson's old friend Damon Runyon was there covering the story for his paper. The trial itself was filled with sensational testimony. New Jersey attorney general David Wilentz personally prosecuted the case.

During opening arguments, he outlined the state's case as developed by the police, showing for the first time publicly how Hauptmann kidnapped the child, how the ladder broke under the additional weight of the baby as he went down, how Hauptmann dropped the child, who died instantly, and how he buried the body and extorted the money. Wilentz told the jury he would ask them to impose the death penalty for the crime.

Hauptmann's attorney, Edward J. Riley from Brooklyn, argued that his client was innocent, that there was not even a shred of evidence tying him to the crime—that, essentially, the state's case was nothing more than weak circumstantial evidence.

In seeking to elicit the jury's sympathy, Lindbergh himself became Wilentz's star witness. Dressed in a rumpled gray suit and blue tie, Lindbergh took the stand and, remembering his expedition to the cemetery with Condon, identified Hauptmann's voice as the one he heard in the cemetery.

Cross-examining Lindbergh, Reilly came up with an alternative theory of the crime: Neighbors, upset over Lindbergh's decision not to allow them on his property to hunt, had kidnapped and killed the toddler for revenge. O'Brien implied Lindbergh was negligent in not checking on the backgrounds of his servants, any of whom might be the responsible party or parties. Reilly also tried to cast suspicion on Dr. Condon.

The state had an overwhelming case. If O'Brien could raise reasonable doubt in the jury's mind, he might be able to get an acquittal. The way to do that was to cast blame anywhere but on his client. Betty Gow, a Scottish maid who was the last person in the house to see Charles Jr. before he was snatched, took the stand. O'Brien implied that Gow and accomplices were in on the crime, which, of course, she denied. Walking back to her chair in the courtroom after her time on the stand, Gow fainted.

The prosecution next called state trooper Corporal Joseph Wolf to the stand. Wolf described seeing a large footprint in the mud near ladder marks by the nursery window. He estimated the footprint to be larger than size nine. On cross-examination, Wolf was ridiculed for not measuring the footprint, and for not knowing whether the print came from a left or right shoe.

A second trooper who testified identified a ladder in the courtroom as the one he had discovered on the night of the kidnapping, 75 feet from the Lindbergh home. Then came an 87-year-old area resident, Amandus Hochmuth with particularly incriminating testimony. Hochmuth testified that Hauptmann was at the wheel of a car that drove by his home the day of the crime. In the car was a ladder.

On top of that testimony, O'Brien had to contend with Condon's. He came to the stand and positively identified Hauptmann as John, the man to whom Condon gave the ransom money. On cross-examination, O'Brien pointed out that Condon had failed previously to identify the defendant in a line-up. Condon skirted the question. He explained that he identified Hauptmann but stopped short of a declaration of identification.

On the trial's eight day, Colonel Norman Schwartzkopf testified. He said that the state police had gotten handwriting specimens from the defendant to compare with the ransom notes. Handwriting expert John Tyrell, who had previously testified at the Leopold and Loeb trial, testified that Hauptmann had, beyond doubt, written the notes. A second handwriting expert who testified, Clark Sellers, said, "He [Hauptmann] might as well have signed the notes with his own name."

Medical testimony followed about the child's death, including the autopsy report that he died from a fractured skull. The coroner told the jury that "the blow [that caused the fracture] was struck *prior* to the death of the child."

At the defense table the defendant listened, ashen faced. As for Lindbergh, for the first time in the trial he appeared emotionally shaken. Following testimony from police about Hauptmann's passing of the gold notes, Wilentz called a balding 47-year-old xylotomist (wood expert) from Madison, Wisconsin, named Arthur Koehler. He identified the board in the kidnapper's ladder as having come from the wood in Hauptmann's apartment. Then the prosecution rested.

Reilly's first witness was the defendant. Speaking in halting English, Hauptmann attempted to elicit the jury's sympathy with testimony of his struggle to make it in America financially. He denied kidnapping Charles Jr. and asserted again that the notes came from his deceased friend Isidor Fitsch.

On cross-examination, Wilentz tried to show how the poor spelling in the notes was consistent with Hauptmann's problems spelling in English. For two days Hauptmann tried not to wilt under Wilentz's caustic questioning. Wilentz wondered why Condon's phone number was found in Hauptmann's closet, about the attic's missing board and, most important, about the more than $13,000 in ransom money found in his apartment.

Comedian Jack Benny, who watched intently from the visitor's gallery, told the press afterward, "What Bruno needs is a second act."

Hauptmann tried. From his wife Anna to others who claimed they saw Hauptmann someplace else on the night of the kidnapping, all spoke in his defense. After his alibi witnesses testified, O'Brien rested.

During summations, Wilentz called Hauptmann "the lowest animal in the animal kingdom," and "public enemy number one of this world." After reviewing the facts of the case implicating the defendant, Wilentz told the jury, Hauptmann is "either the filthiest, vilest snake that ever crawled through the grass, or he is entitled to an acquittal." But he made it clear there should not be mercy if the jurors were convinced of Hauptmann's guilt.

For the defense, O'Brien said that the crime was an inside job. The Lindbergh baby kidnapping was a conspiracy involving Condon, Fitsch, and Sharpe, among others. Unfortunately, like most conspiracy theorists, he could offer no evidence to support his theory. After Judge Trenchard's final instruction, the jury retired to deliberate at 11:21 A.M. on February 13. At 10:28 P.M., after 11 hours and seven minutes of deliberations, the courthouse bell rang. The jury had a verdict. After reconvening, jury foreman Charles Walton announced the verdict:

"We find the defendant, Bruno Richard Hauptmann, guilty of murder in the first degree."

Judge Trenchard asked Hauptmann to stand.

"The sentence of the court is that you suffer death at the time and place, and in the manner specified by law," the judge intoned.

Two reporters talked to Hauptmann the next day. They asked him if he was afraid to go to "the chair."

"You can imagine how I feel when I think of my wife and child," Hauptmann replied, "but I have no fear for myself because I know that I am innocent. If I have to go to the chair in the end, I will go like a man, and like an innocent man."

Hauptmann subsequently lost all his appeals to higher courts. Hauptmann's advisers tried to convince him to confess, figuring that if he took responsibility, his sentence would be commuted. Hauptmann refused and continued to declare his innocence.

On April 3, 1936, at 8:44 P.M., Bruno Richard Hauptmann was strapped into New Jersey's electric chair and 2,000 volts of electricity were sent through his body. His corpse was released to his widow, Anna.

In the wake of his execution, doubts still lingered about Hauptmann's guilt, with many speculating it had to be a conspiracy, that it was too much for one man to pull off. No evidence, though, was ever presented to prove this theory.

Lindbergh never recovered fully from his son's death. He drifted into Fascist politics, eventually lost favor with the American people. But so great was the public's memory of the crime that when Lindbergh died in 1974, obituaries remembered him as much for his son's kidnapping and death as his transatlantic achievement.

Lester M. Gillis, a.k.a. "Baby Face Nelson," a.k.a. "Big George Nelson" (1908–1935)

Lester M. Gillis was one of the few Chicago kids who were not surprised when the "Black Sox" threw the 1919 World Series. He did not believe in heroes. Age 11 at the time, Gillis was already a member of a street gang that specialized in stealing cars.

As he grew up, Lester's body did not. He stood all of five feet, five inches, tall on his tiptoes. He felt that his height or lack thereof would make him a target of the men in his profession who preyed on weakness, so he took the alias "Big George Nelson."

Lester had a baby face. Behind his back, his criminal associates called him "Baby Face." The name stuck, and for the rest of his criminal career, he was known as Baby Face Nelson.

In 1922, at age 14, Nelson was finally convicted of auto theft. Committed to a boy's home (reform school), he served two years and was released on parole. Five months after that, he stole another car and was thrown back in the pokey. He spent the next few years in and out of prison for various crimes and parole violations.

Helen Wawzynak, a salesgirl, found Nelson attractive enough to marry in 1928. As later events would prove, there was something about her husband's criminal life that appealed to her.

Nelson moved up the criminal ladder to bank robbery, and in January 1931 he was sentenced to a prison term of one year to life for robbing a bank in his hometown. After serving his first year in Joliet Prison, he was taken out to stand trial for another bank robbery charge in Wheaton, Illinois. While being returned to Joliet on February 17, 1932, Nelson broke from his guards and made his escape.

Nelson made his way west to Reno, Nevada, then to Sausalito, California. There, he met John Paul Chase. At the time, Chase was a 31-year-old bootlegger. He employed Nelson as a bodyguard, and the two became lifelong friends.

By 1933 Nelson and Helen had taken up residence in Sausalito. Leaving Chase with his wife, Nelson

Mug shot of Lester M. Gillis, a.k.a. "Baby Face Nelson" (National Archives)

went east to Long Beach, Indiana, where he stayed for several months, during which time he made contact with Homer Van Meter, a member of the Dillinger Gang. Later that year, Dillinger, short on gang members—many were already behind bars— recruited Nelson with some reluctance.

Nelson had a reputation as a hothead. He liked to shoot first and ask questions later. Dillinger liked a cooler operative, but he had no choice. In April 1934 Nelson, his wife, and Chase went to Chicago, where they joined the Dillinger Gang. As celebration of their criminal partnership, the ever-effusive Dillinger took Nelson, his wife, and the rest of the gang on vacation to Wisconsin's Little Bohemia Lodge. It was off season, but Dillinger was counting on that fact to deflect attention from the gang's whereabouts.

He was wrong. According to FBI files, the agency learned of "the gang's location on April 22, 1934 and Special Agents proceeded to the Bohemia Lodge. Barking dogs alerted the gangsters to the impending FBI raid," and Dillinger and his men slipped out the back without firing a shot. Not so Nelson.

Nelson resented Dillinger because he had a bigger reputation than he did. The FBI raid was the perfect opportunity to show the bureau who was the top dog when it came to gunplay. During his escape from the lodge, Nelson got himself separated from the main group. Alone Nelson fled to a nearby home, where he took two hostages.

Accompanied by a local constable, Special Agents J. C. Newman and W. Carter Braun of the FBI pulled up in front of the house where Nelson was holed up with his hostages. As soon as the car stopped, Nelson was out of the house and running down the steps, yelling for the car's occupants to get out. The men never had a chance. Nelson opened fire and killed all three men instantly. Nelson had just upped the ante—killing a federal lawman was a capital crime.

Back in Chicago Nelson's wife Helen was arrested, tried, and convicted, all in the space of one month, on a minor charge. Released on parole in late May or early June 1934, she rejoined Nelson near Lake Geneva, Wisconsin. On June 23 Attorney General Homer S. Cummings offered a reward for Nelson's capture or information leading to his arrest.

One week later, on June 30, the Merchants National Bank in South Bend, Indiana, was robbed. A policeman was shot and killed during the robbery. Witnesses identified the bandits as John Dillinger, Homer Van Meter, and Baby Face Nelson.

On Wolf Road outside Chicago, two cops approached a car that they suspected contained the gang. Suddenly, the muzzle of a pistol stuck out the window and belched fire and flame. It was Nelson's finger on the trigger. He shot the cops dead.

Dillinger's reluctance in recruiting the diminutive outlaw had proven justified. Nelson never hesitated to kill. "Inevitably, Dillinger's capers became bloodier after the arrival of Nelson, who often needlessly shot down bank guards and bystanders," Carl Sifakis writes in *The Encyclopedia of American Crime*.

Before he could do something about the "mad dog," Dillinger was betrayed by "the Woman in Red" and killed by FBI agents. After Dillinger's death, his men Tommy Carroll and Homer Van Meter were gunned down by authorities. Eddie Green was arrested. That left only Nelson, who became "Public Enemy Number One."

Nelson and Chase stayed together through all those months, keeping surprisingly low profiles considering their proclivity for violence. And then, on November 26, 1934, Nelson and Chase stole a car in Chicago and drove to Wisconsin.

Inspector Sam Cowley of the FBI's Chicago office, who had been instrumental in killing Dillinger, and his assistant Herman E. Hollis, tracked Nelson and Chase to Barrington, Illinois. When they caught up with the outlaw's car, he was accompanied by his wife as well as Chase.

The agents chased the outlaws until Nelson, at the wheel, turned around suddenly and got on the agents' tail. Chase opened up with five rounds from his automatic rifle. One of the agents returned fire, and a shot pierced the radiator of Nelson's car, causing it to stall.

Stopping their vehicle, Crowley and Hollis leaped for the cover of a nearby ditch. Hollis had a shotgun, good for short range use, while Cowley had an automatic pistol. For the next four or five minutes, a heated exchange of gunfire took place.

Then Nelson tired of the battle. According to Sifakis, he announced, "I'm going down there and get those sons of bitches."

Nelson took 17 bullets to the body from the FBI agents and kept coming, blazing away with his pistols until he had shot Cowley and Hollis dead. Then he got into their car and backed it up. Chase and Helen piled in.

At 8:00 P.M., Baby Face Nelson died from the wounds he had received in his gun battle with the G-men. Helen and Chase stripped his body to make identification difficult and left it near a cemetery outside Niles Center, Illinois.

Helen Nelson would eventually be captured and returned to prison on a parole violation charge. She served a sentence of one year and one day in the Women's Federal Reformatory in Mila, Michigan, and was released. From there, she faded into history.

Nelson's best friend, John Paul Chase, was eventually arrested by the FBI without a struggle on December 27, 1934, in California. Extradited to Illinois, he was the first person to be tried under the law that made it a federal crime to murder a special agent of the FBI in the performance of his duties. He was found guilty of the charges against him and sentenced to life at Alcatraz Prison, where he began his stay on March 31, 1935.

See also CLYDE CHAMPION BARROW AND BONNIE PARKER (1909–1934); JOHN DILLINGER (1903–1934); CHARLES ARTHUR FLOYD, A.K.A. "CHOC" FLOYD (1906–1934).

Brooklyn, New York (1930–1940) Murder, Incorporated

One day in 1929, a 12-year-old Jewish immigrant named Murray Rosen was playing in the playground of the grade school he attended. After only one year in the United States, the Polish immigrant was an orphan, being attended to by his older brothers and sister.

"So I had this accent and when kids would make fun of me, Georgie would step in. Georgie Seitz. He was my best friend," Rosen would later recall.

Georgie was another first-generation American, a tough street kid who was good with his fists. Years later, Rosen said, "Georgie comes to me one day in this pool room. He says 'Mendel—my Yiddish name—hold this for me.' And he gives me this ruby ring. Well, what do I know? I take it and hold it a few days when Georgie comes back for it."

That's when Georgie put in the quid pro quo.

"He asked me if there was anything he could do for me. I said, 'As a matter of fact, there's this guy who owes me five bucks.' Georgie said he'd go collect it for me."

Then Rosen put two and two together.

"I realized that Georgie was one of the 'boys.' What he was going to do for me was beat the guy until he gave him my money. I stopped him before he could do that."

Georgie eventually graduated from loan-sharking.

"Georgie went to work," Rosen continued, "for Murder, Incorporated. He later went to the chair for killing a guy."

The very name brings chills to those still alive who remember it. It was a group formed from the tough Jewish kids of the street like Louis "Lepke" Buchalter, Mendy Weiss, and Abe "Kid Twist" Reles. These were men who readily killed with gun, knife, or whatever was handy in order to make a crooked buck. But they left their own alone. Jewish citizens of the Brooklyn neighborhood of Brownsville who were not in the mob knew how to look the other way.

Authorities would later estimate that in the period from 1930 to 1940, executioners from Murder, Inc., were responsible for 400 to 500 murders nationwide. What made the group so interesting was they were not available to the highest bidder.

Murder, Inc., was the enforcement arm of the Five Families. When someone needed to be killed, Murder, Inc., got the contract to do it. Killers would be dispatched anyplace in the United States and time and time again, as the mob's tentacles spread out through the West, they were called upon. It was as successful a scam as the mob has ever run before or since.

In Brooklyn a multistory brick edifice stands along the Coney Island Boardwalk. It is now a senior citizen's facility. In 1940, it was the Half Moon Hotel, the location where the Brooklyn District Attorney's office stashed witnesses in sensitive criminal cases. In 1940 "Kid Twist" Reles found himself cooped up in a room there, with the D.A.'s men and uniformed New York City police officers as bodyguards. Reles had decided to turn state's evidence before one of his own did. He confessed to 200 killings in which he had either participated or been an accessory.

Reles's information later led to the conviction and execution of Louis "Lepke" Buchalter, Mendy Weiss, Pittsburgh Phil, Louis Capone, Happy Malone, and Frank Abbandando. By November 1941 Reles still had one more story to tell. Reles had information that Benjamin "Bugsy" Siegel, one of the architects of the modern mob, was responsible for an unsolved murder in New York City. That marked the end for "Kid Twist," but much is open to conjecture. Someone in the hotel room with Reles threw him out the window. When he hit the concrete seconds later, the fall broke every bone in his body. Who was responsible for the killing still remains a mystery.

Regardless, Reles's death did nothing to stop the Brooklyn District Attorney's office from prosecuting cases against the boys. By the early 1940s Murder, Inc., was no longer a viable "corporation."

Los Angeles, California (1943–Present) the rise of modern urban gangs

Los Angeles's proximity to Mexico has fostered a dense and culturally rich Latin community in the city. During the 1940s, a generation of young Mexican Americans co-opted the zoot suit, a style of oversized suit, from African-American jazzmen. Some of these zoot suiters, or pachucos, organized into clubs with initiation rituals, typical of which was the "jumping in." During the jumping in, the initiate is surrounded by a circle of club members who proceed to beat him. Standing for the beating was taken as resilience; membership in the club was then offered. The initiate felt he was entering not just a club but a surrogate family.

Pachucos lived by a code of honor and respect similar to that of the Old West gunfighter. Fights inevitably broke out among the pachucos for reasons of love, honor, money, turf, sex, and so on, and eventually the various clubs evolved into rival gangs. Politics, too, would play a significant role in modern gang life.

During the 1960s, brown pride groups arose within the Hispanic communities. White Fence and Maravilla became two of the most powerful Hispanic gangs of East Los Angeles. They had many offshoots and remained rivals for decades. Like other East Los Angeles gangs, they chose to enter the lucrative drug trade and violent crime in Los Angeles spiked. Where once pachucos rumbled with knives, chains, and fists, the modern gangs used handguns and rifles to kill their competitors.

The barrio of East Los Angeles became a desolate, drug-infested landscape, breeding and rebreeding new gangs and gang members for generations.

During the 1940s, African Americans had migrated from the politically and economically repressive South to what they hoped would be a more hospitable place: California. Many settled in south-central Los Angeles. But throughout the 1960s, tensions in the area were high, highlighted by the Watts riots. The streets were patrolled by white police officers who were often brutal. At the same time, it was the Civil Rights era, and African Americans were fighting for their political and social rights. Within this maelstrom, African-American street gangs began to form. The template for these gangs was one part James Boys and one part Mafia. They had the audacity of one and the brains and ruthlessness of the other.

The Crips were founded in 1969 at a south-central Los Angeles high school and now number up to 35,000 members. Gang initiation rites involve activities like committing armed robbery or a drive-by shooting, submitting to group sex (for female members), or some derivation of the above. Part of the Crips' gang code involves using the letter "C" to replace the letter "B" in conversation. Members often wear blue—the gang's color—and their hand signal or gang sign is a "C."

The Crips' rivals are the Bloods, whose signature color is red. The Bloods number up to 20,000, and their initiation involves drawing blood, beatings, and group sex for girl initiates. Unlike the Crips, they never use the letter "C."

The Crips and Bloods engage in the drug trade to finance their activities. They also maintain well-organized arsenals of weapons employed for warfare with rival gangs and the police. By the early 1970s, the Crips and Bloods were organized enough that they could export their criminal activities to other states. By the 21st century, the Crips and Bloods had established beachheads in many major American cities. They were arguably as integral a part of the popular culture as the Mafia. Gangster-style baggy clothing became trendy, and popular athletes could be seen "throwing signs" (making gang hand signs) on national television broadcasts.

Gangs and drugs spread easily from city to city via the national transportation system. Using the interstate highway system, as well as trains and planes, gangs moved north from Los Angeles, spreading the drug trade and emerging as problems in cities all along the coast, including San Francisco, Seattle, and Portland. They have also reached cross-county to penetrate major urban centers like Chicago, New York, and Miami.

In recent decades gangs have continued to grow and spread, and some have developed connections with other types of organized crime, such as the Mafia, or international crime groups, such as the Triads, for purposes of drug trafficking. Some currently active gangs include Folk Nation, the Latin Kings, the Sureño (Mexican Mafia), and the Aryan Brotherhood. Related gangs include motorcycle gangs such as Hells Angels and the Pagans, groups that also have established ties to the drug trade, organized crime, and other criminal enterprises.

DRIVE-BY SHOOTINGS

A by-product of gang rivalries and increased competition for the drug trade was the spread of violence in areas dominated by gangs, and as tensions among gang members increased, violence flared and escalated, often striking those who had no connections to gangs but who were caught in the crossfire. For instance, a promising young film student in Los Angeles, Tom Bush, was the victim of an unsolved drive-by shooting. Tom Bush was a friend of the author's.

Unlike the Chicago mob's use of the automobile running board and machine gun in the 1920s, drive-by shooting involved someone who was not involved in gang life at all. The day Tom was killed, he was simply a random target in some kid's initiation into gang culture, a ritual that had evolved from gang members beating prospective members to the initiates killing at random to prove their worth to the gang.

SOLUTIONS

Opinion differ as to the best way to respond to the gangs that pursue criminal activities. Punitive approaches—arresting and convicting gang members and sentencing them to long prison terms—tend to reinforce the gang lifestyle. Prison can harden gang members, who often fall back on their gang affiliation for protection behind bars. Some notable criminal gangs have even sprouted in prisons, where groups of inmates band together and then spread outward into cities when those prisoners are released. Often, these prison-formed gangs adhere to some form of racist dogma. In 1996, the Federal Bureau of Prisons found that prison disturbances soared by approximately 400 percent in the early 1990s.

One study argued that taxpayers' money could be better spent on a more enlightened approach than imprisonment. The study favored supporting "user end" programs—educational programs, drug counseling, and treatment programs—that help gang members move away from their violent lifestyle. In one study employed gang members as research assistants under the principle that gang members would be more likely to respond truthfully to one of their own. In general, gang members proved reticent to discuss their former activities, especially female members, perhaps because many now have children; they are married and their husbands know nothing about their former lifestyle.

Los Angeles, California (1947) "the Black Dahlia"

In the history of unsolved murders in America, the Black Dahlia case remains one against which all others are measured.

The murder of Elizabeth Short, "the Black Dahlia," came at a time when Raymond Chandler's Philip Marlowe mysteries were widely popular. They showcased the seamy side of Los Angeles and the human heart, as seen through the eyes of the "shopworn Galahad," a detective named Philip Marlowe.

When Short's murder case happened on "Marlowe's turf," journalists were eager to capitalize on the opportunity to write like Chandler. Noting the victim's black hair and dress, the first thing they did was give her a snappy name.

The Black Dahlia was born.

Short may have been a beautiful woman in life, but her death was singular. The killer had cut her body in half and left both parts in a vacant lot in Hollywood. She had been sodomized. It was the most brutal killing the Los Angeles Police Department had ever seen.

The newspapers reported every graphic detail, and the public ate it up. Yet, despite an intensive investigation by the police at the time, the killer of the Black Dahlia was never caught, and the case remains unsolved to this day.

EIGHT
1950-2000

Introduction

In the second half of the 20th century, crime in America picked up speed. As the millennium approached, it was almost as if crime were feeding on the nation's energy. The 1950s was the pivotal decade in announcing the future of America's most deadly crime: terrorism.

Politically, the country was still fighting its way through a "red scare." The development of the Eisenhower Interstate Highway System made it easy for criminals to move from place to place, contributing to the rise of a criminal underclass—serial killers. Using the interstate highway system, criminals began to move from place to place quickly and easily, leaving a trail of bodies wherever they went. While Ted Bundy is probably the country's best-known serial killer who expertly used the roads to get from place to place to commit his crimes, there are many others.

Assassination became a relatively common event. And when it looked like criminals had exhausted their creative repertoire, spectacular new crimes would be committed to shock society. Criminals discovered what Jesse James had known: The media could be manipulated to further their nefarious goals.

Washington, D.C. (1950) terrorist attack on Blair House
The 1948 election had been close, and when the smoke cleared, Thomas E. Dewey had been defeated and Harry Truman elected to his first term as president. Two years later, in 1950, the White House was due for restoration and the Missouri native was forced to vacate the premises and take up temporary quarters across the street in Blair House, which usually serves as the vice president's quarters.

November 1, 1950, President Truman was seated at his desk in Blair House when he heard gunfire from outside his window. The president, who had served in combat during World War I, did not hesitate—he stuck his head out the window to see what was going on. Secret Service agents pulled him back inside.

Outside, a terrorist lay wounded on the ground. His name was Oscar Collazo and he was from Puerto Rico. Collazo was a Puerto Rican nationalist who believed the island was being enslaved by the United States. Near Collazo, a second man lay dead.

His name was Griselio Torresola. He, too, was a Puerto Rican nationalist. Across from him lay a Blair House guard whom Torresola had killed with his pistol. Had it not been for the swift action and careful aim of the Secret Service agents who responded to the shooting, the matter might have gotten a lot worse.

As it was, great damage had been done and not just to the man who has killed. The assassination plot was a deliberate attempt to strike terror into the heart of the Republic, to make the people of the United States understand that certain Puerto Rican nationalists were willing to do anything, including murdering innocents, to achieve their goal of Puerto Rican independence from the United States. It was considered by the federal government to be the same kind of sedition the Union had once gone to war over.

By refusing to single out civilians as noncombatants, and making them as inherently responsible for the state of political affairs as the president, the terrorists had formed their moral justification for killing. This rationale would resurface many times in coming years. The

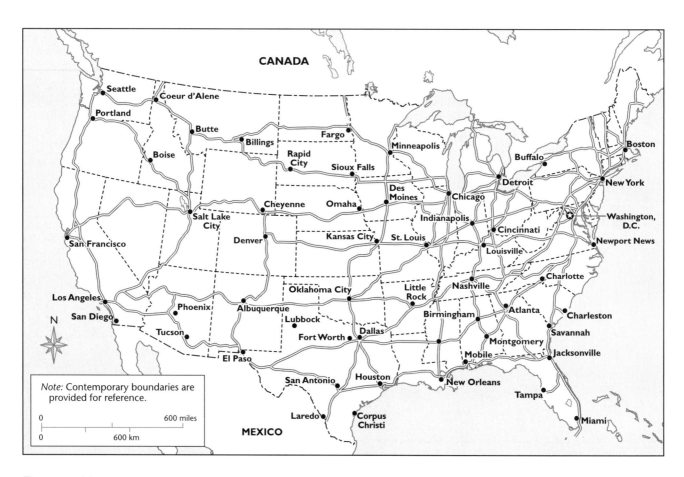

The general location of routes of the recommended interregional highway system. Total length of the system is 33,920 miles.

seditionists were trying to apply a new template that the Confederates had not—targeting civilians.

As for the surviving terrorist, Oscar Collazo, he was tried on murder charges, convicted, and sentenced to death. Ironically, it was his intended target, Truman, who commuted his sentence. Collazo served 29 years before President Jimmy Carter released him in 1977.

San Juan, Puerto Rico (1952) a constitution adopted

After 54 years under U.S. rule without a clear definition of itself as a political entity, Puerto Rico adopted a constitution and officially became a part of the U.S. commonwealth. Despite this, the island continued to be denied representatives in Congress and did not have power to vote in national elections, although on the plus side, Puerto Ricans did not pay income tax. But terrorists on the island would not be satisfied with anything short of complete independence from the United States.

Interstate Highway System (1952–1960)

When Dwight Eisenhower was elected president in 1952, he brought with him the idea conceived by Pershing for an interstate highway system. During World War II, as Supreme Allied Commander in Europe, Eisenhower had seen just how efficiently the Germans could move their troops and supplies on the high-speed autobahns. He envisioned something like that for America.

There was a lot of opposition both in and out of government because many people thought the private sector was better equipped to carry out such a plan than the federal government. Eisenhower did not really make any progress until his State of the Union address in January 1956, when he used his time before Congress and the American people to show what was wrong with the old system and what was right with the new one he was proposing.

Finally persuaded, Congress passed the Federal Aid Highway Act of 1956. Under this legislation, the

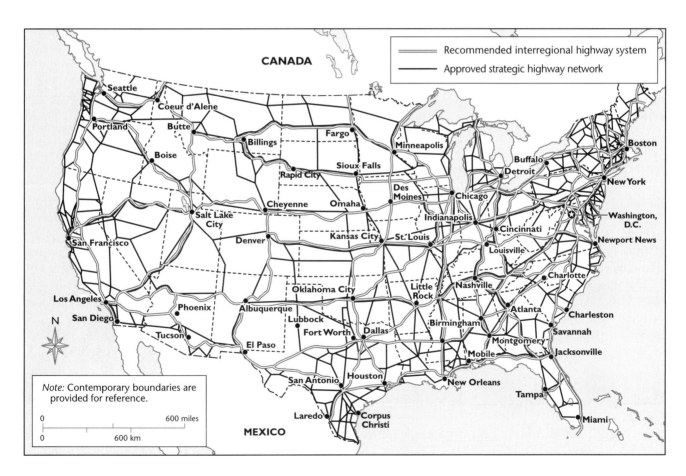

Relation of the recommended interregional system to the strategic network of principal routes of military importance approved by the secretary of war, as revised May 15, 1941

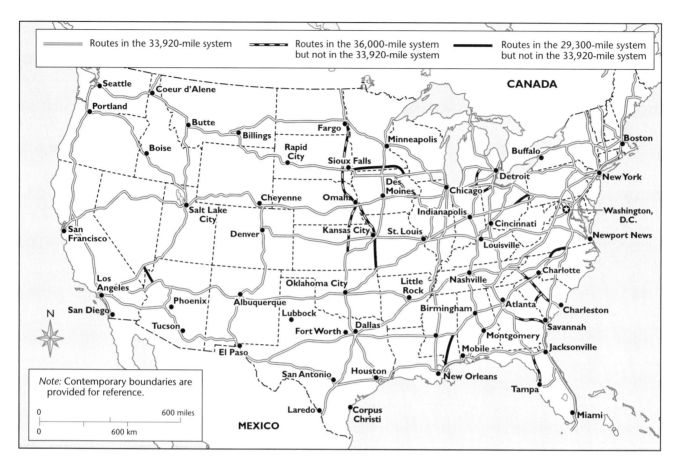

The 36,000-mile additional system investigated by the committee

federal government committed to pay 90 percent of the construction costs for the new system. The money would be raised by increased taxes on gasoline. The other 10 percent, as well as the cost of upkeep, would come from the state governments. Traditional boundaries of time and distance were about to be broken.

The plan was put into force and the federal interstate highway system was begun. By the end of the century, the system comprised 46,677 miles. It proved a boon to criminals, who could now travel with alacrity across the country.

Washington, D.C. (1954) Puerto Rican terrorists attack Congress

Their names were Lolita Lebron, Rafael Cancel Miranda, Irving Flores, and Figeroa Cordero. On March 1, 1954, they entered the visitors gallery in the House of Representatives as anonymous Americans and left as terrorists.

The quartet took automatic weapons out of their coats and opened fire on the floor below. "Long live a free Puerto Rico," the terrorists shouted. Five members of the House of Representatives were wounded in the spray of bullets before Lebron, Miranda, Flores and Cordero were restrained by bystanders and capitol police. Charged with attempted murder and sedition, they were eventually convicted and sentenced to life in prison.

Luckily, no one died, but once again, the United States had been the victim of a terrorist assault. If congresspeople could be targeted, anyone could.

Brooklyn, New York (1954) Julius Rosenberg, atomic spy

The House Un-American Activities Committee (HUAC) was still hard at work in Congress when Joseph McCarthy came along in the Senate. Senator McCarthy of Wisconsin claimed, without evidence, that almost 200 employees of the State Department were communist agents—and people believed him.

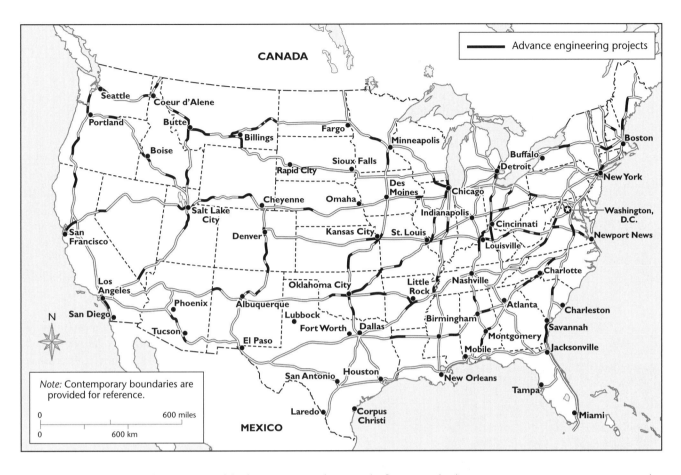

Map of the recommended interregional highway system showing the location of advance engineering projects; approved October 31, 1943

McCarthy became a demagogue determined to rid the country of the "red menace." Into this paranoid powder keg, the Rosenbergs walked an equally serpentine trail. Their criminal case would become the most remembered of the 1950s.

With the detonation of the two atomic bombs in 1945, the United States emerged as the world's superpower. Russia, 28 years into the Communist regime that had executed the czar, could not let the Americans maintain that superiority.

Klaus Fuchs was a British physicist who worked on the Manhattan Project developing the atomic bomb. In 1945, on two different occasions, he met with a Soviet agent named Raymond. Mr. Fuchs provided Raymond some key information about the design of the atomic bomb. But Fuchs did not realize the sophistication of the American intelligence apparatus.

American cryptanalysts had successfully deciphered intercepted cables from the Soviet consulate in the United States to the KGB in Russia. One of the

cables was a report by Klaus Fuchs on how the bomb's development was progressing.

The FBI called Fuchs in for questioning and showed him what they had. Fuchs confessed. He told the G-men about his meetings with Raymond. Three months later, the FBI found a fortyish, bookish chemist named Harry Gold. Gold was another soft case; he readily offered a confession.

According to the FBI's theory, it was Gold who, as Raymond, got the top-secret information for the atomic bomb from Fuchs. But had Fuchs been at the top of the chain of traitors, or was there someone above him? By June 1, 1950, authorities began to focus on a soldier at Los Alamos, New Mexico, who Gold paid $500 specifically for information about the implosion lens for the atomic bomb. The problem was that Gold did not know his name.

Gold thought that the man's wife "may have been Ruth," and he also remembered that the man came from New York City. The feds investigated further.

Two days later they showed Gold a picture of a man, and Gold said he resembled the soldier. It was a picture of a man named David Greenglass, and Gold said that was the man who had paid him.

After agents questioned Greenglass, he admitted that he was the Los Alamos soldier who bought the information from Gold. He also said that his wife Ruth and his brother-in-law, Julius Rosenberg, were part of the spy ring that worked for the Soviets.

By the time he was 16, Julius Rosenberg was a passionate member of the City College of New York's Young Communist League. The son of Polish Jewish immigrants, he had grown up on Manhattan's Lower East Side. He met his future wife, Ethel, at a union fund-raising party. Graduating from college with an engineering degree, Rosenberg began work as a civilian employee of the army's signal corps in 1940.

Ethel and Julius Rosenberg in a lighter moment by the pool (National Archives)

According to Greenglass, late in 1943 he began talking to his brother-in-law Julius Rosenberg about espionage. Shortly after their initial conversation, Rosenberg dropped his Communist Party affiliation. Greenglass claimed Rosenberg needed to do this so he would not be a target once he began active spy work for the Soviets. Rosenberg later denied this.

According to Greenglass, in 1944 Rosenberg approached his wife and asked if his brother-in-law would give him notes on Manhattan Project research. Greenglass agreed. For the next year, he fed Rosenberg information, sometimes directly, sometimes through intermediaries, about the high-explosive lens mold being developed at Los Alamos for the atomic bomb.

Rosenberg learned through his KGB contacts in 1949 that American intelligence was on the trail of Soviet spy Klaus Fuchs. If the trail were followed to its natural end, Greenglass realized, it would lead to him, Gold, and Rosenberg. Julius, seeing the proverbial handwriting on the wall, told Greenglass to get his passport as soon as possible and leave the country.

When Fuchs got arrested, Rosenberg became more anxious for everyone to leave. Greenglass declined. His wife Ruth was six months pregnant. She was also recovering from burns she received in an apartment fire.

On June 16, 1950, FBI agents went to Brooklyn, New York, where Rosenberg lived with his wife and two boys. They asked him to come in for questioning. Rosenberg had no choice, but the FBI soon found him a tough nut to crack. Unlike the others in Greenglass's alleged spy ring, Rosenberg gave a vigorous defense.

Confronted with Greenglass's charges, he said, "Bring him here—I'll call him a liar to his face." Rosenberg was released without being charged, but he knew that was just a matter of time. Realizing the trouble he was in, Rosenberg hired prominent defense attorney Emmanuel Bloch.

By mid-July Greenglass and wife Ruth had offered the FBI additional information about Rosenberg's complicity. On the basis of that information, the FBI went to his Brooklyn apartment and, in full view of his young sons, slapped Rosenberg into cuffs and took him away. As he was hustled out of his apartment, a backup team entered to search for incriminating evidence.

Curious about wife Ethel Rosenberg's complicity, the FBI questioned the Greenglasses, who maintained that Ethel was present during certain conversations. They also claimed she typed up notes on classified information. There was no hard evidence to prove these charges. The government, though, could make enough of a circumstantial case against Ethel to at least charge her. But why bother with Ethel at all if she was such a "small fish?" In public comments, FBI director Hoover stated that "There is no question" that "if Julius Rosenberg would furnish details of his extensive espionage activities, it would be possible to proceed against other individuals. [P]roceeding against his wife might serve as a lever in this matter."

The Feds arrested Ethel on August 11, 1950. Like Julius, Ethel was denied bail and she denied any involvement in the atomic conspiracy. For his part, Julius Rosenberg held to his story. The government's lever was not working. There was nobody for him to roll over on; he was innocent. There was no conspiracy.

The government's strategy had not worked, but now they were committed to it. They could not back off and suddenly drop the charges on Ethel. How would that look, especially to Julius Rosenberg, who they were definitely going to face in court?

While the Rosenbergs were facing their own problems, their friends were facing theirs. The FBI systematically investigated all of the Rosenbergs' associates and friends. Many left the country rather than face federal scrutiny. One of those Rosenberg friends who got out successfully was Morton Sobell, who escaped south of the border.

During this roundup, a Rosenberg acquaintance, Max Flitcher, told the FBI that Rosenberg had tried unsuccessfully to recruit him to work for the Soviets in 1944. He also described a meeting with his friend Morton Sobell in which Flitcher was supposed to serve as a go-between. Sobell would give him a can of film that he was supposed to turn over to Rosenberg.

The American government called the Mexican government and asked them to find Sobell. They did. The federales took Sobell to Laredo, Texas, just over the border from Mexico, and turned him over to the FBI.

The trial of the Rosenbergs and Morton Sobell began in federal court in Brooklyn, New York on March 6, 1951. The charges were conspiracy to commit espionage. It was a capital crime, punishable by death.

During his opening statement, U.S. attorney Irving Saypol told the jury that the defendants "have committed the most serious crime which can be committed against the people of this country." They had conspired to provide the Soviet Union with "the weapons the Soviet Union could use to destroy us."

Defense attorney Bloch declared in his opening statement that the defendants were innocent. He urged the jury to give his clients "a fair shake in the American way," and not to "be influenced by any bias or prejudice or hysteria."

Saypol then called Max Flitcher to the stand. Flitcher went over his association with Sobell, including a car trip the two took together in 1948 to a mysterious location where they delivered the can of film to Julius Rosenberg. Next was 29-year-old David Greenglass, who testified that he had passed sketches of the high-explosive lens mold to Julius Rosenberg. Greenglass's testimony was cut short when the prosecution called Walter Koski to the stand. An Atomic Energy Commission physicist, he explained how the sketches Greenglass passed could help the enemy develop an atomic bomb.

It was a brilliant strategy. The prosecution had now shown the jury, in layman's terms, the true importance of the sketches: if the Soviets had the bomb, like America, they would be capable of wholesale annihilation. The implication was that the people responsible for that betrayal, the Rosenbergs and Sobell, were guilty as charged. Returning to the stand, David Greenglass continued his incriminating testimony.

He told the jury the arcane details of spying. There were meetings on dark streets with half-illuminated figures in dark cars. A Jell-O box was cut in half so the two pieces could be used by Soviet agents as identification. Notes were burned in a frying pan. Finally, Greenglass recalled, he felt the FBI closing in and contemplated an escape to Russia. The FBI caught him before he could flee.

Next, Ruth Greenglass testified that she was approached by Julius Rosenberg to act as an intermediary for her husband. Julius wanted her to see if David would give him various pieces of information on the progress of the Manhattan Project. When David agreed, Julius told her how to handle a courier from Albuquerque. Soon Harry Gold was knocking on her door. In his hand was half a Jell-O box. Ruth's final piece of testimony damned Ethel. Ruth Greenglass claimed that she was present when Ethel Rosenberg typed up some of her bother David Greenglass's notes from the Manhattan Project.

Harry Gold was called to the stand. Gold said that he had numerous meetings with Anatoli Yakovlev, head of the Soviet delegation to the United Nations and the KGB's chief of U.S. spy operations. During a 1945 meeting in particular, he remembered being in a Manhattan bar when Yakovlev gave him a piece of onionskin paper with "Greenglass" and an Albuquerque address typed on it.

Gold's orders were to go to New Mexico, locate the typed address, and announce to the person who opened the door, "I come from Julius." Gold went on to say that Greenglass provided him with handwritten notes and sketches relevant to the development of the atomic bomb.

Most trials with large public impact have something unexpected. In the Rosenberg case, that was Elizabeth Bentley. Bentley had been labeled "the Red Spy Queen" by the press when she marched to the stand at the trial. An attractive former spy for the Soviets and ex-lover of the Soviets' chief U.S. spy, Bentley had switched to the capitalist side in 1945 and made a profit doing it. With a flair for publicity, she had written books about her experiences in the spy game.

Bentley testified that it was she who set up the contact between Julius Rosenberg and Jacob Golos, chief of the KGB's American operations until his death in 1943. She said that five or six times, she got early morning calls from some man identifying himself as "Julius." "Julius" used her as an intermediary in setting up meetings with Golos.

And then, the prosecution rested.

No matter how dramatic the testimony sounded, it was pretty damning stuff. While Sobell and Ethel Rosenberg appeared to be at the fringes of the spy ring, if all the testimony was believed, Julius Rosenberg was the driving force to get the information on the development of the atomic bomb into the hands of the Soviet Union. That would make him the most infamous spy in U.S. history.

The defense needed to show reasonable doubt to save the defendants. In effect, they needed to show that one or more prosecution witnesses lied. The entire country followed the story through radio and newspapers. The few who had televisions watched the evening newscasts for word on what happened next.

The defense decided that the Rosenbergs were their own best witnesses. Using a risky tactic, the defense chose to have only the accused testify in their own defense. Sobell demurred. Perhaps wisely, he kept his silence.

Julius Rosenberg testified that he was a man of modest means who lived an ordinary life, far from the super spy the prosecution was attempting to show he was. As for the charges against him, Rosenberg denied them all. He had never received information from Greenglass about the lens mold or

anything else, for that matter. He knew nothing of cut-up Jell-O boxes. What he did know was that in 1950, Greenglass approached him for money to leave the United States.

Ethel Rosenberg's testimony supported Julius's version of events—she knew nothing and said nothing. She never directly denied the one piece of evidence that damned her—typing up Julius's spy notes.

The defense had shut Ethel up. She testified dispassionately instead of emotionally. By making her into a taciturn woman instead of a victimized woman, she seemed more independent, more self-assured, more capable of committing espionage.

On rebuttal, the prosecution called photographer Ben Schneider to the stand. The operator of a small photo shop near the Brooklyn courthouse, Schneider testified that the Rosenberg family came to his store in June 1950. They wanted three dozen passport-type photos. Rosenberg said they were planning a trip to France, where they had inherited property.

Schneider was a good witness: He remembered the Rosenbergs, he said, because it was an unusually large order and they had two boys who were difficult to control. Details like that were what swayed a jury.

It would later be revealed that the FBI found Schneider through a jailhouse informer named Jerome Tartakow. Tartakow had been Julius's chess partner and confidant since his incarceration eight months before.

The month-long trial ended with passionate summations from both sides. After being charged by the judge the 11 man, one woman jury retired to their deliberations. Reaction was swift: 12 to 1 for conviction. Inside the jury room, several hours were then spent trying to convince the lone hold-out. That person was concerned how Ethel's execution would affect her family. When the jury told the judge they were ready, they reentered the courtroom and delivered a verdict of guilty.

At sentencing, Judge Irving Kaufman characterized the defendant's crimes as "worse than murder." He blamed them for the 50,000 American soldiers killed during the Korean War.

Sobell got 30 years. The Rosenbergs were sentenced to death.

Over the next two years, the Rosenbergs appealed their death sentences, with celebrities speaking out for them. There was passionate public support for mercy. Confined at Sing Sing Prison in Ossining New York, the Rosenbergs watched each and every step, alternating between hope and dread.

Their sons, Robert and Michael, marched at rallies holding aloft signs that read "Don't Kill My Mommy and Daddy." Defense attorney Emmanuel Bloch took his case through the courts and at each turndown went to a higher court. Finally, he was allowed to plead his clients' case before the Supreme Court. He needed a majority of five justices to stay the execution. He got four.

Shortly after 8 P.M. on June 19, 1953, Julius Rosenberg was strapped into the electric chair. He died quickly. Not so his wife. The first 57-second charge of 2,000 volts of electricity did not kill her. Unfortunately, the state did not discover this until Ethel was unstrapped from the chair. So, the guards strapped her in again, unconscious, and she was given two more jolts to finish the job.

Ethel Rosenberg was the first woman in almost a century to be executed by the federal government. The last was Mary Surratt, who had been hanged for her role in the Confederate plot to kill President Lincoln.

In 1997, after the collapse of the Soviet Union, Alexander Feklisov, Julius Rosenberg's Soviet "control," was allowed by his government to finally come forward and describe his meetings with Julius in the 1940s, thus corroborating evidence from a reliable source that Julius Rosenberg was guilty as charged. As for Ethel, Feklisov knew nothing of her espionage activities.

Hollywood Hills, California (1959) the suicide of "Superman"

In the 1950s there was one television show every kid watched—*The Adventures of Superman,* starring George Reeves as "the Man of Steel." Based upon the DC comic book character, the TV show had been spun off in a way that was unusual for the time. A feature film, 1952's *Superman versus the Mole Men* with Reeves in the title role had been successful. It was the second attempt to translate the Son of Krypton to the screen. The first, two serials in the late 1940s, had received only moderate attention. But the Reeves film "had legs," so a decision was made to spin it off and make a TV series. If anything, the TV show was more popular than the movie. George Reeves, journeyman actor, had struck pure gold. Much as the Interstate Highway System physically connected the nation, television brought Americans closer together through widely shared popular culture. By the late 1950s TV was in the majority of American homes, and millions of people watched the same shows, such as *Superman.*

As far back as 1939, when Reeves had played one of the Tarleton twins in *Gone With the Wind,* Reeves had yearned for stardom. As a contract player for the studios during the 1940s, he had achieved only a modicum of success. *Superman* was different.

From 1952 to 1957 Reeves played the Man of Steel to a huge audience of millions of kids watching at home. This was the first era of kids raised on TV. Some were not sophisticated enough to separate the actor from the role, and believed literally what they saw on screen: George Reeves was Superman. His numerous public appearances in costume just served to blur the line between actor and character.

For Reeves the actor, the role was a double-edged sword. He had become the idol of millions, but as Superman, not George Reeves. As an actor, he was stymied. People would not believe him as anything else.

In 1953, shortly after *Superman*'s initial success, Reeves took a major role as Burt Lancaster's sergeant in Fred Zinneman's *From Here to Eternity.* During previews, audiences shouted "There's Superman!" when Reeves's character came on screen. Zinneman realized that Reeves's appearance distracted people, so he cut most of Reeves's part.

By the end of the *Superman* run in 1957, Reeves was severely depressed and drinking heavily. His personal life was a mess. He was engaged to one woman while a former lover pined away for him.

On June 16, 1959, while his fiancée and some friends partied downstairs in his Hollywood Hills home, Reeves went upstairs and took out a .30 caliber Luger. With one carefully placed shot into his head, "Superman" died instantly.

The cause of death was officially ruled as suicide resulting from severe depression. The actor's mother for years questioned the Los Angeles Police Department's lack of investigation. She offered an alternative theory of the crime, in which Reeves was murdered.

Hollywood Kryptonite, the book by Sam Kushner and Nancy Schoenberger advanced the theory that Reeves was killed by Eddie Mannix, a Fox studio executive with mob connections. Reeves had had a long-term affair with Mannix's wife. In revenge, Mannix had the mob "bump off" Reeves and make it look like suicide.

While this is an intriguing theory, it remains just that. The real significance of Reeves and the character he played was brilliantly captured by the authors in the opening to their book:

For those old enough to understand, and for those who would one day come to know what happened to Superman, the world would never again be the same, nor feel as safe. . . . Because he stood on top of the world in that thrilling opening . . . he had seemed invincible. But with George Reeves's death how can you trust anything any adult told you about the world in which not even Superman was safe?

See also CALIFORNIA (1972–1975).

Holcomb, Kansas (1959) *In Cold Blood*

After World War II, many Americans in the 1950s lived in a bubble of sunshine and optimism, convinced that any threat to their security would come from without, never from within. As such, the massacre of the Clutter family has rightly taken its place alongside other legendary crimes. It caused America to finally acknowledge that some social cancer was at work producing home-grown monsters that could commit such a crime. Kansans, though, should not have been surprised.

In a sense, Kansas had forgotten its history and so had the rest of the country. When the Clutter family massacre became public knowledge, the sharp recoil of horror blotted over the fact that the crime had occurred in the very place that had once been referred to as "Bleeding Kansas." Mass murderers like Quantrill and the Benders may have been in the past, but they were still there in spirit, lurking in the recesses of the state's criminal history.

Perry Smith and Dick Hickok fit in well with that bunch. Perry and Dick were ex-cons who separately were just petty thieves but, working together, became mass murderers.

Dick had heard in prison from a cellmate about farmer Herb Clutter's hidden safe that reportedly contained thousands of dollars. When his friend Perry Smith was released from prison, they joined forces to steal into the Clutter house and burgle the safe. Unfortunately, there was no safe, Smith was a schizophrenic, and Hickok was a paranoid who urged Smith to kill all four members of the family.

With knife and gun, the Clutter family was massacred. Hickok and Smith fled south on the roads to Mexico, stayed there for a while, then came north over the burgeoning interstates by car. Were it not for the extensive road system they exploited, they would have been captured earlier. They were finally captured in Las Vegas and extradited after one year on the road, traveling through two countries. In the end, they were tried, found guilty, and sentenced to die by hanging. It is here that once again art collided with real life.

Novelist Truman Capote, seeking a nonfiction story to rejuvenate his failing career, found it in the Clutter family massacre. He spent more than two years reporting the story, getting friendly with the killers. The result, 1964's nonfiction book *In Cold Blood* began a new literary genre called true crime.

Where once cases had been reported by hard-to-get pamphlets, Capote brought crime out to the forefront as a symbol. He saw the Clutter case as indicative of an adverse change in American society. The age in which a family could feel safe in its own home was over.

The Radical Sixties (1960–1977)

The 1960s are sometimes known as "the Radical Sixties" because of the rise of violent, politically motivated gangs. The Weathermen, the Black Panthers, and Venceremos were among the best-known, with many splinter groups abounding. They purported to pursue socially acceptable goals, such as black integration and getting out of Vietnam, but stopped at nothing, including violence, to gain their goals. Such radical gangs continued to have an influence on American society well into the 1970s.

Dallas, Texas (1963) the assassination of President Kennedy

Up until that time, no American crime, with the exception of the Lincoln assassination, provoked such a massive outpouring of public grief than the assassination of John Fitzgerald Kennedy. From coast to coast, Americans young and old, black, white, and Hispanic, rich and poor, felt like they had lost a member of the family.

As president, Kennedy actually achieved very little in the way of social reform and, if anything, his policies served to further mire the United States in what would become the Vietnam War. But he had been the first president to use television effectively. His polished, cool performance on camera during the 1960 presidential debates, as opposed to his opponent Nixon's sweaty, shifty gaze, catapulted him into the Oval Office with a margin of only 100,000 votes. It has been alleged by reporters that his father, Joseph "Old Joe" Kennedy, used his mob connections to rig the vote count in Cook County, Illinois, to provide his son with the slight margin of victory.

Kennedy was just finishing up his third year in office when he decided to visit Dallas in November 1963.

John "Jack" Kennedy was the son of the bootlegger "Old Joe" Kennedy. Besides bootlegging, Old Joe made a fortune through what today would be termed "insider trading." Old Joe used his odiferous wealth to buy legitimacy. He was a supporter of President Franklin D. Roosevelt, who appointed Old Joe U.S. ambassador to the Court of St. James, from 1938 to 1940. But there was a limit to how Joseph Kennedy could go with his background, and that meant his sons needed to take that next step.

Son Joe Jr. was supposed to be the family's political heir, but he was killed in combat during World War II. Instead, the hero's mantle fell onto the broad shoulders of his younger brother Jack. Jack was a war hero too. That made him politically viable.

Soon after exiting the service, Old Joe decided Jack would run for Congress. "We're going to sell Jack like soap flakes," he famously said before the 1946 election. Sure enough, Jack was "sold like soap flakes" to the voters of Massachusetts's 11th District and elected to Congress. He served in the House until 1953, when he was elected to the Senate.

The Kennedy brothers (from left): Bobby, Ted, and Jack, in 1963. Two out of the three would be assassinated before the decade was over. (Photo № St 398-3-63, John F. Kennedy Library)

While a Massachusetts senator, Kennedy published the Pulitzer Prize–winning book *Profiles in Courage* in 1956. It told the story of great Americans who had sacrificed for honor and country. By the time he ran for president in 1960 against Richard M. Nixon, Eisenhower's vice president, Kennedy was as seasoned as any political pro despite his tender age—42.

After besting Nixon, Jack soon became a popular president. The young, vital JFK, as he became known, had a disarming, warm attitude that projected well on television. The Cuban Missile Crisis in 1962, in which JFK stood up to the Russians and would not let them install missiles in Cuba aimed at the United States, established him as a leader. While he was in office, a movie came out about his World War II naval exploits. Called *PT 109,* starring Cliff Robertson as JFK, it was a hit and served to further bolster his mythic status.

That Kennedy was actually an inveterate womanizer would not come out publicly until much later. Journalists, predominantly male, reportedly knew what was happening but chose to look the other way. Revelations in 2002 also showed that Kennedy had a myriad of medical problems for which he took heavy doses of prescription medication, including narcotics.

It was this man, a dashing, womanizing, heroic writer and family man, who made his way to Dallas on November 22, 1963, aboard Air Force One. Waiting for him was a former marine named Lee Harvey Oswald.

Oswald was a criminal right out of central casting. He was a loser, a boy who was abused by his parents and then decided to take out that abuse and hurt on the world. He joined the marines, only to find that he did not fit in. But he was very good at one thing: firing a rifle and hitting the target.

As a marine, Oswald qualified repeatedly as a marksman. In the marines, that was no great shakes. But among the civilian population, that was superior. Armed with a telescopic sight, Oswald could be lethal. But he did not spend all his time on the range.

While serving his country, Oswald began reading Communist Party propaganda. He agreed with the principles of life in the Union of Soviet Socialist Republics and wanted to be a part of it. Oswald subsequently left the service and defected to the USSR in 1959.

The Soviets did not know what to do with him. As far as knowing any valuable defense secrets, he was no Julius Rosenberg. The Soviets decided he should go home and told him to leave. Oswald responded by attempting suicide in his Moscow hotel room. Fearing a public incident that would reflect badly on them, the Soviets chose to let him stay rather than reject him one more time. They did not want him trying to kill himself again. Next time, he was fully capable of doing it in front of the cameras.

Oswald stayed in the USSR and tried to fit in. But he spoke poor Russian and soon tired of the boring factory work to which he had been assigned by the government. It was in the factory that he met his future wife Marina. They fell in love, married, and had a child named June.

Disenchanted with life in the Soviet Union, Oswald petitioned the government to let him and his family leave. They were only too happy to get rid of him. Oswald and his family left the USSR in June 1962 and returned to the United States, where they moved in with Oswald's brother Robert in Fort Worth. Gradually, Oswald's mental state deteriorated. He beat his wife. He argued with his family. At the same time, so did his economic prospects.

The FBI sent agents to interview him about his time in the USSR. They wanted to make sure he was no longer actively involved with the Soviets. Oswald actually convinced the agents he was not. He began to feel paranoid, believing the feds were looking into every nook and cranny of his life. His physical abuse of Marina escalated as Oswald's mind deteriorated.

On March 12, 1963, using the alias "A. Hidell," he bought by mail an Italian-made military rifle, the 6.5mm Mannlicher-Caracano. He acquired a telescopic sight. In the hands of a marksman like Oswald, it was as deadly as any automatic weapon.

Over the next few months, as Oswald immersed himself in Communist Party literature, he saw himself as a champion of Cuba. He moved to New Orleans, where he thought could do some good for the Communist cause. He worked for an organization called "Fair Play for Cuba." A local radio show invited him on to share his views.

The host had done his homework. He confronted Oswald on air about his defection to the USSR and his return home. The paradox was obvious. If communism was so great, why had Oswald come home? Oswald got flustered and never recovered his composure.

Oswald was humiliated by his performance. He began to talk about hijacking a plane to get to Cuba. By November Oswald was withdrawn and more moody and surly than ever. On November 22, 1963, Lee Harvey Oswald entered the Texas School Book Depository in Dallas. Taking up a position in a sixth-floor window, Oswald assembled his mail-order rifle and scope. He waited patiently for the president's motorcade to arrive.

JFK was in the back of an open limousine with his wife Jacqueline. Nellie Connally, wife of Governor John Connally of Texas, sat in the front on the left, her husband on the right. Taking careful aim, Oswald fired three times in rapid succession.

"Most people did not realize the first loud crack was gunfire," writes Gerald Posner in his 1993 book *Case Closed*. "Some thought it was a firecracker or a backfire from a police motorcycle. By the second shot, many realized it was too loud to be anything but gunfire."

The impact had jerked Kennedy's arms up. With the third shot, the president's head seemed to burst apart, "sending a red mist of blood, brain tissue and skull fragments upward and to the front." Shocked, Jacqueline Kennedy cradled the head of her dying husband in her lap. In the front seat, Governor Connally slumped forward, wounded.

Oswald escaped, only to be stopped by a local police officer, J. D. Tippit, a few blocks from the book depository. He shot Tippit dead and then sought refuge in a movie theater. Dallas police tracked him to the theater and gave him a chance to surrender. Oswald took it and was arrested and booked for the president's murder. On November 24 while being transported into the county sheriff's custody, Oswald was gunned down by nightclub owner Jack Ruby, less than two days after Oswald killed Kennedy. The incident was captured on live television.

Despite all the speculation afterward that Oswald was working for somebody else—everybody from the Mob to Cuba was suggested—no credible evidence exists to support this claim. Oswald was certainly capable of firing off the three shots in the allotted time. As for the theory that more than one gunman killed the president, it is a theory based largely on what has come to be known as the Zapruder film.

Abraham Zapruder was a Dallas dressmaker who was filming the president's motorcade as it pulled into Dealey Plaza in front of the depository. His 8mm color film "followed the President's car from the moment it made the turn from Houston onto Elm and stayed with it through the entire assassination," writes Posner in his book.

Posner continues,

Viewing the film with the naked eye, it looks like the president responds to shots from two different angles.

But in 1963, the technology did not exist to fully analyze the film versus the actual trajectory of the bullets.

In March, 1975, Geraldo Rivera aired, for the first time, the Zapruder film on ABC's Goodnight America. Millions were shocked by its graphic detail and especially the image of Kennedy's head snapping back and to the left after the final shot.

If there was more than one gunman, most conspiracy theorists at least allow that Oswald was one of them. The fact remains that no one really knows why Lee Harvey Oswald assassinated John Fitzgerald Kennedy. Oswald was not a die-hard Loyalist like Booth, or an anarchist like Czolgosz. He had more in common with Guiteau, who was simply insane.

See also ASSASSINATION OF PRESIDENT GARFIELD (JULY–SEPTEMBER 1881); JOHN WILKES BOOTH (1838–1865); BUFFALO, NEW YORK (1901); MIAMI, FLORIDA (1933); WASHINGTON, D.C. (1835); WASHINGTON, D.C. (1982).

Montgomery, Alabama (1968) the assassination of Dr. Martin Luther King, Jr.

Martin Luther King, Jr. stands as the preeminent civil rights leader of American history. No one comes close. During the 1960s, when a series of federal and state laws giving African Americans equal rights were fought tooth and nail by the former Confederate states, King was a voice of reason, moderation and eloquence. King espoused Gandhi's philosophy that nonviolent civil disobedience was more effective than violence in effecting social change. King was already making progress doing just that in Memphis in 1968 when he was cut down by a bullet fired by his assassin, James Earl Ray.

In the wake of King's death, conspiracy theorists had a field day. No one could imagine anyone as stupid as Ray, who left the murder weapon behind, covered with his fingerprints, and then fled to Europe. It all seemed too obvious; it *had* to be a conspiracy, many thought then. And many are still trying to prove it, despite hard evidence to the contrary.

James Earl Ray came from a poor family that moved around a lot. As a child in the sixth grade he was first accused of theft. At age 15, he dropped out of school. When he came of age, he joined the army and was sent to Germany right after World War II.

During his army service, Ray showed a propensity for drunkenness. He got thrown in the stockade on a drunk and disorderly charge and served 90 days.

In this photo from a June 22, 1963 civil rights meeting at the White House, Martin Luther King, Jr. (front row, third from left) casts a suspicious eye around him, while Attorney General Bobby Kennedy beams beside him. Vice President Lyndon Johnson (first row, third from right) looks on bemusedly. (Photo № AR 7993B, John F. Kennedy Library)

After he was discharged, Ray did not waste much time in getting into further trouble.

In 1949 Ray drifted out to California. After a burglary went awry, he was captured, tried, convicted and served eight months in jail. By 1952 he had graduated to armed robbery. Captured again, he spent two years in state prison. In 1955 Ray finally graduated to the big time.

He stole and forged postal money orders, a federal crime. Once again, he was caught, tried, and convicted, only this time, he was sent to the federal penitentiary in Leavenworth, a maximum-security facility. When Ray was released from Leavenworth in 1958, his federal parole officer wrote, "He was approved for our Honor Farm but was never actually transferred to the Farm due to the fact that he did not feel he could live in an Honor Farm dormitory because they are integrated . . ."

Ray was a racist who had made his feelings known to the authorities. One year later, on October 10, 1959, Ray held up a grocery store. Arrested for the armed robbery 20 minutes after he did it, he was sentenced as a repeat offender to 20 years in the Missouri State Prison at Jefferson City. As a working criminal, Ray was a complete failure.

For the next two years, Ray acted like a model inmate, never getting in trouble, but he was secretly plotting escape. His first attempt, in 1961, failed and he was condemned to time in solitary confinement. In 1966, with 14 more years to go in his sentence, Ray suddenly claimed schizophrenia. There were voices in his head. He needed therapy and so the prison got him a therapist.

It had seemed like a con, because therapy was a pretty easy way to spend the time in prison, but Ray may have legitimately felt he needed help. The opinion of medical personnel was that Ray was too disturbed to be let out of jail. The system worked; no parole for Ray. That made Ray extremely angry and determined to escape.

Ray got himself assigned to the prison bakery. Every day, a bread truck would stop by the prison, load up, and then go out to the remote sections of the county to service farmers. He determined to make his escape by curling up in a four-foot-square bread box.

On April 23, 1967, bread boxes bound for the farms at the edge of the county were being loaded into the truck. Inside one was James Earl Ray. If any of the guards had bothered to peek into Ray's, all they would have seen were loaves of bread. And in fact, the truck passed out of the prison with Ray undiscovered.

Ray had developed a con's smarts from the men who tutored him in prison. Ray secretly used some wood to make a false bottom. He got into the box, curled up on the bottom, had the fake bottom put over him, then had another inmate put bread over that. Even had the guards looked closely, they never would have found him. It was an absolutely brilliant escape.

After his escape, Ray moved around a lot, mostly between New Orleans and Los Angeles. He used the alias "Eric S. Galt" frequently. By 1968 he had settled in Las Vegas, where he took dance lessons and enrolled in a locksmith course. The latter would be especially useful to a man with a record of burglary and robbery. As for the dance lessons, Ray was a social sort.

Taking a page out of Dillinger's book, in February 1968 Ray went under the plastic surgeon's knife for some changes to his appearance, making identification by law enforcement more difficult. On March 17, 1968, using his Galt identity, he filed a change-of-address form with a Los Angeles post office. The forwarding address was care of General Delivery, Atlanta, Georgia. Within the week, Ray was in New Orleans, dropping off a package of clothing with an acquaintance.

Ray would later admit to writer William Bradford Huie, who paid to interview him, that he began tracking King's movements at this time. King was getting ready for a civil rights march on Washington, D.C. Unobserved, Ray tracked him through Alabama, from Selma to Montgomery to Birmingham, then to Atlanta. Ray stayed there until March 28.

On March 29 Ray showed up at a gun store in Birmingham and asked the salesperson if he could look at some high-powered hunting rifles. Posing as "Harvey Lowmeyer," Ray picked out a Remington Game Master Model 760. The small, .243-caliber rifle was fitted with a pump action, John Browning's invention. The gun was powerful enough to knock down a deer from 330 yards away.

For help in aiming, Ray picked up a Redfield variable scope, 2x to 7x power. Completing his selections, Ray bought some ammunition: hollow-point 75-grain bullets. Contemporary gun laws did not require a waiting period or identity check. Ray paid $250 for the whole package and walked out the front door, happy with his selections.

By the next day, Ray had changed his mind. The gun did not have enough power. He exchanged the Remington Game Master for a more powerful .30-06 caliber rifle, on which he mounted the Redfield scope.

Birmingham to Memphis is a 146-mile trip, over a strip of the federal Interstate Highway System.

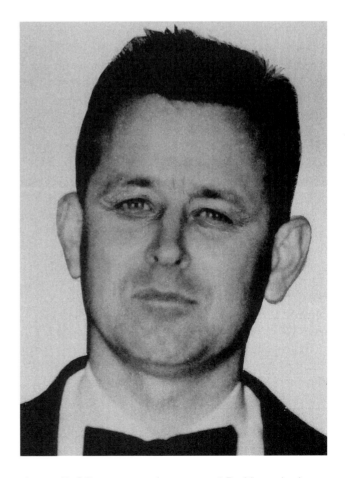

James Earl Ray, convicted assassin of Dr. Martin Luther King, Jr. (National Archives)

253

Because the road was so quick—it was easy to travel faster than 70 miles per hour without a cop stopping you—Ray spent a few days getting there. He could afford to. He read the newspapers. He knew King's schedule in advance and knew when he would be in Memphis.

On April 3, 1968, Ray arrived in Mephis. He rented a room in a downtown hotel. The next day, he moved to 422 1/2 Main Street, a place known as Bessie Brewer's Rooming House. Across the street was the Lorraine Motel.

King had previously been in town to help organize a labor union with a predominantly black membership. He had stayed at the Lorraine Motel. Ray knew that, which was why he staked out the place when King returned to Memphis for a march in support of the union.

King arrived in Memphis on April 3. He and his party checked into the Lorraine, but no sooner were they in town than they were served with a restraining order to prohibit a planned march. Later that evening and into the wee hours of the morning, Dr. King and his advisers brainstormed how to combat the restraining order the next day in court. They also talked about the upcoming demonstration in Washington that King was planning. This one would rival the huge 1963 March on Washington. It would be composed of all those Americans who felt disenfranchised by the government.

At about 4:30 A.M., the meeting broke up. After a few more meetings, King fell asleep in his motel room and did not emerge until midday, April 4. Sometime between 5:30 and 5:45 P.M., King and an aide, Ralph Abernathy, went back to the room they were sharing on the Lorraine's second floor to change for dinner. Freshly dressed, they walked out together from their room at 6 P.M.

King spoke with his driver, Solomon Jones, about the weather. Jones recommended that King take a coat. It would be a cool evening. King nodded, turned, and started back to the room. There was a sound like a single firecracker going off. King fell with a bullet through his jaw. It was a true kill shot that severed the jugular vein, the vertebral and sub-clavian arteries, and finished up by smashing into neck and back vertebrae.

Like Lincoln, King had sustained too much damage. There was nothing the doctors could do. A short while later, King was pronounced dead at a nearby hospital.

After he shot King, Ray slipped through the federal dragnet. The feds tracked him to Canada where he obtained a phony passport under the name "George Ramon Sneyd." He used it to cross the Atlantic to England. Sneyd/Ray traveled from England to Portugal and then back again.

On June 8, 1968, British agents stopped James Earl Ray while he was attempting to board a Brussels-bound jetliner. After a protracted period, during which Ray fought extradition, he was extradited back to the United States. In Alabama he faced murder one charges punishable by death. Ray gave police a cock and bull statement that he was actually working for a mysterious gunrunner named "Raoul" when he pulled the trigger. No evidence was ever presented by Ray to prove "Raoul" existed as anything but another con in a life full of cons and bizarre schizophrenic moments of violence and criminal brilliance.

Ray changed lawyers a number of times as his trial date drew closer, finally settling on Percy Foreman, the renowned defense attorney. Foreman looked over the evidence and realized that he had no defense: Ray was guilty. He then convinced Ray to plead guilty in return for a life sentence. Foreman worked out a deal with the government: Ray would plead guilty, in return for a sentence of 99 years in jail.

Appearing in court before Judge Preston Battle, Ray pleaded guilty to killing King. He affirmed to the judge that his plea had not been coerced; he was entering it on his full volition. He waived his right to trial. And then Ray said he "was not saying there had been no conspiracy, because there had been." Again, he offered no evidence that "Raoul" or any conspiracy to kill King existed.

On Monday, March 10, 1969, Ray was scheduled to be sentenced. Instead, he fired Foreman and wrote Battle that he intended to change his plea back to not guilty. The prosecution appealed on the grounds that it had made a binding agreement with Ray that he now had to honor. After taking it all the way through the court system, Ray's case was heard before the Supreme Court.

Ray lost. He had to take the deal. From 1969 when he first entered prison until he died in 2001, Ray claimed that he was the patsy for a conspiracy with "Raoul" as a central character. Eventually, Ray actually had the chutzpah to claim to King's son's face that he didn't shoot his father.

But for some reason, Ray could not give King's son Martin III a plausible explanation for why his fingerprints were found on the murder weapon recovered across the street from where his father fell. Up until his death in 2001, Ray maintained a Web site touting his innocence. To date, no factual evidence has ever been presented of conspiracy.

Washington, D.C. (1970) the RICO Act passes

The original idea of the Racketeer Influenced and Corrupt Organizations (RICO) Act was to give the federal government broad power to fight organized crime, defined as gangsters, mobsters, or members of a drug ring.

Section A of RICO defines a criminal act as "any act or threat involving murder, kidnapping, gambling, arson, robbery, bribery, extortion, dealing in obscene matter, or dealing in a controlled substance or listed chemical (as defined in section 102 of the Controlled Substances Act), which is chargeable under State law and punishable by imprisonment for more than one year."

RICO would subsequently be used to prosecute members of the Mafia in the 1980s and 1990s to such an extent that the traditional power of the centuries-old Sicilian-born criminal brotherhood lost much of its power in America. Over time, though, the government realized that the RICO Act could be used against corporations for distributing false advertisements. They could go after lawyers, bankers, accountants, and other professionals for helping clients organize fraudulent schemes. Even, individuals could use the RICO Act.

The RICO Act enables people financially injured by a pattern of criminal activity to sue for damages in state or federal courts. For example, RICO has been used to sue spouses for concealing marital assets in divorce proceedings. The act is so elastic that individuals have used it to sue white supremacist groups who have injured them physically, financially, or both.

While its critics say the broader uses of the act have stretched it to its legal limits, RICO is, arguably, the most critical criminal justice legislation in the latter part of the 20th century.

Portland, Oregon (1971) D. B. Cooper, skydiving skyjacker

The Wright brothers' invention gave rise to a peculiar form of crime in the 1970s—skyjacking. Most often, a political dissident would "skyjack" a jetliner at gunpoint and force the airline to accede to some sort of ransom demand, which usually involved transporting the malcontent to some country that would harbor him.

In response, the Federal Marshals Service dispatched armed marshals dressed in civilian clothes to ride "shotgun" on random airliners. They became known as sky marshals. By the end of the decade, skyjacking seemed to have died out, and the sky marshals program was largely abandoned until after September 11, 2001.

The only 1970s skyjacker remembered by name today is D. B. Cooper—and with good reason. Cooper was a true American original. What he did, no one has done before or since. His crime remains one of the most novel uses of transportation technology to commit a robbery in U.S. criminal history.

On November 24, 1971, Thanksgiving Eve, a man calling himself Dan Cooper boarded a Northwest Orient Flight in Portland, Oregon. Wearing a dark suit, dark tie, white shirt, and sunglasses that he never took off, he took seat 18F in coach. Chain-smoking, he ordered a bourbon and water, then handed the flight attendant a note. She did not read it until after take-off. The note said, "Miss, I've got a bomb, come sit next to me—you're being hijacked."

Cooper then gave the flight attendant some messages for the cockpit. He wanted $200,000 in used $20 bills and four parachutes put on at the next stop. He showed the flight attendant a briefcase he carried, containing what looked like a bomb—a couple of red cylinders, wire, and a battery.

During the next stop, Seattle-Tacoma Airport, the money and parachutes were loaded on the plane. In return, the 36 passengers and two flight attendants were released. Cooper ordered the pilot to fly to Mexico. After the plane had been about 40 minutes in the air, Cooper donned one of the parachutes. Then he opened the rear door of the plane. He was pulled out into the darkness of a freezing rainstorm at 10,000 feet. Outside, the temperature was 25 degrees with a wind chill of 70 below due to the plane's speed.

Cooper parachuted over the mountains of the Pacific Northwest; no confirmed trace has ever been found of him or the money. When he was identified to the press, a law enforcement official called him "D.B." instead of "Dan" and the mistake stuck.

California (1972–1975) the Symbionese Liberation Army

The Symbionese Liberation Army was one of the most amateurish and vicious gangs to emerge from the 1960s and explode into the 1970s. Their feeble attempt to masquerade as social reformers did not disguise what they really were—a 20th-century version of the James Gang.

Their leader, Donald "Cinque" DeFreeze, was born in 1943 in Cleveland, Ohio. Physically abused by his father, DeFreeze grew up to become a gangster. He spent the rest of his short life alternating between committing felonies on the outside and going to prison for those crimes. Sometimes he worked both sides of the fence as a police informant. This would later support the rumors that DeFreeze was actually a CIA agent bent on discrediting the leftist movement on the basis of his violent actions.

While serving a five-years-to-life sentence in California's Vacaville prison for robbery and a shootout with police, he became active in the Black Cultural Association. On December 11, 1972, he was transferred to Soledad Prison. The following year, he walked out of prison and before anyone noticed, had made his escape into San Francisco's radical underground. DeFreeze collected around him a like-minded group of "radicals," though "disenchanted, alienated, and violent youth" was probably a better description. They called themselves the Symbionese Liberation Army (SLA). Within a year, SLA membership included Thero Wheeler, Patricia "Mizmoon" Soltysik, Nancy Ling Perry, Russell Little, Willie Wolfe, and Vietnam veteran Joseph Remiro. Associates were Angela Atwood and Bill and Emily Harris.

Accumulating weapons from successful burglaries DeFreeze took his recruits into the Berkeley hills and began molding them into fighting condition. The SLA developed an odd hit list of bombing targets, including Avis Rent-a-Car, and an even more arcane list of people to assassinate, including the director of the California Department of Corrections.

As Thero Wheeler recalls:

We was sitting around the house one day drinking wine and somebody started talking about this dude Foster. At the time there was a lot of feeling against him in the community. Bobby Seale [the Black Panther leader] was raising hell about him and all. All of a sudden DeFreeze sits up and says, "Man, we're gonna waste that nigger!"

The SLA's first target was Marcus Foster, the African American superintendent of the Oakland, California, school district. The SLA disagreed with some of Foster's policies, so they shot him eight times. Foster's associate Robert Blackburn was also shot but eventually recovered.

With the city of Oakland in mourning, the SLA released "Communiqué No. 1" three days later, taking responsibility for the crime. Gang members

Remiro and Little would subsequently be captured on minor charges. Once their identity as SLA members was known, they were held without bail.

On Friday, February 4, 1974, the SLA kidnapped Patty Hearst, heiress to the Hearst media empire. For the next two months, using brutal psychological as well as physical tactics, DeFreeze and the rest brainwashed Hearst into joining them. By the middle of April, the SLA was ready to deploy its newest recruit, who was now known by her revolutionary name, Tanya.

Automatic weapons at the ready, the SLA robbed a San Francisco branch of the Hibernia Bank on April 15, 1974. One person was wounded. In one of the most famous photos taken during the 20th century, Patty Hearst was photographed by the bank's cameras holding an automatic rifle that she used to cover her compadres. There she was, the scion to one of North America's largest fortunes, holding up a bank.

After escaping a police dragnet, DeFreeze moved the group's activities south to Los Angeles, where they got a safe house in the predominantly black neighborhood of Watts. DeFreeze sent out his soldiers in war games practice in groups of three. Basically, these were raids to help support the fugitives. That is how Patty Hearst and Bill and Emily Harris, wound up working together. Their mission was to shoplift from a sporting goods store without getting caught.

Harris was caught shoplifting and pulled to the ground by bystanders. Patty opened fire from their waiting van. Harris broke free. He and Emily jumped in the van and Patty drove off.

Back at the sporting goods store, Emily had stupidly managed to drop a parking ticket issued to an address on West 84th street in Watts—the SLA's safe house. A police raid of the house shortly afterward turned up nothing. DeFreeze had eluded them again.

Employing the traditional police tactic of canvassing the neighborhood, they soon discovered that DeFreeze and the SLA were now hiding at a house on East 54th Street. By 5:40 P.M., on May 17, 1974, police had the place surrounded. They announced that fact at least 19 times on bullhorns. The people inside the house were told to come out with their hands up and no one would be harmed.

Only two people emerged, a boy and a man who had nothing to do with the SLA. Los Angeles's vaunted Special Weapons and Tactics Team (SWAT) moved in. In terms of rounds expended, what followed was the greatest gun battle between police and outlaws in U.S. criminal history. Some 9,000 rounds of ammunition were expended by both parties in a little less than one hour.

Los Angelenos crowded around their televisions to see the shootout live. That included the Harrises, who had checked into an Anaheim motel after their escape. Patty had taken off by herself. For perhaps the first time, Americans watched and listened to a crime taking place on live TV—the SLA firing on the LAPD, and the cops' fusillade in response.

At the end of the hour-long battle, police lobbed tear gas canisters into the house. They exploded and caught fire and the place became an inferno. Camilla Hall and Nancy Ling Perry made their way to the outside where they were confronted with the armed might of the LAPD. Hall fired and took a slug to her forehead for her trouble that killed her instantly. Perry fired quickly, but the SWAT team was faster, killing her.

When the smoke cleared and the cops moved in, they found that every member of the SLA in the house, including DeFreeze, had been killed. Bill and Emily Harris, of course, had gotten away. Determined to continue their activities, they hooked up with a wannabe radical named Kathy Soliah. They later added Jim Kilgore, Mike Bortin, and Steven Soliah (Kathy's brother).

The reconstituted SLA robbed the Guild Savings and Loan Association in Sacramento. Luckily, no one was hurt. Next up was the Crocker National Bank in Carmichael, California. What happened next cemented the SLA's fate. From the *Sacramento Bee,* April 22, 1975:

OFFICERS CALL FATAL BANK ROBBERY WELL PLANNED, POORLY EXECUTED

Sheriff's detectives believe yesterday's $15,000 robbery of a Crocker Bank branch in Carmichael and the murder of a customer had all the earmarks of a well-planned crime, which in execution was botched-up and amateurish.

One of the robbers, armed with a double-barreled shotgun, for no apparent reason fired a blast which fatally wounded a customer, Mrs. Myrna Opsahl, 42, who had come to the bank with two other women to deposit the weekend collection from the Carmichael Seventh-Day Adventist Church. It was Emily Harris who inexplicably blasted Opsahl in the face.

After the robbery/killing, the SLA followed up with a series of bombings, with varying degrees of success. Patricia Hearst, Jim Kilgore, Steven Soliah, and Wendy Yoshimura went underground as roommates, renting a San Francisco apartment on Morse Street. Cops tracked them there and raided the residence on September 18, 1975, capturing Patty Hearst and Wendy Yoshimura.

In a statement issued on January 2, 2002, Sacramento County District Attorney Jan Scully revealed, "After her arrest, Patricia Hearst gave investigators detailed statements about the Crocker National Bank robbery, admitted her participation and named her seven accomplices and the roles they played. In summary, she stated that the four individuals who entered the bank were Emily Harris, Kathleen Soliah, Michael Bortin and James Kilgore. According to Hearst, it was Emily Harris who fired the fatal shot into Mrs. Opsahl. She identified the two armed lookouts as William Harris and Steven Soliah, Kathleen Soliah's brother. Hearst indicated that she was one of the two switch car drivers with Wendy Yoshimura being the other."

Despite her defense that she had been brainwashed, Patricia Hearst was convicted of bank robbery and sentenced to 35 years in prison. She was, however, given a 90-day psychiatric evaluation, after which her sentence would be finalized. A new judge gave her seven years. She had served approximately three years of that term when, on January 29, 1979, President Jimmy Carter commuted her sentence to time served. President Bill Clinton pardoned her in 2001.

Steven Soliah was subsequently tried in federal court for his involvement in the Crocker robbery. He was acquitted in April 1976. But soon after the jury reached its verdict, it was discovered that Soliah's alibi was false.

After Kathy Soliah went underground in 1976, she drifted into Minnesota, where she started a whole new life as wife, mother, and social activist Sara Jane Olson. Finally tracked down and captured in 1999 by the LAPD Cold Case Squad, Soliah plead guilty in 2001 in Los Angeles to a charge that she had attempted as part of her SLA activities to bomb LAPD police cars. She was sentenced to 20 years behind bars.

District Attorney Scully then went back and reviewed the facts of the Carmichael robbery that had led to Myrna Opsahl's death. Scully then issued arrest warrants for Bill and Emily Harris, Michael Bortin, and Jim Kilgore.

They all took deals for guilty pleas on second-degree murder charges. On November 2, 2002, Bill and Emily Harris, Kathy Soliah, and Mike Bortin were sentenced. Emily Harris, who had since divorced Bill and changed her name to Montague, got eight years. Her former husband, Bill, got seven years. Soliah and Bortin got five years each.

As for the last SLA member still at large, Jim Kilgore, he was tracked down to Cape Town, South Africa, where he was living under the name Charles William Page. Kilgore/Page had done very well for himself—he had become a professor at the University of Cape Town. It was a tremendous surprise to his students when he turned out to be one of America's "Most Wanted."

December 14, 2002, Justice Minister Penuell Maduna of South Africa, signed Kilgore's extradition papers. Five days later, Kilgore was back in the United States, facing a federal charge of possessing a pipe bomb. And California had not forgotten about the murder of Myrna Opsahl during the 1975 bank robbery. The Associated Press reported on December 19, 2002, "Before his arrest, Kilgore had been negotiating through a New York attorney to receive a similar sentence [to other SLA members] in exchange for his surrender." But Kilgore had not arranged his surrender; he had forced the cops to come after him. The authorities in Sacramento County were looking forward to seeing him again.

See also HOLLYWOOD HILLS, CALIFORNIA (1959).

Queens, New York (1975) terrorists bomb LaGuardia Airport

To this day the bombing of LaGuardia Airport on December 29, 1975, remains an unsolved crime, one of the worst terrorist attacks on U.S. soil, in fact, worse than the 1993 bombing of the World Trade Center. At 6:30 P.M., a bomb blast in the TWA terminal at LaGuardia Airport blew out floor-to-ceiling plate glass windows along 360 feet of frontage. A group of lockers exploded, sending razor-sharp shrapnel through the terminal into human targets. After the explosion, there was a 12-by-15-foot hole in the eight-inch thick concrete slab of a ceiling in the baggage area.

Port Authority police had not been trained for such a devastating attack and did little or nothing to evacuate the building. Witnesses would later report only one announcement on the terminal's public address system confirming the attack and asking people to leave. Yet no one took charge to make it so.

Eleven people were killed and more than 80 injured. An FBI investigation turned up nothing. No one was ever caught; no one was ever charged; no one ever took responsibility for the crime. While authorities suspected Croatian nationalists to this day, the murders remain unsolved.

See also TIMOTHY MCVEIGH (1968–2001); NEW YORK, NEW YORK (1993); NEW YORK, NEW YORK (2001).

New York, New York (1978) the Lufthansa robbery

All of the famous "five families" of New York, the modern Mafia, had crews at John F. Kennedy Airport, taking a piece of the action on all the freight going in and out of the airport. The Lufthansa robbery at Kennedy was therefore no surprise. The organized crime presence made anything possible. What was a surprise was the take, for the Lufthansa robbery stands as the single largest robbery in United States history.

It was pulled off by James Burke, also known as Jimmy Conway, also known as "Jimmy the Gent." Jimmy was a member of Paulie Vario's crew, a group of Mafia soldiers who worked in the Lucchese crime family. Burke was born on July 5, 1931; he never knew his parents. By the time he was two, he was in foster care. Going from one foster home to another, he was beaten and sexually abused. When he was 13 years old, in 1944, his then current foster father turned in his seat to beat Jimmy in their car. The man lost control, crashed, and died on impact; Jimmy survived unharmed, but his foster mother decided he was responsible and beat him unmercifully. Burke began his criminal career in his teens.

Constantly in trouble with the law for a variety of crimes, he spent most of his time from age 16 to 22 in confinement. As he got older, Burke latched onto Paulie Vario's crew as a feared enforcer and "earner." Committed to hijacking shipments from Kennedy Airport, like all soldiers he "kicked upstairs" (paid money) to his capo, Vario.

A feared killer and expert hijacker, Jimmy had an appreciation for his criminal forebears. Jimmy named his two sons Frank James Burke and Jesse James Burke. His daughter Cathy married Anthony "Whack Whack" Indelicato, one of the murderers of legendary mob boss Carmine Galante.

Throughout the 1970s, Jimmy continued his life-long pattern of going in and out of jail. Convicted on the federal crime of extortion in 1972, Burke was not paroled until October 25, 1978. He wasted little time getting back to business. On Friday, December 8, 1978, Burke and his crew stole $5 million in cash and $850,000 in jewelry from the Lufthansa Airlines terminal at the airport. It was the largest take in United States criminal history.

Allegedly Burke then began murdering members of the crew to keep their mouths shut. Afraid he would be killed next, gangster Henry Hill, who was on Burke's crew, turned informant. Burke was indicted and convicted on racketeering and sports-bribery charges. In January 1982 Burke went behind bars for the last time. Jimmy the Gent died in federal prison on April 13, 1996. He was 65 years old. Except for $20,000, the money and jewels have never been recovered.

Washington, D.C. (1979) FALN commandos pardoned

President Jimmy Carter pardoned the FALN terrorists behind the 1954 attack on Congress, in 1979. Upon his release, Rafael Cancel Miranda, head of the "commando squad," told the press that he was ready to do it all over again, though this time, they would use grenades instead of bullets.

Since that time, the four terrorists have lobbied for the release of 15 other Puerto Rican terrorists who are members of the National Liberation Armed Forces (FALN) and Macheteros who are interned in U.S. jails for "bombings and revolutionary thefts" on the island of Puerto Rico and on the U.S. mainland.

New York, New York (1979–1984) the global drug trade and the "Pizza Connection"

Of all criminal operations, drug trafficking, even with its high transportation overhead, is by far the most lucrative criminal enterprise. Yet, the Mafia, which has never been known to turn its back on a illicit dollar, has always frowned upon drugs. Until the 1960s, the Five Families of New York kept drug dealing to a minimum for the simple reason that it attracted too much police scrutiny. Crime thrives in the dark; the bosses could do without drugs and the attendant attention affecting their other profitable criminal enterprises. The exception was the Bonanno family.

Through a series of power struggles in the 1960s, boss Joe Bonanno lost power to Philip "Rusty" Rastelli. When the latter was convicted in 1976 on a federal racketeering conviction, Carmine Galante began to gain power. The biggest supplier of drugs to the East Coast, Galante used Rastelli's absence to expand operations. Using his "zips," tough Sicilian Mafiosi he imported for "muscle," Galante became

the country's biggest supplier of heroin. Despite Galante's financial success, drugs were still looked at as the kiss of death by the mob. Its ruling body, the Commission, on which all the five families are represented, met and decided that Galante had to go. He was assassinated on July 12, 1979. But that didn't stop the Bonannos from staying embroiled in the drug business. The Bonannos just didn't seem to get the message.

After Galante's death, Caesar Bonaventre cornered New York's drug trade in the early 1980s. The youngest capo in the mob, the 20-something Bonaventre used pizzerias all over the city to distribute the "dope." Police officers stopped Bonaventre while he was making a drop at a pizzeria on Long Island because he was acting suspiciously by circling the lot before he parked. Searching his car, they found a gun and took him in. Subsequent investigation exposed Bonaventre's racket, which became known in the tabloits as "the Pizza Connection."

The Pizza Connection was just one small slice of the international drug trade focused on smuggling illicit drugs into the United States, where the term "drug trafficking" was coined. In China, it's called *jing san jiao* in Chinese, and in Thailand, *sam liam thiong kham*. These countries are in Asia, and so is the Golden Triangle, the place where Laos, Burma, and China meet, where armed drug traffickers rule and where poppies are grown. Physically isolated within the almost impenetrable jungles of Southeast Asia, the Golden Triangle is sort of an Asian version of Hole in the Wall. The place is home to lawbreakers, but instead of Hole in the Wall's robbers and murderers, the Golden Triangle shelters drug dealers who are in the business of manufacturing poppy-derived opiates, such as heroin and cocaine, that are sold on America's streets.

Pack trains loaded with opium make their way out of the Golden Triangle escorted and protected by the Chin Haw, an ancient society of Chinese Muslims that maintains a stranglehold on all of the region's transportation systems. Once out of the Golden Triangle, the drugs reach the United States over land, sea, and air, making full use of all modern transportation systems.

During the later decades of the 20th century and at the beginning of the 21st, much of the cocaine making its way onto America's streets started to come from Colombia in South America. American law enforcement had to confront such deadly criminal gangs as the Colombian Medellín cartel. But regardless of where the drugs originate, drug traffickers rely on sophisticated American air transportation, highways, and waterways to distribute their products.

The U.S. borders with Canada and Mexico stretch across the continent, a total of 6,000 miles. All that is necessary to get the drugs into the country is to penetrate the border successfully at any one point and escape detection. Considering how easily a drug like cocaine can be bought on thousands of streets corners in America's cities, it's obvious that the drugs are getting in more often than they are stopped.

Drug traffickers use both sophisticated and unsophisticated methods, such as human "mules." The "mules" ingest condoms loaded with heroin or cocaine at the embarkation point. They then penetrate U.S. security by simply walking across the border or flying in on a commercial airliner and going through customs like anyone else. Once inside the United States, the "mule" then goes to a prearranged meeting point, where he or she meets with a courier. The courier will stay with the mule in a safe house or hotel room until the condoms are excreted. The courier then takes the drugs to the next step along the stage on the way to street distribution.

Smuggling drugs through the air can be a riskier proposition. The United States is sensitive to unauthorized foreign aircraft that penetrate U.S. airspace, especially after the terrorist attacks of September 11, 2001, but it is relatively easy to fly a small plane across the border, land at a prearranged site, and offload the drugs. While customs will sometimes interdict such flights, enough get in to keep the drug trade going.

Whatever the source—the Colombian drug cartels, Mexican drug traffickers, or American organized crime—the sale of cocaine and heroin in the United States has become a multibillion-dollar industry with millions of customers. What is particularly troubling is how throughout the 1990s and into the 21st century, drug trafficking has become a revenue source to finance terrorism. "There often is a close connection between terrorism and organized crime, including drug trafficking. This nexus takes many forms, ranging from facilitation—protection, transportation, and taxation—to direct trafficking by terrorist organizations themselves," according to the Federal Bureau for International Narcotics and Law Enforcement Affairs.

By trafficking in drugs, terrorist organizations can make huge amounts of money to finance their operations.

"Drug traffickers benefit from terrorists' military skills, weapons supply, and access to clandestine organizations. Terrorists gain a source of revenue and expertise in illicit transfer and laundering of money for their operations. Like traffickers and other organized crime groups, they make use of those countries and jurisdictions where banking regulations are weak. Both groups corrupt officials who can provide fraudulent documents, such as passports and customs papers," the Federal Bureau for International Narcotics and Law Enforcement Affairs continues.

A 2003 UNESCO report called "Criminal Prosperity" says: "The mirror of history clearly shows us the impact of the drug trade in the colonization of Asia. The post cold war geopolitical context reproduces elements of this colonial past, with new opportunities for drug trafficking in the globalization process. This movement marks the renewal of an illicit economy, of drug trafficking and corruption in emergent countries and those in transition."

Washington, D.C. (1982) attempted assassination of President Ronald Reagan broadcast on television

John F. Hinckley Jr. grew up in a loving and close family, with two siblings.

His father, John W. Hinckley, was the wealthy president of the Vanderbilt Energy Corporation, while his mother, Joanne, was a housewife. Popular during junior high school, John became increasingly moody as he aged. He spent the 1970s finishing high school, going in and out of college and following his dream of being a songwriter in Hollywood. Failing at that, he went to movies for escape, seeing *Taxi Driver* 15 times by his own count. The film features Robert De Niro as a cab-driving would-be assassin who wants to "take out" a Presidential candidate and Jodie Foster as a teenage prostitute.

Becoming fascinated by guns, Hinckley bought a .38 caliber pistol in August 1979. During the next few years, Hinckley acquired more guns and exploding-head Devastator bullets. He later admitted that he stalked President Carter during fall 1980, following him to Nashville, where, on October 2, he was stopped at the airport trying to board a plane with two guns in his suitcase. The weapons were confiscated, and Hinckley was fined $62.50 and let go.

Alarmed at their son's behavior, his parents sent him to a psychiatrist, who claimed that John's problems came from emotional immaturity. By that time, John had enrolled in a Yale University writing course to be near *Taxi Driver* actress Jodie Foster, also a student there. Hinckley had two phone conversations with Foster in New Haven, where he assured her he was not dangerous. Foster, apparently, was not convinced; there is no record of any further contact.

Undaunted, Hinckley figured that the notoriety of committing a presidential assassination would gain him the actress's love. He became determined to shoot Carter's successor, President Ronald Reagan.

The morning of March 30, 1982, Hinckley wrote a letter to Foster in which he described his plan to assassinate the president. A few hours later, he stepped from the assembled throng to watch the president depart from a speaking engagement at Washington's Park Center Hotel. Live television cameras tracked the President, who was scheduled to deliver a speech before a labor convention

At 1:30 P.M., John Hinckley aimed and fired six shots from a Rohm R6-14 revolver loaded with Devastator bullets. Reagan, not realizing he was shot, was hustled back into his limo by Secret Service agents and whisked off to the hospital, where it was discovered he had been wounded in the chest. All of this was caught on camera and broadcast on live TV and repeatedly afterward.

Back at the crime scene, Hinckley had been subdued, but not before Devastator bullets had struck press secretary James Brady in the temple, Officer Thomas Delahanty in the neck, and Security Agent Timothy J. McCarthy in the stomach. All would eventually recover, including the president. Brady, though, suffered severe brain damage.

Hinckley's trial on attempted assassination charges began on May 4, 1982, and ended on June 21, 1982, when he was found not guilty by reason of insanity. As of this writing, John Hinckley is still held in St. Elizabeth's Mental Hospital in Washington, D.C. In April 2000, after responding positively to psychiatric treatment, he was allowed unsupervised furloughs outside the hospital grounds. In May 2000 guards found a book about Foster in his cell. Since he is not allowed any material relating to Foster, his furlough privileges were revoked.

Ferdinand Waldo Demara Jr., a.k.a. "the Great Impostor" (1921–1982) the father of identity fraud

Fred Demara was the father of identity fraud. Many years later, when his name was forgotten, "the Great Impostor's" place in criminal history was assured. Ferdinand Waldo Demara Jr. was born in Lawrence, Massachusetts, in 1921. He appears to have had an untroubled childhood with good parents. As a teenager, he attended Central Catholic High School but dropped out before graduation.

Demara would later describe his reasons for his many masquerades as "pure rascality." Whatever his motivations, he decided to pose as a monk. As "Brother John," he entered a monastery as a novitiate. While he was there, he made the acquaintance of Dr. Joseph Cyr, a Canadian. Leaving the monastery before being ordained, Demara showed up in Nova Scotia in March 1951, posing as "Dr. Joseph Cyr."

It was a time of war, with the Korean conflict in full throttle, with a United Nations peacekeeping force doing all it could to stop communism from spreading across the Korean peninsula and beyond. In this time of war, the Canadian military accepted Demara without checking his credentials because they needed all the help they could get.

Commissioned as a surgeon-lieutenant and assigned to the naval hospital in Halifax and subsequently to HMCS *Cayuga,* Demara joined the ship in Esquimalt for its second tour of duty in Korean waters. "Dr. Cyr," of course, had no training as a doctor. But Fred Demara was a brilliant man with a photographic memory. He crammed through medical books, memorizing procedures, doing whatever was necessary to convince people he was a real surgeon. At first he had only minor cases, and then his mettle was finally tested.

A commando-style raid off the west coast of Korea brought three seriously wounded South Korean guerrillas aboard the *Cayuga.* "Cyr" removed a bullet from a man's chest and amputated another's foot. Not only did his patients survive, Cyr's fellow officers were so impressed with his abilities that they planned to recommend him for a medal.

But the last thing an imposter wants is publicity. War correspondents picked up the story and it went out over the wires. The real Dr. Cyr's mother read of the plan to award her son a medal, only the picture in the paper was not of her son—it was Demara. The genuine Joseph Cyr, then practicing in Grand Falls, New Brunswick, soon figured it out. When Demara had been a novice monk, the two had struck up a friendship. Demara stole Cyr's medical credentials and passed himself off as Cyr.

Fred Demara eventually appeared before a Canadian court and was released from service without charges being filed. Over the next decade, Demara went back to the United States and successfully posed as a law student, prison warden, cancer researcher and, finally, a teacher. It was this last, when he was found out, that netted him six months in prison.

Author Robert Crichton later wrote a book about Demara's life. Called *The Great Impostor,* it spawned a hit 1961 movie of the same title that starred Tony Curtis. Demara later decided to write a memoir, but never did. When he died in 1982, he felt that much of his life had been wasted.

Considering Ferdinand Waldo Demara Jr.'s obvious talents, that is true. His legacy in the world of crime, however, was that he was the first to assume another's identity, brilliantly and with panache. The record is also clear that his medical skills saved lives.

Arizona and California (1987) the Keating Five and white-collar crime

Throughout the 1980s, the booming stock market and correlating greed resulted in the rise of corporate outlaws, men who swindled unwitting investors out of billions of dollars. Prominent among these swindlers, practitioners of what is known as white-collar crime, were men with thousand-dollar suits who owned savings and loans (S and L's), financial institutions where people deposited their hard-earned money because it was backed by the full faith of the federal government. When the owners of these S and L's began defrauding their customers, the government moved in to make good on their losses, totaling in the tens of billions.

Prominent among these S and L crooks was Charles Keating, the powerful, charismatic owner of a financial empire built on junk bonds. He ran Arizona's American Continental Corporation, which owned California's Lincoln Savings and Loan, an S and L the government was about to seize because of mismanagement. Keating had allegedly siphoned off some of the company's money into his personal accounts. When government regulators were closing in, Keating turned to his political contacts to keep him out of trouble.

Senator Dennis DeConcini had seen his coffers grow over the years from Keating's campaign contributions. Now Keating asked him to arrange a meeting with the federal regulators who were breathing down his neck. He wanted DeConcini to go to bat for him. DeConcini turned to Arizona's junior senator, John McCain. McCain, a Medal of Honor recipient for his heroism in a Vietnamese POW camp, was reluctant to intervene for Keating. He agreed to attend a meeting to make sure that Keating, a constituent and campaign contributor, got a fair shake. It was an action McCain would later regret.

The meeting took place in DeConcini's office on April 2, 1987. Besides McCain, DeConcini had brought in his colleagues, Senator John Glenn, the first American astronaut to orbit the Earth, and Senator Alan Cranston. Also present was Ed Gray, chairman of the Federal Home Loan Bank Board. He offered to set up a meeting between the senators and the San Francisco regulators in charge of auditing Keating's bank.

The second meeting took place exactly one week later in San Francisco on April 9. Besides DeConcini, Glenn, Cranston, and McCain, Senator Don Riegle joined them. These men would later be dubbed "the Keating Five" by the media. Keating was also present for the meeting, along with William Black, deputy director of the Federal Savings and Loan Insurance Corporation, James Cirona, president of the Federal Home Loan Bank of San Francisco, and Michael Patriarca, director of agency functions at the Federal Savings and Loan Insurance Corporation.

According to an article in the *Arizona Republic* on October 3, 1999,

> . . . Black said the meeting was a show of force by Keating, who wanted the senators to pressure the regulators into dropping their case against Lincoln. The thrift was in trouble for violating "direct investment" rules, which prohibited S&Ls from taking large ownership positions in various ventures.
>
> "The Senate is a really small club, like the cliche goes," Black said. "And you really did have one-twentieth of the Senate in one room, called by one guy, who was the biggest crook in the S&L debacle."

According to transcripts later released, Patriarca said "We're sending a criminal referral to the Department of Justice. Not maybe, we're sending one. This is an extraordinarily serious matter. It involves a whole range of imprudent actions. I can't tell you strongly enough how serious this is. This is not a profitable institution."

Eventually news of the meeting leaked out, and all five senators were forced to account for their activities on behalf of Keating. The Keating Five received intensive media coverage as well as having to answer to their peers. For their activities on behalf of Keating, the Senate Ethics Committee cited their actions as imprudent.

In April 1989 the federal government finally seized Lincoln Savings and Loan, which was forced to declare bankruptcy. Lincoln's losses would eventually total $3.4 billion. It would be the most expensive failure in the national S and L scandal. Keating would spend the next decade defending himself from federal and state charges that he had defrauded his investors. Eventually, he was put behind bars in 1998 when a federal appeals court reinstated state security fraud convictions.

John McCain later became a cosponsor of the McCain-Feingold Bill in the Senate that passed and became law in 2002. The bill enacted a new law that disallowed so-called soft money. Someone like Keating would never again have the opportunity to openly corrupt senators.

Illinois (1989) first DNA reversal of a criminal conviction

The discovery of DNA is the single most significant event in the history of American criminal identification.

Francis Crick and James Watson of Cambridge University and Maurice Wilkins of King's College, London, are usually given credit for the discovery of the "double helix," the molecule that forms the building block of life commonly called DNA. While these three men would win the Nobel Prize in 1962 for their discovery, scientist Rosalind Franklin also contributed to the breakthrough.

Beginning with New York and Oklahoma in 1987 and extending into all 50 states by the end of the 1990s, one state after another allowed DNA testing to be introduced as evidence during a criminal trial.

Like fingerprints, DNA is unique to each individual. Unlike fingerprints, DNA is statistically more reliable and can be identified even if a suspect has left only a microscopic amount at a crime scene. Blood, hairs, and saliva are common DNA sources found at crime scenes, aiding greatly in identifying or excluding suspects.

Following acceptance of DNA evidence, many convictions that had previously been decided on the basis of circumstantial physical evidence have been thrown out when the defense used state-of-the-art DNA testing to prove a mistake had been made. Since most law enforcement offices keep physical evidence in property rooms and courthouses for at least 10 years after conviction, lawyers can use DNA testing to reopen old cases and make a bid for their clients' freedom.

The first instance of this came in connection to a crime committed more than a decade before DNA evidence appeared in courtrooms.

On the evening of July 9, 1977, Margaret Hamilton (a pseudonym) was walking home from work.

She later claimed that two men forced her into the back seat of a car and raped her. One of the men, she would later testify, tried to write words on her stomach using the sharp edge of a broken beer bottle. Somehow, she managed to survive this ordeal and was then pushed from the car onto the street. Her assailants drove off.

Hamilton's story had one basic problem—she never quite explained how she escaped. Nevertheless, police accepted her story. Hamilton was examined at the hospital as a rape victim. A rape kit is administered to any victim of a sexual crime, or anyone who presents themselves as such. The victim's clothing, including undergarments, is identified and bagged; swabs are taken from the genital area and mouth; fingernails are clipped and scraped; blood is drawn; both pubic and scalp hair are clipped, identified, and bagged. From the hospital, Hamilton was taken to police headquarters, where she assisted police artists who drew a sketch of her assailants.

Hamilton went through the mug books, files that contain the pictures known as mug shots. There are the booking and/or sentencing shots taken of suspected and convicted criminals where they pose in profile, facing forward. In looking through the mug books, Hamilton identified Gary Dotson as one of the men who had assaulted her.

Dotson was immediately brought in and placed in a police line-up. Hamilton viewed Dotson and other men in the line-up through a one-way glass, and she picked Dotson. He was formally charged but protested his innocence.

During Dotson's trial in summer 1979, the state's expert serologist testified that the semen on the victim's undergarment came from a type B secretor and that the defendant was a type B secretor. It was later reported that the state's serologist failed to disclose that the *victim* was also a type B secretor. The other seemingly damning piece of physical evidence was a pubic hair removed from the victim's underwear. It was similar to the defendant's and dissimilar to the victim's.

Convicted of aggravated kidnapping and rape, Dotson was sentenced to not less than 25 and not more than 50 years in state prison. He served time, still protesting his innocence, until March 1985, when Hamilton recanted her testimony. She admitted she had made up the rape story to hide a night she had with her boyfriend that she didn't want anyone to know about. Dotson and his attorneys filed court papers contending that the victim's recantation of testimony constituted grounds to vacate the original sentence. At the hearing on Dotson's motion for a new trial, the judge refused to either vacate the verdict or order a new trial. He felt that the complainant was more believable in her original testimony than in her recantation.

Dissatisfied, Dotson pressed his case for justice. Finally, Illinois's attorney general accepted responsibility for the case, stating that he did not believe the victim's recantation. He refused to pardon Dotson. On May 12, 1985, however, the governor commuted Dotson's sentence to the six years he had already served, pending good behavior.

In 1987, Dotson's parole was revoked after his wife accused him of assaulting her. The Appellate Court of Illinois affirmed Dotson's conviction on November 12, 1987. On Christmas Eve 1987, the governor granted Dotson a "last chance" parole. Two days later, Dotson got into a barroom fight. He was arrested again and his parole was revoked.

By 1988, Dotson's new attorney decided to have DNA tests done that were not available at the time of the alleged rape. A sample of semen from Hamilton's underwear was sent to England for DNA analysis. The results were inconclusive due to degradation of the sample. Trying again, the defense sent samples to Forensic Science Associates in Richmond, California. The lab performed then state-of-the-art DNA tests that showed that the semen on Hamilton's underwear could not have come from Dotson. It could, however, have come from Hamilton's boyfriend.

Armed with this new evidence, the chief judge of the Criminal Circuit in Cook County, Illinois, ruled that Dotson should get a new trial. The Illinois State Attorney's Office then made the decision not to prosecute, given the victim's lack of credibility and the results of the DNA test.

On August 14, 1989, Dotson's rape conviction was finally overturned and expunged from his record. It was the first time in U.S. history that DNA had been used to free an innocent man from prison.

Seven years later, a new type of DNA evidence led to a criminal conviction in a murder case, when Paul Ware was found guilty on the basis of mitochondrial DNA (MDNA) evidence. Until Ware's August 1996 trial for murder and rape in Tennessee, mitochondrial DNA evidence had never been introduced in a courtroom. Prior to this, conventional DNA evidence was based upon identification using hair, semen, or blood samples and testing concentrated on the genetic material from the nucleus of the cell—those genes that form the road map of inherited traits. In contrast, MDNA testing is applied to the genetic material in the mitochondria, the energy-producing structures in cells, which are inherited from the female parent. MDNA testing not only compares the samples at 600 places on the DNA strand where differences often occur, it can distinguish between hair and bone samples, which conventional DNA testing cannot.

In the Ware case, a single hair removed from the victim's throat was matched to Ware using MDNA testing. The victim's blood was not found on Ware; neither was Ware's semen found on the victim, yet the jury was convinced. Paul Ware was convicted of rape and murder in a case that successfully established the precedent for using MDNA testing in criminal trials.

Kansas City, Kansas (1989–2000) John Edward Robinson, first Internet serial killer

The Internet, which gained popularity as a communications medium in the 1990s, managed to transcend geography that in the early part of the 20th century took months or years to traverse. For criminals, the Internet was just a new way of committing crimes, particularly wire fraud and identity fraud.

Federal law 18 U.S.C. 1343 makes it a federal crime for anyone to use interstate wire communications facilities in carrying out a scheme to defraud. The crime is known as wire fraud. Examples include Dr. Cecil Jacobsen's use of the telephone to convince infertile couples to be treated at his infertility clinic; the passing to offshore banks of huge sums from the illegal drug trade; and inviting someone to come someplace where they will eventually be swindled.

Identity theft and identity fraud are terms used to refer to all types of crime in which someone wrongfully obtains and uses another person's personal data in some way that involves fraud or deception, typically for economic gain. The Internet has become an especially appealing place for criminals to obtain identifying data, such as passwords and banking information.

In their haste to explore the exciting features of the Internet, many people respond to "spam," unsolicited e-mail that promises them some benefit but requests identifying data, without realizing that in many cases, the requester has no intention of keeping his promise. Criminals have used computer technology to obtain large amounts of personal data.

With enough identifying information about an individual, a criminal can take over that individual's identity to conduct a wide range of crimes:

false applications for loans and credit cards, fraudulent withdrawals from bank accounts, fraudulent use of telephone calling cards, or obtaining other goods or privileges that might be denied the criminal if he were to use his real name. If the criminal takes steps to ensure that bills for the falsely obtained credit cards or bank statements showing the unauthorized withdrawals are sent to an address other than the victim's, the victim may not become aware of what is happening until the criminal has inflicted substantial damage on the victim's assets, credit, and reputation.

Consider the "Slavemaster" serial murder case. It represents the first time the Internet was used to commit serial murder. Before the "Slavemaster," no one had ever used the Internet to lure victims to their doom via cyberspace, as far as is known.

John Edward Robinson, the "Slavemaster," was a prolific serial killer who trolled chat rooms for victims. The third of five children, Robinson was born in Cicero, Illinois, in 1943. A Boy Scout by age 12, in two years he achieved the highest scout rank: Eagle. By 21, Robinson was married and working in the back office of a hospital. Things started going wrong when Robinson was accused of embezzling money from his employer, but the charges didn't stick.

Robinson moved west to Kansas City, Kansas, and in 1965 got a job as an X-ray technician. Later fired from that position because he was incompetent, Robinson charmed his way into running the lab at Fountain Plaza X-ray Laboratory in 1966, where he embezzled approximately $200,000 of the company's money. This time charged and found guilty of embezzlement, he received a suspended sentence.

Robinson then set up his own business, Professional Services Association, Inc., which was supposed to provide financial consulting to doctors in the Kansas City area. He used it as a cover for a forgery business. In 1975, Robinson was caught forging signatures and letters in an attempt to claim thousands of dollars via a stock scam. The U.S. Securities and Exchange Commission charged Robinson's company with securities fraud, mail fraud, and false representation. Robinson pleaded to a lesser charge and was fined $2,500 and placed on probation.

In 1977 Robinson invented an award, "Kansas City Man of the Year," and not only did he claim it in its first year, he tricked a state senator into presenting him with the plaque, a scam later exposed in an exposé in the *Kansas City Star*.

In June 1981, Robinson faced charges of felony theft from a former employer. As a result of a plea agreement, Robinson pleaded guilty to stealing a check worth $6,000. He was ordered to pay back $50,000 to Guy's Foods. He charmed his way into a light sentence: 60 days in jail and five years probation. He was released in July 1982.

Soon afterward, Robinson's scams started to turn decidedly weird. He started up a prostitution service out of a shabby Kansas City apartment building. He kept several mistresses at once, often putting them up in low-rent apartments. He sexually abused some of them.

John Robinson had been working his way up to murder. He finally found his first victim in Lisa Stasi. A pretty, curly-haired 19-year-old Alabaman with a baby daughter, Stasi had split with her unemployed husband Carl. On New Year's Eve 1984, she checked into a battered-women's shelter in Independence, Missouri. Lisa made Osborne/Robinson's acquaintance. He promised to get her a job and a place to stay, and she was more than willing to accept his offer to help. Lisa figured she'd finally caught a break.

Robinson rented Room 131 for Lisa and her daughter Tiffany at the Rodeway Inn in the Kansas City suburb of Overland Park. Lisa noticed that other women at the Rodeway Inn seemed to know him. Robinson told Lisa they were other "outreach moms," but Lisa thought that they looked like prostitutes.

After Lisa and Tiffany had been missing for a while, letters sent from the shelter to family members carried Lisa's signature and explained that she was fine and her baby was healthy. But the letters were typewritten and Lisa could not type. Her sister-in-law, Kathy Klinginsmith, went to the police station in Overland Park to file a missing-persons report on Lisa and Tiffany. The Overland Park detectives began to suspect John Robinson because he had paid for the room that Lisa stayed in with his American Express card in the name of his business, Equi-II. The cops discovered that other women close to Robinson had suddenly gone missing. Amongst them was 19-year-old Paula Godfrey, a sales rep for Equi-II. She vanished in 1984.

Another missing woman was Korean-born Catherine Clampitt, 27, another Equi-II employee. She was reported missing in June 1987. As with Godfrey and Stasi, no physical evidence of a crime could be found. Due to the lack of forensic evidence, the investigation against John Robinson stalled.

In 1986, Robinson, then 43, was sentenced to serve five to 14 years for swindling investors in a partnership. The missing-persons investigations were dropped. Robinson went to prison for three years for fraud. Released in 1989, Robinson discovered the new world of the Internet. He saw it as just another technology he could exploit.

Robinson began to frequent chat rooms and discussion groups that appealed to people interested in sadomasochism and bondage. He felt comfortable in the milieu. It was one he particularly enjoyed, especially what were known as "subs," or "submissives," who were Robinson's real prey.

Using "Midwest Slavemaster" as his screen name, Robinson trolled the Net. Robinson conned lonely, vulnerable women he met in chat rooms and arranged meetings. He would seduce them and have their mail directed toward a mailbox that he controlled. After he killed them, he made a substantial income from cashing their government checks, alimony payments, and whatever other checks were sent to them.

Between the mid-1990s and 2000, John Robinson murdered seven women whom he had met online or through newspaper personal ads. He disposed of most of his victims in metal drums that he buried in Missouri and Kansas. But he began to sloppy. He began to kill more frequently as his insatiable urges could no longer be quieted. Meanwhile, the mother of one of Robinson's victims, Suzette Trouten, received several typed letters from her daughter. They had Kansas City postmarks and were uncharacteristically mistake-free; Suzette was a poor speller and never typed.

Carolyn Trouten called the telephone numbers her daughter had given her. Robinson answered the phone. That was odd. According to Trouten's letters, she was traveling abroad with Robinson, who promptly denied this. Robinson claimed she had run off with another man. Police got warrants to wiretap Robinson's phone and monitor his online activities. The cops now felt Robinson was their prime suspect. Mrs. Trouten's complaint helped that process along. For his part, Robinson picked out his next victim, one of Suzette Trouten's online friends named Susan Kennedy. She lived in western Canada.

Susan met "J. R. Turner," as Robinson called himself, in a bondage chat room. He charmed her into meeting and agreeing to go off with him. Their phone conversations were picked up by the police wiretaps. The Lenexa, Kansas, police contacted Susan and told her they were investigating John Robinson. Not explaining what the investigation was about, they asked her to continue her relationship with him.

Robinson made vague offers about meeting her in person, but he had other fish he was trying to catch. He met local women daily, and online he was quick to strike up conversations that later became telephone relationships. One telephone friendship was with a Texas woman, Sally Russell, an unemployed psychologist who suffered from depression. Robinson picked up on her vulnerability and convinced her that he was a powerful community leader. He encouraged her to move to Kansas City, and when she told him she couldn't afford to move, Robinson said he would pay for it.

Tapping the call, the cops knew Sally Russell might be Robinson's next victim. Robinson wired her the money for her train ticket and Sally traveled to Overland Park.

Robinson tied up Sally and photographed her despite her pleas not to. He slapped her with a lot more strength than she expected. He took her money and then threw her out before she was scheduled to return home. After returning home, Susan had a chance to reflect on recent events and wrote Robinson an e-mail, breaking off their relationship.

Again, Robinson lost little time in finding a new victim in an S and M chatroom. He lured an unemployed dental hygienist named Laura to Overland Park, where Robinson promised to give her a job as an executive assistant in his business. Taking lodging in the same motel where Sally had stayed before her abrupt exit, Laura waited for Robinson.

When he arrived a few days later, he demanded she strip. He forced her to stand naked in the corner. When she refused, Robinson beat her, raped her, and photographed the bruises on her body. Following his usual pattern, he gave Laura $100 and sent her home. He ordered her to put her possessions in storage and then return to Overland Park.

Laura did as she was ordered. But when she returned, Robinson left her alone in the motel, and this time Laura called the police. By that time, a 30-man task force had been formed to capture Robinson. Task force members broke into the motel room and rescued Laura before Robinson could kill her. They got an arrest warrant, picked Robinson up and charged him with murder.

To avoid the death penalty, Robinson pleaded to five murder counts in Missouri and got a life sentence. He was convicted of murder in Kansas, on January 21, 2003, and sentenced to death. He was transferred to El Dorado Correctional Facility outside of Wichita, Kansas, where he awaits execution for his crimes.

The location of three of his victims still remains a mystery.

Alexandria, Virginia (1992) the greatest con in history

Dr. Cecil Jacobsen is American history's greatest con man. That he was a doctor made his actions that much more devious. The level of duplicity he attained to actually con his way into creating life is unparalleled.

Jacobsen was a true con man because he did not look the part. Middle-aged and rotund, he seemed more like a next-door neighbor with a civil service job. He looked positively benevolent, and in fact he believed himself to be so.

At Jacobsen's Vienna Reproductive Genetics Clinic, located in Vienna, Virginia, Jacobsen specialized in helping infertile people. Whether through in vitro fertilization or artificial insemination, with the husband's own sperm or that of an anonymous donor, Jacobsen was determined to give his patients what they wanted: a child of their own.

What makes Jacobsen so unique in the criminal universe is his reputation as a good guy. Jacobsen was the first doctor in the United States to introduce amniocentesis, the now-standard test in which fluid is extracted from the womb for the purpose of detecting birth defects.

Maybe it was that "first" going to his head or just some other character flaw that made the 55-year-old Jacobsen feel like he was above it all. Jacobsen began to think himself a god.

The Virginia Board of Medicine would later charge that Jacobsen injected some women with hormonal doses large enough to simulate pregnancy, but in reality, they would still be infertile. Jacobsen then convinced them that their bodies had mysteriously and sometimes repeatedly "reabsorbed" the dead fetus when it failed to appear in the womb.

Jacobsen might have continued his con were it not for more than 20 former patients who suspected the truth and sued him in civil court to prove it. All the cases were settled in 1988 and Jacobsen was forced by the Federal Trade Commission to reimburse a several defrauded patients. His medical license was also suspended indefinitely. However, under the terms of his agreement with the state medical board, Jacobsen could ask for reinstatement at a later date.

Federal investigators alerted to the case strongly suspected that there was more to Jacobsen's scam. They believed he was secretly impregnating patients with his own sperm. It was the perfect crime, undiscoverable until well after the baby was born and grew up to resemble Jacobsen.

The criminal case might have died were it not for a group of federal prosecutors who felt that Jacobsen's crimes were criminal—that he should answer for them in criminal rather than civil court. There was, however, one problem.

Jacobsen had committed no crime.

There were no laws on the books that prohibited a doctor from impregnating a woman with his own sperm, let alone not telling her. As for the simulated pregnancies, the medical community disagrees as to what level of hormonal treatment is proper for an infertile woman.

Criminal fraud charges involving the U.S. mail and telephones are frequently used to get indictments in cases that fall into this gray area between civil and criminal. Since Jacobsen had used the mails and phones to make medical appointments with patients whom he allegedly defrauded, prosecutors realized they had the statutes under which to charge him.

Often, the victims of con men hate to go public, even if it means financial restitution because they are so embarrassed that they fell for the scam in the first place. They rarely want to testify in open court. What couple would want to admit that Jacobsen had secretly fathered their child?

Months and months of meetings with Jacobsen's victims followed, and hundreds of hours of discussion took place between government prosecutors, guided by medical ethicists, social workers, geneticists, and other health care professionals. The government could have used its subpoena powers to force the victims to testify in court, but a cooperative witness is much better than a hostile one.

The decision was made that no one would be force to testify. The idea was to bring the victims forward and slowly give them the information. The central question was how to approach the con man's targets. Innocent people were at risk of having their lives shattered by the truth.

Another consideration was even more elementary. Without Jacobsen's progeny knowing their true identity, there was always the possibility they would meet and procreate. That would be incest. Even worse, what if Jacobsen had passed on some genetic defect his unknown children could protect against, and they did not know who their biological father really was?

Well aware of the uncertainties, the government proceeded slowly.

During spring 1991, letters began arriving in the mailboxes of Jacobsen's victims from the U.S. Attorney's office. The letters were all the same. Each letter was registered, which meant only the person to whom it was addressed could sign for it, and therefore, only the person it was meant for could open it. The government simply requested an interview with the addressee about Dr. Jacobsen's infertility programs.

"My husband was out of town [when I got the letter]," one of the mothers, Sally Rogers [name changed], later told the *New York Times*. "So the first time I went by myself. The lawyers started talking in general terms about why I went to Jacobsen—and little by little, the wheels started turning in my head."

"My husband and I had chosen not to tell our child she was donor inseminated. It was a big secret in my head. Suddenly I realized, 'They know, they know,' and I wished my husband wasn't out of town. I wished he were sitting there beside me."

At about the same time Sally Rogers was receiving her letter, Mel and Connie Franklin (names changed), parents of three, received theirs.

"I remember a feeling of dread when we first got it," Franklin recalled in the *Times*. "My wife's first reaction was 'no way.' She felt we should not get involved in any way, shape or form. But I said let's hear them out because I never thought in my wildest dreams it would lead to something like [the prosecution of Jacobsen]."

This game plan brought parents and prosecutors together in stages. Information about Jacobsen was distributed in bits and pieces. Parents absorbed each bit of news before deciding whether to go forward into the criminal phase.

Dozens of Jacobsen's patients never called the prosecutors, but most did. Once they did, the government told them there was more information for them, but that it meant disclosing the identity of the anonymous sperm donor. The parents then had to ask the million-dollar question.

The kind of resources the state can legally use to see someone convicted is frightening. When that strength is used to bring about justice, it is that much more formidable.

Prosecutors, preparing for the final showdown with Jacobsen in court, gave each family a pseudonym to protect their identities and a list of social workers they could consult for free counseling.

Some of the families who knew about the scam were unwilling at first to testify in open court. But that was before the government requested they go with their child for DNA testing. If the DNA tests of the children matched those of Jacobsen, it would prove irrefutably that the doctor, and not some anonymous sperm donor as he had claimed, was the father.

At this point, close to the indictments, the government took off the kid gloves. The couples were informed that while the DNA testing would not obligate them to testify against Jacobsen, the results of the test, should they prove positive, would be evidence and therefore might be disclosed publicly by Jacobsen's defense team.

The DNA tests indicated that Jacobsen had fathered 15 children. The prosecution then asked those parents to be listed in the indictment. While some were reluctant, anger and rage and an old-fashioned desire to see justice done convinced them all to go forward.

After months of careful planning, the government finally acted. Jacobsen was charged with 32 counts of mail fraud and 10 counts of wire fraud for using the phone to make medical appointments and then deceiving these same patients. The icing on the prosecutorial cake was an additional four counts of travel fraud because patients crossed state lines to reach the Vienna, Virginia, clinic he operated until his civil liability problems in 1988.

The last counts in the indictment, six perjury charges, had to do with testimony Jacobsen gave to the Federal Trade Commission in a 1988 civil suit brought against him by a former patient for the bogus hormone injection treatments.

The trial of Dr. Cecil Jacobsen opened in Virginia to worldwide publicity in February 1992. In the United States alone, it made the front page coast to coast. Television news ate it up, with updates on the national nightly newscasts as the trial progressed.

The government had a total of 11 parents testify before the jury. Witness after witness, they all detailed Jacobsen's con game, then spoke painfully about their shock, dismay, and anger when they learned that their children were not the product of anonymous sperm donors as Jacobsen had said, but of Jacobsen himself. Others testified about Jacobsen's practice of deliberately misdiagnosing pregnancies.

One parent who testified told a hushed courtroom how Jacobsen had convinced her that she was pregnant when he pointed to a sonogram and said, "There's Junior." But there was no "junior" for many of the others who came to Jacobsen to get pregnant.

For its part, the defense claimed that Dr. Cecil Jacobsen was a humanitarian. His deception was out of a sincere desire to help people. As for the deceit involving his secret parenting, they claimed he used his own sperm only when anonymous donors failed to show up at his clinic. Unfortunately for Jacobsen, that claim was repudiated by three former receptionists at his Vienna clinic and a laboratory technician, all of whom testified that there were never any anonymous sperm donors at the clinic.

The verdict came on March 4, 1992. Cecil Jacobsen sat impassively, his arms crossed across his chest in a protective gesture as the jury foreman said "guilty" to 46 of the fraud counts and six perjury counts. On the rest of the indictment, he was found not guilty.

Despite the verdicts, Jacobsen's ego was still operating on all cylinders.

"It's a shock to be found guilty of trying to help people. I didn't break any law. I spent my life trying to help women have children. If I felt I was a criminal or broke the law, I would never have done it," Jacobsen told the *Times* afterward.

Richard Cullen, U.S. attorney for the Eastern District of Virginia, countered, "It speaks loudly that doctors who lie to their patients for profit are going to be dealt with as criminals."

He added:

"We wanted to make sure that we did everything we could to protect the parents. In the final analysis, though, this was a case of classic, basic fraud. But it was an unusual case and we were faced with a situation where there was no precedent."

At his sentencing hearing on May 5, 1992, Jacobsen told Judge Cacheris:

"I was totally unaware of the anger, anguish and hate I have caused—until these proceedings." Speaking of his former patients and their families, he continued, "I ask for their forgiveness so that the healing process can start. . . . But I helped a great deal of other people. I did not wish to hurt these people. I wished to help," Jacobsen added, as if this would release the burden of pain he had imposed on so many people.

Judge James C. Cacheris sentenced Jacobsen to five years in prison. He let Jacobsen out on bond pending appeal. In the "truth is stranger than fiction" department, Jacobsen still had his medical license. He could continue practicing medicine while his appeal wound its way through the courts. On May 28, 1992, the Commonwealth of Virginia revoked Jacobsen's license to practice medicine.

See also JEFFERSON RANDOLPH "SOAPY" SMITH (1860–1898).

New York, New York (1993) the bombing of the World Trade Center

It was a cold Friday in February and John DiGiovanni was going to work. John was a dental supply salesman. It was a job that had given him stability in a life that had not had all that much of it.

In his early 20s John had gotten a job as a part-time instructor of communications at Hunter College of the City University of New York. Just a few years older than some of his students, young and handsome, he was inspiring in his lectures about the communications medium. He gave direction to students who really needed it, including the author.

John had married a beautiful woman with whom he was deeply in love. But their marriage did not work out and they eventually divorced. As the years went by, John found it difficult to parlay his part-time teaching job into a full time one. Academic politics were harsh and competition was at a premium.

Eventually, John drifted away from teaching and got a job as a dental supply salesman. He moved back in with his mother for a while in their Long Island home, met a girl, and got engaged. His life was finally back on track.

On February 21, 1993, John left his house to go on a sales call for his company in the city. He parked his car in the garage of One World Trade Center and walked the few blocks to his appointment. After he finished, he walked back to pick up his car. Whether or not he saw the truck sitting unattended near the building is hard to say. Certainly, he could not have known its significance.

John was walking through the garage when he was blown to bits. Or he may have been vaporized; it's hard to know. What authorities were able to positively piece together about how John died was this:

On February 26, 1993, Middle Eastern terrorists bombed the World Trade Center. The unattended truck turned out to contain enough explosive to blow a 30-square-meter hole into the underground parking garage where John DiGiovanni was walking. Along with John, Robert Kirkpatrick of Suffern, New York, Steve Knapp of New York City, Monica Smith of Seaford, New York, William Macko of Bayonne, New Jersey, and Wilfredo Mercado of Brooklyn, New York, lost their lives.

In the wake of the bombing, all 110 floors of the north tower filled with smoke and the building had to be evacuated. The authorities began investigating, but it would be eight years before they realized that this had been the first shot in a new kind of war.

See also TIMOTHY MCVEIGH (1968–2001); NEW YORK, NEW YORK (2001); QUEENS, NEW YORK (1975).

Midwestern Bank Bandits (1994–1997) white supremacist bank robbers

Both robbers wore a ski mask, sunglasses, and a white hard hat. The leader clicked the slide back on his silver 9mm automatic and ordered everyone to lie face down on the floor.

The leader vaulted the counter, reached into the teller's drawer, and scooped bills into bags he pulled from his pockets. His partner, also holding a firearm, did the same thing. In less than a minute, the looting was finished.

They had just reached the front doors when the leader pulled a smoke grenade out of his coat. He pulled the pin and threw it behind him. Smoke plumed from the grenade and masked their retreat.

Outside, the two robbers removed their masks. They hid their weapons under their long coats, then calmly walked to a car that was idling at the curb. They got in and the driver took off, taking care to observe the speed limit. A block away, they picked up another man who had served as the lookout and then headed to the outskirts of town, where they switched to another automobile. Then they headed west on the interstate.

The robbers had used the "Lamm Method" to perfection. The date was October 25, 1994, the place, Columbus, Ohio. In the ashtray of the ditched car, the FBI later found a copy of the Declaration of Independence.

At first, it was just a strange series of bank robberies, about one month, in Iowa, Wisconsin, Missouri, Ohio, Nebraska, and Kentucky. By the end of 1995, the robberies totaled 22. Not since the 1930s, when the Dillinger Gang terrorized the Midwest, had one gang simultaneously inspired fear among the populace and been so successful in its criminal endeavors.

The job of discerning a pattern in the seemingly random robberies and eventually capturing the culprits fell to one man: Jim Nelson, special agent in charge of the FBI's St. Louis office.

After the Columbus robbery in 1994, masked bandits robbed the Westport Commercial Bank of St. Louis. Jim Nelson arrived on the scene to interview witnesses and calm the bank employees, who were scared out of their wits.

There were four robbers, the witnesses said. Armed with automatic weapons and disguised in Richard Nixon masks, the robbers snatched the cash themselves, never giving tellers time to rig payroll bags with dye bombs. Before running outside, they left gas grenades to cover their tracks. Then they cruised off in junk cars bought for the occasion with bogus identification.

There had been an almost military-like precision to the operation, and Nelson felt there was something familiar about it. Nelson looked through his database of wanted posters and came upon a description of a group of four bank robbers who had already hit Iowa, Wisconsin, Ohio, Nebraska, and Kentucky. The modus operandi was exactly the same. Only the costumes differed.

Sometimes it was ski masks, other times Nixon masks; once it was Santa Claus, with a hearty, "Ho, Ho, Ho, turn over your dough," to the tellers. What fascinated Nelson the most were the robbers' political leanings.

The bad guys stuffed a copy of the Declaration of Independence in the ashtray of their Columbus getaway car. On other robberies, they wore caps and bandannas with the logo of the Department of Alcohol, Tobacco and Firearms (ATF), a sore reminder of the botched ATF attempt to seize the Branch Davidian compound in Waco, Texas in 1993.

During their second of three robberies of a St. Louis bank in 1995, the gang got even more brazen. They bought a Ford Fairmont for a getaway car using the name of a retired FBI agent who had worked white supremacist cases in the Northwest. When the Ford was abandoned, Nelson found an article about Timothy McVeigh, the Oklahoma City bomber, on the front seat.

Unlike other agents, who viewed the robbers' political motivations as a decoy, Nelson took them seriously. The antigovernment rhetoric and mocking imitation of the G-men reminded Nelson of the Order, a white supremacist group that pulled off a $3.6 million armored-car robbery in California in 1984. Nelson decided to go public with his theory. The reply was swift.

Midwestern newspapers received letters from the bandits themselves, nominating Nelson for an award for "honesty and demonstrating patriotism." They called themselves the "Mid-West Bank Bandits" and were "proud to appoint Jim Nelson as our new spokesman for 1996."

"They knew I had hit the nail on the head," Nelson later said.

He sent case agent Gary Feuer to Hayden Lake, Idaho, to the Aryan Nations white supremacist compound, to gather information on white supremacists who financed their cause through robbery. Feuer came back with two names: Peter Langan and Richard Lee Guthrie Jr.

In 1992, when robbers held up a Pizza Hut in Lavonia, Georgia, childhood friends Peter Langan and Richard Lee Guthrie Jr. were suspected of committing the crime. Langan was eventually caught in Cincinnati and escorted back to Georgia by Franklin County sheriff Hugh Roach.

During their time together, Roach would later recall, Langan told him he was an Aryan Nations supporter, who ". . . said he wanted to tie up the court system so it couldn't operate." Guthrie, though, remained free and up to no good.

In 1993 the Secret Service heard that Guthrie had made threats against President George Bush. Langan was offered a deal: If he were released, he would have to help the government track down his old buddy. Langan agreed. He was released and returned to Cincinnati. After a few perfunctory calls to the Secret Service, he went underground.

In August 1994 Sheriff Roach in Georgia received a card postmarked Syracuse, New York. It said, "Life is so unpredictable. Remember that tyrants never rule forever. And those traitors do eventually end up at the end of a rope. Commander Pedro sends his regards."

That November, Roach received another card, this time from Cincinnati.

"The fishing has been good and I have remembered our time together. Thanks for your help and good luck with your trials and tribulations. . . . Be strong and never let them see you cry. By Commander Pedro."

Roach was baffled. He could not figure out who the cards had come from. One of his investigators said it sounded like Peter Langan. They communicated this information to the Secret Service, and the puzzle eventually found its way to Jim Nelson's desk at FBI headquarters in St. Louis.

Nelson looked for Guthrie and Langan's Achilles' heel. He found it in Guthrie's girlfriend. She bore Guthrie a grudge and eventually tipped Nelson off as to his whereabouts. On January 15, 1996, Guthrie was captured in Cincinnati without a struggle. To help his case, he made a deal and decided to finally turn on his friend.

Three days later, January 18, FBI agents and local police were waiting on a south side street in Columbus, Ohio, when a slight, red-haired man—Peter Langan—bundled in winter clothes stepped into a white Chevy van. Langan did not give up without a fight. Nearly 50 shots were fired, and 30 riddled his van. Langan had the luck that Bonnie and Clyde did not. He escaped with only scratches.

In July 1996 Richard Lee Guthrie Jr. pleaded guilty to 19 counts of bank robbery. Soon after, he reneged on his deal to testify against his old friend when he hanged himself in his cell.

Peter "Commander Pedro" Langan was convicted on February 10, 1997, on bank robbery charges in Columbus, Ohio. He is expected to be in jail for the rest of his life. Jim Nelson has since retired from the FBI.

Miraculously, no one was ever injured during all 22 of the bank robberies.

See also COBB COUNTY, GEORGIA (1914); TIMOTHY MCVEIGH (1968–2001); STONE MOUNTAIN, GEORGIA (1915).

Timothy McVeigh (1968–2001) the Oklahoma City bomber

Timothy McVeigh is the second most prolific mass murderer in U.S. history. For such a dangerous man, his beginnings are rather average. McVeigh was born on April 23, 1968, the middle child of three children, in the suburbs of Buffalo, New York, just miles from the Canadian border. His father Bill worked at the General Motors radiator factory. When McVeigh was 10, his mother, Mildred "Mickey" McVeigh, abandoned the family. After that, McVeigh, normally talkative, turned quiet. He did well in high school, but his quiet demeanor made him the butt of jokes. His classmates sarcastically voted him "Most Talkative."

After high school he decided to forgo college. Instead, he briefly studied computers at a local business school. He soon found work as a security guard. Growing tired and bored with his limited opportunities as a civilian, he joined the army in 1988 when he was 20-years old.

Military life agreed with McVeigh. He was a good and loyal soldier and was promoted to the rank of sergeant. During the Gulf War, McVeigh was a gunner who won a Bronze Star for shooting an Iraqi tank commander from more than a mile away with his favorite weapon—small cannon. He would later tell his biographers that the army taught him how to switch off his emotions.

Despite his performance as a soldier, McVeigh still had major social problems. Simply put, he was not accepted. Soldiers teased him. A woman he dated during his time in the service would later say that all he wanted to talk about was guns, how he mistrusted the government and his high regard for Adolf Hitler. He was virulently anti-semitic.

"He said he didn't necessarily agree with all those Jews being killed," said the woman. "But he said Hitler had the right plan."

What McVeigh really wanted was to become a Green Beret, one of the elite fighting group of the American Special Forces. In order to join up, he had to first undergo a three-week-long Special Forces Assessment and Selection Course in 1991. He washed out in two days. That seemed to change him. McVeigh's dream had been shattered. He no longer liked the military and when the time came to re-enlist, he decided to leave the service instead.

Returning to upstate New York, he found work once again in security. McVeigh felt that the government no longer represented the people as the Constitution guaranteed. In particular, McVeigh was bothered by the killing of white supremacist Randy Weaver's wife and son in 1992; the 1993 50-day standoff in Waco between the FBI and the Branch Davidians, which resulted in a bloodbath when the FBI raided their compound; Congress's passage of the Brady Bill in 1993, which established a five-day waiting period for handgun ownership; and 1994's Omnibus Crime Bill, which banned 19 types of semi-automatic assault weapons. After the passage of the Omnibus Crime Bill, McVeigh wrote Michael Forbes, an Army friend, "What will it take?" to stop the government from infringing on his civil liberties.

McVeigh became a drifter. He took dead-end jobs and followed gun shows around the country. Concerning his future criminal actions, McVeigh would later write to a British newspaper, "I reached the decision to go on the offensive—to put a check on government abuse of power, where others had failed in stopping the federal juggernaut running amok. Borrowing a page from U.S. foreign policy, I decided to send a message to a government that was becoming increasingly hostile, by bombing a government building and the government employees within that building who represent that government."

And that was why, on April 19, 1995, Timothy McVeigh drove a rented Ryder truck full of homemade explosives—fuel oil and fertilizer—and parked it on the street in front of the Alfred P. Murrah Federal Building in Oklahoma City. A few minutes later, when the bomb exploded, 168 people were dead. Among the people blown to bits were 19 children, 15 in a day care center. By that time McVeigh was fleeing the city in a getaway car. What's strange is that for a man who planned meticulously, he had left one thing out that was sure to attract attention—McVeigh had failed to put license plates on the car.

Less than 90 minutes after the bombing, he was stopped by a traffic cop for driving without plates. In searching his vehicle, the cop also found firearms for which McVeigh had no permits. He was jailed for almost two days while they checked on him. During his stay, police did not know who they had in custody. It was only on April 21, just as he was about to be released, that McVeigh was finally identified as the Oklahoma City bomber and formally charged with the crime.

Timothy McVeigh was tried in June 1997 on federal charges of murder and conspiracy to commit murder. Convicted on both counts, he was sentenced to death. Even to the end, he showed no remorse for his crime. He was executed by lethal injection on June 11, 2001.

See also COBB COUNTY, GEORGIA (1914); QUEENS, NEW YORK (1975); STONE MOUNTAIN, GEORGIA (1915); WASHINGTON, D.C. (1950–1954).

Theodore Kaczynski, a.k.a. "the Unabomber" (1978–1997) mail bomber

The Unabomber was a criminal genius who managed to elude capture while spreading terror and misery over two decades by using the national postal system and modern explosives technology. Born in Chicago in 1942, Kaczynski had one younger brother named David. Kaczynski was viewed as a bright child and was later described by his mother as not being particularly comfortable around other children and prone to displaying fears of people and buildings. Kaczynski's high school claim to fame occurred when he constructed a pipe bomb in chemistry class, giving him his 15 minutes of popularity.

He had trouble getting along with women, a problem that haunted him from his teenage years, when a woman complimented him on his good looks. Dr. Sally Johnson, who conducted a psychological evaluation of the Unabomber after his capture, said in her 1998 report, "Kaczynski could not reconcile his attractive self-image and his inability to have sustained relationships with women."

A brilliant student, Kaczynski was accepted into Harvard at age 16, but social ineptitude kept him from making friends. At age 20, he went to the University of Michigan for graduate work. In his fifth year of graduate study Kaczynski began "experiencing several weeks of intense and persistent sexual excitement involving fantasies of being a female" and reached out for psychiatric assistance. Kaczynski initially wanted advice about a sex change operation but could only bring himself to talk about a common anxiety of young men in the 1960s—getting drafted and going to Vietnam.

Johnson reported that "Mr. Kaczynski describes leaving the office and feeling rage, shame, and humiliation over this attempt to seek evaluation. He refers this as a significant turning point in his life."

After graduating, Kaczynski took a series of odd jobs. He experienced persistent "delusional thinking involving being controlled by modern technology" and eventually withdrew to a Lincoln, Montana, cabin where he became a "mountain man" who lived off the land.

At the age of 26, in 1978, Kaczynski began acting out. His first bombing took place on May 25, 1978, when an unmailed package was found in the parking lot of the University of Illinois, Chicago. Addressed to an engineering professor at Rensselear Polytechnic Institute in Troy, New York, it was returned to its alleged sender, engineering professor Buckley Crist Jr., who taught at Northwestern's Technological Institute. Crist, who did not recall sending it, turned the package over to campus security. When Northwestern police officer Terry Marker opened it, a bomb exploded, and the officer was slightly injured.

Over the next 20 years, the Unabomber, as he came to be known to the public, was responsible for a nationwide bombing spree from California to New Jersey that caused three deaths and maimed and injured 23 people. His last bombing occurred 17 years later and showed how far he had come in mastering bomb construction. Sent to the California Forestry Association in Sacramento, California, it was opened by the timber lobbying group's president, Gilbert B. Murray, on April 24, 1995. The package exploded, killing Murray instantly. The explosion was so powerful, it dislodged nails from adjoining offices and drove them further through the walls.

In 1995 Kaczynski offered to cease his bombings in return for publication of his lengthly manifesto, which appeared in a special section of the *Washington Post* that September. It was then that Kaczynski's brother David recognized the work, bringing the Unabomber to ground. David Kaczynski convinced the government not to seek the death penalty against his brother in exchange for his invaluable assistance. With David's help, Kaczynski was arrested on April 3, 1996, and eventually pleaded guilty to 13 counts of bombing and murder in 1998. Kaczynski is now serving several consecutive life sentences.

PART FIVE

THE TWENTY-FIRST CENTURY

NINE
2001 and Beyond

Introduction

Unique among all crimes, terrorism uses criminal means in pursuit of a political goal. A terrorist relies on the criminal underworld of forgers for fake documents; arms smugglers to obtain weapons and explosives; drug deals and any other type of criminal activity necessary to finance operations. Whatever the terrorist's political goal, the terrorist will kill babies and other innocents to achieve it.

In that respect, terrorism is the most cowardly of crimes. Relying for its effectiveness on spreading fear among the targeted populace, the terrorist looks to commit some dramatic act of human and physical destruction.

Terrorism is not a new crime on American shores that begins and ends with 9/11. Some might make the argument that John Brown was America's first terrorist because of his political agenda and the criminal means he used to try and achieve it. Pancho Villa certainly had a political agenda and was willing to use murder to achieve it. Terrorists in the 1950s were willing to risk their own deaths, and some did indeed die, as they attacked Blair House where President Truman was staying. Later in the decade, another group of terrorists shot up the House of Representatives. The first attack on the World Trade Center, Timothy McVeigh's bombing of Oklahoma City's federal building—these were major terrorist crimes of the 1990s.

More than any other crime, modern terrorism in the United State exploits the nation's sophisticated transportation system to get from one target to another. Because of his ability to seemingly infiltrate any place, no matter how tight the security, the terrorist has taken on the air of a modern highwayman, who appears out of nowhere with his dramatic demands. Highwaymen like Joseph Hare were home-grown commodities; with exceptions, including Timothy McVeigh and some white supremacist groups, the modern terrorist usually has origins outside the United States.

Foreign terrorists have been committing crimes for more than 30 years. As early as the Munich Olympics of 1972, when eight Arab terrorists belonging to the militant Black September faction of the Palestine Liberation Organization

(PLO) murdered 11 Israeli athletes, Americans have seen terrorist acts on live television. At the end of the 1970s 66 Americans were taken hostage in Iran, and TV covered it live.

By the time of the second attack on the World Trade Center, Americans were used to viewing terrorism in other countries on their TV screens, but did not fear stateside attacks. And then 9/11 happened.

New York, New York (2001) the second World Trade Center attack

A portent of things to come was a memo written to FBI Headquarters in Washington from the bureau's Phoenix office. Dated July 10, 2001, the memo recommended that the agency begin an investigation into flight schools as a possible place of terrorist activity. The following month, the Minnesota FBI office sent a memo to Washington detailing its frustrations in the investigation of alleged terrorist Zacarias Moussaoui.

Clearly, something was up. Billionaire Osama bin Laden's terrorist network was humming but no one, not the FBI, the DEA, the CIA, not one national agency knew what was going to happen. Meanwhile, relying on forged documents, an untold number of terrorists in the employ of bin Laden had entered the country. Bin Laden used his financial abilities to supply them with money to execute his plan.

Bin Laden's place in American criminal history was assured when he conceived of the brilliant criminal stroke of using the U.S. transportation system to his own criminal ends. He would make airplanes into deadly missiles and use them to strike a metaphoric and physical blow right into the heart of the American economy. Forevermore, his name would be spoken with that of America's most notorious criminals: Big Harp and Little Harp, John Wilkes Booth, Jesse James, Dillinger, and now, bin Laden.

Bin Laden's target would be what he had failed to bring down before: the World Trade Center. Only this time, he would go after both towers, not just one. And he would add one more target: the country's military center, the Pentagon in Washington, D.C.

Early on the morning of September 11, 2001, three groups of five hijackers each and one with four men boarded four jetliners. They had passed through security with box cutters in their pockets. Later that morning, ABC News reported the story as follows:

In a horrific sequence of terrorist violence, four U.S. passenger planes were apparently hijacked and crashed today, including two jets that flew into the twin towers of the World Trade Center in New York City, causing both to collapse.

In Washington D.C., another plane had crashed into the Pentagon, causing part of that building to collapse. A fourth passenger plane, with skyjackers who were part of bin Laden's terrorist network, went down near Pittsburgh. The Federal Aviation Administration ordered all airports around the country closed in the first such nationwide shutdown.

John O'Neill, retired former head of the FBI's New York counterterrorism office, had taken a job as the World Trade Center head of security. He was in his 34th-floor office in the north tower at 8:46 A.M. when American Airlines flight 11 crashed into it. Escaping, he called a friend from outside the building and told her, "Val, it's horrible. There are body parts everywhere." A few seconds later he told her, "Okay, I'll call you in a little bit." Then he found his way to the command center that the police and fire department had set up. FBI agent Wesley Wong was there and later told *Esquire* magazine:

He was in FBI mode. Then he turned and kind of looked at me and went toward the interior of the complex. From the time John walked away to the time the building collapsed was certainly not more than a half hour or 20 minutes.

A week later, O'Neill's body was found in the debris of the south tower. He was given a hero's funeral. O'Neill was among approximately 3,000 people who died during the single largest terrorist attack in U.S. history.

The United States subsequently invaded Afghanistan, looking to capture bin Laden and destroy his terrorist network. In 2003 that was followed by an invasion of Iraq that toppled the government of Saddam Hussein. In the United States, in the wake of what would become known simply as "9/11," New Yorkers walked around in a daze for months afterward, many recovering from post-traumatic stress disorder syndrome. Some New Yorkers chose to leave the city rather than live where they would be constantly reminded of the trauma and the attacks. Counties north of the city suddenly saw their populations grow as, out of fear, people left New York City in droves.

All around the country, Americans were traumatized by the events in New York City and Washington D.C. The 9/11 attacks scared Americans into believing they could be next if they were in the wrong place at the wrong time. But it is only over the long term, from the vantage point of history, that the attack's success, or failure, can be truly evaluated.

See also NEW YORK, NEW YORK (1993); QUEENS, NEW YORK (1975).

Maryland and Virginia (2002) the Sniper and geographic profiling

Using geography to track serial killers is nothing new. Dr. Stuart Kind, the late British forensic pathologist, developed the first-ever geographic profile of an active serial killer, the Yorkshire Ripper, in 1981. A navigator for the RAF during World War II, Kind was intimately familiar with using calculations to fix positions on a map. He decided to apply those same skills toward catching a murderer. Using graph paper and a pencil, he plotted the killer's murder sites, attempting to find his "center of gravity" or "safe zone," the place where the killer felt most comfortable and where the Bobbies might catch him.

Kind then ran his calculations through a computer that determined the killer lived in the Bradford area of Yorkshire. The investigation shifted focus to previous suspects in the Bradford area. Finally, Scotland Yard zeroed in on Peter Sutcliffe, who was then arrested, tried, convicted of murder, and sentenced to life.

A few years later in 1987, geographic profiling was used to track down an English serial rapist/murderer named John Duffy. Yet despite its successes in England, American law offices remained reluctant to accept geographic profiling as an effective law enforcement tool. That changed in October 2002.

That month national news followed the story of a mysterious sniper operating around Maryland and Virginia. The sniper was shooting people with what police figured was some sort of hunting rifle fitted with a telescopic sight. The killer kept to the highways to evade capture. Throughout October 2002 the sniper killed people in Virginia and Maryland, operating in what criminologist Dr. Maurice Godwin described as a wedge-shaped pattern, with northern Virginia as its apex. Godwin was a geographic profiler, trained in a one-of-a-kind criminology program at the University of Liverpool.

Godwin created his geographic profile of the sniper using a complex series of mathematical equations, similar to the ones Kind had used. He plotted out on a map where the sniper had already struck, trying to determine the area in which he operated and where he might strike next. Godwin already had a computer program of his own design called Predator that combined the information from the current case with hundreds of others.

"I was the first and only individual to predict that the sniper would move south along I-95, which I first stated nationally on CNN on October 8," Godwin writes in his 2005 book *Tracker*. "During that CNN interview, I predicted based on my analysis of serial killers, that Fredericksburg, Virginia, would likely be the next target area—which it was, three days later."

Godwin also predicted that the killer was really two men, not one as police suspected. Meanwhile, the FBI employed their own geographic profiler, who did not lead them anywhere. Instead, just as Godwin predicted, the sniper struck just south of Fredericksburg on October 11, gunning down Kenneth H. Bridges at an Exxon station.

The break in the case finally came when two motorists spotted a suspicious-looking car parked at a rest stop off the Maryland interstate on October 22. Investigating officers arrested John Allen Muhammad, 41, an army veteran of the Persian Gulf War, and 17-year-old Lee Boyd Malvo, a Jamaican citizen. Recovered from the Chevy Caprice they were driving were a Bushmaster .233-caliber rifle, a scope, a tripod, and a sniper platform. They had drilled a hole in the trunk to make it easy for whoever was firing to stick the barrel out. In all they had killed 10 people and wounded three.

Tried in 2003, Muhammad was sentenced to death, and Malvo, a minor, to life imprisonment.

Bibliography

GENERAL

Ackerman, Kenneth D. *Dark Horse*. Carroll & Graf, 2003.

Ambrose, Stephen E. *Undaunted Courage*. New York: Touchstone Books, 1996.

Coates, Robert M. *The Outlaw Years: The History of the Land Pirates of the Natchez Trace*. New York: Literary Guild of America, 1930.

Connell, Evan S. *Son of the Morning Star*. San Francisco, Calif.: North Point Press, 1984

Godwin, Grover Maurice. *Hunting Serial Predators*. Boca Raton, Fla: CRC Books, 1997.

Helmer, William, with Rick Mattix. *Public Enemies: America's Criminal Past*. New York: Facts On File, 1998.

Posner, Gerald. *Case Closed*. New York: Random House, 1993.

Sifakis, Carl. *The Encyclopedia of American Crime*. 2d ed. 2 vols. New York: Facts On File, 2001.

Stiles, T. J. *Jesse James: Last Rebel of the Civil War*. New York: Alfred A. Knopf, 2002.

Chapter One
1587–1650

"The Establishment of the Colony." State Library of North Carolina. Available online. URL: http://state library.dcr.state.nc.us/nc/ncsites/english2.htm. Downloaded August 11, 2004.

Fort Raleigh National Historic Site. "The First English Colony." National Park Service. Available online. URL: http://www.nps.gov/fora/first.htm. Downloaded August 11, 2004.

Grymes, Charles A. "Roanoke Colony: Prelude to Jamestown?" Virginia Places. Available online. URL: http://www.virginia places.org/settleland/roanoke-colony.html. Downloaded August 11, 2004.

"Pocahontas." Association for the Preservation of Virginia Antiquities. Available online. URL: http://www.apva.org/history/pocahont.html. Downloaded August 11, 2004.

Chapter Two
1650–1700

Bradford, Will. "Blood will out, or, An example of justice in the tryal, condemnation, confession, and execution of Thomas Lutherland: who barbarously murthered the body of John Clark of Philadelphia, and was executed at Salem in West-Jarsey the 23d of February 1691/2," February 23, 1691–92. University of Michigan: James V. Medler Crime Collection, William L. Clements Library.

Cook, Elisha. "Death Sentence of William Ledra by the Massachusetts Court of Assistants," March 5, 1660. University of Michigan: James V. Medler Crime Collection, William L. Clements Library.

Hawthorne, John. "Warrant for the arrest of Mary Green and Hanah Bromage [Brumidge], both of Haverhill, for witchcraft, Countersigned by Constable William Sterling," July 28, 1692. University of Michigan: James V. Medler Crime Collection, William L. Clements Library.

"Salem Witch Trials, Documentary Archive and Transcription Project." University of Virginia. Available online. URL: http://etext.lib.virginia.edu/salem/witch craft. Downloaded August 11, 2004.

Chapter Three
1700–1750

Smoot, Fred. "The Natchez Road a.k.a. The Natchez Trace." TNGen Web Project. Available online. URL: http://www. tngenweb.org/maps/tntrace.htm. Downloaded August 11, 2004.

Chapter Four
1750–1800

Channing, Henry. "God admonishing his people of their duty, as parents and masters: a sermon, preached at New-London, December 20th, 1786: occasioned by the execution of Hannah Ocuish, a mulatto girl, aged 12 years and 9 months, for the murder of Eunice Bolles, aged 6 years and 6 months," 1786. University of Michigan: James V. Medler Crime Collection, William L. Clements Library.

Coates, Robert M. *The Outlaw Years: The History of the Land Pirates of the Natchez Trace.* New York: Literary Guild of America, 1930.

Cochrun, Simon. "The life and confession of Charles O' Donnel, who was executed at Morgantown, June 19, 1797, for the willful [sic] murder of his son: though he had murdered a woman about 27 years before that time," 1797. University of Michigan: James V. Medler Crime Collection, William L. Clements Library.

Daggett, David. "Sketches of the life of Joseph Mountain: a Negro who was executed at New-Haven on the 20th day of October 1790, for a rape committed on the 26th day of May last: (the writer of this history has directed that the money arising from the sales thereof, after deducting the expence of printing, &c. be given to the unhappy girl, whose life is rendered wretched by the crime of the malefactor.)," 1790. University of Michigan: James V. Medler Crime Collection, William L. Clements Library.

Harpers Ferry National Historic Park. "Guide to Harpers Ferry History." National Park Service. Available online. URL: http://www.nps.gov/hafe/history.htm. Downloaded August 11, 2004.

Mallery, Caleb. "A brief narrative of the life and confession of Barnett Davenport: under sentence of death for a series of the most horrid murders ever perpetrated in this country, or perhaps any other, on the evening following the 3d of February 1780: is to be executed at Litchfield, on the 8th of May," 1780. University of Michigan: James V. Medler Crime Collection, William L. Clements Library.

U.S. Marshals Service. "George Washington Appoints First Marshals—1789." U.S. Department of Justice. Available online. URL: http://www.usdoj.gov/marshals/usmshist.html. Downloaded August 11, 2004.

Wilson, Elizabeth, "A Faithful narrative of Elizabeth Wilson: who was executed at Chester, January 3d, 1786: charged with the murder of her twin infants: containing some account of her dying sayings, with some serious reflections: drawn up at the request of a friend unconnected with the deceased," 1786. University of Michigan: James V. Medler Crime Collection, William L. Clements Library.

Chapter Five
1800–1850

Ambrose, Stephen E. *Undaunted Courage.* New York: Touchstone Books, 1996.

Blackfoot, Emery. *Chance Encounters.* Boston: Serendipity Press, 1987.

Block, W. T. "Pirate Lafitte, Bowie dealt in slave trade via SE Texas," Beaumont *Enterprise,* May 22, 1999. Available online. URL: http://www.wtblock.com/wtblockjr/slavetra. htm. Accessed November 3, 2004.

Coates, Robert M. *The Outlaw Years: The History of the Land Pirates of the Natchez Trace.* New York: Literary Guild of America, 1930.

Fikes, Gordon. "Catherine McCarty, the Mother of Billy the Kid." SouthernNewMexico.com. Available online. URL: http://www.southernnewmexico.com/Articles/Southwest/Grant/Silver_City/Catherine McCarty-TheMothe.html. Updated January 6, 2003.

Geringer, Joseph. *Jesse James: Riding Hell-Bent for Leather into Legend.* Court TV's Crime Library Website, 2004. Available online. URL: http://www.crimelibrary.com/americana/jesse. Accessed November 3, 2004.

Geringer, Joseph. *Jean Lafitte: Gentleman Pirate of New Orleans.* Court TV's Crime Library Website. Available online. URL: http://www.crimelibrary.com/americana/lafitte/ main.htm. Accessed November 3, 2004.

Hare, Joseph. "Dying confession of Joseph Hare, alias Joseph T. Hare, one of the mail robbers: who was executed at Baltimore on the 10th of September 1818." Boston: Printed by N. Coverly, 1818. University of Michigan: James V. Medler Crime Collection, William L. Clements Library.

"John H. Hall," National Park Service. Available online. URL: http://www.nps.gov/hafe/people.htm. Accessed November 3, 2004.

Lake, Stuart. *Wyatt Earp, Frontier Marshal.* Boston: Houghton Mifflin, 1931.

"Richard Lawrence," Wikipedia. Available online. URL: http://en.wikipedia.org/wiki/Richard_Lawrence. Accessed November 3, 2004.

Chapter Six
1850–1900

A&E Television Networks. "December 1, 1884: Elfego Baca Battles Anglo Cowboys." History Channel. com: This Day in History. Available online. URL: http://www.historychannel.com/tdih/tdih.jsp?month=10272964&day=10272966&cat=1 0272948. Accessed November 3, 2004.

Apodaca, Patrick. *Memorandum: Conviction of Dr. Samuel Mudd.* Washington, D.C.: National Archives, May 24, 1978.

Simkin, John. "John Brown." Spartacus Educational. Available online. URL: http://www.spartacus.

schoolnet.co.uk/USASbrown.htm. Updated May 2, 2002.

———. "Dalton Gang." Spartacus Educational. Available online. URL: http://www.spartacus.schoolnet.co.uk/WWdaltongang.htm. Accessed November 3, 2004.

Smith, David Paul. "List of names of men that served under W. C. Quantrill and what happened to them after the Civil War." Red River Authority of Texas. Available online. URL: http://www.rra.dst.tx.us/c_t/people/wcQUANTRILL. cfm. Accessed November 3, 2004.

"Sources for John Brown Information, Documents, and Images." The Institute for Advanced Technology, University of Virginia. Available online. URL: http://www.iath.virginia. edu/jbrown/sources.html. Accessed November 3, 2004.

Spicer, Wells, Justice of the Peace. *The Spicer Decision,* December 1, 1881. Available online. URL: http://meenterprises.talkoftheplanet.com/TRANSCRIPTS.html. Accessed November 3, 2004.

Stiles, T. J. *Jesse James: Last Rebel of the Civil War.* New York: Alfred A. Knopf, 2002.

Taylor, Troy. "The Bloody Benders: Mass Murderers from the history of Kansas." Prairieghosts.com. Available online. URL: http://www.prairieghosts.com/crime.html. Accessed November 3, 2004.

University of Missouri—Kansas City. "Wirz, Henry. Letter to Louis Schade." November 10, 1865. Washington, D.C.: Federal Prison. Available online. URL: http://www.law.umkc.edu/faculty/projects/ftrials/Wirz/Impact1.htm. Accessed November 10, 2004.

University of Missouri—Kansas City. "Wirz, Henry. Letter to President Johnson." November 6, 1865. Washington, D.C.: Federal Prison. Available online. URL: http://www.law.umkc.edu/faculty/projects/ftrials/Wirz/Impact1.htm. Accessed November 10, 2004.

"Wyatt Earp's Life in Lamar." Tombstone Historical Page. Available online. URL: http://members.tripod.com/~Tombstonehistory/wyattearp.html. Accessed November 3, 2004.

Chapter Seven
1900–1950

Aiuto, Russell. *The Case of Leo Frank.* Court TV's Crime Library Website, 2004. Available online. URL: http://www. crimelibrary.com/classics/frank. Accessed November 3, 2004.

Bardsley, Marilyn, and Allan May, *John Dillinger.* Court TV's Crime Library Website, 2000. Available online. URL: http://www.crimelibrary.com/americana/dillinger/dillingermain.htm. Accessed November 3, 2004.

Brown, R. J. "Alexander Graham Bell and the Garfield Assassination." HistoryBuff.com. Available online. URL: http:// www.historybuff.com/library/refgarfield.html. Accessed November 3, 2004.

Dinnerstein, Leonard. "Leo Frank Case." *The New Georgia Encyclopedia.* Available online. URL: http://www.georgiaencyclopedia.org/nge/Article.jsp?id=h-906&pid=s-58. Updated October 10, 2003.

EyewitnesstoHistory.com. "Train Robbery, 1899." Available online. URL: http://www.eyewitnesstohistory.com/cassidy. htm. Posted 1999.

FBI. "Baby Face Nelson." FBI Electronic Reading Room. Available online. URL: http://foia.fbi.gov/foiaindex/nelson.htm. Accessed November 3, 2004.

———. "Bonnie and Clyde." FBI Electronic Reading Room. Available online. URL: http://foia.fbi.gov/foiaindex/bonclyd.htm. Accessed November 3, 2004.

———. "John Dillinger (Summary)." FBI Electronic Reading Room. Available online. URL: http://foia.fbi.gov/foiaindex/dillnger.htm. Accessed November 3, 2004.

———. "FBI History." Available online. URL: http://www. fbi. gov/fbihistory.htm. Accessed November 3, 2004.

Fowler, Joseph M.D., Crego, Floyd S., M.D., et al. Official Report of the Experts of the People in the Case of *The People v. Leon F. Czolgosz. Philadelphia Medical Journal* (1901): 1–6. University of Michigan: James V. Medler Crime Collection, William L. Clements Library.

TheFreeDictionary.com. "John Browning." Available online. URL: http://encyclopedia.thefreedictionary.com/John%20 Browning. Accessed November 3, 2004.

Geringer, Joseph. *Baby Face Nelson: Childlike Mug, Psychopathic Soul.* Court TV's Crime Library Website, 2000. Available online. URL: http://www.crime library.com/americana/babyface. Accessed November 3, 2004.

Geringer, Joseph. *Charles Arthur Floyd: "Pretty Boy" from Cookson Hills.* Court TV's Crime Library Website, 1999. Available online. URL: http://www.crime library.com/gangsters/prettyboy/index.html. Accessed November 3, 2004.

Griffith, Joe. "In Pursuit of Pancho Villa, 1916–1917." *Journal of the Historical Society of the Georgia National Guard* 6, no. 3–4 (summer/fall 1997). Available online. URL: http://www.hsgng.org/pages/pancho.htm. Accessed November 3, 2004.

Linder, Douglas. "Famous American Trials, Bruno Hauptmann (Lindbergh Kidnapping) Trial, 1935." Famous Trials Website. Available online. URL:

http://www.law.umkc.edu/faculty/projects/ftrials/ Hauptmann/Hauptmann.htm. Accessed November 3, 2004.

———. "Famous American Trials, *Illinois v. Nathan Leopold and Richard Loeb,* 1924." Famous Trials Website. Available online. URL: http://www.law. umkc.edu/faculty/projects/ftrials/leoploeb/leopold. htm. Accessed November 3, 2004.

———. "Famous American Trials, The Black Sox Trial, 1921." Famous Trials Website. Available online. URL: http://www.law.umkc.edu/faculty/projects/ ftrials/blacksox/blacksox.html. Accessed November 3, 2004.

———. "Famous American Trials, The Trial of Sheriff Joseph Shipp, et al., 1907." Famous Trials Website. Available online. URL: http://www.law.umkc.edu/ faculty/projects/ftrials/shipp/shipp.html. Accessed November 3, 2004.

MacGowan, Douglas. *Butch Cassidy and the Sundance Kid.* Court TV's Crime Library Website, 2004. Available online. URL:http://www.crimelibrary.com/americana/ butch. Accessed November 3, 2004.

Noe, Denise. *Fatty Arbuckle.* Court TV's Crime Library Website, 2004. Available online. URL: http://www. crimelibrary.com/notorious_murders/classics/fatty_ arbuckle/1.html. Accessed November 3, 2004.

O'Connor, John J., and Edmund F. Robertson. "Francis Galton." MacTutor History of Mathematics archive, School of Mathematics and Statistics, University of St. Andrews, Scotland. Available online. URL: http://www-history.mcs. st-andrews.ac.uk/Mathe- maticians/Galton.html. Posted October 2003.

O'Connor, Richard. *Bat Masterson.* New York: Double- day, 1957.

Park, Edwards. "Pictures of a Tragedy." *Smithsonian Magazine,* February 1999. Available online. URL: http://www.smithsonianmag.si.edu/smithsonian/issue s99/feb99/object_feb99.html. Accessed November 3, 2004.

PBS Online. "Evelyn Remembers," *Murder of the Cen- tury,* American Experience. Available online. URL: http://www.pbs.org/wgbh/amex/century/sfeature/ sf_nesbit.html. Accessed November 3, 2004.

Sharpe, Philip B. "The Thompson Sub-Machine Gun." *Journal of the American Institute of Criminal Law and Criminology* 23 (1932–33): 1098. Second Amend- ment Foundation Online. Available online. URL: http://www.saf.org/LawReviews/PSharpe1.html. Accessed November 3, 2004.

Stein, Alan J., and Chris Goodman. "Tracy, Harry: Trail of the Northwest's Last Desperado Cybertour." History Link.org. Available online. URL: http://www. historylink.org/cybertour/index.cfm?file_id=7059. Accessed November 3, 2004.

U.S. Department of Transportation, Federal Highway Administration. "FHWA by Day: January 7." Available online. URL: http://www.fhwa.dot.gov/byday/fhbd 007.htm. Accessed November 3, 2004.

———. "Highway History." Available online. URL: http://www.fhwa.dot.gov/infrastructure/history.htm. Accessed November 3, 2004.

———. "Logan Waller Page." Available online. URL: http://www.fhwa.dot.gov/administrators/lpage.htm. Updated July 3, 2003.

Weingroff, Richard F. "Building the Foundation." *Pub- lic Roads* 60, no. 1 (summer 1996), Available online. URL: http://www.tfhrc.gov/pubrds/summer96/p96 su2.htm. Accessed November 3, 2004.

Chapter Eight
1950–2000

Bowman, John. "Timothy McVeigh." CBC News Online. Available online. URL: http://www.cbc.ca/ news/indepth/ mcveigh. Updated June 2001.

California Secretary of State. "Robert F. Kennedy Assassination Investigation Records." California State Archives. Available online. URL: http://www. ss.ca.gov/archives/ level3_rfkappe.html. Accessed November 3, 2004.

Capote, Truman. *In Cold Blood.* New York: Random House, 1965.

Collins, Kimberly, Gabe Hinkebein, and Staci Schorgl. "John W. Hinckley, Jr., A Biography." Famous Trials Website. Available online. URL: http://www.law. umkc.edu/faculty/projects/ftrials/hinckley/HBIO. HTM. Accessed November 3, 2004.

The Editors. "Justice for Mrs. Opsahl." Lektrik Press. Available online. URL: http://www.lektrik.com/ feature/justice. htm. Accessed November 3, 2004.

Gribben, Mark. *James Earl Ray: The Man Who Killed Mar- tin Luther King, Jr.* Court TV's Crime Library Website, 2003. Available online. URL: http://www.crime library.com/terrorists_spies/assassins/ray/1.html. Accessed November 3, 2004.

Kashner, Sam, and Nancy Schoenberger. *Hollywood Kryptonite.* New York: St. Martin's Press, 1997.

Linder, Doug. "Famous American Trials, The Rosen- berg Trial, 1951." Famous Trials Website. Available online. URL: http://www.law.umkc.edu/faculty/ projects/ftrials/rosenb/ROSENB.HTM. Accessed November 3, 2004.

Posner, Gerald. *Case Closed.* New York: Random House, 1993.

Smith, Elbert B. "Shoot-Out on Pennsylvania Avenue." *American History* magazine, June 1998. Available online. URL: http://americanhistory.about.com/library/ prm/blpennsylvania1.htm. Accessed November 3, 2004.

Springer, John. "LaGuardia Christmas Bombing Remains Unsolved 27 Years Later." CNN.com, December 24, 2002. Available online. URL: http://www.cnn.com/2002/LAW/12/24/ctv.laguardia. Accessed November 3, 2004.

"War on Terror: Terrorist Attacks on the United States since 1970." *Globe and Mail.* Available online. URL: http://globeandmail.com/special/attack/pages/terror.html. Accessed November 3, 2004.

Weingroff, Richard F. "Creating the Interstate Highway System." U.S. Department of Transportation, Federal Highway Administration. Available online. URL: http://www.tfhrc.gov/pubrds/summer96/p96su10.htm. Accessed November 3, 2004.

General Index

Page numbers in **boldface** indicate main treatment of a topic. Page numbers in *italic* refer to tables, photos, or illustrations.

Y

Z

Geographic Index

Page numbers in *italic* indicate maps; those preceded by *i* indicate maps in the color insert section.

A

Alabama 67, 72, 25, 251–255, 265

Alaska *i8*, 115–116, 156, 158–159, *158*

Arizona 125, 130, 132, 136–139, 227, 262

Arkansas 71–73, 155, 189, 208–209, 220–221

B

Barataria Bay 54–55, 57, 59–60

Big Moose Lake (New York) 174

Bolivia 186

C

California 94, 117, 130, 151–152, 156, 204, 233, 235–237, 247, 251, 255–258, 262, 264, 270, 273

Canada 64, 82, 110, 169, 179, 189, 221, 254, 260, 266

Cave-in-Rock (Illinois) 19, 34, 36, 38

Chisum Trail 127

Coffeyville (Kansas) 118, 151, 152, 155

Colorado 80, 129–130, 144, 157–158, 169, 188

Connecticut 10, 26–27, 30–31, 81, 132

Custer's Hill 127

D

Dakota Territory 94, 117, 121, 125

Deadwood (South Dakota) 125

Delaware 11

District of Columbia *i6*, 30, 51–52, 58, 75–76, 80, 85, 87, 97, 103, 105–106, 109, 110–112, 114, 116, 119, 121, 132–135, 143, 173, 180, 190, 207, 218, 223–224, 227, 240, 242, 255, 259, 260–261, 279

Dodge City (Kansas) 78, 115–116, 127–132, 187–190, 208

E

England 3–6, 11, 30–31, 99, 133, 172, 254, 264

Europe 5–6, 9–10, 31, 65, 98, 173, 191, 24, 251

F

Florida 20, 64, 75, 111, 216, 227

France 49, 53, 59, 176, 194, 246

G

Georgia 68, 77, 98, 100, 112–113, 128, 156, 192–197, 219, 219, 253, 271

Glenwood Springs (Colorado) 130

Grand Terre Island 53, 55, 59

H

Harper's Ferry (Virginia) 42, 50, 65, 85–90

I

Idaho 50, 151, 271

Illinois 19, 34–35, 42, 50, 53, 56, 94, 124, 126–127, 130, 134–135, 197, 209, 212–214, 217, 233–235, 248, 263–265, 273

Indiana 101, 118, 210, 223, 225–227, 229, 234–235, 248

Interstate Highway System 173, 236, *240–243*, 247, 253

Iowa 80, 130, 145, 147, 149, 152, 156, 270

J

Jamestown (Virginia) 5–7

K

Kansas *i7*, *i14–i15*, 26, 67, 80–85, 88, 93–97, 115–116, *116*, 118–119, 124–125, 127–128, 131–132, 143, 145–146, 149, 151–152, 155–156, 188–189, 208, 220–224, 248, 264–267

Kentucky *i10*, 17, 19–21, 33–36, 39, 41, *57*, 72, 97–98, 102, 143, 146, 149, 270

Kitty Hawk (North Carolina) 172